Breach of Trust

Breach of Trust

How the Warren Commission
Failed the Nation and Why

Gerald D. McKnight

 University Press of Kansas

Published by the University Press of Kansas (Lawrence, Kansas 66049), which was organized by the Kansas Board of Regents and is operated and funded by Emporia State University, Fort Hays State University, Kansas State University, Pittsburg State University, the University of Kansas, and Wichita State University

Library of Congress Cataloging-in-Publication Data

McKnight, Gerald.

Breach of trust : how the Warren Commission failed the nation and why

/ Gerald D. McKnight.

p. cm.   *U94500c*

Includes bibliographical references and index.

ISBN 0-7006-1390-0 (cloth : alk. paper)

1. Kennedy, John F. (John Fitzgerald), 1917–1963—Assassination.

2. United States. Warren Commission. 3. Oswald, Lee Harvey. I. Title.

E842.9.M273   2005

364.152'4'092—dc22

2005009136

British Library Cataloguing-in-Publication Data is available.

Printed in the United States of America

10 9 8 7 6 5 4 3 2 1

The paper used in this publication meets the minimum requirements of the American National Standard for Permanence of Paper for Printed Library Materials Z39.48-1984.

To my wife, Barbara L. McKnight,
who, like most Americans her age,
remembers where she was and what she was
doing when the news of JFK's assassination
stunned the world

Contents

Acknowledgments

During the research and writing of this book I incurred many debts. I am grateful for the assistance of many librarians and archivists, especially the National Archives in College Park, Maryland, the Lyndon Johnson Library, and the Richard B. Russell Memorial Library. The library staff at my teaching institute, Hood College, were always helpful, especially Jan Samet O'Leary and Cindy Feher. My thanks go out to people at the University Press of Kansas, especially Mike Briggs, whose unflagging support and gentle prodding throughout the whole process were most appreciated. They all worked with the kind of friendly commitment that comes from a first-rate press. A book project with no problems and no entangling complications. What could be better?

Jim Lesar, president of the Assassination Records Center in Washington, D.C., pointed me to critical primary materials that I otherwise might have overlooked. Cherished friends and trusted colleagues like Tom McGurn, Nick Kotz, and Len Latkovski took time to read early manuscript drafts and made constructive criticisms that I incorporated in almost every instance. Other close friends and subject-matter experts like Dave Wrone and Clay Ogilvie provided guidance and insights from their vast knowledge of the Kennedy assassination. One of the people who sustained me over the years I worked on this project was my literary agent, Leona Schecter. I owe her a very special debt of gratitude.

Finally, without exaggeration, I would never have undertaken this work if it were not for Harold Weisberg (1913–2002). Harold made available to me, as he did to all who asked, access to his voluminous records on the JFK assassination then located in his home in Frederick, Maryland. This archive is now housed at Hood College; I am currently the co-director, with Clay Ogilvie, of this collection, which contains about one third of a million pages of government documents. Harold encouraged me to undertake this work, and I was the beneficiary of his unique insights into the crime of Dallas and his unmatched knowledge of the documentary sources. Harold was my "Harvard" and "Yale" in preparing me in this attempt to pose new challenges to the official record of the assassination of America's thirty-fifth president.

Introduction

It has been more than forty years since President John F. Kennedy was gunned down in the streets of Dallas. If polls about the Kennedy assassination are any guide, most Americans believe either that the government was never fully forthcoming about the real facts of Dallas or that the official version of those facts, the Warren Commission Report, was simply a cover-up of the real truth behind JFK's death.[1] *Breach of Trust* is based mostly on the government's own documents to answer lingering national questions about the Kennedy assassination: Are the content and conclusions of the Warren Commission Report credible? Did the Commission undertake a truly good-faith, thorough, and controlled investigation, or did politics infiltrate the investigative process? Were the Commission's conclusions shaped by the way the Commission was formed, the Commission's methodology, or the actions and priorities of key participants and politics?

When the Warren Commission Report along with twenty-six volumes of Hearings and Exhibits first reached the public in 1964, with its more than seventeen thousand pages of testimony and more than ten million words, it was initially celebrated as the most comprehensive criminal investigation ever undertaken in all of history. Surprisingly, during the ten months that the Commission was in session there was little or no criticism from the media or political commentators about the wall of secrecy behind which the Commission conducted its investigation. Although the Commission had no authority to classify anything, it classified the transcripts of its proceedings "Secret" except when it classified them "Top Secret." Even the Commission's staff was not privy to what went on behind the closed doors of the executive sessions. When proceedings were leaked, it was almost always in the form of "authorized leaks," disclosure of information planted in the media by either the Commission or the FBI to prepare the public for the eventual release of the official explanation of the Kennedy assassination: that Lee Harvey Oswald was the lone assailant and there was no foreign or domestic conspiracy. There was no public opportunity to objectively examine anything relating to the evidence, evaluate witness testimony, or question the Commission's conclusions or the scope of its investigation until the report was made public ten months later.

Most of the fifteen volumes of witness testimony were taken by a staff lawyer, with only the court reporter and the witness present and no member of the Commission in attendance. Except for the former director of central intelligence, Allen Dulles, whom Kennedy had replaced after the Bay of Pigs debacle, all of the commissioners were burdened with heavy demands on their time. As a group they were present for less than 20 percent of the testimony of the hundreds of witnesses questioned.[2] When it first appeared, the magnitude of the report and the twenty-six volumes of appendices achieved what it set out to accomplish: to distract attention from the severe limitations of the investigation.

Richard Whalen, an early critic of the Warren Commission, astutely noted that the report "tells us too much about too little."[3] Only about 11 percent of the 912-page report deals with the alleged facts of the assassination. The report spends considerably more time on the Secret Service and the protection of the president than on the Kennedy autopsy. Most of the report is given over to a detailed biography of the alleged assailant, Lee Harvey Oswald. Commissioner Dulles insisted on this inclusion, and the Commission's general counsel, J. Lee Rankin, embraced Dulles's suggestion, noting, "Some of it will be necessary to tell the story and to show why it is reasonable to assume that he did what the Commission concludes that he did do."[4]

Obviously, biographical information about the man charged with Kennedy's murder was necessary for the Commission in order to settle on the question of motive. But it raises justified suspicions that the reason why the overwhelming majority of the report is on the life and times of Lee Harvey Oswald was to create a state of unquestioned acceptance in the public mind of Oswald's guilt when the concrete forensic evidence proved his innocence. As for the question of Oswald's motive, the Commission ultimately fell back on painting Oswald as having "an overriding hostility to his environment." The day the Commission held its last executive session, President Lyndon Johnson asked Commissioner Richard Russell the "why" of Dallas. Understandably curious, Johnson wanted to know what the Commission had concluded regarding Oswald's motives after ten months of investigation. "He was just a general misanthropic fellow," Russell explained. "He had never been satisfied anywhere he was on earth—in Russia or here. And," the Georgia senator continued, "he had a desire to get his name in history." Former Commission counsel Burt Griffin, who worked on this section of the report, had a different view: "We ducked the question of motive," the then judge Griffin admitted years later.[5]

This is not to suggest that everything in the official accounting is wrong, that none of it had been established as fact even without that marvelous machine for establishing truth: scrutiny of evidence and cross-examination of witnesses. But there are countless examples of the Commission placing special twists or interpretation on the facts. The Commission had a selective attitude toward testimony: It favored witnesses who strengthened the case for Oswald's guilt and discounted or even suppressed testimony (and evidence) of those who jeopardized the prosecution case the government was building against a dead man. A few examples confirm this assertion. The irreconcilable discrepancy between the FBI report of the Dealey Plaza shooting and the scenario found in the Warren report is a striking example.

On the evening of November 22, 1963, when the now president of the United States, Lyndon B. Johnson, returned from Dallas to Washington, he placed FBI Director J. Edgar Hoover in charge of the investigation. Over the weekend following the assassination the two discussed what would be included in the FBI report. According to an FBI document, Johnson "approved the idea that [the FBI] make a report showing the evidence conclusively tying Oswald in as the assailant of President Kennedy." The president and Hoover had agreed on the "official solution" of the crime before any evidence was tested, any witness was questioned, or Kennedy's remains were interred at Arlington National Cemetery. That Sunday (November 24), LBJ told Hoover that he wanted the report on his desk by Tuesday, November 26. Hoover agreed on the timetable and ordered the bureau's General Investigative Division to "wrap up investigation; seems to me we have the basic facts now."[6]

Because of unanticipated intervening events, the FBI's report on the assassination (Commission Document Number 1, or CD 1) was not ready until early December. Due to White House pressure, CD 1 was so hastily thrown together that the FBI never acquired a copy of the official JFK autopsy protocol before putting together its 833-page report. In fact, the FBI initially refused a copy of the autopsy protocol when the Secret Service offered to provide a copy (see Chapter 1). CD 1 asserted that Oswald fired three shots at the presidential motorcade. The three bullets were consistent with the three spent hulls found in the vicinity of the alleged sniper's nest on the sixth floor of the Book Depository Building overlooking Elm Street. According to CD 1, two bullets hit Kennedy and a separate missile struck Texas Governor John B. Connally. The Secret Service agreed with the FBI's three-shots-and-three-hits scenario.

Initially, the Commission satisfied itself with the FBI's construction of the shooting until seven months later, when it was forced to account for a nick in a curb that was made by a bullet where bystander Jim Tague was standing. The Commission's response to this problem was to invent what in time came to be designated as the "single-bullet" theory, in which it postulated that JFK and Connally were hit by the same nonfatal missile. The Warren Commission Report allowed, with studied vagueness, that "one shot probably missed the car and its occupants."[7] The only common ground the two official reports shared was the assertion that only three shots were fired. Neither the Commission nor the FBI could allow for a fourth shot because their own imposed time restraints and the mechanical features of the alleged murder weapon permitted only three shots. A fourth shot meant that there was at least a second gunman and that Kennedy had been the victim of a conspiracy.

The Commission and the FBI disagreed radically on the shooting, basic evidence in any homicide. There is no way to refine this disconnect or explain it away as some inconsequential, idiosyncratic glitch. The Warren report's accounting of the shooting is crucial to its findings that a single gunman killed President Kennedy. There is nothing in the released official record or any subsequent public disclosure of admission by the FBI to show that the bureau altered its conclusions to bring them into alignment with the Warren report. Both could not have been right. (In fact, neither was.)

In 1966, when the media drew attention to the irreconcilable discrepancy in the two reports, Hoover insisted that the FBI's construction of the shooting—three shots, three hits—was the correct one. Since the FBI's file on the Kennedy case was marked "closed," despite the FBI's continued public pledge that it "would remain open for all time," the director's was the last word.[8] According to the official record, the FBI, the Commission's investigative arm in the Kennedy case, made no bones about the fact that it believed the Commission's explanation of the shooting was impossible. In the final accounting, Hoover's bureau and the Warren Commission arrived at conclusions that could only have made sense if they were reporting on two separate and unrelated homicides.

Another example, one directly related to the conflicting shooting scenarios, involved the suppression of evidence that refuted the Commission's no-conspiracy assertion. It was essential to the Commission's no-conspiracy case that there was only one shooter in Dealey Plaza. In carefully brokered language and misstated facts, the report asserted that while it was not necessary to determine which shot hit Connally, "there is very persuasive evidence from the experts to indicate that the same bullet which pierced the President's throat also caused Governor Connally's wounds." The problem was that none of the Bethesda Naval Hospital doctors who performed JFK's autopsy believed that Kennedy and Connally had been hit by the same bullet. Even more dismaying was the fact that the two most experienced ballistics and wounds experts whose advice and special expertise the Commission solicited agreed with the Bethesda prosecutors.[9]

The problem was the alleged history of the single bullet that the Commission insisted had struck both Kennedy and Connally. The path assigned to Commission Exhibit 399 (CE 399) defied the science of forensic medicine. The report contended that CE 399 was the bullet that came from Governor

Connally's stretcher at Parkland Memorial Hospital. According to the report, CE 399 produced all seven of the nonfatal wounds on both shooting victims. It passed through JFK's neck, without striking bone, and entered Connally's back, demolishing four inches of his fifth rib, before exiting his chest. It then, the report asserted, smashed the radius bone (one of the densest bones in the body) in Connally's right wrist before burying itself in his left thigh just above the knee. Despite the trauma it left in its wake, the report described the condition of CE 399 as "only slightly flattened but otherwise unmutilated."[10]

The near-pristine condition of CE 399 convinced the trio of Bethesda doctors that CE 399 could not have produced all of Kennedy's and the governor's seven nonfatal wounds. The two Parkland Memorial doctors who were most responsible for treating Connally's wounds agreed that CE 399 could not have produced this kind of havoc in the human body and remained virtually unscathed. The most qualified ballistics expert the Commission consulted was Dr. Joseph Dolci. At the time Dolci was the chairman of the U.S. Army's Wound Ballistic Board. He had years of experience with wounds inflicted by missiles, beginning as a battlefield surgeon in the Pacific Theater during World War II. Dolci did not mince his words. He told the Commission that the case it was making for this bullet was forensically impossible. But since the politics of the assassination and not medicolegal expertise topped the Commission's scale of priorities, it ignored all of the doctors.

The "experts" referred to in the report were Dr. Alfred G. Olivier, a veterinarian, and Dr. Arthur J. Dziemian, a physiologist. Dr. Olivier was chief of the Wounds Ballistics Branch at the Edgewood Arsenal in Maryland, a branch of the Department of Defense (DOD). The Commission authorized Olivier and Dziemian to run some experimental tests using Oswald's rifle and one hundred rounds of the 6.5-mm ammunition alleged to have been used in the assassination. Olivier and Dziemian set up an experiment that involved firing rounds into horsemeat, gelatin blocks, goat carcasses, and wrists of human cadavers. They reported back that their tests had proved that CE 399 could have inflicted all of the seven nonfatal wounds without exhibiting any marked deformation.[11]

The Olivier-Dziemian report (filed as CRDLR 3264) does not appear in any of the Commission's twenty-six volumes of exhibits. The Commission dared not publish it because page 35 of the fifty-seven-page report contained pictures of 6.5-mm bullets after they had been fired through the radii of cadaver wrists. All of the samples showed the classic mushrooming of bullet metal after striking hard wrist bone. By no stretch of the imagination could any of the bullets be described as near pristine.[12] The Commission had to make certain that the results of the Edgewood Arsenal tests were suppressed. In 1965 the DOD's director of classification management permitted all but one of the twenty DOD documents used by the Warren Commission to be made available to the public upon the approval of the National Archives. The "exception," according to the director's letter, "is the Edgewood Arsenal Technical Report CRDLR 3264, March 1965, which must remain Confidential." The Olivier-Dziemian report was not declassified until March 1973, eight years later.[13]

Over the weekend of the assassination, the government had on hand credible evidence that ruled out the lone-assassin, no-conspiracy explanation that the White House and FBI Director Hoover were settling upon as the solution to the crime. Several days after the assassination the CIA received from the Secret Service a copy of the Abraham Zapruder film. Zapruder's name will be remembered in history as that of the producer of the greatest amateur movie ever made: He captured the shooting death of President Kennedy on film. The CIA had an interest in the film because it was conducting its own investigation of the assassination. In return for a copy of the film, the Secret Service received an analysis of the film from the agency's National Photographic Intelligence Center (NPIC) in Washington, D.C. NPIC enjoyed the well-deserved reputation within the government as the finest photo-interpretation center in the world. The center's interpretation of the film of those terrible six seconds in Dallas came to two conclusions: First, the first shot at the motorcade had not come from the sixth-floor "sniper's nest" where Oswald had allegedly secreted himself. Second, there had been at least two gunmen in Dealey Plaza shooting at the motorcade. The results of NPIC's analysis of the Zapruder film were suppressed. Both agencies engaged in a conspiracy of silence because it was already clearly apparent during the weekend of the assassination that the "official truth" would be that Kennedy had been murdered by a lone sociopath with Marxist sympathies.[14]

The most striking example of the suppression of facts—what defense lawyers colloquially refer to as "bad facts," that is, evidence or witness testimony likely to result in the conviction of their client—was the witting omission of the official JFK death certificate from the Commission's report and the twenty-six volumes of testimony and exhibits.

President Kennedy's personal White House physician was Admiral George G. Burkley, who was with the presidential party in Dallas on November 22, 1963. Dr. Burkley was with the moribund Kennedy in Trauma Room 1 at Parkland Memorial Hospital, and it fell to him to pronounce the president dead. Burkley signed the death certificate before the "official facts" of the assassination had been settled upon. Kennedy's death certificate places the nonfatal rear wound at the third thoracic vertebra. The official death certificate destroyed the Commission's essential assertion that JFK and Connally had been struck by the same bullet. A missile entering

Kennedy's back at a downward angle of 45 degrees and not striking bone could not have altered its trajectory to exit from his throat and then enter Connally's back. This single-bullet construction was the sine qua non of the Commission's single-assassin explanation of the Kennedy assassination. The official death certificate was a "bad fact" and had to be suppressed. Burkley himself was a "bad fact" and was never called as a Commission witness or deposed by a staff lawyer. In effect, Kennedy's personal physician, who should have been one of the Commission's first witnesses, was dropped down the "memory hole."[15]

We are well past the time when all critics of the Warren Commission Report can be responsibly and fairly lumped together as "assassination buffs" and casually dismissed as that element found in any population who indulge in weird hobbies. The reality is that the burden of proof regarding credibility and sound reasoning rests squarely on the shoulders of those defenders of the report, the official mythology of the Kennedy assassination. Relying largely on the government's own documents, *A Breach of Trust* contends that the Warren Commission Report was a shoddily improvised political exercise in public relations and not a good-faith investigation into the Kennedy assassination. Now, after forty years, it is time that we pulled the plug on the Warren report's life-support system. The intolerable alternative is to remain imprisoned by the report, an interim fabrication that was intended only to satisfy immediate political needs and not to answer the questions of the "who" and "why" of Dallas.

1   Assembling the "Official Truth" of Dallas

The facts are often "developed" to support a predetermined outcome. In the perhaps apocryphal exhortation attributed to J. Edgar Hoover, "Fire that man! No. Get the facts. Then fire him!"
—Christopher Kerr (a veteran FBI agent), "Ruby Ridge Investigation Astray," *Washington Times,* September 15, 1995

For a year Texas lingered like a black cloud over President John F. Kennedy when he took time to strategize about his 1964 reelection campaign. According to the midterm election results the celebrated JFK mystique had virtually bottomed out in the Lone Star State. The faction-ridden Democratic Party had lost Dallas by more than sixty thousand votes. Cold War defense spending in the state had spawned a newly emergent corporate elite that propelled Texas, especially Dallas, in a rightward political direction. Texas right-wingers viewed Kennedy's handling of the Cuban missile crisis as a sellout to Castro's Cuba rather than a last-minute reprieve from nuclear disaster. After considering the 1962 election results, a disgruntled Kennedy told Texas governor John Connally, "I don't know why we do anything for Dallas." The equally glum Democratic governor retorted, "I'm telling you, they just murdered all of us." The following November President Kennedy made his fateful trip to Texas to try to heal his party's factional wounds and give a boost to his approval ratings, which were languishing under 40 percent in the polls.[1]

Air Force One touched down at Love Field, Dallas, at 11:40 A.M. (CST) on Friday, November 22, 1963. The weather, as if by executive order, had turned fair for the presidential party. The November sky was a sparkling blue, and the only hitch to a perfect day was a wind that was gusty at times. Dallas turned out to welcome the thirty-fifth president and to get a close look at the First Lady. This was the first time she had accompanied her husband on the campaign trail. As the motorcade made its way through a gauntlet of 250,000 cheering spectators, Mrs. Connally turned to the president and remarked, "Mr. President, you can't say that Dallas doesn't love you." The throng of well-wishers delighted the Kennedys, but for the Secret Service members detailed to protect Kennedy and Vice President Lyndon Baines Johnson, it was an unsettling assignment.

Just a month earlier U.S. Ambassador to the United Nations Adlai Stevenson had been physically accosted in Dallas by a mob of right-wing hecklers. Roy H. Kellerman, the Secret Service agent in charge of Kennedy's Texas outing, told his FBI debriefers a week after the assassination that security arrangements for the trip had been "the most stringent and thorough ever employed by the Secret Service . . . to an American city." However, Kennedy's decision to give politics priority over security made protection for the president and his party even more complicated for the critically under-manned Secret Service White House detail. The fastest and safest route for the presidential motorcade from Love Field to the Trade Mart, where the president was to speak, was only four miles, but this route was rejected for a longer (ten miles) and more circuitous drive through downtown Dallas to allow more people to see President and Mrs. Kennedy. Politics also persuaded JFK to order the Secret Service to remove the plastic bubble from the presidential limousine. The plastic dome was not actually bulletproof, but the Secret Service took some comfort in the notion that it might serve to deflect bullets fired at certain angles.[2]

The presidential limousine slowed almost to a stop in taking a sharp left-hand turn from Houston onto Elm Street, heading for the Dallas Trade Mart, where President Kennedy was scheduled to speak that afternoon. William Greer, a thirteen-year Secret Service veteran who was JFK's driver, recalled that the massive blue-black Lincoln Continental was just picking up speed when shots rang out. Sitting next to Greer, Kellerman turned to his left and heard Mrs. Kennedy cry out, "What are they doing to you?" Within seconds Secret Service agent Clint J. Hill jumped from the left running board of the backup car, which was "tight close at hand," and sprinted to the presidential limousine, narrowly escaping being run down and crushed by the backup car. Hill climbed onto the rear bumper of the Lincoln in time to push Jackie Kennedy, who had climbed out of her seat and was reaching to the right rear of the slippery trunk lid (it had rained earlier that day) for a piece of her husband's skull. Hill pulled Mrs. Kennedy back and forced her to the floor of the limousine. He recalled that she gasped, "They've shot his head off." Kellerman had already radioed the lead car: "We've been hit, lead us to a hospital immediately." As Greer floored the Lincoln, he noticed that Governor Connally had slumped over onto his wife's lap. Kellerman then made a quick check on "Lancer," the Secret Service's code name for JFK, heard him gasping and struggling for breath, and then faced front for the five-minute dash to the hospital, praying that it was not too late.[3]

Back in Washington at "Seat of Government,"[4] FBI director J. Edgar Hoover had just returned from lunch when a call came from J. Gordon Shanklin, the FBI special agent in charge (SAC) of the Dallas office, that the president had been shot.[5] Hoover spent the afternoon on the phone to Dallas and Washington officials. His first call was to the president's brother, Attorney General Robert F. Kennedy, who was holding a luncheon meeting at his Hickory Hill home in McLean, Virginia. Hoover informed the attorney general that his brother had been shot. Kennedy remembered this first of two Hoover calls as clipped, coldly official, and without a hint of sympathy.

What is historically important about the director's second call to Hickory Hill, which came at 4:01 P.M. (EST), was that the director told RFK that the assassin was in custody. "We," Hoover grandly announced, "had the man," overlooking the fact that it was the Dallas police who had arrested Lee Harvey Oswald.[6] Hoover also made calls to James J. Rowley, the head of the Secret Service, and Norbert A. Schlei, assistant attorney general, Office of Legal Counsel.

Cartha D. "Deke" DeLoach, the assistant director in charge of the Crime Records Division, the bureau's well-oiled and effective public relations machine, leaves us with the image of "the Director" as a natural leader able to rise to the occasion and surmount any crisis. DeLoach's Hoover faced national traumas with "a cold and analytical eye," transforming himself into a high-performance machine "spitting out orders . . . measuring his words with the precision of a jeweler."[7] Nevertheless, on the day of the assassination DeLoach's unerring, machinelike director unaccountably broke down. Before that shattering day was over, virtually every fact he reported to high government officers was wrong. He had shots coming from the fourth and fifth floors of the book depository building and a Winchester rifle as the murder weapon rather than the now familiar Mannlicher-Carcano allegedly owned by Oswald. He had Oswald shuffling back and forth to Castro's Cuba, when in fact Oswald's one effort to get to Cuba from Mexico in the fall of 1963 had proven futile. There is no FBI or any other government record made public that documents Oswald ever being in Cuba. Hoover told Rowley that the assassin had gunned down a Secret Service agent when it was actually a Dallas cop, J. D. Tippit, who was killed.[8]

Before the day was over, Hoover, despite his record of factual error, had envisioned the solution to the crime—Oswald, "a nut of the extreme pro-Castro crowd," was the lone assassin.[9] The director's tenuous grip on the facts was partly because the FBI's Dallas field office was in a state of wild confusion, relaying erroneous information back to Seat of Government. One FBI report had Vice President Johnson down with a heart attack and near death. FBI Washington headquarters' (FBIHQ) first information on the alleged assailant came from military intelligence in San Antonio and not from the Dallas field office. The 112th INCT Group's releases from its intelligence file on Oswald alerted FBIHQ that Oswald was an ex-marine, a defector to Russia, and married to a Russian woman. According to the military's Oswald file, when he had returned to the United States with his wife and child he had denounced capitalism and praised communism. The releases also noted that the suspect in the Kennedy assassination was on record with military intelligence in New Orleans for distributing "Hands off Cuba" literature in that city.[10]

Hoover was not happy that his agency was lagging behind army intelligence on the information curve. The FBI had a fairly extensive preassassination file on Lee Harvey Oswald, but the first reports on Oswald to cross the director's desk originated with military intelligence. Hoover imposed his own interpretation on the army's intelligence reports on Oswald that fitted neatly into his version of assassination history. Two hours later, while on the phone with Assistant Attorney General Schlei, Hoover gave the Justice Department official the benefit of his reading of U.S. history and the political leanings of presidential assassins. It was the director's considered opinion that such killers were always either "anarchists" or "communists." Later in the day the Dallas field office, after prodding from FBIHQ, started compiling biographical material from Oswald's FBI file and interview sessions at Dallas police headquarters with the alleged assailant. An FBI agent lifted some of this material from Oswald's wallet when the suspect left the interrogation room to relieve himself. One of the items receiving special attention was a "Fair Play for Cuba, New Orleans Chapter" membership card issued to L. H. Oswald by chapter president A. J. Hidell, which was assumed to be a fictitious name for Oswald himself. Later that same day FBIHQ had a chance to review the agency's preassassination file on Oswald. The salient biographical data in the file strengthened Hoover's conviction that Oswald was the assassin: In 1959 Oswald had told U.S. Embassy officials in Moscow that he was a "Marxist" and wished to renounce his American citizenship. In exchange for Soviet citizenship, he offered to tell the Soviets what he knew about the U.S. Marine Corps and his specialty as a radar operator. The ex-marine had distributed pro-Castro "Fair Play for Cuba" literature in New Orleans and, according to a "confidential informant," Oswald subscribed to *The Worker,* the East Coast organ of the American Communist Party.[11]

Before the day was over the biographical details about Oswald were fitted to Hoover's profile of a presidential assassin. That same day, the word went out from FBIHQ to the Dallas field office that Oswald was not just the principal suspect; he was the only suspect. A Richardson, Texas, law officer called the FBI Dallas office the afternoon of the assassination with the name of a possible suspect, Jimmy George Robinson, and other members of the white supremacist National States Rights Party because of their open hatred for President Kennedy. Before the office memo recording the call was serialized and filed—and it was filed the day of the assassination—it carried the handwritten notation: "Not necessary to cover as true suspect located." In short, within a few hours of the assassination, the FBI was not interested in any possible conspiracy or any suspect other than Lee Harvey Oswald. No action was taken on the lead from Richardson, although the call came in before the Dallas authorities charged Oswald with killing President Kennedy. He was not charged with JFK's murder until 11:25 P.M.

Given Hoover's administrative style, where the line of command from the director's office to all fifty-six field offices was uncompromisingly rigid, it is inconceivable that a supervisor or street agent in the Dallas office would have consigned this lead to archival oblivion without FBIHQ's direct approval. The dismissal of the Richardson alert indicated that the lines of communication from FBI Washington to FBI Dallas carried one directive: The Hoover bureau was interested only in Oswald with a smoking rifle and nothing else. By late morning of the following day, the FBI's New Orleans office, which held a considerable preassassination file on Oswald, was directed to drop all contacts with "informants and other sources with respect to bombing suspects, hate groups and known racial extremists." The New Orleans office was to concentrate only on "*Lee Harvey Oswald* or anything possible on his background; to obtain handwriting, records; all personnel and all Agents should be made to obtain this immediately."[12]

It is puzzling why Hoover felt compelled to rush to judgment when the situation called for cautious reticence until he could be more positive about any information he reported to official Washington. In large part the explanation may rest in the fact that Hoover was a captive of his own carefully cultivated public image of supranational hero above politics, and in this moment of national confusion and profound distress he feared that his and the FBI's reputation would suffer unless there was a quick resolution of the crisis. A related concern growing out of Hoover's tireless public relations campaign of FBI omniscience and infallibility in combating crime and political subversion and rooting out conspiracies was that the public might blame the FBI for failing to prevent JFK's assassination. If Oswald was part of a Communist conspiracy, and nothing that Hoover learned about him that day and the following week argued against that possibility, then the FBI had been caught unawares. Part of the storied reputation of the Hoover bureau during the height of the Cold War was its celebrated sleepless vigilance in protecting the nation by thwarting the nefarious domestic plots of the Red Menace at every turn. But even a worshipful public could not expect Hoover to anticipate and frustrate the sick fantasies of a lone nut. The director's rush to judgment in identifying Oswald as the lone assassin would preserve the Hoover legend built on his FBI's ability to penetrate any conspiracy.

Long before the nation was neck deep in the media age, the Hoover FBI public relations machine operated under the assumption that image always triumphed over reality. Hoover's influence derived from his iconic hold on the popular imagination, and Kennedy's murder posed an immediate threat to the director's "nation savior" image. Hoover received hundreds of letters from deeply distraught Americans. Most craved assurance that the government was not going to hell in a handbasket. Others were bitterly angry and wanted to know how the government, especially the vaunted FBI, could have allowed the head of state to be brutally gunned down in broad daylight.

Most of the letters could have been filed in the "Take care of yourself. We need you in America" category.

But there were also many letters blaming the FBI for failing to prevent Kennedy's foul murder and, unfairly, compounding this dereliction by not keeping the alleged assassin alive so he could be brought to trial. A letter from a woman in Irvington, New Jersey, telling the director, "The FBI has lost the confidence of the nation" was not an isolated reaction. A man from Whitehall, Michigan, asked Hoover, "How could the FBI have goofed" by failing to have a man with Oswald's record under "surveillance until President Kennedy was safely on his plane back to Washington?" A telegram from an outraged citizen from Santa Monica, California, unloaded on the director: "What were you doing today playing golf or looking for Communists." An Allentown, Pennsylvania, resident asserted that if Hoover "was doing his job the President wouldn't be dead today." Some telegrams demanded that Hoover resign immediately. A few were downright nasty. A telegram from the American heartland, Wichita, Kansas, upbraided the sixty-eight-year-old director: "Now old man do you realize the danger always was . . . [that] this right wing thing was every bit as dangerous as the Communists you have talked so profitably about. Now let's see your people get cracking or you get out and let another man in."[13]

National syndicated columnist Drew Pearson, who spent more time at the top of Hoover's "son-of-a-bitch list" than most other media types, wrote a column blaming both the Secret Service and the FBI for "squabbling over jurisdiction and headlines" and leaving the protection of the president to fall between the cracks. DeLoach's immediate instinct was to unleash the FBI's "news media friends" to "take Pearson apart." Uncharacteristically, Hoover restrained his assistant director, confessing, "Unfortunately we are not in a position to completely contradict Pearson." Hoover's hesitation to launch a counterstrike against the offending columnist was not rooted in any debilitating or paralyzing reaction from JFK's brutal slaying. The FBI director was fearful that the FBI, especially the Dallas office, had failed to alert the Secret Service to potential threats in Dallas to President Kennedy, in particular by failing to provide the Secret Service with the information from the FBI's preassassination file on Lee Harvey Oswald.[14]

The day of the assassination, as soon as Hoover and Associate Director Clyde Tolson had an opportunity to review Oswald's preassassination file, they knew the FBI had a monumental problem. Oswald's Dallas field office files carried the slug line "Internal Security—R (Russian)—Cuba case." These early incomplete and raw files revealed that the only suspect in the JFK assassination case was a defector to the Soviet Union; he had threatened to turn over military secrets to his Soviet hosts in exchange for citizenship;

he was a self-declared Marxist; and after his return to the United States in 1962, Oswald had started a Fair Play for Cuba Committee (FPCC), a pro-Castro organization, in New Orleans. These salient facts prompted the director and his top executive officer to ask why Oswald was not on the bureau's "Security Index." Had Oswald been indexed as a security threat the Secret Service would have been alerted and he would have been placed on an "alert list" and denied any access to President Kennedy when he visited Dallas. Hoover and Tolson knew immediately that the FBI was involved in an intelligence failure that had had history-altering consequences. On November 23, Hoover and Tolson met with Assistant Director James H. Gale, the head of the bureau's Inspection Division. Hoover tasked Gale with conducting a secret, in-house investigation to assign responsibility to bureau personnel— from assistant directors to street agents—for letting Oswald slip through the cracks and possibly exposing Hoover's FBI to irreparable damage.[15]

Hoover's nightmare was that this dereliction of responsibility might become known to the public and compromise the FBI's public image. The fastest way the FBI could regain the nation's confidence was to wrap up the case in a tidy, plausible package and present it to the American people as quickly as possible. Hoover's interest in rapidly settling the dust of Dallas was shared by the new occupant in the White House, Lyndon B. Johnson.

As mentioned earlier, the handwritten note regarding the call from Richardson, Texas, could mean only that the director had decided it was in the bureau's interest to identify Oswald as the assassin; all that remained was for the FBI to make its case. No one else in the highly centralized and autocratic Hoover bureau would have dared limit the investigation to the twenty-four-year-old ex-marine and depository employee without Hoover's approval. Hoover responded to the assassination by rushing to judgment to protect the FBI's image and maintain his power. It was the task of the FBI to build the case against Oswald so that the predetermined conclusion decided upon over the weekend would become the "official truth" of the Kennedy assassination.

Although the murder of a president was not a federal crime in 1963, the FBI moved in quickly to take over the investigation. Months after Kennedy's assassination, Hoover boasted to the author William Manchester, who was writing a book on the assassination, that the FBI had seized the case without jurisdiction.[16] With the FBI controlling the investigation, the only leads regarded as promising were those that pointed to Oswald as the lone assassin. While FBI field offices around the country were filing reports under the heading "Threats Against the Life of President Kennedy and Others," the Dallas office, the office of origin, bore the brunt of building the case against the suspect in custody. Many of the fifty-odd names on the FBI "Threats" list were from Texas, but Jimmy George Robinson's name was not on that list.[17]

On December 12, 1963, all of the other fifty-six FBI field offices were brought in line with the reporting procedures already in place with the Dallas office. That is, FBI Washington notified all agents not to investigate the case and to restrict all communications "to information pertaining to him [Oswald] and to allegations that a person or group had a specific connection with him in the assassination." An FBI teletype from FBIHQ sent to all fifty-six state offices stated, "Oswald conclusively established as assassin of President Kennedy." The memo itemized a list of questions related solely to Jack Ruby, Oswald's assassin, that still needed to be investigated. It was clear that Hoover harbored suspicions about Ruby and whether he had had assistance from some Dallas police officers to gain access to Oswald in the basement of the Dallas Police Department.

Ruby was one of the FBI's "tender spots" in the investigation because the Dallas nightclub owner had been a provisional criminal informant (PCI) for the Dallas FBI for at least seven months back in 1959. FBI Washington's instructions to all the field offices to limit the investigation to Oswald came just three days after the Warren Commission, President Johnson's appointed blue-ribbon commission, received the FBI's report on the assassination. Limiting the investigation from the outset to the alleged lone assassin would have consequences: All the evidence allowed to come forward in the case—ballistics, fingerprints and palm prints, fiber analysis, and other technical data—would be slanted and misrepresented to establish that Oswald, and only Oswald, fired the shots that killed Kennedy and wounded Connally.[18]

Hoover's assertion to Manchester that the FBI seized the case without jurisdiction was no idle boast. Without waiting for instructions from the new president, the director immediately launched his agents into the investigation. FBI agents were interrogating Oswald less than two hours after the commission of the crime, even before Lyndon B. Johnson, the newly sworn-in president, was back in the nation's capital. The FBI director ordered about 150 agents to take up the case and begin to immediately question witnesses and prepare reports from the field and back at Seat of Government.[19] All witnesses were warned to maintain strict silence, which precluded any variation of what these witnesses said or could have said from what the FBI chose to represent as their sworn statements. The upshot of this pattern of control of the investigation was so immediate and thorough that it even forestalled the Secret Service, which did have jurisdiction because it was vested with the responsibility for the president's security and protection.

For instance, the day following the assassination the Secret Service, having traced the alleged murder weapon to the seller, Klein's Sporting Goods Company, sent agents to that company's Chicago office. However, Klein's officials refused to share any information with the Secret Service even after they were informed that the agency had primary jurisdiction in the case. It was not until the agent in charge exerted great pressure on William J. Waldman, the company's senior vice president, that he finally was persuaded to be forthcoming. In his report, the agent noted that the FBI had already met with Waldman and that the shaken executive officer "kept reiterating" that the FBI had impressed upon him "not to discuss this investigation with *anyone*" (emphasis in the original report). As a result of stellar investigative techniques or an informant, the FBI had traced Oswald's Mannlicher-Carcano, the alleged assassination weapon, to Klein's the day of the assassination. By 10 P.M. on the night of the assassination, FBI agents had located the sporting-goods store's officials and ordered them to return to their place of business and make available the company's records. A team of FBI agents went through the records and did not leave until 5 o'clock the next morning.[20]

Two weeks after the assassination the FBI discovered that Oswald, the alleged loner charged with Kennedy's murder, had had help running his bogus New Orleans chapter of the pro-Castro FPCC. On May 29, 1963, a white "husky type" male with the "appearance of a laborer" and without a Cuban accent using the name "Osborne," as described by Douglas Jones, the proprietor, had placed an order with the Jones Printing Company for hundreds of "Hands off Cuba" handbills. That person with a "husky" build was clearly not Oswald. The Jones Printing Company was located opposite the side entrance to the William B. Reily Coffee Company, where Oswald worked. A week later the same person picked up the handbills and paid off the balance of the bill in cash. When the FBI questioned Jones and Myra Silver, his secretary, neither one could identify the picture of Oswald as the man who had ordered the handbills. The FBI had to tightly contain this information. If it became known outside the Hoover agency that Oswald, the FBI's only suspect in the assassination, had an accomplice in New Orleans, the news might ignite further speculation that President Kennedy had been a victim of a conspiracy.

On December 6, 1963, blinking red lights went off at FBIHQ when it was learned that the Secret Service was looking into the matter of Oswald's FPCC handbills. FBI New Orleans alerted Joseph A. Sizoo, the assistant to William C. Sullivan, the assistant director of the Domestic Intelligence Division, that a New Orleans Secret Service agent, John Rice, the Service's agent in charge of the New Orleans office, had requested the identity of the company where Oswald had his FPCC handbills printed. FBI Washington immediately contacted the FBI's liaison with James J. Rowley to request that Rowley have his agent stand down. That same day, December 12, Rice received instructions from Secret Service headquarters in Washington to drop his investigation into the matter. He was informed, in effect, that he was poaching in an area of the investigation that was exclusively the FBI's domain. Rice was clearly dumbfounded. That same day he had a phone conversation with the SAC of the FBI's New Orleans office in which he said that he thought his agency and the FBI had a common interest in trying to determine whether the assassination had been the result of a conspiracy that "might extend" to President Johnson, whose protection was the Secret Service's responsibility. Rice was simply not aware that by December 6, 1963, the FBI was already leaking to the press its conclusions that Oswald was the lone assassin and there was no conspiracy, either domestic or foreign.[21]

On the Monday after the assassination Charles Leslie Bronson, a metallurgist and chief engineer with the Varel Manufacturing Co. in Dallas, offered the Dallas FBI copies of a motion-picture film and stills he had taken at the time of the assassination. Bronson was one of the thousands of spectators who filmed the president's visit that day. He was on Houston Street experimenting with his new 8-millimeter Keystone Olympic K-35 camera so as to be ready when the presidential motorcade passed. About six minutes before the presidential limousine passed under the Texas School Book Depository (TSBD) building, Bronson, intending to try out his new telephoto lens, actually panned the area with his wide-angle lens and captured on film the sixth floor of the southeast corner of the TSBD, showing the window where all the shots allegedly originated. Although the movie was a little underexposed, Bronson's was one of only two known films of that window just minutes before the shooting started. He was also filming the motorcade at the exact moment that the fatal shot struck Kennedy.

The Bronson film conclusively proved that the alleged sniper's window was the only open window in the southeast corner of the TSBD at 12:24 P.M. (CST). Bronson had the film developed by the Eastman Kodak Company in Dallas and sent the 8-mm Kodachrome film and 35-mm Leica colored slides with a letter to the Dallas FBI. His letter noted that the film showed the instant President Kennedy was assassinated. Bronson also said he was certain that the film showed the TSBD and the window where the alleged shots originated. Dallas FBI agents Milton D. Newsom and Emory E. Horton reviewed the film and the slides and filed a report that stated, "These films failed to show the building from which the shots were fired. Film did depict the President's car at the time shots were fired; however, the pictures were not sufficiently clear for identification purposes. One of the 35 mm color slides," Newsom's report continued, depicted "a female wearing a brown coat taking pictures from an angle, which would have, undoubtedly included Texas School Book Depository in the background of her pictures." Newsom wrote that "her pictures were taken just as the President was shot" and went on to note, "Approximately five other individuals in the photo were taking pictures at the time."[22]

FBI Dallas never sent the Bronson film and slides to the Washington headquarters. In fact, it treated the film and slides like poisonous snakes.

Despite this potentially valuable information, Dallas SAC even declined free copies of Bronson's slides and film. The FBI returned the slides and film to Bronson. Either FBI Dallas never bothered to let FBIHQ know they existed or the field office received instructions from headquarters not to send them on. Since they were never part of the FBI's investigative record, Bronson's film and slides remained unknown to the Warren Commission and consequently played no part in its investigation into the Kennedy assassination.[23]

It was not until 1978 that the public became aware of Bronson's film and slides. Kennedy assassination researcher Harold Weisberg used the Freedom of Information Act to force the FBI to release the Dallas field office's assassination files. The release included Newsom's report on Bronson's film and slides, a decade and a half after the assassination. The film ignited a flare-up of attention in the Dallas press, the very kind of exposure that the FBI had successfully avoided in 1963. Questions were raised about why this important photographic evidence had not been turned over to the Warren Commission. The *Dallas Morning News* ran four full pages about Bronson; three of the pages were devoted to the reproduction of his stills and frames. Contradicting Newsom, the *News* reported, "Bronson's still photographs of the motorcade were crisp and clear." Bronson's film showed President Kennedy at the moment that he was fatally struck in the head. The slides were clear enough to reveal that there had been nobody at the sixth-floor window seconds before the assassination. There were ninety-two frames of that window—the alleged "sniper's nest"—alone![24]

Clearly, Bronson's film and stills were of immense evidentiary value. Bronson's name should have been paired with that of Abraham Zapruder for capturing on film "the crime of the century." His images showed when JFK was hit and his position in relation to others in the presidential limousine. Dozens of witnesses could be identified in his films who should have been questioned by the authorities. In any genuine investigation Bronson's film and stills would have been treated as crucial material evidence. Instead, the FBI clearly resorted to outright subterfuge in concealing the Bronson film. Agent Newsom's deliberate misrepresentation of the evidentiary value of the film is additional confirmation that the Dallas office knew it was expected to put Oswald in the frame as the lone assassin, to the point of excluding any evidence that pointed in another direction. By Monday, three days after Kennedy was cut down and a day after Oswald was assassinated, Shanklin and the Dallas office probably needed no directive from FBIHQ to suppress any evidence that might exculpate Oswald.[25]

President Lyndon Johnson's weekend after the assassination demanded every waking minute of his time. The circumstances of his ascendancy and the attendant responsibility to ease a grieving nation over the transition would have laid low most mortals. Johnson proved he was more than ready to take on the burdens of the office as he wasted little time in trying to heal the wound of Dallas, taking charge with such consummate skill that even his detractors would come to agree that this was his finest hour. Attention had to be given to settling into the White House; there were endless outreach phone calls to prominent national politicians to enlist their help; and a delegation of state officials from Texas was squeezed into an already overscheduled Sunday, the day before the nation officially mourned its martyred president and tried to make peace with the tragedy in Dallas.[26]

That same weekend Johnson, Hoover, and Deputy Attorney General Nicholas deB. Katzenbach settled upon the "official truth" of the assassination, the politically accepted version fabricated for public consumption. Johnson spoke to Hoover on Saturday morning and the director, anxious to impress the new president, his friend and longtime Washington neighbor, summarized the FBI's case against Oswald. Hoover's phone briefing was disjointed, and his grasp of the facts had not improved over the previous day, but he was candid in admitting that the evidence against Oswald was "not very, very strong."[27] On Sunday, November 24, the man charged with JFK's assassination was shot and killed in the basement of the Dallas police department by Jack Ruby, a local nightclub owner. A nation already reeling from Friday's events in Dallas was shocked anew by Oswald's assassination, which was viewed on public television by millions of Americans. The murder of the alleged assassin of President Kennedy was even more surreal because it happened on police premises while the suspect was surrounded by more than seventy of Dallas's finest. Oswald's death, of course, meant that there would be no trial. The twenty-four-year-old ex-marine, father of two young daughters, would not have his day in court, where the evidence against him could be cross-examined by a determined and forceful defense team.

This startling and unanticipated turn of events had an immediate impact in Washington. On Sunday evening there were a series of short phone conversations involving Johnson, presidential aide Bill Moyers, Hoover, and Katzenbach. Moyers called Johnson at 8:50 P.M., and they spoke for five minutes. The president immediately rang up Hoover, and after a brief conversation LBJ called Katzenbach. The president formally assigned the FBI to take over the investigation into Kennedy's assassination. Johnson wanted Hoover to move quickly on the FBI's report. He approved Hoover's idea of the report "showing the evidence conclusively tying Oswald in as the assailant of President Kennedy," according to the reporting FBI official, Inspector James R. Malley, "along the lines we previously discussed." LBJ also wanted a second report on the Ruby killing of Oswald. LBJ's phone conversation with the director lasted only two minutes.

The president was in a monumental hurry. He wanted the report finished and delivered to the Justice Department by Tuesday, November 26, the day after the one LBJ had set aside as "a national day of mourning." He also sought to inflict on Robert Kennedy the wrenching task of reviewing the FBI's evidence in the assassination of his own brother.[28] Having the attorney general release the report would give the FBI's conclusions an authenticity that would go a long way toward silencing the rumors of conspiracy, including the loose talk and zany allegations that Johnson himself was somehow involved. As a southerner in the 1960s with little prospect of reaching the presidency on his own merits, compounded by the fact that JFK had been killed in his home state, this gifted but accidental president was deeply tormented by these allegations. If his actions were insensitive and unforgivable, they were at least understandable. Insisting that Robert Kennedy release the FBI report would take the political heat off the White House. That Attorney General Kennedy had little or no control over Hoover even on his good days and knew little or nothing more about what had happened in Dallas than the rest of the country did not deter Johnson, who simply wanted to trade on the Kennedy name.

Hoover, according to Malley's record of the conversation, noted that the Tuesday deadline "would be a burden," but he told Johnson he would do his best. It's useful to recall that the aging director was only two years from mandatory retirement. If FBIHQ could quickly throw together a politically safe report on the Kennedy assassination, a grateful LBJ might waive federal guidelines and extend Hoover's directorship beyond the compulsory retirement age. On Tuesday, the day after Kennedy's funeral, Hoover fired off a memo to the General Investigative Division saying, "Wrap up investigation; seems to me we have the basic facts now." Hoover wanted the report on Oswald and Ruby "completed here at Seat of Government" by November 29, a week after the assassination, even though he knew the agency's case against Oswald was full of loose ends. For example, on the day after the assassination Hoover learned from the Dallas office that the paraffin test on Oswald's right cheek showed no traces of nitrates. Paraffin testing was the standard forensic procedure in the 1960s to determine whether a suspect had handled or fired a weapon.[29]

Before the weekend was over FBIHQ dispatched Inspector James R. Malley of the General Investigative Division along with forty-nine agents and forty support personnel to Dallas. Malley was Hoover's man on the ground to supervise the rush job on the FBI report LBJ needed to put the public mind at ease. The lone-assassin explanation for the tragedy of Dallas was the quickest and surest way to calm the waters and dissipate all the rumors and conjectures of conspiracy with possible foreign policy implications. With Oswald's death, immediate political considerations brushed aside any chance for a good-faith investigation into the true reality of the Kennedy assassination. On Tuesday, November 26, Alan H. Belmont, the professionally smooth and savvy assistant to the director, the number three man in the Hoover bureau, perfectly caught the need of the moment. Belmont noted, "This report is to settle the dust, in so far as Oswald and his activities are concerned, both from the standpoint that he is the man who assassinated the President, and relative to Oswald himself and his activities and background, et cetera."[30]

Robert Kennedy was not absent from Washington over the weekend, but all his attention and energies were, understandably, concentrated on trying to provide comfort and solace to the grieving family. Katzenbach was his stand-in at Justice and would continue as "very nearly acting Attorney General" in all matters relating to the government's handling of the Kennedy assassination, from which the attorney general remained detached. Years later, when testifying before the House Select Committee on Assassinations, Katzenbach recalled that the president's murder had left Bobby prostrate. His "world just came apart . . . with that shot."[31]

On Sunday afternoon, November 24, the dean of the Yale Law School, Eugene Victor Rostow, called Bill Moyers, in part because he was worried about Katzenbach. Rostow told the presidential aide that he had spoken three times that day with Katzenbach, who seemed unfocused and "so groggy" that Rostow thought Moyers should know. The nightmare of JFK's violent death compounded by the assassination of his alleged assailant had taken its toll on Katzenbach. A Robert Kennedy loyalist, Katzenbach was concerned after Dallas about restoring the U.S. image as a beacon to the Free World of a nation enjoying the blessings of orderly government under the rule of law. The horror of Dallas projected that image through a glass darkly, fostering a perception at home and abroad that the United States was the biggest banana republic on the planet. Katzenbach had reason to feel burdened and uneasy about containing the impact of Dallas on the public mind. Most of the flood of mail on the assassination coming into Justice fell into the conspiracy camp. There was almost complete agreement that Oswald was not acting alone, whether the writer opted for a conspiracy from the right or the left. The most frequently mentioned suspects for the role of likely masterminds were Fidel Castro, H. L. Hunt, Jimmy Hoffa, General Edwin A. Walker, and Madame Nhu.[32]

When Oswald in turn was murdered that nightmarish weekend, the world reaction hit a ten on the conspiracy-theory meter. As might have been expected, Oswald's televised execution fueled the communist world press's campaign attributing President Kennedy's assassination to a rightist conspiracy. This was matched by a wave of apprehension and question-raising in the free media. Stockholm radio observed that those responsible for Oswald's safety and solving the assassination "appear, to say the least, in a strange and even negative light." America's southern border neighbor, Mexico, speaking through the government-controlled paper, the *Daily Excelsior,* sharply commented, "Was there fear that Oswald would talk and compromise persons or institutions interested in the death of the political chief of the most powerful country on earth?" Oswald's killing received heavy front-page coverage with large pictures of the actual shooting in the London press. The *Guardian* opined, "This grotesque episode is piling more confusion on the shame of Dallas." The *Daily Herald* wrote, "Lynch law has followed assassination. The corruption of this high tragedy by the personal vengeance of a Dallas club owner has brought total fantasy to the American scene." Chile's *El Mercurio* hinted that Oswald's murder "involved more than a man taking justice into his own hand." The two largest Paris evening papers raised the question of whether Oswald's death was part of a larger conspiracy and "whether he was killed to keep him from talking."[33]

It was right after his Sunday-night phone "discussion with the Director," notably after Oswald's own assassination, that Katzenbach composed in longhand his memorandum to President Johnson through Moyers. Hoover received a copy of the memo the next day. The Katzenbach memo was the direct outgrowth of the conversations among the three men over the weekend. It laid out what Johnson, Hoover, and Katzenbach had settled on as the "facts" of Dallas that they deemed safe for the ordinary understanding of the American people. The most salient points in the administration's contest for the "hearts and minds" of a nation plunged into inconsolable grief and numbing despair were the memo's points 1 and 3:

> The public must be satisfied that Oswald was the assassin; that he did not
> have confederates who are still at large, and that the evidence was such that he
> would have been convicted at trial.

> I think this objective may be satisfied by making public as soon as possible a
> complete and thorough FBI report on Oswald and the assassination.

Katzenbach went on to lash out at the Dallas police for issuing statements "on the Communist conspiracy theory" and holding the nation up to the world in the "image of the Dallas police," who failed to protect the only suspect in the case from being murdered while in their custody. He thought that matters could be set right on the strength of the FBI report on the assassination, given the reputation the Hoover agency enjoyed with the American public. The flood of rumors and speculations in the press and telegrams sent to the Justice Department asserting that the crime was too complicated for one man and that Oswald must have had accomplices had Katzenbach on edge. He appointed a departmental task force to prepare counterarguments to these allegations.[34]

President Johnson was also counting on the FBI report to "settle the dust" of Dallas so he could move forward with his own ambitious presidential programs. Along with the FBI report was the pending investigation by the Texas authorities. Legally, Kennedy's murder was not a federal crime, so it was incumbent on the Texas criminal system to treat the assassination as a homicide in Dallas County. Johnson met with the Texas attorney general, Waggoner Carr, Lieutenant Governor Preston Smith, and other state dignitaries on Sunday for a short picture-taking session. As Texas attorney general, Carr would head a state court of inquiry into the Kennedy and Oswald murders. Later that same day Johnson had Carr travel to the White House, and, according to syndicated columnist Joseph Alsop, LBJ spent an hour and a half explaining to the attorney general what he expected from the Texas investigation. It is almost certain that LBJ resorted to the "arts of the Hill"— Johnson's legendary powers of persuasion—to convince his fellow Texan that the FBI had a rock-solid case against Oswald and that the president was counting on Carr's full cooperation in the investigation. It's hard to resist the speculation that LBJ's idea of "cooperation" was couched in the sweet reasonableness of the proposition that all that was expected of the Texas inquiry was simply to endorse the findings of the upcoming FBI report.[35]

By Tuesday, the "not very, very strong" case against Oswald the day before his murder was, according to Assistant Director Courtney A. Evans, FBI liaison with the Justice Department, conclusive, "beyond any doubt showing Oswald was the man who killed President Kennedy." Associate Director Clyde Tolson, the director's alter ego and the number two man in the FBI hierarchy, was satisfied that they had "the basic facts" and approved sending the report over to the Justice Department. Hoover spoke to presidential aide Walter Jenkins on Monday and assured Jenkins that the report would be laid out in such convincing detail and with exhibits that "it would speak for itself." Hoover set Wednesday, November 27, as the date on which the report could be sent to Justice or the White House. But FBI executive officers closer to the investigation convincingly argued for more time until the investigation into Oswald's possible links with either the American Communist Party or pro-Castro organizations could be thoroughly checked out.[36]

Katzenbach became frantic when he learned that the FBI report would not be ready by Wednesday as promised because of the unanticipated fast-moving developments in the case. For the acting attorney general, "time was of the essence." He was counting on Hoover's credibility to put to rest all the rumors and speculations in the U.S. and world press that Kennedy's death was the result of a conspiracy. Katzenbach had the fixed opinion that Hoover's great prestige would assure the American public that the facts of the assassination sent out over his name were accurate. He and the president were both counting on a statement from Hoover to discourage early stirrings in Congress and the press calling for a presidential commission to investigate the crime.

Two days after the assassination, Katzenbach urged Assistant Director DeLoach to put out a public statement saying, "We are now persuaded that Oswald killed the President; however, the investigation by the Department of Justice and the FBI is continuing." For the next week Katzenbach kept up a steady drumbeat of coaxing and pleading to get Hoover to release a statement that Oswald was the lone assassin, and there was no foreign or domestic conspiracy. The director adamantly refused to release any statement. The bureau's policy, Hoover stoutly asserted, would be to turn over the report to Justice when it was completed and adhere to an official policy of "no comment." Unofficially, however, Hoover authorized the leaking of the report's conclusions to "friendly" journalists before the report was released to the White House and the Justice Department. Coordinating his efforts with the FBI, Katzenbach arranged for Justice's Criminal Division to prepare a tentative outline of the Kennedy assassination. The outline was on his desk on Wednesday, November 27, and the only suspect named in the five-page summary outline was Lee Harvey Oswald.[37]

This assertion of rock-hard certitude on the part of the FBI and the Justice Department about Oswald as the lone assailant and no conspiracy was in defiance of the early disclosed evidence in the case and fast-breaking developments originating with U.S. government sources in Mexico City. On Monday, November 25, the White House received a cablegram from Mexico City claiming that JFK was the victim of a Red plot. The sources of this assertion were highly placed government officers, so it could not be dismissed as wild rumors and assassination-generated hysteria. The Monday telegram was only the first of a series of messages from the U.S. ambassador in Mexico and the CIA's Mexico City station chief that peppered the upper reaches of the executive branch over the next several days. Ambassador Thomas C. Mann reported to the White House, FBI, and Justice Department that he and the CIA station chief, Winston ("Win") Scott, had uncovered evidence that Castro, with possible KGB complicity, had paid Oswald to assassinate President Kennedy. Johnson was already aware of possible foreign entanglements in the assassination. On Sunday, Hoover had provided him with a summary of the FBI's investigation and background information on Oswald. Citing CIA sources, Hoover noted that someone impersonating Oswald had been in contact with the Soviet embassy in Mexico City at the time Oswald was allegedly visiting Mexico's capital, just weeks before Kennedy was murdered. The implications of these disclosures shook the foundations of the Washington establishment.[38]

On Monday, November 25, Hoover sent a "top secret" cablegram to the FBI legal attaché in Mexico City, Clark Anderson, to explore all aspects of any "false Oswald" machinations and "possible Russian direction assassination." The unanticipated Mexico City allegations thwarted earlier plans to have the FBI report in the president's hands by Wednesday. Instead, on Wednesday Hoover's and Katzenbach's top priority was to "settle the dust" in Mexico City as quickly as possible. The acting attorney general suggested that the bureau send an agent to Mexico City "with all the facts." For Katzenbach the "facts" was code for instructing the ambassador and the CIA station chief that the White House and the FBI were convinced that Oswald was the assassin and that he had acted alone. On Tuesday, Hoover spoke with CIA Director John McCone and told him what the FBI report concluded and the areas it would cover. The following day the director ordered Agent Laurence Keenan, a Spanish-speaking supervisor from the Domestic Intelligence Division, to leave that evening for Mexico City, "by Air Force," Hoover added, "if he can get there quicker." Keenan's task was to get Mann and Win Scott on message, to alert them to the "facts" of the case: that the White House and the FBI were convinced of Oswald's guilt and that there had been no conspiracy. To assure that the ambassador and the CIA station chief were clear about Washington's instructions, Keenan brought with him two FBI "dossiers," one an eleven-page memorandum with exhibits setting out the "official" case against Oswald and the other dealing with Jack Ruby's assassination of the president's assailant.[39]

President Johnson's weekend push for a speedy and contained investigation ran into a wall of opposition from official and unofficial Washington. Bobby Kennedy loyalists in the Justice Department were engaged in behind-the-scenes lobbying against the White House's plan to have the attorney general rubber-stamp the FBI report. Other Washington insiders had informally caucused over the weekend to derail LBJ's plans in favor of a broader investigation. On Monday, November 25, the *New York Times* carried a column by James "Scotty" Reston calling for a "Presidential or some other objective commission" rather than leaving the investigation solely in the hands of the FBI and the Dallas police. Johnson's ire was piqued by a tip that the *Washington Post* was preparing an editorial calling for a blue-ribbon committee to evaluate the anticipated FBI report.[40]

That Monday morning Johnson called Hoover to rail against the lobbying from Justice and the anticipated *Post* editorial. LBJ did not want to give an inch. He told Hoover that he wanted to go ahead with "your suggestion" about submitting "a full report to the Attorney General" and then make it available to the public in whatever form Hoover deemed desirable. He thought a blue-ribbon commission was a flat-out bad idea because a presidential commission would put the investigation right into the White House. He continued to unload on the director, who had remained silent while the president vented: "Now we can't be checking up on every shooting scrape in the country." Johnson, of course, was preaching to the choir, and the director managed to break into his rant with the interjection: "It's a regular circus then." Johnson finally got to the purpose of his call. He wanted Hoover to try to kill the *Post* editorial before it appeared in the Tuesday edition. Hoover agreed to try but could guarantee nothing since he had little influence with the paper. The director told Johnson he rarely read the *Post* because "I view it like *The Daily Worker.*"[41]

After getting off the phone with the White House, Hoover assigned Deke DeLoach to lobby the *Washington Post.* During Hoover's directorship the Crime Records Division, currently headed by DeLoach, had cultivated "friendly" or "cooperative" relations with over three hundred newspaper reporters, commentators, and television news investigators. These media sources could usually be counted upon to get the "FBI story" out to the public. DeLoach called Al Friendly, the vice president and managing editor of the *Post,* to explain Hoover's "grave concern" about the paper going ahead with an editorial advocating a presidential commission. It was the director's view, DeLoach told Friendly, that such an editorial at this time would "muddy the waters" and create more confusion and hysteria. Friendly proved a congenial and sympathetic listener and, according to DeLoach, agreed to talk to Russ Wiggins, who was in charge of the paper's editorial page, and try to get him to kill the editorial. But Friendly had some advice he wanted DeLoach to take back to Hoover. He struck the same note that had rung so clearly in Scotty Reston's piece in that day's *New York Times:* He told DeLoach that unless some independent group of prominent public figures endorsed the FBI report, other than just the attorney general and that "boob" Waggoner Carr, Texas's attorney general, all the dark suspicions about Dallas might never dissipate. When Katzenbach learned of this behind-the-scenes maneuvering, he offered to call Wiggins. Though he had originally supported the idea of a presidential commission, Katzenbach's first priority was to stay on good terms with the Hoover agency. He called Wiggins and urged him to leave it up to the Justice Department to get "all the facts" out to the American people. Confronted by the White House, the FBI, and the acting attorney general, Wiggins pulled the editorial. Hoover called Walter Jenkins to tell him the good news.[42]

Hoover dug in his heels and refused to release the FBI report until "all allegations and angles" were thoroughly investigated, despite pressure from the White House and Katzenbach at Justice. This incessant importuning for a release of the report understandably irritated Hoover, who responded to one of Katzenbach's requests for a specific date by scrawling on a memo, "If they will leave us alone we will meet our responsibilities." Finally, on December 5, 1963, Assistant Director Evans turned over to Katzenbach the FBI's report on the JFK assassination. Katzenbach spent that evening going over the report, and the next day he called Alan Belmont, the bureau's executive officer in charge of the investigation, and pronounced the report "spectacular." Katzenbach recommended no changes in the document and got clearance from Belmont to send copies to "high officials of CIA, State, Secret Service."[43] Katzenbach's unbounded enthusiasm derived from the document's two basic conclusions: that Oswald had killed the president and that he had acted alone. This satisfied the "Katzenbach imperative"—or what more accurately can be described as tantamount to national policy—laid out in his November 25, 1963, memo to Bill Moyers.[44]

When Hoover told Walter Jenkins that the report would speak for itself he was being prophetic, but in a manner he never intended. The report was largely a vilification of Oswald. It spent fewer than sixty words describing the assassination. Although this section of the report was, to put it charitably, paper thin, the FBI concluded that three shots had been fired, two of the shots had struck President Kennedy, and a separate third shot had wounded Governor Connally. The FBI's three-shots scenario was consistent with the three rifle shells found on the sixth floor of the book depository building. The report ignored the missile that struck a curbstone and wounded a bystander, James T. Tague. The FBI suppressed the Tague bullet because having to account for a fourth shot elevated the possibility that there had been at least two gunmen at Dealey Plaza to a near certainty. The FBI was aware of the curbstone shot the day of the assassination. Tague reported it to the police, and photographs of the curbstone clearly revealed that a bullet had struck the concrete with enough force to spray fragments, one of which struck Tague in the face.[45]

Were Kennedy's wounds consistent with all the shots coming from above and behind the motorcade? The report made no effort to make this case. It even failed to describe all of Kennedy's wounds or to give the cause of death. There is not a word in the report about Governor Connally's wounds. The heading "Autopsy" or "Autopsy Report" did not even appear in the document's index because FBIHQ never requested a copy of the official autopsy report and submitted its "basic facts" about the assassination without even a cursory reading of the quintessential official medical evidence. FBI Washington turned down the Secret Service's offer of the autopsy protocol, X-rays, and medical photographs. Assistant Director Alex Rosen of the FBI's General Investigative Division wrote Belmont that "it does not appear that we shall have need for this material." It was not until two weeks after the FBI submitted its report (CD 1) to LBJ's blue-ribbon commission formed to investigate the crime that the FBI liaison officer with the Secret Service, Orrin Bartlett, requested a copy of the autopsy report from his Secret Service counterpart.[46]

The X-rays and autopsy pictures left Bethesda Naval Hospital with the Secret Service the night of the autopsy. Even the military prosectors who conducted the autopsy were denied access to the X-rays and the photographs for writing their official autopsy report. The bureau's failure to examine the best evidence in the violent death of President Kennedy cannot be attributed to the terrible time pressure FBIHQ was under to release its report. The only credible explanation for this omission was that the report's raison d'être was to "settle the dust" of Dallas with a political solution to the crime that suited the interests of the men who had taken charge of the government at this terrible moment in U.S. history. Since the official version of the truth of Dallas had already been agreed upon over the weekend (and after Oswald's own murder), there was no real need for the FBI to review the official autopsy report.

As expected, Hoover's name was on the title page of the report, set off with a handsome plastic cover, large print, and wide margins to amply accommodate any necessity for the director's marginal note-making. Wide borders on all FBI memos and reports that might land on the director's desk were obligatory in the Hoover bureau. However, as late as a week after the assassination and even with the Oswald section of the report completed, Hoover was still spectacularly disconnected from a basic understanding of the facts of Dallas that would appear in his agency's report. When Hoover spoke to LBJ on November 29, Johnson steered the conversation to the shooting, and Hoover mentioned the three shots all striking either Kennedy or Connally. He then went on to explain that "one complete bullet rolled out of the President's head" after it tore a large part of his head off. "In trying to massage his heart," the director continued, "on the way to the hospital they [doctors] loosened the bullet which fell on the stretcher and we have that." Hoover also assured Johnson that Oswald's $12.88 bolt-action rifle with a shoddy scope could "fire those three shots in *three* seconds." FBI arms experts, Hoover assured Johnson, "have proven it could be done by one man." None of the above details was true, or even possible, as will be covered in the following chapters.

LBJ wanted to know how Governor Connally had been hit if Oswald, this crack shot, was aiming only at President Kennedy. Hoover had a ready answer: The governor was struck by the second shot when he turned to the rear of the limousine upon hearing the first shot. When Johnson asked if JFK would have been hit by the second shot if Connally had not been in the jump seat in front of Kennedy, Hoover assured LBJ that he would have. Of course, the only way Hoover's account could be accurate is if the second shot had come from in front of the motorcade. Although this was an assertion that many critics of the Warren Commission who believed that JFK had been the victim of a conspiracy would insist upon, Hoover was never wittingly in that camp. As at the time of the first news of the assassination,

Hoover was focused on the political issues and, as the released public record revealed, never troubled to master the facts and the evidence of the crime.[47]

The sixty-eight-year-old director had internalized one great truth about staying on top of the Washington power game: Control was the name of the game. This need to control any situation prompted Hoover to order the leaking of the conclusions of the FBI report on the JFK assassination to the media before Johnson's blue-ribbon Warren Commission held its first executive session. Hoover and his executive officers at FBIHQ intended to control the Commission to assure that it ratified the solution to the assassination decided upon by the government over that first weekend.[48]

2   Creating the Warren Commission

"Don't take responsibility unless you can control the situation."
—Lawrence E. Walsh quoting Hoover in *Firewall: The Iran-
   Contra Conspiracy and Cover-Up*

President Johnson received bouquets from every quarter for his masterly performance during the first few days after the assassination. National political columnist and Washington insider Joseph Alsop effused, "You've already made a marvelous start . . . you haven't put a damned foot one-quarter of an inch wrong. . . . I've never seen anything like it." Democratic Congressman Hale Boggs was equally effusive, judging the president "utterly magnificent." The dead president's youngest brother called to express appreciation for Johnson's outreach to the grieving family. National black leader Whitney Young assured the president that the "Negroes . . . have one hundred percent confidence in you."[1] Despite the chorus of hosannas, Johnson was aware of the mounting opposition to his policy of containing the investigation by limiting it to the FBI report and the Texas Court of Inquiry (TCI), as it became known.

Along with the *Washington Post*'s Russ Wiggins and Al Friendly and possibly Scotty Reston of the *New York Times,* influential figures in this camp were Eugene V. Rostow, Joe Alsop, and former Secretary of State Dean Acheson. Although none of them was in government at the time, they all agreed that some kind of high-level commission was essential to review the FBI findings and report them to the nation. The three did not leave a documented record of their collaboration or the reasons for their actions. However, it is certain that they joined together to lobby the White House and the Justice Department to persuade Johnson that the course he and Hoover had set for the investigation was politically unwise.[2]

Oswald's murder made all the difference in terms of what was to follow. He died at 2:07 P.M. (EST) Sunday. Katzenbach wrote his memo to LBJ via Moyers after he learned of Oswald's death and discussed this new development with Hoover. That same day, November 24, the acting attorney general had three phone conversations with Rostow, then dean of the Yale Law School. Dean Rostow had known Katzenbach when he was a law student at Yale and later in the 1950s when Katzenbach joined the law school's teaching faculty. Rostow expressed concern about the burdens his former student and colleague was under when he called Moyers Sunday afternoon, shortly after Oswald's assassination, to alert Moyers to Katzenbach's "groggy" state of mind. The Yale dean might have been calling from a Washington residence since it was during the Thanksgiving semester break. In any case, he mentioned to Moyers that "I've got a party here" and that they had been "pursuing the policy, you know, that people need to come together at this time." Rostow went on to recommend that "in this situation, with the bastard killed, my suggestion is that a Presidential Commission be appointed" that was bipartisan, above politics. He advanced some names of prominent men who might be approached to serve: "Tom Dewey and Bill Storey from Texas . . . maybe Nixon." Columnist Joe Alsop spoke to Moyers on Sunday morning, and it is safe to assume that their conversation covered some of the same ground.[3]

Despite his rattled and unfocused state on Sunday, Katzenbach picked up on the presidential commission idea, almost certainly from his old mentor and Rostow's like-minded but unnamed associates who were anxious to "settle the dust" of Dallas. He included the notion in his memo to Moyers as a possible alternative to an FBI investigation. However, as his memo revealed, Katzenbach was still counting on the public release of the FBI report (CD 1) as the first order of business. He trusted in the country's unquestioning trust in J. Edgar Hoover and the FBI to "head off public speculation or Congressional hearings of the wrong sort."

That same Sunday, Hoover, after speaking to Katzenbach, put in a call to the White House and spoke with presidential aide Walter Jenkins. Hoover told Jenkins that he shared Katzenbach's concern "in having something issued so we can convince the public that Oswald is the real assassin." Hoover noted that the deputy attorney general thought LBJ was going ahead with a "Presidential Commission of three outstanding citizens to make a determination." With a lifetime of gauging the direction of the political winds on Capitol Hill, the savvy director was already a step ahead of Katzenbach and resigned to the fact that Johnson was going to have to appoint a blue-ribbon committee to review the FBI's investigation. On November 23 Hoover had met privately for two hours with Assistant Director Alan H. Belmont, who was in overall charge of the JFK investigation, and Assistant Director James H. Gale, the head of the Inspection Division. Hoover told both men that he anticipated that the White House would appoint a commission, and with that likelihood in mind he wanted Gale to undertake a secret, in-house investigation into the bureau's handling of the JFK case.[4]

In his effort to reach Johnson, Joe Alsop did not stop with Moyers; he went directly to the Oval Office. In 1963 Alsop was one of an elite group of journalists—the others in that very select company were Walter Lippmann and Ben Bradlee—who could pick up the phone and call the president directly. Johnson had a long memory and was receptive to those who carried his colors in political battles, and he could not forget that Alsop had pressed

JFK in 1960 to take the Texan as his running mate. Alsop spoke to the president on Monday morning and listened to Johnson recite all the reasons why a high-level commission would be counterproductive.

When LBJ finished, Alsop started to pinpoint the political flaws in the president's thinking. Alsop mentioned that he and Dean Acheson had given considerable thought to the matter. Although the columnist never confided to Johnson regarding whom else he had spoken to about the investigation, Alsop slipped in the elder statesman Acheson's name three more times during their conversation. When Alsop raised doubts about the controlling role of the FBI in the process, Johnson bristled and shot back, "Why can't the FBI transmit [the report]?" Alsop was ready with "the left won't believe it and the FBI doesn't write very well." Alsop continued pressing his argument for Johnson to appoint a blue-ribbon commission. He wanted Johnson to see that there was a "missing key" in the White House–FBI approach to the investigation. What was needed, he insisted, was for a small group of men of unimpeachable integrity, preferably outside government, like Acheson, to summarize "the result of the FBI inquiry in a way that will be completely coherent, detailed, and will carry unchangeable convictions" to the American people. Johnson promised he would speak to Acheson about the commission idea. He followed through, calling Acheson before November 29, when he signed Executive Order 11130 establishing the Warren Commission.[5]

By November 28 those championing the commission idea helped make up President Johnson's mind for him. It was a decision he had resisted, but once it was forced upon him he moved swiftly to appoint the commissioners. There was an upside to a presidential commission that was not lost on Johnson. A presidential body charged with evaluating the FBI's investigation and reporting to the nation would make the separate proposals circulating through Congress for Senate and House inquiries into the tragedy of Dallas redundant. LBJ was quick to seize the moment and convinced the chairman of the Senate Judiciary Committee, Democrat James Eastland of Mississippi, to drop all talk of a Senate investigation. The Democratic leader of the House, Speaker John McCormick of Massachusetts, was equally obliging. Johnson did not have to resort to arm-twisting to make the case that five separate investigations—FBI, Texas Court of Inquiry, the president's commission, and two from Congress—was an over-the-top response and a certain blueprint for confusion and ridicule. It should be noted that the uncertainty about an alleged Cuban-Soviet plot to assassinate JFK helped persuade Johnson to accept the idea of a White House commission.[6]

The news that the White House was going to appoint a presidential commission came as neither a surprise nor a bitter pill for Hoover and his assistant directors responsible for the investigation. Katzenbach explained the president's decision to the FBI as a preemptive move to forestall an investigation by the Senate Judiciary Committee. Hoover understood that the politics behind the president's decision went deeper than simply heading off a Senate inquiry, and he assured Johnson of the FBI's full cooperation. As mentioned above, as early as November 23 the director had anticipated that Johnson would opt for a commission, and by November 27 he had "not the slightest doubt" that the conclusions in the FBI's report would have to stand up under the scrutiny of a congressional committee.[7]

The announcement that the White House was establishing a high-level committee was met with unfeigned relief at FBI Washington. The idea of a presidential commission appealed to Hoover's operational instincts and played to his agency's strengths and talents in situations where control was the name of the game. A Senate or a joint Senate-House inquiry into the assassination increased the odds that some committee members might bring to the investigation personal or political loyalties to the murdered president and a forceful determination to uncover the facts behind the assassination. The FBI's report would have been castigated, if not demolished, if subjected to sharp cross-examination by men of courage and integrity in a public hearing. Hoover, of course, would have preferred the original game plan: Submit the FBI report to the attorney general's office and be done with it. Considering the alternatives, the Hoover bureau soon warmed to the idea of a presidential commission. Like the curate's fabled egg, it could have been better, but it could have been a lot worse.

Three days after the Warren Commission received CD 1, Hoover explained to J. Lee Rankin, the newly appointed Commission's chief counsel, that CD 1 was not the final word on the assassination. The director felt it was safe to be frank with Rankin because Hoover had sabotaged Chairman Earl Warren's choice for the position in favor of Rankin, as will soon be discussed. Hoover blamed the lapses in CD 1 on the pressure coming from the Justice Department for an early release before the director was satisfied that all the conclusions were supported by the evidence. Hoover told Rankin that he was convinced that Oswald was involved in the assassination, but he was not certain at this time whether Oswald might have had confederates. He assured the chief counsel that the bureau was still working on this angle and was checking on a CIA story about a Cuba-Oswald connection. In his lengthy accounting Hoover glossed over the fact that he was the one, just hours after the assassination, who had identified Oswald, "a nut of the pro-Castro crowd," as the assailant in the shooting. Hoover mentioned other lines of inquiry that the FBI was still pursuing, especially whether Jack Ruby and Oswald had known one another. Also, although it was critical to the shooting sequence and material to the investigation, the director never mentioned the Tague bullet, the missed shot, and why it was not included in the FBI report.[8]

Johnson's choice of men who would serve on this august commission went a long way in easing Hoover's concerns. The bipartisan panel included Chief Justice Earl Warren, former CIA director Allen W. Dulles, former high commissioner to Germany and prominent foreign policy adviser John J. McCloy, Senator Richard B. Russell (D–Ga.), Senator John Cooper (R–Ky.), Congressman Gerald R. Ford (R–Mich.), and Congressman Hale Boggs (D–La.). These were all men with solid reputations, the kind of men for whom the word *eminent* was coined. With the exception of Warren, whom the president knew that Hoover detested, LBJ ran all their names by the director—as a matter of courtesy, but a vetting nonetheless. Hoover gave his laconic appraisal with "good man" to all the selections with the exception of McCloy, who he thought was "garrulous" and something of a showboat.

With Hoover on board with Johnson's selections, a grateful LBJ showed his deep appreciation by referring to the director as "my brother and personal friend," a recognition and recommitment to a friendship of thirty years. Johnson also appreciated Hoover's assigning Deke DeLoach as the new FBI liaison with the White House. DeLoach had a talent for ingratiating himself with those in power. Johnson liked DeLoach and would come to rely on him to carry out many White House assignments. DeLoach replaced Assistant Director Courtney Evans, a twenty-year veteran. Hoover had come to suspect Evans's loyalty to the agency because he believed Evans had grown too close to the Kennedys. Evans saw the handwriting on the wall and resigned soon afterward to work for the Justice Department.[9]

The day Johnson went public with his Commission he called Joe Alsop to get his reaction. Obviously pleased with his creation, he recited the list of his appointees to assure the columnist that it satisfied the requirements of bipartisanship and sectional representation. After receiving Alsop's approbation, LBJ, not Alsop, alluded to the majority of Republicans on the Commission—his "nest of Republicans," as he phrased it—and joked, wondering if he could "trust that many."[10] In most respects Johnson did follow the informal Washington guidelines for selecting a commission, although the press and other commission watchers might have pondered why a Democratic president, especially LBJ, who had a reputation on the Hill for being a consummate political animal, felt the need to load the Commission with members who identified with the opposition party. More deserving of question was that not one of the commissioners, with the possible exception of Hale Boggs, was identified politically with President Kennedy and the liberal wing of the Democratic Party. The two Democrats on the Commission, Russell and Boggs, both southerners, respected Kennedy but had opposed much of his domestic legislation, especially his civil rights initiatives.

Fundamentally, LBJ viewed the creation of the Commission as a public relations triumph.[11] The men he appointed were politicians, not investigators, and that was their redeeming strength in Johnson's eyes. As politicians they were versed in the "art of government," experienced in handling or neutralizing difficult problems through politics, not necessarily resolving them. At this point in time the Johnson White House viewed the Kennedy assassination as a delicate exercise in politics and public relations. During the first week after Dallas most of what Johnson knew about the assassination originated with Hoover. Although the director confided that there were still some angles in the case that his agency was checking on—Oswald's alleged Cuban connections in Mexico were receiving the FBI's closest attention—Hoover had convinced LBJ that the evidence against Oswald was so overwhelming that the case would take care of itself.[12]

With the exception of the former CIA director Dulles, who had been eased into retirement by President Kennedy after the Bay of Pigs debacle, all of the commissioners were overscheduled with many claims on their time. For example, Warren and Russell both tried to beg off this assignment by pleading with Johnson to excuse them because of the demands and responsibilities of their offices. Johnson brushed their entreaties aside. It was imperative for him to have Warren, Russell, and the others on the Commission; he was basically trading on their reputations. These were all honorable men whose credentials placed them above suspicion in the public eye, and whatever they concluded would be immune to criticism. Johnson tempered their anxieties, reminding them that, after all, the Commission staff would do most of the work. He also sweet-talked them, insisting that the case against Oswald was so airtight that whatever sacrifices they would have to make would not drag on interminably. Johnson assured Russell, his long-time mentor, that the whole thing would "not take much time." When sweet reason was not enough for Warren and Russell, Johnson trumped their protestations by forcing them to think about the unthinkable if there was any truth to the allegations from Mexico City about a Red plot behind the assassination. Their resistance melted away when Johnson warned that forty million American lives were in the balance. The president was not coy about letting the commissioners know that he wanted the investigation over and well behind him before he would need to set out to win the White House in his own right. Conscious of the president's expectations, Warren and Rankin initially planned to finish the Commission's work in June, before the 1964 presidential campaign heated up.[13]

With Congress deferring to the Warren Commission, the only remaining obstacle to containing the investigation in federal hands was the Texas Court of Inquiry. Initially, President Johnson had requested the convening of the court. The day of Kennedy's funeral he told Hoover he had met with Waggoner Carr, the attorney general of Texas, for ninety minutes. That afternoon Carr held a press conference at which he read a statement announcing that the Texas authorities would hold an investigation. The "brilliant" Texas jurist, as LBJ had puffed him up to Joe Alsop, anticipated that the press conference would be limited to a handful of Texas pressmen who covered the Washington scene. It apparently never occurred to Carr that the JFK assassination was not just the biggest story in town; it was the only story. When he entered the conference room at the Statler Hotel he was faced with a sea of people, TV cameras, the foreign press, and an array of microphones on the podium. It looked like the entire media world had turned out primed with questions. Confronted by the entire Washington press corps and foreign journalists, a stunned Carr quickly read his statement and then beat an ignominious retreat through a gauntlet of irate reporters who screamed questions and hurled insults at him and the state of Texas as he fled back to his hotel room. The FBI report of the incident concluded that the press conference was an unmitigated disaster. Whether triggered by the Statler Hotel fiasco or a follow-up of LBJ's conversation with Carr, Katzenbach sent Assistant Attorney General Herbert Miller to speak to Carr and the Texas officials. The acting attorney general wanted Miller to convince the Texans to "restrict their hearing . . . showing merely that Oswald killed the President." According to FBI Assistant Director Evans, Katzenbach was concerned that the Texas court might turn up "some pertinent information not now known" or "try to resolve the communist angle." In short, Katzenbach, speaking for the White House, wanted no deviation from the official story that Oswald had done it and acted alone.[14]

After Johnson established the Warren Commission, Washington decided to scuttle the Texas investigation into the Kennedy homicide. During the first week of December Carr and Leon Jaworski, a prominent Houston attorney (who would become a household name during the Watergate scandal investigation), came to Washington at the invitation of the White House. Jaworski and Robert G. Storey, a past president of the American Bar Association and dean emeritus of Southern Methodist University Law School, were the other jurists who made up the Texas Court of Inquiry. Storey, a resident of Dallas, was out of the country at the time and did not make the trip. Johnson invited them with the understanding that they meet with Earl Warren to work out a cooperative arrangement between the Texas court and the Commission. Carr claimed he was shocked when he heard from Katzenbach that Warren wanted Texas to drop all plans to investigate the crime and give up any expectation of participating with the Commission's investigation. The Texas attorney general asserted that he dug in his heels and told Katzenbach that the chief justice's terms were not acceptable. Carr carried a large chip on his shoulder where Warren was concerned. He was furious when he learned that Warren had been overheard commenting during the viewing of the dead president's casket that Texas was to blame for the assassination because it seethed with right-wing anti-Kennedy fanaticism.[15]

Although Carr's account cannot be taken completely at face value, there is no question that there was a two-day standoff that required the fine hand of LBJ to end the impasse. On December 6 Carr released a press statement announcing that the state of Texas was postponing its inquiry into JFK's death until the Warren Commission completed its investigation. Leaving nothing to chance, the Justice Department prepared Carr's press release. The quid pro quo from Warren's end was assurance that the Commission would cooperate fully with the Texas attorney general to see that he received all the information necessary to make "a proper presentation to their public." The Texas Court of Inquiry would have access to the FBI report but would not publish it. Court representatives also had the right to be present at the Commission's closed-door hearings and direct questions to the witnesses, to have access to depositions, and to see the final draft of the Commission's report. This arrangement was really a trade-off: The federal authorities would allow for nominal Texas participation in the investigation, and Carr, after the Commission's findings were made public, would use the published report as his excuse for not proceeding with the state inquiry.[16]

LBJ, through Katzenbach, arranged for Carr and Jaworski to meet with Hoover. At first the FBI refused, telling Justice that the director was too busy putting the final touches on the FBI's report. When Hoover learned that the request had come from the White House, that LBJ was "anxious that Carr be given attention," the director granted the two Texans a fifteen-minute "stand-up" audience. The meeting was vintage Hoover: The director talked for the entire time about his fond memories of visits to the Lone Star State and the "keen softness in his heart for Texas." Following the meeting with Hoover, DeLoach gave the two visitors a tour of FBI headquarters and introduced them to an Inspector Suttler who had once spoken at a Texas youth rally at Carr's invitation. According to DeLoach, the Texans were tremendously impressed and came away from their brief meeting with the director convinced that "he is a man of great integrity and energy." The wily Johnson knew that Carr would regale Rotary Club luncheons and voters back home in his upcoming election with this memorable session with America's legendary lawman and Hoover's kind words about Texas.[17]

Carr's three days in Washington were not an unalloyed success. When he was not encased in the administration's carefully managed and scripted situations, he repeatedly brushed up against smoldering hostility toward everything Texan. This animus was as pronounced in the nation's capital, especially with the press corps, as anywhere else in the country. It was generally overlooked that on November 22 some 250,000 people had turned out in Dallas to welcome President Kennedy and the First Lady. The prevailing image of Texas, and Dallas in particular, was that of a society steeped in hysteria and wild-eyed ultrarightists drenched in the politics of Cold War anticommunism. Right-wing elements in the state hinted darkly at a Washington plot to cover up a Soviet or Castro conspiracy behind the assassination. The violent reception United Nations Ambassador Adlai Stevenson had received in Dallas a month before the Kennedy assassination was recalled in all its hateful and ugly details. The "impeach Earl Warren" billboards that littered the Texas landscape were a testament, detractors of Texas's political lifestyle were quick to point out, to the sick, wall-to-wall political paranoia investing the state. All of this was the grotesque backdrop to the assassination of the president and the murder of Oswald while in police custody and on police premises. To many Americans, Texas was an alien, forbidden zone of free-floating violence and crackpot politics, deserving of national calumny and pariah status.

None of this, of course, was lost on Carr.[18] In his December 5 letter to Chief Justice Warren, Carr pointed out that the people of Texas "shared with their fellow countrymen the loss of a great President." He went on to stress that "the integrity of Texas justice is deeply involved." Carr's letter underscored that it was the responsibility of state officials to "do everything possible to uncover all the facts."[19] However, in his further dealings with the Commission it became clear that the great tragedy of Dallas, as far as Carr was concerned, was the blighted image of his home state in the wake of the assassination. For him, like his fellow Texan in the White House, the Kennedy assassination was in large part a public relations problem. Carr was dubious that non-Texans undertaking the investigation in Washington could be entrusted to look after Texas's interests.

Over the next ten months the relations between the Warren Commission and the Texas Court of Inquiry were at times uneasy and tension-ridden. The first evidence of friction occurred when Carr learned from Rankin that the chief justice was apprehensive about speeches the Texas attorney general was making in Texas about the assassination. Carr wrote to Warren that the people of Texas trusted him to keep them informed about the progress of the investigation and to assure them that it was "fair and equitable to Texas." Short of Texas filing its own report, Carr told Warren he did not know how else he could keep his state informed.[20]

Relations moved from mutual suspicion to threat when the Commission scheduled its first witness, Marina Oswald, Lee Harvey Oswald's widow, and failed to notify the Texas Court of Inquiry. Carr shot off a scorching letter to Warren Commission general counsel Rankin condemning the oversight and reminding Rankin that it was a violation of their December 6 agreement. A copy of the letter was sent to Horace Busby's home address in Washington, D.C.; Busby was LBJ's favorite speechwriter. This breach in their understanding hit Carr's tender spot, and he warned Rankin that if it was repeated he would convene the Texas court and hold open hearings. There is no record of Rankin's response, but on March 18 Carr received the Commission's schedule of witnesses for that month. With that, relations between Washington and the Texas Court of Inquiry were back on track.[21]

In August there was a renewed rash of dissension when Texas submitted a request for the depositions of twenty-five witnesses only to have Rankin politely decline because of security concerns. (There had been a rash of embarrassing leaks of witnesses' testimony that month.) Rankin proposed that the Texas court review the depositions in Washington. On August 14 Carr responded with a long letter. The gist was that under these trying circumstances Carr felt duty-bound to file a Texas report. The Warren Commission capitulated. That same month the process repeated itself when the Texas court requested a draft copy of the Commission's final report. Rankin declined; Carr threatened; the Commission reversed itself and agreed that the Texans could examine the galley proofs of the final report.[22]

On October 5, 1964, the Texas Court of Inquiry released its long-awaited report. It was really only a gloss on the Warren Commission Report, that is, not really an investigative report at all. Carr's final product addressed to Texas Governor John B. Connally was a tablet-sized twenty-page document with large type, wide margins, and fewer than four thousand words. It was more reminiscent of a college undergraduate's term paper, only without sources, than an official accounting of the most important political crime ever committed in the sovereign state of Texas.

The reason Carr gave for not conducting an independent investigation was straightforward enough: The "exhaustiveness" of the Warren Commission Report left nothing about the assassination open to question. Carr had "not the slightest hesitancy in concurring in its conclusions" that Oswald had been the lone gunman who shot JFK, Connally, and Dallas police officer J. D. Tippit, and that he had acted alone. Carr did not neglect his obligation to rush to the defense of Texas officialdom and redeem the image of his home state. The Texas report deflected some of the criticism leveled against Dallas officials, especially the police, by shifting blame onto the "Federal authorities" for failing to notify the police of Oswald's past procommunist activities. Carr took comfort in the fact that the Warren Report rejected the notion that Dallas was "the Southwest hate capital of Dixie" and instead played up the great outpouring of goodwill and excited anticipation at the news of the president and First Lady's visit. The Commission's report noted at some length the reasons for the breakdown of police security that had cost Oswald his life. Although the report made no excuses for the Dallas police, it did not fail to criticize the FBI and Secret Service for allowing agency rivalry to take precedence over security for the president.[23] The Commission's exercise in Solomonic balance was the down payment assuring that Carr and the TCI would not hold open hearings and file a separate report on the Kennedy assassination.

Carr did neglect, however, to include in his report his significant observations about a key piece of the evidence, Oswald's reputed Mannlicher-Carcano rifle. Carr joined some of the commissioners when they finally came to Dallas in May 1964 to examine the assassination scene, and he had occasion to examine the alleged assassination weapon. The Texas attorney general noted that the telescopic sight was "of poor quality and did not bring the objects in very close." After hefting the weapon, operating the bolt action, and sighting through the scope, Carr concluded that "Oswald had to be a crack shot to fire as many times as he did in a period of a few seconds with no more help than he had from the scope."[24] One has to wonder if this was the only residual mystery of the Kennedy assassination that the Texas attorney general held back from his twenty-page summary report. If he had paid any attention to Commission witnesses or read certain depositions, he knew that the most convincing testimony on the subject was that Oswald was a duffer and not a "Buffalo Bill" with a rifle.

The chief justice never wanted to serve on Johnson's presidential commission. He turned aside a delegation from Justice on November 29, when Bobby Kennedy, Katzenbach, and Solicitor General Archibald Cox invited him to take the chairmanship of the president's commission. Late in the afternoon of that same day, LBJ summoned Warren to the White House to renew the request. Warren was equipped with some sound historical precedents regarding why he should not be appointed. In 1941, when Justice Owen B. Roberts chaired the five-man committee that investigated the Japanese attack on Pearl Harbor, his absence from the Supreme Court produced a judicial backlog and resentment among his fellow justices. The same was true in 1945 when Justice H. Robert Jackson jumped at the opportunity to serve as U.S. representative and chief of counsel in preparing the prosecution's case against Nazi war criminals at the Nuremberg trials after World War II. In Justice Jackson's case the legacy of bitterness among some of his brethren, namely Justices Hugo Black and William O. Douglas, may have cost him the chief justice title. Warren was also mindful that if the Jack Ruby case reached the Supreme Court he would have to recuse himself. With history as their guide, most, if not all, of Warren's high-court colleagues opposed his appointment.

Warren's meeting with Johnson is a much-told story about how LBJ appealed to his patriotism, reduced him to tears by some accounts, by confiding that the assassination might have international implications that could threaten the lives of forty million Americans. The president, giving full scope to the legendary "Johnson treatment" few on the Hill could ever resist, also raised the specter of the Texas inquiry that would have all the dignity of a carnival sideshow. Before the meeting was over the chief justice was in full retreat and had agreed to subordinate his views and serve as chair of the Commission. Although LBJ's first choice for his Commission had been Dulles, he needed Warren to deflect any future criticism of the investigation from the liberal establishment.[25]

On December 5, 1963, the Commission held its first executive session. It was devoted to organizational matters and other issues that were foremost on the members' minds as they prepared to make their record for history. When the session turned to selection of a chief counsel, Warren quickly volunteered the name of Warren Olney III. The chairman had a long-standing professional and personal friendship with this son of a former state supreme court justice. In the 1930s Olney had been one of Warren's deputies when Warren held the office of district attorney for the city of Oakland, California. When Warren was governor of the state he appointed Olney as the chief counsel to his commission to study organized crime. They complemented each other perfectly: Warren the public figure and Olney quietly content to work in the background to accomplish their shared progressive political goals. In the 1950s, when Warren was elevated to the Supreme Court, Olney was in the Justice Department, assistant attorney general in charge of the Criminal Division. Warren's choice of Olney was a natural one in view of their shared history.[26]

As head of Justice's Criminal Division Olney also had a shared history with FBI Director Hoover that was altogether different. Hoover despised Olney. As one FBI agent remarked, "Olney was the only guy who had balls enough to stand up to Hoover."[27] For example, the Criminal Division head publicly stated that organized crime was on the increase in the 1950s, when the Hoover bureau reported figures that showed it was on the decline. This butting of heads inspired a lengthy feature story in *Fortune* magazine in which a University of Pennsylvania professor of criminology flatly pronounced that the United States "undoubtedly has the poorest [criminal] statistics of any nation of the free world." Hoover, who had been in a state of denial that there was any organized crime in his America, seethed. "This shows Olney in his true colors," he wrote across the bottom of a bureau memo. He ordered Assistant Director Louis B. Nichols, DeLoach's predecessor, then head of the Crime Records Division, the FBI's propaganda machine, to "promptly and adequately handle this matter." *Handle* was Hooverese for straightening out *Fortune*'s editors regarding the "true facts" of the matter.[28]

The Hoover bureau and Olney clashed over an incident in 1957 that drew international attention, especially from Latin American observers. In 1957 a Dominican Republic national, Jesus de Galindez-Suarez, a professor at

Columbia University and an outspoken political foe of the repressive Trujillo regime, was kidnapped off the streets of New York City by the dictator's agents. He was spirited out of New York and returned to his native country, where he was tortured and murdered. When the FBI failed to show any interest in his abduction, Olney dashed off another of his "outrageous" (Nichols's characterization) memos accusing the FBI of sitting on its hands in the Galindez case. Hoover's dyspeptic marginalia on the memo read, "What an eel this character Olney is!" Olney's liberalism on race (he helped push through Congress the 1957 Civil Rights Act) further widened the divide between the two men, since Hoover viewed the burgeoning civil rights movement as just another front in the Kremlin's conspiracy to destabilize America.[29]

Two days before the Commission's first executive session Hoover learned through Katzenbach that Warren was serious about pushing Olney's name forward for the general counsel position. The acting attorney general wanted to know if the FBI had any ideas on how to block this appointment. Olney's reputation as a boat-rocker unnerved Katzenbach. He was so overwrought at the prospect of Olney steering the Commission that he planned to get his own man from the Criminal Division, Howard P. Willens, to serve on the staff to keep an eye on Warren's protégé. Hoover, of course, was equally aghast as his one-word reaction on the FBI memo—"Horrible"—attested. Immediately, Katzenbach and Hoover initiated a "dump Olney" campaign, for which DeLoach was the point man. The Crime Records Division resorted to the "gray art"—as opposed to the "black art" of outright blackmail—of collecting tidbits of information on Olney; pitching them with the calculated derogatory spin; and, in DeLoach's words, identifying a "number of sources to confidentially brief" the commissioners on why the candidate was unfit for the position. For those who opposed his appointment, Olney's greatest offenses were his integrity, independence of mind, and political liberalism. Congressman Ford was probably the first commissioner to get a phone call from DeLoach's office.[30]

When Johnson called Hoover the day he announced his presidential commission, Ford was one of the names LBJ ran past the director. Hoover responded that he knew Ford only by name but that he had seen the congressman on TV and "he handled himself well." Actually, Hoover knew the seven-term Michigan congressman and House minority leader much better than he was willing to admit. In 1946 Hoover spotted Ford as a potential FBI asset and gave him covert assistance in his congressional campaign. Congressman Ford reciprocated in his maiden speech by asking Congress to increase Hoover's salary.

Over his fifteen years in the House Ford had developed a solid relationship with the Hoover agency. DeLoach noted that "relations were excellent," and that over the years Ford had been "in touch with my office on numerous occasions." Early on, Hoover assigned DeLoach to cultivate Ford, knowing that DeLoach's conservative views would be congenial to the politically like-minded Michigan congressman. That Ford was a valued FBI asset was amply demonstrated by the fact that he was given an autographed copy of Hoover's ghosted book *A Study of Communism,* written by FBI personnel on government time. A week after the Commission's first executive session Ford invited DeLoach to his office to unburden himself, complaining about Warren's general ineptitude and attempt to force Olney on the Commission as chief counsel. During their long session on December 12, 1963, according to DeLoach, Ford volunteered "that he would keep me thoroughly advised as to the activities of the Commission." Five days later DeLoach met his source again in Ford's office in the Cannon Building. They covered a range of topics. Ford reported that there had been no criticism of the FBI in the previous day's executive session. DeLoach, in turn, accused the chief justice of leaking the FBI report to the press. All this was grist to Hoover's control mill, and he acknowledged DeLoach's coup with a succinct "Well Handled."[31]

The House minority leader's readiness to act as a secret informer about what transpired in the Commission's executive sessions won him the bureau's gratitude along with a few perks. At Ford's request, DeLoach loaned the congressman an FBI briefcase with a security lock so he could take the FBI report along on his family's Christmas skiing vacation. Although the Commission was still in session, DeLoach arranged for an intimate dinner at his home for the Fords and the director. The occasion allowed Ford and Hoover to huddle for a long time and discuss, as Hoover noted, "vital issues of interest to you as well as the FBI." The day after their social evening, Hoover wrote an invitation to the congressman and Mrs. Ford to drop by FBIHQ for "a special tour of our facilities." The director closed his letter with an assurance that his door was always open "any time our help is needed or when we can be of service." Politicians enjoying the FBI's favor knew that when reelection time rolled around, the Crime Records Division would be ready with information about their opponents: what backing they had and what skeletons were hidden in their closets.[32]

In 1978, when former President Ford appeared before the House committee investigating the Kennedy assassination, he was asked about his relationship with DeLoach during the time that he had served on the Commission. Most of the questioning was in a hail-fellow spirit. Many on the committee were Ford's former House colleagues; none was after the former president's scalp. Ford assured them that he had met with DeLoach on just two occasions while the Commission was in session. He left the impression that the relationship had been short-lived, business as usual, and above suspicion. It was clear that the committee gave the former president a free pass, wishing to spare embarrassment to Ford and themselves by delving into behavior that some of his former colleagues might have regarded as devious and dishonorable.

At the beginning of 1978, months before Ford appeared before the House committee, the FBI had released more than fifty-eight thousand pages of documents. Some provided a context that exposed the true extent of Ford's relations with the Hoover bureau.[33] For example, it was most certainly Ford who smuggled a copy to DeLoach of an early draft of the Commission's report in July 1964. Assistant Director Rosen noted, "There will be a fourth and final draft made available through a source by July 23, 1964, which will contain the final conclusions and recommendations of the Commission." Only a Commission insider like Ford would have been privy to this kind of information. FBIHQ was acutely uneasy—and with good reason—about any criticism in the Commission's final report about the FBI's failure to notify the Secret Service about Lee Harvey Oswald.[34]

It was certainly no radical departure from long-standing traditional Washington guidelines for an appointed chair to place his own man at the head of a commission staff. In discharging his heavy responsibilities in the Kennedy assassination it was doubly important that Warren have total confidence in his general counsel. He had to be someone who was familiar with the processes of government; had some experience in dealing with agencies like the FBI, Secret Service, and CIA; and would be able to assemble a crack staff that would do most of the Commission's heavy lifting. On every count, given his record and experience, Olney would have admirably filled the role. The very fact that Olney was independent-minded and not under Hoover's rubber stamp when he headed Justice's Criminal Division would have been, as the history of the Commission would bear out, his greatest attribute. Had Olney served as chief counsel it is very likely that the Warren Commission Report would have been an entirely different historical document.

When Warren put forward Olney's name before the Commission, Ford was the first to voice concerns. The Michigan congressman thought they should look for someone without close ties to government. His chief objection, however, was that Olney was too close to Warren, providing cause for future critics to level the charge that the Commission was a "one-man show" with the Chief Justice and his protégé dominating the proceedings. McCloy followed close on Ford's heels, urging that they open the search by considering other candidates. It just so happened that McCloy had prepared his own list of names, one of which was J. Lee Rankin, McCloy's unspoken choice. Cooper and Russell, both Senate veterans familiar with the informal ground rules about commission chairs selecting their own general counsels, found nothing objectionable in Warren's choice. Russell wanted to preserve a semblance of cooperation with Warren given the momentous task they had

both been thrust into against their wills. It was no secret that the segrega-
tionist Georgia lawmaker held the chief justice in contempt for the decisions
of the Warren Court on the country's race relations. Every exchange between them was an ordeal for both men. With the commissioners at an impasse, it was agreed that an all-Republican subcommittee composed of
Warren, Dulles, Ford, and McCloy would meet that same day after lunch to
select a chief counsel.[35]

The four-member subcommittee agreed on J. Lee Rankin. Years later,
when reporting on this critical decision to the Commission staff historian,
the chief justice gave the impression that Rankin had clearly been the best
man for the job. Warren knew Rankin as the former solicitor general in the
Eisenhower administration and respected his principled stand in the so-
called Dixon-Yates case that had embarrassed the Eisenhower White
House.[36] However, Ford secretly reported to DeLoach that the selection of
Rankin had not occurred without bitter internal discord. According to Ford,
during the subcommittee's deliberations Warren fought hard for Olney, only
to back down when Ford and Dulles threatened to resign from the Commission if the chairman insisted on his candidate. Hale Boggs also told Warren
that he could not work with Olney.[37]

The choice of J. Lee Rankin, a conservative Republican, was greeted at
FBI headquarters with elation. When the Justice Department requested a pro
forma name check on Rankin before he was offered the position, the director noted, "Relations between Rankin and the Bureau have been excellent."
As U.S. solicitor general from 1956 to 1961, Rankin had been the FBI's
lawyer in cases that went before the Supreme Court. He knew Hoover on a
first-name basis, and, unlike Olney, there is no indication that there was ever
any animus or clashing of wills between them. If he did not know at the outset, Rankin was in a position to learn that his former client at Seat of Government had engineered this high-profile appointment. Rankin was a
supremely cautious bureaucrat, a consummate insider, not a boat-rocker like
Olney.[38]

As general counsel his management style was rigidly centralized. One
former assistant counsel complained that staff contact with the Commission
members "was all done through Rankin." All staff contact and communication with the FBI had to be approved or was channeled directly through
Rankin's office.[39] During the life of the Commission, Rankin proved re-
sourceful at every turn, steering the Commission away from problems with
the FBI and the CIA and successfully guiding the whole enterprise toward
the predetermined destination laid down in the November 25 Katzenbach
memo. The heading that Rankin followed for nine months virtually without
deviation was lifted right off Hoover's chart, and it pointed to Oswald and
only Oswald as the assassin.

Congressman Gerry Ford contended that the Commission received its first shock on January 22, when Rankin called an emergency meeting to discuss the revelation from Texas Attorney General Carr that Oswald was an FBI "undercover agent."[40] Ford was misleading on both counts. The first jolt to hit the Commission came on December 5, 1963, when Katzenbach confirmed the commissioners' suspicions that the leaking of the conclusions of the FBI report had originated with the Hoover bureau. The Commission had not even taken up permanent quarters in the Veterans of Foreign Wars Building at 200 Maryland Avenue, N.E., when the press started reporting that the FBI had solved "the crime of the century." Details varied in each accounting, but they all reported that the FBI had concluded that Oswald was the lone assassin and there was no foreign conspiracy.[41] Hoover had placed Oswald in the frame when he envisioned his guilt on the day of the assassination. Leaking the conclusions was part of the FBI's campaign to put the Commission in a box and force it to endorse the FBI's findings.

Even before Senator Russell knew that the president had drafted him to serve on the Commission, he was skeptical about the FBI's rushing to judgment with the investigation and its haste to release its report. At the Commission's December 5 executive session, the senator, his sarcasm barely muted, asked Katzenbach, "How much of their findings does the FBI propose to release to the press before we present the findings of this Commission?"[42] Even though he might have wanted to rush to the FBI's defense, Katzenbach knew that he could not argue with the facts. All the press stories appeared before the FBI's CD 1 was released to the White House, the Justice Department, and the Warren Commission. Katzenbach received his copy of the FBI report on December 5, and the commissioners did not get their copies until four days later. The FBI, of course, was not the only agency in Washington that resorted to the self-serving politics of leaking, but the bureau could have covered its tracks by holding back on leaks to the press until CD 1 had been distributed to the other designated government agencies. But FBIHQ chose to be conspicuously out in front with its leaking to convey a clear message to the Commission. In the crudest terms Hoover was signaling that the FBI had solved the case, and all that was expected from this august body was a report that ratified the bureau's findings. Katzenbach tried to soften the impact with the promise that it would not happen again, but he had to admit to the Commission, "with candor . . . I can't think of anybody else it could have come from, because I don't know of anybody else that knew that information."[43]

Katzenbach may not have been a completely innocent bystander in the leaking of the FBI report, if only in the sense that a wink was as good as a nod. He had worked feverishly to get either the White House or the FBI to release a public statement "to put a stop to the many rumors" circulating about a Dallas conspiracy. But Warren threatened to resign if the FBI publicly released its report before the Commission finished its investigation. Hoover insisted that all the bureau would do would be to turn its report over to the Justice Department and continue to "adhere to a 'no comment'" policy.

Not to be rebuffed in his efforts to still the waters, Katzenbach prepared, "in the public interest," a press release for the White House stating that the FBI "through scientific examination of the evidence and testimony, establishes beyond a reasonable doubt" that Oswald was the assassin and that he had acted alone. Katzenbach went so far as to write each of the newly appointed commissioners urging them to issue a press release stating that the FBI report, which had just been submitted to the Warren Commission that same day, proved beyond a shadow of a doubt that Oswald was the lone assassin and there had been no international conspiracy. Abe Fortas, LBJ's longtime political confidant, threw his full weight behind Katzenbach's initiative, arguing that the rumors of conspiracy "should be hit hard now" regardless of Warren's objections. The Johnson White House's speechwriter, Theodore Sorenson, a holdover from the Kennedy administration, was just as adamantly opposed, and the idea of the press release was dropped. It is safe to assume that President Johnson killed the idea, not wanting to chance Warren's resignation. The FBI, whose director had had almost a half century to refine the practice of influencing policy with press leaks, did not need any additional incentive to achieve its desired political ends. In the end, however, the FBI's unauthorized press releases accomplished exactly what Katzenbach had lobbied so sedulously to achieve.[44]

The bureau followed up its leaking offensive with a campaign to blame the unauthorized disclosures on everybody but the FBI. DeLoach took the lead in the blame game. He assured Ford that the leaks had originated in the Justice Department and quite possibly that "members of the Commission were beginning to leak the report." Aware of Ford's suspicions and his low regard for the chief justice, DeLoach accused Warren of leaking to curry favor with the liberal establishment at the *Washington Post*.[45] To ease Russell's apprehensions, DeLoach told the senator that the FBI's policy line was "no comment," and it never broke with that policy. He prefaced his assurance with flattery, one Georgia boy to another, telling Russell of the director's great respect and Hoover's fervent wish to dispel the senator's "misimpression" that the FBI would stoop to leaking information for any self-serving advantage. DeLoach trotted out the Dallas police as another likely culprit. When Russell mentioned Katzenbach's December 5 statement accusing the FBI, DeLoach called Katzenbach a liar who was "cover[ing] up his own guilt by blaming others." When Hoover learned what Katzenbach had told the Commission, he probably thought he had another budding

Warren Olney on his hands. He scrawled across the DeLoach memo, "This certainly shows Katzenbach's true colors."[46]

Although Katzenbach praised the FBI's report as "spectacular," he did point to one shortcoming in CD 1 dealing with the assassination attempt on General Edwin A. Walker. Walker was the officer whom President Kennedy had removed from his command in West Germany for indoctrinating his troops with Birchite right-wing propaganda. Retired from the military in 1961, Walker took up residence in Dallas, where he continued to flagrantly propagandize for extremist right-wing political causes and white supremacist resistance to civil rights campaigns in the South. Katzenbach's reservation was couched not as criticism but rather as a missed opportunity.[47]

The FBI report on the Kennedy assassination asserted that on the evening of April 10, 1963, Oswald had fired a shot into Walker's Dallas home, narrowly missing the general, who was sitting in his study going over his income tax forms. The only supporting evidence for this assertion was a note Oswald had allegedly left for his wife, Marina, and her testimony that her husband had admitted to her that he had made an attempt on the general's life. Katzenbach was aware that Marina had lied to the Secret Service and the FBI, denying that Lee had recently made a trip to Mexico. Katzenbach called Alan H. Belmont, the assistant to the director and the executive officer Hoover had placed in charge of the investigation, to establish whether the Dallas police considered Oswald a suspect in the Walker case. If the accused assassin of President Kennedy was a suspect, Katzenbach mused, "it would place a different aspect on this case." The acting attorney general wanted to reinforce in the public mind the government's image of Oswald as a violent sociopath, the kind of person who could turn his murderous hatred against any public figure. However, Belmont told Katzenbach that as far as he knew, the Dallas authorities did not consider Oswald a suspect.[48]

Katzenbach's call to Belmont was prompted by the flood of inquiries from reporters who were calling Ed Guthman, the Justice Department's press chief, to ask if Oswald had been the sniper in the Walker shooting. Katzenbach told Belmont that *Chicago Sun-Times* reporter Sandy Smith had called several times for confirmation. Smith was one of Deke DeLoach's trusted bureau sources in the "Mass Media Program" that the FBI had built up over the years of Hoover's directorship. Since the *Sun-Times* reporter could be counted upon to put the FBI spin on any story, it is likely that DeLoach fed Smith and other "cooperative" media sources Marina's account of her husband's confession that he had made an attempt on Walker's life.[49]

Belmont was accurate when he told Katzenbach that Oswald had never been a suspect in the Dallas police's investigation into the Walker case. All of the Dallas police's witness testimony pointed to two or three conspirators with cars using a high-powered rifle and steel-jacketed ammunition. Oswald did not drive and had no known access to a car, his Mannlicher-Carcano rifle was not high-powered, and the ammunition he allegedly used to kill Kennedy was copper-jacketed.

The bullet the Dallas police recovered from Walker's home had passed through the center wood strip of the outer screen of the general's study, through a copper weather strip, and penetrated an inside masonry wall reinforced with solid tin and metal lathing, finally falling onto a pile of papers in the adjoining room. Because the bullet was completely mutilated and deformed by such obstruction, the Dallas police claimed they had run no ballistics test on the recovered slug.[50] Taking into account the missile's path, one of the police officers who responded to the Walker shooting reported in the Dallas press that he assumed it had been fired from a .30-06-caliber rifle, a high-velocity weapon with considerable penetrating power.[51]

Whatever weapon was involved in the Walker shooting incident, it was highly unlikely that a 6.5-mm bullet fired from Oswald's rifle could have penetrated a cinder block, as did the projectile recovered from Walker's house. During his first appearance before the Warren Commission, Robert A. Frazier, the FBI's chief firearms expert, repeatedly stressed that Oswald's Mannlicher-Carcano had a "very low velocity and pressure, and just an average-size bullet weight." Frazier's testimony was to establish for the record that a low-velocity weapon would improve the shooter's marksmanship by reducing the rifle's recoil, allowing the shooter to keep his eye on the target under rapid-firing conditions. According to Frazier, Oswald's rifle was capable of allowing him to get off three accurately placed shots in 5.5 to 6 seconds without losing the target in his scope.[52] The government never came forward with any evidence that Oswald owned or had access to a rifle other the Mannlicher-Carcano.

The Commission relied heavily on Frazier's testimony to tie Oswald's rifle to the Kennedy assassination. Just before he concluded his March 31 Commission testimony Frazier was asked about the Walker bullet (FBI designated Q-188). Commission assistant counsel Melvin A. Eisenberg asked whether Q-188 could have been fired from Oswald's Mannlicher-Carcano. According to Frazier, the Walker slug was a 6.5-mm copper-jacketed bullet, but because of its distorted condition he could not answer conclusively. However, on the basis of "its land and groove impressions," the FBI's firearms expert left open the likely possibility that it could have been fired from Oswald's rifle.[53]

What Eisenberg carefully avoided and Frazier did not volunteer were the results of the FBI's spectrographic analysis of Q-188. A week before Frazier appeared before the Commission, Eisenberg met with him and Agent Henry H. Heilberger to review the FBI lab results for the Walker bullet. Eisenberg could not have been encouraged by what he learned from Heilberger, the one who ran the tests. Heilberger concluded in his report (PC-78378) that the lead alloy in the Walker bullet was different from the lead alloy of the two large bullet fragments recovered from under the left jump seat of the presidential limousine. Although determined to construct a convincing prosecution case against Oswald, the government could not have it both ways. Heilberger's report was persuasive evidence that the ammunition Oswald allegedly used to kill Kennedy could not have been involved in the Walker shooting. The only way the Commission and the FBI could transform ambiguity and uncertainty into presumptive evidence of guilt was to suppress from the record the results of Heilberger's spectrographic analysis. Heilberger was never called as a Commission witness.[54]

Not having irrefutable smoking-gun ballistics evidence that Oswald had been Walker's assailant, the government had to rely on Marina Oswald's December 3 revelations. For instance, during the Commission's April 30 executive session Dulles asked Rankin what the Commission had on the Walker shooting. Rankin brushed aside the FBI's ballistics evidence in the case as unconvincing. McCloy, however, immediately chimed in, noting that the Commission had "Marina's testimony," implying that was all the Commission needed. In February, a Dallas newsman asked Dallas Police Chief Jesse E. Curry about the status of the Walker shooting investigation. Curry responded that he was prepared to close the file on the case, not on the strength of the ballistics evidence but solely on Marina Oswald's testimony.[55]

General Walker was quick to place the FBI on notice that he did not intend to sit idly by while assertions attributed to "official sources" (read FBI leaks) were circulating in the press naming Oswald as his assailant. Four days after Marina's confession about Lee's attempt on the general's life, the FBI heard from two of Walker's attorneys, Clyde J. Watts and A.V. Grant. Watts raised the possibility that there might have been others involved in the attempt on his client's life. Concerned for the general-cum-politician's safety—at the time of the April 10 incident Walker was a candidate for the governorship of Texas—Watts wanted to review the results of the bureau's investigation into the shooting and to obtain permission to interview Marina. Although the FBI denied that it was the source of the leaks, it took steps to avoid a rebuff of Watts's request and to assure the Walker camp that the bureau was conducting a thorough investigation. Hoover ordered that a "mature and experienced" agent personally contact Watts at his Oklahoma City offices and explain why FBI policy prevented the dissemination of confidential records of an ongoing investigation.[56]

Hoover's attempt at quiet diplomacy did not work with Walker. The FBI was alarmed to learn that the general had authorized Watts to hire two private detectives to investigate the shooting. The object of their investigation was William MacEwan Duff, a disgruntled former employee who had left

Walker's service several months before the April 10 incident. Watts told the FBI that the investigation had not ruled out the possibility that Duff knew Oswald and that the two might have been involved in a conspiracy to kill the general.[57]

Having no persuasive physical evidence to tie Oswald to the Walker shooting, the FBI was forced to take action to demonstrate it was on top of the investigation. This required interviewing General Walker, something the bureau had hoped to avoid. Actually, Walker forced the FBI's hand. On February 12, during an interview on a Dallas radio station, the general charged that Oswald "was working with a communist cell in Dallas"; Walker further claimed that a Dallas lunchroom owner had reportedly seen Duff and Oswald together in his establishment. Walker's public revelations prompted Belmont to recommend that FBI Dallas interview the general and "pin him down." Hoover reluctantly agreed but noted, "I hope we are right and this is not another gap." The "gap" was the failure of the Dallas FBI to have explored the Duff angle in the Walker case. This was an example, one of many in the matter of the JFK assassination, of the FBI standing around with its pockets open waiting for evidence to drop in.[58]

A week after Walker went public on the radio, the FBI interviewed him. The agent reporting on the encounter claimed that Walker's remarks "were rambling and incoherent." The general insisted that Oswald was working with Dallas communists and that further investigation would probably reveal that Marina Oswald was a KGB agent. It was clear from the report that Walker was angry and frustrated with the FBI, convinced that it was blocking his access to information about the attempt on his life. After the interview FBI Washington instructed the Dallas office to have no more contact with Walker.[59]

Given Walker's extreme right-wing political views, he may have been genuinely convinced that he had been targeted by some vast communist conspiracy with roots in Dallas. It is also possible that gubernatorial candidate Walker calculated he could get a bounce in his polls if enough voters were convinced that the "communist" who had killed Kennedy was the same assailant who had tried to assassinate him. What is certain is that after Walker failed in his bid for political office he continued to take an active interest in the Kennedy assassination and the contradictory facts surrounding the attempt on his own life. His dogged refusal to let the matter drop was important because other than government officials and government-appointed commissions and experts, Walker was the only independent witness who actually examined the bullet that narrowly missed his head.

In 1970, after reading former Police Chief Curry's self-published debunking treatment of some of the evidence in the Warren report, Walker contacted Senator Richard Russell. He told the former Commission member that he had never repaired the bullet hole in the copper strip around the window of his study. He thought the senator should know because this "perfect bullet hole" was the best evidence to determine the caliber of the bullet that had been so mutilated and deformed after it penetrated a masonry wall. Russell forwarded his letter to the FBI and received a prompt reply basically informing Russell that Curry's book was full of errors and that Marina Oswald's testimony and "other evidence" left no doubt that Oswald had been Walker's assailant.[60]

On July 23, 1964, Walker appeared before the Warren Commission, where assistant counsel Wesley Liebeler conducted the questioning. Walker recounted the events of the evening of April 10, 1963, when at about 9 o'clock a bullet had come crashing through the window to his study. When he ran to the window he saw the taillights of a car at the bottom of the alley that ran behind his house before it turned off onto Turtle Creek Boulevard. Liebeler elicited from the general that he no longer believed that there had been any connection between Oswald and William Duff. The session ended without adding any information that was not already available in the Dallas police's investigative reports of the Walker shooting. The one area where Walker's testimony could have added persuasive weight to the Commission's contention that Oswald had been his assailant was conspicuously avoided: Walker was never asked to offer an opinion about Commission Exhibit 573 (CE 573), the mutilated remains of a 6.5-mm metal-jacketed bullet that the government maintained had been recovered from Walker's home on April 10, 1964. Never once during the two-hour session while a cooperative and responsive Walker answered Liebeler's questions did the assistant counsel or any of the commissioners in attendance mention CE 573.[61]

In 1979 Walker was watching a televised session of the House Select Committee on Assassinations when Robert Blakey, the committee's chief counsel, held up CE 573 as a visual aide to augment his narrative on the firearms evidence in the Kennedy assassination. Walker, a thirty-year career army officer with extensive combat experience in World War II, and with more than a passing familiarity with military weaponry, was stunned. According to Walker, what Blakey represented as the bullet fired into his home bore no resemblance to the piece of lead the police had recovered, which he had held in his own hand and closely examined. Walker started a campaign to get the government to "withdraw the substituted bullet" from all records and files relating to the Kennedy assassination. He never contested the official account that Oswald had been his assailant, only the fact that CE 573 was the bullet the Dallas police had recovered from his house. Walker wrote to Blakey; Griffin Bell, the U.S. attorney general; and the Dallas police chief, protesting what he regarded as a grievous error compromising the integrity of the record of the Kennedy assassination. All of Walker's decade-long efforts came to nothing.[62]

If the note (referred to as the "Walker Note") Oswald had left his wife on the evening of April 10, 1963, and the circumstances surrounding its timely discovery were legitimate, then Oswald should have been a prime suspect in the Walker case. Pressing the point even further, if Oswald had written the note, then it was the most damaging evidence the government ever came up with connecting him with the assassination of President Kennedy. As the Warren report pointed out, this attempt on General Walker demonstrated Oswald's "determination and the other traits required to carry out a carefully planned killing of another human being and was willing to consummate such a purpose if he thought there was sufficient reason to do so."[63]

The official story was that on the evening of April 10 Oswald had left his Dallas Neely Street apartment to attend typing classes at the Dallas Evening School. Marina thought nothing about his leaving, but she was not aware that Lee had dropped out of the class a week earlier. According to Marina, when Lee left the apartment he did not have a rifle. Marina grew anxious when he did not return from typing class at the usual time. She went into the room in which he kept his personal things and discovered a note on a small end table. The note contained a list of instructions and courses of action for her to take if he did not return. It informed her that the rent and the gas were paid and told her where to find the post office box, and to send any news clippings to the Soviet consulate, where she might get help after Soviet officials learned "what happened to me." The note's last paragraph provided directions to the "city prison" in the event that "I am still alive" and under arrest.

When Lee returned home that evening Marina confronted him with the note, and, according to her account, he admitted that he had shot at Walker. Lee told her that he had smuggled the rifle out of the apartment three days earlier and hidden it in some bushes on the grounds near Walker's home; after the shooting, he buried the rifle. Marina said she kept the note as a kind of insurance policy against any further "crazy " behavior, warning her husband that if he did anything like this again she would go to the police. According to the official account, Marina slipped the note between the dust covers of a Russian-language book of housekeeping tips for new wives that Lee had given her as a birthday gift. For the next seven months the incriminating note remained hidden until it surfaced, fortuitously and very timely, during the investigation into the Kennedy assassination. Two weeks after the reported attempt on Walker's life, Oswald moved to New Orleans in search of employment.[64]

At about 3 o'clock in the afternoon of November 22, two hours after Kennedy was pronounced dead, four detectives of the Dallas Police Department's

Homicide-Robbery Bureau showed up at the home of Ruth H. Paine in Irving, a Dallas suburb. Marina and her infant daughters had been staying with Paine since the Oswalds had left New Orleans and returned to the Dallas area, where in mid-October Lee had found work at the Texas School Book Depository. Lee rented a small room in Dallas at a rooming house at 1026 North Beckley Street and visited Marina and the children on weekends.

The four Dallas detectives, joined by two Irving policemen, spent the next two to three hours searching Paine's home. According to Detective Richard S. Stovall, who supervised the search, the six officers went through the entire house—Marina's bedroom, Ruth Paine's bedroom, the den, the kitchen, and the closets. The next day they returned and spent four hours searching Paine's garage. Since Lee's room at the North Beckley address was very small, accommodating only a bed and a small chest of drawers, most of the Oswalds' possessions were stored at Ruth Paine's modest but comfortable Irving home. Stovall recalled that the searchers took "one Russian book" from Marina's bedroom, and John P. Adamcik, one of the detectives on the search team, told a Commission staff lawyer that they had found a lot of Russian-language books in the garage. The FBI's compiled inventory of all the items that the Dallas authorities recovered from Oswald's bandbox of a room and Ruth Paine's house and garage was forty-nine pages long, leaving the unavoidable impression that very few of the Oswalds' possessions did not end up in Dallas Police Captain Will Fritz's evidence room. Amazingly, however, despite the exhaustive two-day search the Dallas police did not discover the "thick book of Russian housekeeping advice" where Marina had secreted the incriminating note between the "book's chartreuse covers."[65]

As Ruth Paine related to the author Thomas Mallon, it was on November 30 that she sent to Marina, via the Irving County police, the Russian housekeeping book, some letters, and baby clothes, thinking it would make her close friend less homesick. When Secret Service agents examined these articles they discovered the note "written in very poor Russian." At this time Marina and her two children, one of whom was barely two months old, were under the protective custody of the Secret Service at the Inn of the Six Flags in Fort Worth. During the first week or two of what turned out to be a three-month regime of protective custody after the assassination, Marina Oswald was under intense government pressure.

On November 28 the FBI moved in a team to begin interrogating Marina to clear up some of the loose angles in the case, such as Lee's Mexico trip and whether her husband had ever made any threats against General Walker. Assistant Director William C. Sullivan, chief of the bureau's Domestic Intelligence Division and the official in charge of handling Oswald's widow, told the team to "bear down" on her. FBI headquarters dispatched an Immigration and Naturalization Service (INS) agent to Fort Worth to join the FBI team. The INS agent's assignment was to impress upon Marina that now that her husband was dead, she was an alien with a permanent visa and could face deportation if she did not cooperate with the government. Marina had already forcefully made it clear to the Dallas police through Ruth Paine that she wanted to remain in the United States with her two children and did not want to be sent back to the Soviet Union.[66]

After the Irving police turned the Russian book (English translation: "Book of helpful instructions") with the chartreuse dust cover over to the Secret Service, the note was discovered on December 2, just three days before the FBI sent its report on the Kennedy assassination to Katzenbach at Justice. The note was not dated and was not signed. According to the Secret Service's Russian-language expert, Leon I. Gopadze, it was Marina who translated the note and confirmed that her husband had written it and confessed to her that he was the one who had made an attempt on General Walker's life.[67]

On December 3 the FBI Dallas office sent the "Walker Note" to bureau headquarters, where it was examined by Sebastian Latona, the FBI's fingerprint expert. During his Warren Commission testimony Latona reported that he had lifted Oswald's palm prints and fingerprints from the suspect's wallet, pictures, and personal papers. However, during his appearance before the Commission he was never asked about the "Walker Note." The explanation for this omission may rest in the fact that before he appeared before the Commission, staff assistant counsel Melvin Eisenberg, who went over the FBI fingerprint expert's testimony, learned that Lee's and Marina's fingerprints and palm prints were not on the note. Latona had noted in his report to his supervisor that he had lifted seven latent fingerprints from the letter, but none were "identical with the fingerprints of Lee Harvey Oswald or Marina Nikolaevna Oswald." There could have been many innocent reasons why the Oswalds' prints were not on the "Walker Note." The absence of evidence does not automatically translate into the absence of proof. In any case, handwriting evidence in document identification is more important than the presence or absence of fingerprints. And James C. Cadigan, the FBI handwriting expert, was certain, based on comparisons of documents in Cyrillic print known to have been written by Oswald, that Oswald had written the "Walker Note." Nevertheless, there lingers a cloud of suspicion as to why the Commission never had Latona provide reasoned explanations for the historic record as to why Lee's and Marina's prints were not on the "Walker Note."[68]

While the Oswald note appeared to be convincing evidence that he was the sniper in the Walker shooting, the government's assertion was saddled with some glaring contradictory flaws and suppressed witness testimony that pointed to Oswald's innocence. On December 3 the Dallas office sent the alleged Oswald letter to bureau headquarters, where it was examined by

Sebastian Latona, the FBI's fingerprint expert. As he testified before the Warren Commission, Latona had lifted Oswald's palm and fingerprints from his wallet, pictures, and personal papers. But when it came to "the letter written in the Russian language by Lee Harvey Oswald," as described by Latona, the FBI's top fingerprint expert reported that he had lifted seven latent fingerprints from the letter, but none were "identical with the fingerprints of Lee Harvey Oswald or Marina Nikolaevna Oswald." It is not certain whether the Commission was aware of Latona's report, and he was never asked to render his expert opinion on the "Walker Note." Four days after the discovery of the Oswald note, Katzenbach told Pierre Salinger, President Johnson's press secretary, to go ahead with a White House press release confirming that Oswald had been the sniper who took a shot at the general. That same day, December 6, twenty minutes after Katzenbach spoke with Belmont, FBIHQ Section Chief James L. Handley informed the head of the FBI's Dallas office, J. Gordon Shanklin, that he could expect a memorandum on American Airlines flight 307, with an express receipt to Captain Ed Bachner of the Dallas Police Department. Almost certainly the memorandum contained a copy of the "Walker Note" with Marina's account and instructions to Bachner that the FBI's report would conclude that Oswald was the sniper in the Walker case and that the bureau expected the Dallas police to fully support the official version. It was imperative that FBI headquarters move quickly to tie up all loose ends because the Dallas police were not privy to the conclusions in the FBI report and there was still uncertainty about whether Carr and the Texas Court of Inquiry could be trusted to hew to the official line.[69]

As much as the Commission tried to distance itself from openly espousing the theory that Oswald's attempt on Walker had been the rehearsal for his assassination of Kennedy, the inference did slip into the final report. The Warren report concluded that based on the "Walker Note," Marina's testimony, some pictures of Oswald with the rifle, and the testimony of firearms identification experts, Oswald had "attempted to take the life of General Edwin A. Walker." The report went on to note that Oswald's attempt on Walker "was considered of probative value in this investigation, although the Commission's conclusion concerning the identity of the assassin was based on evidence independent of the finding that Oswald attempted to kill General Walker."[70]

As developed earlier, what the Warren report failed to disclose was that the FBI ballistics experts had no more success than the Dallas police in their efforts to forensically connect Oswald with the Walker shooting. In February 1964 Chief Curry told a reporter from the *Dallas Times-Herald* that the police were ready to name Oswald as the assailant in the Walker case based not on the ballistic evidence but solely on Marina Oswald's testimony. Several months later Rankin wrote Hoover a six-page letter complaining that Marina's testimony on the Walker shooting to the FBI and Secret Service was giving the Commission lawyers fits because it was riddled with contradictions. The Commission requested that the bureau undertake an "extensive investigation concerning the Walker allegations." Rankin's letter spelled out in detail six areas that needed clarification and asked the director to have Marina questioned again. Shanklin, though he had believed that the Walker case was finally closed, had to assign two agents to interview Marina all over again because "her statements just don't jibe."[71]

Hoover's response to Rankin's May 20 letter came about a month later, and in it he pretended to resolve the general counsel's concerns. The director concluded the letter with steely finality: "This concludes our inquiries in this particular matter." However, Rankin was not privy to the addendum to the letter written by one of the agents Shanklin had assigned to the case, Ivan D. Lee, reflecting the FBI's hitting-a-brick-wall frustration in the Walker shooting. Lee's note concluded, "Our investigation did not establish whether Oswald did or did not make an attempt on General Walker's life."[72]

On June 10, the same day that Hoover curtly informed Rankin that the FBI was closing its investigation into the Walker case, the two agents that Shanklin assigned to carry out the "extensive investigation" on the attempt on the general's life reported the results of their investigation. Dallas agents Lee and Robert M. Barrett spent a week interviewing witnesses already identified by the Dallas police. One promising witness was a fifteen-year-old named Walter Kirk Coleman, who was one of Walker's neighbors. On the evening of April 10 he had been working with his godfather, who was helping him build shelves in his room, when he heard a shot sometime between 9 and 10 P.M. He immediately ran from his first-floor bedroom and looked over a stockade fence into the parking lot of the Mormon church that adjoined General Walker's residence at 4011 Turtle Creek Boulevard. He spotted two men getting into their cars and leaving the church parking lot.

When Lee and Barrett questioned Coleman, the youth was able to describe the cars and the two fleeing individuals. The church parking lights were on, so Coleman had had a good look at the men and their vehicles. One of the cars was a white or beige 1950 Ford and the other was a "black over white, two-door Chevrolet." Coleman described the man who left in the Ford as "a white male, about 15 to 20 years of age, about 5 ft. 10" in height, and weighing about 130 pounds. He stated," the FBI report recorded, "this man had dark, bushy hair, a thin face with a large nose, and was 'real skinny.'" When Lee and Barrett showed him numerous photographs, including some of Oswald, Coleman told them that neither of the men looked like Oswald and "that he had never seen anyone in or around the Walker residence or the church before or after April 10, 1963, who resembled Lee Harvey Oswald."

Coleman's account was supported by Robert A. Surrey, a Dallas business-man and a Walker supporter. Surrey told Lee and Barrett that on April 8, two days before the incident, he had arrived at Walker's house and noticed two "well dressed men in suits and ties" looking into Walker's windows. The men did not see him, so he continued to observe them from a position in one of the neighboring yards. After about thirty minutes the men left in a Ford that had no rear license plate. Surrey said he had never seen the intruders be-fore and that neither looked like Oswald.[73]

The FBI agents noted in their report that the two suspects had not yet been identified, but Lee and Barrett were impressed enough with Coleman's de-scription of the two men and their cars to ask whether FBI Washington wanted them to pursue the investigation any further. Their report noted, "It appears only logical" that the two men had either been involved in the as-sault on Walker or had been witnesses to the shooting and were reluctant to come forward and report what they saw. Aware, however, that Oswald was the only official suspect in the case, they ended their report with the caution-ary note that any further investigation would necessitate interviewing Gen-eral Walker, who, they were quick to point out, would "immediately alert the press or call a press conference and publicize the inquiry." With this ad-monition Lee and Barrett were simply preaching to the choir. Hoover had al-ready closed the FBI's investigation into the Walker shooting and had no interest in uncovering any new information that could weaken the govern-ment's case against the only charged assailant in the Kennedy assassination. There is no indication that the FBI ever made Walter Kirk Coleman's testi-mony available to the Warren Commission, and Coleman was never called to testify before the Commission.

Even by applying the most charitable standards it could not be claimed that the government met the criteria Katzenbach set forth in his November 25 memorandum: "The public must be satisfied . . . that the evidence was such that he [Oswald] would have been convicted at trial" when it came to the Walker case. And the Walker case, as used in this instance, was just a mi-crocosm of what was to follow in the government's investigation into the Kennedy assassination. In trying to connect Oswald with the attempt on Walker's life the FBI had dug a dry hole. Had Oswald lived to face a trial with competent defense it would have been risky, at best, for the authorities to try to make the claim that the physical evidence conclusively linked Os-wald to the Walker shooting. The Warren Commission, not having to con-tend with any forceful review of the forensic evidence or cross-examination of witnesses, was free to conclude that Oswald's attempt to kill Walker demonstrated "his disposition to take human life." What is not in the Warren report is any allusion to the strange career and timely appearance of Oswald's alleged "Walker Note" to Marina, a possible forgery, or the progress of the presumption that Oswald was the sniper in the Walker shooting from planted FBI stories in the press to a White House press release and finally into the government's officially sanctioned historical record of the assassination of America's thirty-fifth president.

3   Oswald in Mexico—Seven Days That Shook the Government

The Ambassador in Mexico is acting like a Sherlock Holmes.
—J. Edgar Hoover, November 27, 1963

In life, and for that matter in death, Lee Harvey Oswald remained a mystery. By nature or conscious design, or both, this former marine and expatriate was highly secretive. He confided even in Marina, his wife and the mother of his two children, only on rare occasions. For the rest of the world he never let down his guard; he trusted no one with his secrets. He was capable of taking dangerous risks and openly identifying himself with unpopular views, but he never actually committed himself to any party, political front group, or movement of the right or left.

Surveying the most prominent aspects of his personality shown in the biography of his adult years suggests that Oswald harbored a secret ambition to be a spy or an informer for some government agency. His older brother Robert recalled that as a young child Lee preferred the fantasy world to the drab reality around him. In his early teen years Oswald's favorite television program was *I Led Three Lives,* the story of Herbert Philbrick, an FBI informer who posed as a communist spy. He never missed the weekly telecast of Special Agent Philbrick's derring-do and his double life of intrigue and adventure. When Robert left home to join the marines, Lee was still transfixed in front of the TV watching the reruns. In July 1964 the Warren Commission assembled three psychiatrists to try to divine the mainspring of Oswald's motivations. After a full and taxing day of largely vacuous psychobabble, Dulles, Rankin, McCloy, and the Commission staff lawyers were still in the dark about what made JFK's alleged assassin tick.[1]

Nonetheless, the Commission concluded that Oswald's Mexico trip, in sharp contrast to all the mystery surrounding the rest of his life, was an open book and had no bearing on the subsequent events in Dallas. The Warren report lays out in a wealth of detail the purpose behind Oswald's seven days in Mexico City. The basis for the report's confident assertion in this area of the investigation rested on the FBI's mammoth investigation into Oswald's travel to and from Mexico and the Commission's staff report on Oswald's Mexico City trip. Most of what the Commission's staff lawyers learned about Oswald's alleged contacts with the Soviet and Cuban diplomatic missions originated with the CIA's Mexico City station. Contrary to what the Commission concluded about Oswald's Mexico City trip, there are credible

grounds for believing that Oswald's seven days in Mexico's capital were inextricably tied to President Kennedy's assassination. After forty years there
are lingering dark areas in the Mexico City picture and deeply troubling
questions about the activities of the Mexico City CIA station.[2]

About midday on September 25, Oswald boarded Continental Trailways
Bus Number 5121 leaving New Orleans for Houston, Texas, on the first leg
of his trip to Mexico City. Early Thursday morning (2:35 A.M.) he took
Trailways Bus Number 5133, transferred to Mexican Flecha Roja (Red Ar-
row) Bus Number 516 at Nuevo Laredo, Mexico, and arrived in Mexico
City on September 27 at midmorning.[3]

As presented in the Warren report, the purpose of Oswald's trip was to get
a transit visa to Cuba and then a reentry visa to return to the Soviet Union.
He spent most of his time shuffling back and forth between the Cuban and
Soviet diplomatic compounds trying to get his paperwork in order. Before
Oswald left for Mexico he had done some investigating. His U.S. passport
proscribed travel to Cuba, but Mexican immigration officials did not recog-
nize passport entries prohibiting the bearer's travel to Cuba. Oswald was
aware that if he could get a Cuban in-transit visa he could board a Mexican
flight to Cuba and (still relying on the Commission's account) spend a few
weeks touring Castro's Cuba until his Soviet visa came through. Oswald had
planned and budgeted carefully for his Mexican trip, but it was all for nothing. During his first full day in Mexico City he ran into snags he had not
anticipated.[4]

One of the mysteries surrounding Oswald's Mexico City trip that the
Commission never addressed was whether he ever actually intended to return to the Soviet Union. On the face of it, the notion that Oswald went to
Mexico to ultimately return to the Soviet Union via Cuba made absolutely
no sense. There was something else at play that the Commission failed to investigate. Although he professed to be a Marxist, Oswald was anti-Soviet. If
Oswald ever truly harbored pro-Soviet sympathies, the former defector
joined the legions of one-time true believers who had seen the "workers-
peasants paradise" up close and realized the perverted nature of this claim.
Had he wanted to return to the Soviet Union he would have gone to Canada,
not Mexico. He had no interest in returning to Russia, and by all indications
the Soviet state had no interest in allowing the anti-Soviet Oswald back into
the country. Additionally, the Soviets were not known to issue permits to
travel to Cuba without prior authorization from the Ministry of the Exterior
in Havana, and Oswald had probably investigated this policy before he left
for Mexico. Inarguably, Oswald's purpose in going to Mexico was to make
contact with Cuban consular officials in his effort to get a Cuban visa so he
could spend some time examining Castro's ongoing revolutionary experiment. Before he turned up in Mexico City Oswald had gone to certain

lengths to publicly advertise the fact that he was a convert to Castroism and an enthusiastic supporter of the first self-proclaimed Marxist-Leninist government in Central America.[5]

The rub was that Oswald did not have the resources to underwrite plans for any extended stay in Cuba. He did not have the funds to fly from Mexico City to Havana and then sustain himself sightseeing and taking in the promised wonders of this new socialist state. The Commission was aware that Oswald was on a tight budget. He had been without work for about two months before his Mexico sojourn. Marina left New Orleans and returned to Ruth Paine's home in Irving, Texas, because Lee was so financially strapped that she was not getting the proper prenatal attention. Either Oswald was a moon-walking fantasist with only the flimsiest grip on reality, or he was being handled by sources that had plans for him.

Without question the Commission's task in plumbing Oswald's motives was made more difficult by his assassination. Nonetheless, the Commission should have used all its powers to probe this area of the investigation rather than falling back on the oversimplified explanation that Oswald was committed to "Marxism and communism," a handy idea but largely erroneous. The revelation that JFK's charged assassin, a former defector to the Soviet Union, had been actively seeking a Cuban visa in order to travel to Castro's Cuba just weeks before Kennedy's murder was so significant that the Commission needed to do all in its power to assure that there was no connection between Oswald's Mexico City trip and Kennedy's assassination.[6]

More than a decade after the Warren Commission issued its report, the speculation that Oswald was being manipulated achieved credence from the House Select Committee on Assassinations (HSCA) staff report, "Lee Harvey Oswald, the CIA, and Mexico City." This three hundred–page report was written by two of the HSCA's best investigators, Dan Hardway and Eddie Lopez, and is generally identified as the Lopez Report. Among other revelations, the Lopez Report makes a convincing case that someone was impersonating Oswald in telephone calls and visits to the Soviet and Cuban diplomatic compounds during the week that Oswald was in Mexico City. The strong likelihood that there was an ongoing intelligence operation attempting to link Oswald to a "Red plot" will be developed later in this chapter.[7]

After Oswald's arrival in Mexico City, he wasted no time in getting on with the business at hand. According to the Warren report, he made three visits to the Cuban Consulate and a visit to the Soviet Embassy before the day was over. His first stop was at the Cuban Consulate, where he learned that he could not get an in-transit visa to Cuba unless he could prove that he had a Soviet visa. Silvia Duran, a twenty-six-year-old Mexican national, sent Oswald to the Soviet Embassy to verify that he had a travel visa to the USSR. When Oswald returned to the consulate he told Duran that he had his

Soviet visa. After Duran checked with the Soviet Embassy she found out that Oswald was lying. Confronting the American with his deception, she informed Oswald that he could expect to wait four to five months before word came from Moscow about a visa. The American's reaction was anger tailing off into despair. Oswald had shown Duran some newspaper clippings and a Fair Play for Cuba Committee membership card attesting to his pro-Castro sympathies. Duran recalled that Oswald, confronted with plans gone awry, was on the verge of tears. At that point, she called the Cuban consul, Eusebio Azcue Lopez. When Azcue tried to mollify the now irate Oswald, explaining that Cuba had to be careful about whom the government let into the country without a close security check, all attempts at civility gave way to a shouting match. Duran recalled that the exchange was so loud that people outside the consulate were startled by the uproar. Azcue ordered the American out of the consulate, declaring that he was "not a friend of the Cuban Revolution." Oswald left, and according to Duran, that was the last the Cuban Consulate staff heard of him until the world press carried the story of Kennedy's assassination and the name of his accused assassin.[8]

The Commission's two assistant counsels responsible for the report on Oswald in Mexico were W. David Slawson and William T. Coleman, Jr. With few exceptions, the information in their reports dealing with Oswald's contacts with Cuban and Soviet diplomatic officials was filtered through the CIA and consequently served a single point of view, especially the one advanced by the Mexico City station.[9] This filtering was symptomatic of the inherent weakness of the Commission in undertaking any successful investigation into the possibility of a conspiracy. The development of any plausible conspiracy theories and reasonable suspects was predicated upon the existence of a Commission staff that was knowledgeable about the most likely suspect groups: pro-Castro and anti-Castro groups in the United States and Mexico; Soviet counterintelligence and espionage organs; or even organized crime and its links to the CIA, FBI, or the Dallas police force. There were no Commission staff lawyers with this kind of expertise; only two of the assistant counsels had any substantial background in the area of organized crime, and neither of them was Coleman or Slawson. Understandably, then, the Commission was completely dependent upon the CIA for all of its information on Oswald's activities in Mexico City.

The agency's station in Mexico City had the most comprehensive electronic surveillance system of any CIA station in the world. All the outside lines from the Soviet and Cuban embassies and the Soviet Military Attaché's office were tapped; only the telephone lines at the Cuban Consulate were uncompromised. The agency had two cameras covering the front entrance of the Soviet Embassy and a photo-surveillance post at the rear of the embassy. The entrance to the Cuban Consulate was under photographic surveillance.

The Mexico City station had a base house across the street from the consulate, and pulse cameras located on the second and third floors of an apartment house at 149 Francisco Marquez Street. This photo-surveillance system was in operation through September and October 1963.[10] CIA operative David Atlee Phillips, who was the station's covert action chief of the Cuban section in 1963, admitted that he had a human source inside the Cuban Embassy. During proceedings growing out of a 1984 libel case, Phillips acknowledged under oath that he knew Oswald had visited the Cuban Consulate based on "reports from a Cuban Embassy source that we had inside." It was almost certain that Phillips was referring to a human asset.[11]

The Warren report's rather uncomplicated and straightforward version of Oswald's Mexico trip, more specifically his alleged contacts with Soviet and Cuban diplomatic officials, is far removed from the ominous and murky reality. In this matter the Commission might be excused for allowing itself to be deceived by relying with unquestioned confidence on what the CIA confided about Oswald's activities and intentions. The Commission must be credited, at least, for correctly reporting that Oswald was in Mexico City from September 27 to October 2, 1963. Much of the rest of the Warren report's treatment of Oswald in Mexico City cannot be safely assumed to be an accurate account. A striking example is the fact that the persuasive evidence that there was an Oswald imposter in Mexico City creating a false biography of the man who would soon be accused of assassinating President Kennedy is not in the Commission's "open-book" version of Oswald's 1963 Mexico sojourn.

According to HSCA investigators Hardway and Lopez, all the evidence they examined indicated that during his seven days in Mexico City Oswald visited the Soviet and Cuban diplomatic compounds a combined total of five times. Over that same period, the CIA electronic intercepts disclose that someone who was identified as "Lee Oswald" but was not Oswald was in telephone contact with both Communist embassies. On September 27, his first day in Mexico City, when Oswald was apparently shuttling back and forth between the Soviet Embassy and the Cuban Consulate, CIA phone-tap logs record that an unidentified man (whom the CIA would later identify as Oswald) called the Soviet Military Attaché's Office and the Soviet Embassy twice about a visa to Odessa, USSR. In all three instances the CIA transcriber noted that the conversations were in Spanish.[12] Commission witnesses who had had occasion to observe whether Oswald spoke Spanish all reported that he had no command of the language. Lieutenant John E. Donovan, the officer in charge of the radar squadron in which marine PFC Oswald had served at El Toro Air Base in California, did not remember ever hearing Oswald use Spanish. Donovan's memory carries some weight because the marine air controllers were always having trouble with Mexican ham operators cutting in on the squadron's radio transmissions; when this occurred, someone in the outfit who knew Spanish would be called in to warn them off. According to Donovan, Oswald was not one of the men in his command with any facility in Spanish.[13]

During this same seven-day period a CIA transcriber's log noted that on Saturday, September 28, an American citizen at the Cuban Consulate had had a phone conversation with an official at the Soviet Embassy. Every indication was that the man was at the Cuban Consulate to follow up on his attempts of the previous day to get an in-transit visa to Cuba. Consular employee Silvia Duran was on the phone with an official at the Soviet Embassy explaining that an American was at the consulate who had previously visited the Soviet Embassy. The Russian asked to speak to the man. The CIA transcriber's notes read that the man "speaks terrible, hardly recognizable Russian." Several days later, on October 1, a caller rang up the Soviet Consulate to find out whether the Soviet Embassy in Washington had heard from Moscow about his Soviet visa so he could travel to Odessa. The caller introduced himself as "Lee Oswald" and during the short exchange said he thought that he had spoken earlier with consular official "Kostikov." Before the caller was abruptly cut off he managed to repeat that his name was Oswald. When the CIA translator wrote up the log of the conversation he noted that the October 1 caller was the same man who had called on September 28. The CIA translator based his identification on the caller's "broken Russian" on both occasions. Although the best evidence is that Oswald had no command of Spanish, there is no question about the fact that he was fluent in Russian.[14]

The most likely explanation of these episodes is that someone was impersonating Oswald. In time the Mexico City station linked all the phone calls in September and on October 1 to Oswald.[15] The business Oswald was trying to transact could not have been exclusively conducted over the telephone; he had to present himself at the Cuban and Soviet diplomatic compounds. There is no question that he was at the Cuban Consulate on September 27. His signed application for a visa to travel to Cuba, with a full-frontal snapshot attached, is part of the Commission's record for history.[16]

If the HSCA's estimate that Oswald visited the Cuban and Soviet embassies at least five times is dependable, there should have been pictures of him either entering or leaving the compounds. The Mexico station had full photo-surveillance coverage of both Communist embassies and therefore had ten opportunities of capturing Oswald on film, so it strains credulity that the CIA station reported it had no photographs of Oswald. The agency insisted that the pulse camera covering the entrance to the Cuban Consulate had not been working during the period that Oswald was in Mexico City. The CIA stonewalled the HSCA investigating team on the photographs produced by the other cameras, especially pictures from the base house the station identified as "LILYRIC," located directly across the street from the front gate of the Soviet Embassy.[17]

The HSCA investigators concluded that the CIA had at least one photograph of Oswald entering the Cuban Consulate on September 27. The team interviewed several CIA officers who had been stationed in Mexico City, and all three were in agreement that the station had pictures of Oswald. One of the career agents, Joseph Piccolo, said he had seen a picture of Oswald, a left profile, taken at the entrance of either the Soviet or the Cuban Embassy. Stronger verification came from the private safe of Win Scott, who was the chief of station in Mexico City at the time that Oswald was in the capital. When Scott died his private safe was cleaned out by James Jesus Angleton, the chief of the CIA's Counterintelligence Branch. One of the items from Scott's safe was a manuscript titled "Foul Foe." On page 273 of the manuscript Scott had written, "Oswald's visits and conversations are not hearsay; for persons watching these embassies photographed Oswald as he entered and left each one; and clocked the time he spent on each visit."[18]

The Lopez Report concluded that the CIA was hiding the truth about pictures of Oswald but resisted speculating about reasons for the suppression. A possibility is that some of the Mexico City station's pictures of Oswald showed him in the company of people who had agency connections. During the entire ten months that the Commission went about its investigation, the only photograph that the Mexico City station produced as evidence that Oswald had visited Communist embassies was a fraud. The CIA station chief knew it was bogus. The matter of the so-called Mexico City Mystery Man will be discussed later in this chapter.

During his first week in office President Lyndon B. Johnson entertained the strong likelihood that there had been a plot to assassinate Kennedy. Historian Robert Dallek wrote, "Johnson had a suspicious cast of mind that caused him to see a conspiracy behind every major mishap." A catastrophe like Dallas, which he had witnessed, was guaranteed to adrenalize his conspiratorial view of public affairs.[19] On Saturday, the day following the assassination, Johnson spoke with the two agency heads who could provide the most updated intelligence briefing on the assassination. CIA Director John McCone met twice with the president on November 23. The director used the time to brief Johnson on the Oswald and Mexico City developments. McCone related what the Mexico City station had forwarded to headquarters about Oswald's visits with Soviet diplomats, especially his alleged contact with the Soviet consular official Valery V. Kostikov. Mexico station officials suspected that Kostikov was a sabotage and assassination expert. Since Chief of Station (COS) Win Scott had been an alarmist about Kostikov in his cables to CIA headquarters in Langley, it is safe to assume that during his afternoon meeting with LBJ, McCone sketched out the CIA's suspicions of a Kremlin conspiracy to take the life of John F. Kennedy. Earlier that morning Tennent H. Bagley, the acting chief of the CIA's Soviet Russia Division, notified the FBI's liaison officer about the Oswald-Kostikov contact.[20]

That same day Johnson had a midmorning phone conversation with FBI Director J. Edgar Hoover. He wanted to know whether Hoover had any more information about Oswald's visit to the Soviet Embassy in Mexico City. Obviously they had spoken earlier about this angle in the case the FBI was making against Oswald, even though Hoover admitted that the evidence so far was "not very strong." Hoover then related some news that must have captured the president's attention—there was evidence that someone in Mexico City had been impersonating Lee Harvey Oswald, the charged assassin of President Kennedy. In his fractured syntax, the FBI director gave Johnson the following account: "We have up here the tape and the photograph of the man who was at the Soviet Embassy, using Oswald's name. The picture and the tape do not correspond to this man's [Oswald's] voice, nor his appearance. In other words, it appears that there is a second person who was at the Soviet Embassy down there." Later that day Hoover sent a memorandum to James J. Rowley, the head of the Secret Service. Hoover told Rowley about the CIA photographs and the tape, adding that the Dallas agents who had interrogated Oswald were of the opinion that the photographs and the "recording of his voice" were not those of Lee Harvey Oswald.[21]

Instead of clearing up some of the mystery concerning Oswald's activities, the facts surrounding the voice tape and the photographs only throw a wider shadow of suspicion over the CIA's Mexico City station. On the day of the assassination there was a meeting in the office of Thomas C. Mann, the U.S. ambassador to Mexico. Joining Mann were the FBI's legal attaché (legat), Clark D. Anderson, and Win Scott. During the meeting, arrangements were made to deliver the tape and the photographs to the Dallas FBI field office, where agents were interrogating Kennedy's charged assassin. What was noteworthy about the November 22 meeting in Mann's office was that this was the first time the FBI learned of Oswald's visits to the Cuban Consulate. Legat Anderson was taken aback by this development because it was a clear breach of a long-standing FBI-CIA understanding that the agency would report on the activities of any American who visited Soviet and Cuban embassies.[22] From the bureau's point of view this breach was doubly serious because the ex-marine and former defector's FBI preassassination file carried the slug line "IS" (internal security), which meant that the FBI regarded Oswald as a potential security threat. Mexico City station's withholding of information about Oswald's contacts with the Cuban Consulate was too serious a failure to be dismissed as a case of bureaucratic oversight. COS Scott had notified Anderson in an October 18 memo classified "Secret—Not to Be

Disseminated" about an Oswald contact with Soviet Vice Consul Valery V. Kostikov. It follows that CIA Mexico must have had its own reasons for keeping the FBI in the dark about any real or alleged Oswald contacts with the Cuban diplomatic community.[23]

When the news of Kennedy's assassination reached Mexico City, U.S. officialdom shifted into overdrive. Ambassador Mann volunteered to have his naval attaché use Mann's plane to fly FBI agent Eldon D. Rudd to the United States with two copies of six photos of the man entering and leaving the Soviet Embassy on October 1 and a tape of Oswald's alleged phone conversation with Kostikov. That evening Agent Rudd and the evidence package were flown to Dallas, where Oswald, the only suspect in the case, was in custody and undergoing interrogation.[24] When FBI Dallas reviewed the pictures it was clear that the individual in the photographs was not Oswald. The man in the photographs was about thirty-five years of age, six feet tall, with an athletic build and a receding hairline, balding at the top. At the time of his death, Oswald was twenty-four years old, five feet nine inches in height, and of slight build, weighing 150 pounds.[25]

Of course mistakes can be made even by agency stations that are administered by career professionals such as Win Scott, who had a stellar reputation for being a stickler for details and a "hard taskmaster."[26] But none of the Mexico City station's explanations for the misidentification of this man were plausible. Mexico City station assigned several reasons for the mistaken identification. The man in the photo was the only non-Latin to visit the Soviet Embassy on October 1, and the caller who spoke to Kostikov to arrange an appointment on that date was identified as Oswald: Ergo, the station connected these two converging events and concluded that Oswald was the man who visited the embassy. According to the station this mistake was not detected because Mexico City CIA had no pictures of Oswald to compare with the man captured by the photo-surveillance base house across the street from the embassy's entrance.[27]

The station also stressed the point that beginning on October 23 it made repeated requests to the Office of Naval Intelligence (ONI) for a photograph of former U.S. Marine Lee Harvey Oswald, but the request was never honored. According to CIA Mexico City it was not until November 22, 1963, that the station obtained a picture of Oswald when it picked his photograph off the press wire with the story of the Kennedy assassination.[28] CIA Langley was successful in convincing the Commission that this misidentification could have been avoided but for the navy's noncompliance. When Commission staff lawyer Samuel Stern raised this issue of the ONI's noncompliance, he noted that the Commission had "gigged" the navy on other matters relating to the investigation and planned to take up with the navy the business of its failure to supply a photo of Oswald in a timely manner.[29]

None of these explanations can stand up to critical scrutiny. It is clear that the Mexico City station was engaged in a bold deception. First, the Lopez Report noted that the photo-surveillance logs from a second base house, "Limited," the primary photo base across the street from the Soviet Embassy, recorded that the picture of the man in question had been taken on October 2 and not on October 1, when Oswald allegedly visited the embassy and spoke with Kostikov. Additionally, FBI Washington notified CIA Langley that when the Dallas agents examined the evidence package Agent Rudd brought from Mexico City they had reported that the man in the pictures was not Oswald. On November 23 Langley notified COS Scott about the discrepancy, adding, "Presume MEXI has double-checked dates."[30] The CIA's contention that it depended on the navy for a photograph of Oswald cannot be taken seriously. Even if we set aside the above-mentioned HSCA investigative team's disclosure that COS Scott's "Foul Foe" manuscript proved that the station had pictures of Oswald entering and leaving the Soviet and Cuban embassies, the contention that the CIA was dependent on the navy for a photo is baseless. If Mexico City did not have pictures of the president's accused assassin, the Counter-Intelligence/Special Investigation Branch at Langley had at least two pictures of Oswald in the CIA's preassassination 201 Oswald Personality File. In 1959, when Oswald defected to the Soviet Union, several Washington newspapers carried the story along with pictures of the former U.S. marine.[31] To belabor the obvious, all CIA Mexico City had to do to satisfy the urgent need for pictures of Oswald was to cable CIA Langley and ask for a copy of Oswald's 201 file.

What was the reason behind Mexico City CIA's deception? There can be no innocent explanation for the CIA station's making a case for Oswald calling and visiting the Soviet Embassy and meeting with Kostikov on October 1 despite all evidence to the contrary. The man caught on film entering and leaving the embassy was not Oswald, and the caller spoke "broken Russian," according to the CIA transcriber, whereas Oswald was fluent in that language. A conclusion that deserves consideration is that the CIA in Mexico City was attempting to tie Oswald to Kostikov, a KGB agent under diplomatic cover. CIA Mexico City painted Kostikov as a possible operative with the KGB's notorious Thirteen Department, the section of Soviet security and intelligence service whose "special tasks" were sabotage and "wet acts," the Russian euphemism for assassination. If Oswald was the subject of an intelligence operation it was doubly ominous in light of the role in which he would be cast two months later.

If Kostikov was a Thirteen Department agent, and CIA station Mexico City only assumed that he was, it is likely that he was posted to Mexico to implement Moscow's intention to give the United States another "bloody nose" in the Caribbean by aiding a second Marxist movement to seize power and broaden the revolutionary beachhead in the U.S. sphere of influence. The CIA had either failed to realize or ignored for its own self-serving purposes that the Center (KGB Moscow), beginning in 1961, had deemphasized assassination as a political tool in favor of sabotage missions, especially in the Western Hemisphere. Thirteen Department's new role was to work closely and covertly with the newly emerging national liberation movements inspired by the Cuban revolution. At the top of the list of these movements was the Sandinista National Liberation Front (NLF) in Nicaragua, dedicated to the overthrow of the repressive pro-American dictator Anastasio Somoza.[32]

Kostikov was probably KGB, but then all the senior embassy officials were KGB. He was fluent in Spanish and had served as an interpreter at international conferences at Madrid and Barcelona in 1958 and 1958. In early September 1963 U.S. State Department sources reported that Kostikov, under cover of purchasing cotton, had had meetings with local representatives of Communist front organizations in Tijuana, Ensenada, and Mexicali.[33]

In addition to the occasional political foray outside Mexico City, Kostikov seemed to be wasting his alleged special skills in Mexico City, setting up dental appointments for the Soviet ambassador, arranging transit visas for visiting Soviet artists, making up quest lists for embassy bashes, and answering the telephone. The day after Kennedy's assassination CIA Director McCone instructed Mexico City station to place Kostikov under close surveillance and report his whereabouts hour by hour and the names and background of all his contacts. For the next week the CIA reported that Kostikov did not travel outside Mexico City, and it found no unusual deviation from his normal activities or the "activities of the entire Soviet Embassy compliment [sic]."[34] Eventually the CIA would drop the pretense of any Oswald-Kostikov connection when the White House unmistakably signaled that it was not interested in any "Red plot," real or manufactured. In July the deputy director of plans, Richard Helms, the number two man in the CIA, disclosed to Rankin that when Oswald visited the Soviet Embassy he met with Pavel A. Yatskov, not Kostikov. Helms noted that the CIA's source for this detail was regarded as "reliable."[35]

If Oswald was a Soviet contact recruited by the KGB's "wet acts" section, he was a strange one indeed. He blazed a trail a mile wide to his alleged Soviet controllers in Mexico City. The very openness of his visits and phone calls to the Cuban and Soviet embassies spoke convincingly against any secret role. He traveled to the Mexican capital on a fifteen-day tourist visa and registered in a hotel under his own name. The KGB, like the CIA, made mistakes and could be insecure in its methods, but it rarely persisted in making such glaring errors. Moreover, it was common knowledge within America's intelligence community that it was long-standing KGB practice to forbid its agents serving outside the USSR to have contact with Soviet embassies or consulates.

The KGB would have known that Oswald, as a redefector from the Soviet Union with a Russian wife, would immediately be suspected and placed under surveillance by the FBI. When Soviet authorities, acting on the advice of the KGB, had rejected Oswald's request for citizenship, he presumably attempted to commit suicide by slashing his left wrist in his room at the Hotel Berlin in Moscow. If the KGB had had reason to suspect that Oswald was unstable, his suicide attempt was convincing evidence that he was not agent material.[36] Instead of cultivating a low profile upon his return from Russia, Oswald had gone to great lengths to advertise his political preferences. He subscribed to the *Daily Worker,* corresponded with the American Communist Party headquarters in New York City, openly wrote to the Soviet Embassy in Washington, and established a fake Fair Play for Cuba Committee chapter when he resided in New Orleans for five months during the summer of 1963.[37]

On Monday, November 25, the federal government's first workday of the post-Kennedy New Frontier period, the new chief of state was facing another strenuous, event-packed day. The governing and somber public event was the scheduled funeral procession for the slain thirty-fifth president of the United States and the nation's last chance to honor its fallen leader. One of President Johnson's pressing concerns was the need to preempt all talk about a presidential commission to investigate the assassination. At midmorning he called Hoover to complain about "some lawyer in Justice" who was lobbying the *Washington Post* to come out for a commission "because that's where the suggestion came from." (Johnson was probably confusing Yale Dean Eugene V. Rostow with the marplot over in Justice.) Hoover agreed that they wanted to stick with what they and Katzenbach already agreed to on Sunday: The FBI would make a full report to the attorney general, who would then release the report.

Before noon that Monday Hoover, in three separate conversations, promised Johnson, Katzenbach, and LBJ's White House aide Walter Jenkins that he would have the FBI report finished by that Wednesday, November 27. Alex Rosen, the assistant director of the FBI's General Investigative Division, recalled, "Our basic investigation was substantially completed by November 26, 1963," the day after Kennedy was laid to rest. According to Hoover, the only angle in the case that required a little more time to nail down was how Jack Ruby had breached Dallas police security to get to Oswald.[38]

On Tuesday, November 26, the CIA's Mexico City station dropped a "bomb" on ground zero in Washington, D.C. The CIA's classified message reported that an agent of Somoza's Nicaraguan Security Service, Gilberto Nolasco Alvarado Ugarte, who had furnished information to the CIA for over a year, claimed he had seen Oswald receive $6,500 from a black Cuban with red hair at the Cuban Consulate. The money, according to the Nicaraguan, was payment in advance for the assassination of President Kennedy. A copy of the two-page message went to National Security Adviser McGeorge Bundy at the White House as well as the FBI and the State Department. It was clear that the report had the strong backing of Ambassador Thomas C. Mann.[39]

The Monday after JFK was assassinated and his accused assailant was murdered, Alvarado walked into the U.S. Embassy in Mexico City and recounted a chilling tale. Alvarado had been in and out of the Cuban Consulate during September under the pretext that he was a Nicaraguan Communist and pro-Castro sympathizer anxious to get to Cuba to study guerrilla warfare tactics. On September 18, 1963, he was at the consulate working the Cubans with this story and false documentation. While hanging around the lobby, he claimed that he saw a consular employee, after leaving Consul Azcue's office, hand a package "which appeared to contain money" to a youngish "red haired Negro," tall and solidly built, wearing a brown suit with a red-striped tie. At that time Alvarado said he went to the restroom that was located off a passageway to the patio. When he came out of the bathroom he saw three men in the patio a few feet away. One was the Cuban with the red hair, obviously dyed, talking to two white men. Alvarado would later identify one of them as Lee Harvey Oswald. The Nicaraguan watched while the Negro counted out $6,500 and gave it to the North American, who he noticed was wearing a "shoulder holster like gangsters use."

Alvarado continued to spin his tale, claiming that he was in earshot of the following conversation:

NEGRO: "I want to kill the man."
NORTH AMERICAN: "You're not man enough, I can do it."
NEGRO: "I can't go with you. I have a lot to do."
NORTH AMERICAN: "The people are waiting for me back there."

The Cuban then gave the North American the money in U.S. bills and two hundred Mexican pesos, remarking, "This isn't much." Alvarado claimed that he tried to alert the U.S. Embassy that some important figure in the United States was targeted for assassination, but a secretary or official who took his call berated him for "wasting their time." It was not until after the JFK assassination, when Alvarado saw Oswald's picture, that he realized the enormity of what he had inadvertently witnessed at the Cuban Consulate.[40]

Over the next seven days the Mexico City CIA and Ambassador Mann peppered the White House, State Department, and FBI with twenty-seven cabled reports about Oswald and the Mexico City "Red plot." A November 27 cable added more detail to Alvarado's story about what had transpired between Oswald and the red-haired Negro on September 18 at the Cuban Consulate. In this rendition the Nicaraguan alleged that he saw "a pretty girl, believed to be a consulate employee," give Oswald the "abrazo" and give him her address "where he could find her." The cable noted that the girl's manners "reminded Subj. of prostitute [sic.]." The cable did not identify the woman by name, but there is no doubt that the reference was to the twenty-six-year-old Silvia Duran. Possibly on his own, but more likely taking his cues from the CIA station, Alvarado was hyping up his account with this tidbit to give authenticity to his fragile story. During the height of the Cold War, sexual entrapment, the so-called honey trap, was a favorite ploy used by the clandestine services of the rival Cold War intelligence services. The four-page cable concluded with a glowing affirmation of Alvarado's bona fides: "Subject is young, quiet, very serious person who speaks with conviction." This was a significant upgrading from a few days before, when Mexico City station had evaluated his reliability as "questionable" although he had "not been wholly discredited." The agency's dramatic reassessment of Alvarado's credibility was not unrelated to the news of Oswald's own assassination.[41]

By Tuesday, November 26, the Johnson-Hoover-Katzenbach plan to issue the FBI report concluding that Oswald, acting alone, had killed President Kennedy and to have Justice release it was all up in the air. The CIA's releases about Kostikov and Alvarado eclipsed Hoover's boast to Walter Jenkins on November 25 that the "report would speak for itself." It was the FBI director who had ordered the Dallas FBI, the office of origin, to limit its investigation to Oswald. Now the CIA, the chief rival of the Hoover agency, was advancing a story that Dallas was the result of a "Mexico City plot" that, if true, had unthinkable international implications. Hoover, who did not trust the Nicaraguan agent's story from the beginning, ordered his agency to "explore all angles thoroughly & promptly."[42]

For the White House, the "Red plot" allegations suddenly conferred an unanticipated political appeal on the idea of a presidential commission. This accidental president with Texas-sized ambitions was hardly installed in office before he was confronted with rumors and allegations that, if true, could cause a tremendous storm on the international scene. Much more than JFK, Johnson dreamed big dreams about improving American society, tackling poverty, illiteracy, homelessness, and the corrosive forces of racism. It was essential that rumors of the "Mexico City plot" be contained until the situation had been thoroughly investigated. If the public learned of these rumors, outraged Americans might demand an immediate retaliatory strike against

Castro's Cuba. U.S. military action against Cuba would almost certainly force Moscow to respond with a counteraction. Just what that might be was anybody's guess. Johnson did not want to inaugurate his presidency with another "missile crisis." To prevent a course of action being forced on him with almost certain ruinous consequences, LBJ saw the practical wisdom in appointing his own carefully handpicked commission of prominent and discreet Americans who commanded the nation's respect and trust.

Once President Johnson opted for the commission idea, he moved quickly to head off any concurrent investigations in Congress or with the Texas authorities. He appealed to the speaker of the House, Massachusetts Democrat John McCormick, to do everything he could to discourage any investigation in the House of Representatives. LBJ told McCormick that mayhem could prevail if some "fellow . . . coming up from Dallas" testified that "Khrushchev planned this whole thing and he got our President assassinated." He used the same approach with the House Republican leader from Indiana, Charles Halleck, holding out the ultragrim prospect of forty million dead Americans unless the Mexican rumors could be contained and investigated by tested statesmen.

Johnson had his way with a recalcitrant Senator Russell when the Georgia lawmaker pleaded that he was too busy to serve on any commission. LBJ went ahead without Russell's permission and publicly announced his appointment. When Russell protested, LBJ pulled out the Mexican card with the prospect of American megadeaths. Georgia's senior senator capitulated before the stronger argument, as Johnson knew he would. When a delegation from the Justice Department headed up by Bobby Kennedy approached Chief Justice Earl Warren about serving, Warren gave them a resounding "No!" Two hours later Warren was summoned to the Oval Office. When Warren mustered all the legitimate reasons why he should not serve, Johnson said he showed him two FBI reports about "a little incident in Mexico City" and read aloud from one. When LBJ started in on the forty million American deaths, Warren, according to Johnson, started crying and agreed to chair the commission.[43]

How much of this was the legendary Johnson treatment in which he used the "Red plot" allegations to cynically maneuver others to do his bidding? Did he at any time consider that he might become a prisoner of these fast-moving calamitous developments, forcing him to order a nuclear strike on the Soviet Union, his first act as president and commander-in-chief? What the record does reveal is that the Alvarado story, aggressively pushed by the CIA and Johnson's Mexico ambassador, did not unravel until November 29, after LBJ announced his blue-ribbon commission. During his first week in office the new president had to be mindful at every waking moment of the searing reality that the Cold War could turn hot.

Alvarado's tale had "self-destruct" written all over it. Governments that traffic in assassination of leaders, especially the head of state of the most powerful nation on the planet, do not publicly conduct their machinations and dirty business within earshot of unknown bystanders. Although the CIA had a checkered history of intelligence successes and operational blunders, CIA professionals, especially chiefs of station, did not rise in the agency because they were bubbleheads. It raises suspicions as to why Mexico City station did not take the time to check on the facts instead of treating Alvarado as the soul of probity by immediately releasing his story to the upper reaches of the government in Washington. COS Scott and Ambassador Mann should have made every effort to determine whether Oswald was in Mexico City on September 18, when Alvarado allegedly saw him receive "blood money" to assassinate JFK, before raising the specter of a Castro conspiracy.

CIA Mexico City was the most sensitive of all the agency's stations in terms of intelligence gathering—telephone taps, surveillance teams, and photographic operations. No other CIA station in the world had operations as good. Win Scott, an Ivy Leaguer with a Ph.D. in mathematics, was a former FBI agent and was respected, if not liked, for being a stickler for details and running a very tight operation. FBI Legat Anderson could simply have been called upon to employ his good offices, requesting that FBI Washington contact its New Orleans field office for information on Oswald's movements during September. CIA Mexico City could have had this information in several days, if not sooner. It is inherently incredible and therefore suspicious that this basic routine action was not taken. The CIA knew its business much better than the record reflected. Boneheaded hysteria can be discounted; the only credible explanation is that some senior agency players at Mexico City station had planted the Kostikov and Alvarado stories to attract the attention of higher authorities, especially the highest authority occupying the White House.

According to his Mexico City CIA handlers, the twenty-four-year-old Alvarado had served in the Nicaraguan Army before he was recruited into Somoza's Secret Service. Despite his youth, by 1963 he had been on Somoza's payroll as an agent for four years. Alvarado reported to Major Roger Jerez, the Nicaraguan military attaché in Mexico City. His tradecraft specialty was penetration of pro-Castro groups in Nicaragua and Mexico. For more than a year he was a CIA "walk-in," providing Mexico City station with intelligence about pro-Castro activities for which he received compensation.[44]

It is not likely that Alvarado was freelancing, independently peddling his Oswald story to the CIA for American dollars. The Somoza regime was one of the CIA's most dependable assets, having allowed the agency to use Nicaragua as a training base for the next planned invasion of Cuba. Settling the "Castro problem" was a top priority for both Somoza and the CIA, and the Mexico City station was on the front lines in the agency's no-holds-barred campaign to topple the Cuban dictator. Circumstances strongly suggest that Alvarado was part of a joint counterintelligence operation to create a deliberate provocation in order to incite a punitive military response by the United States against Castro's Cuba. There was, after all, no Latin American figure with a stronger motive to want Castro and his revolution crushed under the heel of a vengeful America than Anastasio Somoza.[45]

It was equally true that there was a sizable element of Castro-haters and hard-line Cold Warriors within the CIA ready to lock onto any opportunity, real or manufactured, to spark a war of revenge against Castro as payback for the humiliation of the Bay of Pigs. For these hard-liners the "Mexico City plot" was a ready-made opportunity to grasp the nettle and finish what they felt a weak and irresolute President Kennedy had twice failed to accomplish during the Bay of Pigs and the Cuban missile crisis—the violent uprooting of the first Communist beachhead in the Western Hemisphere. The CIA had like-minded allies among the senior officer class that made up the Joint Chiefs of Staff who were secretly engaged in extreme contingency planning aimed at fomenting a war with Cuba.[46]

The Monday after the assassination the CIA's Win Scott and Ambassador Mann had this exclusive and "startling information" in the form of Alvarado's story (unchecked) and Oswald's meeting (nonexistent) with "wet acts" specialist Kostikov. When they assembled this information, instead of a kaleidoscope of contradictions and negative indicators, a different pattern emerged: a monstrous conspiracy involving Castro and his Soviet patrons in the Kennedy assassination.

Ambassador Mann did not need much persuasion. The day of the assassination Mann confided to FBI Legat Anderson that he believed Dallas was more than the work of a "nut." The ambassador's suspicions hardened into a certainty when on November 22 he saw the CIA photo of someone COS Scott led him to believe was Oswald entering the Soviet Embassy on October 1. On Saturday, November 23, Mann notified U.S. Secretary of State Dean Rusk that he had ordered all border patrols to check Mexican immigration records for information on Oswald's movements across the border. Mann announced in a "Top Secret" cablegram to Rusk that "circumstances already developed here point to the possibility that Oswald may have been Castro's agent." This was two days before Mann ever heard of Alvarado and was based solely on Oswald's visits to the Cuban Consulate and the photograph.[47]

In short order Mexico City station took a backseat and allowed Ambassador Mann to lead the charge in persuading Washington of the Mexico City "Red plot" to assassinate Kennedy. Like the president, Mann was a Texan. The president knew Mann, and when LBJ visited Mexico Mann always served as his interpreter. Although Mann may not have been a close friend of LBJ's, he was on the same wavelength when it came to their attitudes about Latin Americans. Johnson believed that the Latino personality was combustible and erratic, and that the only way to deal with them was to set strict and unambiguous limits, to assert early and often just who was boss in any joint dealings. Tom Mann, a former executive officer for United Fruit, could not have agreed more. For instance, two days after Alvarado related his account of Oswald at the Cuban Consulate, CIA Director McCone sent a priority cable to Mexico City station strongly indicating that the Nicaraguan's story did not pass the smell test. Aside from some small "incorrect items," such as Alvarado's statement that Oswald wore glasses, the director thought it "incredible that the Cubans would brief and pay an assassin in front of a stranger."[48]

Mann, on the other hand, found nothing in this to cause him to question Alvarado's account. It squared exactly with his imagined "Latin type" psychological profile. "Castro," he wrote to Rusk, "is the kind of person who would avenge himself in this way. He is the Latin type of extremist," the ambassador lectured the secretary, "who reacts viscerally rather than intellectually and apparently without much regard for risks." Alvarado's account surprised him not at all. "The unprofessional and lackadaisical way" in which the transaction took place, Mann assured Rusk, "fits with the way Cubans would be expected to act if the Russians were not guiding them." Even after Alvarado's story fell apart upon further investigation, Mann never changed his tune. To the very end the ambassador insisted that Castro would be reckless enough to hire "an unstable person like Oswald" in reprisal for CIA-sponsored raids against Cuba.[49] For Mexico City CIA the hard-charging and opinionated Mann was the ideal front man to plant the seed of a Castro conspiracy in LBJ's mind. For the CIA operatives who were building the Oswald "legend" or false biography that he was a paid Communist agent, Mann's greatest asset was that he firmly believed that Oswald was working for Fidel Castro.[50]

During the week following Kennedy's assassination, the CIA and Ambassador Mann pulled out all the stops to build their case for a Castro conspiracy. On November 23, two days before CIA headquarters in Langley, Virginia, learned of Alvarado's "startling information," DCI McCone cabled Mexico City to have Silvia Duran arrested. Duran was targeted because she was the one at the Cuban Consulate who had put Oswald in touch with the Soviet Embassy to clear up his visa problems. McCone wanted the Mexican authorities to take full responsibility for her arrest and to interrogate her "to extent necessary." The CIA head insisted that her arrest and interrogation be kept "absolutely secret." COS Scott, who enjoyed close relations with Mexico's President Adolfo Lopez Mateo, requested that the Mexican government arrest Duran. Mateo ordered Luis Echeverría, the acting minister of

Gobernación (internal security), to arrest Duran, adding, "Proceed and inter-rogate forcefully."[51]

Mexican officials responded to McCone's request that same day. Saturday afternoon when Duran returned home from the consulate for lunch, Mexican security personnel were waiting for her. She was arrested and held incom-municado for the next twenty-four hours. Her interrogators went at her, she later claimed, over and over again, accusing her of having sexual relations with Oswald, of being his mistress and conspiratorial "baby-sitter" while he was in Mexico. The line of questioning originated with COS Win Scott. The CIA was trying to force Duran to confess to entrapping Oswald, luring him with sexual favors into a Cuban conspiracy to kill JFK.

During this ordeal with the security police Duran was not beaten, but she was roughly handled to the point where she had bruises on her arms and shoulders. According to her Gobernación interrogators, Duran was coopera-tive and insisted that her only contact with Oswald had been at the Cuban Consulate, and that when he left after the row with Azcue she never saw him again. The Mexican security people released her the next day.[52]

Ambassador Mann was convinced that Mexico City was the heart of Cold War darkness, where the Soviets and their Castro henchmen had hatched one of the most heinous plots of the twentieth century. It never occurred to Mann, caught in the grip of this fixation, to question whether it might have been more than coincidence that Alvarado surfaced the same day that *Excel-sior,* the Mexico City morning paper, carried a front-page story about Os-wald's September visits to the Cuban Consulate and his failed efforts to get to Cuba and to obtain a reentry visa to the Soviet Union. The story's lead in-terest was Oswald as the accused assassin of President Kennedy. However, Silvia Duran's name was mentioned as the Cuban Consulate employee who had handled his application, followed by an account of Consul Azcue's con-frontation with an irate Oswald. CIA station officials suspected that the story had been leaked by Mexican authorities to put to rest any suspicions that JFK was a victim of a conspiracy hatched in Mexico. According to the government-controlled paper, Oswald's visit to Mexico City held no more mystery beyond the account carried in *Excelsior*'s early-morning edition. For a few pesos, Alvarado, at the instructions of his Nicaraguan-CIA han-dlers, had enough information from the newspaper account to gin up a tale about the mafialike Oswald outfitted with a shoulder holster, the red-haired Negro paymaster, and an attractive and willing floozy. It had all the pre-dictable ingredients of a Grade-B Hollywood Cold War spy thriller.[53]

On November 26 Mann and Scott requested permission from CIA head-quarters and the State Department to have Gobernación re-arrest Duran and confront her with Alvarado or his revelations. Having picked her name out of the paper, the Nicaraguan identified Duran as the young woman who had embraced Oswald and been present at the payoff. Duran was especially vulnerable at this time, having lost her job at the Cuban Consulate. On November 25 the Cuban cultural attaché Teresa Proenza forced Duran to resign, most likely under instructions from Havana. All the attention Duran was receiving from the Mexican security police made her a political liability. After her first arrest CIA Mexico City intercepted several phone conversations between Cuban President Osvaldo Dorticos and the Cuban ambassador to Mexico, Juaquin Hernandez Armas. Dorticos was concerned about whether the Mexican police had offered Duran money to testify that Oswald was linked with the Cuban intelligence service. Havana was on edge, suspecting that the CIA and right-wing elements within Gobernación were conspiring to lay the blame for Kennedy's murder at Castro's doorstep.[54]

On November 27 Interior Minister Echeverría had Duran arrested again on the trumped-up charge that she might flee to Cuba. COS Scott prepared the line of questioning. The plan was to break Duran by confronting her with the details of the alleged deal between Oswald and his coconspirators at the Cuban Consulate. Duran's interrogators confronted her with Alvarado's charge, without revealing their source, that she had witnessed the transfer of money to Oswald. Since she was the only non-Cuban to witness the payoff, her interrogators threatened, her only chance of staying alive was to come clean with the Mexican authorities. If she refused to corroborate Alvarado's story the government could not guarantee her safety, and she could expect to be silenced in the same manner as Oswald. During her second interrogation Duran never deviated from her original account of her dealings with Oswald, and Gobernación, fearing a diplomatic rupture with Havana over her incarceration, released her the next day. However, Duran was kept under close surveillance at the request of COS Scott.[55]

On November 26, the same day that the American ambassador acted to have Duran rearrested, he requested that the State Department intercede with the Mexican government and urge it to arrest all the Cuban Consulate officers before they fled to Havana. Mann acknowledged that this was a large order freighted with difficulties, but the ambassador felt "obliged to point out again that time is of the essence here." The action-oriented Mann was ready to chance precipitating a diplomatic crisis even before he had confirmation from Washington about Oswald's whereabouts on September 18, 1963, the day Alvarado placed him at the Cuban Consulate collecting his blood money.[56]

The FBI director initially refused Ambassador Mann's request that he send an agent who was thoroughly familiar with the FBI's file on Oswald to Mexico City. As always, Hoover's operational imperative was control. Hoover was not about to insert the FBI into the Mexican labyrinth to do the bidding of the American ambassador, whose judgment he did not trust.

However, the cable traffic from Mexico City crossing his desk forced Hoover to change his mind. FBI Legat Anderson reported that Mann had misrepresented his request to State for an FBI agent, claiming that it had Anderson's support when, in fact, the legal attaché, as well as two senior embassy officials, had recommended against the request. Anderson did not question Mann's motives, but the subtext of his cablegram was clear enough: The ambassador was so obsessed with the certainty that Oswald was a Castro agent that he was verging on hysteria.

Hoover realized he could not remain on the sidelines while the American ambassador was "acting like a Sherlock Holmes." Anderson's concern that Mann was veering out of control was received with dead seriousness back in Washington. The FBI Mexico City attaché had a stellar reputation within the bureau and was one of LBJ's favorite FBI agents. Anderson was a fellow Texan and an alumnus of Southwest Texas Teachers College, Johnson's alma mater. After Anderson's cable reached FBI Washington, Supervisor Laurence Keenan, a Spanish-speaking agent with experience in internal security, was flown that same day to Mexico City in an army jet. Anderson met him at the airport, where he was rushed through customs and taken directly to the U.S. Embassy. When the two FBI agents reached the embassy COS Scott and Mann were waiting for them. The meeting was short and tense. The instructions Keenan brought with him were terse but unmistakable: Mann was told to stop his conspiracy theorizing. The FBI had correctly identified the man who had killed JFK, and Oswald had acted alone—there was no conspiracy. It was also made clear that President Johnson was in complete agreement with the Hoover bureau on the basic facts of the assassination.[57]

The State Department could not remain indifferent to the diplomatic fallout between Mexico and Cuba over Silvia Duran's arrest. On November 26 Cuban Minister Raul Roa fired off a sharp note to the Mexican ambassador protesting Gobernación's high-handed treatment of Duran, which violated the basic guarantees owed to employees of a consular office. Havana accused Mexico of conspiring with U.S. reactionaries and using the Kennedy assassination to promote a war policy by fabricating a case against Cuba. Mexico rejected the protest on the grounds that the language of the note was unacceptable. One U.S. Embassy official in Mexico City characterized the exchange as "the most acrid on record between the two Governments since Castro came to power." The diplomatic flap over Duran was reported in the Mexican press, evoking strong nationalistic reactions among public groups. A Mexico City paper, *Últimas Noticias,* carried the acerbic statement from one of these groups that "the bosses of the firing squad had nothing to teach Mexicans about individual guarantees." The embassy official did not anticipate a break in diplomatic relations, "barring, of course, further developments of a similar nature." Mann, on the other hand, was of another mind. He cabled Rusk that the diplomatic fallout over the Cuban note "could bring about a serious deterioration and possible break in relations between the two countries," indicating that this might be an unexpected but highly desirable outcome.[58]

Once the FBI was on the case it took only two days to begin the unraveling of the Alvarado hoax. The New Orleans field office was able to establish that Oswald had been in New Orleans from September 17 through September 24. On the 17th he picked up his tourist card from the Mexican Consulate in New Orleans and filled out forms for unemployment compensation. On September 19 Oswald withdrew several books from the Napoleon Branch of the New Orleans Public Library. FBI Washington wanted solid confirmation that Oswald was in New Orleans on September 18, the day that Alvarado had him accepting a payoff in the Cuban Consulate in Mexico City. A check of airline passenger manifest lists turned up neither Oswald's name nor any of his known aliases for September 17, 18, or 19. FBI headquarters was certain it had exploded Mann's theory of a Mexico City conspiracy when Marina Oswald was able to definitely place her husband in New Orleans on September 18.[59]

By November 28 the Mann–CIA station "Red plot" was flaming out. In light of the FBI report that Oswald was not in Mexico City on September 18, McCone directed COS Scott to start "walking back the cat." It was imperative that Duran and the Cubans not suspect that the CIA was behind her arrests. McCone wanted the Mexican government "to take responsibility for the whole affair." CIA Langley now suspected that Alvarado was "delusional and needs psychiatric treatment." It was the CIA director's view that Alvarado's champion, Ambassador Mann, was "pushing the case too hard," and McCone worried that it "could create a flap with Cubans which could have serious repercussions." State's U. Alexis Johnson informed Mann that Washington was certain that Alvarado's story was a hoax; consequently, Johnson notified Mann there would be no further arrests of Cuban Consulate staff. Mann, of course, had to resign himself to Washington's directive, but he was still convinced that Oswald was a Castro tool, and he therefore wanted to "respectfully record" his disagreement with Johnson's instructions "to take no further initiative to encourage the Mexicans to arrest and interrogate."[60]

Once the FBI ended Ambassador Mann's Mexico City witch hunt, the bureau took control of the Alvarado affair. FBI Washington insisted that the CIA turn over the Nicaraguan to the Mexican security police for interrogation.[61] After forty-eight hours of interrogation Alvarado signed a statement admitting he had never seen Oswald in the Cuban Consulate and had never seen any money exchanged. He even failed to identify a photograph of

Silvia Duran. When his interrogators asked about his motives, Alvarado expressed his hatred for Castro and his desire to induce the United States to take action against the Cuban revolutionary state. Alvarado later complained to the U.S. Embassy that during his grilling he was "treated like a dog." The Mexican security forces discovered that he had entered the country illegally. Gobernación set December 4 as the date it planned to send Alvarado back to Nicaragua.[62] No one in the U.S. government protested the decision.

Hoover wanted to be certain that all loose ends in the Alvarado case were tied up before the Nicaraguan intelligence officer was deported. The FBI report on the JFK assassination, CD 1, was scheduled for release to the White House and the Warren Commission in early December. The politically salient conclusions of the report—that Oswald was the lone assassin and there was no conspiracy, foreign or domestic—were slated to be leaked to friendly media sources before CD 1 was delivered to Johnson's blue-ribbon commission. FBI Washington wanted to make certain that neither Mann nor the CIA attempted to resurrect Alvarado's story or some altered version of the hoax for their own nefarious purposes.

To this end, Hoover insisted that Alvarado be submitted to a polygraph examination before being deported. CIA Langley opposed "fluttering" Alvarado (CIA jargon for a polygraph examination). The FBI's liaison with the CIA, Sam J. Papich, informed the chief of the CIA's Special Investigation Unit, Birch D. O'Neal, that the FBI wanted CIA Mexico to "flutter" Alvarado before he was deported. O'Neal tried to stall with the excuse that the CIA station in Mexico City could not come up with a polygraph operator in time. The actual situation was somewhat different, as a CIA cable disclosed that COS Scott had "seasoned operators available on short notice." In any case, Papich made it clear to O'Neal that either the agency would submit Alvarado to a polygraph test or the FBI "will have to determine what other steps might be taken to see that this is done."[63]

Confronted with the FBI's nonnegotiable demands, the CIA made arrangements to have Alvarado undergo a polygraph examination. Always sensitive about protecting its sources and method, Langley found the need to cloak the whole operation in pretext and deception. The polygraph operator, a "Mr. Davis," was dispatched from CIA headquarters at Langley. Mexico City station used some ruse or connection to clear "Davis," who was traveling under cover as a tourist, and his equipment through Mexican customs without incident. The agency rented an apartment set up "for visiting Americans" through a CIA front. FBI Legat Anderson and Joseph B. Garcia, both proficient in Spanish, questioned Alvarado over a two-day period. After two days with the polygraph machine, Davis concluded that Alvarado was lying. Hoover ordered Domestic Intelligence Division head William C. Sullivan to "press" the CIA for the results of the polygraph. The FBI would send the

Warren Commission a detailed report on the bureau's role in discrediting Alvarado's story and other hoaxes and false reporting related to Oswald and his Mexico trip.[64]

Three days after Kennedy's assassination a CIA source tried to get the *Washington Star* to run with the Alvarado hoax, linking Oswald in the public mind with Castro. When the newspaper, at the prodding of its FBI-friendly reporter Jeremiah O'Leary, first checked with FBI headquarters and learned that the story was a suspected hoax, it killed the story. Even after Langley accepted the fact that Alvarado's story was bogus, the hawkish director of the CIA was still pushing the "Mexico City plot" on Capitol Hill.

In early December McCone came to House Minority Leader Gerry Ford's office to confide that the CIA had uncovered some "startling information" in the Oswald case. McCone, unaware that the Michigan congressman was Deke DeLoach's source on the Commission, related the Alvarado story about Oswald as Castro's paid assassin. Ford reported the incident to De-Loach. McCone's attempts to beat a thoroughly dead horse went as far as trying, unsuccessfully as it turned out, to entice syndicated columnist Drew Pearson, a long-standing Hoover nemesis, with the Alvarado story. The CIA chief's provocative meddling aroused the demons of interagency animosity and suspicion. A senior official of the FBI's Domestic Intelligence Division, D. J. Brennan, Jr., wrote his boss that McCone "has attacked the Bureau in a vicious and underhanded manner." Brennan went on to characterize Mc-Cone's statement as "sheer dishonesty" in light of the fact that the CIA "was fully informed" that the Mexico City story was "completely discredited." Firmly convinced from past experience that the only way to deal with the CIA was with "firm and forthright confrontation," the superheated Brennan urged that the bureau confront McCone and demand a denial.[65]

The White House and the FBI director moved to divert attention away from Mexico City and silence all the agitation originating with the U.S. ambassador and the CIA about a Havana-Kremlin plot to assassinate President John F. Kennedy. In mid-December Tom Mann's days as U.S. ambassador to Mexico came to an end. President Johnson appointed him to head the Alliance for Progress, while also serving as special assistant to the president and assistant secretary of state for inter-American affairs. This lofty elevation could hardly be interpreted as a reversal of career fortunes. One historian of the Johnson presidency saw this appointment as a result of LBJ's desire to transform the Alliance and give it a more aggressive probusiness orientation by turning its direction over to Mann, who was a free-market zealot.[66] But an unspoken and deeper reason was to remove him from an overheated cloak-and-dagger environment rife with false reports, rumors, and disinformation operations. Of topmost importance was to remove Mann from the influence of the Mexico City CIA and its efforts to provoke U.S.

military action against Cuba. Mann's new multiple responsibilities in Washington were the best prescription to divert him from his obsession with Castro and his theorizing about the Kennedy assassination.

During the first week of December the White House sent a clear signal to the CIA to end all its agitation about a "Havana-KGB plot" behind the tragedy of Dallas. On December 6, 1963, Acting Attorney General Katzenbach invited CIA representatives to review a copy of CD 1 even before it was released to the White House and the members of the Warren Commission. The CIA sent John Whitten, a senior agency professional and chief of Western Hemisphere, which included Mexico and the Caribbean, and Birch O'Neal, of the Special Investigation Unit of the CIA's Counterintelligence Branch. Whitten and O'Neal were logical choices because each of them was involved in the CIA's own in-house investigation into JFK's murder.[67]

Katzenbach's invitation to Langley was couched as a courtesy, but the true purpose was to caution the CIA to get in step with the official version of the Kennedy assassination. By December 6 Langley knew that the "official truth" of the assassination would be that Oswald, acting alone, had killed the president. CD 1 carried the equivalent weight of a policy statement of national importance issued from the Oval Office and was therefore tantamount to a presidential decree. Using the FBI report LBJ acted to impress upon the higher reaches of the government, especially the CIA, that he wanted all rumors and allegations about a "Red plot" immediately squelched. If Langley needed any more assurance of the administration's "no-conspiracy" solution to the crime, then the leaking of CD 1's conclusions to selected newspapers even before the report was released to the Warren Commission should have been the clincher. The CIA and every intelligence service in the world worth its keep could have predicted what the Warren Commission would conclude before it even held its first executive session or heard its first witness. Once the powerful and feared director of the FBI, clearly with White House backing or at LBJ's direction, publicly committed the bureau to a "no-conspiracy" explanation, Hoover had effectively boxed in the Commission and set the limits for the immediate days and months ahead on what the American people would be conditioned to accept as reasoned and balanced public discourse about the Dealey Plaza assassination.

The experienced and top-echelon professionals at the FBI and the CIA saw that it was in their mutual interest to shift attention away from Oswald, Mexico City, and any hint of the imposter or false Oswald. The first phase of the cover-up began with the FBI report. The CIA review team of Whitten and O'Neal recorded in their memo to McCone, "There was absolutely no mention of the CIA in the report," assuring Langley that the Oswald imposter angle was secure and, as the CIA intended all along, would be kept from the Warren Commission. With the FBI's cooperation, the CIA developed a cover story to explain away the early FBI reports that the voice on the tape identified by CIA Mexico City as Oswald's was actually that of an imposter. As mentioned earlier, Hoover had reported evidence of a false Oswald in Mexico City to President Johnson and Secret Service Chief James Rowley the day after the assassination.[68]

The CIA's improvised account was that FBI Dallas was mistaken. The evidence package that Rudd had brought from Mexico City station contained, the CIA contended, the photographs of a man who was clearly not Oswald and a transcript, not a tape, of Oswald's alleged October 1, September 28, and September 27 phone conversations with Soviet Embassy official Valery V. Kostikov. Kostikov was the embassy official who had allegedly met with Oswald on September 28, according to the CIA's transcriber. According to Mexico City station the tape recordings of Oswald's preassassination conversations had been routinely erased for recycling or destroyed outright. However, the HSCA investigative team convincingly challenged this assertion, pointing out that the tapes were almost certainly available as late as October 16 for comparison purposes. Clearly, the key concern was whether the voice on the tapes was Oswald's, linking Oswald to the CIA's KGB "wet acts" expert, Kostikov, or that of the Oswald imposter. The grounds for the Lopez Report's ruling out of CIA Mexico's claims that the tape was recycled were that Langley had notified COS Scott on October 10 that the Oswald purported to be in contact with Kostikov was the former marine who had defected to the Soviet Union in 1959 and threatened to turn over to the Russians what he knew about highly sensitive U.S. radar capabilities. After this alert, any information about Oswald took on increased, actionable significance during the period from October 11 to October 16, which was reason enough for Mexico City station to retain the tapes.[69]

FBI Washington went right along with Mexico City station's fabrication about the recycled tapes. Hoover held up his end of the cover-up by directing the FBI's Dallas field office to "correct" its representation that the voice on the tape was not Oswald's. On November 23 the head of the Dallas office, Gordon Shanklin, informed the director that "the *actual tape*" from which the transcript had been made had been erased—that, in fact, there was no tape, just a transcript of a conversation.[70] Hoover settled for having the record indicate that the nation's premier law enforcement agency could not distinguish between a transcript and a tape recording of a live conversation. The director's decision to conspire with the CIA in suppressing evidence of an Oswald imposter was consistent with the no-conspiracy case the FBI was building over the weekend to explain Kennedy's assassination. Any admission that there was a second person posing as Oswald in Mexico City carried the attendant and inescapable inference that either Oswald had an accomplice or he was being manipulated as part of an intelligence operation.

Under Hoover's direction the FBI's handling of Oswald's Mexico City activities was simply a repetition of the way the director and bureau elites dealt with the larger, controlling issue of the assassination itself. That is to say, the politically determined theory of the crime—Oswald acting alone took the president's life—took iron-clad, unamendable precedence over all the evidence and witness testimony. President Johnson and Hoover had agreed on the "official truth" of Dallas over the weekend following the assassination. When LBJ, anxious to "settle the dust" of Dallas, asked that the FBI report on the assassination be on his desk by Tuesday, November 26, the day after Kennedy was buried, Hoover notified the General Investigative Division "to wrap up investigation; seems to me we have the basic facts now."[71] Only two developments delayed for the moment this rush to judgment: The first was Hoover's suspicion regarding Oswald's assassin, Jack Ruby, and his easy access to Oswald in the basement of the Dallas police department. The second unanticipated development was the revelation from Mexico City about an Oswald imposter and a possible KGB-Castro conspiracy to assassinate Kennedy.[72]

As soon as FBI Washington had proved that the Alvarado story was bogus and conspired with the CIA to suppress from the Commission any revelations about an Oswald imposter, Hoover closed the book on any further FBI investigation into the "potential Cuban aspects" surrounding Oswald and his seven days in Mexico City. It would have been expected that the FBI's General Investigative Division (GID) would carry the major responsibility in any legitimate investigation into the Kennedy assassination. Up to a point, this was true. The FBI report that LBJ wanted on his desk by November 26 was prepared by the GID. According to Assistant Director Alex Rosen, the head of that division, the "basic investigation was substantially completed by November 26, 1963," to meet the White House's expectations.[73] After the GID turned in its thrown-together report the division was relegated to the margins of the investigation. Rosen himself was assigned to the bureau's bank-robbery desk. The GID head would later characterize the FBI's investigative efforts into the Kennedy assassination as "standing around with pockets open waiting for evidence to drop in." Even more telltale was Hoover's order on November 23 to cancel all bureau contacts with Cuban sources. He followed this up by excluding the FBI's Cuban experts and supervisors in the bureau's own Cuba Section of the Domestic Intelligence Division from any investigation into Oswald's Mexico City activities. The director focused the probe away from Mexico and the Caribbean to the Soviet Union. Investigation into Oswald's political activities and associations was turned over to the bureau's Soviet experts.[74]

In concert with the FBI, CIA Langley pulled the plug on an honest investigation into any Cuban aspects of the Kennedy assassination. In the CIA's case, the process was more indirect and devious, but the end result was same. Initially, the CIA's deputy director of plans, Richard Helms, appointed John Whitten to undertake the agency's in-house investigation into the assassination. Whitten was a senior career officer with twenty-three years in the clandestine service. In 1963 he was the head of WH-3, the agency's designation for the Western Hemisphere Branch that comprised Mexico and the Caribbean. The WH-3 head had a staff of thirty officers and about an equal number of clerical staff. What Whitten did not suspect at the time was that Helms and the chief of the CIA's Counterintelligence Branch, James Jesus Angleton, had set him up for failure. There is good reason to believe that Hoover was part of an interagency scheme to thwart any good-faith investigation into the suspicious machinations surrounding the activities of the CIA's Mexico City station.

Theoretically, Whitten had the experienced area professionals, staff, and informers to conduct a sweeping investigation into Oswald's activities in Mexico City, but during the short time that Whitten was in charge of the investigation he ran into a stone wall. The FBI deluged his branch with thousands of reports containing bits and fragments of witness testimony that required laborious and time-consuming name checks. Whitten characterized most of the FBI information as "weirdo stuff."[75] None of this mountain of paper contained vital information that was critical to any legitimate probe into the assassination. For example, Whitten knew nothing of Oswald's alleged pro-Castro activities in New Orleans during the summer of 1963, Oswald's so-called Historic Diary with insights into his years in the Soviet Union, or the FBI's assertion that JFK's charged assailant had attempted to take the life of General Edwin Walker. Whitten knew none of this until, at Katzenbach's December 6 invitation, he was allowed to read CD 1. By that time Helms and Angleton were preparing to pull the investigation out from under him.[76]

In the chain of command for WH-3, COS Win Scott was under Whitten and, in the bureaucratic scheme of things, expected to report directly to Whitten. But Scott, Whitten's subordinate, never told him about Oswald's contacts with the Cuban and Soviet embassies until the day Kennedy was assassinated. Equally remarkable was the fact that Whitten had never heard of Lee Harvey Oswald until November 22, 1963, even though the CIA had a restricted 201 preassassination file on Oswald held by the Counterintelligence/Special Investigative Group, indicating that this branch of the CIA confined to sensitive counterintelligence operations may have had a special interest in former marine PFC Lee Harvey Oswald.[77]

Compounding Scott's insubordination were the station chief's suspected furtive efforts to undermine Whitten and get him removed.[78] Whitten was never privy to his agency's tightly controlled, ultrasecret "Executive Action

Program," the CIA's euphemism for sabotage and assassination operations against foreign leaders, including the more than a handful targeted against Fidel Castro. If his mandate from Helms had been legitimate, this piece of the intelligence picture would have been essential. To borrow a contemporary idiom, Whitten, on all counts, was kept "out of the loop," assuring that the draft of his report on the assassination would be the subject of ridicule.[79]

Several days after Whitten had reviewed the FBI's CD 1 in Katzenbach's office, Helms called a meeting to evaluate Whitten's report. Whitten realized after reading CD 1 that his report was hopelessly irrelevant. Angleton, who had seen an early draft of the report but ignored Whitten's invitation to comment, used the meeting to tear Whitten's efforts to shreds while Helms looked on, making no attempt to stop the mauling. Whitten remained silent throughout the ordeal but suspected he had been set up by the deputy director of plans and the formidable counterintelligence chief. Right after the meeting Helms took the investigation away from Whitten and turned it over to Angleton and the Counterintelligence Branch.[80]

Whitten suspected that Hoover had fed Angleton vital information that the FBI had withheld from him. His suspicions were probably warranted. Despite the director's long-standing hostility and famous turf battles with the CIA—he even once broke off all liaison with the CIA out of sheer pique—Hoover still maintained a close professional relationship and direct ties with the CIA's counterintelligence chief.[81] Once Angleton, with Helms's connivance, had wrested the investigation away from Whitten, any significant CIA interest in Cuban aspects of the Kennedy assassination vanished. With Angleton in charge the investigation was placed in the hands of the agency's Soviet Division, and after that the only serious focus of the investigation was directed at the Soviet Union.[82]

The Warren report's assertion that Oswald's Mexico City venture had no relevance to the assassination cannot stand up under scrutiny. The Mexico City mysteries and unexplained developments reanimate the suspicion that Oswald's bizarre political odyssey, which defined his adult life, was more than just the acting out of an absurd, self-absorbed, and rebellious young man. It was the Warren Commission's obligation to investigate this aspect of the Kennedy assassination. It was a responsibility, as will be discussed in later chapters, that the Commission went to great lengths to avoid.

4 The Warren Commission Behind Closed Doors

*To investigate, lay to rest rumors and convince the public of the
validity of one particular set of facts. The Warren Commission is
the most outstanding example of this type of commission.*
—Elizabeth B. Drew, "How to Govern (or Avoid It) by
Commission," *Atlantic Monthly,* May 1968

When the commissioners first met they all knew what
was expected of them. They were to go through the motions of an inquiry
and release their report in quick order. There was no element of suspense as
to where their inquiry might lead and what their final report would conclude. The FBI's strategic leaking of the conclusions of its investigation to
the press made this incandescently clear to the commissioners. The records
of the executive sessions disclose that the Commission's prestructured task
was to support the FBI's conclusions: Oswald was the assassin, and he had
acted alone.[1]

Chairman Warren underscored the secondary, almost remote connection
of the Commission with the inquiry into the assassination during the first
executive session. He proposed that the Commission avoid public hearings
and resist calling any live witnesses. The chief justice saw no gain in asking
for subpoena power. The Commission, Warren opined, "could hold our
meetings and take any evidence or any statements in camera, and eventually
make our report without any great fanfare throughout the country." Warren
thought that these steps would expedite the process. He was comfortable relying on the FBI, CIA, Secret Service, and other government agencies to
carry out all the investigative functions. Senator Russell, who had no confidence in Warren and rarely, if ever, allied himself with the chief justice, favored all of Warren's proposed procedural ground rules. General Counsel J.
Lee Rankin contributed to this penchant for containment and secrecy by assuming without legal authority the right to classify all Commission documents. Rankin saw to it that all the Commission's executive sessions were
classified "Top Secret" despite their historical value and the absence of any
indication that the records could aid a foreign government or threaten national security.[2]

Warren's proposal that the Commission restrict itself to simply evaluating
the evidence fed to it by government agencies elicited a forceful demur from
John J. McCloy. McCloy's reputation as the country's "most influential private citizen," a respected member of that select fraternity of "wise men"
presidents frequently called upon for advice, was well deserved. During
World War II he had served as Secretary of War Henry Stimson's right-hand

man; he had been president of the World Bank and then chairman of the Chase financial empire before returning to private practice at a large Wall Street law firm. McCloy's towering achievements in public life resonated not only at home but also with the international community.[3]

McCloy was the only commissioner to at least entertain the possibility that Kennedy's assassination might have been the result of a domestic conspiracy. He cautioned Warren about relying solely on government agencies where there was "a potential culpability," and when those agencies' reports "may have some self-serving aspects in them." Recognizing the pressure on the Commission "to lay the dust, dust not only in the United States but all over the world," he alerted the chairman about "the amazing number of telephone calls I have gotten from abroad." McCloy expressed his concern about the number of his friends in Europe who believed that there was a conspiracy behind the Kennedy assassination. History would be an unforgiving judge, McCloy admonished, if the Commission failed "to show the world that America is not a banana republic, where a government can be changed by conspiracy."[4] With this in mind, McCloy urged that Warren reverse his position and support the right of the Commission to subpoena documents and witnesses when the need arose. The force of McCloy's argument persuaded Russell to backtrack and come out in support of subpoena power.[5]

As the ranking member of the two-member Senate Oversight Committee for the CIA, Russell knew more about the agency's secrets and "black arts" than anyone else on the Hill. Consequently, he had little confidence that the agency would volunteer much, if any, useful information, especially if it hinted at the CIA's sources and methods. When Dulles suggested that the CIA might be able to fill in some of the record of Oswald's activities in the Soviet Union, Russell retorted that the former spymaster had "more faith in them than I have. I think they'll doctor anything they hand us." The Georgia lawmaker nursed his own suspicions about a foreign conspiracy to take Kennedy's life, the threads of which ran from Dallas back to Castro's Cuba. If Russell had even an inkling of the CIA's attempts to assassinate Castro, he never disclosed it to the rest of the commissioners. Dulles, on the other hand, had been the director of the CIA during the Eisenhower administration, when the agency began targeting Castro for assassination. But Dulles's first loyalties were to the CIA and its secrets, and he never revealed anything about this anti-Castro scheming and the agency's "Executive Action Program" to his Commission colleagues.[6]

If the Hoover bureau's leaking of Commission Document (CD) 1 to the press was the Commission's first jolt, the FBI's report itself came as a startling aftershock. Katzenbach had made a special point of being present at the Commission's first executive session on December 5, 1963. Even before he had read the FBI document, he had assured the members that the report would contain only the facts but have "no conclusions in it." Four days later, in his letter of transmittal of CD 1 to Warren, Katzenbach, without breaking stride, characterized the report as virtually definitive, "establishing beyond a reasonable doubt" that Oswald had been the assailant and that all indications were that he had acted alone. Katzenbach was not coy about the purpose behind his cover letter to the Commission's chairman. In view of the groundswell of rumors and dark suspicions about a conspiracy in Kennedy's death, the acting attorney general hoped the Commission would release a statement supporting the conclusions that, in fact, the FBI had already leaked to the press. His assurance that CD 1 was the end product of an "exhaustive investigation" would ring hollow once the commissioners had the FBI report in hand.[7]

During the December 12 executive session, the first meeting after the commissioners had a chance to review the 833-page FBI report, it was evident that DeLoach's campaign to exonerate the FBI for the leaking had made no headway. Twice during this session Warren mentioned that he had not found "anything in the report that has not been leaked to the press." In the discussion that followed, no one rushed to the defense of the FBI. Russell found himself again in total agreement with Warren. Even Ford, DeLoach's key source inside the Commission, had developed a tender spot about the leaking "from some agency of the Federal Government" with the intent to "confirm by Commission action what had been leaked previously." The Michigan congressman opined that "somebody ought to check on that."[8]

Although the commissioners were agitated over the FBI's preemptive leaking, it was the investigative report itself that drew their heaviest fire. The "loopholes," McCloy's charitable characterization, in the FBI report on Kennedy's wounds were the greatest source of the Commission's confusion. The FBI had never asked for a copy of the official autopsy protocol when preparing CD 1, relying solely on the report from the two FBI agents, James W. Sibert and Francis X. O'Neill, who had been present at the Bethesda Naval Hospital morgue when the autopsy was performed.[9] The Sibert-O'Neill report stated that a missile had entered Kennedy's back about six inches below the shoulder to the right of the spinal column at a 45- to 60-degree angle. The two FBI agents, who were scrupulous in their attentiveness to every step in the procedure, reported that when one of the prosecutors probed the back wound with his finger, he could not find an exit path. Their report described JFK's fatal head wound but failed to mention the wound in his throat. The official autopsy protocol placed the back wound at the base of Kennedy's neck, high enough to allow the bullet to exit Kennedy's throat below the Adam's apple. The Bethesda autopsy report recorded that the nonfatal missile that entered Kennedy's back emerged from his throat without striking bone.[10]

The Commission was understandably confused. It was as if they had been handed autopsy reports on two different homicide victims. Boggs was surprised that the FBI report made no mention of Governor Connally's wounds. McCloy hoped that the Secret Service report on the assassination would fill in the gaps of the "very unsatisfactory" and "poorly written" FBI document Katzenbach had praised as "sensational" and the White House wanted made available to the public without delay. The Secret Service report did not answer McCloy's questions about JFK's wounds. A month later, his mind still "muddy as to what really did happen," McCloy suggested that the Commission turn to Dr. Winfred Overholser to reconcile the differences between the FBI report and the official autopsy protocol. Dr. Overholser was a psychiatrist, not a forensic pathologist. He was the former head of St. Elizabeth's Hospital, a psychiatric institution in Washington, D.C. The Commission retained him on a part-time basis largely to take advantage of his psychiatric skills in trying to plumb Oswald's motivations for shooting the president.[11]

If McCloy and the Commission were seriously looking for expert opinion to untangle the muddled and contradictory reports on Kennedy's wounds, experienced medical forensic pathologists were just a phone call away. At some point in their inquiry the Commission should have interviewed Sibert and O'Neill about their observations that had gone into the FBI report on the Kennedy autopsy. The Commission never called them as witnesses or had the staff depose them. Ultimately, as the documentary record discloses, the Commission colluded with the Bethesda naval prosecutors in endorsing an autopsy report that was prepared to satisfy political needs instead of the true forensic facts of the assassination.[12]

Given the glaring inadequacies of CD 1, the commissioners unanimously settled on several initial courses of action. They agreed that the FBI report not be made public. They supported a resolution introduced by Warren that they request all raw materials and reports from the agencies reporting to the Commission. Rankin, conceding that "the report has so many holes in it," went so far as to suggest that the Commission consider hiring its own independent investigative staff.[13]

It was clear that the commissioners were beginning to feel as if they were standing on shifting sand. The airtight case against Oswald as represented by Katzenbach and the FBI was, if not coming apart at the seams, at least suspiciously porous in critical evidentiary areas. A perceptible, if subdued, tension and uneasiness among the commissioners surfaced when Dulles passed out a ten-year-old book dealing with attempts on the lives of seven past American presidents. The author's thesis was that presidential assassins were typically loners and social misfits. Dulles's purpose was to bring his colleagues back onto firmer, politically safer ground, assuring them that they would find the same pattern "in this present case." But Boggs and McCloy were not willing to let Dulles impose his predisposition about the assassination on the rest of the Commission. Perhaps only for the sake of argument, they both recommended an essay in the December 21 edition of the *New Republic* titled "Seeds of Doubt." The authors were Staughton Lynd, a Yale historian, and Jack Minnis, a political scientist. As the essay's title implied, the piece raised some serious questions about the assassination and the official explanations that had appeared in the press. Kennedy loyalist and special assistant to the murdered president Arthur Schlesinger, Jr., received a prepublication copy of "Seeds of Doubt" and thought the essay's arguments were persuasive and troubling enough to send a copy to Bobby Kennedy.[14]

It was clear that McCloy had read the Lynd-Minnis piece and that it reinforced his own misgivings about discrepancies in accounting for JFK's wounds. For example, "Seeds of Doubt" reported that two of the doctors who performed a tracheotomy on the moribund president identified the wound in Kennedy's throat as a wound of entrance. Obviously conflicted but still clinging to the official version that all shots had come from the "sniper's nest," McCloy believed it was imperative that the Commission visit the *locus in quo*—the scene of the crime—"before the evidence gets too dusty." Although his lawyer's mind did not seem to trip on the contradiction, McCloy wanted to see firsthand "if it was humanly possible for [JFK] to have been hit in the front from a shot fired from that window."[15]

When Hoover learned that Rankin was considering employing an independent investigative staff for the Commission, the news went down like battery acid. Dulles passed on this meaty tidbit to James Jesus Angleton, the CIA's counterintelligence chief, confident that it would find its way to Hoover's desk. Angleton's staff served as the liaison between the CIA and the Warren Commission and kept in close contact with the FBI about the Commission's executive sessions through Sam Papich, the bureau's liaison with the CIA. Papich immediately informed Assistant Director Belmont of this development. Papich's report contained what had to be more unsettling news when he noted that the Commission "will be in business for a long time . . . cover a broad field and may even talk to some of our Agents who conducted investigation of the assassination and the Ruby case." Belmont's recommendation to Hoover was that "Rankin should be discouraged from having an investigative staff" and James R. Malley, Hoover's liaison with the Commission, "should make it clear to him."[16] It is safe to conclude that little or nothing that went on behind the Commission's closed doors—its "Top Secret" executive sessions—remained privileged information when these agencies' interests and operations were at stake.[17]

Hoover anticipated smooth sailing after he successfully conspired to get Rankin the post of Commission general counsel. As mentioned earlier, he knew Rankin quite well—they had communicated on a "Lee" and "Edgar" basis when Rankin was solicitor general—and Hoover expected that Rankin would keep the Commission in tow long enough to rubberstamp the FBI's report on the assassination. In a December 12 conversation with Rankin, the director, while amiable and vowing that he would do everything possible to make Rankin's "job easier," reminded the chief counsel of their distinct roles. It was Hoover's understanding that the FBI was to collect the facts and the Commission would evaluate them and submit its conclusions to the White House. In Hoover's mind there was no question about the facts and what the Commission would report. He told Rankin that the FBI had established that the shooting attributed to Oswald posed no problem because the ex-marine was a skilled marksman. Hoover continued to inventory the case-closing evidence: The FBI had Oswald's fingerprints on the rifle, the bullet found in Connally's stretcher that came from the assailant's rifle, and "all the photographs."[18]

For the Hoover bureau, if the Commission was going to spin out the inquiry, investigate the investigators, and reexamine the evidence, then dumping Olney for Rankin was not cause for complacency. Hoover and his assistant directors had good reason to worry. Over the weekend following the assassination Hoover was already arranging for a secret in-house investigation to determine why Oswald's name was not on the FBI's Security Index. On the strength of the agency's raw intelligence alone, the FBI should have alerted the Secret Service that Oswald posed a potential risk to Kennedy while the presidential party was in Dallas. The FBI not only failed to pass Oswald's name along to the Secret Service but also covered up its bungling by destroying incriminating evidence after the assassination.[19]

Another skeleton in the bureau's closet that it was desperate to keep hidden had to do with Jack Ruby, Oswald's assassin. In 1959 the FBI had recruited Ruby as a provisional criminal informant (PCI). There was nothing suspicious or unusual in employing a nightclub owner as an informant; for the FBI this was business as usual. Ruby's livelihood brought him into contact with the kind of people and information that law enforcement agencies feed upon. Ruby's status as a PCI had lasted for almost eight months until the FBI dropped him because he was largely a dry well, providing little useful information on Dallas's criminal element. The FBI did not volunteer information about Ruby's PCI status to the Commission until February 1964, when Rankin asked for the FBI's Ruby file. In short order Hoover honored Rankin's request, trusting that the chief counsel would keep this sensitive intelligence under wraps. Rankin did not disappoint him: There is nothing in the Warren report about Ruby's FBI connections.[20] Had either or both of these FBI secrets—the criminal destruction of evidence and Ruby's informer status—found their way into the public domain, the proud, towering image of the Hoover bureau would have suffered a devastating, perhaps even an irreversible, blow to its image under the weight of the scandal.

Hoover needed a cooperative and compliant Rankin and not a nascent Warren Olney at the helm of this blue-ribbon commission. The director was certain that Chairman Warren could not be trusted. Hoover cautioned Malley to be careful with the chief justice because Warren was "hostile" to the FBI. Hoover's paranoia about the Commission's chairman only deepened when Warren reported to the press that the FBI report was in "skeletal form" and the Commission would need to examine the raw materials and reports to evaluate it properly. Furious with Warren for implying that the FBI had been less than thorough, Hoover responded on a copy of the news story, "Certainly a needless dirty dig by the Chief Justice."[21]

Papich's report on the Commission's December 16 executive session spurred the FBI headquarters to feel out Rankin about the Commission's intentions. A late-afternoon phone call from Assistant Director Rosen to the general counsel must have relieved the FBI's apprehensions. Rosen explained that the Bethesda naval autopsy record had been excluded from the FBI report to the Commission because the Kennedy family wanted to keep the autopsy material confidential, and Rankin accepted this line of reasoning. This was the first salvo in the FBI's campaign to blame the Kennedys for suppressing material evidence that was crucial to the investigation. If this lame and spurious excuse did not sit well with Rankin, he never let on. In time, Rankin, McCloy, and some of the other commissioners would adopt the same stratagem to justify the Commission's own suppression of the medical evidence.[22] The purpose behind Rosen's call was to smoke out from Rankin whether the Commission was serious about employing its own investigative staff, an idea that the general counsel himself had floated. As Rosen reported, Rankin allowed that some of the members favored this course, but he assured Rosen that he was not one of them. Personally, the general counsel told Rosen, he had every confidence that the agencies were best qualified to handle their own responsibilities, and he wanted to put Rosen's mind at ease on this score. Rankin gave every impression that he was a team player, and Rosen reciprocated by promising full bureau cooperation in all matters relating to the investigation.[23]

In the absence of any firm evidence it is not possible to know whether Malley or anybody else from FBIHQ aside from Rosen tried to "discourage" Rankin from hiring an independent investigative staff. Threats were not necessary because in any overt contest of wills the Commission would come out on the very shortest of ends. Warren and his colleagues could not even hope to make a pretense of carrying out their solemn charge if Hoover ordered his agents in the field to sit on their hands. Rankin and the commissioners did not need to have this problem spelled out for them.

It was well known among both lesser and greater power brokers in Washington political circles, who traded chilling tales—some informed, others hearsay—that Hoover used files kept in cabinets outside his office to punish his enemies. To be sure, Hoover's private files inspired some unwarranted paranoia. But the files were real, and one federal judge who recently perused them revealed that they held thousands of documents containing "scandalous material on public figures to be used for political blackmail."[24] The commissioners knew that Hoover had used these files to destroy reputations and wreck more than one political career. Hoover and his private files cast a long shadow, and the enduring director, if crossed, was the most formidable and unrelenting of adversaries.[25]

Rankin's exchange with Rosen cleared the air with the director, at least for the short run. Hoover told Tolson that he wanted to cultivate "the closest and most amicable relationship" with the general counsel. Still smarting over Warren's "skeletal form" comment, Hoover wanted to impress Rankin with FBI efficiency and mastery of investigative detail and at the same time twist the dagger in the offending chief justice. He ordered *all* reports and "raw" materials to be sent to the Commission, even the so-called nut reports. For example, Rankin requested that the FBI interview a Marshall, Texas, man who wrote Warren that he had information that would crack the JFK case. FBI agents talked to the man and reported that he was an obvious "mental case." Rosen recommended that they bury the interview in the "nut file," but Hoover overruled him and wrote on the memo, "Expedite." The director intended to bury the Commission under an avalanche of bureaucratic paper.[26]

There were a few other items of business generated by the Commission's executive session of December 16 that Papich learned through the Dulles-Angleton pipeline and that Hoover wanted settled. The director wanted to discredit the "Seeds of Doubt" piece in the *New Republic,* not with forceful and persuasive rebuttals but by attacking the authors. DeLoach contacted Ford and fed him derogatory information from FBI files to destroy Lynd's and Minnis's credibility. The FBI's argument regarding Lynd was that "he had associated with known communists." There were so many links among activists in the 1960s that it would have been surprising if the Yale history professor had not "associated" with Communists. In 1963 Lynd was a Quaker and a confirmed pacifist. A year later, while holding an assistant professorship at Yale, he took on the duties of editing the *Liberation,* a pacifist journal. Minnis's fall from grace was a contact he had made with the Soviet Embassy in Washington in 1959, though he "had reported this fact to the Bureau." In Minnis's case it was debatable whether he had erred in the first or second instance. Rankin was sent a summary of their backgrounds to ensure that the Commission would dismiss "Seeds of Doubt" as communist-inspired propaganda.[27]

The other piece of information in Papich's report that caught Hoover's attention was the fact that the Department of Defense was submitting Adam Yarmolinsky's name as its liaison with the Commission. Hoover had a history with Yarmolinsky that went back to 1961, when the director had tried to block his appointment as Defense Secretary Robert S. McNamara's aide. Yarmolinsky, the Jewish son of Russian émigré parents of distinguished intellectual achievement, was suspected because of his "leftist" views. Yarmolinsky had pushed for integration of off-base military facilities and as a consequence was anathema to southerners in Congress, who were some of Hoover's staunchest supporters. He was also a stand-up Kennedy loyalist, and it had been rumored that JFK was thinking of appointing him as Hoover's successor when the director reached the mandatory retirement age. On all counts, Yarmolinsky's appointment had to be scuttled. Hoover had DeLoach "handle" this matter with White House aide Walter Jenkins, but to no avail. Yarmolinsky's appointment stood, probably at Secretary McNamara's insistence.[28]

Determined to impress the Warren Commission with FBI thoroughness in preparing its cases, Hoover authorized the bureau's Exhibits Section to prepare a model of the assassination site. When the Exhibits Section was not adding improvements to the director's home, its primary function was to construct courtroom mock-ups, charts, maps, and training aids. The technical skills and accomplishments of Inspector Leo J. Gauthier's Exhibits Section were inarguably first-rate. In just five weeks Gauthier's technicians assembled a three-dimensional scale model of Dealey Plaza containing all the physical features of the *locus in quo*, which covered a 480-square-foot area. The mock-up with its accompanying charts and the aerial view of Dallas proper was so impressively complete and extensive that it could not fit in the Commission's conference room. Rankin arranged to have it housed in the large assembly room several floors below the conference room in the Veterans of Foreign Wars Building.[29]

Hoover had his own private walk-through of the exhibit and was properly impressed with the consummate skill and exactitude that had gone into the model as a demonstrative courtroom aid. He urged Gauthier to make it available to the Commission as soon as possible. Proud of the Exhibits Section's handiwork and anxious to put it on display, Hoover could not resist a little dig at the chief justice when he noted, "Better have some extra wood & nails as Warren may want to see the 'raw' materials." By the end of January the FBI's scale-model version of Dealey Plaza was open to the Commission, its staff members, and Secret Service agents. From that point on Commission staffers and Secret Service agents used the model extensively along with the accompanying visual aids to reconstruct the timing and the sequence of the shooting in the Kennedy assassination. With the FBI's model up and running, McCloy's initial concern about getting to Dallas before the "evidence gets too dusty" no longer seemed so pressing. Actually, it was not until May that some of the commissioners visited the scene of the crime.[30]

The painstaking detail and careful workmanship that went into the mockup could not help but fascinate and add weight to its claim of authenticity. The model presidential limousines, the Secret Service follow-up cars, and the vice president's car were miniature replicas of the real motorcade reduced to a scale of one-quarter inch to the foot. The roof of the model Texas School Book Depository (TSBD) was removable, allowing the viewer to sight out of the "sniper's nest" at the presidential car below as it moved toward the Triple Underpass. All of this impressive and seductive miniaturization was intended to underscore one big construct: the FBI's version of the shooting of the president. The exhibit was a three-dimensional reiteration of the conclusions presented in the FBI report: three shots and three hits. According to the model, President Kennedy was hit by the first and third shots; a separate bullet, the second shot, struck Governor Connally. All of the shots came from the sixth floor of the TSBD, the location of the so-called sniper's nest. To highlight the line of fire, Gauthier's technicians attached three strands of luminescent string from the "sniper's nest" to each model of the presidential limousine at the presumed approximate location where each shot had struck a target. Except for some disagreement about the exact location of the presidential limo when each shot was fired, the Secret Service was in basic agreement with the FBI's scenario of three shots and three hits.[31]

Although the Dealey Plaza three-dimensional model was a tribute to the Exhibits Section's model-building skills, it was fundamentally and willfully flawed. It failed to account for the missed or so-called wild shot that had struck the curb on the south side of Main Street and wounded bystander James T. Tague. The FBI knew about the curbstone shot the day of the assassination because Deputy Sheriff Eddy R. "Buddy" Walthers had filed an investigative report on the Tague bullet with the Dallas County Sheriff's Department. Walthers had James Underwood of KRLD-TV, a Dallas station, and Tom Dillard of the *Dallas Morning News* take photographs of the point of impact on the curbstone where Tague was standing when he was hit in the face by either a piece of cement or a bullet fragment. One of Dillard's photographs appeared in the *Dallas Morning News* the following day with the caption "Concrete Scar." The short narrative under the photo read, "A detective points to a chip in the curb. . . . A bullet from the rifle that took President Kennedy's life apparently caused the hole." At the insistence of Walthers and a Dallas motorcycle police officer, Tague reported his minor wound to the Homicide Section of the Dallas Police Department that same day. Clearly, the Tague bullet was not an assassination event that went unnoticed and unrecorded.[32]

The FBI did not get around to interviewing Tague until he called the Dallas office. The interview took place on December 14, 1963, more than three weeks after the assassination and five days after the FBIHQ had submitted its report to the Warren Commission. The FBI report of the interview noted that Tague, after being struck in the face, "looked around the curb and near where he was standing there was a chip missing." Later, when FBI agent Robert P. Gemberling wrote up the Dallas field office report on the assassination, section B of the report read, "One Bullet Fired During Assassination Went Wild, Crashed into a Curb and Struck Jim Tague." In June 1964, just when the Commission originally expected to end its inquiry, a set of circumstances beyond its control and unanticipated by the FBI forced the Commission to radically revise its treatment of the shooting. It was forced to reject the FBI and Secret Service's three-shots, three-hits scenario in order to try to account for the missed shot. Even an FBIHQ internal memo allowed for the possibility "that one of the shots fired by Oswald did go wild."[33] The FBI didn't get around to examining the curbstone until August 1964, and then only after the Warren Commission requested an investigation, only to report that any evidence of a missile impact had been patched over.[34]

Gauthier's imposing model was another calculated maneuver in the FBI's campaign to control the investigation and defend the official solution to the crime. Inconvenient facts, such as the Tague bullet, did not survive the FBI's procrustean method of determining materiality in the Kennedy assassination. Oswald had been the lone assassin, and the mock-up in the assembly room, the charts, the maps, and the impressively bound visual-aid manual allowed for no other possibility. The three discharged cartridge cases found at the "sniper's nest" were consistent with the official version of the three shots fired from that window. The time frame dictated by Abraham Zapruder's film of the assassination allowed for only three shots from Oswald's bolt-action Mannlicher-Carcano rifle. According to FBI calculations, it took at best a little more than two seconds just to cycle the rifle, with no leeway factored in for the shooter to keep the scope fixed on the moving target. The manual that accompanied the model determined that all the shooting had occurred within a span of 6.4 to 8.0 seconds. Given these specific physical conditions, a fourth shot could be explained only by a second gunman, an alternative that was politically unacceptable.[35]

It is impossible to avoid concluding that the FBI's suppression of the "missed shot" is a more damaging self-accusation of the Hoover bureau than any of its critics could devise. The FBI ignored Tague and the scar on the curbstone. It filed its supposedly definitive five-volume report without mentioning either the missed shot or, for that matter, the wound in the front of

JFK's neck. It was eight months after the assassination before the FBI took any evidentiary interest, perfunctory as it was, in the Tague curbstone shot, and that was only because it was compelled to investigate. Hoover pretended that the model in the assembly room, like CD 1, spoke for itself. He bristled when Commission staff lawyers wanted to employ additional tests with the Zapruder film and other films of the assassination to pinpoint the intervals between the three shots. On one memo Hoover grumped, "It sounds like a lot of poppycock to me." When Melvin Eisenberg, the Commission's assistant counsel responsible for the shooting sequence in the final report, decided that it was necessary to conduct an on-site inspection in Dallas, Hoover reluctantly agreed to provide FBI support but privately accused Eisenberg and the Commission of "playing games." Ultimately, as relations between the FBI and the Commission became sharply adversarial, the director balked at assisting the Commission in any on-site reenactment of the Dealey Plaza shooting.[36]

On June 4, 1964, the Commission held its most unusual executive session, which was atypical in several ways. Although Rankin was present, he never spoke a word. It was the only one of the Commission's thirteen executive sessions in which two staff members, Rankin's protégé and special assistant Norman Redlich and Arlen Specter, were in attendance.[37] When Rankin opted to classify all of the Commission's executive sessions as "Top Secret," the classification extended to the staff. Under this provision, staff were excluded from all executive sessions, were kept in the dark about what transpired there, and were not privy to the division of responsibility between Commission members.[38] This ruling was relaxed on June 4 to permit Redlich and Specter, representing all the assistant counsels, to enter the holy of holies. The occasion was to hear Commissioner Ford read a prepared statement.

Without waiting for a nod from the chairman, Ford launched into his prepared text. Although the Michigan congressman privately held Warren in low esteem, he meant no disrespect in this instance. Both Warren and McCloy, the only other commissioner present at the start of the session, already knew and had agreed to what Ford was going to say. The June 4 session was convened for no purpose other than to permit Congressman Ford to read into the record a strong statement disassociating himself, and the rest of the Commission by extension, from a spate of stories circulating in the press. Ford, who was doing his fair share of leaking to the FBI, feigned outrage at recent articles in the *Christian Science Monitor* and the *New York Times* that the Commission was on the verge of releasing its report concluding that Oswald had been the lone assassin and had not been an agent of a foreign government. He strenuously protested these assertions, claiming that the Commission "as a Commission . . . had not made any final judgment."

Ford's spongy and equivocal language that there had been no discussion "as a Commission" was meaningless and a confession of informal discussion and agreement by the Commission that Oswald had been the lone assailant.

Ford was exercised over the fact that each of these news stories cited a "Commission source, or a source close to the Commission" as the basis for the report. Warren and McCloy chimed in, registering like concerns, each citing similar stories obviously planted in both wire services and *U.S. News and World Report.* All three commissioners were properly aghast at the accelerated volume of leaks and thoroughly condemned the practice. Ironically, only Ford inferentially nudged the discussion in the direction of finger-pointing, noting that in December Katzenbach had importuned the Commission to release a statement to the effect that Dallas had not been the work of a conspiracy, that Oswald had acted alone. The Commission had refused, Ford reminded his colleagues, and opposed any similar release from the Justice Department. Ford, naturally, never mentioned the FBI as a possible source of these planted stories. The upshot of the session was a joint decision that Warren would release a statement to the press to the effect that the Commission was still considering its report and had made "no final conclusions as a Commission."[39]

The June 4 session was a sham, with self-serving statements written in advance. Its purpose was to launch a preemptive strike at public opinion and history. Rankin had cautioned the staff that its work would be more closely scrutinized than any work ever done by any staff members in the past. The government's report on the Kennedy assassination, Rankin predicted, would come under close examination for the next fifty years.[40] It was a heavy responsibility for the assistant counsels, most of whom were just beginning to carve out careers in the legal profession and the criminal justice system. The press leaks attributing sources close to or inside the Commission should have alarmed the entire staff and its boss, the general counsel. Reputations would have been tarnished and careers cut short if the public came to believe that the Commission had reached its conclusions before it heard all of its witnesses.

The spate of press leaks coincided with Warren and Rankin's original target date of June 1964 to turn over the finished report to the White House. The media probably learned of the June deadline from either the FBI or a source inside the Commission. Modern American political life offers countless examples of secret releases by the government when it wants to influence and control public opinion about political and diplomatic events. The converse is equally true: When there are unauthorized and unwanted leaks to the press, something is done about it. The government does try to identify and punish officials who preempt this long-held executive prerogative for their own purposes.

If the commissioners were genuinely apprehensive about these leaks, they would have called on Rankin to take preventative measures to try to stop them. He could have shaken down the staff and launched a real inquiry to find out if the leaks were coming from inside the Commission. For instance, it was common knowledge among some of the staff that Assistant Counsel Albert E. Jenner, Jr., was a habitual leaker, holding court with reporters over lunch at Hogate's, a fashionable seafood restaurant in the D.C. Wharf area. Sam Stern, a Commission staff lawyer, recalled that some of his colleagues came up with a nifty little ditty about Jenner that started out: "Down at the tables of Hogate's where old Jenner dwells." Jenner left the Commission to return to his Chicago law firm before September 1964, when the final report was released. There was no indication that his "tutorials" at Hogate's had anything to do with his early departure. Regarding the leaks issue, the truth was that Rankin never initiated an in-house investigation into the source of these planted press stories. The Commission was not worried because it was the beneficiary of these leaks. These secret releases conditioned the public mind and molded editorial opinion to accept that Oswald was the unassisted assassin long before the Commission went public with its findings setting out the "official truth" of Dallas.[41]

Ford's pious denials aside, the Commission members did not have to discuss "as a Commission" to reach a conclusion. The Commission began its work with a predetermined solution to the assassination. On January 11, 1964, Rankin, at Warren's request, had prepared a very detailed nine-page working outline for the staff presenting the Commission's case against Lee Harvey Oswald. Section II of the outline was titled "Lee Harvey Oswald as the Assassin of President Kennedy." Under this section is a subheading H, "Evidence Implicating Others in Assassination or Suggesting Accomplices." Point 5 under H is "Refutation of Allegations."[42]

This working outline was prepared three weeks before the Commission interviewed its first witness, Marina Oswald. In the first four weeks of its nine-month tenure, without benefit of hearing one witness and with scant time to acquaint itself with the physical and medical evidence, the Commission, without hesitation or investigation, had arrived at the conclusion that Oswald—it allowed for no other possible outcomes—had on his own killed President Kennedy. The Commission's January 11 working outline was the final major piece on the board setting out how the government was going to explain to the ordinary understanding of the American people the tragedy of Dallas. The president's Commission dutifully aligned itself with Hoover's instant vision of Oswald's guilt, the imperatives laid out in Katzenbach's November 25 memo to Bill Moyers, and the FBI's "definitive" report (CD 1). It was now left up to the Commission and its staff, working with the FBI, to run the investigation backward to reach its preordained conclusions.

Although the commissioners had charted their course, they were not naïve in believing that it would be all smooth sailing. From the outset Commission members in their "Top Secret" executive sessions were frank in expressing some of their deep and nagging misgivings. McCloy had legitimate concerns about "a potential culpability" of the FBI and Secret Service in the assassination. He felt that since the Secret Service and the FBI had some overlapping responsibility for protecting the head of state, then bad judgment, gross incompetence, or even perfidy—it could not be ruled out—might have sealed JFK's fate. How could the Commission investigate the investigators? Reports to the Commission from these agencies, McCloy ventured, would be slanted and self-serving to cover up unforgivable agency sloppiness or even worse.[43]

None of McCloy's fellow commissioners cared to join him in this line of speculation. They were, however, ready to jump all over the FBI report for being "skeletal," "full of holes," "hard to read," and "badly written." Rankin summed up their frustrations best when he observed, "It just doesn't seem like they're looking for things the Commission has to look for in order to get answers that it wants and is entitled to."[44] They were all aware that the FBI had written its report without benefit of examination of JFK's autopsy protocol. Then there was Oswald's mysterious seven-day trip to Mexico City, with his visits to the Soviet Embassy and Cuban Consulate. Hoover had rushed CD 1 out before the FBI had followed up all its leads into a possible foreign conspiracy. All of the commissioners expressed their resentment over the FBI's leaking of CD 1's conclusions to the press even before the commissioners received the report. McCloy was livid upon learning from Boggs and Russell that the FBI had leaked Rankin's name to the press as the front-runner in the Commission's search for a general counsel. With Hoover playing politics to get his man in position to steer the Commission, Warren fretted that all appearances of an independent Commission would be compromised in the public mind.[45]

The responsibility for easing the commissioners' deep misgivings about the trustworthiness and competence of the FBI fell squarely on Rankin's shoulders. At one point he hinted at employing an independent investigative staff whose first loyalty would be to the Commission. This proposal had a very short shelf life. It received no warm follow-up endorsement from the commissioners, and Rankin quickly distanced himself from the idea, citing the "expense and so forth" in setting up a "lot of new staff."[46] Rankin knew that Hoover had been largely responsible for his selection as the Commission's chief counsel. He also knew that if the lines of cooperation between the FBI and the Commission were not to be tied into knots by an obstructionist FBI, a truly independent investigative staff was out of the question. As mentioned before, when Assistant Director Rosen queried him about this matter, Rankin assured him that the Commission had no such plans.[47]

The Commission's general counsel, mindful that this blue-ribbon committee was tasked with making a record for history and would be judged accordingly, was careful not to antagonize the FBI director. However, short of unconditional capitulation to Hoover and his assistant directors and their control over the investigation, Rankin and his staff soon found themselves sailing against the wind. In short order, relations between the Commission and the Hoover bureau became adversarial.[48]

Relations between FBI Washington and the Commission began their downward slide in March 1964. In order to fill in some of the glaring gaps in the FBI report, Rankin submitted to Hoover a five-page document containing thirty specific questions with the request that the FBI provide "a reasoned response . . . in reasonable detail," including "such substantiating materials as seem appropriate." The thirty questions could be boiled down to three basic categories: What did the FBI know about Oswald? When did it have this information? Last, what had the FBI done with the information in its Oswald file? Working under the assumption that Oswald was the lone assassin, the commissioners could not accept the fact that he had had such easy access to President Kennedy and had been able to escape the scene of the crime without apprehension. Allowing for its untested and unproven presumption of Oswald's guilt, the Commission's skepticism was reasonable. Long before the Commission's thirty questions reached Hoover's desk, Rankin and the commissioners knew that the FBI had had certain critical knowledge about Oswald that it had not shared with the Secret Service. Rankin spoke to this point when he mentioned to the Commission that the Hoover bureau was "certainly tender" about the fact that it had not shared its knowledge of Oswald with the Secret Service before President Kennedy's Dallas trip.[49]

The fact that Oswald had made contact with the Soviet Embassy and the Cuban Consulate in Mexico City was grounds enough for the FBI to have advised the Secret Service to place him on its alert list. Had it not been for FBI bungling, the Dallas field office would have been able to pass on firsthand information about Oswald and his potential for violence that should have made him a prime candidate for the Secret Service's attention. A month before the assassination Oswald had written a threatening note to the Dallas field office that his case officer, James P. Hosty, Jr., had quietly filed away in his Oswald file. The Commission never learned about Oswald's note to Hosty and its subsequent destruction during the course of its investigation.[50]

FBIHQ received Rankin's March 26 request with exasperation and suspicion. Rankin's request came in the wake of sixteen pending Commission requests dating back to January 1964 that the bureau was still trying to address. This backlog did not mean that the FBI had been sitting on its hands. The bureau had turned over to Rankin and his staff almost thirteen thousand pages of investigative results and prepared more than 2,400 photographs for the Commission. Even before Rankin's March 26 letter reached FBIHQ, assistant directors were complaining that the Commission was unreasonable and presumptuous in its flood of requests. Rankin's thirty questions changed the mood at FBI headquarters from frustrated contentiousness to deep suspicion. William Branigan, the number-two man in the FBI's Domestic Intelligence Division, characterized the questions as "those of a cross-examining attorney." The questions, in Branigan's view, ran the gamut from childishly petty to unfairly accusatory, implying that the FBI had held back information (which, of course, it had) from the Secret Service about Oswald that fatally compromised President Kennedy's security. There was a sudden chill in the air at Seat of Government that the Commission was contriving to build a case against the FBI for gross ineptitude in the assassination of America's thirty-fifth president. Hoover ordered headquarters to give Rankin's request "top priority" and to prepare responses "to these obviously loaded questions," in Hoover's words, with great care.[51]

Rankin knew that he would have to use his staff to investigate some areas of the case where he knew the Commission would not get answers from the FBI because they were, as he delicately put it, bureau "tender spots." He knew Hoover would treat Commission lawyers interviewing witnesses and digging for evidence in Dallas, New Orleans, and Mexico City as hostile interlopers and unwelcome trespassers on FBI turf.

When Rankin notified the bureau that four assistant counsels were scheduled to arrive in Dallas to interview witnesses, FBIHQ dashed off a teletype message alerting the Dallas office that it could expect "a bunch of real crackpots" during the next few days. "Be extremely cautious," the teletype warned, "keep quiet and [do] not volunteer any information." Two of Rankin's investigators, Joe Ball and Albert Jenner, FBI Washington headquarters pointed out, were undergoing a "loyalty investigation." The other Commission staffer, Norman Redlich, special assistant to the general counsel, according to the Hoover-inspired teletype, "has been over in Russia and is on the borderline." Hoover issued a hard and fast rule: Any Commission request made to the Dallas office had to be cleared first through the director's office. There would be no exceptions. For example, Harold Barefoot Sanders, Jr., U.S. attorney for the northern district of Texas, offered his good offices to help Commission lawyers with the witnesses they intended to depose. Sanders called on the Dallas office to locate the witnesses and set up times for them to appear in the office to help expedite the process. When the FBI raised one bureaucratic hurdle after another, Sanders finally gave up and turned to the Secret Service for help.[52]

When Commission assistant counsel Wesley J. Liebeler showed up in New Orleans to interview Dean Andrews, who later would attract national attention during Jim Garrison's Clay Shaw fiasco of a trial, he was also blindsided by Hoover's rules on Commission engagement. William C. Sullivan, head of the FBI's Domestic Intelligence Division, advised the New Orleans field office to invent some excuse to deny Liebeler access to the FBI's Andrews file. Hoover tried to persuade Rankin to curtail his staff interviewing, arguing that the Commission was engaging in senseless duplication since the FBI had already covered this ground. When Rankin was singled out for one of the director's harrumphing memos his tactic was to apologize for the "misunderstanding," then assure Hoover that the Commission was immensely grateful for the tremendous job the bureau was doing. Rankin did not want to antagonize Hoover; at the same time, he did not want to surrender all control over the investigation. From March to September 1964, there were many occasions when a deferential Rankin tried to smooth the director's ruffled feathers. His placatory efforts never mattered in any fundamental way because the director and his agency perceived the Commission as an adversary and a threat that had to be contained. When Rankin gushed about the superior quality of FBI testimony before the Commission, Hoover dismissed the compliments. "They were looking for FBI 'gaps,'" he huffed, "and having found none yet they try to get 'syrupy.'"[53]

Commission staff members, especially the younger lawyers, who may have harbored some romantic notions rooted in the mystique of the crime-busting Hoover FBI, discovered a different FBI in their close-up dealings with the agency. They were worn down by the "exasperatingly bureaucratic" way the Hoover bureau did business. All requests for information and assistance had to go through "channels," wasting time and impeding the investigation. Commission staffers complained that agents would never volunteer information other than what was specifically asked of them. Despite the flood of FBI investigative reports, important facts were not reported. Sam Stern and other staffers had a very low regard for Inspector Jim Malley, the FBI's liaison with the Commission. Stern depicted him as a "big jovial insurance salesman, without any great intelligence" who took delight in "hustling" the staff, always pumping them for information but never reciprocating. "The FBI was like a bunch of clerks on roller skates" was the lasting impression Stern carried away from his Commission experience.[54]

These newly minted, bright, and self-assured young lawyers were, in fact, being hustled, but in ways they never suspected. Their explanation for these "communication problems" (Rankin's words) stemmed from what Stern claimed was the FBI's "crazy" and "impotent" system of fiercely centralized headquarters control and its outmoded system of internal management. The reality, of course, was that the Commission lawyers were caught up in the FBI's covert and systematic efforts to control their investigation.[55]

This was especially true in Dallas, where the FBI was hypersensitive about so many "tender spots" in its investigation of the assassination. There was the willful suppression of the Charles Bronson film showing, among other things, the president being assassinated. The FBI had deliberately ignored Jim Tague and the curbstone shot that was, at least, prima facie evidence of a fourth shot and therefore a possible second assassin. There were witnesses whose FBI statements were altered to make them compatible with its Oswald solution to the tragedy. There were witnesses whom the FBI purposely overlooked because of what they might have reported. The most tender of these FBI "tender spots" was Oswald's threatening note to Special Agent Hosty and FBIHQ's subsequent instructions to suppress and then destroy the note.

The Hoover bureau wisely understood that any exposure of these cases of suppression and corruption of the evidence could result in irreparable damage to its image and pride of place in the public mind. FBIHQ's radar screen closely monitored the movements of Commission lawyers whenever they were in Dallas to pick up signals of where they went and whom they spoke with. Alarm bells went off when FBI Washington learned that Commission lawyer Burt W. Griffin had questioned a local Alcohol, Tobacco and Tax Unit agent, Frank L. Ellsworth, about Hosty to find out whether Ellsworth was aware of any instances of the FBI withholding information that should have been disseminated. This piece of news only confirmed the director's suspicions that the Commission was out to crucify his agency. He scrawled across the bottom of the memo, "I hope you now realize what Commission investigators are seeking." Hoover's comment circulated among the top rung of bureau officialdom and to Inspector Malley, the FBI liaison with the Commission.[56]

5   The Warren Commission
   Confronts the Evidence

He emphasized that the Commission had to determine the truth,
whatever that might be.
—Melvin A. Eisenberg's memorandum on Chairman Warren's
   charge to the staff at the first Commission staff conference,
   January 24, 1964

Placing Oswald at the sixth-floor window—the "sniper's nest"—at the time of the assassination was one of the Commission's biggest fizzles. The Warren report banked heavily on a single witness, Howard Leslie Brennan. The report stated that Brennan identified Oswald as the man who "fire[d] the shots from the sixth-floor window of the Depository Building" and stressed that Brennan "was in an excellent position to observe anyone in the window." He was no more than 120 feet away and, according to the Commission, was "an accurate observer," whose description of the shooter was the one that went out over the Dallas police radio minutes (12:45 P.M. CST) after the assassination. In a statement made to the Sheriff's Department immediately after the shooting, Brennan swore he saw a "white man in his early 30's, slender, nice looking, slender and would weigh about 165 to 175 pounds. He had on light colored clothing but definitely not a suit."

The Commission gave Brennan top billing in its report since it had no other witnesses willing to swear that they had seen Oswald with a rifle at that sixth-floor, southeast corner window at the time of the assassination. Congressman Gerald Ford focused on Brennan in an article in *Life* magazine as the Commission's most important witness. In his article Ford unequivocally stated that Brennan was "the only known person who actually saw Lee Harvey Oswald fire his rifle at President Kennedy." When Brennan testified before the Commission, McCloy asked him if he had seen "the rifle discharge, did you see the recoil or the flash?" Brennan's response was an unequivocal "No."[1] This kind of disconnect was exemplary of Brennan's Warren Commission testimony. Besides, as we will see, if any rifle was fired as Brennan testified, the bullet or bullets would have had to penetrate two panes of glass, neither of which had a bullet hole.

Despite the weight the Commission gave to this testimony, Rankin was nervously aware that almost all of Brennan's evidence was shaky, if not impossible. A number of articles were being published that pointed out the contradictions in Brennan's testimony as it appeared in the Warren Commission's report. Two weeks after the report was made public Rankin wrote Hoover twice, on December 2 and again on the 18th, requesting that the FBI determine "a complete chain of information from Brennan to the police dispatcher" to show that Brennan's description of the shooter was the source of the suspect alert that went out over the police radio.[2]

Hoover's response provided scant solace for the general counsel. All Hoover could confirm was that according to the Dallas police, the information came from an "unidentified citizen." The FBI had never bothered to track down specific information to confirm the precise origin of the description of the suspected assassin or descriptions of where the shots had originated. To leave it hanging like that meant accepting the inability of the police to provide their source when there was only one official alleged eyewitness to the actual crime.[3] Rankin knew his way around the criminal law enough to realize that this kind of specific information was essential to the investigation and reconstruction of the crime scene. It was also essential to combat any suspicion that the assassination was the result of a conspiracy and that the conspirators were the source of the description, which did match Oswald. More than a month after the Warren report became a public document, Rankin asked the Commission historian, Dr. Alfred Goldberg, to renew the request. Goldberg contacted FBIHQ and pointed out that it could be to the advantage of the Commission and "to the Bureau's advantage" to ascertain the "full facts" to answer future critics in the most unequivocal and positive terms. Hoover, smarting over the Commission's mild criticism of the FBI in Chapter VIII of the Warren report and caught up in preparing the bureau's "counterattack" against the Commission, was not inclined to give the request top-priority attention. In response to Goldberg's appeal, Hoover grumbled, "They never have shown before any concern about the Bureau's advantage." In the end the FBI, in effect, told Rankin that he would have to be satisfied with Brennan's contradiction-ridden sworn statement to the Sheriff's Department as the source of the identification of the assassin on the sixth floor of the Texas School Book Depository (TSBD) that had gone out on the police radio.[4]

No matter how much the Warren report massaged the facts, it could not establish Brennan's credibility as a witness. Given the immense tragedy witnessed by onlookers along Elm Street and the attendant confusion in Dealey Plaza, most of the statements given to the Sheriff's Department were, as might be expected, vague, general, and more often than not in error. However, Howard Leslie Brennan's statement was a model of specificity. He reported that he had seen the shooter "sitting up and looking down apparently waiting for the same thing I was, to see the President." To reiterate, Brennan described the man as white, "in his early 30's, slender, nice looking, slender and would weigh about 165 to 175 pounds." After the last explosion, Brennan stated, "he let the gun to his side and stepped down out of sight."[5]

His "stepped down out of sight" added another non sequitur to his already impossible and trifling account, since FBI pictures showed that the windowsill was only a foot above the floor. Brennan went on to say that he "could see this man from the belt up." The report was obliged to come to Brennan's rescue, explaining that "he [Oswald] most probably was sitting or kneeling" while aiming at the president. In Brennan's account the standing gunman would have been shooting through a double-paned window. Even allowing for the report's self-serving correction of the "accurate observer's" claims, the sitting or kneeling gunman's face would have been pressed against a double thickness of dirty window from which the sun was reflecting. If the gunman was sitting or kneeling, then how to account for Brennan's description of his height, weight, and the clothes he was wearing? In stressing that Brennan's "description most probably led to the [police] radio alert of the suspect," the report failed to explain how the star witness had arrived at these physical characteristics, especially the suspect's height if he was sitting.

The Warren report unintentionally went a long way toward subverting both Brennan and its own revision of Brennan's account with Commission Exhibit 1311. Exhibit 1311 revealed that the distance from the floor to the windowsill at the so-called sniper's nest was approximately one foot. In this Commission reconstruction the window was opened about fourteen inches, approximating its height on the day of the assassination. The FBI photograph, made at Rankin's request, makes a mockery of Brennan's claim that the assassin was standing when he fired at the presidential motorcade. At the same time, it inspires no more confidence in the Commission's redacted version of a kneeling gunman for the same reasons.[6]

Having no other witnesses who would testify that they had seen Oswald with a rifle, the Commission had to shore up Brennan's testimony at every turn. "Brennan also testified," the report asserted, that Oswald, "whom he viewed in a police lineup on the night of the assassination," was the same man he had seen at the sixth-floor window of the book depository building. It is true that Brennan viewed the lineup, but he never positively identified Oswald. The unadorned fact was that Brennan at no time during the lineup made any identification. Brennan even told the FBI that he "could not positively identify Oswald as the person he saw fire the rifle," and this was after Brennan had seen Oswald's picture on television.[7] The staff writer responsible for Chapter IV of the Warren report was using words to convey meaning that was the opposite of the truth. For example, the report stooped to cheap deception to convince that Brennan was an "accurate observer" who only declined to make a positive identification of Oswald "when he *first* saw him in the police lineup," implying that he ultimately did make a positive identification. The report then went on to compound this deception with a self-refuting claim that the "Commission, therefore, does not base· its conclusions concerning the identity of the assassin on Brennan's . . . identification of Lee Harvey Oswald as the man he saw with the rifle." Having made this retraction, the report then mentioned some other witnesses, none of them any more credible than Brennan.[8]

Sheer immobilizing fear was Brennan's explanation for his failure to identify Oswald in the police lineup. He explained that he believed that the assassination was a "Communist activity," and since he was the only eyewitness (although at the time he had no way of knowing this), he feared for his safety and that of his family. If Brennan was no great shakes as a witness, he did have one memorable quality—an irrepressible talent for unintentional self-mockery and self-subversion. Shortly after explaining to the Commission how his fear, which he admitted was suggested to him by the Secret Service, had overcome his sense of public duty at the police lineup, Brennan reversed course, startling David Belin, the assistant counsel who was questioning him. He asked Belin if the Commission had the television coverage of his interview with Secret Service agents at the crime scene. Belin was thrown completely off stride. Here was Brennan going on record to, in effect, boast about his instant celebrity. Brennan's face and name and what he allegedly saw had been all over Dallas television before he showed up to view the police lineup.[9]

Having no credible witness to place Oswald at the sixth-floor southeast corner window at the time of the crime, the Commission stumbled headfirst in another critical area of its prosecution case. The Commission was never able to prove that Oswald had brought the alleged assassination weapon into the book depository building the day of the assassination. It merely concluded that he had despite testimony to the contrary. The only person who had seen Oswald enter the building that morning was Jack E. Dougherty. Dougherty had been working at the TSBD for eleven years with the general job description of shipping clerk. Employees began their workday at 8 A.M., but Dougherty's regular routine was to be on the job an hour earlier to take care of "some extra chores." On the morning of November 22 he had finished those chores and was sitting on the wrapping table when Oswald entered the back door of the building at about 8 o'clock to start his workday. It was the Commission's contention that Oswald had brought the Mannlicher-Carcano into the building that morning, broken down and disguised as curtain rods hidden in brown wrapping paper. The report contended that Oswald had disguised the contents of the package with the cover story he had given Wesley Frazier (who had driven Oswald to work that day), that he was carrying curtain rods for his Dallas apartment at 1026 North Beckley Avenue.[10]

Commission assistant counsel Joseph Ball walked Dougherty through his testimony. After some preliminary questioning that seemed scripted to show that Dougherty was not the brightest crayon in the box, Ball got to the root of the matter:

MR. BALL: Did he come in with anybody?

MR. DOUGHERTY: No.

MR. BALL: He was alone?

MR. DOUGHERTY: Yes, he was alone.

MR. BALL: Do you recall him having anything in his hand?

MR. DOUGHERTY: Well, I didn't see anything, if he did.

MR. BALL: Did you pay enough attention to him, you think, that you would remember whether he did or didn't?

MR. DOUGHERTY: Well, I believe I can—yes, sir—I'll put it this way: I didn't see anything in his hands at all.

MR. BALL: In other words, your memory is definite on that, is it?

MR. DOUGHERTY: Yes, sir.

MR. BALL: In other words, you would say positively he had nothing in his hands?

MR. DOUGHERTY: I would say that—yes, sir.[11]

Although he was an experienced lawyer, Ball made a rookie courtroom slip by asking one question too many. He got Dougherty to say under oath and on record that he was positive Oswald had come into the building that day empty-handed. The Commission, of course, would have its own way in the end. The report ignored Dougherty's testimony and concluded that Oswald had carried the disassembled rifle into the depository building the day of the assassination in a package disguised as curtain rods.

Although the government featured Brennan and ignored Dougherty, other key witness testimony relating to Oswald's movements was fraudulently dismissed, altered, or willfully suppressed. The Commission ran into problems trying to make a convincing case that after shooting the president Oswald had time to cross the sixth floor from the southeast to the northeast corner, stopping on the way to hide the rifle behind a barricade of book cartons, and take the stairs down to the second floor. According to the Commission's reenactment scenario, he had to reach the vestibule to the second-floor lunchroom before encountering Superintendent Roy S. Truly and police officer Marrion L. Baker. The Commission estimated that in order for Oswald to narrowly miss being spotted rushing pell-mell down the back stairs by Truly and Baker, who were running up the same stairwell, he had to have arrived on the second floor in about seventy-five seconds.

To stack the odds in favor of their own reconstruction of Oswald's alleged movements after the shooting, the FBI and the Commission ignored the time it would have taken him to hide the rifle. Seymour Weitzman and Eugene Boone, two Dallas County deputies, discovered the rifle. When Joseph Ball deposed Weitzman, the deputy constable exposed the fallacies in the Commission's reenactment of Oswald's movements. Weitzman stated that the rifle was so well hidden, "I would venture to say eight or nine of us stumbled over the gun a couple of times before we thoroughly searched the building." Boone's testimony went even further in denying the Commission a soft landing on the business of the rifle's discovery. He was even more graphic in his account of the location of the weapon: They "caught a glance of the rifle," Boone told Ball, "stuffed down between two rows of boxes with another pulled over the top of it." It is clear from Weitzman's and Boone's testimony that precious, time-consuming seconds had gone into the hiding of the Mannlicher-Carcano rifle. It was not just tossed behind a wall of cartons by a fleeing Oswald desperate to place as much distance as possible between himself and the sixth-floor "sniper's nest." It does not stretch credulity too much to speculate that the rifle may have been planted even before the attempt was made on President Kennedy's life. There is nothing in the Commission's report that could categorically rule out this possibility.[12]

Although the Commission ignored the hiding of the rifle in its reconstruction of Oswald's movements, it could not so easily dismiss witness Victoria E. Adams, a depository employee who was watching the presidential motorcade from an open window in the fourth-floor office of the Scott, Foresman Publishing Company where she worked. Adams, a former novice of the Ursuline Order in Ohio and Catholic schoolteacher, testified before the Commission that within thirty seconds to a minute after witnessing the shooting she ran down the back stairs from the fourth to the first floor and did not meet a fleeing Oswald or hear anyone running down the stairs because Oswald was not escaping down the stairs. Adams contended that if Oswald was fleeing down the stairs, she would have seen or heard him. If her testimony had been allowed to stand, it would have indicated that Oswald had not been on the sixth floor at the time JFK was shot![13]

Immediately after the assassination Adams gave the same account to Dallas police detective James R. Leavelle. She told Leavelle that immediately after the third shot she ran down the stairs and noted that the "elevator was not running and there was no one on the stairs." When she reached the first floor she started to run toward the railroad tracks, but "a police officer stopped me and turned me back." Despite the horror of what Adams had just witnessed, she was emphatic about her movements and appeared to be a credible witness. Sandra Styles, a coworker who had also witnessed the shooting, joined Adams in her rapid descent down the stairs to the first floor. Adams testified that when she reached the first floor she also noticed William Shelley and Billy Lovelady, both book depository employees, and told them that the president had been shot.[14]

The Warren report concluded that Adams was mistaken about the time she came down the back stairs. The report cited the April Commission testimony of Billy Lovelady and William Shelley, who stated that immediately after the shooting they left the front steps of the depository building and ran toward the railroad yards to the west to watch the police search the cars; they did not return to the building until minutes later. According to the report, when Adams encountered Lovelady and Shelley on the first floor they had already been to the railroad yards and had returned to the book depository. Therefore, minutes had elapsed, explaining why Adams did not see Oswald when she came down the back stairs. The twenty-four-year-old Scott, Foresman employee, the Commission would conclude, was simply confused about exactly when she descended the stairs and when she saw Lovelady and Shelley.[15]

What the Warren report failed to point out was that Lovelady and Shelley's April testimony was contradicted by the sworn affidavits both men had executed for the Dallas police the day of the assassination. Lovelady's affidavit states that after the shooting stopped, "we went back into the building and I took some police officers up to search the building." This was consistent with what he told the FBI the day of the assassination. According to the FBI's FD-302 interview form, Lovelady reported that after hearing shots, "he and Shelley started running toward the President's car, but it sped away west on Elm Street. . . . He and Shelley then returned to the Texas School Book Depository Building." Shelley reported to the police that after the shooting, "I went back into the building and went inside and called my wife and told her what happened. I was on the first floor and I stayed at the elevator."[16]

In their initial accounts there is nothing about railroad yards. Their police affidavits and Lovelady's FBI interview were sworn when events of that day were still fresh and accurate recall more likely. Their original statements are perfectly consistent with Victoria Adams's testimony, and that has to be the reason that the Commission had to ignore them. Lovelady's and Shelley's altered April Commission testimony was essential to discredit Adams's account and pull the Commission's case against Oswald back from the brink of disaster. Unless we can discount any suspicion that both men forgot to mention the railroad yards, only to independently and conveniently remember them in April, then there is reason to suspect that the FBI or the Commission persuaded them to alter their testimony to allow the Commission to salvage the official and predetermined version of the Kennedy assassination.[17]

Carolyn Arnold, who worked at the book depository as a secretary, was certain she had seen Oswald on the first floor at 12:25 P.M. Arnold told FBI agent Richard E. Harrison that as she was leaving the building to watch the presidential motorcade, she spotted Oswald "between the front door and the double doors leading to the warehouse on the first floor." When Harrison wrote up her statement he changed the time on the FD-302 form from 12:25 to "a few minutes before 12:15 PM." The FBI tweaked her statement to provide the necessary plausible interval to allow Oswald to get into position at the "sniper's nest" on the sixth floor. The Commission never called Arnold as a witness. It also failed to call any of her five coworkers who had joined her on the front steps of the building to catch a view of President Kennedy and the First Lady and who might have corroborated her sighting of Oswald on the first floor at 12:25 P.M.[18]

Fifteen years later an investigative reporter for the *Dallas Morning News,* Earl Golz, sought out Carolyn Arnold to ask her about what she had told the FBI in 1963. She had remarried (she was then Carolyn Johnson) and had become secretary to the vice president of the TSBD. According to Golz's story, she was shocked when he pointed out to her that the FBI had not mentioned her sighting of Oswald at 12:25, five minutes before President Kennedy was shot.[19]

Oswald's story was that he had been on the first floor watching the presidential motorcade when the shooting happened. He gave the same account to the Dallas police, the Secret Service, and the FBI. When Dallas police captain Will Fritz questioned him, Oswald said he was leaving the building shortly after the shooting when two men, one with a crew cut, approached him, identified themselves as Secret Service agents, and asked for the location of the nearest telephone. Fritz passed this information on to Forrest V. Sorrels, the head of the Dallas Secret Service. Oswald repeated this account to Secret Service Inspector Thomas J. Kelley. According to Kelley's report of his private interview with the suspect, Oswald said he was standing outside the depository building right after the motorcade was fired upon when a "young crew-cut man" rushed up to him, identified himself as a Secret Service agent, and asked for directions to the nearest telephone.[20]

More than a month after the assassination, Sorrels's agents interviewed the two men, Pierce M. Allman and Terrance S. Ford, employed as program directors by the Dallas TV and radio station WFAA. Both programmers were in Dealey Plaza that Friday. They were standing near the corner of Elm and Houston Streets watching the presidential motorcade when shots suddenly rang out. Allman and Ford immediately started running toward the TSBD to find a phone to report the shooting. They reported to the Secret Service that a man in front of the depository building matching Oswald's description directed them to a phone. The interviewing agents neglected to ask how much time had elapsed between their hearing the shots and reaching the depository. Later, when he executed an affidavit for the Dallas police, Allman reported that it was only a "few moments" before he and Ford entered the building. The Secret Service report of its interview stated that after being shown photos of Oswald, neither man was able to positively identify him as the person who directed them to the phone on the first floor. However, the report noted that Allman had a "crew cut" and "carried his press pass in a leather case similar to cases carried by Federal agents and police officers." By the time the report was filed on February 3, 1964, the Secret Service was satisfied that Allman and Ford were the men "referred to by Oswald in his interview." The report concluded, however, that since there was no indication that either Allman or Ford had "identified themselves as Secret Service Agents," the investigation was closed![21]

The most charitable reaction to the Secret Service's suppression of Allman's and Ford's statements is that their accounts, standing alone, might have been of limited interest and should have been filed and forgotten along with hundreds of other assassination reports. But in light of what the government heard from Adams, Arnold, Dougherty, and sheriff's deputies Weitzman and Boone, the Commission's investigation should have taken a different turn. The combined weight of the statements and testimonies of these witnesses provided grounds for the exculpation of the government's only suspect in the assassination. Had the intentions of the Commission and the FBI been to uncover the truth of Dallas, the accounts of these witnesses would not have been knowingly misrepresented, altered, and swept under the rug.

Never at any time did the Commission have as much as a single investigator of its own. The commissioners, Rankin, and the staff lawyers relied totally on the FBI to collect the evidence. The FBI's record of collecting evidence in the case was marred by sloppy and indifferent procedure when the Commission's investigative arm was not avoiding it altogether. On the surface, the impression left was that bureau agents and the vaunted FBI Crime Laboratory (BuLab) were parodies of the Keystone Kops, incapable of handling a crime scene and even grasping the rudimentary principles of forensic science. The reality was, of course, almost entirely different. The Hoover bureau, having settled on a politically safe solution to the Kennedy assassination, did not want to deal with unruly and contrary evidence that broke ranks with the predetermined official solution.

In March 1964 Commission lawyer Melvin Eisenberg made what could only be characterized as a strange request of BuLab concerning the ballistics report about the murder of Dallas police officer J. D. Tippit. According to the official account Oswald gunned down Officer Tippit less than an hour after he slipped away from the book depository building. The FBI retrieved several cartridge cases from the Tippit crime scene as well as the one bullet Dr. Paul Moellenhoff removed from Tippit, who was dead when he arrived at Methodist Hospital in Dallas. BuLab was satisfied that the cartridge cases matched up with Oswald's revolver. However, because of severe mutilation of this one bullet, there were not sufficient marks to determine whether it came from Oswald's handgun. FBI Washington had this ballistics report the day after the assassination. It was not until almost four months later that Eisenberg pointed out that the FBI might find it advantageous to obtain the three other bullets recovered by Dr. Earl F. Rose, the Dallas County medical examiner, from the body of the luckless Tippit when he was brought to autopsy on November 22, 1963.[22]

Eisenberg's reference to the three bullets Dr. Rose removed from Tippit's body could not have come as breaking news to the FBI. The FBI's report to the Commission (CD 1) noted on page 2 that Tippit was shot three times (one of the bullets hit his belt and did not penetrate his body but was recovered at the crime scene). The Dallas field office just never bothered to collect these slugs removed by Dr. Rose. There should have been raised eyebrows when Eisenberg and the other Commission lawyers realized that the FBI had pinned the cop-killer label on Oswald without any hard ballistic evidence. The FBI's conspicuous indifference toward testing the other slugs for a ballistic match underscored the bureau's single-minded determination to insist that Oswald was the lone assailant. Moreover, the FBI never asked for a copy of Tippit's autopsy report until more than three months after Dr. Rose released it to the Secret Service on December 10, 1963. December 10 was the day after the FBI report (CD 1), including a section on Oswald's alleged murder of Tippit, was released to the Warren Commission.[23]

The FBI's crime lab and the Dallas field office concocted a cover story to feed the Commission, blaming the Dallas Police Department for dragging its feet on the bureau's request for the three bullets. The hard truth was that FBI Dallas did not contact the Dallas police until two days after Eisenberg made his request. The upshot of this extraordinary episode was that the bullets eventually turned up in Captain Will Fritz's evidence file, unbeknownst to the captain because the detective who placed them there did not identify them for the record. Captain Fritz, chief of homicide, was laboring under the impression that the one slug taken from Tippit at Methodist Hospital was the sum total of bullets removed from the body. As soon as the three slugs were resurrected from Fritz's file, they were turned over to the Dallas field office.[24] Had Oswald lived to stand trial, the prosecution would have seriously stubbed its toe in trying to explain to a jury this chain of evidence. This is not to imply that Oswald would necessarily have been exonerated on the charge of killing Tippit or, for that matter, assassinating President Kennedy. The image planted in the public mind of Oswald as a cold-blooded cop-killer (Tippit left a wife and three young children) was a defining and validating precursor to the accusation that he was the monster who had taken the life of an American president.

The FBI lab's deception and cover-up with the Tippit bullets did not work with Rankin and his staff. There were no Commission memos castigating the bureau for its apparent sloppy and inadequate work ethic; this was not Rankin's way. Moreover, the Commission could not afford to openly antagonize Hoover, not knowing how he might retaliate. Nevertheless, the course

Rankin took was unprecedented. FBIHQ was politely placed on notice that the Commission was going to have an independent examiner go over some of the firearms evidence. In the long history of the Hoover bureau, the FBI lab had never been subjected to any external scrutiny. Because of sedulous public image-building and aggressive lobbying on Capitol Hill, the FBI lab enjoyed the unquestioned reputation as the best forensic laboratory in the world. The FBI was used to having defense lawyers take what BuLab said at face value. Most lawyers often simply stipulated to vital trial information when they learned that someone from the FBI lab was going to testify.[25]

Hoover's gorge rose when he learned of the Commission's plans to call on outside examiners. "It is getting more and more intolerable," he vented, "to deal with the Warren Commission." Disgusted with what he regarded as the Commission's vote of no confidence, the director toyed with the idea of pulling the FBI laboratory out of the investigation. Rankin heard from Assistant Director Alex Rosen about Hoover's displeasure, accompanied by an unveiled threat that the FBI was ready "to step out of the picture from the standpoint of laboratory examinations." According to Rosen's account of the discussion, Rankin was taken aback. The Commission's general counsel iterated that he had the utmost confidence in the FBI lab. Rankin insisted that he had just been following instructions from the seven commissioners in this matter. This immediate "crisis of confidence" did blow over in the sense that it never went public. It did nothing, however, to relieve Hoover and his assistant directors' distrust of the Commission. Hoover would have the last word because he insisted that any material earmarked for the independent examiner be delivered to the Commission and that the Commission make all the arrangements for handling and delivery. After negotiating this speed bump, Rankin, in the Commission's name, gave the FBI carte blanche for its subsequent treatment of the physical and firearms evidence.[26]

In April 1964 Rankin made a request for the FBI lab results on Governor Connally's clothes. As in any homicide investigation, the victim's clothes contained many valuable forensic clues. Analysis of the gunshot holes in Connally's clothes was important to the Commission staffers in reconstructing the shootings of President Kennedy and the gravely injured governor, who was in the jump seat of the presidential limousine just in front of the mortally wounded president. President Kennedy's clothes had been flown to Washington and examined immediately by the FBI Crime Laboratory. An examination of Connally's clothing took on added importance several months after Rankin's April request when the Commission was forced to conjecture that the governor had been struck by the same nonfatal bullet that allegedly exited Kennedy's throat. This so-called single-bullet construction was absolutely essential to the Warren report's contention that all three shots came from the rear of the motorcade and were fired by a lone gunman.[27]

Hoover's written response to Rankin's request about Connally's clothes was both astonishing and inaccurate. Most of the text was lifted directly from the April 22, 1964, report submitted by the FBI laboratory. The key portion of Hoover's memo to Rankin read, "Nothing was found to indicate which holes were entrances and which were exits. The coat, shirt, and trousers were cleaned prior to their receipt in the Laboratory, which might account for the fact that no foreign deposits of metal or other substances were found on the cloth surrounding the holes." Not mentioned in Hoover's letter but included in the FBI lab report was the crushing conclusion: "It was not possible from an examination of the clothing to determine whether or not all the holes were made by the same projectile or projectile fragments." In short, the dry cleaning of Connally's clothes compromised much of their value as physical evidence. Hoover made no apology and gave no explanation as to why the FBI, once again, had apparently been so dilatory and slipshod in gathering vital physical evidence. In addition, Hoover failed to mention that there were two holes in Connally's shirt.[28]

There really was no mystery attached to the whereabouts of Governor Connally's shirt and coat. They were held at Parkland Memorial Hospital, and when neither the FBI nor the Secret Service showed up after a reasonable interval to claim them, they were turned over to Texas Congressman Henry Gonzales. They remained in the congressman's closet in Washington until he eventually returned them to Mrs. John B. ("Nellie") Connally. Mrs. Connally later reported that she notified the FBI and the Secret Service that she had received the bagged and bloody clothes, "but nobody seemed interested." After almost two months of official inaction, Nellie Connally, understandably, sent them to the dry cleaners.[29]

If the FBI made any effort to locate Connally's clothes it was cursory at best. A week after the assassination James Rowley, chief of the Secret Service, passed on a request from Connally's office in Texas to the FBI as to the whereabouts of the governor's clothes and the personal effects in his suit coat pockets. Gordon Shanklin, the agent in charge of the Dallas field office, notified FBIHQ that he had checked around and come up empty. Shanklin's memo suggested that the missing objects of interest were Connally's "glasses, cigarette lighter, and a bunch of papers." It was not until April 1 that BuLab received the governor's cleaned clothes for examination and then another three weeks before the FBI lab furnished its findings to the Commission. This was the same masterful FBI that on the day of the assassination identified the sporting goods store in Chicago where Oswald had purchased his Mannlicher-Carcano.[30] This slapstick, Dogberry-like routine of avoiding essential evidence for four months had to be intentional. Even on its worst days the FBI was much better than this. The only plausible explanation was that the FBI was simply not interested in identifying witnesses or uncovering evidence that might jeopardize its prefabricated case against Oswald.

The Commission had Connally's dry-cleaned clothes. The Warren report clearly stated that there was one gunshot hole in Connally's coat but two holes in his shirt.[31] Two of the Parkland Memorial Hospital doctors who worked on Connally had experience with gunshot wounds. They both suspected that the bullet in Connally had fragmented—a possibility that BuLab could not reject—thereby accounting for the two holes in the shirt. Dr. Charles F. Gregory, who treated Connally's wrist injuries, when questioned by the Commission urged that "someone ought to search his belongings and other areas where he had been" to uncover the fragments. Dr. Robert Shaw, Connally's chest surgeon, remained convinced long after the Commission had reported its findings that the bullet had fragmented and that two of the largest fragments found on the limousine's floor were from the Connally bullet.[32] All the plausible conjecturing by these experienced surgeons was rendered moot by the failure of the FBI to collect Connally's clothes on the day of the assassination. Since the FBI had immediately seized the case from the Secret Service, as Hoover had boasted to author William Manchester, along with the top billing went the responsibility to conduct a fair and complete investigation.[33]

If Drs. Gregory and Shaw were right about the fragmenting of the Connally bullet, then the Commission's "single-bullet" assumption would have passed from the realm of highly improbable to the categorically impossible. The nonfatal bullet that struck Connally, according to the Commission's construction, had first gone through Kennedy before creating the massive wounds in the governor. It left lead deposits on Connally's shattered fifth rib and in his wrist wound and a piece embedded in the femur of his left leg. Some of the wrist fragments were debrided (washed away) when the doctors cleaned the wound, which the Commission conveniently ignored. Yet this bullet, CE 399, which the Commission described as "pristine" despite the trauma it had produced and which lost less than three grains (the weight of a postage stamp is one grain), is the missile of single-bullet fame upon which the Commission rested its case of a lone shooter. Had the two holes in Connally's shirt been made by fragments from this bullet, it would have endowed CE 399 with more magic than even the Commission would have dared claim it contained. (A detailed critique of the Commission's so-called single-bullet theory is developed in Chapters 8 and 9.)

The cleaning of Connally's clothing prevented other textbook forensic examination of the physical evidence. Once the clothes were dry cleaned it was impossible to conduct a fiber analysis to determine beyond a scientific doubt whether the governor had been hit by a single bullet and whether that bullet had entered or exited his back. The cleaning and pressing of the coat destroyed the orientation or position of the fibers around the bullet hole. In addition, when a bullet strikes material it leaves a deposit of residue of metal (called "bullet wipe") on the cloth surrounding the hole. With refined scientific testing an examiner can make calculations about the metallic composition of the bullet. Spectrographic analysis tests run on the "bullet wipe" taken from JFK's coat could have been compared against the metal deposits from Connally's unlaundered clothes to determine whether the holes were made by a missile that came from the same batch as the fragments found in the presidential limousine from the fatal bullet that disintegrated as it passed through Kennedy's skull.[34] If the concentration of the trace elements (e.g., antimony, bismuth, silver) in the "bullet wipe" from both Connally's garments and the head fragments proved to be the same or nearly the same in parts per million, then the Commission's case for a single shooter could have stood virtually unchallenged. The cleaning of Connally's clothes ruled out the possibility of any comparative testing.

Most astonishing and conspicuous by its absence in the Warren report is any reference to the FBI lab's conducting a cotton-swab test on the alleged assassination rifle. The most basic ballistic testing is to run a cotton swab down the barrel of a weapon to determine whether it has been recently discharged. If the FBI did go ahead with the swab test on the Mannlicher-Carcano, Oswald's alleged murder weapon, then the results from BuLab's cotton-swab test were likely inconclusive or even negative and therefore were quietly suppressed. It was extraordinary that Robert A. Frazier, the FBI's leading firearms expert, never mentioned a swab test. He told the Commission that in his years with the FBI he had undertaken about 50,000 to 100,000 firearms comparisons. Certainly some, if not all, of these examinations must have included the basic swab test. Even more remarkable was that none of the Commissioners ever asked him about the results of such a test. Commissioner McCloy, who owned guns and was familiar with firearms, tentatively touched on the subject when he asked Frazier whether there were "metal filings in the barrel?" When Frazier responded, "I did not examine it for that," the matter was instantly dropped and McCloy shifted to questions about the homemade sling on the Mannlicher-Carcano.[35]

The Commission had no more legitimate success with the ballistics evidence than it did in placing Oswald on the sixth floor of the TSBD at the time of the assassination. Undeterred, the Warren report relied on the meaningless and misleading testimony of FBI firearms experts to build its case against Oswald.

At the beginning of July 1964, after all but one of the FBI crime lab experts had testified, a dismayed Norman Redlich, Rankin's special assistant, sent off a memo to Commissioner Dulles. In summary, Redlich noted that at that point in the investigation it had not been established beyond a doubt that

Oswald had killed policeman Tippit because it was not clear whether he had fired his revolver. Even more problematic, according to Redlich, was whether Oswald had even fired a rifle the day of the assassination. The first indication that Oswald's .38 Smith and Wesson revolver was defective surfaced in the Warren report's account of his arrest in the Texas Theatre. The report stated that while Oswald was scuffling with one of the arresting officers, "a click" was heard, which the report identified as the sound of Oswald's handgun misfiring.[36] Later, when the FBI crime lab examined the four empty .38 hulls retrieved from the Tippit crime scene, none of the cartridges bore firing-pin indentations. Based on the physical evidence, BuLab surmised, "the firing pin would not strike one or more of the cartridges with sufficient force to fire them."[37] The FBI was confronted with the strong likelihood that Oswald's pistol was so hopelessly defective that it could not have been used in the Tippit shooting. This could explain why the FBI was so conspicuously indifferent about collecting and testing the three slugs Dr. Rose had removed from the slain policeman's body.

As mentioned earlier, it was not until months later, after Assistant Counsel Eisenberg prodded the FBI, that it located the three bullets and subjected them to ballistic testing and spectrographic analysis. Despite the bureau's efforts to put the best evidentiary face on the outcome, the results were at best inconclusive and in actuality forensically meaningless. The results of the ballistic testing were summed up in one thudding sentence: "No conclusion could be reached as to whether or not they were fired from Oswald's revolver." At the end of March Hoover wrote Rankin a two-page memo explaining why BuLab's tests were inconclusive. At the same time, the director was not about to let Oswald out of the frame for the Tippit killing. The organic connection of the assassination of JFK and the ruthless murder of a law officer was perceived as essential for the public validation of the "official truth" of Dallas, an ongoing collaborative FBI-Commission enterprise that was still in progress. With this as his subtext, Hoover reported that the FBI laboratory's spectrographic unit had found that the lead alloy in the Tippit slugs was "qualitatively similar" in composition to the lead alloy in the six live shells recovered from Oswald's revolver.[38]

In limiting his report to the results of the qualitative tests, all Hoover was saying was that all the specimens tested spectrographically were bullet metal. This disclosure was anything but earthshaking. The FBI already knew that the specimens taken from Tippit's body and the six live rounds in Oswald's handgun were "qualitatively similar" in that they were all bullets. It is not clear whether Hoover was trying to mislead Rankin into believing that "similar" was a forensic synonym for "identical" or prepping the general counsel for the future appearance of FBI firearms experts who were scheduled to provide testimony before the Commission.

Lead alloys used in the manufacture of bullets contain an assortment of trace elements. When the FBI was forced to examine the curbstone associated with James Tague and the missed shot the work was assigned to the Physics and Chemistry Section of the FBI laboratory. John F. Gallagher, an eighteen-year FBI veteran, with most of those years spent in the bureau's spectrographic unit, was the special agent in charge. Part of his examination included running a quantitative spectrographic analysis on the alleged Oswald rifle bullet (CE 399) and bullet fragments recovered from the presidential limousine. Gallagher reported that the bullets used in the Kennedy assassination contained eleven trace elements.[39] Since there are literally hundreds of different compositions of trace elements found in commercially manufactured bullets, it is not enough to say that two or more bullets are qualitatively similar. Quantitative analysis can determine in parts per million the percentage of chemical trace elements in bullet metal, which allows the forensic examiner to say with scientific exactitude that two bullets or bullet fragments, to the exclusion of all others, are a match or "hit" because they have a common origin.

Commission staff lawyer Melvin A. Eisenberg learned firsthand from the FBI's most experienced firearms expert about the difference in FBI terminology between *similar* and *identical.* The difference, to borrow Mark Twain's analogy, is as great as the difference between the lightning bug and the lightning. In his March 31, 1964, exchange with Robert A. Frazier, Eisenberg asked Frazier several times about "apparent matches." Frazier confided, "We don't actually use that term in the FBI." Frazier went further with his "tutorial," stating, "Occasionally we say that some of the marks were similar in nature. They were not sufficient to substantiate an identification." He noted, however, "That type of terminology is not entirely accurate." Frazier's last comment is worth emphasizing: *"Unless you have sufficient marks for an identification, you cannot say one way or the other as to whether or not two bullets were fired from a particular barrel."* Frazier, of course, was speaking about his own line of specialty, ballistic testing, but what he had to say about the general meaninglessness of terms such as *apparent match* and *similar in composition* applied equally to crime lab emission spectroscopy.[40]

Rankin made a point of bestowing encomiums on all the FBI witnesses who testified before the Commission. According to FBI Assistant Director Rosen, Rankin conveyed the view of the Commission members in attendance that "the testimony of the Bureau personnel was far superior to testimony received from anyone else that has appeared before the Commission." Rankin singled out Frazier as the FBI expert whose confidence and professional manner were so impressive that "any possible doubt that anyone had, had been completely removed by the Bureau experts' testimony."[41]

High praise indeed; however, the fact that Frazier lent himself to at-length questioning about areas in which he had no personal knowledge—the spectrographic evidence—perhaps warranted special acknowledgement in Rankin's view. In Frazier's May 6, 1964, Commission testimony he assumed the role of surrogate for John F. Gallagher, the senior member of BuLab's spectrographic unit. Frazier freely admitted to the Commission that his job was to analyze all the bullet and bullet fragments found in the presidential limousine "except for the spectrographic analysis of the composition."[42] This admission should have prompted at least one of the Commissioners to wonder out loud why Gallagher was not present to field questions in this highly specialized area. Frazier's expertise in ballistics was obviously not the reason that he was selected to lead the commissioners through this evidentiary mine field. Frazier was doubtlessly picked because he was a polished and accomplished professional witness, specially trained by the FBI to testify in court cases. Considering the troubling questions surrounding whether Oswald had discharged any firearms the day of the assassination, the Commission and its staff looked to Frazier to dispel any doubts.

Commission Assistant Counsel Arlen Specter choreographed Frazier's May 1964 session before the Commission. Specter first wanted to establish the relationship between the three bullet fragments found in the rear of the limousine and CE 399 (the so-called magic bullet), allegedly found on Governor Connally's stretcher at Parkland Memorial Hospital. Frazier prefaced his response by noting that he did not have Gallagher's results with him to place in the record. He went on, "I did ascertain that it was determined that the lead fragments were similar in composition." When Specter pressed him further about whether this meant conclusively that they had a common origin, Frazier replied, "No, sir." Specter's next series of inquiries was designed to elicit the results of spectrographic analysis comparing the scrapings of the bullet smear on the limousine's windshield with CE 399. Frazier's response was, "The lead was found to be similar in composition." All that was left was for Specter to establish for the record the relationship between the fragments removed from JFK's head wound and Connally's wrist wound and the lead smear from the windshield of the president's car. Frazier did not disappoint. His response was the standard rhetorical trope, devoid of any evidentiary value: "And they were found to be similar in metallic composition." At that point, Specter asked again whether Frazier could state "with any more certainty" whether all of these fragments had a common origin. Sticking to the script, all the FBI firearms expert could vouch was that they "are all of similar composition."[43]

When Frazier completed his May 1964 testimony he advised the Commission that any detailed information about the spectrographic analysis would have to come from John F. Gallagher.[44] Clearly, it was fundamentally essential for the Commission to question Gallagher, the one man with first-hand, personal knowledge, about the quantitative readout on CE 399, the lead scrapings from the windshield, and the fragments from Kennedy's and Connally's bodies. In addition to Kennedy's autopsy, this was the best forensic evidence in the case. However, it was never presented.

Gallagher was the last witness to testify. He appeared before Commission Assistant Counsel Norman Redlich on September 15, 1964, when the report was already in galley proofs and one week before the Commission's findings were sent to the U.S. Government Printing Office. Not a single Commission member was in attendance at this short session. It was simply one on one, Redlich and Gallagher. Even more revealing about this ritualistic, for-the-record-only nature of the session was the fact that Redlich never deviated from his prepared script to ask Gallagher a single question about the results of his spectrographic analysis of CE 399 and the fragments.[45] Redlich, Rankin's most trusted Commission assistant, studiously avoided interrogating Gallagher on the results of his quantitative examination—the only results that mattered.

According to Frazier's May 1964 testimony, the FBI had these test results as part of its permanent record. However, the FBI never volunteered them to the Commission and the Commission never asked for them. The curious will search in vain through the 912-page Warren report and the twenty-six volumes of Hearings and Exhibits and will have to be content with Frazier's assurances to the commissioners that these quantitative test results were "a part of the permanent record of the FBI."[46] That the Commission treated this critical evidence as though it were plague-ridden can only be interpreted to mean that it resolved Redlich's uncertainty back in July as to whether or not Oswald actually shot President Kennedy. The answer, to Redlich and the Commission's dismay, was not one they could live with, so the results were omitted from the official record.

Like the FBI, the Commission had its share of worrisome "tender spots," and for good reason. Since it had begun its investigation into the assassination with a prefabricated conclusion, there was the danger that its ex parte findings would ignite more controversy in the public mind rather than a tranquilizing state of acceptance. The commissioners made no secret of this in their "Top Secret" executive sessions, for they all understood what was expected of them, even when it was unspoken. The language was always polite, as befits men of imposing gravity, men for whom the term *honorable* was coined. When discussing the configuration of their final report, Dulles suggested that a detailed biography of Lee Harvey Oswald be included in the main report rather than tucked away in an appendix. Rankin liked the idea. The general counsel thought it would help to tell the Commission's story and "show why it is reasonable to assume that he did what the Commission concludes that he did."[47]

Even standing alone, the Commission's April 30, 1964, executive session is instructive as a self-portrait of these "honorable men." By the end of April the Commission had heard from only about half of the witnesses who would ultimately be called for questioning. One of the most important would be Abraham Zapruder, and he was not questioned until July, almost three months later. To be fair to the Commission, and to place the April 30 session in context, Warren and Rankin expected to finish the investigation and have the final report out by June, months before the 1964 presidential campaign started in earnest. These plans were aborted largely because the Commission was forced to retool its findings to account for Jim Tague and the curbstone bullet, the missed shot.[48]

The April 30 session was given over to musings about the need to tidy up some of the perceived loose ends in the investigation and, more importantly, what actions the Commission could take to prepare the public for its published conclusions. Warren suggested that they cultivate the heads of the Associated Press and United Press International, the two large news services from which most publications and the electronic media got their news. The chairman's idea was to invite them "to examine their [the Commission's] reports and files . . . and discuss on a confidential basis—not for publication— anything that might be in their minds as to what should be investigated." Warren hoped that this little exercise in news management would win the support of the media barons. "I am of the opinion," he went on, "that we could get a statement from them that would be of a confirmatory nature so far as our report is concerned." McCloy supported the idea as a quick fix for stifling adverse overseas opinion that viewed Kennedy's murder as a dark and bloody conspiracy.[49] Had Hoover been privy to this executive session he would have recognized in Warren, at least for the moment, a kindred spirit who understood that politics and image were the only things that really mattered. As it turned out, Warren's idea never went any further than the Commission's conference room.

Once the chief justice got the ball rolling others chimed in. McCloy suggested calling a witness from the State Department to testify that Foggy Bottom was satisfied that there had been no conspiracy. Apparently adrenalized by the unanimous approval of his first suggestion, the chief justice dragged Robert Kennedy's name into the discussion. Warren asserted that if Bobby was to testify as "a brother" and not as attorney general, "it would have tremendous force." Rankin was quick to give his stamp of approval about corralling the testimony of the dead president's brother. The general counsel thought it would work wonders in quashing all the conspiracy talk if

Bobby Kennedy would agree to testify that he was satisfied that Oswald was the lone assailant. "It's hardly believable," Rankin opined, "that the brother of the President would stand by if there was some conspiracy in the United States to dispose of his brother." Then Warren did what at this point in the session would seem impossible—he took the discussion to an even lower level by suggesting that the Commission trade on the name of Sargent Shriver, the brother-in-law of the murdered president. It was at this point that McCloy and Dulles reined in the chief justice, but not because their sense of decency was offended. Dulles was quick to point out the practical flaw in Warren's suggestion when he noted that Shriver "had no government position which could bring him in touch with the records and files and information on the subject."[50]

The Commission was aware that Bobby Kennedy knew nothing about the assassination. He had disassociated himself from the investigation, relying largely on Acting Attorney General Nicholas Katzenbach, a close political ally and family friend, to oversee the proceedings. If he were to testify, it would be testimony without any honest meaning. But the American people would assume that as attorney general he knew all the details of the case and that, as the bereaved brother, he would have seen to it that truth was indeed the Commission's only mission.

Contemplating trading on Robert Kennedy's name was a shabby deception by men intent on deceiving the nation. As far as the public record reveals, none of these suggestions raised during the April 30 session went any further than the talking stage. But the fact that the Commission contemplated going to these lengths is the best self-indictment that it did not have much confidence in the case it was building against the dead Oswald.[51]

6 The Warren Commission's "Smoking Guns"

We have a dirty rumor . . . and it must be wiped out insofar as it is possible to do so by this Commission.
—J. Lee Rankin, Warren Commission transcript,
    January 27, 1964

Contrary to the old maxim, it was January and not April that proved the cruelest, most agonizing, and most self-revealing month of the Commission's life. During January 1964 the commissioners met on three occasions: January 22, 24, and 27. The terrible question that plagued these eminent public men was one they could no longer ignore—was Lee Harvey Oswald an agent or informer for a government agency? This "Agent Oswald" question was the theme for all three meetings. Moreover, the extraordinary lengths to which Rankin, Warren, and the commissioners went to suppress the record of these meetings reveals a self-accusatory "smoking gun": the Commission and its general counsel's unswerving determination to join with the FBI in an alliance to impose a counterfeit solution on the American people. Before the Commission even heard its first witness it had already abandoned any intention to carry out a good-faith search for the underlying facts surrounding the assassination of President John F. Kennedy.

In summary, before the commissioners and Rankin went off the record during their January 22 meeting, the commissioners, terrified by the prospects of Oswald having government connections, agreed to destroy all evidence of the meeting.[1] Two days later Rankin and Chairman Warren met in a secret session with members of the Texas Court of Inquiry, the court's general counsel, and the Dallas County district attorney and his assistant. Chief Justice Warren and Rankin viewed this session on January 24 as so sensitive that no transcript was made. The only record of this meeting is Rankin's six-page summary.[2] Rankin and Warren even deemed it necessary to hold back from the rest of the Commission a disclosure that Oswald may have been linked in some way with the Central Intelligence Agency. Years later, when Rankin was serving as corporation counsel for the City of New York, he was a government affiant in a Freedom of Information suit challenging the government's withholding of the Warren Commission executive session transcript for January 27, 1964. In this case, Rankin attested that he was instructed by the Commission to classify the transcript "Top Secret" under the authorization of Executive Order 10501, as amended. Rankin made this claim before a court knowing there was no such authorization in that executive order. He risked court-imposed penalties for false swearing and damage to his reputation to keep the January 27 transcript out of the public domain. Rankin had his reasons. Not the least of these could be that the January 27 transcript might qualify as one of the most dishonorable documents in the entire corpus of government-disclosed Kennedy assassination records.[3]

On January 22, 1964, Chairman Warren called a meeting of the Commission at 5:30 P.M., when most government employees were preparing to sit down to dinner. The reason he gave for this emergency session was "because of something that developed today." "Something," the chief justice continued, "that you shouldn't hear from the public before you had an opportunity to think about it." At this point Warren turned the meeting over to the general counsel to explain to the other four commissioners in attendance, Dulles, Ford, Boggs, and Cooper, why it had been necessary to interrupt their plans for the evening. Rankin proceeded to give an account of a phone conversation he had had that morning with Waggoner Carr, the attorney general of Texas and head of the Texas Court of Inquiry. Carr had called to tell Rankin that "the word had come out" that Oswald was "acting as an FBI undercover agent" from "September 1962 until the time of the assassination." According to Carr, the story even asserted that Oswald had an FBI "badge" (Number 179) and that he was "being paid two hundred a month" by the Hoover agency. Carr felt compelled to call, Rankin continued, because the source of this story was not some off-the-wall crank but the district attorney of Dallas County, Henry Wade.[4]

The "something" that prompted Warren and Rankin to call this emergency session was not breaking news. As the Texas attorney general had mentioned in the morning phone conversation, there were already "25 to 40 different versions" of the "Agent Oswald" story being bruited about by the Texas press corps. At the beginning of the year the *Houston Post* had run a two-column story by staff reporter Alonzo "Lonnie" F. Hudkins, "Oswald Rumored as Informant for U.S." Hudkins made no claim that the story was anything more than a rumor at that stage, but he noted that it was "a question being asked by many people in responsible positions here."[5] It was clear that the "Agent Oswald" story had had legs long before the Commission's January 22 emergency session. Moreover, on December 17 Hudkins had informed Lane Bertram, special agent in charge of the Secret Service's Houston office, about a conversation he had had with Allen Sweatt, chief of the Criminal Division, Sheriff's Office, in Dallas. According to Bertram, Hudkins told him that Sweatt had information that Oswald was an FBI informer receiving $200 a month for information relating to subversive activities. Inexplicably, Bertram did not file this report until January 3, 1964, and held the report back from Rankin until the day after the January 22 emergency session.[6] Although Rankin and the commissioners were unaware of the Secret Service report, Boggs and Cooper acknowledged during the January 22 meeting that they had already been aware of the "Agent Oswald" stories because they had seen FBI reports refuting this rumor.[7]

Given the fact that the FBI and the Commission did not know what had happened in Dallas, the Commission was working in the dark. The last thing the commissioners wanted to wrestle with were any surprises that would contradict the "official truth" assembled over the weekend of the assassination. Rankin had convinced Warren to call the January 22 meeting because these rumors could no longer be ignored, especially when a respected and responsible Texas official such as Wade appeared, if not to embrace them, then at least to treat them with a degree of seriousness. Rankin might have dismissed Carr's phone conversation as just Texas tall talk, as Carr's December visit to Washington had not done much to inspire confidence. When Carr left the nation's capital the general opinion regarding the Texas attorney general was: caliber light, range limited. Still, it certainly crossed Rankin's mind that Texas officials, such as Carr and Wade, could see a light at the end of a very dark tunnel if there was any truth to the "Agent Oswald" story. If it could be proved that Kennedy's assassin had been in the pay of an agency of the federal government, then Texas and the city of Dallas would be exonerated in the public mind. A tidal wave of public outrage would swamp the government in Washington while it raised Texas to safe ground. After Rankin spoke to Carr that morning he called the Texas Court of Inquiry's general counsel, Leon Jaworski, to elicit from the prominent Texas jurist his opinion about District Attorney Wade. Jaworski told Rankin that if Wade "did not have substantial evidence to support" these allegations he would never identify himself with them because "it would ruin him for future public life."[8]

The commissioners were aware of certain tidbits of intelligence in Oswald's record that suggested there might be some substance to the rumors. For instance, Rankin learned from the U.S. Navy's file on the Schrand case (the shooting of an eighteen-year-old marine in Oswald's outfit who had died of a gunshot wound while guarding the crypto van at Cubi Point) that marine PFC Oswald had had to have "Crypto" clearance to enter the highly secret crypto van. There was the tantalizing mystery of Oswald's command of the Russian language, which the Commission never attempted to explain. Just how had a high school dropout been able to master such a difficult language without special instruction and tutorial assistance? When Marina first met Oswald in Minsk she was puzzled by his accent before she learned he was an American and that Russian was not his native language. "He did use postal boxes practically every place he went," Rankin pointed out, "an ideal way to get money to anyone you wanted as an undercover agent." Ford noted from the FBI mail cover on Oswald that he was "writing to both elements of Communist parties": the Moscow-oriented American party and the breakaway, dissident Trotskyites. "Playing ball," as Ford put it, with implacable ideological enemies locked in a death struggle over Lenin's legacy. The Michigan congressman had hit momentarily on a clue that should have been followed up but never was. Then Warren raised the "strange thing that happened" when Oswald applied for a passport in New Orleans: That Oswald, a professed defector to the Soviet Union, was able to obtain a passport in the 1960s was highly unusual. That he received his passport overnight stunned even Warren, who, among all the commissioners, showed over the life of the Commission an unflinching readiness to accept some of the more ridiculous claims supporting Oswald as the lone-nut assassin.[9] Rankin steered the commissioners back from the periphery of their speculations to the vortex of their troubling problem: Was Oswald an undercover FBI informer? The chief counsel's words held no relief for the Commission. "I am confident," Rankin asserted, "that the FBI would never admit it, and I presume their records will never show it."[10] With that, Rankin essentially told the Commission that its deeply vexing problem was insoluble.

After more than thirty years it still remains a mystery why Rankin misled the Commission on this critical issue. As solicitor general for eight years Rankin had to have some idea, albeit limited, of the FBI's record-keeping system and how it identified its informants. As solicitor general he represented the FBI in its cases before the Supreme Court. It might be that despite his close and cordial working relations with Director Hoover, Rankin was not trusted to be privy to the names of the agency's informers. However, by January 1964 he already had access to thousands of pages of FBI investigative reports dealing with the assassination. Many of these documents, especially those the FBI termed "Letterhead Memoranda," were accompanied by tear-away pages containing the names and the symbols of the informers who had provided the intelligence. If not during his years in the Justice Department then surely as chief counsel responsible for the day-to-day progress of the Commission, Rankin had to have operational knowledge of the FBI's informant system. He had to be aware that the names of its informers were recorded in a comprehensible and retrievable manner; otherwise the FBI, which relied heavily on its informers, could not function.

Contrary to what Rankin told the Commission, if Oswald had been an FBI informer there would have been a record in at least three places: FBIHQ, FBI Dallas, and the New Orleans field office. For example, if Oswald was being handled by the Dallas field office as a "symbol informant," that is, a part-time FBI employee receiving $200 a month, as the rumors had it, then he would have had a number, not a "badge." His informant number would have consisted of the FBI's abbreviation for the field office (DL) plus an arbitrary four-digit number followed by a symbol "S" for "Security" if he was being run as a political informer (e.g., DL1268S).[11] In view of these facts, laying to rest the "Agent Oswald" rumor should not have been an impossible task for the Commission when in fact the FBI could have reported the truth quite readily. Under Commission direction, FBIHQ could have been compelled to order its agents with firsthand knowledge of the files in Dallas, New Orleans, and FBI Washington headquarters to conduct a proper search and submit proper attestation as to whether or not Oswald was ever an FBI informer. If the bureau proved recalcitrant, the Commission had the authority to initiate an independent search. But as the January 22 transcript reveals, like two halves of the same walnut, the commissioners were too afraid of what they might uncover and too intimidated by Hoover to take either course of action.

More than midway through the emergency session Senator Cooper finally went to the root of the matter when he asked, "How do you propose to meet this situation?" All heads must have turned in Rankin's direction. They expected him, as the Commission's chief counsel and the one who had called this emergency meeting, to have some answers. Rankin proceeded to limn for the Commission his perception of their nightmarish dilemma:

> The FBI is very explicit that Oswald . . . was the assassin, and they are very explicit that there was no conspiracy, and they are also saying in the same place that they are continuing their investigation. Now in my experience of almost nine years, in the first place it is hard to get them to say when you think you have got a case tight enough to convict somebody, that that is the person that committed the crime. In my experience the FBI don't do that. They claim that they don't evaluate, and it is uniform [words missing in transcript] prior experience that they don't do that. Secondly, they have not run out all kinds of leads in Mexico or in Russia and so forth . . . and they could probably say—that isn't our business.[12]

Commissioner Dulles, who in his former official capacity as director of the CIA had had access to many FBI reports, agreed with Rankin that this was a great departure from standard FBI practice. Then Rankin took the commissioners a step back from the abyss, adding that it "is just circumstantial evidence," of what he did not say, "and it don't prove anything about this ['Agent Oswald' story] but it raises questions." It was his and the staff's responsibility to come up with the answers to these questions, Rankin promised the commissioners, and "report it to you."[13] After providing the commissioners a brief reprieve, Rankin yanked them back to the lip of the abyss: "But when the Chief Justice and I were just briefly reflecting on this we said if that was true and it ever came out and could be established, then you would have people think that there was a conspiracy to accomplish this assassination that nothing the Commission did or anybody could dissipate."[14]

It was at this point in the unscheduled emergency session that the Commission came to the crossroads. More than a week earlier the Commission had already indicated its adoption of the FBI's solution to the assassination even before it heard its first witness. This was adumbrated in its January 11, 1964, tentative outline for its report on the assassination with the all-controlling but unconfirmed presumption that Oswald had been the lone assassin and no one else had been involved.[15] Nor could the commissioners overlook the fact that the FBI had sent them a clear message with its preemptive leaks to the press of the conclusions of its report (CD 1). The only conceivable purpose behind the calculated use of this blunt method was to box in the Commission before it even selected a chief counsel, hired a staff, and plugged in its copying machines. Now the Commission was confronted with the dilemma that if it was established that Oswald had worked for the FBI or, for that matter, any other government agency, it could not get away with a report that there had not been a conspiracy. There was, of course, an alternative proposition that the Rankin-dominated Commission never entertained: that Oswald did have some low-level association with a government agency but was not President Kennedy's assassin.

Even before the Commission dismissed the Ward & Paul stenotypist from its "Top Secret" January 22 session and went off the record, the commissioners made clear which fork in the road they would travel now that they felt the ground quaking under their feet. Congressman Boggs started the chain reaction of barely controlled terror that blanketed the session after Rankin's chilling sentence setting out the impasse facing the Commission:

BOGGS: You are so right.

DULLES: Oh, terrible.

BOGGS: The implications of this are fantastic, don't you think so?

RANKIN: To have anybody admit to it, even if it was the fact, I am sure that there wouldn't be at this point anything to prove it.

DULLES: Lee, if this were true, why would it be particularly in their interest? I could see it would be in their interest to get rid of this man but why would it be in their interest to say he is clearly the only guilty one? I mean I don't see that argument that you raise particularly shows an interest.

BOGGS: I can immediately.

RANKIN: They would like to have us fold up and quit.

BOGGS: This closes the case, you see. Don't you see?

DULLES: Yes, I can see that.

RANKIN: They found the man. There is nothing more to do. The Commission supports their conclusions, and we can go home and that is the end of it.

DULLES: But that puts the man right on them. If he was not the killer and they employed him, they are already it, you see. So your argument is correct if they are sure that this is going to close the case, but if it doesn't close the case, they are worse off than ever by doing this.

BOGGS: Yes, I would think so. And of course, we are all even gaining in the realm of speculation. I don't even like to see this being taken down.

DULLES: Yes, I think this record ought to be destroyed. Do you think we need a record of this[?]

The Commission had established from the outset that it would have a court reporter make a transcript of every executive session. It was up to the chair whether to make an exception in this case and consign the record of the January 22 session to archival oblivion. Chairman Warren, hearing no objections, immediately agreed to have the record destroyed.[16]

An hour before the Commission convened on January 22, Rankin called Carr and requested that the Texas attorney general come to Washington and bring Wade, Wade's assistant Will Alexander, Jaworski, and former Southern Methodist University Law School dean Robert Storey to meet with Chief Justice Warren. Rankin was especially interested in confronting the Dallas County district attorney to find out his source for the "Agent Oswald" story and what he intended to do about this rumor. The machinery was set in motion by Rankin and the chief justice to contain what Rankin would later characterize as "the dirty rumor." Rankin was nervous about Wade and what he might know. A day or two before the secret meeting with the TCI contingent on January 24, a lengthy piece by the investigative reporter Harold Feldman appeared in the *Nation* in which Feldman inferred that Wade, a former FBI agent, had been Hudkins's source for his "Agent Oswald" story in the *Houston Post.* Wade was reluctant to join the Texas representatives, but Carr passed the word on to him that it was a summons and not an invitation that could be brushed aside. Since the meeting was ultra-hush-hush, it was initially arranged for the Texans to be flown to Washington in a U.S. Air Force plane. However, this plan was inexplicably cancelled, and the five-member Texas delegation arrived in the nation's capital by commercial air the following day.[17]

On the morning of January 24 the Texans met with Rankin and Warren for almost three hours.[18] There was no court reporter present, and, according to Wade, the Texans were "sworn to secrecy" about what took place during that session.[19] The only record of the January 24 session is Rankin's memorandum to the files. He was so intent to control what was on paper that he did not even date his memorandum. The chief counsel identified the subject of the meeting as "Rumors that Oswald was an undercover agent."[20] It must be kept in mind that Rankin had every reason to believe that his six-page summary of the meeting would be the only record that would exist of this session. Since Warren had agreed to the destruction of the record of the Commission's Wednesday, January 22, executive session, Rankin was assured that the "Agent Oswald" rumors were now contained. He had no way of knowing that the stenotypist's tape of the Wednesday emergency session would escape destruction and find its way into the public record. Moreover, he had no reason to suspect that Ford was Deke DeLoach's source on the Commission and would convey an accurate account of what had transpired behind closed doors on the evening of January 22, when the five commissioners realized that the FBI wanted them to simply rubber-stamp the FBI report. Rankin was so confident about his rewriting of history that he did not bother to classify his memo for the files. He expected that his document would be the only record of those two sessions: a false record showing the exact opposite of what he knew to be the truth.

Rankin's memo states that the Commission "regarded seriously" the allegation that Oswald was an undercover agent and "agreed . . . to take whatever action necessary to pursue the matter to final conclusion." He noted that according to Lane Bertram's report of his interview with *Houston Post* reporter Lonnie Hudkins, Hudkins had asserted that his source for the story of Oswald's alleged FBI connection was Allen Sweatt of the Dallas Sheriff's Office.

Rankin did not comment on the fact that it had taken the Secret Service three weeks to get Bertram's report to the Commission, or why five weeks into the investigation the Secret Service still had not interviewed Sweatt. The general counsel noted that he requested that this oversight be corrected and that the Secret Service interview Sweatt, the chief of the Dallas Sheriff's Office Criminal Division.[21]

If it is puzzling why the Secret Service ignored Sweatt, it is doubly confounding why Sweatt was never called as a Commission witness or why Rankin never saw fit to have a staff member take his statement. If pursuing the "Agent Oswald" matter "to final conclusion" was what the Commission was all about, then Sweatt should have given testimony under oath. There were numerous compelling reasons why Sweatt should have been called before the Commission. He was in charge of the sheriff's investigation into the Kennedy assassination. The crime had been committed almost directly outside his office. Minutes after the assassination police and sheriff's deputies had crowded witnesses into his office, where statements were taken and sworn to under oath. Sweatt identified and spoke to witnesses who were unknown to the Commission and promptly collected all available pictures of the assassination and the crime scene. There is no question that Sweatt could have been a source of additional useful information.[22] Lane Bertram's name, as the agent in charge of the Secret Service's Houston office, should also have been on the Commission's witness list. But the Commission was not interested in Bertram either, for reasons that will be suggested later.

The FBI learned from a Dallas source of the Friday session with the Texans and was keenly interested in what transpired. In one FBI memo Hoover characterized the Friday meeting as "pretty slimy tactics upon the part of Warren and Rankin." FBIHQ learned that Wade had been summoned to Washington from a source in the Dallas Police Department who informed Robert F. Gemberling, the FBI's Dallas case officer for the Kennedy assassination. As soon as Hoover learned that the Commission wanted to speak to Wade he ordered FBI Dallas to interview both Wade and his assistant, Will Alexander. The director was certain that the article in the *Nation* was responsible for the Commission's sudden urgent need to meet with the Texans, especially Wade and Alexander, whose names appeared in Feldman's story. Where Chief Justice Warren was concerned, Hoover's paranoia hovered close to the surface. He was worried that Feldman's story might push the Commission's chairman around the bend on the "Agent Oswald" allegations because, in Hoover's view, "the *Nation* was Warren's Bible." When the Dallas district attorney returned to Dallas that Friday night he had a call from SAC Shanklin of the FBI Dallas office insisting on a meeting to discuss what had taken place during the January 24 session.[23]

Wade was actually interviewed by the Dallas office on two occasions about this meeting. Wade asked Shanklin to treat what he had to say in the strictest confidence because he and his fellow Texans at the January 24 meeting had been sworn to secrecy. If Shanklin agreed to these conditions for their first interview, he knew, even if he was a principled man, that FBIHQ would never permit him to honor them. In due course everything Wade told the Dallas FBI about the January 24 meeting was reported to Hoover and his assistant directors.[24]

As a consequence, Wade's accounts of the meeting serve as a valuable and instructive cross-check against Rankin's self-serving summary memorandum. According to Wade, as filtered through Shanklin, there was only limited discussion about Oswald being an FBI informer. Wade acknowledged at the meeting that he had spoken once with Hudkins, but he protested that he had never told the reporter that Oswald was linked with the FBI, CIA, or any other government agency. When the discussion turned to Oswald's possible government connections, Wade made the interesting revelation that most of the speculation centered on the CIA. Rankin's memo made a fleeting reference to this; he noted that Wade "was aware of an allegation to the effect that Oswald was an informant for the CIA and carried Number 110669."[25]

Unlike the fictitious FBI "badge" numbers "S172" and "S179" that cropped up in the "Agent Oswald" stories, 110669 had a ring of authenticity because it was consistent with the CIA's system of identifying its informers and sources. According to Wade, Robert Storey took this occasion to hold an impromptu forum on the CIA's identification system, assuring the meeting that this was a legitimate CIA number. Storey had been associated with the War Crimes Commission in Germany after World War II and had worked with the CIA in postwar Europe, so his contribution to the discussion was grounded in firsthand knowledge and not mere speculation. None of this, of course, appeared in Rankin's carefully controlled accounting of the Friday session. He did not even reveal Wade's source, if he shared that with the others, for the allegation that Oswald "carried Number 110669." The only other reference to 110669 in the released Commission records is in a memo from Lane Bertram to the head of the Secret Service. It is not certain, but this may be the reason Bertram was never called as a Commission witness or asked to provide a statement.[26] What is certain is that three days later, when the Commission held a scheduled meeting to decide just how it would "pursue this matter to final conclusion," Rankin and Warren withheld the number 110669 from the rest of the Commission.

The FBI had more than a month's head start over the Commission in trying to track down the source of the "Agent Oswald" stories. The Commission, on the other hand, ignored them until confronted with the traumatizing possibility that press stories might build a fire under Texas authorities, especially Carr and the Texas Court of Inquiry, and that the Texas court might feel pressured to launch its own independent investigation. The FBI did not have the luxury of waiting around until these rumors lost their appeal and the public's attention shifted to other and fresher sensational breaking news. Whether Oswald had ever been an FBI source or informer was only one of several "sensitive areas" in which the FBI had zero tolerance for protracted investigations and public scrutiny. There were other aspects of the Kennedy assassination that the bureau could not afford to have exposed: FBIHQ's ordering of the destruction of the so-called Hosty note and the fact that Jack Ruby, the assassin of the alleged presidential assassin, had been a probationary FBI informer, or provisional informant (a distinction that would have hardly softened public reaction if it was ever disclosed). It was in the FBI's interest to identify the source of the allegations quickly and subject the suspect to an intimidating grilling. To assure someone's silence, it was standard FBI practice to subject them to an undisguised "put up or shut up" interview.

The FBI's first indication that a reporter was working on an "Agent Oswald" story came through a tip from Jim Lehrer of the *Dallas Morning News.* Lehrer told Agent Shanklin that Joseph Goulden, a reporter for the *Philadelphia Inquirer,* had contacted him for the correct spelling of Dallas FBI agent James P. Hosty's name. Goulden confided to Lehrer that he was preparing a story on Hosty's efforts to recruit Oswald to inform against the pro-Castro Fair Play for Cuba Committee (FPCC). At this point Hoover ordered a search of the bureau's files to determine whether Oswald had ever been developed as an informer. The report back stated that at no time during the agency's three interviews with Oswald had a pitch ever been made to develop him as an informer.[27] The FBI took no further action until Goulden wrote a piece in the *Philadelphia Inquirer* stating that Oswald had been contacted by the Dallas FBI to inform on the FPCC. The FBI interviewed Goulden twice. The Philadelphia reporter admitted that he knew Hudkins in both a professional and a social capacity; their association had begun when Goulden worked for the *Dallas Morning News.* In December 1963, when Hudkins came to Philadelphia to cover a convention of the National Council of Churches, he had come to dinner at Goulden's home. During this social evening the two journalists had discussed the assassination, but Goulden insisted that Hudkins was not his source. All Goulden would volunteer was that his source was a Texas government official who had told him that Oswald was on the payroll of either the FBI or the CIA and that his payroll or voucher number was 179.[28]

The subsequent FBI interview with Hudkins was almost a reprise of Goulden's first interview. Hudkins offered that his source was a Texas government official who had provided him with reliable information in the past, but, like Goulden, he refused to give a name or to furnish a signed statement. He noted that the official had not shown him any supporting documentation to substantiate the charge that Oswald was on a government payroll and was receiving $200 a month. Hudkins did add that he had heard from Goulden that Oswald "might be a symbol informant" whose payroll or voucher number was different from the 179 that Goulden had reported during his first FBI interview, but Hudkins claimed he could not recall the number.[29]

The FBI finally settled on William Alexander as the Texas government official who was spreading the "Agent Oswald" rumors. Although the FBI interviewed the assistant district attorney on two occasions, Alexander never admitted to anything. It was the accumulated weight of circumstantial evidence and hearsay that pushed his name to the top of the list of likely suspects. From all indications, the FBI had the right man. For instance, when Wade reported to the FBI about the January 24 session, he repeated to Shanklin what he had confided to Rankin about his assistant: that Alexander could not be trusted because he was a loose cannon. "Anything that Alexander said concerning the FBI," Wade told the chief counsel, "had to be taken with a grain of salt." Wade, a former FBI agent with strong positive feelings about his agency service, told Shanklin that Alexander distrusted and despised the FBI and the Justice Department. In addition, Joe B. Brown, the judge presiding over the Ruby case, bumped into Shanklin at the Dallas County Courthouse and proceeded to vent about Alexander. He called Wade's assistant a "mental case" and let the FBI SAC know that Brown was "burned up" over Alexander's leaking the results of Ruby's psychiatric tests to the *Dallas Morning News.* In high dudgeon, the judge speculated that it was Alexander who was spreading rumors about Oswald as an FBI undercover informer. The flamboyant courtroom personality and celebrity attorney Melvin I. Belli, who was Jack Ruby's lawyer, told the FBI that he was "damn tired" of Alexander "planting rumors" about Oswald and Ruby being paid FBI informers and expecting Belli to run with them.[30]

During his second interview with FBI agents, Alexander "was vigorously interviewed in depth" by Dallas agents Vincent E. Drain and W. Harlan Brown. Although "shaken and extremely nervous," according to the FBI report, Alexander insisted that he was not the source of the allegations and had no idea who was planting them. The day after the interview, Hoover instructed Shanklin to break off all contact with Alexander. "This fellow," the director concluded, "was a low s.o.b." and an inveterate troublemaker. FBIHQ was satisfied that Alexander was the source of "Agent Oswald" rumors. Assistant Director William C. Sullivan called Shanklin and told him to instruct Wade to put his assistant on notice: "Alexander should either put up or shut up; that we insist upon it."[31] Unmasked and probably somewhat the worse for wear from his FBI grilling, Alexander doubtless took some quirky satisfaction from having had the last laugh at the FBI's expense. This had to do with the flimflamming connected with the fabrication of Oswald's alleged voucher or payroll number, variously cited in the press as S172 and S179.

Sometime in early 1964 Alexander became convinced, despite FBI denials, that the agency was tapping his office and home telephones. Lonnie Hudkins and Hugh Aynesworth, then a reporter for the *Dallas Morning News,* both friends of the assistant district attorney, shared the same suspicions. All three were avidly looking into the "Agent Oswald" rumors circulating among Lone Star State officials and the Texas press corps. The trio arranged a conference call to spring a story that was so wild it would bring the FBI running. According to Hudkins's reconstruction of their jape, Alexander started the three-way phone conversation by asking if either party remembered Oswald's payroll number. Hudkins said he thought it was "S172." Alexander, on cue, shot back that he was sure it was "S179." Within half an hour FBI agents, flashing their badges, showed up at the offices of all three of these marplots asking what they knew about Oswald's government payroll number.

Years after Hudkins left Dallas to go to work for a Baltimore, Maryland, newspaper, he felt compelled to reveal the story behind the story of these phony numbers that had stirred up so much misplaced attention in the wake of the Kennedy assassination. After his one piece in the *Houston Post,* Hudkins had refrained from writing again about the tragedy in Dallas. He was prompted to break his silence when he saw comedian-cum-assassination guru Dick Gregory on a TV talk show referring to "S172" as proof that Oswald was an FBI agent. Somewhat red-faced that after more than a decade this baseless fabrication was still bandied about by critics of the Warren Commission, the politically conservative Hudkins decided to write one more story on the assassination, this one divulging the true origins of the bogus "badge" numbers rumored to be proof of Oswald's connections to the FBI.[32]

On Monday, January 27, 1964, the Commission met to decide how it was going to deal with the allegations that Oswald was affiliated with a government agency. According to Rankin, it was Warren's decision to call a Monday session "to present the results" of the January 24 meeting with the Texas delegation to the entire Commission.[33] Although Warren called the meeting, it was Rankin who deftly steered the Commission over the course of the three-hour meeting to ensure that the Commission's version of Dallas was not compromised and that Hoover and his FBI would not be embarrassed.

Rankin opened the meeting by reporting what he and the chief justice had learned from the Texas officials. From the very start the chief counsel deliberately misrepresented what had taken place at the ultrasecret Friday meeting. He gave the commissioners the impression that the all-absorbing issue of the Friday meeting had been whether there was any substance to the rumors that Oswald was an FBI undercover informer. Rankin even dredged up the bogus number 179, Oswald's alleged FBI payroll or voucher number, and paraded it before the Commission. Rankin had to know that 179 was bogus even if he was in the dark about its true origins. If he needed further confirmation, District Attorney Henry Wade had told him at the Friday meeting that 179 was not, in his four-year experience in the FBI, like any designation the FBI used to record the identity of an informer.[34] Although Rankin dangled 179 before the Commission, the chief counsel never once mentioned 110669, the number that Wade had introduced at the January 24 meeting. Unlike 179, a meaningless and mischievous invention, 110669 was consistent with the CIA's numbering system for its informers. Moreover, according to Wade, the Friday meeting with the Texas delegates was focused mostly on speculation about whether Oswald had worked for the CIA, not whether he had been an informant for the FBI, as Rankin led the Commission to believe. Rankin's omission of 110669 did not stem from dismissal of Wade as a garrulous lightweight of limited intelligence. Leon Jaworski, the Texas Court of Inquiry's special counsel, had confirmed that the Dallas district attorney was a man of probity and sound political judgment. Rankin's own impression of Wade was that he was a "very canny, able prosecutor." The generally well-informed Senator Russell readily shared this opinion about Wade's bona fides.[35]

It is not altogether clear why Rankin suppressed 110669 and deliberately manipulated the Commission. However, it is clear that he wanted to limit the "Agent Oswald" allegations to the FBI to the exclusion of all other government agencies. Rankin was graphically open with the Commission about his own views of Oswald as a government informer. Before the session was very old and the commissioners had had time to wrap their minds around the problem, the general counsel laid out the course of action he thought the Commission should follow: "We do have a dirty rumor," Rankin announced, "that is very bad for the Commission . . . [and] very damaging to the agencies that are involved . . . and it must be wiped out insofar as it is possible to do so by this Commission."[36]

Some of the Commission members were doubtlessly at sea wondering why their chief counsel was just now bringing this issue before them. Russell asked what steps Rankin had taken to determine whether there was any truth to the rumors. Rankin's lame response was that he and the chief justice had spent the weekend after the meeting with the Texas officials discussing the matter. He wanted to use the January 27 meeting to share their thoughts and receive the commissioners' instructions "on what you want us to do." In short, Rankin and Warren had done nothing about the "Agent Oswald" allegations. The rumors and stories had been circulating in the national press for almost two months before the general counsel saw fit to make them Commission business. Then, once these allegations became a formal agenda item, Rankin prejudiced their seriousness by characterizing them with the picturesque phrase *dirty rumor,* fit only to be summarily eradicated.

Rankin, of course, was aware of the early Joe Goulden and Lonnie Hudkins "Agent Oswald" stories, as were most of the commissioners. Moreover, as general counsel he had access to thousands of pages of FBI reports on the assassination. The Hoover bureau had begun looking into the rumors about Oswald in early December 1963, beginning with Joe Goulden's story in the *Philadelphia Inquirer.* Since it was FBI practice to deliver its reports to Rankin and the staff promptly and by courier, Rankin knew that the agency was taking these allegations seriously and was digging deep to uncover their source.[37] It is most likely that the chief counsel was relying on the FBI to "wipe out" the rumors and speculations before they became a problem for the Commission. The last thing that Rankin wanted was for the Commission to be saddled with what he could only have imagined as a political nightmare in having to investigate the FBI, the Commission's own investigative arm. Rankin and Warren might have continued their policy of abdication on the "Agent Oswald" issue if they had not been brought up short by the disturbing signals emanating from Texas. When elected officials such as Carr and Wade proved reluctant to brush aside these allegations as idle and baseless rumors, Rankin knew he had to bring the issue before the Commission, if only to make a record for history.[38]

Since Rankin had effectively narrowed the scope of the problem to Oswald as some kind of undercover source or informer for the FBI, the commissioners agonized over how to approach Director Hoover without "impeaching his testimony" and earning his enmity.[39] Hoover had already written forcefully to the Commission to deny that Oswald had ever been on the FBI payroll in any capacity. In addition, a story in the *New York Times* on January 26, 1964, had reported that a bureau spokesman had registered a categorical denial to all speculation that Oswald had ever served as an FBI informer.[40]

There was no question that the formidable FBI director cast an enveloping shadow over the January 27 session. For example, some of the members explored the idea of calling Hudkins, Sweatt, and Alexander before the Commission in executive session to try to get at the facts. They were dumbfounded, momentarily at least, when Rankin disclosed that the FBI knew about the secret Friday meeting with the Texas officials. Rankin's source for this revelation was the FBI itself. It was also relayed to him that Hoover took a dim view of this meeting, but the general counsel was probably spared the full bore of the director's acrimony. The Commission spent most of the January 27 executive session exploring ways to make a pro forma effort to get at the facts of the Oswald allegations without offending or embarrassing the FBI. For all their efforts to tread softly around the "Agent Oswald" question, the commissioners would have been dismayed to learn that from the very outset of the official investigation Hoover and his executive elites had privately treated the relationship with the Commission as adversarial. Dismay would have given way to shock had they ever learned that Director Hoover had had the bureau's Crime Records Division prepare dossiers on the Commission members and staff.[41]

By the end of the January 27 session Rankin and the commissioners arrived at a consensus on how they would go about trying to confirm or refute the Oswald rumors. The strategy they adopted was a marriage between proposals offered by Rankin and Warren. The general counsel opted for first calling on Hoover, explaining their problem, and asking the director for documentary verification that Oswald had never been an FBI informer. The chief justice's idea was to first work from the other end: to bring Hudkins, Sweatt, and Alexander before the Commission at the same time and question them about their source for the allegations about Oswald's FBI connections before going to Hoover.[42]

Rankin initially resisted this approach. For reasons that can only be guessed at, he took it upon himself to convey to the Commission members that the Texans believed Hudkins was the sole source of the rumors. However, pinpointing Hudkins was Rankin's own construction and, by his own private admission, was never an accusation leveled by the Texas delegation.[43] The general counsel used Hudkins as a red herring, arguing that if they brought him before the Commission the newsman would use the occasion as a springboard for another splashy "Agent Oswald" story. It was Dulles who politely punctured Rankin's rationale by citing Jack Langguth's story in the previous Sunday's *New York Times,* suggesting that the story had already "gone a little further in the press" independent of Hudkins's efforts.[44] In the end all of the commissioners except Ford, who was not in attendance, concluded that Rankin's approach would not clear the stones from the road. They agreed that the American people would expect nothing less of them than to try to run down these rumors so the Commission could be assured that Oswald was not an informer for any government agency. Rankin led the commissioners to believe that he was comfortable with their decision. It was decided that the general counsel and his staff would proceed with the two-track strategy: Rankin would speak with Hoover, and his staff would interview Hudkins, Sweatt, and Alexander.[45]

The next day Rankin met with Hoover in the director's office. He wasted little time in breaking faith with the agreement struck the previous day. According to Hoover, Rankin stated that the Commission did not want to launch an "outside investigation, such as the calling of Mr. Hudkins, who was the originator" of the Oswald rumors. He assured the director that the commissioners wanted to avoid any appearance that the Commission was investigating the FBI. Hoover must have surprised Rankin when he opined that the Commission should call Hudkins, place him under oath, and demand answers. However, as Hoover pointed out, he was certain that Hudkins would be uncooperative, claiming as a reporter that his sources were privileged. Hoover was probably aware of what had taken place at the Monday executive session, courtesy of the Dulles-CIA-FBI pipeline. He would have known of Rankin's reluctance to investigate the FBI, and was likely having a little fun at the general counsel's expense. As on other occasions when Rankin found himself boxed into a corner, he turned to Hoover for help. Not surprisingly, the director was more than ready to oblige. Hoover's proffered solution to Rankin's "problem"—wiping out the "dirty rumor"—was to volunteer to go on record with an affidavit and appear before the Commission under oath to give an accounting "as to what the facts were." Hoover noted that Rankin was profuse in his appreciation for all the help and cooperation that the FBI had extended to the Commission.[46]

In some ways Hoover was one of the most predictable political operators in Washington. He could not resist using the meeting to lecture Rankin on the unfairness of the chief justice's "carping criticism" of the FBI report (CD 1). He launched into a defense of CD 1 against Warren's public characterization of the report as "skeletal" and his implication that the Commission was forced to spend valuable time filling in the "gaps" in the investigation. Hoover's memo does not indicate how Rankin parried this onslaught or whether he just hunkered down until the storm subsided.[47] The truth of the matter was that in calling CD 1 "skeletal," Warren was, unintentionally of course, praising it. In all five volumes of more than nine hundred pages, CD 1 devoted ten words to the shooting of JFK and only forty-two words to his wounds. As mentioned earlier, it did not account for all of the known shots, it failed to mention Governor Connally's wounds, and it neglected to even record the cause of the president's death. Most of its narrative thrust was a relentless diatribe against Oswald. This was the report that Hoover held up before Rankin as an exemplary product of FBI investigative expertise.

In the end, the FBI report was of so little use to the Commission that it ignored it entirely. The Commission did not publish CD 1 in any of the twenty-six volumes of its report, nor did it ever mention it as "evidence" or as anything else. There was no public access to the FBI report until the Commission's records became available at the National Archives long after the Warren report had taken its place in national history as the official account of President John F. Kennedy's assassination. This same grossly inept and slipshod report, hastily thrown together in response to White House pressure, with its built-in prestructured conclusions, had been selectively leaked to the press to put to rest all rumors of conspiracy. That the Commission, given its own deplorable record in the investigation, felt compelled to suppress the FBI report because it was so demonstrably flawed was a resounding rebuke indeed. This blunt and unceremonious dismissal of CD 1 was not lost on Hoover. It would be a factor in the FBI's political counterattack against the Warren report after it was released to the public.[48]

In the meantime, Hoover's sworn affidavit attesting that the FBI had never employed Oswald in any capacity carried the day, as Rankin expected it would. As soon as FBI Assistant Director Alex Rosen delivered Hoover's affidavit to Rankin's office, the general counsel and Warren were satisfied that the "dirty rumor" had been properly exorcised. Apparently Hoover's sworn word had such great "cash value" with the chief justice that he saw the wisdom of Rankin's resistance to calling Hudkins, Sweatt, and Alexander before the Commission. None of the three would ever be Commission witnesses or even be questioned by Rankin's staff. The two-track strategy that Warren had insisted upon during the January 27 session collapsed like a rope of sand. If it would later be judged necessary to question any or all of the three to nail down the truth of the Oswald allegations, Warren and Rankin were satisfied to leave it up to the FBI. In addition to the director's affidavit, Rankin asked and received affidavits from FBI agents who had interviewed Oswald and from the special agents in charge of the field offices where the interviews had been conducted.

The pro forma Hoover affidavit did not slide by without comment. Assistant Counsel Leon D. Hubert, Jr., a law professor at Tulane University, felt the need to point out to his boss that the FBI affidavits did "not constitute a complete refutation." Hoover's affidavit, Hubert remarked, covered only the director's knowledge and therefore fell short of a convincing blackout of the rumor. In order to make "a perfect record rumor," Hubert suggested that the Commission get firsthand knowledge by asking for a sworn affidavit from the division chief in charge of FBIHQ's Security Division. This was the source inside FBI Washington headquarters that had access to all FBI records on informers, their numbers, and their payroll vouchers. Hubert was right on the law of the matter; he was simply uninformed on the politics. Had Rankin wanted to establish for the record as complete a refutation as possible, he would have asked for a search of FBI informant files for FBIHQ, Dallas, and New Orleans field offices. Nothing ever came of Hubert's suggestion. There may or may not have been a connection, but Hubert returned to private life months before the Commission's report was finished. The morning after Rankin received Hoover's affidavit, Allen Dulles had a chance meeting with FBI Assistant Director William C. Sullivan at the annual Boy Scout breakfast at the Statler Hotel in downtown Washington. The old spymaster confided to Sullivan that the Commission "was not having any major problems and that from the standpoint of the FBI there were no worries."[49]

Having satisfied itself that Hoover's affidavit rebutted rumors that Oswald was an FBI informant, the Commission turned next to establishing a record to exonerate the CIA of the same allegations. On March 12, 1964, Rankin and a few selected members of his staff met with Richard Helms, the CIA's deputy director of plans. The general purpose of the meeting was to discuss how the agency could assist the Commission in its investigation. During the course of the lengthy meeting Howard P. Willens, one of Rankin's assistant counsels, asked Helms whether Oswald had been a CIA agent. Helms responded that he had not been and that the Commission "would have to take his word" for it since he was an officer of the "Clandestine Services" and would know whether or not Oswald had been an agent for the CIA while he was in the Soviet Union. Rankin, noting that the Commission had not adopted this procedure with the FBI, wanted this point clarified more effectively for the record. Before the meeting was over Rankin and Helms settled on the "Hoover formula": CIA Director John McCone would submit an affidavit. This took place about six weeks after former CIA director Allen Dulles had told his Commission colleagues in a secret session that the CIA would not admit that someone had been an informant or agent even under oath, except at the specific direction of the president. At the end of April Rankin wrote McCone and requested that he submit an affidavit to the effect that Oswald had never been a CIA agent even though he knew that any pro forma denial was worthless.[50]

Warren's easy acquiescence in this whole affair was indicative of his incremental slide into an almost spectatorlike passivity as the Commission took its lead more and more from the general counsel. The chief justice seemed resigned to drift, leaving Rankin to steer the Commission unopposed. It is possible that Warren had convinced himself that the greater good would be served if the Commission could spare the nation greater pain and heal the great wound of Dallas with the politically comforting balm of the "official truth." A contributing, if not dominating, factor in explaining Warren's puzzling passivity was his allowing Hoover's ringers on the Commission to ride roughshod over him in the matter of Warren Olney. Once Chairman Warren mistakenly surrendered his prerogative to insist on his own general counsel in the interest of Commission unity, he lost any real opportunity to bend the Commission to his will, if indeed that was what he desired. With Olney as general counsel the government's report on the assassination might have been a document of great historical value, heightening the political awareness of the American people regarding the tragic costs of the Cold War's deep politics. The official report on Dallas should have been the proud culmination of Warren's stellar career of selfless public service. Instead, the Warren Commission Report, in truth, better merits the title "The Rankin Commission Report."[51]

There can be no innocent explanation why Rankin maneuvered to avoid placing Hudkins, Sweatt, or Alexander under oath and have the Commission or his staff question them. It was Rankin, after all, who insisted at the January 27 executive session that Hudkins was the source of the "Agent Oswald" allegations. At the same time, in his summary notes for the session with the Texas delegation Rankin cited Secret Service agent Lane Bertram's report that Hudkins had advised him that Allen Sweatt was Hudkins's source for the rumors.[52] The only reasonable explanation for why Rankin avoided any or all three of these men is that he was afraid they might say something under oath that the Commission did not want to hear.

Had truth really been the Commission's only agenda, there was absolutely nothing to be lost in calling Hudkins or Sweatt. For example, even if Hudkins had refused to divulge his source, the commissioners—who were all lawyers—could have phrased questions that might have been useful: "Did you make any effort to confirm what your source told you?" Or, "Do you know of any confirmation or refutation to these allegations we can get and, if so, how?" And again, "Do you know of anyone we can speak to with information that will help with these stories?" Warren almost certainly had some such line of questioning in mind when he insisted at the January 27 session that simply going to Director Hoover would not be enough. Even if the commissioners ran into a blank wall they would at least have demonstrated that they had tried. As a lawman and officer of the court, Sweatt most likely would have been forthcoming. Unlike Alexander, he had never expressed anger against the Justice Department, FBI, or any federal government entity. The same argument can be made for the politically conservative Hudkins.[53] This was just another example in the Rankin-dominated Commission of guilty knowledge taking precedence over a good-faith search for the truth, wherever it might lead. Any new and unwelcome information that might threaten the official mythology of Dallas was assigned pariah status and had to be suppressed.

These three January 1964 Commission transcripts disclose that the Commission was confronted with reports that the man they had already decided was the lone assassin had worked for the FBI or the CIA. That possibility raised the unavoidable and troubling question of a government agency conspiracy to kill President Kennedy. Regardless of how unlikely it may have seemed, the Commission was duty-bound to undertake the most vigorous pursuit of these rumors and speculations. Oswald's military security clearances, his atypical U.S. Marine Corps service and dubious discharge, his "defection" and then "redefection" from the Soviet Union, and the strange political odyssey that was his civilian life after returning to the United States should have motivated the Commission to exhaust every means at its disposal to refute or confirm the "Agent Oswald" stories. (See Chapter 12 for more on Oswald as a government agent.)

Settling the dust over the Oswald allegations with Hoover's affidavit was one piece in Rankin's public relations approach, but the master stroke was Director Hoover's Commission testimony in May. The day before Hoover appeared before the Commission the chief justice invited the director to share luncheon with him in Warren's private dining room. "The luncheon," Hoover troubled to note, "was entirely pleasant," suggesting that he was genuinely surprised that any social interaction with the chief justice, whom he despised and distrusted, could be anything other than an ordeal. On May 14 Hoover presented himself before the Commission; only Russell and McCloy missed the performance. For two and a half hours the FBI director fielded questions of the "softball" variety and expatiated at length on a variety of subjects. He established right off for the record that Oswald had never been linked to the FBI in any capacity whatsoever and that there was no credible evidence of any conspiracy, domestic or foreign, involved in the assassination. Hoover moved on to establish that no matter what the FBI and the Commission concluded, there would be "extremists" of every ideological bent who "will disagree violently" with the official findings "without any foundation" for their radical views. It was the FBI director's clear intent to plant in the public mind the notion that any criticism of the official report on the Kennedy assassination would be a vicious thought crime. Careful study had persuaded him, he intoned, that Oswald was a "dedicated Communist" and that the assailant's claim otherwise—that he was a "Marxist"—was just semantic twaddle. In his next breath the director assured the commissioners that the FBI's investigation had "found no indication at all that Oswald was a man addicted to violence."[54]

Hoover's testimony was treated like one of the most treasured documents in the history of the republic. Rankin thought he had done "an excellent job." For Dulles it was nothing less than a "brilliant presentation." Hoover insisted, and Rankin readily agreed, that his twenty-three pages of testimony be reviewed before it became part of the historic record. All six of the FBI's assistant directors reviewed the transcript. Assistant Director Belmont, number three in the bureau hierarchy, assisted by five FBI inspectors and supervisors, went over Hoover's testimony "word-by-word" to catch any misspellings and typographical errors. In actual fact, they cleaned up "the Boss's" syntax and redundancies. The chief reason for this impressive mobilization of bureau manpower was allegedly to remedy the fact that the court reporter "did not record the Director's testimony accurately in some instances," according to Belmont. Since the FBI filmed Hoover's 150 minutes of testimony (none of the other seventy-nine Commission witnesses was ever filmed), there was a film record to check against the Ward & Paul court reporter's stenographic written record.[55]

Rankin also reviewed the transcript and made his own suggestions. In several instances he added his own words, a sentence or two here and there and in one instance an entire paragraph, which Rankin believed more properly represented the director's thoughts. Hoover's May 14 Commission testimony as it appears in the official *Hearings Before the President's Commission,* all but chased in silver, is really the heavily edited FBIHQ version with Rankin's augmentations.[56] The combined years of agency service of all eleven of these senior FBI officials who pored over the director's Commission testimony was well over the century mark. One can only wonder in the final analysis what difference it could have made to the investigation if all this professional experience had been brought to bear on uncovering what really happened in Dallas. This was most poignantly underscored by the head of the bureau's General Investigative Division, Alex Rosen, who privately characterized the whole sorry affair as the FBI "standing with pockets open waiting for evidence to drop in."[57]

Intoxicated by his own infallibility, the director was known to launch into lengthy dissertations about matters of which his knowledge was paper thin or nonexistent. Early in his Commission testimony, this tendency to orate pompously took over. The occasion was innocent enough. Boggs asked Hoover if he could speculate on Oswald's motive for killing the president. At the end of his lengthy and rambling response Hoover saw fit to correct critics who argued that if Oswald was the lone assassin, why did he wait until the presidential limousine turned onto Elm Street when he had a more open and clearer shot as the car approached the Texas School Book Depository (TSBD) building on Houston Street? On the face of it, this was a salient observation, carrying the inference that Elm Street was a "killing zone" where assassins posted themselves for shots from both the rear and the front of the motorcade. Hoover's explanation was as seductively simple as it was monumentally wrong: "There were some trees," the director noted, "between the window [the 'sniper's nest'] on the sixth floor and the cars" as they moved toward the TSBD on Houston Street.[58]

It is hard to imagine that Hoover's grasp of the topography of Dealey Plaza was so tenuous. The FBI's three-dimensional scale model of Dealey Plaza, the impressive 480-square-foot mock-up of the assassination scene that Hoover ordered the Exhibits Section to construct, flatly and unquestionably refuted his contention. The model showed that there were no trees obstructing a gunman lying in wait at the southeast corner of the sixth floor as the presidential motorcade approached along Houston Street toward the TSBD building. In truth, the only tree along the motorcade route that blocked a clear shot from the so-called sniper's nest was a large live pin oak tree in full foliage in front of the depository building on Elm Street. Any assailant lurking in the "sniper's nest" would have had to wait until the motorcade cleared this obstruction for a clean shot. The uncontested fact was that a lone gunman in the "sniper's nest" had an easier shot at the motorcade while it was moving toward him on Houston Street. It was this tree that forced the Commission to conclude that the first shot could not have come until Zapruder frame 210, when the presidential limousine emerged from underneath the cover of the tree.[59] Neither Boggs nor any of the other commissioners called Hoover on this blatant slip-up. Even more astonishing was the fact that none of the senior FBI executive officers responsible for editing Hoover's Commission testimony caught this factual error. Had they picked up on the director's blooper it would have been edited out of his original testimony.

Two years after the Commission report was published, Harold Weisberg, the author of *Whitewash,* the first book-length critique of the report, was interviewed on WTOP Radio in the nation's capital. During the course of the interview Weisberg happened to point out Hoover's howler about the trees on Houston Street. Apparently the FBI, ever diligent with all domestic intelligence channels open to record any criticism, taped the broadcast. Weisberg's remarks became a momentous matter that required the time and thought of the FBI's top echelon. Robert E. Wick, DeLoach's deputy, passed the matter up the line to his boss, who in turn bucked it up to Associate Director Clyde Tolson, the director's trusted number two man in the bureau. Some of the FBI inspectors and supervisors who had gone over Hoover's testimony "word-by-word," such as James R. Malley and Jim Bishop, were included in this exercise in damage control. They had to avoid the unthinkable admission that the director had been in error. "Life in the circus," Assistant Director Sullivan's picturesque characterization after thirty years in the Hoover bureau, was possible only if one unwritten but iron rule was unfailingly observed: The director was always right. The explanation they settled on to prove that Weisberg was "completely off base on this point" was that once the motorcade turned onto Houston Street "it entered the park" (Dealey Plaza), and since there were trees in the park Oswald's view would have been blocked. "The Director's testimony," the FBI brain trust concluded, "was accurate." The director was right even if the photographs and the FBI's own elaborate mock-up of Dealey Plaza proved otherwise.[60]

CIA Director John Alex McCone followed Hoover as the next Commission witness. McCone assured the Commission that Oswald had never had any connection with the Central Intelligence Agency and that the CIA had no evidence of a conspiracy in the Kennedy assassination. McCone's responses to these sensitive questions were prearranged to coincide with Hoover's responses. It was in the interest of both agencies that Hoover and McCone be on the same page when they testified before the Commission. To assure that this was indeed the case, the CIA's James J. Angleton and FBI Assistant Director Sullivan were the responsible parties for arranging this interagency cooperation.[61] This synchronization of Commission testimony had one other common factor: When Hoover and McCone went on the record with the Commission in May, they had known months earlier as a result of the investigations by their own agencies that President Kennedy was the victim of a conspiracy.

At the end of February 1964 the assistant chief of *Life* magazine's Photographic Laboratory, Herbert G. Orth, turned over to the FBI a copy made from the original of Abraham Zapruder's historic six-foot strip of his film that captured the shooting death of President Kennedy. Orth also provided the bureau with the filmstrip from Zapruder frames 171 (Z 171) through 343 (Z 343). At the request of the Commission staff, the FBI Crime Laboratory analyzed the Zapruder film in order to establish the speed of the presidential limousine as well as the distance the car traveled from Z 171 to Z 343. Hoover approved the request but sourly remarked that it sounded "like a lot of poppycock" to him. In its examination of the Zapruder film BuLab went beyond the limited parameters set by Commission staffers. The laboratory analysts, under the direction of photography expert Lyndal L. Shaneyfelt, used the Zapruder film and slides to establish when the shots had occurred. According to FBI photo analysis, the first shot occurred at about Z 170. By the FBI's own calculations, at Z 170 the presidential limousine was hidden from the Commission's designated "sniper's nest" by an oak tree in full foliage located in front of the book depository. The lab photo experts determined that first clear shot from Oswald's alleged "sniper's perch" was at Z 207. The only conclusion that could be drawn from the FBI lab's analysis was that either there were at least two shooters in Dealey Plaza or the shots originated from someplace other than the sixth floor of the southeast corner of the Texas School Book Depository.[62]

The CIA uncovered critical evidence in the assassination before the government's official version was agreed upon and before President Johnson appointed the Warren Commission. Late Sunday, November 24, the Secret Service turned over to the CIA a copy of the Zapruder film. The CIA had a keen interest in the film because the White House had authorized the agency to conduct its own in-house investigation. McCone requested that the agency's National Photographic Intelligence Center (NPIC) in Washington, D.C., undertake a special rush job on the film.[63]

NPIC enjoyed the well-deserved reputation within the government of being the finest photo interpretation center in the world. The report on the center's analysis of those terrible six seconds in Dallas was returned to McCone or Richard Helms, the CIA's deputy director of plans, sometime early Monday morning. The results were presented in tabular frame-interpretation of the Zapruder film, the same historic six feet of film upon which the Commission would rely heavily for its own version of the Kennedy assassination. NPIC's analysis indicated that the first shot came before Zapruder frame 210. In addition, the center's analysis showed that there was a second shot at Z 242, just 1.6 seconds after the first shot. All of the Commission's firearms experts agreed that even the most experienced and skilled rifleman would require at least 2.4 seconds (and this was an optimistic estimate) to cycle Oswald's alleged murder weapon. The 1.6-second interlude between the first and second shots could only mean that there had to be more than one shooter at Dealey Plaza.[64]

The Warren report held that the first shot could not have been fired before Z 210. The Commission's reasoning was clear enough. If Oswald had secreted himself on the sixth floor at the southeast corner of the Texas School Book Depository to prepare for his rendezvous with history, he could not have had a clear shot at Kennedy until at least Z 210. Between frames 166 and 209, the aforementioned live oak in full foliage on November 22 would have blocked a view of the presidential limousine from the so-called sniper's nest. If the first shot occurred before Z 210, as both FBI and CIA photo analysts determined, then, according to the Commission's own construction, Oswald could not have fired it. However, a sniper hidden in one of the buildings on Houston Street, the Dal-Tex Building, for example, would have had a clear shot at Kennedy's back anytime between Z 170 and Z 210.

Since what should have been unthinkable in the investigation into the murder of President Kennedy became commonplace, it is not surprising that the results of the FBI and CIA analyses of the Zapruder film were ignored. The FBI and Rankin and his staff suppressed the results of the bureau's photo interpretation of Zapruder's historic film, and it is not certain whether McCone or Helms ever shared with the Commission the NPIC's analysis of the Zapruder film. What the record revealed was that the FBI and CIA colluded in fabricating a story that the CIA never received a copy of the Zapruder film until December 1964, after the Commission disbanded. Hoover told Rankin that in December 1964 the CIA requested a copy of the film for "training purposes."[65]

7   The JFK Autopsy

*The powerful tell lies believing that they have greater than the
ordinary understanding of what is at stake; very often, they
regard their dupes as having inadequate judgment, or as likely to
respond in the wrong way to truthful information.*
—Sissela Bok, *Lying: Moral Choice in
Public and Private Life,* 1978

Unquestionably, the autopsy was the one area of the investigation in which the Commission should have done everything possible to establish an unimpeachable record. JFK's remains provided some of the best evidence as to what had happened in Dallas. The work of compiling the medicolegal record of the murdered president did not require the cooperation of the FBI and CIA, so in this crucial aspect of the investigation the Commission's efforts were not impeded or distorted by the investigative dishonesties and cover-ups perpetrated upon it by those agencies. The belated anguish professed by J. Lee Rankin, Nicholas Katzenbach, and Commission staffers over the FBI's suppression and destruction of the Hosty note and the CIA's concealment of the agency's derring-do plots with the mafia to assassinate Castro all rang hollow.[1]

When it came to "the autopsy of the century,"[2] it was the Commission itself that sanctioned perjury, connived at the destruction of the best evidence, boycotted key witnesses, and deliberately and knowingly suppressed material medical records and legal documents. This massive corruption of the autopsy records was undertaken with one purpose: to ensure that the medical evidence in the Kennedy assassination was consistent with the official government version of a lone assassin. The overwhelming weight of the evidence supports the view that President Kennedy's official autopsy report was deliberately falsified to suppress the fact that he was the victim of a conspiracy.

It is a joyless irony that the autopsy of Kennedy's alleged assassin, Lee Harvey Oswald, performed by the Dallas County medical examiner, Dr. Earl F. Rose, was worthy of a president.[3] By comparison, President Kennedy received an autopsy unworthy of even the most unfortunate and unlamented derelict. There were never any questions raised about the professional accuracy of Oswald's autopsy, but many questions and dark suspicions surround the one President Kennedy received.[4]

Fifteen years after Kennedy's death a government report revealed that his autopsy had been incompetently conducted, full of gross errors and failures to carry out standard forensic procedures in the investigation of an "unnatural" violent death. In 1979 the report of the medical panel of nine forensic pathologists selected by the House Select Committee on Assassinations to review JFK's autopsy disclosed some startling facts. For example, JFK's fatal head wound was incorrectly described; the official autopsy had the wound one hundred millimeters (four inches) lower than the true point of entry. The lacerated brain was not properly examined and sectioned to determine beyond a forensic doubt that only one missile was responsible for the massive head trauma. The prosecutors did not X-ray JFK's extremities to be certain there were no bullets or missile fragments in those areas of the dead president's body. Another bullet or even additional fragments located in JFK's lower arms, wrists, and hands or lower legs, ankles, and feet would have raised legitimate suspicions that there was more than one assassin. The controversial "neck" wound, as described in the official protocol, was not dissected to determine beyond question the track of this missile and whether all the shots had come from the rear of the presidential motorcade. One of the prosecutors, Lt. Col. Pierre A. Finck of the U.S. Army, was prevented by a superior officer in the morgue from examining Kennedy's clothes.[5] Had Oswald lived to stand trial, any forceful cross-examination of the official autopsy report at the least would have embarrassed the government to no end, assuming it did not leave its case in shreds on the courtroom floor.

Defenders of the Warren Commission Report, though they lament the serious shortcomings of the autopsy protocol, insist that these were innocent mistakes and oversights and that the official autopsy was an honest effort to report on the medicolegal evidence in the death of President Kennedy. This soft reassurance by Commission apologists fails to convince when confronted with the record of corruption of the Kennedy autopsy. There is some element of truth, however, in the charge that the Bethesda Naval Hospital Center was not equipped to do a flawless medicolegal autopsy on the murdered president. Navy pathologist Lt. Comdr. J. Thornton Boswell, one of the doctors involved in the autopsy, thought it was "foolish" to have the postmortem at Bethesda because it was largely a "training school for technologists" and lacked the necessary facilities. Boswell also complained about the noise and distractions the prosecutors had to contend with as they went about their grim business. The only phone in the morgue was located right next to Boswell's shoulder, about three or four feet from the autopsy table. The navy pathologist complained that all during the autopsy he was distracted by the constant conversations of the FBI and Secret Service agents who "stayed on the phone all the time." Lieutenant Colonel Finck noted that there were at least two dozen onlookers, almost all ranking military officers, in the autopsy room, and this overcrowding contributed to the din of background noise that interfered with the work of the pathologists. The navy autopsy photographer, John T. Stringer, Jr., recalled that the scene in the morgue resembled "a three-ring circus." When the prosecutors initially failed to locate the missile that had caused JFK's back wound, Stringer remembered that "some of the military men considered bringing in metal detectors." Adm. David Osborne (then a captain) recalled that there was tremendous pressure on the pathologists to perform "a quick post" and "get out of there."[6]

Osborne had it about right. What should have been a painstakingly methodical autopsy lasting through the night and well into the next morning instead was a bungled rush job. The actual autopsy lasted no more than several hours. The rest of the time, until the remains were released to the family at 5:30 A.M., was occupied in helping the mortician embalm the body and put the skull together. An autopsy in a death by gunshot is not over until the prosectors are satisfied that they have worked out the bullet tracks, along with the entrance and exit paths. This was not done in the Kennedy autopsy. The fact that the autopsy was that of a murdered president and was by any forensic standards an exceedingly complicated one meant, according to Dr. Michael M. Baden, former medical examiner for New York City, that it should have gone on for eight to ten hours. Since the autopsy was conducted under conditions that could be parodied as "Amateur Night at the Bethesda Naval Hospital Morgue," the overriding pressure on the pathologists from the military brass, Secret Service, and FBI in attendance was to find the bullets so they could be matched against the alleged murder weapon found at the scene of the crime. When the chief prosecutor, navy pathologist James J. Humes, probed Kennedy's back wound with his finger and failed to find a bullet, he assumed it had worked its way out during cardiac massage performed by the emergency-room doctors in Dallas.[7]

Humes was mistaken because once a bullet enters the body the track closes behind it, blocking off any possibility of its backing out of the track. Humes's error in judgment was due to the fact that he had never before in his professional career autopsied a gunshot victim. It was only during the later stages of the autopsy that Humes discovered the bullet hole in Kennedy's back "below the shoulders and two inches to the right of the middle of the spine," according to the two FBI agents assigned to report back to headquarters and collect any missiles recovered from the president's body. FBI agent James W. Sibert made a call to the Firearms Section of the FBI Crime Laboratory (BuLab), hoping to get some expert opinion to resolve the dilemma confronting the Bethesda autopsy team—a body with a bullet hole and no bullet to be found. During the call Sibert learned from Agent Charles L. Killion that BuLab had recently received a whole bullet from the Secret Service that had been retrieved from a stretcher at Parkland Memorial Hospital. Killion reported that the missile was a copper-jacketed 6.5-mm rifle bullet that could have been fired from the suspected murder weapon. Humes now felt vindicated in his original conviction that the bullet that had made a wound in Kennedy's back had, indeed, worked its way out during the cardiac massage. The news of the recovered stretcher bullet effectively brought the autopsy to an end. Early in the autopsy the commanding officer of the Bethesda Naval Hospital Center, Adm. C. B. Galloway, had ordered a full autopsy. When Galloway learned about the Parkland stretcher bullet, he, as will be discussed later, prohibited the autopsy team from dissecting the bullet track in the president's back, an essential and basic requirement in any investigation into an unnatural death by gunshot.[8]

Navy Commander John H. Ebersole, M.D., head of the Radiology Division at Bethesda but not yet board certified, admitted that X-rays were not taken of Kennedy's extremities because he was using a portable X-ray machine; the morgue was not equipped with its own X-ray equipment. In hindsight, Ebersole was frank enough to confess that the body should have been taken to the hospital's X-ray room. The problem with the portable machine, as Ebersole explained to the House Select Committee on Assassinations Medical Panel, was that it left much to be desired in "terms of exquisite detail." At the end of his lengthy session with the Medical Panel Ebersole was asked if he had any closing thoughts. The navy radiologist, thinking back on that chaotic night in the Bethesda morgue, expressed an emotion that might have been harbored by his fellow physicians on the panel: "No, except considering your recommendations that you have a team of forensic pathologists when this happens the next time, God help us."[9]

Most of the controversy and mystery surrounding the autopsy could have been avoided had the prosectors been experienced forensic pathologists. Highly qualified and experienced forensic experts were only a phone call away when the public learned of the assassination. For instance, Cyril H. Wecht, coroner for Allegheny County in Pennsylvania and the director of the Pittsburgh Institute of Legal Medicine; Milton Helpern, the chief medical examiner of New York; Russell S. Fisher, the medical examiner of Maryland and professor of forensic pathology at the University of Maryland; Dr. Joseph W. Spelman in Philadelphia; and Dr. Geoffrey T. Mann in Virginia were all within an hour's flying time of Washington, D.C. Between them these doctors had done thousands of medicolegal autopsies and given expert interpretation of violent deaths in courtrooms or at some other point in the justice system.

Because they were some of the most eminent forensic pathologists in the nation, the government had previously invited them to lecture at the Armed Forces Institute of Pathology (AFIP). However, on November 22, 1963, they waited by their phones in vain.[10] Was their exclusion an innocent oversight in the heat and confusion of a national tragedy, or a conscious decision? The one trait they all shared, in addition to their enviable professional renown, was the fact that they were not in the military and thus subject to orders from superiors.

At about 7:35 P.M. (EST), when President Kennedy's body was wheeled into the Bethesda morgue, the military assumed de facto total responsibility for the autopsy, the autopsy records, and the final autopsy report. The autopsy room was immediately placed under tight security by marine guards and Secret Service agents. The only nonmilitary personnel in the morgue were three Secret Service agents—Roy H. Kellerman, who was in charge of the White House detail; William Greer; and William O'Leary—and two FBI agents dispatched from FBIHQ to observe the autopsy and report back to headquarters. The FBI agents, James W. Sibert, a thirteen-year bureau veteran, and Francis X. O'Neill, Jr., who had been with the FBI for ten years, kept a record, not entirely complete, of all those attending the autopsy. The other seventeen people there were all uniformed members of the U.S. Armed Forces. The ranking senior officers were all medical admirals: Edward C. Kinney, surgeon general of the navy (1961–1965); Calvin B. Galloway, the commanding officer of the Bethesda Naval Hospital Center; and George G. Burkley, JFK's personal White House physician.[11]

None of the prosectors qualified as forensic pathologists. Lt. Comdr. James J. Humes was the third of the military pathologists (the others being Boswell and Finck) selected to perform what was perhaps the most important autopsy in U.S. history. Humes was the director of the Naval Medical School at the Naval Medical Center at Bethesda. His experience with forensic pathology had been limited to a one-week course in 1953 at the AFIP. During his Warren Commission interview Dr. Finck reported that he had "reviewed" hundreds of cases of wounds while he was chief of the Wound Ballistics Pathology Branch of the AFIP. However, his work there had been largely administrative and supervisory; it had not included the performance of autopsies. Finck, in short, had never before performed a forensic autopsy. Finck's Commission testimony revealed that he was only able to cite two bullet-wound cases in which he had actually testified in a legal proceeding. The Commission never attempted to establish Boswell's expertise, but it was probably no more extensive than Humes's one-week course at the AFIP. Although all three prosectors were competent pathologists, they were hopelessly out of their depth when it came to a medicolegal investigation into a violent death. New York's chief medical examiner, Dr. Milton Helpern, likened the situation of an ordinary hospital pathologist confronted with a gunshot wound to "sending a seven-year-old boy who had taken three lessons on the violin over to the New York Philharmonic and expecting him to perform a Tchaikovsky symphony. He knows how to hold the violin and bow, but he has a long way to go before he can make music."[12] In addition to being woefully unprepared to conduct a medicolegal autopsy, the other factor all three had in common was that they were career military officers conditioned to follow orders.

On March 16, 1964, the Warren Commission heard the testimony of the three prosectors who had conducted the Kennedy autopsy. Arlen Specter, a Commission assistant counsel responsible for assembling the medicolegal evidence section of the report, opened the session by questioning Dr. Humes. Humes was the logical choice to begin the round of questioning since he was the one who had written the autopsy protocol.

During the course of his testimony Humes made a startling admission. In accounting for the notes and working papers that made up the documentary record of the autopsy, the senior pathologist admitted that he had burned the first draft of the autopsy report "in the fireplace of my recreation room." After a short and innocuous exchange with Specter, Humes further disclosed that he had burned "certain preliminary draft notes."[13] As the government records make indisputably clear, Humes never destroyed any notes taken while the autopsy was in progress. With Specter's connivance, Humes, for specific reasons of deception, was using the lawyerlike construction "certain preliminary draft notes" to refer again to the destruction of the first autopsy draft. The navy pathologist might as well have confessed to changing the ribbon in his typewriter halfway through completing the final autopsy draft for all the response these admissions elicited from Specter and the commissioners in attendance. Not a single commissioner was moved to ask Humes what right he had to destroy these papers or even why he had felt compelled on his own initiative to consign them to archival oblivion.

The Commission, of course, knew beforehand what Humes was going to attest under Specter's questioning. All the prosectors had met frequently with the assistant counsel before they testified. Years later, when they were deposed by the Assassination Records Review Board (ARRB), both Humes and Boswell recalled that they had had "an awful lot" of sessions with Specter before they testified. Humes's best guess was that there had been at least eight to ten meetings.[14] The painstaking and intense handling of these key material witnesses assured that there would be no surprises when they went on record and under oath before the Warren Commission. It had to be a great comfort to Humes to know exactly how Specter was going to choreograph his testimony and to anticipate that the commissioners would not bat an eye when he admitted to the destruction of the first draft of the autopsy report on the slain president.

Unless we are to believe that the military had a very relaxed policy about medical records, Humes had no warrant to destroy autopsy records. These documents were not Humes's property; they belonged to the hospital, and it was the responsibility of the Bethesda authorities to see that all the records were preserved. A hospital that fails to protect its records is considered derelict in its duty. In the civilian medical world there are severe penalties for altering, tampering with, or destroying medical records—suspension of license, possible criminal charges of perjury or obstruction of justice, and charges of fraudulent misrepresentation.[15] Moreover, the U.S. Armed Forces' own manual that set standards for military autopsies is very clear about the importance of keeping complete records. Humes had to have a working hands-on knowledge of this set of governing directives published by the AFIP because it was the standard text used in military teaching hospitals such as the Bethesda Naval Hospital Center.[16]

The Warren Commission's witting decision to deceive the American people about the JFK autopsy began with Dr. Humes's testimony. Assistant Counsel Specter led Humes in establishing for the record that Commission Exhibit (CE) 397 was the documentary basis for the official autopsy report. Nothing could have been further from the truth. In his March 1964 Commission testimony Humes had attested that CE 397 contained "copies . . . of various notes in longhand" made by himself that comprised what Specter represented as part of "a group of documents" used to draft the final autopsy report. CE 397 consisted of three sheets of paper and the fifteen-page handwritten or holographic "revision," according to Humes, of the first autopsy draft that he admitted burning in the fireplace of his recreation room on Sunday, the day Oswald was assassinated in the basement of the Dallas Police Department. One of these sheets of paper was a regulation U.S. Armed Forces autopsy descriptive sheet, or "face sheet," with front and back body diagrams locating the wounds on the president's body with accompanying abbreviated notes and measurements. The other sheets contain a few notes from a phone conversation between Humes and Dr. Malcolm Perry, the Dallas emergency room surgeon who had performed a tracheotomy on the clinically dead president before Kennedy received the last rites.[17]

Even allowing for understandable memory lapses on the part of the prosectors, Humes's representations to the Commission are not consistent with the public record. When he testified before the ARRB Humes recalled making two or three pages of shorthand notes recording certain detailed measurements. Boswell's recall on note-taking at the time of the autopsy varied over the years with the telling. In his March 1979 testimony before the House Select Committee on Assassinations (HSCA) the navy pathologist claimed that he had been the only one taking notes. However, when Boswell appeared before the ARRB he recalled that he and Humes had both taken notes. Boswell was clear and probably correct in his claim that it was his notes that appeared on the autopsy descriptive sheet.[18] The other prosector, Dr. Finck, testified on two separate occasions that he had taken notes on small pieces of paper and turned them over to Humes. A short time after the

Bethesda autopsy Finck was heard by a colleague at the AFIP complaining loudly during lunch that his autopsy notes had disappeared before he left the morgue the night of the autopsy. The army pathologist later testified before the ARRB that he had rewritten his notes from memory before turning them over to Humes.[19]

Clearly, CE 397 did not contain all of the medicolegal documentation of the Kennedy autopsy that Humes and Specter represented before the Warren Commission. Despite Humes's tricky Commission testimony, there is no accounting for Finck's missing autopsy notes, which are but a small part of the official deception. Years later, when a groundswell of criticism of the Warren Commission Report forced the government to reexamine the events of Dallas, the prosecutors found themselves testifying before Congress. In March 1979 Dr. Humes testified before the HSCA that in addition to burning the first autopsy draft he had burned all autopsy notes in his possession because they were stained with JFK's blood and body fluids. However, he assured Staff Counsel Gary Cornwell, before he destroyed the original autopsy notes he "sat down and word for word copied what I had on fresh paper."[20]

Humes's "bloodstain" story as he related it to the HSCA and later to the ARRB is as implausible as the acts of destruction of the original autopsy report and the notes themselves. Sometime before 1963 Humes had been assigned to escort a delegation of visiting foreign naval physicians to various military installations to demonstrate how U.S. Navy doctors functioned in military settings. He took them on a side trip to Henry Ford's Greenfield Village in suburban Detroit, where America's most internationally celebrated industrialist had spent some of his fortune to create his vision of America's idyllic past. One of the feature attractions in Ford's museum village was the chair from Ford's Theatre in which President Abraham Lincoln had sat the night he was assassinated. The back of the chair was stained with a dark substance that might have been the blood of the martyred president. Humes recounted that his guests were appalled by this public display. Years later, when some of Kennedy's blood stained the autopsy notes, Humes said he was determined they would never fall into the hands of some sensation-seeker and placed on ghoulish display.[21]

The official contention that CE 397 represented the documentary basis for the final autopsy report collapses under the weight of objective factual evidence. The autopsy notes in CE 397 consist of four brief notations and five measurements on Boswell's autopsy descriptive sheet and a single sheet of paper with a few brief notes Humes made after a phone call to Dr. Perry at Parkland Memorial Hospital. Humes's notes contain one measurement, Perry's description of the hole in the front of JFK's neck, estimated at 3–5 millimeters in diameter.[22]

According to the Warren Commission, the final official autopsy report, a six-page, single-spaced typewritten document, is based on the above-mentioned notes, represented by Specter, with Humes's confirmation, to be all the notes found in CE 397.[23] Isolating every single fact in the official typed copy against the notes found in CE 397 reveals enough serious and blatant discrepancies to discredit the entire report. Data such as JFK's height, weight, hair color, and other commonplace physical features were counted as autopsy facts. The more important data included physical characteristics such as parts of the body and their condition. Of these facts, the most important involved measurements referring directly to the wounds, their size, and their distance from other parts of the body. A few selected examples illustrate the point:

- The official autopsy report (AR) noted on page 2, "There is edema and ecchymosis of the inner canthus region of the left eyelid measuring approximately 1.5 cm in greatest diameter." The notes made no reference to this damage, not to mention the measurement.
- The AR noted on page 3, "There is an old well healed 8 cm. McBurney abdominal incision." There was an apparent mark on the descriptive sheet indicating this scar but no measurement indicated in the notes.
- The AR noted on page 3, "Situated on the upper antero-lateral aspect of the right thigh is an old, well healed 8 cm. scar." The notes indicated no mark of any nature on the thighs. Likewise, the 8-cm measurement appears nowhere on Boswell's descriptive sheet.
- The AR noted on page 2, "There is edema and ecchymosis diffusely over the right supra-orbital ridge with abnormal mobility of the underlying bone." There was no mention of this in the notes.
- Page 3 of the AR described JFK's back wound as "situated on the upper right posterior thorax just above the upper border of the scapula." Nowhere in the notes was it stated or implied that the rear wound was near the scapula.
- The AR on page 4 spoke of a beveling in a large fragment of JFK's skull retrieved from the assassination scene and recorded that the beveling "is estimated to measure approximately 2.5 to 3.0 cm. in diameter." There was no mention of these measurements in the notes.
- The AR on page 4 described two irregularly shaped fragments of metal found in the right cerebral cortex. "These measure 7 × 2 mm. and 3 × 1 mm. These are placed in the custody of Agents Francis X. O'Neill and James W. Sibert of the [FBI], who executed a receipt therefore attached." The notes contained no mention of these missile fragments, their number, or their location.

There are, give or take, about eighty-eight autopsy "facts" in the official pro-sectors' report. About sixty-four of these "facts" or pieces of medicolegal in-formation (almost 75 percent) cannot be found in either the published notes or CE 397. Some fifteen of these pieces of information involve measure-ments and numbers that are not found in the published record.[24]

It is not possible that Humes, even with the help of the other pathologists, could have drawn from memory those minute measurements referring to bullet wounds, their dimensions and distance from one another, and other medicolegal details with the unerring exactitude expected in the forensic in-vestigation of an assassinated president. Relying on memory would have been made even more complicated by the fact that the autopsy doctors did not have access to the autopsy X-rays and photographs when drafting the of-ficial autopsy report. All these photos and X-rays had been loaded into a cardboard box and handed over to Secret Service agent Roy H. Kellerman the night of the autopsy. Remarkably, it was not until November 1966 that Humes and Boswell first saw the autopsy photos when the Justice Depart-ment requested that they identify and inventory them for the National Archives.[25]

The real mystery of the autopsy notes begins when an attempt is made to trace their chain of possession. In a November 24, 1963, letter of transfer to Humes's commanding officer, Capt. J. H. Stover, the navy pathologist certi-fied that "all working papers" associated with the JFK autopsy "have re-mained in my personal custody" until he turned over to Captain Stover the "autopsy notes and the holograph draft of the final report." Stover signed Humes's certificate, noting that "above working papers" had been received.[26] The following day Stover's boss, Adm. C. B. Galloway, in turn, transmitted the autopsy protocol along with "all the work papers used by the Prosector and his assistants" to Admiral Burkley.[27] On November 26 Dr. Burkley sent Kennedy's autopsy records to Robert Bouck, chief of the President Protective Service arm of the Secret Service. Bouck's receipt was a ten-item tally of everything Burkley transferred to his office. One of the entries read, "One copy of autopsy report and notes of the examining doctor which is described in letter of transmittal Nov. 25, 1963 by Dr. Gallaway [sic]." Bouck's receipt should have been one of the documents in CE 397, but it was excluded be-cause one of the items on the list, in addition to the acknowledged receipt of the autopsy notes, read, "An original and six pink copies of Certificate of Death [Nav. Med. N]." The Commission deliberately suppressed JFK's death certificate from its published records because it was destructive of the official explanation of the crime.[28] The paper trail establishes beyond a doubt that the autopsy notes existed as late as November 26, 1963, when they were turned over to Bouck. After that the trail ends as though the autopsy notes dropped out of the government's database and into some memory hole.

These suppressed receipts and the unaccounted-for number of autopsy facts and statements in the final autopsy report make a convincing case that the original autopsy notes, not just those published in CE 397, were preserved and existed after the final report was completed. CE 397 should have been a historical document uncompromising in its accuracy and completeness instead of the gutted remnant of the medicolegal evidence in an assassination of politically far-reaching and wrenching consequences. After almost four decades the question that still begs an answer is: What was in those suppressed notes and the first autopsy draft that Humes swore he committed to the flames?

Pointedly vague in his Commission testimony about the autopsy note-taking, Humes remembered the time and the circumstances when he burned the first handwritten autopsy draft. During Specter's questioning and later before the HSCA, Humes pinpointed the time as coinciding with the news of Oswald's assassination by Jack Ruby. Before the HSCA's panel of forensic pathologists Humes volunteered that "we interrupted our work to try and figure out what that meant to us."[29] One thing that was clearly apparent to the prosectors and their superiors who controlled the Bethesda autopsy was that Oswald's death changed everything. Now there would be no need to produce all the contemporaneous autopsy notes and the first holographic autopsy draft at a trial of the accused assailant and to defend the autopsy report if it came under cross-examination by any forceful and determined defense attorney. The destruction of the first autopsy draft, which Humes disingenuously described (presumably under Specter's coaching) as "certain preliminary draft notes," and the substitution of the rewritten version for the original took place that Sunday afternoon in Admiral Galloway's office after the nation had been rocked by the TV coverage of Oswald's murder.[30]

The revised handwritten autopsy draft revealed substantive changes of fact from the original draft that Humes told the Commission he had burned. Some of these changes were innocuous enough, although they would not likely be found in any autopsy report conducted by experienced forensic pathologists. For instance, Humes originally described the presidential limousine as "moving at approximately twenty miles per hour." In addition to being incorrect, there was no way Humes could have known this except by having read it in the newspaper or having heard it on the TV or radio. In the revised holograph it was changed to "moving at a slow rate of speed."[31] In the last sentence on the same page the report claimed, "Three shots were heard and the President fell face down to the floor of the vehicle." This was a fabrication. It was revised to read, "Three shots were heard and the President fell forward." Both versions are in error but are consistent with the official "truth" that all the shots originated from the rear of the presidential motorcade. The Abraham Zapruder film of the assassination depicted the fatal headshot with sickening clarity. Upon impact JFK went forward for a split second before being violently slammed back and to his left into Jackie Kennedy's lap.[32]

There were other changes that are more disturbing and raise deep suspicions. In medicolegal terminology the description *puncture wound* usually denotes a wound of entrance. Humes always used *puncture* when referring to a wound of entrance in the handwritten autopsy draft. On page seven, in a single sentence where there were seven changes of fact about the head wound, the term *puncture* was twice eliminated and replaced in one instance with the term *lacerated,* which changed the whole nature of the wound. On pages eight and nine, *puncture* was stricken through and on page nine was replaced with *occipital,* which was entirely different.[33] Over the years the wound that has generated the most controversy about the assassination has been JFK's front neck wound. The solution to the assassination and the validation of the Warren report itself rest on the assertion that this was a wound of exit. On page nine the handwritten autopsy draft was edited to read "presumably of exit." The last sentence on page nine was edited to read "presumably of entrance" when referring to JFK's nonfatal posterior wound. According to Dr. Finck, it was Admiral Galloway who insisted on the term *presumably* in both instances. Although he was a medical admiral, Galloway was not a pathologist. But he was a flag-rank officer and the controlling authority when the three pathologists prepared the final typewritten autopsy report.[34]

Unlike some of the other revisions in the autopsy holograph, this woeful lack of precision about the neck wound was not a technical error that could be chalked up to the prosectors' lack of medicolegal experience. How much authority can the official government report on the assassination command when the autopsy—the best evidence in any homicide—could not conclude with iron-clad assurance that all of the shots had come from behind the presidential limousine? However, there was one almost iron-clad certainty in the revised handwritten autopsy draft: On every page where the term *puncture* was used by Humes to denote a wound of entrance, it was crossed out except in one instance. Page two of the revised draft contained the question-begging sentence: "Dr. Perry noted the massive head wound and a second, *puncture wound,* in the low *anterior neck* [my italics] in approximately the midline." In the final typed version of the report this was changed to read, "Dr. Perry noted the massive head wound and a second much smaller wound of the low anterior neck in approximately the midline."[35]

A natural chronological order manifested itself in this business of destruction of autopsy records, missing notes, and the heavy editing of the first autopsy holograph—later things that necessarily grew out of earlier ones. The rewriting of the Kennedy autopsy records coincided exactly with Oswald's murder and Katzenbach's handwritten memo, Sunday, November 24, to Bill Moyers. After conversations with President Johnson and Director Hoover, Katzenbach laid out for Moyers the official version of the assassination for public consumption. From the very outset of the official investigation Oswald was not just the principal suspect, he was the only suspect.[36]

In 1996, a few years before his death, Dr. Humes testified before the ARRB and was asked why he had burned the first autopsy draft. Humes had no real answers. The "bloodstain" story was not an option because the draft in question had been written in the privacy of his home. When mildly pressed by the board's executive director, T. Jeremy Gunn, Humes became testy and defiant. He offered that it "might have been errors in spelling or I don't know what was the matter with it, or whether I even ever did that." As if caught in the thicket of an elaborate fabrication, Humes used the defense of failed memory. "I absolutely can't recall, and I apologize for that," he floundered along, "but that's the way the cookie crumbles." Gunn reminded Humes of his 1979 HSCA testimony before Gary Cornwell about the rewriting of the autopsy notes on fresh paper before burning the bloodstained originals. Gunn's efforts to get the navy prosector to explain for the record why he had destroyed unsoiled draft notes met with no more success than his questions about the first autopsy draft. Deeply agitated and verging on incoherence, Humes claimed that "it was my own materials" to destroy and said he did not want "anything to remain that some squirrel would grab and make whatever they might." His only thought, he told Gunn, had been to turn over to Admiral Burkley "my complete version. So I burned everything else."[37]

The ARRB was established by Congress to see that hitherto unreleased documentary records material to the Kennedy assassination be made public. Its mandate mentioned nothing about the board assuming the role of advocate for the Warren Commission Report. Gunn had ample opportunity to catch Humes up in these blatant misrepresentations about the destruction of irreplaceable evidence in the Kennedy assassination. The ARRB had in its possession all the receipts for the autopsy records mentioned before. Gunn knew that these records had existed as late as November 26, 1963, when they were no longer in Humes's personal custody. He had Humes's own self-subverting words to refute the pathologist's assertion that he had burned all the autopsy notes in his possession, but he never used the documents. Instead of pressing Humes for the truth, Gunn allowed him to revert to formula and repeat the implausible "bloodstain" story without serious objection.

As it turned out, this was Humes's last under-oath public statement about the JFK autopsy records. During his entire session before the ARRB, Humes enjoyed almost carte blanche in the record he was making for history. His last assertion about the autopsy records was that the final typewritten autopsy report "was the product" of the three pages of notes that appeared in CE 397. Having elicited this response, Gunn, with his keen devotion to orderly procedure, moved on to another area of questioning, thereby conceding what he must have known was an impossible assertion.[38]

In 1998, shortly before the ARRB ended its official tenure, it released a staff report on the Kennedy medical and autopsy records. The report noted that one of the many tragedies surrounding the JFK assassination was the incompleteness of the autopsy report and the "suspicion caused by the shroud of secrecy that has surrounded the records that do exist." The report lamented that after deposing all three prosecutors the board was still uncertain whether Humes had destroyed just the original autopsy draft or the draft and the autopsy notes.[39] Had the ARRB been willing not just to ration the truth but to reveal the full suppression of the autopsy facts, it would have reported that more than 70 percent of the facts and statements in the final autopsy draft do not appear in any published government records.[40] Either they have been memory-holed in some obscure government archive or they underwent the same alleged fate as Humes's first autopsy draft.

As the official solution to Dallas was being assembled over the first weekend after the assassination, one major snag required immediate attention. An inconvenient obstacle to Katzenbach's November 24 imperative that the public be satisfied that Dallas was the act of a lone assassin was the fast-breaking news stories. The one that captured the most national attention was the televised news conference with Drs. Malcolm Perry and Kemp Clark at Dallas's Parkland Memorial Hospital that took place several hours after Kennedy was pronounced dead. Dr. Perry drew most of the newsmen's questions because he was the surgeon who had performed the tracheotomy on the moribund president. While fielding questions about JFK's wounds, Perry, on three occasions, matter-of-factly identified the wound in Kennedy's throat as an entrance wound. Dr. Clark, professor of neurosurgery at Parkland, who was standing right beside Perry, concurred with Perry's description of the puncture wound in Kennedy's neck as a wound of entrance.[41] As an emergency room surgeon in gun-toting Dallas, Perry had seen hundreds of bullet wounds. The thirty-four-year-old surgeon was a keen hunter, familiar with firearms, and even packed his own ammunition. But before this traumatic weekend was over the young surgeon, with a promising medical career still ahead of him, was pressured into backtracking on his initial description of Kennedy's neck wound.[42]

Despite the televised news conference and all the media attention to the assassination, the autopsy doctors have always insisted on the record that they knew nothing about the bullet wound in the front of JFK's throat until Saturday morning, when Humes called Perry. It was only then that Humes claimed he learned that the tracheotomy created by Perry was covering the puncture wound in JFK's neck. With this new information, Humes contends, he was able to write the first autopsy draft. The official story is that the call to Dallas instantly cleared up the perplexing mystery that had baffled the prosectors the night before—they had an entrance wound in the president's back but no known wound of exit. By Saturday morning the Bethesda autopsy team had a track for the nonfatal bullet fired from behind and above the presidential limousine. According to the official account the nonfatal missile, the first shot, entered the back of Kennedy's neck at about a 45-degree downward angle and emerged from his throat just below the Adam's apple.[43]

The Saturday-morning phone call to Dr. Perry and the autopsy report's tracking of JFK's nonfatal posterior wound were, to put it mildly, a towering liberation from the documented truth. Like Humes's "bloodstain" story, these representations by the Bethesda autopsy team were designed to satisfy political needs rather than answer the medicolegal questions surrounding the assassination.

What is beyond dispute in the prosectors' account was their urgency to find the bullet that had made this textbooklike wound located, as described in the final autopsy report, "on the upper right posterior thorax just above the upper border of the scapula."[44] According to Boswell, it was initially understood that the autopsy was to be "limited." The news in the Bethesda morgue was that "they had caught the assailant" and all that was expected of the prosectors was to recover the bullet or bullets in the president's body as essential evidence in a criminal prosecution. As mentioned earlier, there was great confusion when the posterior wound was probed and no missile was discovered. Dr. Ebersole, the acting chief of radiology at Bethesda, recalled being summoned to the morgue to take X-rays when Humes's probing of the posterior wound failed to locate the bullet. When the first set of X-rays failed to locate a missile or bullet fragments, Secret Service agent Kellerman insisted that Ebersole take a second set.[45] The mystery of the vanishing bullet was allegedly solved when FBI agent James W. Sibert called the Firearms Section of the FBI laboratory and learned that a whole missile (later labeled CE 399) had been found on a stretcher at Parkland Memorial Hospital.[46]

Doubtless there was confusion and high stress in the autopsy room, considering the grim business at hand. Nonetheless, the autopsy doctors, even allowing for their own considerable limitations, had to know about the anterior neck wound before they performed the postmortem on their dead commander in chief.[47] The news of the events in Dallas had been on the TV and radio for more than six hours before the autopsy began. If experienced forensic pathologists had conducted the autopsy, they would have immediately called Parkland Memorial Hospital to speak to the doctors who had worked on the stricken president. After the president's corpse was returned to the nation's capital, the members of the Parkland medical team did write out their recollections of what had happened.[48] Their notes were available upon request even though the Bethesda prosectors, as they claimed, did not call before beginning the autopsy. The failure of the Bethesda pathologists to call Parkland earlier had nothing to do with their inexperience or lack of foresight. The most authoritative source with firsthand knowledge of the tracheotomy over the anterior neck wound was the White House physician, Dr. George B. Burkley. Burkley had escorted Kennedy's body back to Washington and remained at Bethesda until the body was released and returned to the White House.

Dr. Burkley had been with Kennedy in the Parkland Memorial emergency room and had observed the futile efforts by the team of doctors and nurses to resuscitate Kennedy. It was Burkley who had formally pronounced Kennedy dead at 1 P.M. (CST) before they pulled the sheet over his head.[49] Since Burkley was just one of a trio of medical admirals in the Bethesda morgue, his statement that he "supervised the autopsy . . . and had complete knowledge of everything that was done" is probably an exaggerated claim.[50] Nonetheless, whether or not Burkley was the medical officer in charge, the president's personal physician certainly must have shared the information about the tracheotomy with the autopsy team. Given the urgent need to find the track for JFK's posterior wound, the autopsy doctors would have turned immediately to the White House physician.

There were calls to Dallas, but not for the reasons that all the autopsy doctors reported. Even the slightly different spin that Admiral Galloway improvised years later, when he insisted that the prosectors "actually suspected" that a tracheotomy had obliterated a neck wound and called Dr. Perry to confirm their suspicions, played fast and loose with the truth.[51] The most direct refutation of the "Saturday morning call to Dallas" story originated with one of the autopsy doctors. In an interview with the *Baltimore Sun,* timed with the third anniversary of the assassination, Dr. Boswell told reporter Richard H. Levine that the prosectors had known the extent of JFK's injuries and what the Dallas doctors had done before the president's remains arrived at Bethesda.[52] Boswell did not mention where this information originated. It might have come from one of the emergency room doctors or the Dallas County justice of the peace office where JFK's inquest had been executed, but the most logical source was Dr. Burkley.

When he appeared before the HSCA's Medical Panel, Dr. Ebersole was clear in his own mind that Humes had made a phone call to Dallas the Friday night of the autopsy. During the course of his testimony, Ebersole made four separate references to Humes's Friday-night call to Dallas, but after fifteen years he could only approximate the time. The navy radiologist's best recollection was that the call had been made between 10 and 11 P.M. The call made a lasting impression on Ebersole because the problem surrounding the search for an exit path for Kennedy's posterior wound appeared to have been solved. After the call Humes returned to the autopsy table, Ebersole recalled, announcing that Kennedy had an *exit* wound under the tracheotomy that matched up with the posterior entrance wound. Although his recollection was not as definite as Ebersole's, the autopsy photographer, John T. Stringer, also thought Humes had made a call to Dallas on Friday night.[53]

Like many of the details related to the JFK autopsy, the question of the Dallas phone calls is rife with contradictory testimony. According to Perry and other Parkland doctors, Humes made two back-to-back calls on Saturday morning before the hospital's scheduled press conference.[54] When Humes testified before the Warren Commission, Specter pointedly asked him if he had discussed the autopsy findings with Perry during his Saturday phone call. Humes's response was an unambiguous "No, Sir, I did not." Perry basically agreed with Humes's version as far as the first phone conversation was concerned. But the Dallas surgeon's account of the second phone call, about thirty minutes later, implied that Humes had discussed in confidence what would appear in the Bethesda autopsy report.[55] Perry's colleague, Dr. Kemp Clark, told the Warren Commission that Perry related to him and two other doctors that he had learned from Humes what the autopsy findings would report; at that point he had asked Clark to take over for him at the press conference.[56]

The Monday following the assassination Perry packed up his family and left Dallas for "a little bit of rest" and to avoid further questioning by the media. When he returned to Dallas he was repeatedly visited by Secret Service and FBI agents who questioned him about his views "as to the origin of the missiles and trajectories."[57] If the government's intention was to instruct Perry about the "official facts" of Dallas, Perry proved an apt pupil. In March 1964, when he first appeared before the Warren Commission, he assured Assistant Counsel Specter that there were "no discrepancies at all" between his observations and the conclusions of the official autopsy report. Perry confessed that he had misspoken at the November 22 press conference because he "did not have that information initially"—an interesting and perhaps tangential allusion to the official medical cover-up—and "as a result was somewhat confused about the nature of the wounds." In his March 1964 Warren Commission testimony, Dr. Clark reported what he characterized as routine questioning by the FBI a few days after the assassination and later by the Secret Service.[58] Dr. Charles A. Crenshaw, one of the trauma-team doctors who worked on the stricken president, would later write that Parkland Memorial Hospital became a zone of silence about the events of November 22, 1963. The hospital administration sent out an unwritten warning that any further media publicity from doctors and staff would be hazardous to their future medical careers.[59]

It was absolutely essential to the Warren Commission Report that the gunshot wound trauma in JFK's throat be forensically established as the exit wound of the nonfatal missile that had struck the president from the back and above. Humes provided a clear verbal description of the trajectory of this bullet during his Warren Commission testimony. The senior prosecutor testified in March 1964 that the bullet hit Kennedy's neck at a 45-degree angle, striking no bone, and exited his throat below the Adam's apple. At one point in Humes's testimony Commissioner John J. McCloy, speaking for the record, asked for a more graphic description of the missile's trajectory. McCloy wanted the witness to attest to the fact that CE 385, a medical illustrator's rendition of the flight of the nonfatal bullet, was consistent with Humes's testimony. Humes obliged, responding that as depicted in Exhibit 385, "the wound in the anterior portion of the lower neck is physically lower than the point of entrance posteriorly, sir."[60] Throughout his testimony Humes proved creative in his anatomical descriptions of Kennedy's posterior wound, variously describing it as "low neck," "lower neck," "base of neck," and "lower posterior neck."[61]

It was four months after the assassination when Humes and the other Bethesda pathologists testified before the Warren Commission, and some of the best evidence, the autopsy photographs and X-rays, was not available for informing the official record of John F. Kennedy's assassination. This lack did not catch Humes up short. Specter had told the prosectors in their pretestimony interviews to bring with them schematic drawings as stand-ins for the autopsy raw materials. T. H. Ryberg, the medical illustrator for the Naval Medical School, made the drawings. Ryberg's illustrations were not made from firsthand observation and study since he had not witnessed the autopsy and had never had access to the autopsy photos and X-rays. The drawings that Specter had Humes introduce into evidence to substantiate the official version of a missile striking JFK in the back of his neck and exiting his throat were actually dictated to Ryberg by Humes. In his ARRB deposition, Humes said he agreed with the Commission's decision to substitute the drawings for the photos and X-rays because the autopsy pictures were terribly graphic and upsetting. As with the "bloodstain" story, Humes said he had been concerned that if the photos were introduced into evidence they might find their way into the hands of people who would exploit them for money or some sick purpose. Humes left the ARRB with the impression that Specter had said it was the wish of the Kennedy family that the autopsy photographs not be used in the hearings.[62] Dr. Finck was more emphatic on this point, claiming that Specter had told the doctors that Robert Kennedy opposed the introduction of the autopsy raw materials into the Commission hearings.[63]

Specter knew that the story about Robert Kennedy and the autopsy pictures was bogus through and through. In an April 1964 memo to Chief Counsel Rankin, Specter urged that the Commission obtain the autopsy photos and X-rays to "determine with certainty whether two shots came from the rear." A month after the prosectors appeared before the Commission, Specter, who was then an assistant district attorney in Philadelphia, knew the Ryberg medical illustrations were no substitute for the best forensic evidence. He noted that he had learned from Secret Service inspector Thomas J. Kelley that "the Attorney General did not categorically decline to make them available." The dead president's brother wanted "to be satisfied that they were really necessary." When he did not hear back from Rankin, the harried assistant counsel wrote again for staff access to the X-rays and the autopsy photos. Specter had good reason to importune the Commission's chief counsel since Rankin had made it known that he expected to wrap up the Commission's work in June.[64]

At the time Specter was apparently not privy to the fact that Rankin and the Commission had the X-rays and the autopsy photos. They had kept this information from the assistant counsels and the staff, though the materials were available to the Commission members. Most of the commissioners were lawyers with prominent legal careers. They knew the rules of evidence but were content to sit through testimony in which key material witnesses were denied the best medicolegal evidence, just as they failed to raise a collective eyebrow when Humes admitted to burning autopsy records.[65]

Several years after the Warren Commission published its report on the assassination, former Commissioner McCloy appeared on CBS's *Face the Nation*. In discussing that fateful day in Dallas, McCloy waxed contrite, expressing his regrets that the Commission, "for the sake of completion," had not looked at the late president's autopsy X-rays and photographs. McCloy told the program's millions of Sunday viewers, "We were perhaps a little oversensitive" to the wishes of the Kennedy family, who "were against the production of colored photographs of the body and so forth." After striking the right tone of repentance, McCloy went on to assure the TV audience that even without reviewing the autopsy pictures the Commission had "the best evidence [on the autopsy] in the sworn testimony of the doctors."[66]

McCloy's subtle exercise in blaming the Kennedys for withholding crucial evidence was all part of the FBI's campaign, mentioned before, to cover up its embarrassing failure to acquire a copy of the official autopsy report before submitting its report (CD 1) on the assassination to the Commission. This confection of lies, misinformation, and blaming the victim was so unpalatable even to Hoover that he scrawled on an FBI memo that belatedly attempted to rationalize this gaffe, "The confusion . . . would never have occurred if we had obtained the autopsy report originally. The Kennedys never asked us to withhold it and if they had we should have disregarded it."[67]

Nothing in the official autopsy is more suspect than the described trajectory of JFK's nonfatal through-and-through neck wound. If the autopsy statement about this wound was a fabrication, then the Warren report is nothing more than official mythology. Is it possible that the autopsy pictures would have generated embarrassing questions about this wound and the report's conclusions that persuaded Rankin and the commissioners to make certain they were repressed? The documentary record goes a long way toward providing an obvious answer to this question.

The first nonmilitary personnel at Bethesda Naval Hospital Center to see JFK's rear wound were FBI agents Sibert and O'Neill. One or the other was always in the morgue observing the prosectors and taking notes while his partner slipped out to grab a bite to eat or go to the restroom. Boswell complained that one or both were always hovering near the phone that was only three or four feet away from the autopsy table. In their jointly submitted report to FBIHQ they described Kennedy's nonfatal posterior wound as "one bullet hole located just below shoulders to the right of the spinal column." The report went on to note that "hand probing indicated trajectory of 45 to 60 degrees with no point of exit."[68] In 1978, when HSCA staffers interviewed O'Neill, his recollection had not changed. He still referred to the wound as a back wound and even executed a body-chart drawing with the wound located at the level of the shoulder girdle, well below the lower neck or base of the neck. The HSCA interviewer noted that O'Neill mentioned being questioned at length by Specter and "felt it was odd that he was not called to give testimony." An explanation might be that O'Neill was so adamant about the location of the nonfatal rear wound that Specter knew he would be a troublesome witness. In an affidavit the FBI veteran executed, along with the HSCA interview, O'Neill remarked, "I do not see how the bullet entered below the shoulder in the back could come out the front of the throat."[69]

Another who supported the location of JFK's rear wound in the shoulder area was Clint Hill, the Secret Service agent who narrowly missed being run down when he leaped onto the back of the presidential limousine to assist Mrs. Kennedy. Hill was called into the morgue by Kellerman to view the body and observed "a wound six inches down from the neck line down the back, just to the right of the spinal column."[70] Kellerman was in earshot of Dr. Finck when the pathologist probed Kennedy's rear wound, and he stated that he heard the doctor comment, "There are no lanes for an outlet of this entry in this man's shoulder." In 1977 Kellerman was interviewed by HSCA staffers and, like O'Neill, was asked to locate the back wound on a rough body chart. The Secret Service man placed the location of the rear wound on the lower right shoulder.[71] Chester H. Boyer, chief petty officer in charge of Bethesda's Pathology Department, observed "an entrance wound in the right shoulder blade . . . just under the scapula and next to it." Bethesda lab technician Jan G. Rudnicki, who had observed about twenty Bethesda autopsies, noticed "a wound in the shoulder blade region" of the president's back.[72]

Even Specter's memos to Rankin referred to JFK's rear wound as a back and not a neck wound. Specter limned for Rankin how Admiral Galloway illustrated the missile's trajectory "by placing one finger on my back and the second finger on the front part of my chest which indicated that the bullet traveled in a downward path, on the assumption that it emerged in the opening on the President's throat."[73] According to the prosectors' autopsy report, confirmed by the Ramsey Clark Medical Panel, the missile that made the rear wound struck no bone and was traveling at a downward trajectory, so it could only be hoped that the admiral's medical skills were superior to his grasp of physics and trajectories. In Dr. Finck's own summary report to his commanding officer at AFIP, the army pathologist described the wound as located "in the upper back . . . to the right of the midline."[74]

In any homicide where the experienced forensic pathologist was confronted with questions about traumas such as JFK's nonfatal wounds, there are two obvious textbook procedures that are called for before any other steps are taken to determine whether one or more missiles were involved. What was medicolegally called for in the Kennedy autopsy was an examination of the president's clothes and the dissection of the anterior and posterior wounds to uncover the track of the bullet or bullets. The Bethesda pathologists finished their autopsy without undertaking either of these procedures. Humes and Boswell claimed that they never saw Kennedy's clothes and were so intensely involved in searching for a missile in the corpse that it never occurred to them to examine the garments. Finck had a different version. In his summary report to General Blumberg, Finck noted that when he tried to examine Kennedy's coat and shirt, an "officer who outranked me told me that my request was only of academic interest."[75] The prosectors did not see Kennedy's clothes until months later, when Specter made them available at their pretestimony sessions. The bullet holes in Kennedy's coat and shirt were in almost perfect alignment, indicating that the same missile had made them. They were about six inches below the top of the collar line and almost two inches to the right of the midline.[76] The alignment was consistent with a wound of entrance in the shoulder, the "upper right posterior thorax," as Humes described in the official autopsy protocol, and not a posterior neck wound.[77]

Humes and Boswell had ready explanations for "the neck wound" when confronted with this inconsistency. Both insisted that Kennedy's custom-made clothes had ridden up on his back as he waved to the cheering Dallas crowd just as the first shot hit him.[78] As it turned out, it was Boswell who had to do most of the heavy lifting in explaining the apparent mismatch between the holes in JFK's clothes and the autopsy report's placement of the posterior wound in the neck region. The original autopsy descriptive sheet, or "face sheet," placed the posterior wound in the region of the shoulder girdle, exactly where you would expect to find the nonfatal rear wound based on the holes in JFK's shirt and coat (see CE 397). There is no dispute that Boswell made all the notes and measurements on this autopsy worksheet while the autopsy was in progress. The position of this wound was crucial in determining the trajectory of the nonfatal missile and, by extension, whether all the shots had come from the rear of the presidential motorcade.

On the third anniversary of Kennedy's assassination there was a flurry of press stories pointing to the conflict between the holes in JFK's clothes, the autopsy report, and Boswell's placement of the posterior wound on the descriptive sheet. The confusion about the exact location of the rear wound was further compounded when attention was drawn to the FBI report on the autopsy. FBI agents Sibert and O'Neill reported to FBI headquarters that the posterior wound was located "just below shoulders to right of the spinal column and hand probing indicated trajectory at angle of forty five to sixty degrees downward and hole of short depth with no point of exit." Both men were veteran agents, trained to observe and report accurately. According to their statements, one or both were always in close proximity to the autopsy table and took notes on what they heard from the prosectors as they examined the body.[79]

Boswell tried to explain away these inconsistencies by claiming that the diagram was quickly drawn as "rough notes" and not intended to be exact. "If I had known that the sketch would become public record," he continued, "I would have been more careful." Boswell shrugged off the Sibert and O'Neill report, noting that "FBI agents . . . were not trained in medicine."[80] Many years later, during an interview with the HSCA, Boswell speculated that his accuracy about the controversial posterior wound "may have been somewhat limited and the neatness lessened by the fact that he was writing with gloves on." When his HSCA interviewers provided Boswell with a fresh copy of the original face sheet he moved the bullet hole from the right shoulder to the lower neck.[81]

The Bethesda pathologist's repositioning of the nonfatal rear wound was the last official adjustment in the intriguing saga of this roving bullet hole that began with Commissioner Jerry Ford. In editing the initial draft of the Warren report, Ford moved the wound in Kennedy's back from "a point slightly below the shoulder to the right of the spine" to "the back of his neck slightly to the right of the spine." Ford's revision brought the posterior wound in line with the Commission's no-conspiracy conclusion, repositioning it to make it consistent with what came to be called "the single-bullet theory."[82]

To lay to rest any question about Kennedy's nonfatal wounds, the neck should have been dissected. The medicolegal technique required that the organs of the neck be taken out and laid open to reveal the track of the bullet from the point of entrance to the point of exit. When pressed by the HSCA's panel of forensic pathologists, Humes and Boswell admitted that this had not been done. Humes took full responsibility for failing to carry out this procedure. He explained that there had been so much going on, and since the pathologists had exposed some of the bullet track they had been satisfied that they had "the two points of the wound and then subsequently the wound of exit."[83]

Dr. Finck, on the other hand, sought refuge in blaming the Kennedys. He told the HSCA's medical panel of pathologists that Admiral Galloway, acting under the direction of the Kennedy family, had instructed the autopsy team not to dissect the organs of the neck.[84] On the face of it, Finck's claim does not ring true. Since the prosectors had removed JFK's brain and executed a modified Y-cut to remove internal organs, what could possibly have been sacrosanct about the organs of the neck? For the Kennedy family the neck organs held no special or exemptive significance, as revealed in the authorization form for the postmortem examination signed by Robert F. Kennedy, acting for JFK's widow. The section of the form stipulating any limitations on the autopsy is blank. The Kennedys placed no conditions on the president's autopsy and clearly cannot be blamed for the prosectors' failure to dissect JFK's neck wound. Even more suggestive is the fact that the authorization form was omitted from the official record.[85]

The failure to dissect the neck wound was a political and not a Kennedy family decision. Testimony from Dr. Finck's own mouth and a pivotal document from the Kennedy White House physician, Dr. Burkley, push the argument to the point of cold conviction that the Warren report is a conscious, knowing, and deliberate falsification of our history. Finck's remarkable testimony in the 1969 trial of Clay L. Shaw in New Orleans, the import of which went largely unnoticed by the press, established to a certainty the fact that the prosectors were under military orders not to dissect JFK's neck wound. President Kennedy's death certificate, signed by Admiral Burkley, refuted the false claim that the wound in Kennedy's throat was the trauma made by the exiting bullet that had first struck him in the lower neck. What other explanation can there be for why the death certificate was suppressed from the official records?

Over two stressful days Dr. Finck was subjected to seven hours of intense and forceful cross-examination by the prosecution in New Orleans district attorney Jim Garrison's showcase JFK conspiracy trial involving a prominent local patron of the arts, Clay L. Shaw. Finck found himself in a New Orleans courtroom when his superiors and the Justice Department granted him permission to be a witness for E. F. Wegmann, Shaw's leading defense attorney. Before leaving for New Orleans Finck spent a day in the office of Carl Eardley, deputy assistant attorney general, where he reviewed Kennedy's autopsy X-rays, photos, and Ramsey Clark's Medical Panel report and may have received some coaching from Eardley.[86]

Assuming airs of shocking arrogance and self-importance, Finck began his first day under cross-examination by spelling out words he used in response to the questioning, such as "abrasion," "entry," and "entrance," as though he were in an elementary school classroom and not a courtroom.[87] Before his first day was over Finck became contentious, sour-tempered, and harried under the prosecution's probing cross-examination, especially about the failure to dissect JFK's neck wound. The navy pathologist began to argue with the judge, ignored the advice of his counsel, and flirted with contempt charges rather than answer questions directed at him by the prosecution. He tried to blame the Kennedys for placing restrictions on the autopsy, but to no avail.[88]

Then, under pressure from the judge's threat to cite him for contempt, Finck made some startling disclosures. He reluctantly acknowledged that there had been uniformed admirals in the Bethesda morgue and made the revealing admission that "when you are a Lieutenant Colonel in the Army you just follow orders." Finck was no longer a cocky witness. He knew he was building a gigantic snowball that could envelop him and the official autopsy report, but he did not want to be slapped with a contempt citation by a judge whose patience he had come close to exhausting.[89]

Finally, during his second day on the witness stand Finck came forward and named names. He disclosed that Admirals Galloway and Kinney, not Humes, had been in charge of the autopsy. Alvin Oser, the assistant district attorney who was conducting Finck's cross-examination, pressed Finck about whether the neck wound had not been dissected because of "direct orders." Trying to salvage what he could, Finck resorted to semantics, taking exception to Oser's phrase *direct orders;* the distressed army doctor preferred instead to characterize them as "suggestions and directions" offered by the two medical flag officers Galloway and Kinney.[90] At that point Finck's two-day ordeal came to an end. Once Oser had Finck on record admitting to military interference with the president's autopsy, the prosecution was satisfied that the national press would run with the story.[91]

Although Finck's admissions drew little press attention, his New Orleans testimony set off bells and whistles at the Justice Department. According to Boswell, an alarmed Carl Eardley called him and pleaded with him to hop on a plane and get to New Orleans "quick." Eardley was beside himself because "Pierre is testifying and lousing everything up." Boswell spent several days in New Orleans at government expense consulting with Justice attorneys, reviewing the transcript of Finck's testimony, and apparently assisting with a government damage-control exercise.[92]

The most obvious, authoritative, and accessible source on Kennedy's wounds and the surrounding events of that dark day in Dallas was Kennedy's personal physician. Dr. Burkley had been in the presidential motorcade and with the dying president in the Parkland emergency room. He was with the body in *Air Force One* in the sad trip back to the nation's capital and accompanied the remains in the ambulance from the Bethesda morgue back to the White House.[93] It is generally agreed that it was Burkley who convinced Jackie Kennedy on the flight back from Dallas that the autopsy should be conducted at a military hospital for "security" reasons. Bethesda, he helped her to see, would be most appropriate because her husband was a former naval officer.[94]

Dr. Burkley's name should have been at the top of the Warren Commission's list of witnesses. Incredibly, JFK's personal physician was never called to testify. Commission assistant counsel Specter never interviewed Burkley or asked him to prepare a statement on his observations of the president's wounds or any information he might have relating to the assassination. The FBI and the Secret Service never interviewed him before or after they submitted their respective reports on the assassination to the Warren Commission. Admiral Burkley's plight was akin to that of the old Bolsheviks who were airbrushed out of Soviet history books and the national narrative after they fell victim to one of Stalin's party purges.

Except for a modest act of initiative on his part, Burkley would have slipped unnoticed and unremarked down the official memory hole. In June 1964 Burkley approached the FBI liaison with the White House, Orrin H. Bartlett, with a request. Obviously puzzled and miffed, according to Agent Bartlett, over the fact that the Warren Commission had not contacted him, he asked Bartlett to use his good offices to get the Commission to accept for the record his statement on the assassination. Burkley's request was sent up the FBI's ladder of command and reviewed by all the need-to-know assistant directors before a recommendation was made to contact the Commission's chief counsel. Rankin, somewhat reluctantly, accepted Burkley's statement and placed it in the record. As it happened, Burkley's nine-page statement contained absolutely nothing of consequence, which may explain Rankin's grudging willingness to accept it for the historical record.[95]

That the Commission, along with the other government agencies ostensibly responsible for investigating the assassination, had no interest in Kennedy's personal physician is a stunning self-indictment. The Commission's systematic campaign to keep Burkley's testimony out of the record established early in the Commission's life that it had decided not to conduct a good-faith investigation into the facts of Dallas. A document that was anathema to the Commission and its predetermined conclusions—one it treated like a poisonous snake—was JFK's death certificate, signed by Dr. Burkley. The death-certificate sheet with the heading "summary of the facts related to death" placed President Kennedy's nonfatal rear wound "in the posterior back at about the level of the third *thoracic* [my italics] verte-bra."[96] It is important to note that Burkley wrote the death certificate a day before he received the Bethesda prosectors' original autopsy report along with the six pink copies; that is, before the official version of the assassina-tion was settled upon.[97]

Burkley's positioning of the rear wound is consistent with the Dallas in-quest report signed on November 22, 1963, at 1 P.M. (CST) by Theran Ward, justice of the peace, Precinct No. 2, Dallas County. Under the heading "Findings of the Justice," it reported the cause of death as "two gunshot wounds," one of which was "near the center of the body and just above the right shoulder." Ward's information came from Dr. Malcolm Perry. This document destroys the generally accepted "folklore" of the assassination that the Parkland Memorial Hospital emergency team never turned the body over and was therefore unaware of JFK's back wound. In an interview with researcher Harold Weisberg, the surgeon Dr. Charles Carrico reported that he ran his hands down the sides of Kennedy's body to determine whether there was a large wound in the back. Carrico noted that this was standard operational procedure in all gunshot cases.[98]

If the political considerations surrounding JFK's autopsy are set aside, there is a medicolegal explanation for the discrepancies between the nonfa-tal posterior wound being reported as a back wound or a neck wound. It is briefly limned in the House Select Committee Medical Panel's critique of the official autopsy report in point 2 under "Examination Procedure." The short sentence read, "The entrance and exit wounds on the back and front neck were not localized with reference to fixed body landmarks and to each other so as to permit reconstruction of trajectories." What this means in plain language is that the Bethesda prosectors' measurements and position-ing of this wound were forensically meaningless, although the HSCA's Medical Panel drew no such conclusion. During the course of the autopsy Dr. Finck located this wound by measuring from the highly mobile mastoid process behind JFK's right ear and the acromion, the tip of the right shoul-der. This measurement was clearly recorded on the autopsy face sheet. These are not fixed body landmarks, and unless the length of the neck and the position of the body on the autopsy table are known, the measurement is forensically useless. The forensically prescribed fixed body landmark used as the point of reference for locating a trauma suspected of being a through-

and-through wound should have been Kennedy's vertebrae.[99] The correct medicolegal procedure would have been to locate the wound by measuring from the top of the head down the midline or the spine of the body. In his ARRB interview Finck conceded to Jeremy Gunn that JFK's spine, a fixed landmark, was the correct and only point of reference to determine the accurate location of this posterior wound.[100]

Some might attribute the Bethesda autopsy doctors' "unorthodox" approach in locating the nonfatal posterior wound to their collective incompetence. They were thrust into a highly charged, sensitive, and grotesque situation, to say the least, with which they were woefully unprepared to cope. However, in light of Dr. Finck's sworn testimony about high-ranking medical officers' interference with required autopsy procedures, it would be naïve to characterize these mistakes as innocent technical errors. Moreover, since most of the contemporaneous autopsy working papers have inexplicably vanished, there is no way to re-create a fully documented medicolegal accounting of the wounds Kennedy sustained, or even a precise understanding of the cause of death. Under these circumstances the most viable conclusion must be that it was necessary to corrupt the autopsy database in order to align the Bethesda prosecutors' findings with the official no-conspiracy conclusion. To help in accomplishing this politically imposed end, the prosectors measured the nonfatal posterior wound from flexible or mobile points on the body to give themselves the anatomical edge they needed to manipulate the location of the wound. The report of what was indisputably a back wound was deliberately altered to position it in the region of the neck.

Burkley's description of the wound is consistent with the holes in JFK's shirt and suit coat and the recorded observations of the FBI and Secret Service agents who were in the morgue and many of the medical orderlies and technicians who assisted at the autopsy. A wound at the level of the third thoracic vertebra severely compromises the Commission's contention that the nonfatal bullet entered Kennedy's lower neck and exited his throat before slamming into Governor John Connally. How was it possible for a bullet traveling at a downward angle, entering the body at the level of the third thoracic vertebra, and striking no bone to exit the throat below the Adam's apple? Kennedy's death certificate goes a long way toward contradicting the Warren report's conclusion that all the shots came from above and to the rear and were fired by a lone assassin. Unless the laws of motion and the science of ballistics were suspended that dreadful day in Dallas, Burkley's death certificate adds greater weight to Drs. Perry and Clark's original and firsthand medical opinion that Kennedy's front neck wound was a wound of entrance.

Since JFK's death certificate struck at the vitals of the Warren report, it was essential that the Commission ignore Burkley and suppress his report on the president's wounds. The Kennedy death certificate does not appear in the report or the twenty-six volumes of hearings and exhibits. It was after all Kennedy's assassination that generated the 914-page investigative report, dressed out with almost seven thousand footnotes and a bodyguard of twenty-six stout volumes of more than ten million words. That a two-page death certificate could threaten to topple this impressive edifice of officially sanctioned truths and conclusions is a scenario worthy of the talents of a George Orwell.

Although Burkley was decidedly marginalized in the official record of the Kennedy assassination, his career did not suffer. Early Saturday morning, after he absented himself from the White House deathwatch, Burkley notified the presidential aide Walter Jenkins that he wished to resign. However, President Johnson wanted Burkley to stay on as White House physician, and what LBJ wanted usually happened. The new president's persuasive skills were legendary. Johnson called Burkley into the Oval Office one afternoon for a chat, and before the day was over Rear Admiral Burkley was Vice Admiral Burkley, the highest-ranking medical officer in the U.S. Navy. George G. Burkley was only the second White House physician in history to carry the rank of vice admiral.[101]

Burkley was neither called to testify before the HSCA nor interviewed by any of its staff. He did go on record in 1967 with Harvard University's JFK oral history project but refused to comment on the Warren report. When asked if he agreed with the report's conclusions, Burkley's terse response was "I would not care to be quoted on that." After he retired in 1968 and before his death in 1991, Burkley broke his silence on at least one occasion about the assassination when he confided to the writer Henry Hurt that he believed Kennedy had been the victim of a conspiracy. When Hurt tried to follow up on their phone conversation with an in-depth interview, Burkley abruptly refused.[102]

8   Birth of the "Single-Bullet" Fabrication

All evidence indicated that the bullet found on the governor's stretcher could have caused all his wounds.
—Warren Commission Report

If there is a Rosetta stone for the Kennedy assassination that exposed the deception of the government's investigation into the crime, it is what in time came to be referred to as the "single-bullet" theory.* The Warren Commission began its investigation with the predetermined conclusion that the crime had been carried out by a lone sociopath. Consequently, over time, the Commission was forced to fabricate a convincing case that a single bullet—Commission Exhibit (CE) 399—had inflicted all seven nonfatal wounds on President Kennedy and Governor John B. Connally. When its own medical and forensic experts asserted that the medical and physical evidence was inconsistent with this one-bullet invention, the Commission ignored them. In one instance the Commission even suppressed the results of experimental tests it had authorized because the results did not substantiate this hypothesis. When the respected and powerful Senator Richard B. Russell, with support from Senator John Cooper, forced a special Commission executive session to register his dissent on this single-bullet theory, Chairman Warren and General Counsel Rankin saw to it that the senior Georgia lawmaker's strongly felt objection was suppressed from the official record.[1]

What the Commission attributed to CE 399 was meant to satisfy the government's assassination-driven immediate political needs and not a let-the-chips-fall-where-they-may effort to uncover what had happened in Dallas on November 22, 1963. The Commission's true priorities were adumbrated in the elliptical language it employed in its report: "Although it is not necessary to any essential findings of the Commission to determine just which shot hit Governor Connally, there is very persuasive evidence from the experts to indicate that the same bullet which pierced the President's throat also caused Governor Connally's wounds. However, Governor Connally's testimony and certain other factors have given rise to some differences of opinion as to this probability."[2]

---

* It is generally accepted that a theory is a well-supported and well-tested hypothesis or set of hypotheses. It is the author's contention that the Commission's one-bullet construction never met these demanding standards. Instead, it was an ad hoc invention or fabrication to meet the Commission's requirements for a lone-assassin, no-conspiracy explanation of the Kennedy assassination.

Despite the report's guarded language it was absolutely essential to the Commission's conclusion that a lone gunman firing from above and to the rear of the motorcade had killed President Kennedy and that JFK and Connally had been hit by the same bullet. The time constraints and the mechanical features of the alleged murder rifle required that CE 399 had inflicted all seven nonfatal wounds on Kennedy and Connally. Otherwise, at least one other rifle and a second gunman were necessary to account for all of the victims' wounds.[3]

The career assigned to this single bullet was little short of fabulous. According to the report, CE 399 hit JFK in the back of the neck, then passed through the neck without striking any hard object and emerged at the front of his throat. It then entered Connally in the back of the right armpit and slid along his fifth rib, demolishing four inches of the rib before it exited the chest below the right nipple. The bullet then allegedly struck and shattered the radius of Connally's right wrist, one of the hardest bones in the body, located just above the wrist on the dorsal side, then exited at the base of his palm and entered his left thigh just above the knee. CE 399 then traveled about three inches beneath the surface of the thigh, hit the femur, and deposited a lead fragment on the bone. Some time later, with a spasm of reverse kinetic energy, it spontaneously exited the hole in Connally's thigh and neatly tucked itself under the mattress of a stretcher parked in a hallway of the Parkland Memorial Hospital that the report asserted was linked to the wounded governor.[4]

Critics of the Warren Commission Report were quick to mockingly dub CE 399 the "magic bullet." They pointed to the fact that after allegedly producing seven wounds, most notably the shattering of Connally's fifth rib bone and the radius of his right wrist, CE 399 was, in the report's own words, "slightly flattened but otherwise unmutilated." CE 399 was turned over to the FBI. It was the bureau's firearms expert, Robert A. Frazier, who identified it as a full-metal-jacketed, military-type bullet weighing 158.6 grains. Frazier testified before the Commission that the original weight of a 6.5-mm bullet, unfired or pristine, was on average about 160 to 161 grains.[5]

In advancing its conclusion for history that the assassination of President Kennedy was the work of a lone assassin, the Commission was forced into buttressing its case on the proposition that a single bullet had passed through two bodies, smashing bone in one, and lost only about two grains of weight in the process. (Two grains are about the weight of a common postage stamp.) Since CE 399 was copper-jacketed, all of the metal lost in the bullet had to come from its exposed lead base. After the Commission published its official findings on the assassination, skeptics insisted that in order to accept the "magic" of CE 399, suspension of common sense and disbelief was mandatory. Supporters of the Commission have been just as adamant in their defense of the single-bullet theory.[6] What can be touted in the Kennedy assassination literature as the "single-bullet wars" is not just a parlor game with each side building up academic debating points against the other. In addition to the Kennedy autopsy, the other crucial evidentiary area upon which the Warren report should either prevail as the historical account of the JFK assassination or be dismissed as official mythology is the final acceptance or rejection of the single-bullet theory.

For much of its life the Commission proceeded under the presumption that Kennedy had been hit by two bullets, the first and the third shots, whereas Connally had been struck by the second shot, a separate bullet. This was the sequence laid out in the FBI's report to the Commission (Commission Document [CD] 1). As mentioned earlier, CD 1 spent less than sixty words on the shooting. It was rushed into print without consulting the official autopsy report, failed to mention any of JFK's or Connally's wounds, failed to give the cause of the president's death, and suppressed any mention of the curbstone shot, or the "missed bullet." Although the FBI's investigative report was a structure of suppression, shoddiness, and dodges, it carried Director Hoover's imprimatur. CD 1 was Hoover's hasty, shake-and-bake solution to the Kennedy murder, an explanation the FBI knew from the start was inconsistent with the physical evidence of the crime. To impose the FBI's investigative "triumph" on the nation and bludgeon the Commission into acquiescence, Hoover had CD 1's conclusions leaked to the press before President Johnson's blue-ribbon commission had even settled into its quarters at the Veterans of Foreign Wars Building.[7]

The Secret Service agreed with the FBI's rendition of the shooting. That agency's official position was that all of the shots had come from the rear of the presidential motorcade. It also concurred that the first and third bullets had hit President Kennedy, and the second shot, a separate bullet, had wounded Governor Connally.[8] By the end of January the FBI's scale model of Dealey Plaza was ready for inspection in the Assembly Room on the first floor of the Veterans of Foreign Wars Building. This elaborate model, with accompanying visuals such as the panoramic aerial view of the entire assassination area and a brochure describing the exhibit's technical details, was a constant reminder to the Commission and the legal staff of the "true facts" of the assassination. The impressive 480-square-foot mock-up was designed as an architectonic testimonial to the Hoover version of the assassination.[9]

From February through June Commission staff lawyers worked intensively with the layout in the Assembly Room to construct the shooting sequence that had killed JFK and seriously wounded the governor. In order to pinpoint as closely as possible the time intervals between "the assassin's three shots," Commission lawyer Melvin A. Eisenberg, the point man for this area of the report, employed the use of some of the assassination films, most notably those taken by Abraham Zapruder, Orville O. Nix, and Mary Muchmore. Along with these films and slides made from the Zapruder film, Eisenberg enlisted the assistance of FBI and Secret Service agents, medical doctors, army ballistics experts, and one veterinarian.[10] During these five months the Commission groped toward validating its preconceived conclusion of one lone gunman despite the fact that a preponderance of the evidence pointed in another direction.

This lengthy exercise was bogus from its inception because the Commission lawyers agreed to ignore the bullet that had struck a curbstone and slightly wounded a bystander. The Tague bullet, or the "missed shot," was not accounted for in the FBI model of three shots and three hits. A fourth shot could only mean that there had been at least two assassins in Dealey Plaza.

The Warren report's own construction of the time span of the shooting realistically left room for no other conclusion. Whether the lapsed time between the second and third shots was 4.8 seconds or 5.6 seconds, as the report concluded, it still required a minimum of 2.3 seconds by the best of professional experts to cycle the alleged murder weapon. This time span does not allow for a fourth shot. The Commission did leave room for a fourth-shot scenario, but only if the first or the third shot missed the motorcade. Then, the report argued, the time span of the shooting had to be stretched to 7.1 to 7.9 seconds.[11] It is clear, however, that the Commission was not serious about a shooting span in excess of seven seconds, allowing for a fourth shot. If Oswald had squeezed off four rounds at the motorcade, how to account for only three spent cartridges, with none left in the rifle, found scattered around the book depository's sixth-floor "sniper's nest"? Would the assassin have delayed making his escape to wildly fire off another round after seeing the president's head explode seconds before with the third and unmistakably fatal shot? Still addressing the alternatives, the Commission posited that the least likely missed shot would have been the first shot because it was the easiest. The target was closest, and the element of surprise favored the assassin. Furthermore, Governor Connally, a witness whose testimony the Commission had to respect, insisted that he had heard the first shot and was adamant that it hit only JFK, whereas the second shot hit him. Mrs. Connally supported the governor's version in her Commission testimony.[12]

Although some of these points may invite debate, there is no question that the Commission knew about the curbstone shot early in its investigation. The Dallas FBI case officer for the JFK assassination, Robert P. Gemberling, included a section on the Tague bullet in a December 23, 1963, report on the status of the investigation. Gemberling titled that section of his report

"Information to the Effect One Bullet Fired During Assassination Went Wild, Crashed into Curb, and Struck Jim Tague." Although the FBI's CD 1 deliberately ignored the curbstone shot, Hoover was quick to remind Rankin that his office was furnished the Gemberling report—the director even cited the appropriate page numbers—when Tague and the "missed-shot" story became news in June 1964. Commission assistant counsel Arlen Specter confirmed this approach of deliberate ignorance when he suggested to Rankin that Tague should be deposed since he was one of two "witnesses mentioned in the early FBI reports" who had knowledge "on where the missing bullet struck."[13] Specter's memo was so understated and self-censoring that he did not even bother to note that Tague had been the third victim of the Dealey Plaza shooting. From the outset of the investigation there was a tacit agreement among the FBI, the Secret Service, and the Commission to leave Jim Tague to bleed in vain. The unspoken arrangement seemed to be that if the "missed shot" was ignored long enough and hard enough, it would go away.

Melvin A. Eisenberg may have been the most put-upon of the Commission lawyers. Tasked with constructing the shooting sequence that was consistent with the FBI model (three shots, three hits), with the physical and medical evidence, and with the Zapruder and Nix films of the assassination, Eisenberg was like a man dropped into the middle of a maze that had no exit. His assigned area of work was crucial for what would be Chapter 3 ("The Shots from the Texas School Book Depository") of the final report, one of the two most important chapters in this historic document. It was in Chapter 3 of the final report that the Commission presented its "very persuasive evidence from the experts" for the so-called single-bullet theory, the sine qua non for a no-conspiracy solution to the crime of Dallas.

Eisenberg had to be ever mindful that Chief Counsel Rankin had originally set a June 1 deadline for all staff reports.[14] The mortifying fact plaguing Eisenberg was that the single-bullet construction was being discredited even as the Commission staff lawyers were dreaming it up. One of the first problems that the staff members tussled with was their inability to account for what had happened to the first shot after it allegedly exited JFK's throat. Under the premise that the first shot penetrated only soft tissue in the president's neck, it should have ripped up the car after exiting his body, but it did not. In an aside to Inspector Thomas Kelley, the Secret Service's liaison with the Commission, one of the staff lawyers offered as "an outside possibility" that the first shot might have gone through JFK with sufficient velocity "to penetrate Connally's body, wrist and leg." Kelley later confided to the FBI's L. T. Gauthier that the idea was "ridiculous" and that a shot under those circumstances would have gone completely "wild."[15]

In April Eisenberg arranged for two sessions to determine which frames of the Zapruder movies captured the impact of the first and second bullets.

He enlisted the support of medical doctors for both sessions. In the April 14 conference the three pathologists who had performed the autopsy, Humes, Boswell, and Finck, viewed Zapruder's 8-mm movie and frames of the assassination for the first time. Since Humes had written the official autopsy protocol, he more or less took the lead in this session. After viewing the Zapruder film and studying the slides, the Bethesda navy doctor hypothesized that Connally had been hit by the first two shots. He thought that the first shot that had exited JFK's throat had then passed through Connally's chest, losing velocity in its flight, lodged itself in the governor's clothing, and later appeared on his stretcher. The second bullet, a separate shot, according to Humes's reconstruction, had hit Connally's wrist with such impact that it had shattered into fragments, one of these fragments causing the wound to the governor's left thigh. Just as they had testified before the Warren Commission a month earlier, Humes and the other two prosecutors had not changed their opinion about Connally's wrist wound. All three were convinced that the near-pristine CE 399 was not mutilated enough to have shattered the governor's wrist bone. Humes, Boswell, and Finck refused to attribute any magic to the "magic bullet."[16]

The Commission arranged for a second conference a week later. Governor Connally and Mrs. Connally were in town and agreed to attend the meeting and view the Zapruder film. The focus of attention for this conference was not on the Texas governor and his wife but rather on two ballistics experts, Dr. Joseph R. Dolce and Dr. Frederick W. Light, Jr., associated with the Biophysics Division at Edgewood Arsenal in Maryland. Dolce and Light were joined by Dr. Alfred G. Olivier, a veterinarian and chief of the division. Not satisfied with the Bethesda doctors' answers about Connally's wounds, the Commission called upon the U.S. Army to make available its most qualified experts on wounds sustained by military-type weapons. Others in attendance at this April 21 conference were two of Connally's Parkland Memorial Hospital physicians, Drs. Shaw and Gregory; several FBI agents; Rankin; McCloy; and Commission lawyers Norman Redlich, Eisenberg's supervisor, and junior counsels Arlen Specter, David Belin, and Eisenberg.[17]

Of the three Edgewood Arsenal resource people, Dolce was the most qualified. During World War II he had spent a three-year tour of duty as a battlefield surgeon in the Pacific Theater; he had retired from the army as a full colonel. In 1964 he was chairman of the army's Wounds Ballistic Board. When the Commission asked the army for its top ballistics man, it sent Dolce. He was regarded so highly as an expert on wounds from high-velocity weapons that it was "army rules," Dolce's words, that in the event of a serious injury to any VIP in Congress or in the administration, he was to "be called to go over the case."[18] Even though Dolce was still in government service at the time of the assassination, he never received a call from

Bethesda Naval Hospital. According to Dolce, the Commission lawyers were up front about what they wanted from him. He was summoned to provide the answers that the Commission wanted, and when he failed, he was ignored.

"Now, doctor," Dolce recalled the moment and his charge at the opening of the conference, "we want you to tell us exactly how this bullet traveled, the velocity lost during the period of travel. And why it came out as an . . . unmarked bullet." After reviewing the Zapruder film and discussing it with the Connallys, Dolce arrived at a conclusion that was unwelcome to the Commission lawyers. He concluded that two bullets had hit Connally: the first and second shots. Dolce's opinions echoed Humes's views expressed during the April 14 session. Dolce asserted, and Dr. Light agreed, that CE 399 could not have shattered the governor's wrist and still retained its virtually pristine condition. All of Dolce's thirty-three years as a surgeon and his work in wound ballistics argued against it.[19]

After the conference ended, Dolce and Light's collective experience and expertise in wounds ballistics did not carry the day with what Dolce referred to as some of the "legal talent" in attendance. The one who battled hardest, Dolce recalled, for CE 399 having produced all the nonfatal wounds in JFK and Connally was Arlen Specter. Only Dr. Olivier of the Edgewood Arsenal contingent withheld a conclusion until he had the opportunity to make some tests on animal tissue and bone with the Oswald rifle.[20]

At the close of the conference the three Edgewood experts were asked to carry out some experiments. They were given Oswald's Mannlicher-Carcano and one hundred 6.5-mm bullets to use for testing. Tests were carried out under the direction of Dr. Olivier, chief of the Wounds Ballistics Branch at Edgewood. Dolce later stated in his 1986 interview with Chip Selby that they had used Oswald's rifle and 6.5-mm ammunition to fire into ten cadaver wrists. He stressed to Selby that in each and every instance the bullet was "markedly deformed."[21]

On May 6 it fell to Philadelphia's former assistant district attorney to neutralize the Commission's most qualified witness's testimony on Connally's wrist wound. Shrewdly, Specter avoided crossing swords with Dolce and thereby allowing his testimony into the permanent record; he simply refused to call him as a Commission witness. Specter was at his masterful best when he led Drs. Olivier, Dziemian, and Light through the minefield that was Connally's wrist wound. Olivier, the veterinarian, and his assistant, Dr. Arthur J. Dziemian, a Ph.D. in physiology, both agreed that CE 399 had inflicted all seven nonfatal wounds on JFK and the governor.[22]

Dr. Light, a forensic pathologist and a young man with a promising future, was more guarded and crafty in his testimony. Dolce had a high regard for Light. He thought Light was "a brilliant man"—a doctor with both a medical degree and a Ph.D. in mathematics from Johns Hopkins University—whose career opportunities in government had been stifled because he was not afraid to speak his mind. It was Dolce's experience in government that in "conferences you cannot disagree too often. . . . Especially when you're discussing bullets before three-and-four-star generals."[23]

Light's very brief stint before the Commission was vintage "Good Soldier Schweik" (Jaroslav Hasek's hilarious account of a lowly wartime draftee who dutifully carried out his orders in a way calculated to subvert his commander's mission). Light began his response to Specter's questioning by agreeing with what his boss and Dziemian had said about CE 399—but not on the basis of "the anatomical findings as much as the circumstances." That is, on what he had been told: the relative positions of JFK and Connally at Zapruder frame 236 and the "appearance of the bullet that was found, presumably, the bullet was the one which wounded the Governor." Light's responses to Specter's questions took on Schweikian overtones:

> MR. SPECTER: And what about the whole bullet [CE 399] leads you to believe that the one bullet caused the President's neck wound and all the wounds on Governor Connally?
>
> DR. LIGHT: Nothing about the bullet. Mainly the position in which they were seated in the automobile.
>
> MR. SPECTER: So in addition to . . .
>
> DR. LIGHT: And the fact that the bullet that passed through the President's body lost very little velocity since it passed soft tissue, so that it would strike the Governor, if it did, with a velocity only, what was it, 100 feet per second, very little lower than it would have if it hadn't struck anything else first.

Either Light misspoke when he referred to the bullet's velocity reduced *to* one hundred feet per second, instead of saying its velocity was reduced *by* one hundred feet per second, or he was putting Specter on. A bullet moving one hundred feet per second might have enough kinetic energy to penetrate paper but not skin, let alone to shatter the radius, the hardest bone in the body to break.

> MR. SPECTER: Then do you think based on only the anatomical findings and the results of the tests which Dr. Olivier has performed that the scales are in equipoise as to whether the bullet passed through the President first and then through the Governor or passed only through the Governor?
>
> DR. LIGHT: Yes; I would say I don't feel justified in drawing a conclusion one way or the other on that basis alone.[24]

Dodging and weaving, Light was careful not to openly repudiate the opinions of Olivier and Dziemian based on their own administered Edgewood Arsenal tests. At the same time he was not willing to concede that it was possible for a bullet, especially at low velocity, to strike a bone such as the radius and remain in virtually pristine condition. He and Dolce had demonstrated this with the tests they had performed by firing 6.5-mm bullets from Oswald's rifle into cadaver wrists. It's important to note that Specter never asked any of these witnesses a single question about the results of the Dolce-Light tests on human cadavers.[25]

After the two April conferences the Commission lawyers drifted, as it were, in a Sargasso Sea, with no sure wind at their back and a nagging uncertainty as to whether landfall was just over the horizon. Contention and an underlying hysteria interfered with the day-to-day work of the Commission staff lawyers. Rankin's June 1 deadline was approaching, and a politically acceptable scenario of the shooting sequence still eluded them. Everything they had learned from Zapruder's movie, the ballistics experts Dolce and Light, the Bethesda doctors, and Governor Connally pushed them inexorably to the conclusion that the governor had been hit no later than Zapruder frame 236. Junior Counsel Specter was the only one who disagreed with this interpretation. There was a consensus regarding the first shot that had hit President Kennedy. The Commission was never able to pinpoint this exactly but assumed that JFK had been hit while hidden from Zapruder's lens when the limo passed behind the Stemmons Highway sign at Zapruder frames 215 to 225. Ultimately, the Commission arbitrarily settled on Zapruder 210 as the point where Kennedy had first been hit. Since the FBI laboratory established that Abraham Zapruder's Bell and Howell zoom-lens 8-mm camera took on average 18.3 frames every second, the lapsed time between the first shot that struck JFK (Z 210) and the last frame in which Connally could have been hit (Z 236) was less than two seconds.[26]

These parameters were not calculated to inspire relief or celebration. FBI firearms experts had established that the Oswald rifle required a minimum of 2.3 seconds to recycle between shots.[27] This inconvenient fact confronted the Commission with a pernicious Hobson's choice of its own making. One explanation was anathema politically: that Connally had been hit by a separate bullet fired by a second assassin. Banning this option, the Commission was left with one surviving alternative: The nonfatal bullet that struck Kennedy from the rear exited his body and continued in a downward trajectory, hitting Connally and causing all of the governor's wounds. In order to exorcise the demon of conspiracy, Rankin and his staff lawyers paid a heavy price in the coin of credibility. The Commission had no recourse other than to brush aside the April conferences and ignore the opinions and testimony of its own handpicked and most qualified expert medical and forensic witnesses.

There was staff pressure on Rankin to enlist the FBI's assistance in a reenactment of the assassination at the scene of the crime. Hoover, whose grip on the facts of the assassination was tenuous at best, regarded the idea of the April conferences as unadulterated "poppycock." The director and his senior assistant directors, Alex Rosen and Alan Belmont, were even more opposed to any reenactment. They knew that the story they had made up was impossible and wanted no part of any inquiry that could prove that their so-called investigation was no better than fiction. Hoover was satisfied that the Commission had the definitive answer to Dallas in that sprawling scale model of the crime scene occupying the Assembly Hall several floors below the room where the Commission went about its business. When Rankin sent out initial feelers about recruiting bureau personnel to help in collecting on-site data to resolve some "technical problems," he was told that the FBI would "prefer not to be involved in any such plan."[28] What Rankin characterized as "technical problems" centered on whether JFK and Connally were aligned at or near Zapruder frame 236, so that a shot from the southeast corner of the sixth floor of the Texas School Book Depository, the alleged "sniper's nest," could have penetrated both their bodies. Tentatively, the groundwork for the counterfeit history of CE 399 that the Commission advanced as an indispensable part of its "factual story" of the Kennedy assassination was being laid.[29]

In preparing for the Dallas reenactment, an issue that the Commission had been dodging finally surfaced as item five on the agenda for the April 30 executive session: "Autopsy Pictures of President Kennedy." Rankin started the discussion by pointing to the conflict arising from the April conferences. He limited his cautionary remarks to the conflicting testimony and opinions of Humes and Connally. Humes had speculated that both JFK and Connally had been hit by the first shot, whereas the governor was anchored in his belief that he had heard the first shot and it was the second bullet that had struck him. The chief counsel noted that he had heard from "the staff" that it was important to clear up this confusion by examining the JFK autopsy photos and X-rays. That same day, before the Commission had convened, Rankin had received a memo from Specter laying out in the strongest terms the argument that it was imperative that the autopsy pictures and X-rays be made available to selected members of the staff before the reenactment. Specter noted that it was "essential for the Commission to know precisely the location of the bullet wound on the President's back so the angle may be calculated." Otherwise, Specter wrote, he could not finish his part of the report with any confidence.[30] Comments made well after the Warren report was published revealed that Specter, Belin, and probably others on the staff were incredulous and resentful over the Commission's treatment of the autopsy material.[31]

The problem of the autopsy materials resided in Chairman Warren's determination to keep them, especially the photographs, out of the official record and thereby out of the public eye. Warren had viewed the autopsy pictures with horror. He was firm on this point, announcing to his fellow commissioners, "We don't want them in our record. It would make it a morbid thing for all time to come."[32] The chief justice's high-minded sentiments were respectful of the Kennedy family and laudable in that he did not want the nation to remember its slain president prone on a dissection table, exposing the enormity of his gaping wounds and his open eyes fixed in death. Rankin, who undoubtedly saw the photos and X-rays since the originals or at least copies were under his care, may have known or at least suspected that they contradicted the Commission's preconceptions about the crime. Although he respected Warren's position, the chief counsel was feeling the pressure from the staff, Specter in particular. Specter, the point man for the upcoming reenactment, had started his campaign in March for limited access to the autopsy material, especially any descriptions of JFK's back wound. Rankin realized that it could be a disastrous decision to forgo examining this crucial evidence and thereby fail to corroborate both the autopsy report and the conclusions of the Commission's own findings. If absolute accuracy was not the ne plus ultra Rankin aspired to in the Commission's investigation, he did want the report to "tell the story and to show why it is reasonable to assume that he [Oswald] did what the Commission concluded that he did."[33]

The facts about what ensued are somewhat muddled, but apparently shortly after the April 30 session the Commission came to some sort of understanding that satisfied Warren but permitted some limited (read "unofficial") access to some of the autopsy material, for key staff members only, during the reenactment at the scene of the crime. This approach meant that the Commission could maintain its public party line that it never saw or used the autopsy photographs or X-rays.

A little more than a week before Rankin, Redlich, and Specter left for Dallas, Specter sent a memo to General Counsel Rankin in which he laid out in detail what should be looked at when the autopsy photos and X-rays were examined. In the second point of his five-point memo Specter urged that the autopsy pictures and X-rays were essential "to confirm the precise location" of Kennedy's "upper back" wound as "depicted in Commission Exhibits 385 and 386." These were schematic drawings of President Kennedy's nonfatal wounds, of which more will be said shortly. It is not certain exactly what Specter saw of the autopsy pictures and X-rays when he was in Dallas during the May 24 reenactment. However, several years after the Commission had concluded its business, he acknowledged, in rather curious, lawyer-like language, that he had seen "one picture of the back of a body which was represented to be the back of the President, although it was not technically authenticated."[34]

Specter's tortured and coded construction is the language of plausible denial. He saw a picture, but he could not say for certain that it was genuine. If asked while under oath, as he was later when appearing before the House Select Committee on Assassinations (HSCA), whether he saw the autopsy pictures and X-rays, Specter could safely shave the truth and deny that they had ever been made available to him.[35] These comments support the speculation that an arrangement was struck between Rankin and Warren after the April 30 Commission executive session. Specter could see one of the autopsy pictures unofficially and surreptitiously to satisfy the needs of the reenactment and permit him to finish his report in confidence. At the same time, this "duplicitous bargain" allowed the Commission to publish its report without the photos and X-rays.

There is a puzzling and pungent irony to all of this Commission hugger-mugger. Using the autopsy picture, Specter was able to accurately pinpoint the precise location of the wound in JFK's back. That the autopsy picture was used in the May 24 reenactment is dramatically attested to by photograph Number 12 found in Chapter 8 of the Warren report. In the photograph two FBI stand-ins for President Kennedy and Governor Connally have chalk patches on their coats representing where the first shot hit JFK and allegedly continued through his body to enter under the governor's right armpit. The purpose of all this was to substantiate the proposition that the two men were in perfect alignment, making it possible for a single bullet to inflict all of their nonfatal wounds. Secret Service Inspector Thomas J. Kelley, who assisted in the May 24 reenactment, recalled that the chalk mark on JFK's stand-in "represented the point of the shot which wounded the President." The chalk mark, Kelley told the Commission, was based on the "medical drawings by physicians and people at Parkland" and an examination of the coat JFK was wearing at the time of the assassination. In this reenactment the coat on "President Kennedy" is not riding up his back.[36]

The chalk patch on "President Kennedy" is clearly located on his back at the level of the third thoracic vertebra, consistent with Dr. George G. Burkley's description of this wound in President Kennedy's death certificate—that same two-page document mentioned in Chapter 7, which the Commission inexplicably failed to include in its report or in the twenty-six volumes of Hearings and Exhibits. There is no mistaking this wound for a neck or lower-neck wound. The endgame of all this Byzantine maneuvering to use the autopsy picture of JFK's back wound was the unintended subversion of the Warren report's single-bullet hypothesis. A bullet entering Kennedy's back at the level of the third thoracic vertebra at a downward angle, not striking bone, could not possibly have exited his throat. The Commission's own reenactment black-and-white Number 12 photograph unmistakably underscored this aberration in its group-grope for a single-bullet, no-conspiracy solution. The reenactment picture allowed for no believable explanation of President Kennedy's throat wound. Furthermore, it had to be perfectly evident to Specter that the autopsy picture of Kennedy's back wound used in the reenactment was anatomically incompatible with CE 385 and CE 386. At this point the only explanation for Specter's insistence on the single-bullet invention was political need rather than fact.

As the Commission pressed forward with its facsimile of an investigation, it took on the appearance of a Rube Goldberg enterprise. In its devious and complex attempt to work through the traps and snares of its predetermined conclusions, it lost track of just how the pieces of its prosecutorial case were supposed to knit together. This defect centered in the fact that the Commission's modus operandi where the single-bullet fabrication was concerned was makeshift and improvisational.

This allegation can be documented best by juxtaposing photograph Number 12 against CE 385 and CE 386. These two Commission exhibits are schematic drawings of the entry and exit wounds to JFK's neck area. Dr. Humes dictated these drawings to a Bethesda naval medical artist. The Bethesda prosectors, essentially Humes, relied on these medical illustrations when testifying before the Commission because they were denied access to the autopsy pictures and X-rays. According to Humes's Commission testimony, the drawings depicted the trajectory of the nonfatal bullet (CE 399) entering Kennedy's lower neck at a downward angle and exiting his throat in the region of the Adam's apple.[37]

During Specter's and the commissioners' March 16 questioning, Humes repeatedly referred to these drawings when describing JFK's neck wounds. When McCloy asked the navy doctor if the bullet's trajectory took "roughly the line which is shown on your Exhibit 385," Humes's succinct response was "Yes, sir."[38] Even to the medically or forensically untrained eye it is patently obvious that the depictions of JFK's nonfatal wounds presumably produced by bullet CE 399 in photograph Number 12 and CE 385 and CE 386 are hopelessly irreconcilable. There simply is no way that these separate representations can coexist in the Commission's own permanent record without inviting skepticism of the deepest die.

Commissioner Jerry Ford spotted this "eccentricity" in the report's third draft where it asserted, "A bullet entered his back at a point slightly above the shoulder to the right of the spine." Ford edited this sentence to read, "A bullet entered the back of his neck slightly to the right of the spine." With just a few facile changes, Ford and the Reediting Committee were satisfied that photograph Number 12, based on Specter's prized autopsy picture, and Humes's much-exploited drawings—stand-ins for the best evidence—were now compatible and would travel well together.[39] The Rube Goldberg contraption of the official findings was now free to chug along into the annals of the nation's history.

It was Norman Redlich, Rankin's "top gun" among the assistant counsels, who pointed out in the strongest terms that the FBI model of the shooting was a rock tied around the Commission's neck. Redlich's memo to the general counsel urging him to abandon the FBI's and Secret Service's assertions that Connally had been struck by a separate bullet was written a week after the April 21 conference. He told Rankin that the FBI and Secret Service reports "were totally incorrect, and if left uncorrected, will present a completely misleading picture." Redlich did not pull his punches: If the Commission adopted the FBI model, it was his opinion that this "would place the report in jeopardy since it is a certainty that others will examine the Zapruder film and raise the same questions which have been raised by our examination of the film." The thrust of Redlich's memo was that the Commission had to go to Dallas and collect its own on-site data to establish that it would have been "physically possible" for Oswald to have accomplished what the Commission intended all along to attribute to him. "Our intention," he briefed Rankin, was "not to establish the point" at which JFK and Connally had been hit with the first shot "with complete accuracy, but merely to substantiate the hypothesis which underlies the conclusion that Oswald was the sole assassin." Since the FBI model of the shooting could not be jiggered to accommodate a single-bullet hypothesis, it had to be jettisoned.[40]

Before Rankin was able to coax Hoover to lend bureau support to a reenactment, a contingent of Commission members made a visit (May 7–9) to the scene of the crime. This was the first time any Commission members had visited Dallas in connection with the investigation. Commissioners John S. Cooper, John J. McCloy, and Allen Dulles were escorted by Junior Counsel David W. Belin. For two days, with Belin acting as guide, the commissioners did a walkabout, essentially familiarizing themselves with the physical layout of the assassination scene. The visit by the three Commission members drew media attention, and they made themselves available for a press conference at the end of the two days. Even Belin's report about the trip did not try to disguise the fact that the biggest payoff was its public relations advantage. Belin did let slip that when the commissioners took up the same vantage point that Howard Brennan, a highly touted key witness, had occupied while a Secret Service agent assumed Oswald's alleged position at the window "where the shots were fired, we could see the problem involved in identification."[41] It's safe to assume that Belin was referring to the fact that Brennan could not have determined the assassin's height, weight, and the clothes he was wearing from the waist down unless the Secret Service substitute was standing and pretending to shoot through a windowpane.

Rankin did get the FBI to cooperate in a reenactment of the assassination at the scene of the crime. The chief counsel promised to supervise the work and bring along certain staff members to help with on-the-spot examination and evaluation. Rankin selected Arlen Specter and Redlich, Specter's supervisor, to accompany him to Dallas. May 23 was the date they expected to arrive. Two days before the reenactment was scheduled (May 24), Rankin called a meeting that lasted three hours. Assistant Director Rosen learned from James R. Malley, the FBI's liaison with the Commission and one of the bureau's representatives at this lengthy conference, that there were still "a few gaps that remain." What Malley brushed aside as a piddling matter, or Rosen chose to downplay to avoid angering Hoover, was the fact that the Commission lawyers were now seriously entertaining the possibility that one of the three shots may have missed the presidential limousine entirely. In fact, this new development was the focus of the three-hour session.[42]

At 6 A.M. (CST) on May 24 the Dallas police cordoned off Elm Street, and for the next seven hours the Commission staff worked with FBI and Secret Service teams as they went through their paces in reenacting the government version of the assassination. The Zapruder film was used extensively in the restaging. The pertinent Zapruder frames were checked against known reference points in an effort to pinpoint the position of the presidential limousine and the relative positions of the president and Connally, especially from frames 207 through 313, the frame that depicts Kennedy's fatal headshot. At the end of the day Rankin, Redlich, and Specter were satisfied that they had discovered their "silver bullet." At or near Zapruder frame 222 JFK and Connally were aligned so that a shot from the "sniper's nest" striking the president could have exited his throat and gone through Connally's chest. It had previously been determined that the angle of the bullet traveling through the body of both victims was 17 degrees. At Zapruder 222 the angle from the "sniper's nest" to JFK's rear wound was also 17 degrees. In demonstrating a perfect JFK-Connally alignment at Zapruder 222, basic trigonometry, it could be said, helped play midwife to the single-bullet theory.[43]

Specter grasped this new piece of information as the keystone evidence supporting the Commission's initial and continuing premise that Oswald had been the lone triggerman. Early on in his Commission appointment the junior counsel had found himself solely responsible for laying out the fundamental arguments to support this conclusion. When the Commission began its work Francis W. H. Adams, a former assistant to the U.S. attorney general and later New York City's commissioner of police (1953–1954), was senior counsel for Area I of the investigation. Adams was Specter's nominal supervisor, tasked to bring together "the basic facts of the assassination." Adams's professional background made him eminently qualified for this section of the report, but by February he was beginning to distance himself from the work, and by May he had left the Commission to return to private legal practice with the Washington–New York law firm of Satterlee, Warfield, and Stephens. Adams was not the only Commission lawyer to leave before the report was in its final draft. When Albert E. Jenner and Leon D. Hubert left early, Rankin and Warren provided the other commissioners with an explanation for their premature departures, but Adams's departure seemed to draw no comment. It could have been innocent enough. Adams's law firm was involved in a major case, and the senior partners might have persuaded Adams to rethink his priorities. Whatever the reason for Adams's early abandonment of the Commission, it unfairly saddled Specter, who was facing demanding time pressures, with sole responsibility for this critical area of the investigation.[44]

By June Specter had finished his Area I draft report and turned it in to Rankin. He and Joe Ball were the only two staff lawyers whose draft reports met Rankin's June deadline. The report leaned heavily on the results of the May 24 reenactment and Specter's selective use of Drs. Olivier and Dziemian's experimental results from firing 6.5-mm ammunition from the alleged murder weapon into horsemeat, gelatin blocks, and goat carcasses. Olivier and Dziemian concluded that their tests results showed that CE 399 could have inflicted all seven nonfatal wounds without exhibiting any marked deformation. In his draft report Specter cited these test results and concluded that "all medical findings established" that one bullet had caused all the governor's wounds. His report took wide liberties with the truth, particularly when he noted that "the Army Wound Ballistics Experts" tests "on the wrists of human cadavers" proved that Connally's wrist wound "was not caused by a pristine bullet."

As mentioned before, these were clearly not the "medical findings" of the most qualified wound ballistics experts, Drs. Dolce and Light. Then again, Dolce's name did not appear in Specter's draft report. Specter's June 10 report was the Commission's in-house enthronement of the single-bullet construction. The results cited in the June 10 draft report were used to support the assumptions and conclusions appearing in the report's critical chapter: Chapter 3, "Three Shots from the Texas School Book Depository." Specter's assertions in the Warren report's Chapter 3 were an egregious distortion of the facts. The Olivier-Dziemian report (filed as CRDLR 3264) showed that when 6.5-mm bullets were fired through the radii of cadaver wrists they all manifested the classic signs of mushrooming. CRDLR 3264 did not appear in the Commission report or the twenty-six accompanying volumes. The Commission dared not print it because it destroyed the single-bullet hypothesis that was absolutely essential to the Warren report's lone-assassin explanation. The Olivier-Dziemian report was not declassified until eight years after the Commission had released its report to the American people.[45]

Some years later, when the House Select Committee on Assassinations re-examined the Kennedy assassination, Dr. Dolce tried to set the record straight on the Edgewood Arsenal tests. Then living in retirement in Riviera Beach, Florida, Dolce wrote his U.S. senator, Lawton Chiles (D–Fla.), to say that he would like to appear before the special committee and "give them his thoughts." Chiles passed this request on to Congressman Richardson Preyer (D–N.C.), a member of the committee, along with Dolce's letter charging that Drs. Olivier and Dziemian had cooked the results of the Edgewood Arsenal tests so they would be consistent with the "one bullet theory." The gravamen of Dolce's charge was that the original "write-up" of the ballistics testing in the original fifty-five-page Edgewood report had been altered before the report was turned over to the Warren Commission. Dolce wanted to share the original report with the House committee.[46] But for its own, unexplained reasons, the special House committee was not interested in learning citizen Dolce's thoughts on this matter. Dolce was never called as a witness or deposed by HSCA staffers.

Even before the May reenactment the Commission and its staff lawyers were no longer hostage to Hoover's and the FBI's three-shots-and-three-hits assassination scenario. In its defense, the Commission had reason not to place unconditional trust in the FBI's investigative record in the case. Aside from Earl Warren's characterization of CD 1 as "skeletal," there were investigative lapses and acts of deliberate suppression of evidence that the Commission had to finesse or explain away in putting its report together. The FBI's failure to retrieve the missing Tippit bullets, the fact that Connally's clothes were ignored until their evidentiary value was largely compromised, and Frazier's admission that the FBI firearms team did not swab the barrel of the suspected murder weapon to see if it had been used in the assassination were reasons enough for the Commission's skepticism about the bureau's investigative methods. In the final accounting, of course, none of the FBI's bumbling—if that is what it was—and deception played a part in the Commission's discarding the FBI's construction of the shooting. The Commission could only live with a scenario that allowed for one assassin. The single-bullet explanation provided this solution. Just as the Commission rejected the opinions of its own expert witnesses, it would abandon the FBI model of the shooting that had Connally struck by a separate bullet.

The Commission's rejection of the FBI's construction of the shooting sequence did not have to mean that CD 1 was flawed in every instance. It is possible that FBI laboratory testing of the evidence made a persuasive forensic case for Connally being struck by a separate bullet. The record revealed that FBIHQ received crime-scene evidence immediately after the assassination. A day after the assassination the FBI Crime Laboratory (BuLab) in Washington, D.C., had a fragment from Connally's right arm, the bullet allegedly found on Connally's stretcher (CE 399), five bullet fragments found in the president's limo, two fragments recovered from the president's head at autopsy, and JFK's clothes. The FBI wasted no time in subjecting this evidence to ballistic and spectrographic analysis.[47] By the Tuesday following the assassination, for example, BuLab had run a spectrographic analysis on Kennedy's clothes, reporting "copper in minute traces surrounding the holes" in his coat.[48] Results of these tests were made available to the Secret Service so it could complete its report of the assassination and file it with the Commission. The Secret Service report, as mentioned before, agreed with the FBI's assertion that three shots were fired and all of them hit either JFK or the governor, Connally being struck by a separate bullet.[49]

After the Commission went public with its report, neither agency about-faced on the Connally bullet and rushed to embrace the single-bullet theory. For instance, on the third anniversary of the tragedy in Dallas, *Life* magazine urged a review of Kennedy's assassination based on Connally's reiteration of his Warren Commission testimony that he had been struck by the second bullet and not the first shot, which hit only the president. When the FBI's clipping service bucked this story up to Hoover, the director wrote at the bottom of the memo, "We don't agree with the Commission as it says one shot missed entirely & we contend all 3 shots hit." (Hoover underlined "it" twice, venting his exasperation with the Commission.)[50] The fact that the Commission and the FBI, the Commission's investigative arm, never arrived at a consensus on this crucial aspect of the assassination means that the government's investigation cannot stand up to doubt. By the Commission's own admission, if JFK and Connally were hit by separate bullets, then the official explanation of the assassination of President John F. Kennedy cannot be true. This disconnect between the Commission and the FBI on the shooting sequence explains why the FBI's five-volume report on the assassination (CD 1) did not appear in the Commission's twenty-six volumes of Hearings and Exhibits. What other explanation can there be for this omission?

Test results from FBI microscopic examinations and spectrographic analysis should have eliminated confusion and distrust about what happened in Dallas. To the Commission's discredit, the evidence it entered into the permanent record, as well as the evidence it ignored, fosters nothing but doubt, disbelief, and distrust. Firearms identification expert Robert A. Frazier spent more hours testifying before the Commission than any of the other dozen or so expert FBI witnesses, including the director, with the exception of photographic expert Lyndal L. Shaneyfelt. Frazier was a twenty-three-year veteran of the bureau and the senior examiner of the Firearms and

Toolmarks Unit of the Physics and Chemistry Section of the FBI Crime Laboratory. Over his two decades in the bureau Frazier had made between fifty thousand and sixty thousand ballistic comparisons and testified for the prosecution in probably hundreds of court cases around the country.

Frazier was trained and practiced in giving testimony that frustrated defense lawyers, and he knew his way around a courtroom.[51] He made two lengthy appearances before the Commission. The first was on March 19 and the second on May 13, about the time that Commission counsels began their early flirtation with the single-bullet invention. In March Eisenberg led Frazier through all the characteristics of Oswald's Mannlicher-Carcano rifle (CE 139). The FBI's ballistics expert testified that despite the fact that the weapon showed "aspects of wear and corrosion" and had a defective scope, it was very reliable and had "very adequate killing power."[52] Frazier asserted in a convincing manner that the defect in CE 139's telescopic sight actually favored the marksmanship of the shooter.[53]

Under questioning, Frazier went on record assuring Counsel Eisenberg that CE 399 had been fired from Oswald's rifle to the exclusion of all other rifles. He discussed the range of weights of 6.5-mm bullets such as CE 399 and noted that the bullet in question had lost only several grains from its original weight. When Eisenberg asked about the defacement of CE 399, Frazier responded, "It is hardly visible," only "slightly flattened or twisted." The ballistics expert was describing the near-pristine bullet that reputedly produced all the nonfatal wounds in two men, shattering Connally's wrist and destroying four inches of his fifth rib. According to one of the governor's surgeons, Dr. Charles Gregory, Connally's fifth rib was "literally shattered by the missile." A few minutes later in his testimony Frazier slipped into an inconsistency when he expanded on the arcane science of ballistics for the commissioners, noting that "even a piece of coarse cloth, leather or some other object" can leave marks on a bullet.[54]

In setting the stage for this line of questioning, Eisenberg asked if Frazier needed to prepare CE 399 in any way for examination. What followed was an exchange that can only be characterized as an exercise in bad faith on the part of the Commission in its professed search for the truth:

MR. EISENBERG: Did you prepare the bullet in any way for examination? That is, did you clean it or in any way alter it?

MR. FRAZIER: No, sir; it was not necessary. The bullet was clean and it was not necessary to change it in any way.

MR. EISENBERG: There was no blood or similar material on the bullet when you received it?

MR. FRAZIER: Not any which would interfere with the examination, no, sir. Now there may have been slight traces which could have been removed just in ordinary handling, but it wasn't necessary to actually clean blood or tissue off of the bullet.[55]

Eisenberg never faltered or showed surprise at this and went on with a new line of questioning. Eisenberg was anything but slow on the uptake. He was a graduate of Harvard Law School, a member of Phi Beta Kappa, and former editor of the *Harvard Law Review*. The assistant counsel had been an associate of a New York City law firm when he came to the Commission. His legal background and expertise may not have been in criminal law, but to compensate for this deficiency, he and Redlich had been burning the midnight oil to familiarize themselves with the finer points of ballistics and firearms identification.[56] He knew that any residue on a bullet such as CE 399 with its storied past should have been sent to BuLab and subjected to analysis to determine whether the material was from human tissue or bone. On the face of it, Frazier's comment that it had been wiped clean so it would "not interfere with the examination" should have provoked some serious questions. How was it possible for CE 399 to have been wiped clean as it passed from the hospital to the Secret Service, then to the FBI? Who was responsible for this destruction of crucial evidence? Eisenberg never faltered or showed surprise at this and went on to a new line of questioning, but he soon returned to the point at issue.

Eisenberg's failure to probe for answers imported into the Commission's investigative record a damaging impression that it should have moved heaven and earth to avoid. Unless there were hidden factors in play, the Eisenberg-Frazier exchange disclosed that the Commission's own firearms expert could not be trusted to properly handle crucial evidence. Earlier the Commission had demonstrated that it would ignore its own medical witnesses and experts in forensic pathology when their opinions failed to support the lone-gunman solution to the assassination. With Frazier the Commission was ready to suspend any doubt or ignore any questions about his bona fides and the credibility of his testimony. Were these inconsistencies accidental? Were they all innocent and explainable?

Eisenberg returned to the matter of the "clean" CE 399 later in his questioning to elicit from Frazier that CE 399 still retained some foreign material:

> MR. EISENBERG: You mentioned there was blood or some other substance
> on the bullet marked 399. Is this an off-hand determination, or was
> there a test to determine what the substance was?
> MR. FRAZIER: No, there was no test made of the materials.[57]

Eisenberg's response to this revelation was no response at all. He simply moved on to another area of questioning. It was as though the assistant counsel was sleepwalking through a minefield, oblivious to all the sirens and bells and whistles sounding an alarm. He never asked why the FBI had shown no interest in the nature of the residue carried in the grooves in CE 399. Why BuLab had not made the necessary tests was never asked. Could the residue be associated with either President Kennedy's or Connally's body? Here was the best evidence to settle the question of whether both victims had been struck by the same bullet. Chairman Warren, Boggs, and Mc-Cloy, who attended this Commission session, proved as incurious as the seemingly distracted and feckless assistant counsel.

Frazier testified that he wiped clean "a slight residue of blood or some other material" adhering to two fragments (CE 567 and CE 569) found in the front seat of the presidential limousine. Both fragments, according to his testimony, had been fired from Oswald's Mannlicher-Carcano to the exclusion of all other rifles. Because of their mutilated condition Frazier said he could not determine whether they had come from one or two bullets. Because of their size and weight they could not have come from the whole bullet (CE 399). The fragment CE 569, found beside the front seat, weighed 21.6 grains. CE 567, found under the front seat cushion, weighed 44.6 grains.[58]

It was clear that Eisenberg and Commissioner McCloy were jolted when Frazier reported that he could not determine whether CE 567 and CE 569 had come from one or two bullets. Since bullets inside bodies do strange things, it is possible that these two fragments were from the fatal shot to JFK's head. However, the medical evidence did not favor this interpretation. Just three days before Frazier testified, the Commission had heard from the Bethesda doctors. Humes noted that the X-ray of Kennedy's brain revealed "tiny fragments . . . dispersed through the substance of the brain . . . extremely minute, less than 1 mm. in size for the most part." Humes estimated that there were "between 30 to 40 dust-like particle fragments" in JFK's head. FBI agent James W. Sibert, who was assigned to the Bethesda morgue during the autopsy, recalled in a more graphic fashion that the JFK X-rays revealed "flecks like the Milky Way." The autopsy doctors, Sibert remembered, were puzzled that a copper-jacketed, military-type bullet such as CE 399 had disintegrated so completely.[59]

The most likely forensic possibility was that these two fragments were from separate bullets. One of these bullets could have been the missile that struck only Connally and was responsible for the shattering of his radius. This would explain why the FBI's and Secret Service's descriptions of the shooting insisted on three shots and three hits, with one of the three bullets hitting only the governor. It satisfied the need to explain the three spent cartridges found in the vicinity of the "sniper's nest" and provided a more plausible, well-grounded inference that a pristine bullet had torn into the governor at full velocity, producing the massive damage Connally's wrist sustained in the shooting. As mentioned previously, the Bethesda prosectors, as reported by the FBI agents Sibert and Francis X. O'Neill, could not find an exit for the bullet that had struck Kennedy in the back.[60] This piece of information favored CD 1's description of the shooting sequence. Laboratory analysis, of course, of the "blood and some other material," to use Frazier's throwaway lines, adhering to the fragments could have resolved this critical impasse—or it could have wrecked the official fabrication beyond repair if the residue proved to be only Connally's blood.

The uncertain history of these two fragments must have produced a pit-of-the-stomach panic among the Commission and its lawyers. If CE 567 and CE 569 were from separate bullets, then elementary math tilted heavily toward a shooting scenario involving at least five shots: the missile that disintegrated in JFK's head, the whole bullet allegedly found in Connally's stretcher, the two bullets that fragmented into CE 567 and 569, and the Tague bullet, or the missed shot, that was not allowed on the table for discussion. Sensing that they were approaching a hidden third rail, McCloy and Eisenberg abandoned their interest in this line of discussion and moved the questioning of Frazier on to other matters.

As will soon be developed, there was no mystery about the origin of these bullet fragments, at least as far as Frazier was concerned. When Frazier testified in March he knew that these fragments along with other physical specimens critical to the case had been subjected to the highly sensitive neutron activation analysis (NAA) during secret tests conducted under FBI auspices at the Oak Ridge National Laboratory in Tennessee. The Commission did not learn about these tests until September, when its report was ready for the publisher. But Frazier knew by December 1963 or January 1964, when the results of the Oak Ridge lab tests were available, that the Commission's case against Oswald and the no-conspiracy conclusion were forensically untenable. Consequently, his only fallback position on CE 567 and CE 569 was to feign uncertainty.

In May, two months later, Frazier was back testifying again. The Commission counted on his testimony to prop up, to use Redlich's words, "the conclusion that Oswald was the lone assassin." This time Specter did the questioning. The purpose of this May 13 session was to establish for the record that all of the recovered bullet fragments in evidence, CE 399, and the lead residue on the inside of the car's windshield had all originated from a common source. Specter painstakingly guided Frazier over this difficult and critical evidentiary terrain. The thirty-four-year-old former assistant district attorney's performance left no doubt that he would have a promising future.

Specter showcased his skills not only in how he structured his questions but with the questions he should have asked but did not. There is every reason to suspect that Specter spent time coaching Frazier before the FBI agent was sworn in and went on the permanent record. Their entire colloquy resonated with that quality of, well, "inside baseball"—nothing either man would want to have to explain to the public or a determined defense lawyer had Oswald lived to have a trial.

Specter used Frazier in this Commission session to introduce into the record secondhand testimony in the area of scientific testing in which Frazier had no expertise. The line of questioning dealt with the results of the analytical spectrographic examination of the bullet fragments entered into evidence in the crime. The spirit of the American legal philosopher John Henry Wigmore was nowhere in evidence when Specter led the FBI's senior ballistics examiner through his May 13 testimony. Wigmore, whose name was synonymous for twentieth-century American lawyers with the law of evidence, was credited with the legal axiom that cross-examination of a witness with firsthand information was the greatest engine for uncovering the truth. The Commission was satisfied to forgo this process and allow Frazier the widest latitude to interpolate the results of these scientific tests. Years later, when Frazier was deposed under oath, he casually explained that his stand-in performance for FBI spectrographic specialist John F. Gallagher was "to save time, as far as I know . . . instead of having Gallagher go up and testify to a very short period of time, I related what his report showed."[61]

Specter began by asking Frazier for the results of his comparative examination of CE 399 and the bullet fragments found in the president's car. Frazier responded that the "lead fragments were similar in composition."[62] The lead residue recovered from the inside of the windshield was also, according to Frazier, found to be "similar in composition" to the lead in CE 399 and the fragments from the limousine.[63] Specter next turned to the fragment removed from Connally's wrist and asked for Frazier's expert opinion. The best Frazier could do with this fragment (CE 842) was to say it was "consistent" with CE 399 and one of the fragments (CE 567) found in the front seat on the driver's side of the presidential limousine.[64] Specter then had Frazier associate the two fragments removed from JFK's head wound in the autopsy room, which were later delivered to FBIHQ by Special Agents Sibert and O'Neill, with the other fragments and the whole bullet. Frazier attested that these fragments (CE 843), when compared with all of the other spectrographically examined fragments, "were found to be similar in metallic composition." This dense and intermittently obfuscating line of questioning culminated with Frazier testifying that all the fragments, the lead smear on the windshield, and the lead he had cratered from the base of CE 399 were "similar in metallic composition."[65]

A question Frazier was not asked was whether the fragment reportedly recovered from Connally's wrist had come from CE 399, the bullet allegedly found on the governor's stretcher. One explanation for this glaring omission is that Specter might have been warned off about asking the veteran FBI agent this question. Frazier may have intimated or told Specter outright when they were preparing for his May 13 Commission testimony that he would not or could not break with the official Hoover FBI position that Connally had been struck by a separate bullet. The cardinal rule of the Hoover FBI, as repeatedly noted by students of the agency, was "Don't embarrass the Bureau." There was a corollary that all FBI personnel, from street agents to assistant directors, were governed by during the Hoover era—in all agency matters, "cover the Bureau's ass and cover your own ass." With any infraction of this "rule" an agent, regardless of seniority, could face summary dismissal or be posted to some undesirable field office. Butte, Montana, was one of Director Hoover's favorite "gulags" for backsliding agents. The other, more incriminating explanation, which Frazier would have not shared with Specter, was that the Oak Ridge NAA test results disclosed that Connally's wrist fragment could not have come from CE 399. (This issue is discussed in more detail later in the chapter.)

As a lawyer and big-city prosecutor in his own right, Specter knew that Frazier's testimony verged on the meaningless. All the FBI witness was really saying was that all the samples he had examined were of lead composition. Specter was certainly aware, as was Frazier, that there are hundreds of different compositions of lead in manufactured bullets. Any probative scientific results that would have stood up in a court of law, where the rules of evidence were in play, would have had to show that the lead in the bullet or fragments came from the same batch of lead and that the composition, beginning with the lead, was therefore the same—identical! Not similar! Specter tried prodding Frazier in that direction when he asked, "Is it possible to state with any more certainty whether or not any of those fragments came from the same bullet?" Frazier's response was not helpful: "Not definitely, no; only that they are of similar lead composition." Frazier was actually testifying that the fragments were *not* from the same bullet. For reasons already mentioned, Specter never quizzed Frazier on his opinions about CE 567 and CE 569 other than to elicit the statement that their lead content was similar to all the other fragments and the whole bullet. Aware of the FBI agent's March Commission testimony, Specter had no interest in opening this Pandora's box again.[66]

Had the government's investigation into the JFK assassination made truth its only goal, the Commission would have conducted its business differently. It would have worked first from the best evidence to build a case for posthumous conviction of Oswald instead of manipulating, screening, suppressing, and retrofitting expert witnesses' testimony and the evidence to accommodate a preordained verdict. The Commission should have heard from

FBI spectrographer John F. Gallagher as soon as Frazier had finished his testimony. In 1964, spectrographic analysis was recognized as a refined scientific technique capable of proving whether tested substances could or could not have a common origin. The technique was used to determine the percentage or quantitative measurement of chemical elements present in a sample, the relative concentrations of these elements, and the absence of detectable concentrations of elements. Frazier testified that Gallagher had run spectrographic analysis on all the fragments, the whole bullet, and Kennedy's clothes the day after the assassination. Gallagher had submitted his findings to Frazier, who "prepared the formal report of the entire examination." It was Gallagher's results that Frazier relied upon to prepare for his second appearance before the Commission; he did not have the report before him during his May testimony. This, of course, did not surprise or deter Specter one bit. Frazier was Specter's indispensable lodestar. If Gallagher had been called as a witness and asked under oath the real meaning of some of those reports, the Warren report's conclusions would have been in jeopardy. The Commission lawyer's strategy and sole purpose was to implant the impression that the FBI's scientific spectrographic results (somewhere out there in the ether) buttressed Frazier's testimony in every instance. Specter did not leave hanging any doubts or questions about the fate of Gallagher's report and Frazier's "formal report." Both, Frazier assured him, would be "a part of the permanent record of the FBI."[67] Nothing, it is almost needless to say, was said about the more specific and scientifically sensitive secret NAA testing.

Neither report can be found in the Commission's documents, the Warren report, or the twenty-six volumes of Hearings and Exhibits. It was incumbent on the Commission, charged with passing judgment and bringing closure to the tragedy of Dallas, to include in its report a complete and lucid presentation of these scientific tests. Is it a safe assumption that this omission meant that Gallagher's supervised tests—both spectrographic analysis and even the more sensitive NAA tests—did not support the incriminating inferences Specter assigned to them with hard scientific evidence? An internal FBI memo went a long way in answering this question.

In July 1964 Ivan W. Conrad, assistant chief of BuLab, was reminded by his assistant that Gallagher's test results "did not permit a positive finding or statement that any given small fragment did in fact come from one of the bullets to the exclusion of the others." The most positive spin that could be placed on the results was "a probability that the fragment from the Governor's arm came from the whole bullet [CE 399] rather than from the mutilated bullet." Since the memo lacked specificity, it could have been referring to either CE 567 or 569, or, generically, to both. The Commission, including Specter, knew long before this that Gallagher's results could not support the burden of proof with positive evidence that Oswald's rifle had been used in the assassination. In early February Rankin asked Hoover for detailed laboratory evidence that Oswald's rifle had been used. Hoover responded that the spectrographic examination showed that the two fragments recovered from JFK's head and the lead core from CE 399 were "comparable in composition" but that this was "not sufficient to definitely establish that they are from a bullet fired from Oswald's gun."[68] Without clear proof that all five fragments found in the car and the two removed from Kennedy's head at autopsy had a common origin, the Warren report is irreparably compromised.

With nothing but inconclusive test results to disclose, there is no mystery about why Gallagher was never called before the Commission to testify. Redlich eventually deposed him on September 15, 1964, in the privacy of the assistant counsel's office. The galley proofs of the report were already prepared for the printer when the Commission solicited Gallagher's firsthand testimony. What prompted the Commission's interest in Gallagher had nothing to do with his examination of the bullet fragments. The sudden urgency to get his comments on record stemmed from test results on the paraffin casts made on Lee Harvey Oswald.

In December 1963 the FBI contracted with a private firm from New York to run NAA tests on the paraffin casts, bullet fragments from the presidential limo, Connally's wrist, JFK's head, and the president's clothes. The New York firm did the testing in secret at the Atomic Energy Commission's (AEC) Oak Ridge National Laboratory in Tennessee. As mentioned before, even the Commission was kept in the dark about the tests and the results. Gallagher brought the samples to the Oak Ridge lab and remained with them until the testing was complete.[69]

Gallagher's September testimony was choreographed to allow him to do some last-minute damage control relating to whether Oswald had fired a weapon the day of the assassination. The "evidence file" on this question was no more conclusive than other physical evidence the Commission worked with as it pursued its investigation. Paraffin tests authorized by the Dallas police on Oswald's right cheek and both hands emerged, in fact, as an overpowering problem for the FBI and the Commission. Dr. Morton S. Mason, director of the Dallas County Criminal Laboratory, had processed Oswald's paraffin casts. The paraffin test was a standard police examination that had been used since 1933 to determine whether a suspect had fired a weapon. If the tests showed the presence of nitrates (gunshot residue) in higher concentrations than might normally be expected on the hands or cheek, then the probability was that that person had recently fired a weapon or handled one that had recently been discharged. The test on the paraffin casts from Oswald's hands showed positive for both hands, "typical," according to the Dallas police report, "of the patterns produced in firing a revolver." But Dr. Mason's report on the cast of Oswald's right cheek showed no traces of nitrates.[70]

The problem confronting the Commission was that paraffin testing is unreliable in that heavier concentrations of nitrates can be accounted for by exposure to common substances including rust, urine, soap, sugar, cloth, and printed matter such as books.[71] Whatever Oswald did or did not do on that terrible Friday, it is certain that he handled books; that was what he was paid to do, fill textbook orders for Dallas County's public schools. A negative nitrate test such as the one on Oswald's right cheek is exculpatory unless it can be proven that the cheek was thoroughly washed before the tests were administered. However, this caveat applies only if the paraffin casts are tested by spectrographic analysis. If the casts are subjected to the more sensitive and highly specific NAA testing, washing the face or hands will not compromise this procedure if the tests are run even two to two and a half hours after initial exposure.

The Commission's dilemma was further complicated by BuLab reports that the firing pin in Oswald's .38 Special was defective and had failed to strike the cartridges "with sufficient force to fire them." The FBI ballistic tests on the three bullets recovered from slain Dallas police officer Tippit could not definitely tie Oswald's revolver to the crime. According to Conrad's assistant, R. H. Jevons, "No conclusion could be reached as to whether or not these bullets were fired from Oswald's revolver."[72]

The issue of Oswald's paraffin casts became a problem for Commission staffers Redlich and Eisenberg, who were responsible for this area of the report. The Commission was counting on the more highly sensitive and discriminating NAA procedure to make a clear determination of whether Oswald had actually fired a weapon. By July, when the staff lawyers were putting together the final draft of the Commission's findings, Redlich found himself in a quandary about how to smooth over test results that pointed more in the direction of Oswald's exculpation than incrimination. He wrote Commissioner Dulles, referring to the NAA results on the paraffin casts, "At best the analysis shows that Oswald may have fired a pistol, although this is by no means certain." But even more deflating for the harried assistant counsel was the fact that "there is no basis for concluding that he also fired a rifle."[73]

Confronted with scientific evidence that tilted strongly in the direction of exculpating Oswald, the Commission's sense of urgency became acute. On September 5, when the report was already in galley proofs, Eisenberg laid out for Redlich a series of questions for the FBI. The first on the list was "A description of the neutron activation tests," followed by the equally revealing and astonishing inquiry "When the test (NAA) was performed on the paraffin cast." The report was already written, and the Commission lawyers responsible for proving that Oswald had fired weapons the day of the assassination had not even seen for themselves the results of these scientific tests. Moreover, it was not until March that the Commission learned from Hoover that NAA tests had been conducted at Oak Ridge National Laboratory in December and early January 1964! If Rankin had asked Hoover at an earlier date for the full information from the Oak Ridge lab tests, he must have been put off and let the matter drop. In March the director notified the general counsel not to expect too much from NAA. The occasion for Hoover's passing judgment on NAA arose when Eisenberg, uneasy because FBI spectrographic analysis failed to show any copper around the slits in JFK's collar that could be attributed to a copper-jacketed bullet such as CE 399, asked Gallagher if the more sensitive NAA would show that a bullet had passed through the perforations in the collar. Hoover, at his stonewalling best, informed Rankin, "It was not felt" that NAA "would contribute substantially to the understanding of the origin of this hole and frayed area."[74]

Hoover had his reasons for trying to convince Rankin that NAA testing was a new analytical technique that FBI Crime Laboratory personnel were convinced promised more by way of scientific exactitude than it could deliver.[75] When the director wrote to Rankin dismissing NAA testing he was aware of the results of the Oak Ridge tests on Oswald's paraffin casts for his hands and right cheek, which had been disclosed in a March 6, 1964, FBI report. The report noted, "The deposits found on the paraffin casts from the hands and cheek of Oswald could not be specifically associated with the rifle cartridges." Lacking any other plausible explanation, the only tenable conclusion that could be drawn from the Oak Ridge tests was that Oswald had not fired a rifle on the day of the assassination. These more scientifically sophisticated results were consistent with the results reported on November 23, 1963, by Dallas's Dr. Morton Mason's testing of the paraffin casts.[76]

Truth to tell, FBI Washington's reluctance to engage the Oak Ridge facilities to run NAA testing had nothing to do with BuLab's reservations about the scientific efficacy of this relatively new analytical technique. The concern at FBIHQ was that the tests would underscore to an even higher degree of scientific probability the likelihood that Oswald had not fired a rifle the day JFK was assassinated. The FBI had a standing arrangement with the AEC that gave the bureau ready access to its facilities upon request. However, it was the AEC, not the FBI, that offered (insisted might be the more accurate characterization) its Oak Ridge facilities for NAA testing of Oswald's paraffin casts and other physical evidence in the case. Jevons laid out the dilemma confronting the bureau when he noted that "highly placed individuals in the AEC charged with developing neutron activation analyses" were anxious to demonstrate the usefulness of NAA testing. Jevons reported that he had already received numerous inquiries from AEC representatives offering the use of their facilities. If BuLab refused this offer, Jevons feared that Oak Ridge would go public with questions about why the FBI had rejected the best opportunity to obtain the most scientifically significant data in the murder of an American president. In view of these developments, Jevons recommended that the Bureau go ahead and authorize NAA testing. Placing the best face on the situation, Jevons noted that "Oswald . . . is now dead and there will be no trial" (and therefore no courtroom examination of the evidence and test results) and the assurance that "the information and dissemination of the results will be under complete FBI control."[77] As we will see, the FBI and the Commission conspired to suppress the results of the NAA testing. They do not appear in the Warren report or in the twenty-six volumes of Hearings and Exhibits.

There was an additional factor that forced the Commission to get the FBI's spectrographic specialist, John F. Gallagher, on record. The prompt came from within the Commission and could not be ignored. In early September Senator Russell notified Rankin and Warren that he could not support the single-bullet construction and requested that a special executive session be convened so he could explain the reasons for his dissent. Russell was firm in his belief that Oswald was involved in the assassination, but he was equally persuaded that the FBI had deceived the Commission on the ballistic evidence. His skepticism about the report's assertion that one bullet had caused all the nonfatal wounds to Connally and Kennedy was heavily influenced by Connally's unyielding contention that he had been struck by a separate bullet. Russell's reservations were shared by Senator Cooper and, to a lesser degree, Congressman Hale Boggs. Rankin, determined that the Commission's findings not raise a shadow of a doubt by any publicized division within its ranks, would devise a way to deceive Russell into believing that his dissent would be incorporated into the report's conclusions. But Russell's disagreement on the ballistic evidence only further underscored the Commission's urgency to strengthen its case against Oswald as the lone assassin.[78]

It was Gallagher's last-minute testimony—he was literally the last witness the Commission questioned—that was imported into the final draft of the Commission's Volume 15 of the Hearings and Exhibits to explain away all of these evidentiary shortcomings. The Commission depended on Gallagher's testimony to insert into the record the explanation that paraffin testing was not reliable. The Commission's purpose could not have been clearer: It wished to neutralize the Dallas police report on the paraffin cast of Oswald's right cheek. The Commission and the FBI felt confident that they could safely control by suppression the Oak Ridge test results, but the independent testing of Oswald's paraffin casts authorized by the Dallas Police Department was another matter. As mentioned above, Dr. Mason's report included the disclosure that the cast of Oswald's right cheek had shown no traces of barium or antimony, nitrate residues that should have been present if Oswald had fired a rifle. Gallagher did not disappoint. He assured Redlich that the Oak Ridge tests showed gunshot residues (barium and antimony) in Oswald's hand casts in greater amounts than one would expect to find on the hands of a person who had not fired a weapon. As for Oswald's right cheek cast, Gallagher's verdict was that it was inconclusive as to whether Oswald had fired a rifle. But during his brief session with Redlich, which only lasted the better part of an hour, Gallagher did not, because he dared not, categorically say that Oswald had fired a weapon. The best Redlich could elicit from this eighteen-year FBI veteran was that Oswald "may have either handled a fired weapon, or fired a weapon."[79]

Gallagher's Commission testimony was carried out in incriminating haste. Gallagher should have been one of the early witnesses had the Commission really been interested in uncovering the truth of Kennedy's assassination. He had supervised the NAA tests that were run at the Oak Ridge National Laboratory. This December-January NAA testing involved more than the paraffin casts, which were the only subject discussed at Gallagher's September 15 private session with Redlich. According to FBI Director Clarence M. Kelley, Hoover's successor at the bureau, other physical evidence central to the crime, such as CE 399 (Connally's alleged stretcher bullet), the bullet fragments from the front and rear seats of the presidential limo, two fragments recovered from JFK's head, and a metal fragment from Connally's wrist, were all subjected to NAA testing at the Oak Ridge National Laboratory. As noted earlier, the results of these tests do not appear in the report or the twenty-six volumes of Hearings and Exhibits.[80] Kelley's list should have included the unfired round left in the chamber of the Mannlicher-Carcano rifle; the Tague curbstone; the scrapings from the car's windshield; Kennedy's clothing, especially the slits in his collar; and even Connally's dry-cleaned clothes, on the off chance that ultrasensitive NAA testing might detect gunpowder residues even after the cleaning.

If Gallagher could have testified that NAA testing disclosed that all this lead had exactly the same chemical composition, then the Commission would have had an airtight, scientifically rock-hard, incontestable case that the fatal bullet had been fired from Oswald's rifle. Had the Commission had the scientific proof to state this case with confidence, then Gallagher would have been one of its first witnesses rather than slipped in at the fag end of the investigation. By September 15 Redlich was certainly aware of Gallagher's work on spectrographic analysis and the NAA tests conducted at Oak Ridge. His knowledge was made clear in his opening questions to Gallagher. It was also clear that they had gone over the ground rules, what would be asked and what would be out of bounds, before they went on record. Redlich carefully limited his questions to the paraffin casts, scrupulously and dishonestly avoiding any questions about all the other physical evidence central to the crime.[81]

This deliberately circumscribed and staged Redlich-Gallagher exercise in half truths willfully and knowingly suppressed evidence from scientific testing on the Oswald paraffin casts that argued strongly that he had not fired a rifle the day of the assassination. This assertion is based on two independent controlled NAA tests run on the alleged Oswald rifle and a Mannlicher-Carcano that was similar to the one found on the sixth floor of the Texas School Book Depository on the day that Kennedy was assassinated. Gallagher was aware of these results when Redlich deposed him.

At the end of February 1964 Dr. Vincent P. Guinn, head of the NAA Section of General Atomic Division, of the General Dynamics Corporation, called Gallagher about the research his division was undertaking for the Atomic Energy Commission. For the past few years, Guinn reported, he and his colleagues had been using NAA to test the powder residues from discharged firearms. He sought out Gallagher to report the results of their tests on a "rifle similar to the one reportedly owned by Lee Harvey Oswald." The triple firing of the rifle, Guinn advised, "leaves unambiguous positive tests every time on the paraffin casts." Because of the inferior construction of the Mannlicher-Carcano, the Italian army's World War II assault rifle, Guinn noted that the blowback from one or three shots deposited power residue "on both cheeks" of the shooter. Guinn's observations about the inferior construction of the Mannlicher-Carcano were consistent with everything the FBI knew about the rifle. The bureau had learned from an informant knowledgeable about the rifle's history that "Model 91s," the type of rifle found at the Texas School Book Depository, were a dangerous weapon to the handler, "many of them bursting, with frequent fatal consequences, and many would not fire." Guinn also reported that "it appears that these results can be obtained even if the paraffin casts are made 2.5 hours after the shooting . . . providing the skin of the shooter has not been washed in the meantime." Guinn was hoping that Gallagher might reciprocate and share some information about the Oswald paraffin casts, only to be told that this information was not available from the FBI or the Dallas police at the time.[82]

There was nothing in Guinn's February telephone conversation with Gallagher that was new or startling. Gallagher, of course, was already aware of the results of the controlled NAA testing at Oak Ridge of Oswald's revolver and the rifle allegedly used in the assassination. The test results that had to be of special interest to the FBI disclosed that every time the Mannlicher-Carcano was fired the paraffin tests showed positive for barium and antimony, gunpowder residues, on the test shooter's hands and right cheek. These repeated tests with the rifle were incompatible with Dr. Mason's report that the paraffin cast from Oswald's right cheek proved negative for the telltale and incriminating nitrates, barium and antimony.[83]

Could the explanation reside in the argument that Oswald washed his face shortly after firing on the presidential motorcade? Mrs. Earlene Roberts, the housekeeper at 1026 North Beckley, where Oswald had a room, testified before the Commission that at about 1 P.M. he rushed into the rooming house and then left about three to four minutes later.[84] In addition to picking up a jacket and his revolver, Oswald could have washed his face and hands. It should be noted that Gallagher did not resort to arguing that Oswald must have washed his face and hands to cast doubt on the reliability of paraffin testing when Redlich deposed him. The reason had to do with the science of neutron activation analysis. NAA is so highly sensitive that it can pick up trace elements such as barium and antimony in parts per billion and trillion. Even if Oswald had used that brief stopover at the rooming house to scrub his skin to remove surface residues, the scientific certainty is that there would still remain enough atoms of barium and antimony deep in his facial pores, especially considering the heavy blowback from this particular type of rifle, to be detectable. Once the hot paraffin is applied to the cheek or hands, the heat will extract any residual nitrates buried in the pores. Short of Oswald spending the afternoon in a Russian steam bath sweating out his pores, the negative results on the paraffin cast of his right cheek argue strongly for his exculpation.[85]

Gallagher had the last word in the Commission's historic report on its representation of the facts of Dallas. But long before the Commission heard from its last witness, it had much work ahead of it to prove that the single-bullet theory explained everything and was not the flawed conclusion of desperate and fatigued men.

9   Politics of the "Single-Bullet" Fabrication

The FBI talked to me for about 15 minutes and seemed mainly concerned about whether I knew Jack Ruby.
—Jim Tague

Once the Commission committed to the "single-bullet" construction it faced a staggering evidence problem. All the physical and scientific evidence confuted the career the Warren report attributed to CE 399, the "magic bullet." In creating the single-bullet theory as a talisman to ward off the unacceptable reality that the Kennedy assassination had been a conspiracy, the Commission's reach far exceeded what it could credibly grasp. All the evidence it confronted—such as the discovery of the so-called Connally stretcher bullet, the slits in the front of JFK's shirt collar, and the number and disposition of the bullet fragments associated with the nonfatal shot—pointed unmistakably in a direction contradictory to the "official truth" of a lone gunman.

Since the Commission was hell-bent on delivering a politically tranquilizing answer to the question of Dallas, evidence was never a weighty consideration. The only serious speed bump the Commission had to negotiate was unanticipated: the sudden insertion into the investigation of Jim Tague and the curbstone shot. With assistance from the FBI, Chief Counsel Rankin and his staff of lawyers were able to finesse this problem before the report went to print.

One of the evidentiary hurdles the Commission had to clear was providing a convincing case that CE 399 was associated with Governor Connally's stretcher rather than any other stretcher in the emergency room. Connally was rushed to Parkland Memorial Hospital and into Trauma Room Number Two at about 12:47 P.M. (CST). He spent about twenty minutes in the emergency room while a team of doctors stabilized his condition and prepared him for surgery. At about 1 P.M. he was transferred to the operating room on the second floor, where anesthesia was begun. During Connally's short stay in the emergency room all his clothes were removed, placed in a paper sack, and left at the bottom of his stretcher when he was wheeled into the operating room.[1]

It is the Warren report's contention that CE 399 went through Kennedy's neck and Connally's chest, then smashed the governor's right wrist before it lodged in his left thigh. At some point, according to the Commission, the "stretcher bullet" came out of Connally's thigh wound and tucked itself under the stretcher mattress. After Connally was transferred from the stretcher to the operating table the cart was placed in an elevator to be returned to the emergency room on the ground level. According to the Commission, the bullet remained hidden under the mattress until Darrell C. Tomlinson, a Parkland Hospital senior engineer, pushed the stretcher up against the wall to clear a path to the elevator and the bullet came tumbling out.[2]

Commission records established the following chain of possession. Tomlinson turned the bullet over to O. P. Wright, the hospital's personnel director of security, who gave it to Secret Service agent Richard E. Johnsen. The night of the assassination, Johnsen hand-carried the missile to Washington, D.C., and turned it over to his boss, Secret Service chief James C. Rowley. Rowley, in turn, alerted the FBI liaison to the White House about the discovery and arranged the transfer of the missile to an FBI agent at the South Motor Entrance of the Executive Offices Building on the west side of West Executive Avenue. The FBI's Washington field office arranged for agent Elmer L. Todd to pick up the bullet, along with a memorandum by Johnsen explaining the circumstances of how it had come into his possession. The time of delivery was about 8:50 P.M. Todd immediately took the "stretcher bullet" to the FBI Crime Laboratory.[3]

Before that earthshaking Friday was over—the day Louis Nizer invoked in his Foreword to the Warren report as "The Day That Will Never End"—Director Hoover had everything he needed to close the book on Lee Harvey Oswald. Oswald, the only suspect, a self-professed Marxist recently redefected from the Soviet Union, was in custody. A rifle allegedly belonging to him had been found at his place of work overlooking the presidential motorcade route. And a bullet that could have been fired from that weapon had been discovered after allegedly having fallen out of the body of one of the victims of the shooting.

The discovered rifle slug, designated as C1 by the FBI, reduced the high stress levels in the Bethesda morgue on the JFK prosectors and medical admirals who were frantically searching for a missile in Kennedy's body. The news of C1 was a godsend to them as well because they now had an expedient explanation for JFK's back wound. Dr. Humes, or his superiors who were in control of the autopsy, had a handy forensic hypothesis: C1 must have fallen out of Kennedy's back during cardiac massage. The discovery of the Parkland Hospital bullet not only reduced the confusion and circuslike atmosphere in the Bethesda morgue, it also provided the medical admirals in charge of the autopsy, Galloway and Kinney, with a ready excuse for not dissecting the back wound to lay open the track of the bullet in Kennedy's body. Wittingly or not, this dereliction of standard textbook forensic procedure would later prove an indispensable aid to the Commission's single-bullet fabrication.[4]

In linking C1 (later designated CE 399) with Connally's stretcher, the Warren report stooped to a dishonest representation of the facts surrounding the discovery of the bullet. The report contended that Tomlinson was unsure which of the two stretchers on the hospital's ground floor across from the elevator had given up C1 when he pushed it up against the wall. The report made the false argument that it had to come from the governor's stretcher because all the "evidence . . . eliminated President Kennedy's stretcher as a source of the bullet."[5]

It was a manipulation of the facts to leave the impression that Tomlinson could not distinguish between the governor's and Kennedy's stretchers because Kennedy's cart was never one of the two stretchers in question. JFK's stretcher, as the report noted, never left Trauma Room Number One in the emergency unit of the hospital until his body was placed in a casket for the trip back to Washington. This was at 2:10 P.M., about twenty-five minutes after Tomlinson discovered the bullet.[6] A second "mysterious" stretcher—mysterious only because the Commission and the FBI chose not to investigate its origins—was lined up with Connally's in a corridor closed off from the emergency room by a door in the north wall.[7] According to Tomlinson, this second stretcher had rolled-up bloody sheets at one end along with "a few surgical instruments . . . and a sterile pack or two." It was this cart that the senior engineer identified as the source of the bullet. For reasons to be explained presently, this could not have been the governor's stretcher.[8]

The day of the assassination Parkland Memorial Hospital admitted, in addition to JFK and Connally, four emergency cases in a period of twenty minutes. Two of these patients were bleeding profusely. At 12:38 P.M. Helen Guycion was admitted, bleeding from the mouth. Sixteen minutes later two-and-a-half-year-old Ronald Fuller was admitted with a deep cut on his chin. It is likely that C1 came from a stretcher that belonged to one of these patients. The Commission, however, opted to leave this possibility unexplored.[9]

It was Commission junior counsel Arlen Specter who did the work-up on the "stretcher bullet." In March 1964 Specter went to Dallas to depose many of the Parkland staff on the events of that tragic day. Tomlinson was the chief focus of Specter's attention. He wanted Tomlinson to testify that C1 had come from the stretcher he brought down from the second floor, which was Connally's stretcher. To avoid confusion, Specter called this cart "stretcher A." Tomlinson could offer Specter no comfort on "stretcher A." He was persuaded that the bullet had come from Specter's "stretcher B," with the "surgical instruments . . . and a sterile pack or two." It was four months since the assassination, memory can fail over time, and the senior engineer would not swear that the bullet had come from "stretcher A." Specter pressed Tomlinson, insisting that he had told Secret Service agent Johnsen that the bullet came from the stretcher he took off the elevator. Tomlinson balked at the notion that he had made a "positive statement to that effect." "The Secret Service man wrote a report," Specter persisted, stating, "the bullet was found on the stretcher you took off the elevator. I called that to your attention before I started to ask you questions under oath." Specter's attempts at intimidation did him no good. All Tomlinson was willing to concede was, "It could have come from two, it could have come from three, it could have come from some other place." Deeply agitated and probably more than a little scared, Tomlinson signaled that the interrogation was over, telling Specter, "I am not going to tell you something I can't lay down and sleep at night with either."[10]

That same day, before Specter deposed Tomlinson, he questioned a few other members of the hospital staff. One was Jane C. Wester, a registered nurse employed by Parkland for almost ten years. Wester's recall of the events of November 22, 1963, was sharp and gave every indication of reliability. She was certain that after Connally had been placed on the operating table, there were various items left on his cart. She ticked off an inventory of medical paraphernalia: "several glassine packets, small packets of hypodermic needles. . . . There were several others—some alcohol sponges and a roll of 1-inch tape." When Specter asked if there were any tools at the end of the stretcher, Wester thought there might have been "a curved hemostat." Before Wester turned the governor's stretcher over to orderly R. J. Jimison, to place on the elevator to be returned to the emergency room, she said she "rolled the sheets up and removed the items from the cart." So when Connally's cart reached the ground floor all it had was a mattress and rolled-up bloody sheets. When questioned by Specter, Jimison confirmed Wester's account. He had noticed "nothing more than a flat mattress and two sheets as usual" on Connally's stretcher, he told Specter, as he pushed it down the second-floor corridor to the elevator.[11]

Wester's testimony, corroborated by Jimison, strongly supported the conclusion that CE 399 had been lodged in "stretcher B," the one Tomlinson designated, and not the governor's cart. Secret Service agent Johnsen's account adds more ballast to this argument. He was the agent who personally delivered CE 399 to the chief of the Secret Service. He reported to Rowley that he had received the bullet a little after 2 P.M., before Mrs. Kennedy and the others from the president's party left the hospital. Johnsen, relying on Tomlinson's firsthand account, identified the cart where the rifle slug was hidden as the "same stretcher" containing items such as "rubber gloves, a stethoscope, and other doctor's paraphernalia." He went on to report, "It could not be determined who used this stretcher or if President Kennedy had occupied it."[12]

The Warren report's misrepresentation of the facts of the "stretcher bullet" leaves the Commission open to the allegation that it chose to ignore evidence of a conspiracy to take the life of President Kennedy. Specter, for instance, during his questioning of Dr. Humes before the Commission in March 1964, categorically stated that C1 had come "from the stretcher occupied by Connally." What other alternative did the Commission leave? If, as the facts strongly argue, C1 did not come from Connally's stretcher, what explanation is left other than the idea that it was planted to incriminate Oswald and divert attention from the real assassins? This strategy would have demanded a conspirator at the hospital who took advantage of the general chaos that reigned at Parkland to hurriedly slip the virtually pristine C1 under the mattress of a cart with bloody sheets that he or she mistook for the governor's stretcher. The facts surrounding the "stretcher bullet" pointed in a direction the government had ruled as off limits for its investigation: that Dallas was more than just the violent acting out of a lone nut who wanted to nail his name in the history books.[13]

Once the single-bullet fabrication calcified into an obsession, the Commission was compelled to select supporting facts while it ignored evidence that refuted the hypothesis. An instructive example of this process was the Warren report's treatment of President Kennedy's clothes. Unlike Governor Connally's clothes, which the FBI inexplicably failed to collect, Kennedy's clothes were treated as essential evidence and rushed to the FBI's laboratory for ballistic, hair, and fiber examination and spectrographic analysis.

The report accurately noted that the bullet hole in JFK's coat was "5 3/8 inches below the top of the collar and 1 3/4 inches to the right of the center back seam of the coat." The relative position of the hole in Kennedy's shirt, the report continued, "indicated that both were caused by the same penetrating missile." The alignment of the holes in coat and shirt made a strong case for a missile striking President Kennedy from the rear. Furthermore, FBI spectrographic analysis disclosed a bullet wipe, or residue of copper, around both perforations, indicating that the bullet was copper-jacketed. These accurate measurements were consistent with Dr. Burkley's death-certificate description of the wound at the third thoracic vertebra, a back wound. The report, taking anatomical liberties with the wound's location, described it as a wound "in the vicinity of the lower neck."[14]

The report's language became more guarded and evasive when it tackled the slits in the front of JFK's collar, for reasons that will be explained later. It was essential to the Commission's case that it present a plausible argument that the slits in the collar and the "nick on the left side of JFK's tie" were caused by a bullet exiting his throat and continuing on in a downward trajectory into Connally's chest. This configuration was essential to make it compatible with Dr. Humes's schematic drawings of the neck wound depicted in

Commission Exhibits (CE) 385 and 386. At the same time, as the reader will recall, these drawings were totally and inarguably in conflict with Specter's reenactment photograph Number 12. The Commission's report spent two paragraphs on the front of JFK's collar in what can only be characterized as shameless "spin-doctoring," in the language of a later age. The report suppressed the results of the FBI's spectrographic and fiber analysis run on the slits in the collar. Was there copper residue deposited around the "holes" or "slits" in the collar, indicating that an exiting bullet made them? The report was mute on this question. As for fiber analysis, all the report could muster was the indecisive statement that "the fibers were not affected in a manner which would shed light on the direction of the missile."[15]

Rankin and the lawyers who assembled this section of the report were not innocent dupes or blissfully unaware that they were adrift on a sea of splendid ignorance. As with the "stretcher bullet," they had to follow the logic of the scenario that the Commission began with: that all the Dealey Plaza shots came from above and to the rear of the presidential motorcade. Therefore, the bullet that entered JFK's back had to exit his throat and enter Connally's body. As iterated, it was critical to the Commission's case that a single missile had struck both President Kennedy and Governor Connally to avoid any suspicion of a conspiracy. To achieve this politically determined end it was necessary to invent the single-bullet theory.

The circumstances, reliable firsthand testimony, and FBI laboratory evidence relating to JFK's shirt collar presented an explanation diametrically opposed to the Commission's claims. When the stricken president was rushed into Parkland Memorial Hospital's Trauma Room Number One, the first doctor to see him before his clothes were removed was Charles J. Carrico. When deposed by Specter on March 21, 1964, Dr. Carrico described Kennedy's condition as "agonal." That is, his breathing was spasmodic and his color was cyanotic, bluish gray, symptoms usually associated with a terminal patient. Carrico's immediate response was to insert a cuffed endotracheal tube to clear the breathing passage. Because time was critical, the attending nurses, Diana H. Bowron and Margaret M. Hentchcliffe, took scalpels and cut off Kennedy's clothes. In their haste to free Kennedy from his clothes the nurses nicked the tie and left two slits in his shirt collar. The use of scalpels, as Carrico explained to Specter, was "the usual practice" in a medical emergency of this nature.[16]

The Warren report's treatment of these slits in JFK's collar cannot be explained away as innocent errors or conflicting interpretations open to honest debate. The report's sophistical and evasive language is a dead giveaway. The Commission asserted, "These two holes fell into alignment on overlapping positions when the shirt was buttoned." What the Commission never provided in its report or the twenty-six volumes of Hearings and Exhibits is a picture of the front of Kennedy's shirt. Commission exhibits do, however, include photographs of Kennedy's coat (CE 393), his shirt (CE 394), and the tie (CE 395). The reason the Commission did not include a picture of the shirt collar was that it dared not. The slit on the left-hand side of the shirt and collar was much longer than the slit on the right-hand side as worn. To claim there was an alignment was patently untrue.[17] This is exactly what one would expect not from a bullet but from a right-handed nurse cutting the tie off at the knot. In fact, this was what happened when Nurse Bowron hurriedly made a single cut downward and a single cut upward while pulling away from the shirt to free the tie from Kennedy's neck.

The fact that the slits were not aligned destroys the Commission's contention that they were made by a bullet. Bullets make holes and not slits unless they are tumbling when they strike flesh or cloth. Carrico described Kennedy's anterior neck wound as "rather round and there were no ragged edges or ostellic lacerations." Carrico used the term *punctate* in describing the wound, another term for puncture, which is more commonly used when describing a wound of entry. Carrico's description of a clean hole about four to seven millimeters wide eliminated the possibility that the wound could have been made by a tumbling or yawing bullet.[18]

Almost two weeks after he was deposed by Specter at Parkland Memorial Hospital, Dr. Carrico was called to Washington to testify before the Warren Commission. Specter took him over some of the same ground covered in his Dallas deposition for the benefit of the attending commissioners. Carrico described JFK's anterior neck wound as a "small wound . . . below the thyroid cartilage, the Adam's apple." Dulles asked him to "show us about where it was." The Parkland doctor pointed to his own neck. Dulles, innocently and for the record, responded: "I see. And you put your hand right *above* [italics mine] where your tie is?" Carrico confirmed that the hole in the front of Kennedy's neck was above the collar.[19]

The Commission's record of Carrico's testimony should have been enough to deter it from attempting to persist with the single-bullet deception. But as we have already seen, with the Commission politics took precedence over the facts. When evidence militated against what it wanted to rule in, the Commission simply pretended it had gotten the results it wanted. For example, the Commission accurately reported the FBI Crime Laboratory's (BuLab) spectrographic results of the copper traces around the fabric surrounding the hole found in JFK's coat and shirt. However, the report failed to mention that BuLab found "no trace of copper or lead" around the knot on the tie or "the front of the neckband" after subjecting these items to X-ray and spectrographic analysis.[20] In suppressing this particular scientific evidence the Commission tipped its hand. It knew that a copper-jacketed bullet such as CE 399 could not have made these slits.

Another familiar Commission tactic was to avoid entering into the permanent record expert testimony that would have countermanded its politically driven preordained conclusions. In an attempt to buttress the case for a bullet having caused the slits in JFK's collar, the report noted that on each of the "vertical, ragged slits" the "cloth fibers [were] protruding outward." The Commission pretended that the orientation of the fibers was virtually proof positive that a missile exiting the collar was responsible. It based these assertions on circumstantial or presumptive evidence, at best, originating with its investigative agency. For example, Hoover assured Rankin that BuLab's hair and fiber expert had examined the shirt collar and found that "the torn threads around the holes were bent outward. These characteristics," Hoover asserted, "are typical of an exit hole for a projectile." There is no indication that Rankin or any of the staff assistant counsels asked to see the report. However, when FBI agent Robert Frazier testified before the Commission two months later, he inadvertently contradicted Hoover. Trained to testify under oath in courtroom situations, Frazier was cautious. He testified that the orientation of the fibers in JFK's collar was indicative of an exit only "assuming that when I first examined the shirt it was—it had not been altered from the condition it was in at the time the hole was made." At best, this was an unproven assumption. He also noted that the slits in the collar "were not specifically characteristic of a bullet-hole to the extent that you could say it was to the exclusion of being a piece of bone or some other type of projectile."[21]

A reader of the report and the twenty-six volumes of Hearings and Exhibits will look in vain for the FBI's hair and fiber report on JFK's collar and tie. Paul M. Stombaugh, BuLab's hair and fiber expert, did testify before the Commission. During Stombaugh's April 3, 1964, testimony, Assistant Counsel Eisenberg asked questions about Oswald's blanket found in Ruth Paine's garage, the fibers of the alleged killer's shirt, and the paper bag Oswald had allegedly used to smuggle the murder weapon into the Texas School Book Depository on the morning of the assassination. During Stombaugh's lengthy testimony not a single question was asked about his fiber examination of Kennedy's collar and tie, or whether it was his expert opinion that the slits in the collar overlapped. In February 1977, when Frazier was being deposed in what could only be described as an adversarial setting, he was asked about Kennedy's collar and tie. Although under oath, Frazier was very much a reluctant and evasive witness, but he did allow that Stombaugh had run tests on the collar and tie. He also admitted that Stombaugh made a report.[22] The obvious conclusion is that the Stombaugh report supported the FBI's spectrographic analysis finding no copper and lead traces on the JFK tie and collar. It was Nurse Bowron's scalpel and not CE 399 that accounted for the slits. Since these FBI laboratory results did not support the Commission's assertions they were omitted from the report.

In the so-called single-bullet wars that pervade the JFK assassination literature, Commission critics usually aim their sharpest blows at the virtually unscathed condition of the "stretcher bullet," or CE 399. According to the Warren report, despite the path of destruction it left behind in two bodies it lost only a minuscule percentage of its weight. Citing BuLab's estimations, the Commission reported that the weight loss of the "stretcher bullet" was only several grains.[23] The threshold question was clear: Did the number and disposition of the bullet fragments from Kennedy's and Connally's nonfatal wounds prove consistent with that figure, or were they in greater excess of weight loss than the single-bullet theory could tolerate? Any attempt at a fair-minded effort to reconstruct the body of evidence that would support or refute what the Commission attributes to CE 399 is an exercise in frustration. Evidence was lost or undetected and misrepresented, FBI interviews were careless and inaccurate or designed to confuse, the Commission ignored key witnesses, and Commission staff lawyers doctored testimony to tilt it in favor of the one-bullet hypothesis. Even if the explanation of these problems rested on shoddy performance and innocent human error, the wholesale confusion centering on the "stretcher bullet" fragments was inexcusable in the investigation of the murder of a president. Almost certainly some of the confusion was intentionally manufactured and imported into the public record to generate confidence in the impossible claims the Commission made for CE 399.

Dr. Charles F. Gregory was the surgeon who worked on Connally's wrist after he was operated on for his more critical chest wounds. According to Gregory, the preoperative X-rays showed seven or eight fragments in the governor's wrist. The normal procedure first undertaken with a wound of this nature was surgical debridement: The attending surgeon removed all the necrotic or contaminated tissue in the wound and identifiable foreign objects such as bullet fragments, cloth, and dirt. The wound was irrigated to further clean it before a decision was made to suture it or leave it open. Gregory noted in his postoperative report that "small bits of metal were encountered at various levels throughout the wound." The larger identifiable bullet fragments were retrieved and sent to the Pathology Department for examination. The Parkland orthopedic surgeon's best recollection was that he collected two or three of the larger fragments, but an uncountable number of the smaller metallic flakes were irretrievably lost in the debridement procedure. Although understandably imprecise, Gregory estimated that the metallic flakes that were dissected or washed away weighed less than a "postage stamp."[24]

Testifying before the Commission on Connally's wrist wound, Gregory made a rather startling statement. After noting that he had recovered two or three of the wrist fragments, he added, almost out of the blue, "the major one or ones now being missing."[25] Specter, who was doing the questioning, brushed this comment aside and moved on with his prepared line of interrogation. We will return to Gregory's missing fragments soon. To point out the obvious, when fragments, the larger or the largest ones at that, went missing they could not be subtracted from the weight of the "stretcher bullet." When Dr. Robert R. Shaw, Connally's thoracic surgeon, first studied the governor's preoperative X-rays, it was his opinion that the metal in the wrist "seemed to be more than three grains."[26] Although Shaw's observation is not conclusive, his estimate must have been based on the larger wrist fragments that showed up in the X-rays.

Little by little, as the number and disposition of the known and reported fragments deposited in Connally's body are accounted for, a picture begins to emerge. It is important to recall that the amount of weight loss attributed to this "magic bullet" was infinitesimal, about 2.5 grains, or the weight of a common postage stamp. To recap, the Warren report asserted, "The stretcher bullet weighed 158.6 grains, or several grains less than the average Western Cartridge Co. 6.5-millimeter Mannlicher-Carcano bullet."[27]

Part of this loss came from the two or three fragments Dr. Gregory retrieved from Connally's right wrist. With any discharge of a weapon, the missile deposits metallic filings in the rifling as it is propelled along the barrel. CE 399 would have left anywhere from 0.3 to 0.5 grains in the barrel. Adding to the "stretcher bullet's" burdens were the tiny metallic flakes of unknown combined weight lost in the debridement procedure. Connally's thigh fragment was problematic, since it was never removed. However, when Specter asked Dr. Gregory for his opinion, the Parkland surgeon described the fragment's size and estimated it was "postage stamp weight." Dr. George T. Shires, Connally's principal physician, was more conservative, estimating the thigh fragment at about "a tenth of a grain."

There were other bullet fragments, ghastly souvenirs, that Governor Connally would carry with him for the rest of his life. Parkland radiologist Dr. Jack Reynolds noted in his postoperative report that Connally's wrist held "two small metallic densities" near the fracture site. They were left because further surgery might have immobilized the wrist. These two wrist fragments and a small postoperative fragment remaining in Connally's chest added to the burden the Commission assigned to the "stretcher bullet." Years later Dr. Shaw, Connally's thoracic surgeon, was interviewed by the House Select Committee on Assassinations (HSCA). Over the intervening years Shaw had had time to think about the nature of Connally's wounds, especially the large exit hole in the chest. Shaw told the HSCA interviewers that during this interval he had changed his opinion about the nature of Connally's chest wound; he now attributed the gaping chest wound to "bullet and rib fragments." These metallic fragments, like those debrided from Connally's wrist, could not be recovered. They were washed out of the presidential limousine along with the blood and other assassination gore.[28]

In addition, there were other metallic deposits that the Commission was presumably unaware of at the time but that need to be factored into any discussion of the threshold question posed by the "stretcher bullet" and the claims the Commission made for it. In 1968 there was a secret government review, the so-called Ramsey Clark Panel, of the Kennedy autopsy photographs, X-ray files, and documents. The four physicians who carried out the review were eminent members of the medical profession with sterling credentials in their respective fields. Three were nationally recognized forensic pathologists, and one was a prominent radiologist. Their review was purposely limited and never intended to cast doubt on the official autopsy findings. The Clark Panel report did, however, contain two disclosures relevant to the single-bullet theory. In reporting on JFK's wounds, it noted, "As far as can be ascertained this missile struck no bony structures in its path through the body." In reviewing the X-rays of Kennedy's neck region the panel reported that "several metallic fragments are present in this region."[29] The "stretcher bullet's" validity, absolutely essential to the Commission's case, was further eroded by this secret government report.

In late April, when Connally's two principal surgeons testified before the Commission, a remarkable consensus was achieved between the Parkland and Bethesda doctors. During their March Commission testimony the Bethesda group, Drs. Humes, Boswell, and Finck, had all agreed that CE 399 was not deformed enough to have produced all the nonfatal wounds on Connally and Kennedy.[30] In March, when Assistant Counsel Specter was in Dallas deposing the Parkland doctors, Gregory and Shaw, both were agreeable to the proposition that the two men could have been struck by the same bullet. Dr. Shaw called the single-bullet hypothesis "perfectly tenable." Four weeks later, when the Parkland surgeons testified before the Commission, they experienced a sea change.

Hours before they testified they had the opportunity to study Connally's clothes and, more importantly, to view the "stretcher bullet" for the first time. Dr. Shaw, the governor's thoracic surgeon, told Specter that his views had shifted from what they had been a month earlier. He now "would have some difficulty in explaining all the wounds as being inflicted by Exhibit 399 without causing more in the way of loss of substance to the bullet or deformation of the bullet." Gregory thought the possibility of CE 399 inflicting all seven nonfatal wounds was "much diminished." He could not ally himself with Specter's "hypothetical circumstances" and related forms of courtroom gamesmanship the assistant counsel indulged in to draw attention away from the physical realities the doctors had observed. Gregory could not accept the fact that a bullet that had passed through so much soft tissue

still possessed "sufficient energy to smash a radius." At this point in his testimony Gregory took the initiative and nudged their exchange in a direction
for which Specter was totally unprepared. He thought that the two large
bullet fragments (CE 567 and CE 569) found under the front seats of the
presidential limousine—those same metallic specters that haunted the Commission and its junior counsel—were the more likely candidates for Connally's wrist wound. When Dulles jumped in to follow up this line of
speculation, a rattled Specter abruptly cut it off and moved the questioning
on to JFK's head wound.[31]

The Commission's April 21 session with the Parkland Hospital surgeons
did not, of course, discourage the Commission from ultimately adopting the
one-bullet construction. Still, this April 21 session was memorable in one
respect. It was the only time in the history of the investigation that both the
Parkland and Bethesda doctors were on record and unanimous in their opinions about the forensic facts and circumstances surrounding the assassination. Admittedly, none of these physicians were forensic pathologists,
although most of them had seen hundreds of bullet wounds in their professional careers in military and civilian medicine. Nevertheless, this unique
consensus over Connally's wrist wound was hardly a vote of confidence in
the Warren report's assertion that "there is very persuasive evidence from
the experts to indicate that the same bullet which pierced the President's
throat also caused Governor Connally's wounds."[32]

Dr. Gregory's mystifying April 21 statement that "the major one or ones"
of Connally's wrist fragments were missing demands exploration. This critical evidence was so poorly handled that it invites suspicion. Either there
was an improbable series of human errors in handling and labeling the Connally fragments, or the wrist-fragment evidence was corrupted. If this evidence was tainted, the only party that could have benefited was the
government and its case for a lone Dealey Plaza triggerman.

Audrey N. Bell, the supervising nurse of the Parkland Memorial Hospital
operating and recovery rooms, was on duty the day JFK and Connally were
shot. She was responsible for collecting the fragments Dr. Gregory retrieved
from Connally's wrist. She placed them in a foreign-body envelope and
turned the sealed envelope over to Texas state trooper Bobby M. Nolan.
Nolan brought the envelope to the Dallas Police Department and handed it
over to Captain Will Fritz. The next day Fritz released the envelope to the
Dallas FBI. The story of the missing fragments starts at this point in the
chain of possession.

On November 23, the day the Dallas FBI assumed custody of the wrist
fragments, FBI agent J. Doyle Williams interviewed Dr. Gregory, Trooper
Nolan, and Nurse Bell. Williams's record of these interviews is almost a
perfect failure in accurate reporting. He confused the fragments removed

from Connally's right wrist with the one that remained in the governor's thigh. In his FD-302 interview forms, Connally's wrist fragments are reduced to one fragment. The FBI designated this fragment as Q9 and assigned it a weight of 0.5 grains. It's possible that when Williams conducted these interviews he was depleted, hung over with exhaustion, considering how the JFK assassination had swept the Dallas office into a twenty-four-hour maelstrom. A discombobulated Williams might have confused the single fragment left in Connally's left thigh with Bell's envelope containing the wrist fragments. It is also possible that FBIHQ edited Williams's interviews at some later date before they were made available to the Warren Commission and ultimately went into the permanent record.[33]

It's worth recalling that Hoover had envisioned the solution to Dallas on the day of the assassination. Before the weekend was over Oswald, the government's only suspect, was assassinated while in police custody. The FBI had his rifle and the "stretcher bullet" that presumably came from that rifle. Over the weekend of the assassination the White House, Hoover, and Robert Kennedy's stand-in at the Justice Department, Nicholas Katzenbach, had established what the government would represent to the nation as the "official truth" of Dallas. With the FBI committed to the official version, it would not hesitate to bend the evidence in any direction calculated to strengthen the official story.

Whatever the cause of this confusion, there is no reason to doubt that Bell's sealed envelope contained fragments. The manila envelope with Bell and Nolan's initials is in the official evidence and exists in the Commission Hearings and Exhibits as part of CE 842. Next to the line "TYPE OF FOREIGN BODY:" are the words *Bullet fragments*. Unfortunately, there is no entry in the space where the number of fragments should have been recorded. The Dallas police evidence inventory listed "Bullet fragments taken from the body of Governor Connally" and recorded the chain of possession from Bell to Nolan to Captain Fritz to the Dallas police crime lab to the FBI. The Warren report noted that there were "two or three . . . very minute" fragments removed from Connally's wrist. This was a laudable effort at accuracy compared to Specter's June draft of Area I of the report, where he recorded, "One of the fragments was removed from Connally's wrist." Specter wrote his June 10 draft weeks after Dr. Gregory told him he had retrieved two or three fragments from Connally's badly damaged wrist.[34]

The Warren Commission never questioned or deposed Audrey Bell. But the House Select Committee on Assassinations questioned her in March 1977, and twenty years later the staff members of the Assassination Records Review Board (ARRB) interviewed her. On both occasions Bell noted that she had placed four or five fragments in a foreign-bodies envelope before initialing it and sealing it. The ARRB staff showed her a Warren Commission photograph (CE 842) reputed to be "a small fragment from wrist of Governor Connally." Either this photo is labeled incorrectly or the Commission was engaged in some trickery. When the HSCA used the photograph (CE 842), the label attached read, "Four lead-like fragments removed from Governor Connally." Three of the reported fragments were almost too small for the naked eye to pick out. The only visible fragment was smaller than a pinhead. These could not be the "major one or ones" that Gregory reported missing. When Bell was shown CE 842 she commented that there had been more than one fragment and that CE 842 was too small.[35] In 1977 HSCA staff member Howard Gilbert asked Bell to humor him by making a pencil drawing of the "smallest size . . . of the foreign objects." She was a little reluctant but agreed. Her sketch from memory of the smallest Connally fragment was significantly larger than the single visible one depicted in CE 842.[36]

There are scattered references to Bell in the HSCA report but no effort to resolve the discrepancies between her account and the official record. The HSCA ignored Bell's testimony and provided no explanation of why her account was suppressed.[37] Her recollections about the number and size of the Connally fragments were consistent with Dr. Gregory's assertion that the "major one or ones" were missing. Bell's account also supported Dr. Shaw's observation that Connally's wrist fragments might have weighed as much as three grains. Bell's recollection about the size of one or some of the governor's fragments is supported by a photograph in former Dallas police chief Jesse Curry's book on the assassination. One of the numerous photos in Curry's *JFK Assassination Files* included a fragment removed from Connally's right wrist. It was clearly far larger than the fragment in CE 842. This was the fragment the FBI designated Q9 and assigned a weight of 0.5 grains. In the Dallas Police Department photo it appeared to be all of 0.5 grains, a hefty one-half grain.[38]

Indicative of the way the Commission stacked its exhibits to virtually drape, light, and set to music its "stretcher-bullet" scenario is that it saw the need to publish nineteen photographs of the controversial Olivier-Dziemian Edgewood Arsenal test results. These included photos of bullet tracks in gelatin tissue models, missile damage to the ribs of goats, bullet holes in goatskin, a photo of a bullet fired through a goat, and the like. The only photo of the Connally fragments was the mislabeled and contested CE 842.[39]

As though there was not enough controversy and confusion surrounding the Connally fragments, a story appeared in the Dallas press about a Texas highway patrolman who claimed he had turned over to the FBI three or more fragments recovered from Governor Connally. Patrolman Charles W. Harbison said he was prompted to come forward with his account after reading in the *Dallas Morning News* about Audrey Bell's HSCA testimony.

Harbison was posted at Parkland Memorial Hospital to provide security for Connally while the governor recovered from his surgery. According to his account, several days after the assassination Harbison was on duty in the hall outside Connally's recovery room when the governor was transferred to a private room. At that point a doctor handed him some fragments. Harbison's recollection was "more than three fragments," which he promptly turned over to an FBI agent whose name he could not recall. Harbison's 1977 tale could be dismissed as vintage Dallas assassination gossip generated to sell newspapers. But in light of the gross official ineptitude and mishandling of this crucial evidence, whether innocent or by design, his account deserves to be part of the record. The Warren Commission never questioned Harbison. When Bell was confronted with the Texas patrolman's story she was mystified. She said she had never heard of Harbison and had no explanation for these additional fragments unless they had been "temporarily misplaced" and given to him later.[40]

Kevin Walsh, a private investigator employed by the HSCA, learned about Harbison from *Dallas Morning News* reporter Earl Golz. Golz was the paper's desk reporter for the Kennedy assassination. Walsh alerted the HSCA staff about the Harbison fragments and told committee staff member Donovan Gay that he had worked with Golz on the JFK case before and found him "to be consistently reliable."[41] As in Bell's case, the HSCA was not interested in Harbison's account of multiple Connally fragments. He was never called before the committee and asked to repeat his story under oath.

In view of the contradictions and questions about the integrity of the official evidence related to the Connally fragments, the most conservative and generous conclusion is that the Commission's claims for the "stretcher bullet" warrant profound doubts. Having said this, there is no possible excuse for all the official mismanagement of the evidence in a case of this political and historical magnitude. Had Oswald gone to trial it is unlikely that this evidence would have been admitted. It would be easier to relocate one hundred cemeteries than to get a credible and reasonably accurate official estimate of the number of fragments associated with the wounds Connally sustained. Perhaps skepticism about CE 399 could be tempered if all the other Commission claims made for the "stretcher bullet" were supported by hard evidence. But the case the Commission made for Connally's "stretcher bullet" and the path of CE 399 through Kennedy's neck collapses under inspection. The only possible verdict is that CE 399 fails the threshold test. The Commission's contention that CE 399 could have inflicted all the nonfatal wounds on JFK and Connally and emerged in a near-pristine condition satisfied the report's political needs but told us nothing about how President Kennedy was assassinated.

The June deadline Rankin and Warren had set to finish the Commission's work was overtaken by events. On June 5 a story appeared in the *Dallas Times Herald* reporting that one of the shots fired at President Kennedy had gone wild and crashed into a curb in front of an onlooker. James T. Tague, the third victim of the Dealey Plaza shooting, was the *Herald*'s anonymous source. United Press International (UPI) picked up the story and ran it as a lead release that same day. Tague was apparently motivated to contact the paper because a week earlier Dallas's KRLD-TV had carried an exclusive story from "a source close to the Warren Commission" saying that the Commission's report would conclude that JFK and Connally had been hit by the first shot and the second shot had struck President Kennedy in the head. Since nothing was said about the missed shot, Tague, who had reported the curbstone shot to the FBI six months earlier, took it upon himself to set the record straight.[42]

The Commission gave every indication that it was still determined to ignore Tague and the curbstone shot despite the stories in the press. In June the Commission's staff prepared two drafts of Chapter 3 dealing with the sensitive topic of the shots from the Texas School Book Depository. Both drafts allowed for a missed shot, but Tague's name was never mentioned and each draft treated the subject with studied vagueness and limp indecisiveness. Both stated that on February 13, 1964, "the Secret Service checked the area where a bullet reportedly struck near the Triple Overpass but could find no indication that a bullet had struck near the street in that area."[43] The fact that the FBI knew about Tague the day of the assassination and had informed the Commission of this missed, or "wild," shot with Robert P. Gemberling's December 23, 1964, report on the assassination went unmentioned in these June drafts. Tague was not deposed until July 23, 1964, and then only because circumstances forced the Commission's hand.

Exactly how these circumstances came into play is a little murky. Apparently Tom Dillard of the *Dallas Morning News* was covering a speech of the U.S. attorney for the northern district of Texas, Harold Barefoot Sanders, Jr. After Sanders finished his presentation and opened the floor for questions, Dillard, who had taken in KRLD-TV's exclusive on the Warren Commission, asked Sanders why the government was ignoring the Tague curbstone shot. Unaware of the missed shot, Sanders was lost for an explanation. But to his credit he did not brush off Dillard and was intrigued when the newsman reported that he had taken photographs of the bullet-pocked curb minutes after the assassination.[44] The upshot of this chance encounter was a registered letter to Commission general counsel Rankin from Sanders's assistant, Martha Joe Stroud. Stroud, assistant U.S. attorney in Dallas, informed Rankin of Dillard's curbstone photograph taken on the day of the assassination and sent him a copy of the picture.[45] For Rankin and Hoover the Stroud letter was a call to general quarters. The Commission and the FBI were forced to abandon their six-month conspiracy of silence about the Tague bullet and scramble to devise damage-control measures to protect the official version of the assassination, and by extension their own reputations.

Rankin wrote Hoover and requested that the FBI locate the curbstone and run tests to determine whether it had been struck by a bullet. Careful to avoid stirring up any more bad blood between Hoover and the Commission, Rankin made no direct comment about the failure of the FBI model of the shooting to address the curbstone shot. But he did ask the director to use "either the model . . . or a diagram" to trace the path of a missile from the sixth floor of the depository building to the point on the curb depicted in the Dillard photographs. Hoover alerted the Dallas office to locate "the nick" on the curbstone using the Dillard pictures and prepare for the "removal of a portion of the curbing." Two days later FBI Dallas reported back that the search had been abortive. FBIHQ responded with a two-page directive with detailed instructions on how to use the Dillard photographs and the pictures taken of the Tague curbstone by James R. Underwood, the news director for KRLD-TV, to locate the correct point on the curb.[46] If the FBI Dallas field office was stalling for time until the curbstone issue dissipated, the two-page directive put it on notice that this was no time for playing games. FBI Washington followed up the directive, alerting Dallas that it should expect FBI Supervisor Lyndal L. Shaneyfelt to arrive in Dallas on August 4 to collect "the desired portion of the curb" containing the "chip marks."[47] After nine months of willful avoidance of the Tague curbstone the FBI was finally forced to take the action it should have taken the day Kennedy was murdered.

The previously ignored Tague, the twenty-seven-year-old fleet sales manager of a Dallas Chevrolet dealership, and the circumstances that plummeted him into this American tragedy finally appeared in the Commission staff's August drafts of the crucial Chapter 3. In both drafts Tague's account of the curbstone shot, corroborated by Deputy Sheriff Buddy Walthers and the Dallas police officer who reported that a bystander had been hit by "a ricochet off the curb," was treated in a limited but accurate manner. The August 25 draft, identified as the "Final Draft," included the intriguing statement that "scientific examination of the mark on the south curb of Main Street corroborated the opinions of Walthers and Tague that it was made by a bullet." Shaneyfelt returned to FBIHQ with the section of the curbstone on August 5, and it was immediately subjected to spectrographic microscopic analysis. The results of BuLab's tests were available long before the August 25 draft was completed. The same statement, for example, was made in the earlier August 14 draft.[48]

Designated "final drafts" are usually never final. In any case, this was true of the Commission's August 25 draft. When the Warren report came to that section in Chapter 3 it noted that "scientific examination of the mark on the south curb of Main Street" by FBI experts disclosed "metal smears," which upon spectrographic analysis were "determined to be essentially lead with a trace of antimony." The absence of copper, according to the report, precluded the possibility that the "mark on the curbing section was made by an unmutilated military full metal-jacketed bullet." The report left open the possibility that the mark had been made by a bullet fragment but was quick to declare that it "cannot be identified conclusively with any of the three shots fired."[49] What the FBI had earlier identified as a "nick" or "chip marks" on the curb was suddenly a "smear." The more decisive language of the August 25 draft, relying on FBI lab results, which did not shrink from asserting that a bullet had hit the curb, was now revised. Citing the same FBI science, the Warren report resorted to inconclusive and fuzzy speculation about long-shot possibilities of a fragment from the headshot or a ricocheting missed shot that first hit some other object before it hit the curb.[50] As will be made apparent, the report's flimsy reasoning and evasive and tortured construction were intended to salvage credibility for the single-bullet theory and to hide evidence of the presence of at least one other Dealey Plaza gunman.

There is no margin for doubt that whatever hit the curbstone where Tague was standing left a mark in the cement. The FBI agents who interviewed him on December 14 reported that after Tague felt a sting on his right cheek he looked down and saw a "chip missing" from the curb where he was standing. KRLD-TV's Underwood, who took pictures of the curb the day of the assassination, observed that the "object that struck the curb had hit it with such force that it left a fresh white mark." The first law officer on the scene was Deputy Sheriff Buddy Walthers. Later that day he filed a report with the Dallas Sheriff's Department noting that "a bullet splattered on the top edge of the curb." Tom Dillard, who was summoned to the spot by Walthers, took pictures of the curb. A Dillard photograph appearing in the *Dallas Morning News* carried the caption "Concrete Scar," and the story line under the photo started with "A detective points to a chip in the curb." The Dallas FBI case officer for the JFK assassination, Robert P. Gemberling, recorded in section B of his report that "One Bullet Fired During Assassination Went Wild. Crashed into a Curb and Struck Jim Tague."[51]

The FBI's Shaneyfelt never bothered to interview any of these potential witnesses with firsthand knowledge during his August stopover in Dallas to collect the section of the wounded curbstone. He might have been in a rush to get the excised section back to Washington and have tests run on this important evidence. The more certain explanation is that Shaneyfelt already knew that the mark on the curb was no longer visible because it had been patched.

This development had already surfaced when Warren Commission junior counsel Wesley J. Liebeler deposed Tague in late July. At the end of May the

Tagues were planning a visit to his parents in Indianapolis. Before leaving, Tague returned to Dealey Plaza to take pictures of the assassination scene and of the storied curbstone where he had had his encounter with history. During his deposition Liebeler, for reasons that can only be guessed at, interjected into the questioning, "I understand that you went back there subsequently and took some pictures of the area." Understandably, Tague was taken aback. "I didn't know anybody knew about that," was all he could manage at that unsettling moment. But it must have been clear to Tague, a stand-up citizen who had broken no laws and held down an important managerial position for a dealership that employed over two hundred people, that the federal government had him under physical surveillance. The government agency with an intelligence interest in Tague was most certainly the FBI. Liebeler's questioning elicited from Tague that when he returned to take pictures of the curbstone the mark was no longer visible.[52]

In attempting to finesse the curbstone shot to salvage the single-bullet theory, the Commission interjected an unintended clarity into the case. Since there cannot be any legitimate question about the mark on the south curb of Main Street, the Warren report leaves open only two possible alternatives. Either Shaneyfelt brought the wrong section of the curb to FBIHQ, or the scar was patched. The FBI's own lab report on the curbstone "smear" eliminated any possibility that a fragment or a ricocheting shot from the depository building's sixth floor could have struck the curb where Tague was standing.

When Rankin and the Commission staffers responsible for Chapter 3 were forced to deal with the curbstone bullet, they had to turn to the FBI for answers to two essential questions about this missed shot. Both parties must have appreciated the irony of the situation. The FBI had not budged from its official position of three shots and three hits, which ran counter to the Commission's adopted single-bullet theory. But the Stroud letter transformed this misalliance into an alliance of necessity to cope with the immediate political pressures.

In a July 7 letter to Hoover, Rankin addressed the Commission's two interrelated concerns about the Tague bullet. By this time the general counsel had two of the FBI's Underwood photos of the damaged curbstone and the one taken by Dillard that Stroud had included in her June 9 letter. Rankin wanted to know at what point or frame in the Zapruder film the "wild" shot passed over the presidential limo and whether the mark on the curb was caused by a bullet.[53] Understandably, all Rankin wanted to hear from the director was that the missed shot could have originated from the "sniper's nest." Unhappily for Rankin, Hoover was not able to accommodate him.

The director's report on the FBI laboratory's findings was a masterpiece, even for Hoover. He was careful not to say that the missile that struck the curb came from the "sniper's nest." Instead, he noted, perhaps to give Rankin at least a thin diet of hope, the FBI had "determined from a microscopic study that the lead object that struck the curb was moving in a *general direction away* [italics mine] from the Texas School Book Depository Building." Any shot fired from anywhere in the depository building—or for that matter anywhere north or east of the Triple Underpass—would have to have been moving "in a general direction" away from the depository. The impact of Hoover's summary of BuLab's results must have left Rankin faltering and desperate. Assuming the shot had come from the sixth floor, Hoover continued citing from the laboratory report, an analysis of the Zapruder film showed that the bullet would have had to pass over the president's car at Zapruder frame 410 at an elevation of "about 18 feet from street level" to have struck the curb where Tague was standing. This was truly a "wild" shot. It refuted the concept the Commission and FBI firearms expert Frazier had worked so hard to establish: that Oswald was skilled enough with a rifle to place two of his three attempts into a moving target. Furthermore, Hoover pointed out, still assuming the shot had come from the "sniper's nest," Z 410 was 5.3 seconds after Oswald would have seen JFK's head explode at Z 313. This time frame was almost double the time permitted by the Commission for the entire assassination to take place. For Oswald to have hung around for more than five seconds after killing President Kennedy meant that he was a crazed killer, and a cool one at that.[54]

When studying Hoover's letter and the attached FBI Crime Laboratory report Rankin must have felt that he had fallen down a rabbit hole and was having tea with Alice and the Mad Hatter. Hoover did not rule out the possibility that a fragment from the fatal shot to the head had caused the smear, but the laws of physics almost certainly did. In order for a lead fragment—it would have had to be sizable—to scar the curb, it would have had to continue down range about 260 feet beyond Z 313 and still have had enough kinetic energy to chip and spray cement. Adding to the absurdities was an FBI lab sketch disclosing the alleged angle of the "smear" as 33 degrees. The angle was oriented from west to east in a downward trajectory, meaning that the shot had come from the right or the front of the motorcade. This orientation could mean only that a shot had come from the Triple Underpass. Assume, however, that this was an unintentional mistake and the sketch meant to depict the angle of the "smear" from east to west. The Texas School Book Depository was located at the north end of Elm Street, and the motorcade was moving from east to west as it passed along Elm Street toward the Triple Underpass. If that 33-degree angle is projected back the more than five hundred feet from the Tague curbstone to the depository building, Oswald would have had to be suspended somewhere in the air above the building and the alleged sniper's perch.[55]

Reporting the complete results of the FBI's laboratory examination of the Tague curbstone would have destroyed the single-bullet theory and the Commission's solution to the assassination. If a bullet had scarred the curb, as the August 14 and the August 25 "Final Draft" had unequivocally stated, then at least one shot had come from somewhere other than the "sniper's nest," and Dallas was a conspiracy. Rankin and the staff carefully selected from Hoover's letter and BuLab's report only what appeared to support the "official truth" and suppressed the rest, which was most of the five-page report. As cited earlier, the most self-serving line from BuLab's scientific examination incorporated into the Warren report was that the absence of copper precluded "the possibility that the mark on the curbing section was made by an unmutilated military full copper-jacketed bullet such as the bullet from Governor Connally's stretcher."[56] This was the assistance from Hoover's FBI, and the Commission ran with it. The Commission made no attempt to explain what had happened to the curbstone mark.

Years later Henry Hurt of *Reader's Digest* was working on a manuscript about the Kennedy assassination that subsequently appeared in 1985 under the short title *Reasonable Doubt.* His research assistant, Sissi Maleski, employed Construction Environment, Inc., to exam the Shaneyfelt curb section housed at the National Archives in Washington, D.C. The chief engineer for the company, Jose I. Fernandez, submitted a two-page report on the results of the examination. Since the exam was only visual in nature (microscopic petrography and other techniques that could do mechanical damage to the curb section were forbidden), the report was necessarily inconclusive. Despite the obvious limitations, Fernandez was willing to offer the opinion that "the dark spot" on the curb that so sharply contrasted with the surrounding lighter gray areas was consistent with a "surface patch" that could "explain all the observed differences."[57]

The FBI never officially closed the JFK murder case. If the Hoover bureau had a pressing need to look into the mystery of the vanishing "chip" or "nick" on the curbstone it could have started by examining the records of the Dallas Department of Public Works to determine whether the city had patched the curbstone. If the Department of Public Works did the repair, where did the authorization originate that resulted in the destruction of critical evidence in the Kennedy assassination? That, at least, would have been the logical place to begin a good-faith investigation. There is one absolute certainty about the patched curbstone: Oswald can be eliminated as a suspect in the firing of that particular bullet. It is not surprising that the patching of the curbstone was an assassination mystery that the FBI and the Commission preferred not to solve.[58]

A shattering public event generates false leads and deranged responses from mentally unhinged elements in any population. The Kennedy assassination was no exception. During the first three weeks after the shootings, the FBI was inundated with reports of false sightings of Oswald in every corner of the United States. Hoover complained to Rankin in a "Dear Lee" letter about these "attempts by unscrupulous individuals to exploit the assassination of President Kennedy."[59] Following the assassination and for several years afterward the FBI's Dallas field office invested considerable man-hours in dealing with bullets found in the vicinity of Dealey Plaza.

One of these was an obvious plant, and the FBI chalked it up as a hoax and made no follow-up investigation. This bogus missile, a .30-caliber U.S. military–type copper-jacketed lead-core bullet, was found in a planter in Dealey Plaza in October 1970. There were, however, other bullets found under circumstances that warranted closer investigation. For example, Rex M. Oliver, a Texas Highway Department employee, discovered a .45-caliber steel-jacketed soft-point bullet in the vicinity of Commerce Street and the entrance to the North Stemmons Freeway. It was sometime in October or November 1968 when Oliver found the partially corroded bullet while working on the highway. He kept the bullet for a time until his supervisor persuaded him to turn it over to the FBI, pointing out that it might be "the third bullet" in the JFK assassination and that it was "found in just about the right place."[60] William A. Barbee from Mesquite, Texas, found a .30-caliber carbine-type bullet embedded in the roof of a building with a Stemmons Freeway address and, according to the FBI, about one-quarter of a mile from the Texas School Book Depository and "in the general line of fire from where Oswald allegedly shot." Barbee found the missile in July or August 1966 and was prompted to turn it over to the FBI after reading an article in *Life* about the "missed shot."[61]

Whatever the true histories of the Oliver and Barbee bullets, they were both discovered in the proximate area of the "killing ground" or "killing zone," as military argot would refer to the area. Both of these bullets were turned over to BuLab's Firearms Unit for examination. Not surprisingly, the full weight of FBI science focused on one concern: Could these bullets have been fired from Oswald's "assassination rifle"? Once it was established that these ammunition specimens could not have been used with the Oswald rifle, the FBI had no further interest in them. FBIHQ authorized the Dallas field office to return them to Oliver and Barbee.[62] In the larger scheme of things, the FBI's dismissal of these bullets was plain vanilla compared to the way it ignored the curbstone shot and mishandled critical evidence such as Connally's clothes and the Tippit bullets. But it gave a hollow ring to Director Hoover's assurance to the Commission that "the case will continue in an open classification for all time. That is, any information coming to us or any report coming from any source will be thoroughly investigated."[63]

Hoover's humbug about the "open classification" status of the Kennedy assassination was even more pointedly underscored by Eugene P. Aldredge's report to the FBI. Aldredge, a resident of Dallas, phoned the FBI at the end of September 1964 to report a bullet scar on the sidewalk on the east side of Elm Street, the side of the street where the Texas School Book Depository was located. He was surprised when he read the published Warren report to find that whereas it mentioned the bullet "smear" on south Main Street, it failed to mention a bullet mark in the sidewalk on Elm Street. The exclusion prompted Aldredge to call the FBI's Dallas office; at the time he called he was ill and confined to his home. Aldredge had first noticed the bullet mark in the sidewalk in early September, when he had given a visiting relative a "Cook's tour" of Dealey Plaza.[64]

According to Aldredge, several days after he reported the bullet mark to the FBI he revisited the scene and found that the bullet hole had been "patched with some sort of plastic-type material." Aldredge described the patch to the FBI as a "sloppy" job, "as only the hole was covered and not the whole area." The day after receiving Aldredge's phone call the FBI sent two agents, Manning C. Clements and Richard J. Burnett, to interview the recuperating witness at his home. According to their report, Aldredge "minutely described the location" of the bullet mark.[65] That same day, September 30, with the help of Aldredge's description, Clements and Burnett inspected the site of the alleged bullet hole. Their report contained the following pertinent information:

> In the sixth large cement square, four feet from the street curb and six feet from the park side curbing, is an approximately four inches long by one half-inch wide dug-out scar, which could possibly have been made by some blunt-end type instrument or projectile. It is noted that this scar lies in such a direction that if it had been made by a bullet, it could not have come from the direction of the window the President's Commission . . . has publicly stated was used by LEE HARVEY OSWALD when firing his assassination bullets at the late President.
>
> This particular scar is in line with the western end of the [Texas School Book Depository], that is, the opposite end of the building from where OSWALD was shooting at the President.
>
> No other mark was found in the area of the second lamppost which might appear to have been made by a bullet.[66]

About three weeks later the FBI sent agents to recheck the Elm Street mark and reported back that "now some sort of foreign material is partially covering this nick in the sidewalk." Scrapings were taken of this patching material and sent to BuLab for possible identification.[67] Nothing more was heard about Aldredge or the second curbstone shot. Apparently this treatment of the mystery bullets and the Elm Street gouged sidewalk was enough to satisfy the Hoover bureau standards of a "thorough investigation."

The Aldredge capper is reminiscent of the FBI's feigned Dogberry-like routine with Governor Connally's clothes, when critical and, for the government, potentially compromising physical evidence was lost or corrupted in the JFK assassination case because of an apparent sudden fit of absent-mindedness on the part of the nation's premier law enforcement agency. Even the most generous-minded would regard the loss of one bullet-scarred curbstone as blatant laxity and ineptitude, but to have lost two crosses the line between carelessness and weighty suspicion of criminal government evidence-tampering. It is almost superfluous to say that the FBI made no effort to investigate whether the Oliver and Barbee bullets or bullets of the same caliber could have been responsible for the Elm Street sidewalk bullet scar. Fortunately for the FBI the matter of the mysterious bullets and bullet mark could largely be handled in house.

However, during the Kennedy assassination investigation the Hoover bureau was not always able to dodge the bullet by hiding or suppressing agency dereliction. In the matter of presidential security and protection, FBI failure to communicate with the Secret Service set in motion a sequence of events that radically altered the history of the assassination in Dallas.

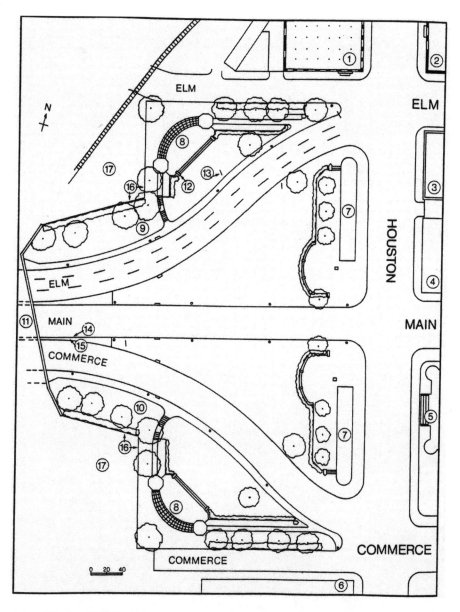

Map of Dealey Plaza by Katherine Guth. Key: (1) Texas School Book Depository; alleged
assassin's lair on the sixth-floor, easternmost window; (2) Dal-Tex Building; (3) Dallas
County Records Building; (4) Dallas County Criminal Courts Building; (5) Old Court
House; (6) U.S. Post Office Building; (7) peristyles and reflecting pools; (8) pergolas;
(9) grassy knoll north; (10) grassy knoll south; (11) triple underpass; (12) position of
Abraham Zapruder; (13) Stemmons Freeway sign; (14) approximate location of curbstone
hit; (15) position of James T. Tague; (16) stockade fences; and (17) parking lots.
(Courtesy David Wrone)

Texas School Book Depository and Dal-Tex Building looking northeast from southwest of Dealey Plaza. (Courtesy Bill Mills)

The presidential limousine in front of the Texas School Book Depository seconds before the first gunshot. (Harold Weisberg Archives, Hood College, Frederick, Maryland)

Associated Press photographer James W. Altgens took the most important still picture of the assassination. He captured the motorcade just after the president and Governor Connally were struck and seconds before the fatal head shot. In the photo, one can see the front of the Depository and a live oak tree in full foliage. The Warren Commission contended that the oak tree blocked any clear view of the presidential limousine from Oswald's alleged "sniper's nest" until about frame 210 of Abraham Zapruder's eight-millimeter film of the assassination. But the FBI's photo-analysis of Zapruder's film indicated that the first shot came at about frame 170. The most likely origin of a shot at that frame was the Dal-Tex Building located at the corner of Houston and Elm Streets. (AP/Wide World Photos)

Frame 260 from Abraham Zapruder's film. President Kennedy can be seen clutching at his throat after having been hit by gunshot. (Copyright 1967, renewed 1995, The Sixth Floor Museum at Dealey Plaza. All Rights Reserved.)

Secret Service Agent Clint Hill tries to restrain Jacqueline Kennedy as she reaches for a piece of her husband's skull. Hill's quick response prevented her from sliding off the rear of the limousine and compounding the horror of that tragic day. (Weisberg Archives)

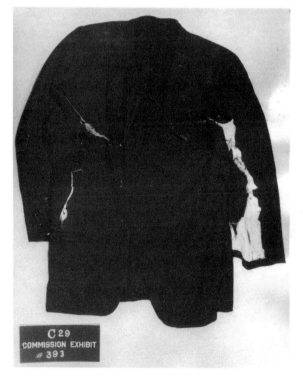

Commission Exhibit 393 shows the front of the suit coat the president was wearing that day in Dallas. The great tears in the coat were made by scalpel-wielding attending nurses Bowron and Henchliffe to prepare Kennedy for emergency medical attention. (Weisberg Archives)

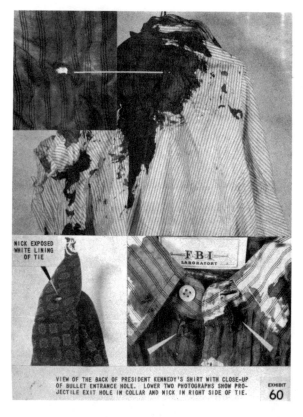

NICK EXPOSED
WHITE LINING
OF TIE

F-B-I
LABORATORY

VIEW OF THE BACK OF PRESIDENT KENNEDY'S SHIRT WITH CLOSE-UP
OF BULLET ENTRANCE HOLE. LOWER TWO PHOTOGRAPHS SHOW PRO-
JECTILE EXIT HOLE IN COLLAR AND NICK IN RIGHT SIDE OF TIE.

EXHIBIT
60

The Commission dared not publish FBI Exhibit 60 because it destroys the official version of the assassination. The hole in Kennedy's shirt aligns perfectly with a shot that entered at the third thoracic vertebra, as confirmed in Dr. Burkley's official death certificate, and not the president's neck. The non-overlapping slits in the president's collar were made by a scalpel and not a missile. When Commissioner Allen Dulles asked Dr. Carrico about the location of Kennedy's front wound, the Parkland physician told him it was above the shirt. All of the FBI's forensic testing of the tie and the shirt collar was omitted from the Commission's Report because it proved that no bullet hit either the tie or the neckband in front of the shirt. (Weisberg Archives)

C 31
COMMISSION EXHIBIT
395

Commission Exhibit 395 was prepared by Special Agent Lyndal L. Shaneyfelt, the FBI's forensic photographer. According to the official account a bullet entered Kennedy's posterior neck and exited his throat, severing his tie before entering Connally's back. The Commission's use of this photograph was to support the so-called single-bullet theory. (Weisberg Archives)

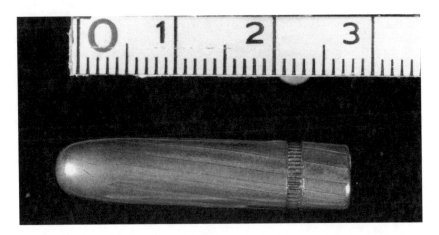

FBI Exhibit 23 (better known as Commission Exhibit 399) is the bullet that allegedly produced all seven nonlethal wounds in President Kennedy and Governor Connally, breaking two of the latter's bones in the process. (Weisberg Archives)

Robert Lee Studebaker's Exhibit D is one of four pictures of the alleged "sniper's nest" taken by the Dallas Police Department on the day of the assassination. The picture refutes key arguments in the testimony of Howard Brennan, the Commission's declared "star witness." In order for Brennan's detailed description of Oswald as the man firing from this window to ring true, Oswald would have had to be standing. If Oswald had been standing upright, he would have had to fire through a double-paned window. (Weisberg Archives)

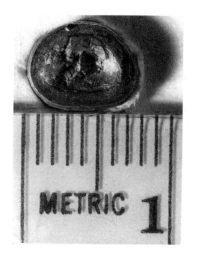

The condition of Commission Exhibit 399 was virtually pristine except for the flattening of the base and the crater of its lead base. FBI ballistics expert Robert Frazier scooped out a lead sample from the base for scientific testing. (Weisberg Archives)

Robert Lee Studebaker's Exhibit C shows how carefully the alleged murder weapon had been hidden under two boxes behind a barricade of book cartons. The picture explains why Dallas deputies Weitzman and Boone's searches for the murder weapon took time and why the FBI and the Commission ignored this in their reconstruction of Oswald's flight from the sixth floor after allegedly shooting Kennedy. (Weisberg Archives)

Dallas Morning News photographer Tom Dillard's picture of a Dallas detective pointing to a chip in the curb on the south side of Main Street near the triple underpass. Either a piece of the curb or a bullet fragment struck bystander James Tague in the face. Tague was the third person wounded that day in Dallas. Dillard's picture appeared in the Dallas newspapers the day following the assassination. (Dallas Morning News)

OPPOSITE PAGE, CENTER:
Committed to a shooting scenario that allowed for only three shots, the FBI and the Commission ignored the "Tague Bullet." It was not until July 1964, eight months after the assassination, that FBI director J. Edgar Hoover ordered FBI agent Lyndal Shaneyfelt to go to Dallas and recover the bullet-scarred curbing. The foot-long section of curbing Shaneyfelt brought back to Washington for analysis strangely showed no damage at all—it had obviously been patched by that time. (Weisberg Archives)

Dallas detectives and police search the area for the bullet that struck the curbstone near James Tague. (Weisberg Archives)

Oswald hands out "Fair Play for Cuba" fliers in front of New Orleans TV station WDSU in August 1963. (Weisberg Archives)

FBI Director J. Edgar Hoover
(LBJ Library)

Deputy Attorney General
Nicholas Katzenbach (LBJ Library)

Warren Commission member
Senator Richard Russell
(LBJ Library)

Earl Warren, Chief Justice of the Supreme Court and presiding member of the Warren Commission, delivers the Commission's official report to Lyndon Johnson at the White House. From left to right are Commission members John J. McCloy, J. Lee Rankin (general counsel), Senator Richard Russell, Representative Gerald Ford, Warren, President Johnson, Allen Dulles, Senator John Sherman Cooper, and Representative Hale Boggs. (LBJ Library)

10   FBI Blunders and Cover-Ups
      in the JFK Assassination

Tell Malley to tell Hosty to keep his mouth shut. He has already
done irreparable harm.
—J. Edgar Hoover

In late 1962 President Kennedy began to gear up the White House planning staff to prepare for a formal visit to Texas the following year. Since his election in 1960 President Kennedy had made only a few brief visits to Texas. Even with the state's putative favorite son, Lyndon B. Johnson, on the ticket in 1960, Kennedy had only narrowly carried the state by less than fifty thousand votes. The Lone Star State's twenty-five electoral votes loomed large in Kennedy's 1964 reelection plans.

The extreme right-wing climate of Texas politics in 1963 did nothing to guarantee that the state would line up in the Democratic Party's column in the 1964 presidential contest. Kennedy's chilly Lone Star State's political fortunes were made even more complicated by an internecine Democratic Party struggle between liberal Senator Ralph Yarborough and Governor John B. Connally, the leader of the party's conservative wing, that threatened to tear the party asunder. In early June 1963 Kennedy met with Johnson and Connally in El Paso, Texas, and a November date was set for his formal visit. All parties agreed that the overarching purpose of the Texas trip was to expose President Kennedy to the greatest number of the state's voters. For the Dallas leg of the trip a ten-mile motorcade through the heart of the city was planned to assure maximum public exposure for the presidential party.[1]

The national nightmare of Dallas began as a security nightmare for the U.S. Secret Service. Several weeks after the assassination the head of the Protective Research Section (PRS) of the Secret Service, Robert I. Bouck, unburdened himself to the agency's FBI liaison. Historically, the perennial plight of the Secret Service anytime the president decided to hit the campaign trail was a toss-up—security versus politics. The Kennedy White House was certainly no exception. But for the Dallas visit Kennedy ruled against even the most basic PRS-recommended precautions. Since the weather was beautiful, Kennedy insisted that the presidential limousine not be outfitted with a quarter-inch-thick Plexiglas "bubble-top." He even refused to permit Secret Service agents to stand on the back of SS-100-X, the agency's designation for the presidential limo. According to Bouck, JFK insisted "that none of the Secret Service men be even near SS-100-X during the motorcade." In hindsight, the deeply distraught PRS head thought these elementary precautions might have foiled the assassination.[2]

It was Secret Service practice to send two members of the White House detail to carry out advance preparations for a presidential visit, but the president's November Texas trip stretched an already overtaxed White House detail too thin. With Kennedy scheduled to visit five cities in two days, PRS could assign only one agent to Dallas. Thirty-five-year-old Winston G. Lawson drew the Dallas assignment. Lawson worked closely with the head of the Dallas Secret Service office, Special Agent in Charge (SAC) Forrest V. Sorrels. The Dallas SAC was a veteran agent who had been helping to protect presidents in Dallas since 1936, when Franklin D. Roosevelt had visited the city.[3]

One of Lawson's many assignments was to choose the motorcade route from Love Field to the Trade Mart, the site of the luncheon for Kennedy provided by Dallas's business and civic leaders. Lawson worked with Sorrels on the most direct route to keep pace with an official schedule that allowed only about forty-five minutes to travel the ten-mile course from the airport to the Trade Mart while still providing Kennedy maximum exposure. As Sorrels pointed out to the Warren Commission, given these constraints, the route pretty much mapped itself.

The procession passed through the heart of downtown Dallas along Main Street to Houston and then made a sharp left-hand turn onto Elm. The hard left forced William R. Greer, JFK's Secret Service driver of choice, to decelerate to below ten miles per hour. This risky slowing was doubly dangerous considering that the limousine was open. Although the Plexiglas cover was not bulletproof, it might have improved the odds against the president receiving a fatal wound. Lawson, Sorrels, and the entire White House detail who accompanied the presidential party to Dallas understood that when politics trumped security, the risks increased exponentially. Sorrels later recalled his sudden panic when the motorcade reached Main Street and he saw the tremendous crowd. Sorrels said he just blurted out, "My God look at the people. They are even hanging out the windows." The motorcade had no alternative other than to turn onto Elm Street to gain access to the Stemmons Expressway, the direct and fastest route to the Trade Mart. On the north side of Elm Street was the Texas School Book Depository (TSBD), where, according to the official story, Oswald lurked, waiting patiently for his rendezvous with history.[4]

Lawson arrived in Dallas on November 13 to prepare for the presidential visit. It was standard Secret Service practice for an agent undertaking such advance preparation to check the PRS trip index files to see if there were any individuals in the area to be visited who might pose a threat to the president. Although there was nothing in the PRS files for Dallas, Lawson checked with Sorrels when he got to Dallas. Three weeks earlier an ugly incident had occurred in Dallas involving Adlai E. Stevenson, the U.S. ambassador to the United Nations. Right-wing agitators had heckled Stevenson during his speech at the Trade Mart, and upon leaving the building the ambassador had been spat on and hit with a picket sign.

Some of these troublemakers were student members of the Young Republican Club at North Texas State University at Denton, Texas, and known satellites of the strident and blustering far-right Dallas agitator, former General Edwin A. Walker. Walker made it known at every opportunity that he regarded President Kennedy as a gutless "commie-symp" intent on handing the country over to his Kremlin masters. The Dallas Secret Service learned from the Dallas police, who received the information from a student informer, that some of Walker's Denton troops were planning something for Kennedy's Dallas visit. One of the suspects that the Dallas Secret Service had identified from the Stevenson rumpus was alleged to have remarked that he and others planned to "drag his [Kennedy's] dick in the dirt." Pictures of this student and others who had been involved in the October 24 incident with Ambassador Stevenson were circulated to all security personnel assigned to the Trade Mart, and a "trip file" was prepared on each subject for use in any future presidential visits.[5] For the Houston leg of the presidential trip, the PRS pulled two file jackets of potentially dangerous suspects. Both of these people were added to the agency's alert list and placed under surveillance during Kennedy's stopover in that city.[6]

In 1963 the PRS was composed of twelve specialists and three clerks. This horse-and-buggy operation might have been effective for the first quarter of the century, but it was not even minimally adequate for the challenges and workload the Secret Service faced beginning as early as World War II. The amount of information relevant to its core mission received by the PRS had tripled between 1943 and 1963.[7] As a consequence, the Secret Service was increasingly forced to rely on dissemination of intelligence from other federal agencies and local law enforcement forces about possible harm to the president, his family, and the vice president.

During the Warren Commission's April 30 executive session the commissioners registered surprise that Oswald's name had not surfaced on the PRS's alert list as part of the security preparations for the president's Dallas visit. Although the commissioners were not looking to embarrass the FBI, Chairman Warren thought it was the responsibility of the Commission to explore the reasons for this oversight in its report to the nation. It was not lost on the Commission that the alleged assassin had been employed for over a month in a building that directly overlooked the route of the presidential motorcade. This, coupled with the fact that the Commission soon learned that the FBI had a substantial preassassination file on Oswald and still had not placed his name on its Security Index, underscored Warren's appeal that the Commission make recommendations on how to better protect the president.[8] The FBI's Dallas field office disseminated only three items to the Secret Service in connection with President Kennedy's Dallas visit. One was the name of a local Ku Klux Klan member who might pose a threat, and the Secret Service was already aware of the other two. Before November 22, 1963, Lee Harvey Oswald's name was unknown to the PRS and all the Secret Service agents in Dallas.[9]

Based on just the raw information in the FBI's Oswald file, it is hard to imagine anyone else living in Dallas—or in any of the other four cities that were on Kennedy's Texas itinerary, for that matter—better qualified to have been on the Secret Service's alert list. Oswald had been a defector to the Soviet Union; he maintained contacts with the Soviet Embassy in Washington after returning from Russia; and he was open about his pro-Castro sympathies and Fair Play for Cuba Committee activities while residing in New Orleans. During his seven-day trip to Mexico City in late September and early October 1963 he had visited both the Soviet Embassy and the Cuban Consulate. Furthermore, Oswald had been court-martialed from the U.S. Marine Corps for possessing an illegal firearm. While stationed in Japan he had lost a stripe for pouring a drink on a noncommissioned officer. The case he made to the Marine Corps for an early hardship dependency discharge was a blatant fabrication. According to his FBI file Oswald drank to excess and beat his wife. The fact that he had defected to the Soviet Union during the height of the Cold War, along with these other characteristics, would have been enough to alert the Secret Service that he was a potential danger and needed to be kept under surveillance. Speculation about the Secret Service's course of action regarding Oswald gives way to certainty when access to the president is considered. Had the FBI alerted the Secret Service about Oswald and his place of employment, every move that Oswald made while JFK was in Dallas would have been carefully watched. "Unusual access," as PRS head Bouck informed the Warren Commission, was the acid test for the Secret Service taking action—"drastic action" were his carefully chosen words to the commissioners.[10]

The FBI had opened a file on Oswald following his defection. The first item in the file was a news story about the twenty-year-old ex-marine announcing that he was applying for Soviet citizenship. Oswald made the statement at a well-attended staged news conference at the Metropole Hotel in Moscow at the end of September 1959. On June 13, 1962, after almost three years in the Soviet Union, Oswald returned to the United States with his Russian wife and infant daughter. The Oswalds took up residence in Fort Worth, Texas, and immediately became the subjects of FBI scrutiny. On July 3, 1961, FBI headquarters (FBIHQ) in Washington, D.C., created a new file on Oswald under the slug line 105 ("internal security"). This action, of course, was entirely proper. The FBI had to try to determine whether Oswald had been recruited at any time by Soviet intelligence to obtain permission to return to the United States with his wife and child. The circumstances of his defection and redefection raised understandable suspicions that he or Marina might be a Soviet "agent-in-place" or "sleeper agent."[11]

John W. Fain was the Fort Worth FBI agent in charge of Oswald's file. Oswald was Fain's first defector, but the twenty-year bureau veteran had spent more than ten years dealing with security-type investigations. Fain's Fort Worth supervisor directed him to conduct a background investigation of the redefecting former marine. Fain, accompanied by a second agent, interviewed Oswald on June 26 and again on August 16, 1962. Although they found Oswald arrogant and evasive—he refused, for example, to take a polygraph—nevertheless, he emphatically denied ever having given his Soviet hosts any information that could be used against the United States. After the second interview Fain reported that Oswald refused to explain why he had gone to the Soviet Union, stating that it was "nobody's business." But he did agree to contact the FBI if approached by any person in the United States under suspicious circumstances.[12]

This pledge came wrapped in a mystery of sorts. Oswald did tell Fain that he had been approached by the Ministry of Internal Affairs while in Russia. Fain left this statement out of his reports and apparently never followed it up.[13] Arguably with some cause, Fain on his own initiative may have dismissed this admission as a fabrication on Oswald's part to feed his inflated sense of self-importance. The FBI had so thoroughly penetrated the American Communist Party (CPUSA) that it knew that Oswald had never been a registered party member. In fact, there is no evidence that he ever had a personal contact with any party or any official connected to the American left, except by correspondence, and then on his own initiative and with no clear significance. What was thoroughly documented by the Warren Commission was Oswald's hatred for the Soviet communist system.[14] Marina Oswald's friend Ruth Paine, whose father-in-law was a dedicated Trotskyite, recalled that when Lee grandly announced that he was a "Trotskyite Communist" she "found this and similar statements illogical and somewhat amusing."[15] In September 1963 Oswald wrote to the New York headquarters of the CPUSA asking how he might contact the party when he relocated to the Baltimore-Washington area. That same day he wrote a similar letter to the Socialist Workers' Party headquarters, the historical nemesis of Soviet communism, making the same request.[16] At the time he wrote these letters he was planning his trip to Mexico City and had no known future plans to resettle anywhere around the Baltimore-Washington corridor.

Oswald's invention of a pro-Castro Fair Play for Cuba Committee (FPCC) in New Orleans followed the same suspicious pattern. In May 1963 Oswald wrote FPCC headquarters in New York City, asking for membership and announcing his intention of starting a chapter in New Orleans. After his arrest as Kennedy's suspected assassin he confessed to being the secretary of the FPCC in New Orleans. In fact, there was no FPCC chapter in New Orleans except the bogus one with only two enrolled members, Oswald and an "A. J. Hidell." Oswald had had the Jones Printing Company make up one thousand "Hands off Cuba" handbills that bore the contact information "A. J. Hidell, P.O. Box 30016." After a quick check, FBI New Orleans discovered that P.O. Box 30016 was nonexistent; whatever Oswald was about, he was not interested in recruiting members. After Kennedy's assassination, the New Orleans FBI agent in charge of Oswald's file, Warren C. de Brueys, found out from Marina that her husband had often used "Hidell" because it rhymed with Fidel, reflecting Lee's fascination with and hero worship of Castro.[17] The Warren Commission never tried to explain the motives or speculate about the reasons for this bizarre behavior other than to attribute it to Oswald's "commitment to Marxism and communism."[18] The Commission's linking Oswald with Soviet communism, which ran counter to the truth, was intended to strengthen the credibility of the report it foisted off on an innocent public.

There were other more obvious explanations that the Commission had no choice but to ignore. Unsuited for Marine Corps life and bitterly disillusioned with Soviet communism, Oswald diverted himself by thinking up escapist forms of political adventure rather than buckling down to change a life he felt was going nowhere. At first glance, Oswald appeared to be a confused and immature young man who was a danger only to himself and the family he put at risk. The other possibility that escaped Commission consideration was that he was some kind of agent or low-level informant trying to penetrate one of these left-wing organizations targeted by a U.S. government agency.

After his second interview with Oswald, Fain recommended, "No further work to be done at this time." As he explained to the Warren Commission, the subject had found a job, was living with his family, and was not a member of the Communist Party. Fain was satisfied that Oswald had no contacts with Soviet intelligence, was no security threat, and showed no propensity for violence. His recommendation to close the case was supported by his field office supervisor and the security desk officer at FBIHQ. There was nothing permanent about a closed file; it was standard FBI policy to reopen a file if there was a perceived need. When Fain retired in 1962 the FBI's Oswald file was turned over to FBI agent James P. Hosty, Jr., of the Dallas office.[19]

Fired from his Dallas job in April 1963, Oswald went to New Orleans to find work. After Oswald found employment as a "greaser" of coffee machines for the William B. Reily Company, he sent for Marina, now three months pregnant, and their infant daughter.

Oswald became a blip on FBI radar again with his overt promoting of FPCC activities—printing and distributing "Hands off Cuba" handbills, speaking on street corners, and debating America's Cuba policy on talk shows on radio station WDSU in New Orleans. Apparently not afraid to take some risks, he exhibited street smarts in drawing attention to himself. In June Oswald stationed himself at the Dumaire Street Wharf, where the aircraft carrier USS *Wasp* was berthed. His handing out of his pro-Castro leaflets to the crew and visitors to the carrier created enough of a protest that the police were called in and Oswald was ushered off the wharf. In August his provocative al fresco pro-Castro politicking and handbill distribution were clearly acts to attract attention. For instance, Oswald was observed wearing a placard around his neck reading, "Hands off Cuba, Viva Fidel," which led, as it was almost certainly intended, to a street scuffle with three anti-Castro Cuban emigrants who were itching to confront this propagandist. Oswald and the three Cubans were arrested for disturbing the peace. Oswald pled guilty and elected to pay a small fine. While biding his time in jail, Oswald, at his own request, was interviewed by FBI Special Agent John L. Quigley. During a rather lengthy discussion Quigley brought up the name A. J. Hidell. Oswald admitted that he knew Hidell. He had spoken with him over the phone, he told Quigley, but had never personally met him. It was Hidell, Oswald maintained, who had recruited him to distribute the FPCC handbills. One of the Cubans involved in the scuffle, Carlos J. Bringuier, would later report that several days before this incident Oswald had come to his place of business and volunteered to work for the anti-Castro movement.[20] This behavior suggested that Oswald either was in free fall in his own dreamed-up fantasy world or was actively cultivating a cover, or a "legend" in intelligence community argot, laying the groundwork for some future venture or assignment.

Back in Dallas a check of Oswald's file disclosed a memo from the New York office that Oswald had subscribed to the *Daily Worker,* the East Coast organ of the CPUSA. This revelation was enough to persuade Agent Hosty to reopen the Oswald file, although the Dallas security supervisor had ignored the New York memo, probably because it was known that Oswald also subscribed to the *Militant,* the Trotskyite publication of the Socialist Workers' Party. Oswald's name on the *Daily Worker* mailing list was enough proof for Hosty that he had lied to Fain about his disillusionment with communism. If Hosty read Oswald's file carefully, he would also have been aware that Oswald had lied to Agent Quigley about A. J. Hidell recruiting him to distribute the FPCC handbills. In September 1963 Hosty added to the Oswald file a report that Oswald "drank to excess and beat his wife on numerous occasions." The report was wrong on the first count—Oswald was a teetotaler—but his relationship with Marina was marred by spousal abuse. His periodic rages and physical attacks on his wife were an ugly reality and evidence that he was capable of violence, at least against the woman he professed to love and the mother of his children. In his published account of the Kennedy assassination, Hosty disclosed even deeper reasons for his mistrust of both Lee and Marina. He did not suspect Marina at first, but as he studied her FBI file he came to the disturbing conclusion that she was a KGB-planted "sleeper agent."[21] That Marina at the time could not read or completely understand the English language gave Agent Hosty no pause in his mission to excavate the "true facts" about the Oswalds. All through his book he referred to the Oswalds as "counter-espionage" cases despite the fact that the FBI files on Lee carried the slug line "Internal Security—R."

After FBIHQ learned of Oswald's visits to the Soviet and Cuban embassies in Mexico City, it decided to probe deeper into the Oswald case. It was Hosty's job to locate Oswald and find out what he could about the suspect's contacts with the Russians and Castro Cubans in Mexico City without tipping Oswald off to the FBI's interest in his activities.[22]

At the end of October 1963 Hosty learned from FBI New Orleans that Oswald had left an Irving, Texas, forwarding address; Irving was a Dallas suburb. On November 1 Hosty showed up at the Irving address, which turned out to be the residence of Ruth Paine. Marina Oswald was staying with Paine until her husband could locate an apartment they could afford. Hosty learned from Paine that Oswald was employed at the Texas School Book Depository, but she did not know where he was living. During the workweek Lee kept in touch with Marina by telephone. Ruth Paine knew the phone number where Lee could be reached at the rooming house on North Beckley Street in Dallas but never volunteered the number to Hosty because it did not occur to the eleven-year FBI veteran to ask whether she had that information. Four days later Hosty, accompanied by a rookie FBI agent, showed up again at Paine's Irving house. His intention was to interview Marina to find out what she knew about the purpose behind Lee's phone calls to the Soviet Union's Mexico City embassy. Marina's due date for her second pregnancy was just days away, and she was not in any frame of mind to be questioned by government authorities. Hosty left a note with his Dallas FBI address and phone number and said he would return at a later date.[23]

November 1 was a Friday, the end of the workweek and a day that Lee usually showed up at Ruth Paine's home to visit Marina and his daughter. On that Friday he arrived in Irving about an hour after the Hosty visit. Oswald was outraged when he learned of Hosty's attempts to interview his pregnant wife. He apparently ordered the women to get Hosty's license plate number if and when he showed up again. Apparently that same evening Oswald roughed out a draft of a letter intended for the Soviet Embassy in Washington, D.C. In the letter Oswald fulminated against the "tactics of the notorious F.B.I." He accused Hosty of threatening him that if he did not drop his Fair Play for Cuba Committee activities, he could expect serious FBI "interest" in his affairs. According to the note, Hosty had encouraged Marina to "defect from the Soviet Union." These allegations almost certainly had no basis in fact and were obviously made to curry favor with the Russians for some self-serving reason. Hosty never came face to face with Oswald before the assassination. Oswald's most likely motive was to prepare for a second attempt to secure a Soviet visa to Cuba, having failed in this project during his recent Mexico City trip. Whatever Oswald was angling for, there is no mistaking his genuine hostility toward the "notorious" FBI and its agent incarnate, James P. Hosty, Jr.[24]

Sometime between November 2 and 9, Oswald entered the Santa Fe Building at 1114 Commerce Street and took the elevator to the twelfth floor, which housed FBI headquarters in Dallas. He carried a note he had written for Agent Hosty. He presented himself before the FBI receptionist, Nannie Lee Fenner, and asked to see Hosty. When Fenner told him that Hosty was not in the office at the moment, Oswald threw an envelope on her desk addressed to "SA Hosty," barked out, "Give it to him," and stormed off toward the elevator. Momentous events often have the most mundane origins, and this was certainly the case with the Oswald note. Inside the unsealed envelope was a note that Fenner would later describe as written in a "large scrawl, very childlike in nature."[25]

Oswald's note carried the potential to have dramatically altered the history of "the Day That Will Never End." It set in motion an FBI cover-up that concealed a terrible, corrosive secret that could have seriously, perhaps irreparably, damaged the public image of Hoover's FBI. This cover-up was orchestrated at the very top levels of FBIHQ and lasted for twelve years. The note was also a persuasive, if not absolutely convincing, countercheck to the official assertion that Oswald assassinated President John F. Kennedy.

Not surprisingly, when the Oswald note finally became public it stirred up a storm of controversy. There is no disagreement over whether there was an Oswald note. Moreover, there is no disputing the fact that Hosty was ordered to destroy the note after Oswald was murdered in the basement of the Dallas Police Department. In 1975 the FBI was forced to go through the motions of an internal investigation into the content of the note and who had ordered its destruction. Harry N. Bassett, an assistant director of internal affairs, was in charge of the 1975 investigation. Bassett reported that it was common knowledge at the Dallas field office that Oswald had written a note to Hosty and, more importantly, that the note had contained a threat.

Bassett's findings were based on more than fifty interviews with FBIHQ officials and Dallas field office supervisors, agents, and staff. Most of the interviews were with Dallas field office agents, both active and retired, and these statements are convincing testimony to the fact that Nannie Lee Fenner was not afflicted with a runaway imagination when she reported that the note threatened violent reprisal against Hosty or the FBI if Hosty did not leave Oswald's wife alone.

Former assistant director William Sullivan stated that he learned from Dallas SAC J. Gordon Shanklin in the aftermath of the assassination that Shanklin had "internal personnel problems" because one of his agents had received "a threatening message" from Oswald just weeks before Kennedy's assassination. Shanklin was initially reluctant to give any details, but during a subsequent phone conversation he told Sullivan that Hosty was the agent who had received the message. He also let drop that Hoover was going to order a disciplinary transfer of Hosty after the agent's Commission testimony. Agent John V. Almon, who was assigned to the Dallas field office at the time of the assassination, noted that it "was common knowledge" that Oswald had left a "threatening note" addressed to Hosty and that the note "was destroyed." Dallas agent Ural E. Horton, Jr., supported Almon's assertion to the extent that he reported that it was bruited about the office that "there was an Oswald note to Hosty and it allegedly contained a threat." Agent Charles T. Brown stated that he learned of the Oswald note from fellow agent Vincent E. Drain a few weeks after Kennedy's assassination. According to Brown, Drain told him that Oswald had left a note for Hosty in which he threatened to "blow up the FBI and Dallas Police Department . . . if the FBI did not stop harassing his wife." Joseph L. Schott, retired former Dallas field agent and author of the lighthearted spoof of the Hoover bureau, *No Left Turns,* told an Associated Press reporter that he understood that Oswald had left a note for Hosty threatening to kill the FBI agent "if Hosty tried to talk to his wife Marina again." The Schott quotation appeared in the *Dallas Times Herald* on August 31, 1975. Schott refused to identify his source when Bassett questioned him.[26]

Hosty has always insisted that the note contained a complaint, not a threat. According to Hosty, Oswald wanted him to stop harassing his wife or he would "take some kind of action against the FBI; I assumed he meant some kind of legal action." So there was an admission of a threat of some kind of action against the FBI. There was little likelihood, however, that Oswald, who was making a dollar and a quarter an hour, would have had the wherewithal to engage legal representation against a federal agency. Moreover, there was no basis for any kind of lawsuit. Hosty was a federal agent doing his assigned duty in a perfectly legal manner. If the content of the Oswald note was as nebulous and innocuous as Hosty represents, what was the pressing reason for its destruction? After Oswald was charged with Kennedy's murder, the note, regardless of its contents, was evidence in the case. Hosty also swore that he had no recollection of a signature and therefore never associated the note with Oswald, whom he had never met. This claim crosses the line separating the trifling from the unbelievable. Anxious as Oswald clearly was to warn off Hosty about harassing his wife, why would he not sign the note? Without identifying himself, what purpose was there in writing and hand-delivering the letter to Dallas FBI headquarters in the first place? How would Hosty know who had sent the note, since he had never met or spoken to Oswald? According to Hosty, after reading this anonymous note he "tossed it in my file drawer at the office and never gave it another thought." But the day of the assassination, he related, he was called into Shanklin's office, where Hosty's supervisor, Kenneth C. Howe, and Shanklin were waiting for him. An extremely agitated Shanklin held up the Oswald letter and demanded, "What the hell is this?" Hosty did not explain how his bosses had gotten the letter or had known where to search for it in Hosty's file drawer. Hosty had thirty-five or more cases; in his absence from the office, how did Shanklin or Howe know how to retrieve the note from his files unless they knew it was from Oswald?

Nannie Lee Fenner's recall of the note's content was worlds apart from Hosty's largely innocuous and improbable version. Since the note was in an unsealed envelope, Fenner swore she read it after Oswald flung it on her desk and abruptly turned and headed for the elevator. According to Fenner, the note said something like the following: "Let this be a warning. I will blow up the FBI and the Dallas Police Department if you don't stop bothering my wife." Fenner was certain that the note was signed "Lee Harvey Oswald." During the FBI's 1975 investigation she signed three affidavits over a three-month period about the Oswald note and never changed her story.[27]

As soon as Oswald left her work area Fenner took the note to Kyle Clark, the assistant agent in charge of the Dallas office. Assuming that terrorist threats by street walk-ins were not common occurrences with the Dallas FBI, Clark must have shown the note to Shanklin, his boss. Sometime that same day Howe must have been alerted. A short time later, Clark returned the note to Fenner and, according to her, said it was from some "nut case" and to give the note to Hosty. Hosty confirmed that Fenner gave him the note when he returned to the office. Sticking to his version that the "unsigned" note was "no big deal," Hosty said he dropped it in his workbox and forgot about it. Not one of his bosses, Shanklin, Clark, or Howe, showed an iota of curiosity about the note writer or directed Hosty to review Oswald's file in light of President Kennedy's upcoming Dallas visit. On Sunday, November 24, after Oswald was murdered, Fenner claimed that Clark told her to "forget about the Oswald letter." Two or three days later, Fenner reported, Ken Howe came over to her desk and said, "Nan—forget the letter."[28]

In time the FBI was forced to make what could be characterized as a public confession about the Oswald note. This carefully hedged mea culpa was forced upon the bureau as a result of a story in the August 31, 1975, edition of the *Dallas Times Herald*. In broad strokes, the story alleged that some days before the assassination Oswald entered the Dallas FBI building and left a threatening note addressed to Agent Hosty. The article went on to allege that the agent never reported the Oswald visit or the contents of the note prior to the president's trip to Dallas or after the assassination. According to the official FBI line, the *Dallas Times Herald* story was the first time FBIHQ learned of these serious allegations. The bureau immediately contacted Attorney General Edward Levi and initiated "an exhaustive internal inquiry." FBI Director Clarence M. Kelley appointed Bassett to conduct the inquiry.[29]

With the integrity of the FBI at stake, it fell to Deputy Associate Director James B. Adams to disclose the results of Bassett's inquiry to the Committee on the Judiciary chaired by former FBI agent Don Edwards (D–Calif.). In his prepared statement Adams was the soul of contrition. He stated emphatically that the "concealment and subsequent destruction of the note . . . was *wrong* [Adams's emphasis]" and a violation of FBI rules. He did not resolve for the Edwards committee and the nation the exact nature of the threat in the Oswald note or who had ordered its destruction. His one certain claim was that the note had contained no threat against President Kennedy or "anything which would have fore-warned of the assassination of the President." After some eighty interviews of current and past Dallas agents and staff, some of whom were interviewed two or three times, Adams conceded to the Edwards committee that serious and regrettable wrongdoing by Dallas field office personnel had, in fact, occurred. In this exercise in damage control, Adams acknowledged certain FBI sins of omission and commission in order to cover up perhaps the most colossal blunder in the history of the Hoover bureau.[30]

The FBI cover-up in the matter of the Oswald note started the weekend of the assassination. As a result of the bureau's mail cover of the Soviet Embassy in Washington, D.C., FBIHQ had a copy of Oswald's November 9, 1963, letter in which he mentioned the note he had delivered for FBI agent Hosty.[31] This intercepted communication had no special meaning until Oswald was accused of assassinating Kennedy. The Sunday after the assassination, after it was learned that Oswald had been murdered and there would be no trial, FBIHQ contacted Shanklin, the SAC of the Dallas office, and directed him to destroy the Oswald note. The order probably came from either Assistant Director Alan H. Belmont or John P. Mohr. It is not clear whether Hoover had known about the Oswald note and ordered its destruction. There were doubtless things that the "palace guard" of assistant directors conspired to keep from the aging director, fearing that his reaction might destroy careers, perhaps even their own.

Hosty recalled that when he returned to the office that Sunday afternoon, "all hell was breaking loose." Ken Howe told him that Shanklin wanted to see him immediately. The Dallas SAC was pacing behind his desk and smoking furiously when Hosty entered his office. By this time Shanklin had the note retrieved from Hosty's workbox. According to Hosty, Shanklin bellowed, "Hosty! Headquarters is going nuts. They have a million questions for you, so sit down and listen." Shanklin ordered Hosty to destroy the note—"To get rid of it. Get it out of here." Hosty recalled thinking that his chain-smoking boss was going to have a nervous breakdown. Hosty claimed that he took the note to the men's room located between the eleventh and twelfth floors, tore it to bits, and flushed it down the commode. This disposal of the note was the inaugural event in what became a twelve-year FBI cover-up.[32]

No doubt Shanklin's panic was triggered by the phone call from Assistant Director Belmont. FBI Washington began circling the wagons when it learned about the Oswald threat. The implications for the reputation of the Hoover bureau were staggering if the Oswald note went public. It was imperative that the Warren Commission be kept in the dark about the note and its destruction. As mentioned before, this was not the only secret FBIHQ kept from the Commission but the note's potential to wreak irremediable damage if exposed gave it primacy. In "spookspeak," the language of the intelligence community, the Oswald note was the Hoover bureau's "family jewels," the FBI's most embarrassing and corrosive secret associated with the Kennedy assassination.

FBI Washington's rapid and decisive action in ordering the note's destruction ended any serious controversy about the content of Oswald's note. It was Fenner's version, not Hosty's, that best explained why FBIHQ, in Hoover's name, ordered the note's destruction. If, as Hosty claimed, the note was unsigned and contained only a mild complaint, it would not have ignited a chain reaction of rapid responses from Belmont's desk to SAC Dallas to Hosty's workbox and finally the flushing of the note down the commode. It was this suppression of evidence, "a violation of firm [FBI] rules," that Adams moralized about when he testified before the Edwards committee. However, in his prepared remarks before the committee Adams confined the wrongdoing strictly to the FBI's Dallas office.[33]

There is still the mystifying and mind-boggling fact of Hosty's inaction after he received Oswald's note threatening violence against the FBI and the Dallas Police Department. The eleven-year FBI veteran had been in charge of the file while the Oswalds resided in Fort Worth and had reopened the Oswald case when he learned of Oswald's subscription to the *Daily Worker.*

It was this information that convinced him that the ex-marine and one-time defector was a communist and a potential security threat. He learned from Ruth Paine during his November 1 interview that Oswald worked at the Texas School Book Depository. He even made a follow-up undercover phone call to the TSBD to confirm that Oswald was indeed employed there. The *Dallas Times Herald* reported on November 15 that Kennedy was scheduled to attend a luncheon in his honor at the Trade Mart. On November 19 and succeeding days, the *Dallas Times Herald* and the *Dallas Morning News* carried detailed descriptions of the planned route of the presidential motorcade. It was hardly a guarded secret that President Kennedy was going to pass close by the TSBD on the last leg of the route to the Trade Mart—except, apparently, to Hosty.[34]

In May 1964, when Hosty appeared before the Warren Commission, he was repeatedly questioned about why he had not alerted the Secret Service about Oswald as a precaution in light of the president's Dallas visit. Although the commissioners had not reviewed all of the sixty-nine items in the FBI's Oswald file, they were familiar enough with some of the more relevant intelligence about the alleged assassin to engage in some sharp questioning. The commissioners were, of course, at a complete disadvantage when questioning Hosty because the FBI had suppressed any acknowledgement of the note and its destruction. The Commission did learn about the note from another source. In her March 1964 testimony before the Commission, Ruth Paine mentioned that Oswald had told her he had "stopped at the downtown office of the FBI . . . and left a note." In the follow-up questioning by Assistant Counsel Albert Jenner, Paine recalled that Lee was "irritated" and "left the note saying what he thought."[35] So four months after Hosty flushed the note down a commode the Commission knew about a note but either saw no need to explore this new information any further or was reluctant to investigate for fear of what it might uncover.

During his lengthy Commission testimony Hosty did little to burnish the Hoover bureau's carefully cultivated image of the FBI agent as the epitome of law enforcement excellence and infallibility, but he managed to get through his Commission ordeal without giving up the bureau's "family jewels." Nevertheless, Hosty set the commissioners back on their heels when he volunteered that a week or ten days before November 22, SAC Shanklin had held a meeting in which he instructed the forty agents of the Dallas office to play the presidential visit by the book. If an agent, Shanklin directed, had knowledge of any uncontrolled individuals who might pose a threat to Kennedy or Vice President Johnson, he should immediately notify the Secret Service. Some of the commissioners wanted to know why Hosty had not informed Sorrels's office about Oswald and the fact that he worked at the Texas School Book Depository. Hosty's carefully rehearsed response, which became the FBI's party line on this question, was that Oswald had never revealed any propensity for violence. Earlier in his testimony Hosty had disclosed that he had received information on October 25 that when Oswald was in Mexico City he had made contact with the Soviet Embassy. When Assistant Counsel Stern asked if he had taken any action on the Oswald case between November 5 and November 22, Hosty replied, "No, Sir." Hosty's testimony, in view of Oswald's Mexico City activities, did nothing for the vaunted public image of FBI efficiency. This was not lost on the Commission, nor did it go unnoticed by members of the bureau elite in Washington, especially Director Hoover.

The impression Hosty wanted to leave with the Commission was that he had never made any connection between Oswald and President Kennedy's visit because there was no connection to make. In a short exchange with Stern and Commissioner Dulles, Hosty hewed to this line to the point of unintended self-ridicule:

STERN: Did you know the route of the motorcade?

HOSTY: No, Sir.

DULLES: Had there been any contact between you or the Dallas office with the Secret Service on this point?

HOSTY: On the motorcade route, sir?

DULLES: Yes.

HOSTY: No.

DULLES: Had not been?

HOSTY: No.

STERN: The newspaper stories did not as far as you can recall tell what the motorcade route would be?

HOSTY: Yes, they did. There was a description of the motorcade route, but as I say, I didn't bother to read it in detail. I noticed that it was coming up Main Street. That was the only thing I was interested in, where maybe I could watch it if I had a chance.

STERN: So that the fact Lee Harvey Oswald was working in the Texas School Book Depository meant nothing.

HOSTY: No.

STERN: In connection with the motorcade route?

HOSTY: No.

STERN: Did you think of him at all in connection with the President's trip?

HOSTY: No, Sir.

Commissioner Ford elicited from Hosty that he had been busy eating his lunch when the motorcade swung onto Elm Street and passed under the shadow of the TSBD. An incredulous John J. McCloy asked Hosty if he would have informed the Secret Service if he had known the motorcade was going to pass by the TSBD. The unabashed Hosty responded, "No, Sir."[36]

The explanation for Hosty's behavior is probably banal. After more than a decade in the Hoover bureau, Hosty, like most of his fellow veteran street agents (as opposed to desk-bound supervisors), was a creature of rigid bureaucratic routine. Staying inside the lines and avoiding embarrassing the bureau were prerequisites for a good fitness report and advancement in the nation's most celebrated government agency. When Shanklin raised the topic of the presidential visit and instructed his agents to "do everything by the book," the Dallas SAC was referring to the FBI Handbook. As an agent in good standing, Hosty knew his handbook and the section that addressed the matter of threats to the president, his immediate family, and the vice president. The language of the handbook, while turgid, was comprehensive: "Therefore, any information indicating a possibility of an attempt against the person or safety of the President, members of the immediate family of the President, the President-elect, or the Vice-President must be referred immediately by the most expeditious means of communication to the nearest office of the U.S. Secret Service."[37] Despite the threatening language of Oswald's note and Hosty's own professional judgment that Oswald was a security risk, the threat had not been aimed at anyone in the presidential party. Oswald did not fit the criteria for informing the Secret Service. Apparently, Hosty treated the Oswald case as just one of the thirty-five or more cases that he was currently juggling.

There are other plausible reasons for Hosty's fateful inaction and the resulting history-altering consequences that followed. Hosty was waiting for the Oswald file to be officially transferred from New Orleans once it was learned that he had relocated to Dallas, the new office of record. According to Hosty, he had deferred any further action on the Oswalds until he had the updated file. This was all standard operational procedure outlined under 105-E in the FBI's Manual of Instructions. The fact that Oswald had made contact with the Soviet Embassy in Mexico City, as the Dallas office and Hosty learned more than a month before the Kennedy assassination, was apparently not regarded as important enough to alter routine procedure. It was not until the morning of November 22 that the Oswald file arrived at the FBI Dallas office.[38] In the meantime, Hosty turned to other matters at hand and simply forgot the Oswald note that was tucked away in his workbox.

If Fenner's memory was accurate on the key points, Hosty's supervisors, Shanklin, Clark, and Howe, knew about the Oswald note two weeks before President Kennedy's Dallas visit and, inexplicably, did nothing. As the Dallas office's supervisory personnel, common sense dictated that they should have sat down with Hosty and reviewed the Oswald file. It was Shanklin, after all, who alerted the office to Kennedy's visit and lectured the agents not to fail to report any possibility of a threat while the presidential party was in Dallas. After reading the Oswald note and failing to take any follow-up action, Shanklin, as well as Clark and Howe, was as culpable as Hosty.

This utter dereliction of responsibility and communication collapse was distressingly typical of the across-the-board FBI security failure associated with the Kennedy assassination. Unless FBIHQ had prior knowledge that Oswald had some U.S. government intelligence connections, his name should have been on the FBI's Security Index. Among other potential threats, the index contained names of persons who might be a threat to the president, and those names would be submitted to the Secret Service. Had Oswald's file indicated that he was on the Security Index, it would have underscored the heightened degree of Seat of Government's (Hooverese for the FBI's Washington headquarters) interest in the former defector and might have galvanized FBI Dallas to ensure that his name was on the Secret Service's "alert list."

Dallas in the 1960s had earned the sorry reputation of "the Hate Capital" of America. Birchites, the Klan, General Walker's Minutemen, and the most radical of the radical right, the National States Rights Party, found aid and comfort from like-minded Dallas cold warriors and dedicated right-wingers. In view of the extremist political climate in Dallas, the Commission registered surprised at the paucity of names Dallas FBI pulled from its files in preparation for Kennedy's visit. Hosty's own case files were made up largely of right-wing extremists, and he sent only one name, a Dallas County Klan member, to Sorrels's office. As mentioned before, it was Dallas police lieutenant Jack Revill, not Hosty, who alerted the Secret Service to General Walker's Denton, Texas, minions who were planning a "reception" for Kennedy. When Dallas's Secret Service chief testified before the Commission about security precautions surrounding Kennedy's appearance in Dallas, Sorrels spoke highly of the assistance his agency had received from the Dallas Police Department. He said nothing negative about the FBI, but he hardly mentioned the bureau at all and only as a trailing afterthought.[39]

It does not require special insight to appreciate how Dallas and the nation's history would have been dramatically different if the Secret Service had had Oswald's name on its "alert list." Although no analogy is perfect, a close parallel from modern U.S. history jumps to mind: the phone call that Watergate security guard Frank Wills made when he discovered tape holding a door unlocked within the complex that housed the Democratic National Committee headquarters. That call changed American history. It precipitated a cascade of events that ended in the resignation of an American president. Had Hosty walked Oswald's file over to Sorrels's office, this ordinary and, considering the circumstances, reasonable and expected action would also have changed history. With Oswald under surveillance, the Secret Service would have made certain that he never had Bouck's "unusual access," or any access at all, for that matter, to President Kennedy. It's a safe assumption that Secret Service agents and the Dallas police would have staked out the TSBD and possibly assigned more manpower in a visible show of force along the Houston–Elm Street stretch of the route to the Trade Mart. A show of force might have deterred any hidden gunmen in the vicinity of Dealey Plaza from carrying out plans to assassinate the president.

Another related momentous and tantalizing "what if" of Dallas rests on the arguable assumption that Oswald never shot anybody that day, that he was an unwitting patsy set up by conspirators who went free. Had Oswald been on the Secret Service's "alert list" Kennedy might still have been killed, but the official history of Dallas could not have been the politically preordained Warren report. The Oswald note perforce raises an essential question: Would someone who was bent on assassinating the president of the United States have left a threatening note with the FBI just weeks before the planned attempt? It is hard to think of any action more likely to draw unwanted attention from the authorities, short of advertising in one of the Dallas newspapers. This argument cannot be lightly shunted aside, even assuming, as Commission apologists maintain, that Oswald was an unstable, combustible personality, a sociopath at war with all authority figures and intent on entering the history books at any cost. The Hosty note still looms as an act counterproductive to Oswald ever realizing his alleged insidious fantasies. Furthermore, the Oswald-did-it-no-conspiracy advocates' only source is the Warren report, a document whose assumptions and conclusions are inconsistent with the Commission's own forensic and physical evidence and cannot stand up to scrutiny.

Before the weekend of the assassination was over James P. Hosty, Jr., became a household name at Seat of Government. In addition to the scandal of the Oswald note, FBI Washington received reports that Hosty had blurted out things to Dallas police and Secret Service agents that, if true, loomed as unmitigated disasters for the Hoover bureau. The mood at Seat of Government must have been dark and despairing. Had Hoover ordered the note's destruction, which is admittedly unclear, he had engaged in a criminal act by ordering the destruction of key evidence that could have destroyed the reputation of his FBI in the public mind. All the early physical evidence of the crime pointed to a conspiracy, and the Dallas agent in charge of the file of the only suspect in the case was proving a wild card, a veritable flap factory.

After learning that Kennedy had been shot, Hosty returned to the FBI Dallas office. He was confronted by Ken Howe, his supervisor, who told him that a Lee Oswald had been arrested for the shooting of Patrolman Tippit in the Oak Cliff area. According to Hosty, the whole awful reality of that day hit him like a ton of bricks: "Oswald was the son of a bitch who shot the president."[40] As Oswald's case officer, Hosty was ordered to get over to the police department and join in the interrogation of the suspect. In the basement garage of the Dallas police headquarters he ran into detectives Lt. Jack Revill and V. J. "Jackie" Brian. As the three men converged and rushed toward the elevator to police Capt. Will Fritz's office on the third floor, where Oswald was being questioned, Hosty and Revill exchanged information on the assassination. The men had worked with one another on criminal investigations for several years and were on a first-name basis. Exactly what was said in those few minutes became a source of sharp controversy and generated a deep and punishing resentment between the FBI and the Dallas Police Department.

Revill claimed that as he and Hosty kept pace with one another as they walked quickly through the garage to the elevator, Hosty blurted out that a "Communist killed President Kennedy" and that the FBI had a file on the assailant, Lee Harvey Oswald. Revill said he was at first stunned by this information and then ready to blow his top at Hosty's revelation just before they entered the elevator. According to the police lieutenant, he understood Hosty to say, "We had information that this man was capable of committing the assassination." In an affidavit executed on April 20, 1964, Detective Brian corroborated part of Revill's account, namely, that Hosty had said the FBI had known that Oswald was a communist and that he worked at the TSBD. But Brian said he missed snatches of the conversation because of the "excitement and commotion" in the basement.[41] Hosty did not deny the encounter with Revill in the garage, but his account was flat and lackluster compared to Revill's alarming version. Hosty claimed that he told Revill that Oswald was a defector, employed at the TSBD, and a suspect in the Kennedy assassination. Hosty contradicted Revill's and Brian's versions in that he insisted that the conversation took place while they were running up three flights of stairs and not facing each other while police, media, and unauthorized persons were passing them pell-mell on the stairwell in both directions. Hosty never mentioned any exchange while waiting to enter the elevator. In depicting a scene of total bedlam, Hosty underscored his contention that in all the confusion Revill simply misunderstood what he said.[42]

Years later, after Hosty retired from the FBI, the account in his book of the chance meeting with Revill was both more colorful and unintentionally more revealing about Agent Hosty. In his *Assignment Oswald* there was a good deal of self-puffery and braggadocio. What also surfaced was his barely disguised contempt for the investigative skills of the Dallas police, especially Revill, and the inadequacy of the Secret Service in general and that agency's Dallas office in particular. In puffing himself, Hosty put down Revill and Sorrels, for example, for lagging far behind the information curve on the day of the assassination. It was Agent James P. Hosty, Jr., whose special insight and acumen in intelligence work allowed him to identify Oswald as the assassin who had been hired to carry out this assignment by the Mexico City KGB. Hosty had intuited all this as a result of his own imagined unique knowledge of the case even before Oswald was charged and placed under arrest.[43]

Reveling in this intelligence leg up on his contemporaries, Hosty might have been tempted to blurt out things that would come back and haunt him and embarrass his own agency. For example, in reconstructing his on-the-fly exchange with Revill, he wrote that the police lieutenant understandably asked why, if the FBI had known that Oswald was a communist and worked at the TSBD, the bureau hadn't notified the Dallas police. Hosty countered with the FBI's "need-to-know rule." Hosty explained in his book that it "was the long-standing policy on espionage cases" that the "Bureau did not consider local police part of the need-to-know group, and this drove Revill crazy."[44] This, of course, made no sense at all other than providing Hosty an opportunity to flaunt an intelligence advantage and enjoy himself at Revill's expense. In the first place, Oswald was not an "espionage case," and second, the FBI did not have to reveal its sources to the Dallas police in order to alert the department to Oswald's presence in town and his place of employment. If what Hosty related was true, then it underscored questions about his fundamental judgment, questions that were very much on the mind of his superiors at FBIHQ as reports filtered in about his alleged reckless and runaway garrulity.

FBI Washington learned from a Secret Service January 23 memorandum that Hosty had let slip to Forrest Sorrels and a few other Secret Service agents in Captain Fritz's office that Oswald had "contacted two known subversive agents about fifteen days before the shooting of President Kennedy." In his book Hosty set the scene of his conversation with Sorrels in the same patronizing way that he depicted his exchange with Revill the same day. As he watched Sorrels interview Oswald, Hosty noted that he was "struck by Sorrels's dazed and distant approach." In Hosty's version, the Secret Service SAC asked questions that had already been asked and seemed hopelessly unprepared for interrogating the suspect. As an investigator of long experience, Hosty had to know that it was necessary for Sorrels to go over the same ground in order for the Secret Service to make its own record. After the questioning was interrupted so Oswald could be taken to a lineup, Hosty stated that he drew Sorrels aside to inform him that FBI Dallas had two pieces of secret information on Oswald's contacts that the Secret Service should know about. Here was Hosty, after Kennedy was gunned down, allegedly by a man whom Hosty regarded as a security risk, going out of his way to get poor, bewildered Sorrels up to speed.

Months later, when Sorrels was before the Commission, Assistant Counsel Stern asked about this meeting. Sorrels remembered that Hosty had spoken not to him but to Secret Service agent William H. Patterson, and Sorrels had no memory of what was said. It was Patterson who wrote the memorandum reporting that Hosty had told him and Agent Warner that Oswald had met with "two known subversive agents" two weeks before the assassination.[45] The "subversive agents" that Hosty was referring to had to be the Russians at the Soviet Embassy whom Oswald had spoken to over the phone while he was in Mexico City. Hosty had just received the updated Oswald file that morning, containing Oswald's November 9 letter to the USSR's Washington embassy in which he mentioned his phone contact with "comrade Kostine" and the CIA's report on its telephone interception of Oswald's call to the Mexico City Soviet Embassy. It was these two documents that apparently inspired Hosty's epiphany on that surreal Friday that Oswald had assassinated Kennedy at the direction of the Mexico City KGB. It would be consistent with his inflated "Hosty-of-the-Bureau" self-image for Hosty to have flaunted his imagined special insights and knowledge in the breaking case by filling in Agents Patterson and Warner on what he had glimpsed from Oswald's file that landed on his desk that morning. However, Hosty denied that he spoke to Patterson at all and insisted that he only told Sorrels that there was "more information concerning Oswald, but he should get it through . . . Washington headquarters." Shanklin sent off a four-page teletype to FBIHQ supporting Hosty's version of what had taken place in Capt. Will Fritz's office.[46]

The attention Hosty drew to himself over the weekend of the assassination persuaded FBI Washington to isolate him from the Oswald case. After Hosty parted company with Revill and Brian, he entered Captain Fritz's office prepared to interrogate Oswald. As soon as he introduced himself, Oswald went ballistic. "So you are Hosty. I've heard about you," was Oswald's opening response after Hosty introduced himself. He then proceeded to rip into Hosty for harassing his wife and not coming to Oswald directly with his questions. According to Hosty, Oswald then launched into a harangue against the FBI and Hoover, adding a final threat: "I'm going to fix you, FBI." Hosty and James W. Bookhout, the FBI agent accompanying Hosty, retreated into the background while Fritz tried to calm Oswald in order to continue with the interrogation.[47]

This brief confrontation revealed a bureau secret: The Dallas police now knew that the FBI had had an interest in Oswald before the assassination. This corroborated part of Revill's account of his exchange earlier that day with Hosty. Revill's boss, Capt. Pat Ganoway, instructed Revill to put his exchange with Hosty in writing for the record. On Monday, November 25, Hosty was taken off the Oswald case and assigned to the team investigating Jack Ruby, Oswald's assassin. This decision came from FBI headquarters. It coincided with the arrival in Dallas of Inspector James R. Malley, the deputy director of Division Six, the criminal division, to supervise the overall investigation into the Kennedy assassination. Malley impressed upon Shanklin that Hosty should be removed from the case for a growing number of embarrassing and potentially damaging reasons. Not the least of these was the fact that Hosty's visits to the Paine residence had upset Marina Oswald, and she was shaping up as the FBI's key witness against her husband, so FBIHQ wanted her in a cooperative frame of mind. Moreover, when Malley arrived in Dallas he learned that Oswald's notebook found at his Oak Cliff rooming house contained Hosty's name, license plate number, and the address and phone number of Dallas FBI headquarters. Having already ordered the destruction of the Oswald note, FBIHQ paled at the prospect of this evidence in the hands of the Commission, possibly inviting a line of inquiry into areas that might unravel the cover-up of the destruction of the Hosty note.[48]

The Hoover bureau hardly appreciated the dimensions of the emerging scandal when it was hit with the first public installment of the "Hosty problem." Saturday morning, the day after the assassination, Dallas police chief Jesse E. Curry made some alarming claims during an interview on NBC TV. He charged that the FBI had known about Oswald's procommunist and pro-Castro leanings and had failed to advise the Dallas police. The police chief also asserted that the FBI had interviewed Oswald several weeks before the president's Dallas visit and had had him under surveillance. Curry did not disclose his sources, but his information came from Lt. Jack Revill's report of his exchange with Hosty the previous day.

Hoover immediately ordered FBI Dallas to demand a retraction, and Shanklin called Curry at once to set him straight. That afternoon Curry was back on NBC TV and apologized for his comments, assuring the public that his statement "was not in accordance with the facts." FBIHQ was not satisfied with Curry's retraction. Back in Washington, Assistant Director Deke DeLoach, the keeper of the FBI's public relations flame, contacted cooperative sources at United Press International (UPI) and the Associated Press (AP) on a "confidential basis" and requested that they instruct their affiliates in Dallas to contact Curry and get him to repudiate his allegations on their wire services. To cover all points on the media compass, DeLoach had *Washington Evening Star* reporter Jeremy O'Leary immediately set up an interview with the Dallas police chief. O'Leary was one of DeLoach's stalwart and willing "friendly sources" in the news business, and a great favorite with Hoover. O'Leary agreed to contact Curry and write a feature story with the embattled police chief on record making another abject apology for spreading, according to the FBI, false allegations.[49]

The day Curry went public with his inference that FBI bungling was responsible for Kennedy's assassination, Hoover ordered an internal investigation into the Oswald case. The FBI headquarters official who drew the short straw was a twenty-three-year-veteran and assistant director of the Inspection Division, James H. Gale. On Saturday, November 23, Gale was called into Hoover's office, where he met with Hoover and Associate Director Clyde Tolson, the FBI's number-two man. During the two-hour meeting Hoover anticipated that there would be a presidential commission that would review the bureau's handling of the Oswald case. He instructed Gale to do a thorough investigation to determine whether there were shortcomings or problem areas in the case. "Leave no stone unturned," Hoover enjoined Gale, "and let the chips fall where they may." According to Gale's account, Hoover repeatedly stressed, "This is undoubtedly the most important responsibility I have given you since you have been in the FBI." In order to distance himself from allegations that he was responsible in any way for what had happened in Dallas, Hoover was prepared to throw some of his underlings overboard. Gale was to investigate the performance of all FBI personnel, up and down the chain of command, from assistant directors to agents in the field, who had any responsibility for the Oswald file. Gale finished his report in about two weeks without ever leaving Washington or personally interviewing a single agent, supervisor, or headquarters official. His conclusion was laid out in the second paragraph of the nine-page report: "It is definitely felt that the subject Oswald should have been on the Security Index." There is nothing in the report about the Oswald note or its subsequent destruction. Fifteen years later Gale would testify that he never learned of the note or its destruction until four years after he retired.[50]

The whole business of the Oswald note and FBI headquarters' orders to destroy it was a closely held secret. Probably only a handful of Hoover's assistant directors were privy to the cover-up. So there is no reason to believe Gale was being untruthful in his denial. The report, which was a secret in-house document and, therefore, not shared with the Warren Commission, never ventured to speculate counterfactually as to whether what happened in Dealey Plaza might have had a different outcome had Oswald's name been on the Security Index.[51]

The report recommended disciplinary action in seventeen cases. The list comprised veteran street agents, including Hosty, field office supervisors, and at least four highly placed agents at Seat of Government, including Assistant Director William C. Sullivan. Sullivan would later claim that he had never seen the Oswald file and never heard of Oswald until after the assassination. But as assistant director of the Domestic Intelligence Division (DID) he was held theoretically responsible. Sullivan had cause for feeling he was unjustly victimized because FBI records disclosed that the head of the DID knew nothing about the Hosty note destruction. According to Gale's report, all of them shared some degree of responsibility for letting Oswald slip through the cracks when he should have been on the Security Index. Not surprisingly, Hoover agreed with the report's recommendations in all seventeen cases. Gale's name was on the report, but it was the director who had set out the results he expected before Gale went through the motions of an investigation.[52]

Hoover's administrative ramrodding of Gale's recommendations for disciplinary action did not go unchallenged. Alan Belmont, the number-three man at FBIHQ and the assistant director overseeing the Kennedy investigation, argued that the officials and agents cited by Gale had not been in error; the problem was that the criteria were not "sufficiently specific" to include Oswald. Belmont wanted Hoover to drop any disciplinary action and have Gale redraft the criteria for the Security Index. DeLoach joined in the dissent. Politics and image were always primary concerns for DeLoach, who fashioned himself after the director. He urged his boss to postpone any disciplinary action until after the Warren Commission's findings were made public. His fear was that the immediate implementation of Gale's recommended actions might reach the Commission and the public and leave the appearance that FBI negligence "might have resulted in the assassination of the President." Hoover initially resisted these appeals, arguing that "such gross incompetence can't be overlooked or administrative action postponed." It was all a "shameful mess" (Hoover's words), and he wanted those responsible to feel the sting of his displeasure.

Some in the FBI hierarchy, such as Assistant Director Sullivan, who were most familiar with the wiles and survival skills of this consummate bureaucrat must have been aware that Hoover was creating a record in the event that the public ever learned that FBI investigative deficiencies had played a critical role in the assassination. If that dreaded moment ever came Hoover could wrap himself in the Gale report and proclaim that he had taken immediate action, fixed the responsibility for what had happened, and punished those who had been derelict in their duties. What purpose was there for an ultrasecret investigation other than to provide the director with an off-the-shelf insurance policy if it was ever needed? If Hoover's purpose was to send a message through agency ranks demanding better accountability in the future, why shroud the whole process in secrecy? For example, the disciplining of Sullivan and other DID officials was kept secret. Some highly placed FBIHQ officials, such as Alex Rosen, assistant director of the General Investigative Division, the division formally in charge of the investigation of the crime, never knew about the Gale report. Ultimately, Hoover agreed to hold back on disciplinary measures until the Commission published its report. The only exception was Hosty, who was censured and placed on probation for three months beginning in December until March 1964.[53]

On April 24 the "Hosty problem" was back in the news. Hugh Aynesworth, a reporter for the *Dallas Morning News,* wrote a two-column story titled, "FBI Knew Oswald Capable of Act, Reports Indicate." Crediting a source "close to the Warren Commission," Aynesworth's story centered on Lieutenant Revill's affidavit reporting his exchange with Hosty in the basement of the Dallas Police Department on the day of the assassination. The Dallas detective's five-paragraph affidavit concluded with the startling assertion that Hosty had told Revill that the FBI "knew he [Oswald] was capable of assassinating the president, but we didn't dream he would do it." Chief Curry had provided the Commission with a photographic copy of Revill's affidavit several weeks before, when he was called to Washington to testify. Rankin assured the FBI that the leak had not come from the Commission. He suspected Dallas assistant district attorney Will Alexander, based on Alexander's undisguised animosity toward the FBI and his close relationship with Aynesworth. Rankin was probably right about Alexander. It had not slipped his mind that these two, in league with reporter Lonnie Hudkins, had cooked up the three-way phone conversation about Oswald's fabricated FBI payroll number, setting agents off on a wild-goose chase, much to the trio's amusement.[54]

Inspector Malley, the bureau's liaison with the Commission, requested copies of Revill's and Detective Brian's Commission testimony. Rankin refused, citing Commission rules, but let Malley know that Aynesworth's news story was faithful to the language in Revill's affidavit. The general counsel tried to ease Malley's concern by assuring him that he, Rankin, "was not concerned too much" about the news story because he "felt certain SA Hosty would not have made the statements attributed to him."

In the meantime, DeLoach arranged through the executive editor of the rival *Dallas Times Herald,* Felix McKnight, a trusted bureau media asset, a platform for Hoover "to set the record straight," categorically denying that Hosty had ever made such a statement. Before the day was over Shanklin's office was flooded with calls from radio, newspaper, and TV journalists asking for his comments on the Aynesworth story. The Dallas SAC gave the bureau's stock response: "No comment. The Director was the spokesman for the FBI at all times." Hosty did not help the situation much by taking a UPI reporter's call in which he ridiculed the story as completely false but, by adding the personal disclaimer, gave the wire story the excuse to repeat Revill's allegation all over again. The Aynesworth story and all that it set in motion confirmed in Hoover's mind that Hosty was a "pop off," a loose cannon that he could neither control nor push over the side, certainly not before the Commission published its findings. When he saw the UPI story the director was beside himself. He wrote in the margin of a copy of the wire story, "I don't believe the UPI would put such words in Hosty's mouth if he hadn't said them."[55]

With all the attention Hosty was attracting, it was certain that he would be called as a Commission witness. This was a development that Seat of Government, at least at the time of Gale's internal investigation, did not anticipate and would not have welcomed. In early April the Dallas field office's number-two man, Kyle Clark, noted that Malley "had no hesitation" in allowing any agent in the office to submit affidavits to the Commission, "with the exception of SA Hosty." Belmont shared Malley's concern and instructed Kyle to make it clear to Hosty that if he was to testify or furnish an affidavit, all the "information . . . be reduced to writing and put in report form." Spelling it out further, Belmont added that it "should be impressed on SA Hosty that he has no personal opinions or observations concerning the investigation of the President's assassination."[56] The day Aynesworth's story appeared, Hoover ordered that Hosty immediately prepare an affidavit for the Commission. Belmont screened Hosty's draft and "advised" that a sentence be added stating that "Hosty had never heard any information indicating potential violence on the part of Oswald." A sentence to that effect appeared on page 4 of the Hosty affidavit. The affidavit was delivered by courier service to Rankin with a cover letter from Hoover assuring the Commission's general counsel that Revill's allegations were completely false. Belmont ended his day by instructing Shanklin, at Hoover's direction, to start dealing with Chief Curry and the Dallas police "at arm's length." The severing of relations and all cooperative functions went into effect immediately, with the Dallas SAC canceling the appointments of Dallas police applicants to the FBI Academy.[57]

The "Hosty problem" not only soured FBI relations with the Dallas police but stirred up deep-seated tensions between the Hoover bureau and the Secret Service. It was no secret, at least among Washington insiders, that Hoover had dreamed and schemed through four administrations to pry the protection of the president away from the Secret Service.[58] Despite official statements and protestations to the contrary from both agency heads, relations between the FBI and the Secret Service during the investigation into the JFK assassination were rent by "turf" issues, mutual suspicions, and finger pointing.

As a harbinger of things to come, a Secret Service agent got physical with an FBI agent almost before President Kennedy had received the last rites. The altercation occurred outside Trauma Room One at Parkland Memorial Hospital. Secret Service agents Andrew E. Berger and Richard E. Johnsen were stationed outside the emergency room where Kennedy's body remained, awaiting the arrangements to take his remains back to Washington. A tall, strapping, unidentified man, shouting that he was an FBI agent but flashing no identification, tried to push by Berger and Johnsen and follow a nurse into the emergency room. He was instantly slammed to the wall and fell to the floor after receiving a haymaker from one of the Secret Service agents.[59] The FBI agent was later identified as J. Doyle Williams.

The fracas would probably have been overlooked in light of the enormity of that day's controlling events except that the incident received some media attention. Both the UPI and the AP included it in their hastily prepared photojournalistic accounts of the assassination. The UPI book, *Four Days,* more addicted to overinflated high drama than to accuracy, described the incident in comic book–like prose: "Suddenly two Secret Service men burst into the room. One of them, his face contorted with anguish, was waving a submachine gun. Staff members dived for cover. A man in a business suit dashed in; this agent slammed him against the wall with one punch. Dazed, the man pulled out F.B.I. credentials and gasped, 'I've got to call J. Edgar Hoover.'"[60]

Caught in the web of his obsession with image, Hoover could not stand by and allow the FBI to be made a laughingstock before the entire nation. FBI Washington lodged a protest with Lyle C. Wilson, UPI's vice president. Wilson informed FBIHQ that two Parkland interns had witnessed the incident, and the description in *Four Days* was based on their accounts. Hoover ordered the Dallas office to send someone to question the doctors and make them "put up or shut up." The director wanted them to retract their version that SA Williams had been "knocked to the floor." Wilson and the UPI apologized for the offending reference and promised to omit the account in future printings of the book. Secret Service chief Rowley heard from FBIHQ about "the Bureau's displeasure" and the uncalled-for rough handling dealt out by two of his agents. Rowley attributed the incident to the "tenseness of the situation" but wanted Hoover to know he was "sincerely sorry the incident occurred."[61]

Although the "knock-down" flap quickly dissipated, the FBI grew increasingly uneasy over the Secret Service's interest in Hosty's preassassination investigation of Lee Harvey Oswald. It was not FBI paranoia or petty turf battles that generated this suspicion. The Secret Service agents responsible for the protection of the president were unofficially attempting to ferret out whether Hosty had withheld any information about Oswald that should have been turned over to the Secret Service. When reminded that the FBI had complete jurisdiction in the Oswald investigation, Rowley assured FBI liaison Orrin H. Bartlett that his agency's interest was solely in "tying up a few loose ends." Rowley pointed out that he had instructed Secret Service agents to turn over to the FBI all pertinent documents and communications relating to Oswald.[62]

FBI Washington was not convinced. A week after Rowley's conversation with Bartlett, Assistant Director Rosen picked up on the theme of the Secret

Service's "more than normal interest" in the FBI's preassassination interest in the alleged assassin. Rosen was vexed by the Secret Service agents who were trying to elicit from Marina Oswald the identity of the FBI agent who had contacted Ruth Paine. Reading between the lines of the transcript of the Secret Service's November 24 interview, Rosen was convinced that Rowley's agents were trying to establish whether the FBI had "more recent personal contact" with both Oswald and his wife than the FBI had set out in its report to the Commission.

Rosen had reason to be concerned because the FBI record of its contacts never mentioned Hosty's November 1 and 5 visits to Ruth Paine's residence. The document listed John Fain's August 16, 1962, interview with Oswald as the agency's last personal contact with the alleged assassin. The only possible official FBI rationalization for these omissions was to create the impression that Hosty had spoken only to Ruth Paine and never tried to interview Marina during either of his visits to the Paine residence. However, in light of the rumors that were flying around Dallas the day after the assassination— Chief Curry's NBC TV interview, for example—the Secret Service had cause and a self-interested motive for suspecting that the FBI had something to hide. Did the FBI's file on Oswald indicate that he might be a danger to the president? If there was a "smoking gun," then the failure to alert the Secret Service fixed the culpability for Dallas on a rival agency whose director had maneuvered for years to take over the job of protecting the chief executive. There was also an outside possibility that Oswald was being run by some agency or was Hosty's own private "hip-pocket" informant. Although these speculations were unproven and probably groundless, if Oswald had had some low-level intelligence connection, it would have gone a long way toward answering some tormenting questions that had to be plaguing the Secret Service: Why did the defector Oswald never have a stop placed on his passport? Why was he not on the FBI's Security Index? And why was his name never submitted to the Secret Service prior to President Kennedy's visit to Dallas? Before the dust of that horrendous day had settled, these questions, dark suspicions, wild tales, and background clatter were rife in Dallas. It would have required superhuman restraint for Secret Service agents to resist being drawn into this undertow of assassination allegation, speculation, and rumor.[63]

The Secret Service had reason to believe that the FBI had had personal contact with Marina before the assassination. According to the Secret Service, this information originated with Hosty. The first joint FBI–Secret Service postassassination interview with Marina occurred on Wednesday, November 27. Hosty was part of the interview team, which also included Secret Service Agents Sorrels and Patterson and Inspector Thomas J. Kelley. While they were discussing interview strategy, Hosty, according to a Secret

Service report, freely confided that he had interviewed Marina "to a great extent." This was probably another instance of the FBI agent's fluent one-upmanship and self-puffery to impress his Secret Service teammates with his unique and intimate grasp of the case. If Hosty had had extensive personal contact with Marina, then he lied to the Warren Commission. When Hosty appeared before the Commission in May 1964 he assured his questioners that he had never interviewed Marina during his November 1 visit to Ruth Paine's house. He testified that when he returned four days later he had a two-minute conversation with Ruth Paine on her front porch and never saw Marina.[64]

Then there was the discovery of Oswald's address book containing Hosty's name, the address and phone number of the Dallas FBI, and the license number of Hosty's car. Most of the information was retrieved from a piece of paper Hosty had left with Ruth Paine during his November 1 visit. Marina, per Lee's instructions, had copied the license plate number of Hosty's car when the FBI agent returned on November 5. The Dallas police uncovered the address book among Oswald's effects at the North Beckley Street rooming house. Hosty claimed that Captain Fritz had turned the document over to him the day of the assassination. There is some confusion about the date on which Hosty received the address book. However, before it became the evidentiary property of the FBI the Secret Service had gone over it and picked out the Hosty citation on page 68. The Dallas Secret Service and the police department enjoyed a good working relationship, and Fritz would have made a point of seeing that Sorrels or someone from Sorrels's office examined the address book before it was turned over to the FBI. When Secret Service agent Leon L. Gopadze, the agency's top Russian-language expert, interviewed Marina in early December he showed her the notation found in her dead husband's address book, and Marina claimed that Hosty had interviewed her.[65]

Ultimately responsible for the integrity of the Kennedy investigation, Hoover must have come to view Hosty as a recurring bad dream. He had censured Hosty and placed him on a ninety-day probation. Hoover's December 13 letter of censure charged that Hosty's investigation of Oswald had been "slipshod," "grossly inadequate," and marked by "exceedingly poor" judgment and "unwarranted delay" in reporting information in a "security-type case" of this nature. Responsibility for interviewing Marina Oswald was taken away from Hosty and assigned to other agents.[66] The message from FBI Washington could not have been clearer: Hosty was an embarrassment to the bureau, and he was being sent to Coventry. The criminal destruction of the Oswald note was reason enough to keep Hosty's name out of the public limelight. But all of Seat of Government's efforts to handle the "Hosty problem" were to no avail. With the discovery of Oswald's address book Hosty's name was back in the news. The "Hosty problem" was like a child's bathtub yellow rubber duck: Every time it was pushed under the water it defiantly popped back up again.

If the Dallas police and the Secret Service knew about the Hosty citation in Oswald's address book on the day of the assassination, it could be expected that Rankin and Commission staffers were, in short order, informed about it as well. But when the Commission received FBI inspector Robert Gemberling's December 23, 1963, report, which purported to include a verbatim reproduction of the address book, the Hosty citation was omitted. Gemberling was the Dallas case officer on the Kennedy assassination, and his voluminous report represented the investigative findings of that office. Rankin's request to Hoover for an explanation of the omission seemed suspiciously delayed and came only after the matter had received public attention. It is possible that the general counsel and Hoover privately agreed to treat this disclosure as "extraneous" to the official investigation, believing it would only provide more fuel for the firestorm of conspiracy rumors circulating in the domestic and foreign press. If there was a mutual agreement to suppress the Oswald address book, it would not have been the first time that an inconvenient fact was covered up. For instance, Rankin and the Commission held back from the American people the fact that Jack Ruby, the killer of the alleged assassin, had been an FBI provisional criminal informant. It was not until twelve years after the Warren report was published that the American people learned that in 1959 Ruby had reported on at least eight occasions to the FBI.[67]

Speculation aside, the disclosed records show that on January 28 Hoover and Rankin had a private discussion about allegations that Oswald was an FBI informant. The upshot of the meeting was a flood of affidavits from all FBI agents connected with the case, in addition to the director's own sworn statement, that Oswald had never reported to the FBI. Rankin's meeting with Hoover was the result of the director's January 27 letter to the general counsel informing him, presumably for the first time in writing, about the Hosty notations in Oswald's address book. It had to be more than coincidence that on that same day the *Nation* carried Harold Feldman's piece, "Oswald and the FBI." In trying to make a case for Oswald as an FBI informer, Feldman disclosed that Oswald's address book contained Hosty's name, business phone and address, and the agent's license plate number. Learning from Congressman Gerry Ford of the Commission's keen interest in Feldman's piece in the *Nation* was probably enough of a prompt to get Hoover to go on record in his January 27 letter to Rankin.[68]

Several weeks after Feldman's story appeared, Rankin wrote Hoover about the omission of the Hosty citations in the Gemberling report. The subject had come up in the Commission's February 24 executive session, and that presumably forced Rankin's hand. Writing for the Commission, Rankin requested a "full explanation" of the "circumstances surrounding this omission." Hoover registered his surprise and mortification about the way the whole affair had been handled. He blanketed headquarters memoranda with his dyspeptic marginalia: "The written record is not one reflecting any credit on the Bureau but rather shortcomings." On another: "In failing to send *all* to the Committee we have created a suspicion we are hiding something." Either the director was writing for the record and employing the charade of distance, or his surprise was genuine. It is possible that Gemberling had decided on his own to omit the Hosty references from the address book when recording the entries for his report in order to protect the Dallas office from Hoover's wrath.[69] Whatever the real explanation, the FBI was forced to explain the omission. The official line was that Gemberling and his assistant, John T. Kesler, were looking for leads in the case when transcribing names and telephone numbers from Oswald's address book. Since Hosty was known to them and was not lead information, his name and related information were excluded. Gemberling and Kesler executed affidavits to that effect.[70]

In March Commission staff reports of rehearsal interviews with Secret Service agents began to filter into Rankin's office. The general counsel was uncomfortable with the overall message being delivered. All of the agents interviewed either directly or indirectly were critical of FBI arrogance, aloofness, and dereliction of responsibility when it came to security precautions for President Kennedy's Dallas visit. Commission staff lawyer Burt W. Griffin had a lengthy conversation with veteran Secret Service agent Sorrels. He was moved by Sorrels's expressed sadness over the assassination and feelings of personal guilt for Kennedy's death. Sorrels commented on the "marked change" for the better in cooperation between the FBI and his agency after the assassination. When the conversation shifted toward Hosty, Sorrels's tone changed. He characterized the FBI agent as being "brusque," "supercilious," and "distrustful with respect to others." He shared with Griffin what Hosty had allegedly told one of Sorrels's agents, which proved to be an accurate preview of Hosty's Commission testimony. According to this hearsay, Hosty had prepared an explanation for his failure to alert the Secret Service to Oswald's employment at the TSBD. Hosty would tell the Commission, Sorrels reported, that "he was so busy he never read the newspapers and did not know where the caravan would travel." When Griffin asked if this was a fabrication, Sorrels replied that "he understood that it could be Hosty's attitude." Griffin's conversation with Sorrels apparently sharpened his interest in Hosty. Griffin was back in Dallas in April to investigate gun-running activities of anti-Castro Cubans to determine if there was any connection with the Kennedy assassination. While interviewing an agent of the

Alcohol and Tobacco Tax Unit, Griffin, accompanied by Secret Service agent Patterson, asked the agent about Hosty and whether he knew of any instances of the FBI withholding information that should have been disseminated. When Hoover learned of Griffin's interest he ordered the FBI liaison with the Secret Service to get Rowley to explain why one of his agents was assisting in a Commission field investigation. At the bottom of the FBI memo he scrawled, "I hope you realize what Commission investigators are seeking."[71]

Commission counsel Sam Stern interviewed Robert Bouck, head of the PRS, and Inspector Thomas J. Kelley to define the topics for their upcoming testimony before the Commission. During their first session both men asserted that in view of what they knew about the FBI's Oswald file they would have expected to have been informed about Oswald, would have regarded him as a threat, and would have placed him under surveillance during the president's stay in Dallas. Bouck and Kelley drew parallels between Dallas and the narrowly unsuccessful 1950 attempt by two Puerto Rican nationalists to break into Blair House and assassinate President Harry S. Truman. The agents told Stern that the FBI had had a file on the Puerto Rican Nationalist Movement but had never alerted the Secret Service about the organization or its potential for violence until after the failed assassination attempt.

In Stern's second rehearsal interview with Bouck, the PRS head brought with him a list of items of information about Oswald that he believed the FBI had had before the assassination. Bouck, according to Stern, was "firmer than ever that this information clearly indicates enough of a threat to the President to have warranted the FBI's advising PRS."[72] Even before Stern's interviews with Bouck and Kelley, he had reviewed the FBI's pre-assassination file on Oswald and developed a set of probing questions about the FBI's handling of the Oswald case. Rankin received Stern's list of twenty-eight detailed questions and accompanying concerns in February. "On the facts now available," Stern wrote the general counsel, it was incumbent upon the Commission to ascertain "why the FBI apparently did not consider that his conduct merited advice to the Secret Service . . . particularly in the liaison activities immediately preceding the President's trip, and why the FBI was not more actively pursuing Oswald in connection with its own direct responsibilities."[73] Completely unaware of the Hoover-inspired secret Gale report, Stern raised the same troubling questions about the FBI's handling of the Oswald case that the FBI's assistant director and chief inspector had addressed back in December 1963.

The Commission's general counsel did not like where this was heading. The last thing the Commission needed was a finger-pointing contest between two agencies of the executive branch, each determined to place the onus of the assassination on the other. As a seasoned bureaucrat Rankin knew that such an internecine battle would soon erupt into the public domain. Unsettling, too, was the fact that some of his own staff appeared to champion the Secret Service and its brief that FBI negligence had compromised the agency's primary mission of presidential protection. No one was more acutely aware than Rankin that in order to accomplish the Commission's mandate and produce a report that would lay to rest rumors and suspicions about Dallas, he had to have the FBI's full cooperation. From the day Rankin took over de facto control of the Commission, a top priority was to avoid alienating Hoover even if he had to bend or break the Commission's rules of procedure.

A week before Bouck's scheduled Commission appearance Rankin alerted Malley, the FBI's liaison with the Commission, that the FBI might have a problem. He confided that a Secret Service agent had told Commission staffers that Oswald would have been under surveillance "had information available been made known to the Secret Service." Malley had been cultivating Rankin all along, but this was the first time the general counsel "has bent a bit . . . and had departed from his strict, official role in so advising Malley." Rankin would not give up the Secret Service agent's name, but FBIHQ had learned from two other sources that it was Bouck. Rankin's purpose was clear enough. He was providing FBIHQ with lead time to prepare a counterstroke.[74]

The FBI's number-two man and Hoover's alter ego, Associate Director Clyde Tolson, directed Belmont to take up the issue with Rowley. When Chief Rowley heard from the FBI's Secret Service liaison that some of his agents were "attempting to dump" responsibility for the JFK assassination on the FBI, he was "shocked and indignant." Rowley had no way of knowing that Rankin had set up this preemptive strike against Bouck, his agency's number-two man. According to Bartlett, the FBI's liaison with the Secret Service, Rowley protested that only he and Bouck could speak for the Secret Service, and he knew of no information that indicated that Oswald was capable of violence; therefore, Oswald would not have been placed under surveillance. Rowley assured Bartlett in light of this development that Bouck would be "thoroughly brief[ed] in advance" of his Commission testimony. On April 22, the day before Bouck's scheduled Commission appearance, Malley relayed Rowley's comments to Rankin. The Commission's general counsel was relieved to learn that Rowley was going to rein in Bouck before he appeared before the Commission. That same day Bartlett met with Rowley to tell him that Rankin had been given Rowley's assurance that Oswald would not have been placed under surveillance. Rowley, according to Bartlett, reiterated that Bouck would be briefed on the Secret Service's "official position" before testifying before the Commission.[75]

The Bouck who appeared before the Warren commissioners was a markedly deflated version of the unflinching PRS chief who had unequivocally told Stern in his rehearsal interviews that the FBI had failed in its responsibilities by not advising the Secret Service about Oswald. The Bouck the commissioners heard from was tentative, evasive, and frustratingly noncommittal. Even when McCloy suggested that the FBI, and the Dallas office in particular, had been less than forthcoming in sharing information with the Secret Service, Bouck refused to connect the dots laid out before him. Assistant Counsel Stern tried to draw out the twenty-four-year agency professional, but to no avail. Whatever tack Rowley had taken with Bouck in laying out the Secret Service's "official position" had left an indelible impression. The only time Bouck came out of his shell was to suggest that Oswald would have met the Secret Service criteria for surveillance based on his "unusual access" to the motorcade route. But he quickly retreated behind a veil of equivocation and indecisiveness. The "unusual access" criterion, he ventured, would only have gone into effect if PRS had known about the derogatory information on Oswald that was scattered through four agencies. Having made this observation, Bouck went into full skedaddle mode, confessing, "I am not aware of how much any one agency or any one person might have known." Bouck never mentioned Hosty and insisted that he knew of no one in the FBI who had known that Oswald "had a vantage point on the route."[76]

On all counts FBI headquarters had every reason to be satisfied with the results of the Commission's investigation into the area of problems and methods of presidential protection. The immediate feedback from Rankin about Bouck's Commission appearance was comforting. Rankin classified the PRS head's performance as a "push," that is, unconvincingly self-serving. The other Commission members, Malley also learned from Rankin, did not "buy" Bouck's testimony and were put off by his evasiveness. Off the record, the FBI learned that Rankin and Chairman Warren did not place much stock in Lt. Jack Revill's deposition about what he alleged Hosty had blurted out to him in the Dallas Police Department's garage an hour after the assassination. They privately assumed that Chief Curry had had Revill and Detective "Jackie" Brian fabricate their sworn accounts to divert any responsibility and national obloquy away from the police and the city of Dallas, pointing out that the affidavits matched each other nearly word for word and had not been notarized until mid-April. On the other hand, the Commission gave weight to Hosty's affidavit, in which he denied Revill's account and swore he had never tried to develop Oswald as an informant or source of information.[77]

During Hosty's two and a half hours before the Commission, he was never asked about the Oswald note, although, as mentioned before, the

Commission knew from Ruth Paine that Oswald had delivered a note to Hosty. It did not escape FBI Washington that the commissioners never asked Hosty a direct question about why his name, license plate, business address, and phone number appeared in Oswald's address book. None of the commissioners evinced any curiosity about whether there was a story behind this story. Assistant Director Alex Rosen, embellishing somewhat, observed that "it appeared apparent to Agent Hosty that all members of the Commission were completely satisfied with the presentation." Rosen was not basing his remarks on Belmont's post-testimony briefing of Hosty. Belmont had his own independent source in Commissioner Gerry Ford, and even possibly Rankin.[78] From Hosty to Hoover, all the way up the line, it appeared as if the cover-up were intact and the "Hosty problem" had vanished.

While he was in Washington to testify, Hosty asked Belmont if he could meet with the director before returning to Dallas. Belmont said he would forward the request, but not until after Hosty had testified. According to Hosty, Hoover did favor him with an audience, and the hour he spent with the director was very upbeat. Hoover had just returned from lunch with President Johnson and was "bursting with good news." Over lunch Johnson had told Hoover that he was waiving the mandatory retirement requirement, thereby allowing the sixty-nine-year-old to stay on as FBI director. Hoover complimented Hosty on his Commission testimony and, according to Hosty, assured him that the Warren Commission would "clear the FBI of any mishandling of the Oswald case." During his hour-long monologue, which included tales about strengths and foibles of past presidents and potshots at Bobby Kennedy, Warren, and McCloy, the director, according to Hosty, never brought up the Oswald note or Hosty's handling of the case. When Hoover ushered him to the door in his "best esprit de corps manner," he told Hosty not to talk to the press or the police when he returned to Dallas. Whatever private plans Hoover had for Hosty, they would wait until after the Commission's findings became public.[79]

11   Senator Russell Dissents

The reputations of all of us are at stake in this thing.
—Senator Richard B. Russell, Warren Commission
Executive Session, December 5, 1963

In May 1964, about the midway point in the Warren Commission's investigation, Director J. Edgar Hoover appeared before the commissioners to provide them with his special insights into the Kennedy assassination and the benefit of his forty years as head of the nation's most prestigious and revered law enforcement agency. Hoover was probably America's most renowned and best-recognized public figure, and the Commission wanted to trade on his éclat.

Hoover was scheduled to give his testimony when the Commission was still working under Warren and Rankin's initial time frame and expected to finish up its work by the end of June. Ford and Dulles did most of the early questioning. What they wanted from America's iconic hero was his assurance that the assassination had been the act of a lone nut. Hoover was quick to oblige, assuring the commissioners that there was not "a scintilla of evidence showing any foreign conspiracy or domestic conspiracy that culminated in the assassination of President Kennedy." Hoover told the commissioners they could expect to be second-guessed and violently disagreed with, whatever their ultimate findings were. He pointed out that the FBI was already inundated with crank letters and calls from kooks, weirdos, crazies, and self-anointed psychics, all alleging a monstrous conspiracy behind Kennedy's violent death.[1] Whether orchestrated or not, his testimony before the Commission provided the director an opportunity to launch a preemptive strike against future dissenters and critics of the Warren Commission and, by extension, Hoover's FBI, the Commission's investigative arm.

Whatever the merits, if any, of Hoover's profiling of future Commission dissenters and critics, its first test was a hands-down failure. The Commission's first dissenter was Senator Richard Brevard Russell, Jr., one of the most conservative as well as respected and admired members of the U.S. Senate. Russell wielded great power in the upper chamber and had earned the title "dean of the Senate." During 1963–1964, when the Warren Commission was conducting its business, no U.S. legislator was at the White House as frequently as the senior senator from Georgia.[2]

On September 18, 1964, a Friday evening, President Johnson phoned Russell, his old political mentor and longtime friend, to find out what was in the Commission's report scheduled for release within the week. Johnson was surprised that Russell had suddenly bolted from Washington for a weekend retreat to his Winder, Georgia, home. Russell was quick to clear up the mystery as to why he needed to get out of the nation's capital. For the past nine months the Georgia lawmaker had been trying to balance his heavy senatorial duties with his responsibilities as a member of the Warren Commission, a perfect drudgery that Johnson had imposed upon him despite Russell's strenuous objections. No longer a young man and suffering from debilitating emphysema, Russell was simply played out. But it was the Warren Commission's last piece of business that had prompted his sudden Friday decision to escape Washington.

That Friday, September 18, Russell forced a special executive session of the Commission. It was not a placid meeting. In brief, Russell intended to use this session to explain to his Commission colleagues why he could not sign a report stating that the same bullet had struck both President Kennedy and Governor Connally. Russell was convinced that the missile that had struck Connally was a separate bullet. Senator Cooper was in strong agreement with Russell, and Boggs, to a lesser extent, had his own serious reservations about the single-bullet explanation. The Commission's findings were already in page proofs and ready for printing when Russell balked at signing the report. Commissioners Ford, Dulles, and McCloy were satisfied that the one-bullet scenario was the most reasonable explanation because it was essential to the report's single-assassin conclusion. With the Commission divided almost down the middle, Chairman Warren insisted on nothing less than a unanimous report. The stalemate was resolved, superficially at least, when Commissioner McCloy fashioned some compromise language that satisfied both camps.[3]

The tension-ridden Friday-morning executive session had worn Russell out. He told Johnson that the "damn Commission business whupped me down." Russell was in such haste to get away that he had forgotten to pack his toothbrush, extra shirts, and the medicine he used to ease his respiratory illness. Although Russell had support from Cooper and Boggs, he was the only one who actively dug in his heels against Rankin and the staff's contention that Kennedy and Connally had been hit by the same nonfatal bullet. Because of Russell's chronic Commission absenteeism he never fully comprehended that the final report's no-conspiracy conclusion was inextricably tied to the validity of what would later be referred to as the "single-bullet" theory. But he had read most of the testimony and was convinced that the staff's contention that the same missile had hit Kennedy and Connally was, at best, "credible" but not persuasive. "I don't believe it," he frankly told the president. Johnson's response—whether patronizing or genuine remains guesswork—was "I don't either." In summing up their Friday-night exchange, Russell and Johnson agreed that the question of the Connally bullet did not jeopardize the credibility of the report. Neither questioned the official version that Oswald had shot President Kennedy.[4]

Russell enjoyed a deserved reputation for devotion to his senatorial responsibilities and mastery of the legislative details of the business that came before the Senate. Consequently, he was sensitive and apologetic about the fact that time constraints had limited him to being only a part-time member of the Commission. As he told Johnson, "This staff business always scares me. I like to put my own views down." When he left Friday afternoon for his Georgia home, he was not at ease in his own mind about McCloy's compromise language. He told Johnson, "I tried my best to get in a dissent. But they came around and traded me out of it by giving me a little ole thread of it." Russell was referring to his less-than-enthusiastic acceptance of McCloy's compromise language.[5] What Russell was not aware of at the time was that wholesale perfidy, not mere pressure for consensus, would stigmatize the Commission's September 18 executive session as one of the most disgraceful episodes in the history of the Kennedy assassination investigation. Rankin suppressed the entire record of the divisions among the commissioners over the single-bullet construction to leave the false impression that the commissioners were in universal agreement on this crucial point. The unreported record revealed that Russell, and by extension the American people, were misled by Rankin's unprecedented deception, whose sole purpose was to hide the fact that unanimous Commission support for the single-bullet "solution" was a fraud.

Russell was more outspoken than any of his colleagues in his displeasure about both the quality of the FBI investigation and the information the FBI and CIA fed to the Commission. He suspected that both agencies were not giving the Commission everything they knew about the assassination. For instance, during the January 27, 1964, executive session the commissioners were wrestling with how to approach FBI director Hoover to help them disprove the rumors and allegations that Oswald had been an FBI source or informant. They discussed the unlikeliness of any possibility that the FBI or CIA, investigating themselves, could be counted upon to be forthcoming with whatever information they had, especially if the allegations were true. Russell was certain that the FBI "would have denied that he was an agent." The Georgia senator was certain the CIA would take the same tack. When he turned to Allen Dulles, the former CIA director agreed with him. Russell, expressing the hopelessness of their quandary, remarked to Dulles, "They [CIA] would be the first to deny it. Your agents would have done exactly the same thing."

"Exactly," was Dulles's curt response.[6]

Russell first suspected that information was not being fully shared with the Commission at the first executive session. Sometime during that December 5, 1963, session Russell made a few cryptic notes that underscored his early uneasiness with Warren and suspicion that the chairman was operating on his own unspoken agenda. At some point, before the commissioners went on record, Warren asked the senator whether the CIA had had anything on the Mexico situation. Russell was one of two senators who served on the Senate Subcommittee on the CIA. McCone had briefed Russell about Alvarado Ugarte, the Nicaraguan intelligence agent, and his story about Oswald allegedly receiving thousands of dollars from a Castro Cuban paymaster to assassinate President Kennedy, though the FBI was quick to prove this story bogus. When Russell related this tale to Warren, "not mentioning sums," he was astonished to find that the chairman knew about the "5 G" payoff and more about the CIA and the alleged Mexico City "Red plot" than the senator did.[7]

Even more troubling to Russell was the appearance, at that same session, that Warren and Katzenbach gave every indication of unquestioned acceptance of the FBI report's conclusion (leaked to the press before CD 1 was released to the Commission) that Oswald was the assassin and that he had acted alone. Russell wrote, "Something strange is happening. W and Katzenbach know all about F.B.I. and they are apparently [illegible] and others planning to show Oswald only one considered." Russell could see no integrity or courage in an approach that saddled the Commission with rubber-stamping the FBI's conclusions. "This to me is [*sic*] untenable position. I must," he noted, "insist on outside Counsel." Before the December 5 session ended Russell moved that a subcommittee composed of three commissioners look into the matter of selecting a general counsel. Russell never questioned the Commission's conclusion that Oswald had shot the president, but he refused to accept the official assertion that Dallas was the act of a lone assailant. Russell first aired his suspicions in a January executive session. To Russell, it was more than just happenstance that after Oswald returned from his "secret Mexico" trip he had quickly settled in Dallas and found a job at the Texas School Book Depository, a prime vantage point that would overlook the route of the presidential motorcade. All this caused Russell to "believe that he had to have someone somewhere to advise him about that."[8]

In a prepared statement that he read at the September 18 executive session, Russell laid out reasons why he believed that "a number of suspicious circumstances" precluded the conclusion that Oswald alone "without knowledge, encouragement or assistance of any other person, planned and perpetrated the assassination." The "several bits of evidence" that the senator thought contested the Commission's "no-conspiracy" conclusion were Oswald's "secret visit to Mexico" and his association with "the large number of Cuban nationals who were students" in Minsk when Oswald and Marina were residents of that city.[9]

As one of the members on the Senate oversight committee on the CIA, Russell probably knew, even if only in the broadest terms, about the agency's Operation Mongoose, the sabotage operations directed against Castro's Cuba with President Kennedy's blessing. He might have had some direct knowledge or heard rumors from reliable sources of the CIA's efforts to assassinate Castro. That he was the principal person in the Senate who had oversight of the CIA and access to secret information, some of it filtered to him from the hawkish CIA director McCone, helps in understanding why Russell suspected that Castro was behind the assassination.[10] He might have bought into the CIA's pet "kickback" theory, that is, that Castro had decided to move against Kennedy before the CIA eliminated him. For instance, Russell was disappointed with what he regarded as Warren and Rankin's rather slack and inconsequential interrogation of Marina Oswald. He suspected that she knew more about her husband's contacts with Soviet agents in Russia, and especially Lee's associations with Cuban students in Minsk, than she admitted when she was a Commission witness.[11]

Russell's most active role as a commissioner occurred when he presided over the September 6, 1964, questioning of Marina Oswald at the U.S. Naval Air Station in Dallas. Russell was determined to interrogate Oswald's widow before the Commission released its findings. He invited Cooper and Boggs to join him. Cooper agreed because he shared Russell's opinion that Marina had not told the Commission everything she knew. That Sunday afternoon Russell subjected Marina to more than forty minutes of strenuous cross-examination. Cooper recalled how impressed he was with Russell's "powerful examination" in his search for "the truth." He wanted to elicit from her whether her husband had had Cuban friends when they resided in Minsk. The city was the home of the Academy of Sciences of the USSR, with its numerous affiliated scientific institutions, including the Lenin State University of the USSR. It attracted thousands of foreign students. Some six hundred to seven hundred Cuban students were living in Minsk when the Oswalds were in residence. Russell's fixation on Minsk apparently stemmed from allegations that the Russians had an intelligence or sabotage school in the city. Russell asked Dulles to persuade the CIA to see what it had in its files on Minsk. The CIA reported back to the Commission that there had been a sabotage school in Minsk until the German invasion in 1941, when the school was moved to Leningrad. The CIA reported that after what it characterized as a "careful review," it had found nothing in the files to indicate that an intelligence school still existed in Minsk when Oswald lived and worked there.[12] Even after Marina's four-hour hearing, the Russell subcommittee had learned little that was not already known.

As mentioned before, Russell forced the convening of the September 18 Commission session to give his reasons why he could not sign a report stating that Kennedy and Connally had been struck by the same bullet. Cooper called Russell's statement "compelling." Commissioner Russell had visited the sixth floor of the Texas School Book Depository and was convinced that Oswald would have had to be highly proficient with a rifle to "shoot with [the] deadly accuracy" the report attributed to him. It made no sense to him that a rapid-firing Oswald could place two shots into his target while completely missing the presidential limo "and even the street" with a third shot. An even more significant factor shaping Russell's dissent was Governor John Connally's testimony. Connally was a strong Commission witness, and his cast-iron insistence that he had been struck by a separate missile struck a strong chord in both Russell and Cooper. Never fainthearted when it came to truth and accuracy as he understood them, Russell told his Commission colleagues, "I'll never sign that report if this Commission says categorically that the second shot passed through both of them." Russell's rejection of the single-bullet construction should not have caught his fellow commissioners unawares. The many comments he had made as he reviewed the rough drafts of Chapter 3, "The Shots from the Texas School Book Depository," were consistent indicators of his refusal to accept the proposition that a near-pristine bullet could have inflicted all seven of the nonfatal wounds on Kennedy and Connally.[13]

Russell said that he would sign the report if it contained a footnote stating that he agreed with the Commission's findings but that he was not in accord with the majority view that President Kennedy and Governor Connally had been hit by the same missile. Russell, naturally, expected that his prepared written statements would be part of the Commission's record and available at some future date for those curious about the reasons for his dissent. As stated earlier, Warren and a majority of the commissioners were insistent that the Commission dared not issue a majority and minority report on a matter of such national importance. In order to iron out a consensus and turn out a unanimous document, Russell, as he told Johnson, was "trade[d]" out of his "little ole" dissenting footnote for some compromise language that all the commissioners could live with. What transpired was, in Commissioner Ford's apt description, "the battle of the adjectives."[14] Ford wanted the report to state that there was "compelling" evidence that the same bullet had hit Kennedy and Connally. Russell thought that "compelling" was claiming more than the evidence would allow and wanted to settle for the more moderate "credible." McCloy finally suggested the adjective "persuasive," which was agreeable to both parties and was used in the report.[15]

It was consistent with the Commission's modus operandi to dodge and weave and resort to lawyerlike language to squelch any in-house dissent that might encourage "ugly rumors" of conspiracy. It was doubly fitting that it was McCloy who alerted his colleagues at the Commission's first executive session that there was extreme pressure on the Commission "to lay the dust" of Dallas, that is, to demonstrate that the assassination had not been a conspiracy, "not only in the United States but around the world." At the end of June, almost three months before Russell called for the September 18 session, McCloy, after reviewing the first draft of the report's Chapter 3, wrote Rankin, "Too much effort is expended on attempting to prove that the first bullet which hit the President was also responsible for all Connally's wounds." He was obviously persuaded that the idea of one bullet striking both JFK and the governor was so flimsy that the better part of valor was not to draw overdue attention to it. An avid sportsman who was knowledgeable about weapons and ammunition, McCloy thought that the assertion that one bullet had inflicted all seven nonfatal wounds on both men was attempting "to prove too much." This hardly sounded like someone in the grip of a conviction that the evidence supporting the view that all of Kennedy's and Connally's nonfatal wounds were caused by the same bullet was "very persuasive."[16]

When the Friday session ended on a compromise note, staff lawyer Norman Redlich, almost certainly with Rankin's guidance, was tasked with rewriting the report's "Summary and Conclusions" section. Time was a factor because the White House expected the finished product on Thursday, September 24.[17] In order to expedite the process and get the finished proof of "Summary and Conclusions" to the government printing office, Rankin's secretary read McCloy's compromise language to Russell over the phone later that same day. The so-called McCloy compromise was embodied in point 3 under the rubric "Conclusions":

> Although it is not necessary to any essential findings of the Commission to determine just which shot hit Governor Connally, there is *very persuasive* evidence from *the experts* to indicate that the same bullet which pierced the President's throat also caused Governor Connally's wounds. However, Governor Connally's testimony and *certain other factors* [my italics] have given rise to some difference of opinion as to this probability but there is no question in the mind of any member of the Commission that all the shots which caused the President's and Governor Connally's wounds were fired from the sixth floor window of the Texas School Book Depository.[18]

This paragraph that was so essential to the Commission's contention that the assassination was the work of a lone assailant was riddled with dodges, obfuscations, and cheap distortions of the facts. It had to be dishonest writing to save the lone-assailant, no-conspiracy conclusion from imploding under the weight of its own irreconcilable eccentricities. Guided by the rule of common sense and the Commission's own assertion that only three bullets had been fired, the only bullet in the Commission's accounting that could have inflicted all the nonfatal wounds on both victims had to be the first shot. The Redlich-Rankin-McCloy lawyer language, "it is not necessary to any essential findings of the Commission," was a superficial accommodation to satisfy Russell and Cooper's strongly voiced opposition to the single-bullet construction, although in fact the paragraph merely restated the basic conclusion to which both refused to agree.[19] In addition to Connally, the fact that three Commission members resisted the conclusion that the same bullet had hit the governor and President Kennedy is lightly dismissed with the passing reference to "certain other factors," a travesty of understatement. When this was called to Russell's attention in 1968, as will be discussed later, he saw immediately that he had been properly gulled.

The two principal experts summoned by the Warren Commission to provide "very persuasive" evidence supporting the single-bullet hypothesis were Dr. Alfred G. Olivier, a veterinarian, and Dr. Arthur J. Dziemian, a Ph.D. in physiology. The report never specified what kind of doctors they were and was singularly mute when it came to Dr. Dziemian's qualifications.[20] Both men were employed at the time by the Biophysics Division of the Edgewood Arsenal in Maryland, a facility operated by the federal government.

The awkward fact confronting the Commission in marshalling so-called expert testimony was that most of the experts the Commission called upon for this critical determination actually disagreed with the conclusion stated in the report. The three Bethesda prosectors, Drs. Humes, Boswell, and Finck, were convinced that a separate bullet had struck Connally. None of them supported the possibility that Commission Exhibit (CE) 399 (the so-called magic bullet) could have shattered the governor's wrist and remained in near-pristine condition.[21] Dr. Joseph R. Dolce, the U.S. Army's expert on high-velocity weapons and the military's top ballistics expert, remained unyielding in his opinion that two bullets had hit Connally, with a separate bullet causing the extensive damage to his wrist. When Dolce told Commission lawyer Arlen Specter that the forensic evidence did not support the contention that both men had been hit by the same missile, he was never again consulted and was not called as a witness.[22] Governor Connally's two principal surgeons, Drs. Robert R. Shaw and Charles F. Gregory, testified before the Commission in late April that Connally's wounds were too massive to have been inflicted by one missile, especially one that was barely mutilated.[23] It is worth noting that it was a unique event in the investigation for the Bethesda prosectors and the Parkland Memorial Hospital doctors to be in agreement about the medicolegal evidence in the Kennedy assassination.

Throughout the remainder of their lives Russell and Cooper adhered to the view that the one-bullet theory was not possible. For all their wisdom, sophistication, and experience gained from successful lives in law, politics, and government, they did not understand the simple truth: If the single-bullet hypothesis was not valid, then without question the crime had been a conspiracy on that basis alone.

The explanation, in part, for this disconnect was the fact that the commissioners in general did not have a command of the underlying facts of the assassination. Most of the basic evidence of the case was introduced into the record at the Commission hearings. Only roughly 30 percent of the hearings dealt with the pertinent assassination facts: the critical medicolegal and ballistics evidence, the source of the shots, Oswald's movements on the day of the assassination. The bulk of the hearings delved into areas that had little or nothing to do with the assassination itself. There is no better example than a comparison of the space the report devoted to the president's autopsy with that given to Oswald's life in Russia. More than 40 percent of the hearings were dedicated to detailing the life of the alleged assassin, underscoring the argument that the Warren report's focus was on Oswald and not the assassination itself.[24]

It was an unwritten but institutionalized expectation on the Hill that when the president established a blue-ribbon commission, most of the work, from investigation to writing the report, would be left to the staff lawyers. Many of the staff lawyers saw no reason to question this truism during the nine months that they were associated with the Warren Commission's investigation into the Kennedy assassination. Joe Ball, Wesley Liebeler, Melvin Eisenberg, and Howard Willens all shared the view that the commissioners, at best, were "not in touch with the investigation at all times."[25] When Liebeler testified before the House Select Committee on Assassinations, Gary Cornwell isolated a comment he had made to the author Edward Jay Epstein that appeared in Epstein's book *Inquest.* When Epstein interviewed Liebeler and asked what the commissioners actually did, Liebeler, taking some liberty with the truth, curtly replied, "In one word, Nothing." Cornwell confronted the former staff lawyer with this quotation, probably expecting Liebeler to back away from a statement he had made more than a decade before. But Liebeler held his ground, explaining to Cornwell that the impression he wanted to convey to Epstein was that the "Commissioners themselves were not directly involved, and they were not."[26]

Most of the commissioners had a multiplicity of responsibilities aside from their work on the Commission and attended only a minor portion of the hearings. Senator Russell's attendance record revealed that he was present, according to Epstein's calculations, for only about 6 percent of the testimony. Russell was probably more diverted and burdened by outside responsibilities than any other Commission member. He would later recall that the time he spent on the Commission was "the most arduous . . . I've ever had in my life and I've had some tough ones." He served as chairman of both the Appropriations and the Armed Services committees, two of the most powerful and time-consuming Senate committees. Russell also divided his time in the Upper Chamber with membership on the Democratic Policy and Democratic Steering committees. But for the first six months of 1964 the senator from Winder, Georgia, concentrated his energies on one overriding objective: blocking the White House's Civil Rights Bill from becoming the law of the land. As the South's most skilled and trusted parliamentarian, Russell spearheaded the fight against President Johnson's determined effort to begin to remedy America's long-delayed promise of equal treatment for its African American population. Russell was the South's point man in its campaign to gag the Senate, but his efforts proved futile when that body voted 71-29 for cloture, ending the filibuster and clearing the way for the passage of the 1964 Civil Rights Act.[27]

In late February, weighed down by his onerous committee responsibilities and irritated that Rankin's office had neglected to notify his office about hearings he was anxious to attend, Russell wrote President Johnson a three-page letter explaining why he could not continue his Commission duties. Russell never mailed the letter for reasons that were unexplained. However, in April his Commission duties were made considerably easier when he retained an assistant, Alfredda Scobey, a law clerk for Judge Robert L. Russell of the Georgia State Court of Appeals, to help him with his Commission responsibilities. Very quickly the talented and dedicated Scobey became the senator's trusted staff assistant. Russell tried to keep up with the Commission's business by evaluating the testimony from the transcripts of the hearings, but his experience as a trial lawyer told him that reading off a page was no substitute for personally hearing and observing a witness's testimony. Moreover, the vast majority of witness statements (458 out of 552) were depositions or were submitted as affidavits. He was very uneasy about having to rely so heavily on the work of the staff; Russell liked to "put his own views down," as he told LBJ, but the circumstances largely circumscribed the chance for firsthand impressions because it was not possible to cross-examine a piece of paper.[28]

It was the nation's great misfortune that Russell found it necessary to absent himself from so much of the work of the Commission. His Senate duties and responsibilities were a heavy burden, to be sure, but he wasted his great talents and most of his first six months on the Commission opposing programs for racial justice. In retrospect, Russell diverted his considerable abilities and energies to the defense of a social system that was indefensible when he could have had a significant—perhaps decisive—impact on the outcome of the government's investigation into President Kennedy's assassination. There was an exasperating irony in Russell's extensive Commission absenteeism. Russell suspected that Johnson had appointed him to the Commission to prevent him from leading the South's fight against the pending civil rights legislation. However, all the evidence suggests that Russell misread LBJ's motives. Johnson's interest was to select eminent and trusted public figures to assure that his blue-ribbon commission's findings would receive ready and uncritical acceptance. But Russell thought he had outsmarted "ole Lyndon," as he confided to assassination researcher Harold Weisberg: "I led the fight and spent little time with the Commission."[29]

During his almost forty years in the U.S. Senate, Russell set an example of honesty, integrity, and rectitude. Even those who were worlds apart politically from Georgia's senior senator, such as Senator Edward Kennedy, held him in high esteem, noting that Russell "established a code of conduct that captured the essence of what the Senate is."[30] Despite Russell's poor attendance, former Commission staff lawyer Bert Griffin was impressed with the senator. He thought Russell "genuinely wanted to conduct an investigation as distinguished from simply an evaluation." Russell used Alfredda Scobey as a countercheck on the staff and had her report back to him. It is almost certain, however, that Russell and Cooper never learned about the missing shot that struck the curb and wounded Jim Tague. Rankin and the staff ignored it until June, when a letter from the assistant U.S. attorney in Dallas, Martha Joe Stroud, forced them to take some action. It was not until July 23, 1964, that Commission staffer Wesley Liebeler deposed Tague in Dallas in the office of the U.S. attorney. There was no one else present when Tague gave his account of the curbstone shot.[31]

Tague's deposition was one of hundreds taken by the staff lawyers, and unless it was brought to Russell's attention, there is no reason to assume he ever heard of James Thomas Tague. The ten-page list of names of those whom the Commission staff lawyers deposed and whose affidavits Russell reviewed did not include Tague's name.[32] Russell never mentioned the Tague bullet or the curbstone shot in the statements he read to his colleagues at the September 18 executive session. In August, after Senator Cooper reviewed a draft of Chapter 3, he wrote to Rankin, "what proof 'probably missed,'" referring to that section of the chapter labeled "The Shot That Missed." Connally's Commission testimony resonated strongly with Russell and Cooper, as the Kentucky senator noted in his dissent: "It seems to me that Governor Connally's statement negates such a conclusion."[33]

Cooper, unlike Russell, did not recruit an assistant to help with the heavy workload his Commission duties imposed. He apparently interpreted Rankin's "Top Secret" classification of Commission executive sessions as reason enough for doing all the work on his own. Cooper recalled later that he spent virtually all his waking hours going over the transcripts of the hearings and trying to read the hundreds of depositions and affidavits. He told an interviewer, "As for being in the Senate at the time, you just as soon not have been there." When he came down with a bad chest cold and his doctor insisted that he take two or three days off with complete rest, Cooper took to his bed but continued plowing through the stacks of Commission reports while his staff "kicked all the time," complaining that he needed to break stride and get his rest.[34] It is possible that Cooper simply breezed over Tague's deposition and all of the other Commission documents and FBI reports on the curbstone shot, or read them but failed to grasp their significance. It is much more likely, however, that since Rankin and his staff lawyers were not forced to deal with the "missed shot" until July, they simply never brought this new development to the attention of the commissioners.[35]

If Cooper never heard of Jim Tague and was kept in the dark about the missed shot until August, when he reviewed the report's Chapter 3, and most certainly knew nothing about the FBI's report on the bullet-scarred curbstone, it is a hands-down certainty that Russell was equally uninformed about the details of the Commission's proof of the missed shot. That Russell was totally unaware of the missed shot until it was sprung upon him at the Friday executive session he forced on Rankin and Warren was revealed in his September 18 phone conversation with President Johnson. In recounting his reasons for his dissent about the same bullet hitting Kennedy and Connally, Russell held to the view that Oswald had not missed with the third shot. "According to that theory"—his dismissive characterization of the staff lawyers' contention that one of the three shots had missed—"he not only missed the whole automobile but *missed the street*. Well," he continued, "that man is a good enough shot to put two bullets into Kennedy, he didn't miss the ole automobile nor the street."[36]

Russell and Cooper were strong in their conviction that all three of the assassin's bullets had hit Kennedy and Connally. Had they been familiar with Tague's affidavit about the missed shot, they would have had to confront the implications of a fourth shot in their understanding of the assassination. A fourth shot was "very persuasive" but, more to the point, very "compelling" evidence of at least a second shooter and a conspiracy. Minimally, it is almost certain that Russell and Cooper, and perhaps even Boggs, would never have signed their names to a report that did not account for all the shots they believed were fired in Dealey Plaza. It was Russell, after all, who cautioned his colleagues at the Commission's first executive session that their reputations were at stake in this difficult but necessary undertaking. He was almost certainly thinking in the long term of history's impartial verdict after they were all gone. A report would have been published, but it would not have carried the same weight of conviction and regard that the Warren report initially bore, which was made possible only by the spurious claim of unanimity among the commissioners. But if Russell and Cooper had insisted on facing up to the evidence of a fourth shot, Warren and Rankin would have had to settle for something that fell far short of the imperatives laid out in the November 25 Katzenbach memo for the common understanding of the American people—Oswald acted alone, no conspiracy. Had the Commission been forced to issue a majority and minority report on the Kennedy assassination, public confidence and acceptance of its conclusions would have been irreparably compromised. There would have been no need to wait for history's judgment that the Warren report was a counterfeit of the nation's history.

When the Friday, September 18, executive session ended, Russell and the Commission had, so to speak, split the difference over his two demurrers. As he told LBJ, he was "traded out" of his objection to Rankin and the staff's conclusion that one bullet had struck both Kennedy and the governor, but he insisted that the Commission's findings include a statement to the effect that it could not categorically claim that Oswald had perpetrated the assassination alone. In this instance Russell had his way. This disclaimer was included in the report: "Because of the difficulty of proving negatives to a certainty the possibility of others being involved with either Oswald or Ruby cannot be rejected categorically, but if there is any such evidence it has been beyond the reach of all the investigative agencies and resources of the United States and has not come to the attention of this Commission."[37]

Russell satisfied himself with half a loaf, believing that with the September 18 executive session transcript and his two prepared statements made for the Commission's record he had fulfilled his obligations to his Georgia constituents and to the record of history. But Rankin, guided by the Katzenbach memo, had his own political reasons for what he would and would not permit into the Commission's record on the Kennedy assassination. Given the fact that the report was already prepared and ready to be printed, the general counsel did not want any evidence of division within the Commission's ranks. So Rankin saw to it that Russell's two prepared statements, along with everything of consequence that took place at the September 18 session, were purged from the Commission's records. There is no clear proof, but it's hard to believe that Rankin did not have Chairman Warren's acquiescence in this act of deception and suppression.

Initially it was agreed that a record of all executive sessions would be kept. Warren had hired the old and respectable Washington firm of Ward & Paul as the official stenographic reporters to produce transcripts of all the Commission executive sessions, hearings, and depositions executed in Washington. It's very likely that it was Russell who recommended the firm. Ward & Paul was the official reporter for the Armed Services Committee when Russell was the chairman.[38] When all the commissioners and Rankin assembled for the 10 A.M. meeting on September 18, Russell expected that there would be a stenographic record of the session. Russell remembered seeing a stenographer in the hearing room and assumed she was the official court reporter. Rankin did arrange to have a woman present who gave every appearance of recording the session, but she was not from Ward & Paul. The firm's records reveal that the last billing date for work for the Commission was September 15, when a Ward & Paul reporter ([first name unknown] Mills) was called for staff lawyer Redlich's deposition of the FBI's John F. Gallagher.[39] The transcript of the September 18 session that Rankin submitted into the record is an unmistakable fraud. It is a six-page document of some housekeeping items and innocuous motions, seconded and carried, about the numbers of copies of the report to be released, who was to get leather-bound copies of the report and accompanying volumes of hearings with their names stamped in gold, and similar inconsequential matters. Russell's prepared statements were lost deep in the memory hole. There is no mention of the Russell-Cooper objections and refusal to agree with the report that was already in page proof. There is not a hint of any exchange that took place among the commissioners and their strenuous reaction to Russell's objections to the lone-bullet construction, his disclaimer to the report's no-conspiracy assertion, or any go-around among Ford, Russell, and Mc-Cloy over compromise language.[40]

This extraordinary deception had Rankin's signature of suppression all over it. It was a reprise of the way the Commission's general counsel had handled the secret January 24 meeting with the Texas delegation, during which most of the three-hour session, according to Dallas district attorney Henry Wade and Dean Robert G. Storey, dealt with Oswald as a possible CIA source. No Ward & Paul court reporter was present then, just Rankin, Warren, and the two Texans. There was no transcript of what was discussed, only Rankin's memorandum for the file titled "Rumors that Oswald was an undercover agent." The Texans were sworn to secrecy about what was said at that Monday-morning meeting. Both Warren and Rankin resisted any impulse to openness with the rest of the Commission about rumors and allegations linking Oswald to the CIA when Rankin broached the subject three days later at the January 27 executive session. The only two Commission members, Russell and McCloy, who ever entertained the possibility that the assassination might have been the result of a conspiracy were present at the January 27 Commission session. Since there was no transcript of the session with the Texas delegation, the commissioners had to rely on Rankin's version of what had taken place. The general counsel's "spin-doctoring" of the January 24 session was perfectly captured by his charge to the Commission: "We do have a dirty rumor that is very bad for the Commission . . . and it must be wiped out insofar as it is possible to do so by this Commission."[41]

Rankin waited until November 5, more than a week after the report was out, before he made available for the commissioners what he falsely represented as "the minutes of the last meeting of the Commission." The general counsel anticipated that since the Commission's legal life had ended the moment the report was issued, none of the overly busy former members had the time, need, or interest to review the transcript and discover his misrepresentation.[42] It was not until the late spring of 1968 that Russell learned of Rankin's fakery. Assassination researcher Harold Weisberg, who had sources on the Hill, found out that Russell had expressed strong doubts about the Warren report's conclusions at the September 18 executive session. At Russell's request, Weisberg wrote to the National Archives in Washington to request a copy of the stenographic transcript of the Commission's September 18, 1964, executive session. The archivist of the United States, James B. Rhoads, responded, "No verbatim transcript of the executive session of September 18, 1964, is known to be among the records of the Commission." The only record in the Archives' possession, Rhoads reported, "is the minutes of which a copy was furnished to you." This meant that Russell's dissent about the draft of the report and the disagreement within the Commission about what the final record should conclude about the Kennedy assassination no longer existed. When Weisberg showed Russell the Rhoads letter, the senator was aghast. This bold deception was outside all his almost forty years of experience in Washington. Shortly after Russell was confronted with this irrefutable evidence of Rankin's suppression, he resigned his chairmanship of the Military Affairs Committee and divested himself of his "oversight" responsibilities on the CIA. Weisberg and Russell, or the senator's legislative aide, C. E. Campbell, exchanged letters over the next seven months. Russell urged Weisberg to continue his work on the Kennedy assassination and to keep him informed of the progress of his investigative efforts.[43]

Russell's interest in the Kennedy assassination never diminished. But as he wrote Weisberg, his time was taken up by his chairmanship duties for the Senate Appropriations Committee and election as president pro tempore of the Upper House. Sometime in 1969 he was diagnosed with lung cancer. Aware that his condition was terminal, Russell agreed to do a series of taped television interviews with Cox Television, headquartered in his home state of Georgia. In effect, the Cox TV series was Russell's "farewell address" to the people of Georgia, who had honored him by returning him to the U.S. Senate for almost four decades. On January 19, 1970, less than a year before his death, Russell again proclaimed his doubts about the Warren report. When asked to speculate about a possible conspiracy, Russell simply stated that he "was not prepared to say, because" the Commission did not have access to "enough evidence to pin it down." Although he agreed with the report that Oswald had been the lone gunman, he still held as strongly as ever that he "never believed that Lee Harvey Oswald assassinated President Kennedy without at least some encouragement from others. And that's what a majority of the Committee wanted to find." He added, "I think someone else worked with him on the planning."[44]

12   Was Oswald a Government "Agent"?

*I don't see how the country is ever going to be willing to accept it
if we don't satisfy them on this particular issue, not only with
them [the FBI] but the CIA and every other agency.*
—J. Lee Rankin on the "Agent Oswald" question,
   Executive Session, January 27, 1964

Whether Oswald had any connection with any U.S. government intelligence operation of any kind cannot be stated with certainty from the official records that are not still kept secret. There was a basis, more than a suspicion, for the government to have investigated that possibility, but it never did. Senator Richard Russell's insistence at the Commission's last executive session on September 18, 1964, that Oswald must have had some assistance in carrying out the crime forced Chief Counsel Rankin and Chairman Warren to make a concession in the report's findings to the possibility of a conspiracy in the assassination.[1] The Warren report concluded, "Because of the difficulty of proving a negative to a certainty," the Commission "could not categorically reject the possibility that others were involved." "But if there was any evidence to this effect," the text continued in Commissioner McCloy's skillfully brokered wording, "it has been beyond the reach of all investigative agencies and resources of the United States and has not come to the attention of this Commission."[2]

On the issue of "Agent Oswald," however, the Commission left no room for speculation. The report concluded with iron-jawed certainty, "All the evidence before the Commission established that there was nothing to support the speculation that Oswald was an agent, employee, or informant of the FBI, the CIA, or any other governmental agency." The report went on to assure the American people that this categorical denial was based on a thorough investigation of "Oswald's relationships prior to the assassination with all agencies of the U.S. Government."[3]

So after the Commission's ten months of thorough investigation the picture of Oswald the report painted varied little, if at all, from the image of Oswald that had become a household name the day of the assassination. Within a few hours after the assassination the suspected assailant was identified by 112th Army Intelligence in San Antonio as a former marine who had defected to the Soviet Union at age twenty and was an active pro-Castro supporter after he returned to the United States. A few hours later that same day, FBI director J. Edgar Hoover had satisfied himself that Oswald, a "nut" of the "extremist pro-Castro group," was almost certainly the lone assassin. The first news reports of the assassination carried accounts of Oswald's quirky political odyssey from former marine to card-carrying member of the Fair Play for Cuba Committee (FPCC), a short-lived and ineffectual collection of left-wing Americans who demanded that the government keep its hands off Cuba. There was nothing in the Warren report to alter the public's first image of Oswald as a former Leatherneck who had forsaken his allegiance to the red, white, and blue and embraced the red banner of international communism.[4]

Based on the Commission's refusal to launch a good-faith investigation into the "Agent Oswald" matter, its assertion that Oswald had no relationship with any government agency colored the truth. When the report dealt with Oswald's U.S. Marine Corps records, it suppressed facts and ignored circumstances that were inconvenient to the Commission's prosecutorial case against the dead suspect. Oswald was not a model marine. He was moody, disrespectful, and occasionally insubordinate to those superiors whom he regarded as his intellectual inferiors. The report covered these incidents and his two court-martials in sufficient detail. At the same time, the Commission never attempted to explain why the corps was so uncharacteristically tolerant of Oswald's consuming and well-known interest in Marxism and the Soviet Union.

While he was a marine Oswald studied the Russian language; played Russian songs in the barracks; and received communist literature such as the *Worker,* the organ of the American Communist Party, and Russian newspapers in the mail. He brushed up on *Das Kapital* when free time permitted. By the time Oswald defected to the Soviet Union, he was fluent in Russian, though by any linguistic standards Russian is a difficult language to master. The report left the impression that Oswald, a high school dropout, had learned the language on his own in his spare time. Oswald's Marine Corps records simply noted that on February 25, 1959, he was tested in the Russian language, as though every marine had to qualify in Russian just as they did on the rifle range. Most of Oswald's stateside duty was in California, where the government ran a foreign-language school in Monterey. Predictably, Oswald's Russophilia drew attention from his fellow "gyrenes." Some of them took to calling him "Oswaldovich" or addressed him as "Comrade," usually at Oswald's insistence and to his genuine delight.[5]

The Commission studiously avoided explaining how Oswald had managed to become fluent in Russian. A clue to this mystery surfaced when Rankin addressed the question of Oswald's clumsy command of Spanish during the January 27, 1964, executive session. The general counsel noted that "we are trying to run that down to find out what he studied at the Monterey School of the Army in the way of languages." Rankin's reference to the Defense Language Institute in Monterey and the fact that the Marine Corps had tested Oswald's Russian-language skills strongly suggested that

Oswald had been a student at the institute while posted at the El Toro marine base. Why would the corps have submitted Oswald to formal testing if he was only dabbling in Russian on his own? Persistent efforts by the researcher Emory Brown to retrieve records of Oswald's language training from the U.S. Marine Corps ran into a stone wall. The Department of the Navy and the Defense Language Institute reported back that Oswald was never enrolled as a student at the Monterey institute. There might be an innocent explanation for this puzzling development, but the Commission never bothered to clarify the mystery.[6]

Oswald's self-professed Marxism and his avid interest in things Russian never interfered with his Marine Corps security clearances. The Warren report hinted that Oswald had a clearance "above the 'confidential' level" with access to certain kinds of classified material. Actually, when he served overseas at Cubi Point, the Philippines, and Atsugi, Japan, Oswald had "Crypto" clearance, probably one of a dozen or more special clearances at that time higher than "Top Secret." His Marine Corps military occupation specialty (MOS) was electronics operator airborne, which meant he worked with rather sophisticated radar equipment and systems. In May 1958 his radar crew played some role in the CIA's covert "Operation Strongback," an abortive attempt to topple the leftward-leaning government of Indonesia's President Achmed Sukarno.[7]

The Warren Commission knew about Oswald's "Crypto" clearance but suppressed it from being included in the record. Rankin never raised this issue in any of the on-the-record executive sessions. The Commission became intensely interested in Oswald's tour of duty in the Philippines when it learned that an eighteen-year-old marine in Oswald's outfit had died of a gunshot wound while guarding the crypto van at Cubi Point. The dead marine was Pvt. Martin D. Schrand. Schrand and Oswald had attended the electronics school at Jacksonville, Florida, and advanced radar school at Biloxi, Mississippi, before being posted overseas in the same radar unit assigned to the ultrasecret crypto van. All six marines, including Lee Harvey Oswald, attached to the crypto van had to have "Crypto" clearance. Commission lawyers probing for information into Oswald's clearances questioned several of his Marine Corps buddies. Kerry W. Thornley, who served with Oswald at the marines' El Toro base in Santa Ana, California, told Commission counsel Albert Jenner that Oswald's clearance was much higher than "confidential." Thornley thought Oswald's duties had required a "secret clearance." At one point, Thornley told Jenner, he thought Oswald "worked in the security files, the S&C files, at LTA or at El Toro." Nelson Delgado agreed with Thornley about Oswald's access to "secret" data. He placed Oswald in the "silent area. That is the war room."[8] This was not where one would expect the Marine Corps to assign a barracks-room Russophile and self-professed Marxist.

Soon after the assassination the FBI went over Oswald's Marine Corps records and came across reports on Schrand's death while on sentry duty in January 1958. The bureau's interest was aroused by the fact that Oswald had served with the unfortunate Schrand and by rumors circulated by several marines in Oswald's outfit that he might have been responsible for Schrand's death. After two criminal investigations into the case the navy's official 1958 verdict had been accidental death "with no other person or persons involved in the incident." After the FBI's own investigation into the rumors came to no different conclusion, Rankin requested that the judge advocate general's (JAG) office review the record on the off chance that the facts of the case just might, upon reexamination, point to foul play. What better collateral evidence of Oswald's criminally violent nature to bolster the Commission's "reasonable" case than tying him to the "murder" of Private Schrand? The JAG forwarded to Rankin two copies of the Schrand investigation, establishing beyond any doubt that Rankin must have been aware of the status of Oswald's security clearance. After a review of the facts and interviews with the marines identified with the rumors of Oswald's involvement, the JAG was satisfied with the correctness of the original verdict.[9]

The Commission's failure to mention Oswald's "Crypto" clearance and access to highly sensitive military secrets cannot be attributed, at least in any conventional understanding, to national security reasons. The U.S. Navy never classified its investigation into the Schrand case. Any highlighting of Oswald's tightly held Marine Corps duties would have been incompatible with the profile of Oswald the Commission was building in its prima facie case against the dead assailant. This was especially true when it came to the matter of motive. According to the Commission, a major factor in Oswald's decision to kill Kennedy was "his avowed commitment to Marxism and communism, as he understood the terms and developed his own interpretation of them." This suppression conformed with the extraordinary circumstances surrounding Oswald's early discharge from the marines and his subsequent defection to the Soviet Union.

With two months of his enlistment remaining, Oswald petitioned the Marine Corps's Dependency Discharge Board for a "hardship discharge." The reason he gave was that his mother had suffered an "industrial accident" and could no longer be gainfully employed. Since she had no other source of income, Oswald requested an early discharge in order to take care of his destitute mother. The request was spurious, and the Marine Corps had to have known that it was a flat-out deception, yet in August 1959 the board agreed to release Oswald from active duty. His discharge was scheduled for September 11, 1959; a week earlier Oswald had applied for a passport from his stateside posting at El Toro.[10]

With the full knowledge and support of the U.S. Marine Corps, Oswald's passport was issued on September 10, 1959, just six days after he had applied. Along with his passport application were standard Marine Corps forms he had to fill out. Oswald noted on these forms that he intended to visit, among other countries, the Soviet Union and Cuba before enrolling as a student at Albert Schweitzer College in Switzerland and the University of Turku in Finland.[11] How did the corps think Oswald was going to support his invalid mother while traipsing around communist countries and attending European institutions of higher learning? Why did alarm bells fail to go off when marine PFC Oswald, with his unrevoked ultrasecret clearance, flatly reported that he was going to spend some time in Russia and Castro's Cuba—at the height of the Cold War—before pursuing a university degree? Add to that the Marine Corps's knowledge that Oswald was a high school dropout, although he did receive his high school equivalency diploma while stationed in Biloxi, Mississippi. Despite his indifferent public school record Oswald was not intellectually impaired. While in the service he achieved a score of 110 on his general classification test, high enough to get into radar school and to qualify him to become a commissioned officer.

Although the Commission included all this in its twenty-six volumes of Hearings and Exhibits, it made no attempt to explain away these suspicious circumstances in Oswald's service records. It was all passed over and ignored as though it were as unremarkable as water running downhill. The Warren report failed to expend a word on his fraudulent discharge and treated the issuance of his passport as administratively routine.[12] The Commission could have gone a long way toward alleviating suspicion if it could have documented just one other serviceman's record from any branch of the military as unconventional as Oswald's before he found his way to Russia and announced his intention of seeking Soviet citizenship to U.S. Embassy officials in Moscow.

On Saturday morning, October 31, 1959, two weeks after he arrived in Russia, Oswald entered the U.S. Embassy in Moscow. He strode up to the receptionist's desk, placed his passport on her desk, and announced that he had come to "dissolve his American citizenship." The receptionist turned him over to Richard E. Snyder, a senior consular official. Snyder was a CIA operative posted to Moscow under State Department cover. A truculent Oswald thumped his passport down on Snyder's desk with a handwritten note laying out his decision to seek Soviet citizenship. According to Snyder, Oswald was visibly nervous, but he had carefully prepared for the encounter and gave every indication that he would not be dissuaded from following through with his decision.

John A. McVickar, another consular official, was seated across the room and heard the Oswald-Snyder conversation. In a memo written sometime after Oswald's embassy visit, McVickar noted that Oswald "displayed all the airs of a new sophomore party-liner." His choice of language and "simple Marxist stereotypes" left McVickar with the firm impression that he had been "tutored" before showing up at the embassy. In a sharp exchange with Snyder, Oswald let drop that he had told Soviet authorities he would furnish them with everything he knew about his military specialty, U.S. radar capabilities. Explaining that the renunciation of citizenship was a complicated and irrevocable action, Snyder asked Oswald to return to the embassy on Monday under the pretext that the consulate could not process his application on a Saturday. After Oswald left the embassy Snyder notified the State Department of Oswald's intention to defect and to turn over to the Soviets information about U.S. radar capabilities. In short order, a State Department telex on Oswald was sent to the CIA, FBI, and Office of Naval Intelligence (ONI).[13]

Oswald never returned to the consulate on Monday and never renounced his U.S. citizenship. He remained in the Soviet Union as a guest of the state. In February 1961 Oswald wrote the U.S. Embassy in Moscow from his residence in Minsk, alerting the consulate that he desired to return to the United States. Before repatriating himself, this American defector set down his own terms: Oswald wanted an iron-clad guarantee that he would not be prosecuted "under any circumstances" should he return. He also wanted assurances that Marina, his Russian wife, and their child would be able to return with him and be admitted to the United States.[14]

The Warren report spent more than thirty pages of tedious detail on the legal intricacies and financial arrangements involved in the State Department's efforts to return Oswald and his family to the United States. It is a classic example of the report's telling too much about too little. To begin with, the State Department could not have assured Oswald that he would not be prosecuted without first clearing this issue with the Justice Department and the U.S. Navy, especially the ONI. By all rights, the navy had a legitimate interest in Oswald on at least two counts: His fraudulent "hardship discharge" and his admission that he intended to compromise secrets about the navy's radar capabilities as the quid pro quo for Soviet citizenship should have assured that the ONI would, at least, have debriefed Oswald once he returned home.

When Oswald was discharged he had signed an acknowledgment of having been informed about the penalties for violating the Internal Security Act of 1950. If Oswald did turn over classified information to the Soviets, as he had threatened, then he had placed himself in jeopardy of a trial and a likely long jail sentence when he returned home. However, nothing was done to the "redefecting" ex-marine when he arrived in the United States. In fact, according to Spas Theodore Raikin, a caseworker for Travelers Aid (TA) in

New York City, the State Department requested that TA have a caseworker meet the Oswalds when their ship, the SS *Maasdam,* docked at Hoboken, New Jersey. Raikin was assigned to meet the returning Oswalds and provide financial assistance to get them to their destination, Fort Worth, Texas. The State Department could have taken adverse action against Oswald by denying him any future passport; that it never did so is suspicious. In June 1963, when Oswald applied for a passport for travel to, among other countries, the Soviet Union, the passport was granted the next day. Unless this was standard State Department policy for redefecting American servicemen, it appears that for unexplained reasons some government elements were anxious to have Oswald back home.[15]

The news of Oswald's defection must have sent every intelligence agency in Washington scrambling for its files on the ex-marine. As a former radar operator with "Crypto" clearance, this twenty-year-old was privy to some of the navy's advanced technologies, information that any foreign government would covet. The Warren Commission learned something about the magnitude of security Oswald threatened when it questioned John E. Donovan, the officer in charge of marine Air Control Squadron 9, the radar crew that Oswald had served with at El Toro. As a crew member of Squadron 9, Oswald knew all the radar and radio frequencies, the location of all the military bases on the West Coast, all the squadrons and each one's relative tactical strength, and the names of their commanding officers. He was familiar with all the authentication codes for aircraft entering and exiting the Air Defense Identification Zone for the West Coast.

When news of his defection reached the United States, all of these codes and signals had to be changed. Donovan allowed that it was navy policy to routinely change these authentication codes and radio signals. He also disclosed that PFC Oswald was knowledgeable about the navy's MPS 16, the newly developed height-finder radar gear, and the technologically advanced TPX-1 system used to transfer radio and radar signals over a long distance. The capabilities of these new online systems, Donovan stressed, could not be changed. Although the Commission never went on the record and asked, Oswald's radar responsibilities as described by Donovan would have required at least a "Secret" clearance. After Donovan left the service he was interviewed by FBI agent James F. Morrissey. Oswald's former section commander at El Toro noted in passing that "Oswald's position required a secret clearance." Donovan also stated that Oswald "had a very high IQ" and was "well read, especially in the fields of world affairs." He characterized Oswald as an "anomaly for a 20-year-old Marine Private with an extensive knowledge and maturing interest in world affairs and politics."[16]

What the Commission did not learn from former marine lieutenant Donovan was that Oswald had been stationed at marine air-traffic-control bases overseas, notably Atsugi, Japan, and Cubi Point in the Philippines, two of the operational locations for the "black lady of espionage," the CIA's U-2 spy plane. Oswald pulled radar duty at both of these bases. Oswald was with the 1st Marine Aircraft Wing at Atsugi Air Facility when he became familiar with some of the U-2's flight capabilities. Most astonishing to the marine radar operators at Atsugi was the discovery that "Race Car" (the CIA's code name for the U-2) could reach altitudes of ninety thousand feet, a height previously believed impossible for any aircraft. During the Eisenhower administration the U-2 was furnishing the government with 90 percent of the hard intelligence on Soviet military, ballistic, and nuclear capabilities. While he was stationed at these U-2 bases Oswald had contact with "Race Car" pilots and other personnel working with the planes. Doubtless, some of his off-duty social contacts were with CIA officers connected with these espionage operations, or "black ops."[17]

The John F. Kennedy Collection Register at National Archives II in College Park, Maryland, lists four boxes of ONI materials. There is nothing in the ONI files indicating that the navy debriefed Oswald upon his return to the United States. Moreover, there are no ONI records regarding any background check on Oswald relating to his security clearances. The ONI files devoted more attention to the activities of a Gerald Patrick Hemming, an ex-marine and soldier of fortune who was training anti-Castro Cubans in New Orleans, than to Oswald.

At the end of January 1964 Rankin requested the navy's Oswald file. Capt. Robert P. Jackson, assistant director of naval counterintelligence, transmitted some twenty documents to the Commission. In his letter of transmittal Jackson noted that the "bulk of this file is comprised of reports from other agencies, copies of which the President's Commission undoubtedly has already." There was nothing in the folders sent to the Commission relating to an Oswald debriefing or any records pertaining to his security clearances. In short, there was nothing in these papers that indicated whether or not Oswald had some connection with the navy's intelligence arm or any other government intelligence entity.[18] The irresistible conclusion is that Oswald's ONI file had been systematically purged.

As would be expected, within hours after Oswald was charged with Kennedy's assassination every intelligence agency in Washington scrambled to review its files on the president's alleged killer. At 5 P.M. on the day of the assassination, Donald R. Paschal, a civilian assigned to the Programs Section of the naval counterintelligence branch, which had "primary responsibility for monitoring the file within ONI," delivered a "supplemental file" to Vice Adm. Rufus Taylor, the director of naval intelligence. Within hours, interest in seeing Oswald's ONI file had spread throughout the corridors of power in Washington. General Carroll, the head of the Pentagon's recently created Defense Intelligence Agency (DIA), requested Oswald's ONI file. Admiral Taylor gave instructions that Carroll "could peruse the file" but that he had to return it to Special Agent Bliss, who delivered it. Bliss carried the file to Carroll's office, where it was reviewed by the DIA director, and "only by the Director," in Bliss's presence. Taylor's extreme caution in this matter suggested that he did not want Carroll to make a copy of the file. The admiral's instructions to Paschal were to "prepare a file," not, it seems, to "prepare copies" or "make a copy." Was this an odd choice of words, or was ONI holding back some of its information on Oswald? It is sheer speculation, but the DIA chief could have been considered an outsider who might cause trouble if he spotted irregularities in the ONI file. At about midnight on November 22, Lt. Patrick D. Molinari, at the Naval Counterintelligence Support Center, received a call from a superior to prepare copies of Oswald's file for the FBI and Secret Service, but "to release no files to anyone except by order" of the center's duty officer.[19]

The Warren Commission did not receive Oswald's military records until the middle of January 1964. By this time the file, with the intriguing title "Intelligence Plot," had circulated to another naval office, then to the State Department, and finally to the Department of Defense (DOD) and its Office of General Counsel, where it apparently remained under the care of John McNaughton, the DOD's general counsel. On February 18, 1964, Rankin wrote McNaughton to request additional records not included in the January 15 release. Rankin was especially interested in the ONI records dealing with Oswald's activities after he left the Marine Corps and "his subsequent trip to the Soviet Union." In an attachment to Rankin's February 18 request, Frank A. Bartimo, the DOD's assistant counsel, noted that there were two documents in Oswald's U.S. Marine Corps records that covered Rankin's request. As the record revealed, both of these documents were not in Oswald's ONI file that was originally sent to McNaughton. These two documents and a third one were sent to McNaughton after he expressed a "strong desire" to see them. By May Rankin had still not heard from the DOD general counsel's office. Rankin and his staff, apparently tired of McNaughton's stalling tactics, contacted Lt. Col. Allison G. Folsom, of the Marine Corps Personnel Department in Washington, D.C., to ask for Oswald's records.[20]

All the available records strongly suggested that there had been a systematic sanitization of Oswald's military records before they were turned over to the Warren Commission. The twenty documents that Captain Jackson represented to Rankin as the ONI's Oswald file were a gross misrepresentation of what the navy was actually holding. The navy initially withheld at least three documents from the DOD and sent them forward only when McNaughton protested. Whatever was in these documents, it is certain that they never reached the Warren Commission; whatever his reasons, General

Counsel McNaughton saw to that. A vexed Commission staff lawyer, Samuel Stern, noted that the Commission was exasperated with the ONI's noncompliance in a host of matters and had "gigged" the navy for failing to cooperate in the investigation.[21]

Nobody knew more about Oswald than the navy. Any detail about the only official suspect in the crime was essential to the investigation, so it cannot be dismissed as simple bureaucratic oversight that the navy suppressed critical details of Oswald's military career. That the navy saw fit to do this, and has still not disclosed any of it, even after Congress passed the 1992 JFK Assassination Records Collection Act, which required full disclosure, places the navy squarely in the dock. It was a party either to the assassination or to the cover-up.[22]

The CIA's preassassination file on Oswald was practically a carbon copy of the ONI files turned over to the Commission. In March 1964 the CIA gave the Commission its "official dossier" on Lee Harvey Oswald. The CIA's preassassination file contained thirty documents, the great bulk of which, some twenty documents, originated from other government agencies and departments. The rest of what the CIA represented as Oswald's 201 file was made up of four newspaper clippings and five internal CIA notes. The last item was a CIA report sent to the Commission after the assassination.[23] Like the ONI, the CIA contended that it had not debriefed Oswald either while the Oswalds ostensibly spent two days sightseeing in Amsterdam before their ship left for America or after he returned to the United States. The largely derivative nature of the agency's preassassination file created the impression that Oswald was a security suspect and therefore the proper subject for handling by the ONI and the FBI rather than the CIA. Equally curious was the fact that the CIA did not open its 201 file on Oswald until a year after the CIA's Snyder notified the State Department of Oswald's visit to the U.S. Embassy in Moscow, when he declared his intention to seek Soviet citizenship and to reveal everything he knew about the navy's radar capabilities.

None of this would ring true even if it were a story line in a pulp-fiction spy novel. The CIA made it its business to debrief American servicemen going and returning from abroad. That business certainly included defectors. The agency's Office of Operations had a Domestic Contact Division all across the United States whose function was to interview American citizens—businessmen, students, artists, and tourists—returning from the Soviet Union or Soviet bloc countries. This was standard CIA operational procedure during the height of the Cold War.[24] Any intelligence agency in the world worth its keep would have debriefed any of its nationals who had Oswald's history and credentials. If Oswald's defection was legitimate, the CIA, as well as the ONI, needed to know what secrets Oswald may have compromised. It seems incredible that the CIA, if it did not already know, did not check with the ONI to find out about Oswald's security clearances and his overseas assignments, especially what, if any, information he might have furnished the Soviets about the CIA's ultrasecret spy plane. Langley, the CIA's headquarters in Virginia, was immediately alerted about Oswald's defection and the threat he had voiced to Richard Snyder. It would have been an inexplicable dereliction of responsibility if the CIA did not debrief Oswald to learn what he might have told his Soviet hosts about the U-2, the jewel in the crown of the agency's espionage arsenal.

The CIA's concerted effort to distance itself from Oswald is contradicted by disclosed facts. For example, a special unit of the agency's Counterintelligence (CI) staff, the Special Investigations Group (SIG), had a preassassination file on Oswald. The SIG was staffed by a select handful of operatives whose mission was to ferret out any foreign attempt to penetrate the CIA. John Whitten, the former chief of the agency's Western Division, noted that the SIG worked on cases that were "so sensitive . . . that they should not be handled by one of the area divisions." Raymond G. Rocca, deputy to the agency's CI chief, James J. Angleton, disclosed to a congressional committee that he was certain the KGB had debriefed Oswald about U.S. radar secrets and any information he had about the agency's top-secret U-2 spy plane.[25]

These revelations indicated that the CIA's attempt to distance itself from Oswald was a tactical charade. Why did the supersensitive SIG have a file on an ex-marine defector? Why did the CIA wait for a year before opening a file on Oswald after learning about his defection? Even more inexplicable is the CIA's contention that it never debriefed Oswald before or after he returned to the United States. If the CIA was certain that the KGB had questioned Oswald about the U-2, then it was in the agency's interest to find out what his Soviet interrogators had wanted to know, where he had been questioned, and much more. That is, if his defection had not been staged.[26]

Assuming Oswald's defection was genuine, the Soviet branch of the agency's CI Division would have needed to know if the redefecting Oswald had been "turned" while in Russia and was returning as a KGB "sleeper," or dormant agent. Angleton, who was famously ensnared in his own web of Cold War paranoia, would never have missed an opportunity to aggressively debrief Oswald if he had indeed breached security. Angleton's suspicions of the Soviet menace were so ingrained that he never retreated from his deep conviction that the KGB was behind the Kennedy assassination.[27] As mentioned earlier, it was Angleton who wrested the CIA's in-house investigation away from John Whitten because he either was convinced or pretended to believe that the purpose of Oswald's trip to Mexico City had been to meet with his KGB handlers to finalize plans to assassinate Kennedy.[28]

Even if Oswald was just an ordinary defector, a "small potato" in the eyes of the American intelligence community, the fact that most of his time in Russia had been spent working in an electronics factory in Minsk would have aroused CIA interest. This was exactly the kind of information Oswald included in the section of his "Historic Diary" titled "Composition on 'The Collective' and Minsk, Russia." It included twenty-five pages describing the Minsk radio and TV plant where he had worked, with detailed accounts of the various shops making up the plant, profiles of individual workers, accounts of demonstrations and meetings, descriptions of the ethnic composition of the workers, production schedules, population figures, and a layout of the city. This section of his manuscript-sized diary indicated both organizational skill and a keen eye for detail. These were the kind of nontravelogue facts and information that the CIA would have found useful.[29]

The CIA's attempts to create an impression for the official record that it had only a casual interest in the defecting and redefecting Oswald failed to satisfy other elements of the U.S. intelligence establishment. On April 6, 1964, an ONI operative, G. R. Wilson, turned over to FBI agent J. M. Fitzgerald a "Confidential" memorandum containing classified information. The memo contained statements made to the ONI by Eugene J. Hobbs, a former marine who was stationed at Atsugi, Japan, from 1956 through 1957. Hobbs contended that it "was common knowledge" that Atsugi was used for reconnaissance flights for the U-2. Having picked up accounts of Oswald's tour of duty from the media, Hobbs was concerned that the former marine radar operator who had served in Atsugi might have furnished valuable information to the Soviets that had led to the May 1960 shoot-down of Gary Powers.[30]

Since the ONI did not object to the FBI sharing Hobbs's "Confidential" statements with the CIA, Hoover wasted little time in contacting Langley. Apparently during the intervening week the FBI did its own investigation into Oswald's Marine Corps records. When Hoover wrote to CIA director McCone a week after Agent Fitzgerald received the Hobbs memo, he was able to cite chapter and verse about Oswald's assignments at Atsugi and Cubi Point. The FBI had contacted at least five marines who had served with Oswald at either Atsugi or Cubi Point. According to Hoover, one of these former Oswald associates recalled that at Cubi Point "the gear of the Squadron was housed there in an airplane hangar which he says he now knows was the hangar for a U-2 airplane." This underscored Hobbs's concerns that Oswald could have had some social contact with the U-2 pilots and maintenance personnel who serviced the U-2s, and that he might have picked up some valuable tidbits of intelligence about the spy plane and passed them on to the Russians. Hoover's three-page letter to McCone was couched in terms of professional courtesy, furnished solely for the agency director's information. However, the FBI director let McCone know that if the CIA felt it necessary "to conduct further inquiry" into Hobbs's disclosures, the "Bureau would appreciate being advised of the results of your analysis and inquiry."[31]

Washington insiders knew that the FBI director was a master of bureaucratic infighting, and more often than not came out on top in interagency power struggles. All veterans and observers of the Washington power game knew that beginning with the Truman administration the Hoover bureau and the CIA had waged bitter behind-the-scenes turf battles.[32] With the assassination and its aftermath, Hoover had some immediate scores to settle with McCone's agency. It would have been understandable if Hoover was unhappy with the CIA for withholding from the FBI Oswald's connections with the U-2. The director would have wanted to know what the CIA had learned from the accused assassin of President Kennedy when it had debriefed him, which Hoover assumed it must have done, as standard intelligence procedures dictated. Since President Johnson had assigned the FBI to investigate the crime, the bureau had every right to information about the assailant from all cooperating agencies indicated in the presidential executive order, including the CIA.

This practice of CIA withholding of information carried over into Oswald's activities in Mexico City. Although the CIA's Mexico City station reported promptly to the FBI about Oswald's contacts with the Soviet Embassy, it withheld information about his visits to the Cuban Consulate until the day of the assassination.[33] No bureaucratic lapse or administrative oversight could explain away this failure in intelligence sharing. The Hoover bureau had a standing intelligence-sharing understanding with CIA Mexico that the FBI would be alerted about any Americans in Mexico who made contact with the Soviet or Cuban Embassy. Whitten recalled that "Hoover used to glow every time that he thought of the Mexico station. This was one of the outstanding areas of cooperation with the FBI." Had FBI Washington's Domestic Intelligence Division been alerted about Oswald's contacts with the Cubans, it would have placed his name on the bureau's "Security Index," thereby avoiding the subsequent criticism it received in the Warren report for failing to notify the Secret Service about Oswald before Kennedy's Dallas visit.[34] This controlling CIA impulse for withholding when it came to Oswald's activities raised suspicions in Hoover's mind that Oswald must have had some kind of relationship with the CIA. As to whether or not the CIA had debriefed the redefecting Oswald, Hoover never believed for a moment the CIA's steadfast denials that it had had no interest in interviewing Oswald.

Hoover's suspicions were not unfounded. An internal CIA document dated February 20, 1964, revealed that the CIA was deceiving the Commission. Eight days before, Rankin had asked Director McCone to turn over the agency's entire preassassination file on Oswald. The informal February 20 document acknowledged that some thirty-seven documents from Oswald's 201 file were withheld. The missing documents included some CIA dispatches, seven FBI memoranda, one CIA counterintelligence document, several State Department documents, and twenty-five agency cables. There was nothing in the internal note that explained the discrepancy between the file Deputy Director Richard Helms forwarded to the Commission as the agency's "Oswald dossier" and the withheld thirty-seven documents. What did these missing documents contain that was so sensitive? One thing is certain: The 201 file that Helms represented to the Commission as the "complete" agency preassassination file on Oswald was sanitized. A key to this deception might be the fact that the CIA, as Hoover expected, actually had debriefed Oswald either before he left the Netherlands or after he arrived back in the United States. Several CIA documents unearthed by the House Select Committee on Assassinations during its investigation into Kennedy's murder indicated that this was almost certainly the case.[35]

Two days after Langley received Hoover's letter Richard Helms, the deputy director of plans (DDP), responded with a three-page letter of his own. Helms's letter deflected, point by point, all of the concerns raised by Hobbs in his "Confidential" ONI memorandum. Helms assured Hoover that the U-2 bases were "closed" and that Oswald could have had no contact with the Joint Technical Advisory Group teams, the men who piloted and the technicians who maintained the CIA's ultrasecret spy planes. Even if Oswald had seen a U-2 aircraft, Helms confidently asserted, "It was most unlikely that Oswald had the necessary prerequisites to differentiate between the U-2 and other aircraft engaged in classified missions which were similarly visible at Atsugi at the same time." The DDP could not have believed his own assertions. Oswald and all the other radar operators at Atsugi had tracked the CIA spy plane on radar. There was not another U.S. airplane in that theater, or the world, for that matter, that could climb to ninety thousand feet. All Marine Corps radar operators were above average in intelligence and would have figured out that the mission of this remarkable aircraft was intelligence-gathering. Helms would not allow that Oswald, Hobbs, or any of the marines in the radar units associated with the U-2 operations would have even been familiar with the term *U-2* or the plane's mission until it gained worldwide notoriety with the ill-fated Powers mission.[36] Helms closed his May 15 letter to the director by noting that a copy of his memorandum was being forwarded to the Commission. Leaving nothing to chance, Hoover sent a copy of the ONI's "Confidential" Hobbs memorandum and a copy of Helms's response to the Commission's general counsel, J. Lee Rankin.[37]

In April 1963 Oswald moved his family to his hometown of New Orleans. During his five months in New Orleans all his known activities were consistent with what is called in the intelligence game "building a cover." From May through August 1963 Oswald assiduously created a false biography in which he pretended to be a recruiter for the pro-Castro Fair Play for Cuba Committee. His carefully planned street demonstrations were calculated to attract the attention of the police, the FBI, and anti-Castro Cuban refugees in New Orleans. These manufactured incidents received extensive press, radio, and TV coverage, which Oswald later used to establish his bona fides when he went to Mexico City and sought admission to Cuba as a "friend" of the Castro revolution. Although he posed as a Castro sympathizer during this New Orleans interlude, all of his real contacts were with militant anti-Castro Cubans and Americans who had connections with or were of interest to the CIA.

In late 1960 and early 1961 New Orleans and the surrounding parishes were a hotbed of CIA-organized anti-Castro activity. The agency was involved in a variety of activities in preparation for "Operation Zapata," the CIA's code name for the planned invasion of Cuba. The CIA ran two secret camps for training anti-Castro guerrillas. One was located on the north shore of Lake Pontchartrain, and the other was situated between Mandeville and Lacombe.[38] In the early spring of 1961 David Atlee Phillips, the agency's psychological warfare expert, made several visits to New Orleans. Phillips was working with E. Howard Hunt at the CIA's main staging area for the upcoming invasion in South Dade County, Miami, code named JM/Wave. Phillips was renowned throughout the agency for his role in the CIA's overthrow of Guatemala's social democratic government, headed by Jacobo Arbenz Guzman, in 1954. Phillips was awarded the agency's Intelligence Medal of Merit for the disinformation campaign he orchestrated in preparation for what the CIA named "Operation Success." Robert M. Gaynor, the chairman of the Honor Awards Board, cited Phillips for an achievement that "had no parallel in the history of psychological warfare."[39]

Phillips held a series of meetings with his New Orleans contacts to crank up a sophisticated anti-Castro media campaign in the city in preparation for the April 1961 Bay of Pigs operation. The sources Phillips relied on all had some links with the agency. Edward Butler, the executive director of the Information Council of the Americas (ICA), an anticommunist propaganda organization, turned out tapes of interviews with Cuban refugees about the horrors inside Castro's Cuba that were played on radio stations throughout Latin America. Some of Butler's tapes were even used in Louisiana schools. The CIA had cleared Butler for "contact use," so whether or not the ICA was an outright CIA "front," Butler was always ready to help the agency in any way he could. Cuban refugee Sergio Arcacha Smith, a spokesman for the New Orleans chapter of the Cuban Revolutionary Council (CRC), a CIA-funded organization, sat in on Phillips's meetings. A young and well-connected New Orleans native recruited by Smith, Gordon Novel, brought to the group his expert knowledge about sophisticated electronics. Novel knew most of the print news media; radio and advertising agency people in the city came under Phillips's tutelage. Novel later claimed he was a CIA operative, but the CIA disputed his claim. Butler and Novel were the mainstays in Phillips's anti-Castro media crusade. Guy Bannister, a former FBI agent, set up the meetings with Phillips. Bannister's main role in the New Orleans part of the planned "Operation Zapata" was to provide security and build up a cache of arms, ammunition, antipersonnel mines, and deadly chemicals. Bannister also assigned Novel to identify former servicemen, especially ex-marines, who had special weapons skills and held strong anti-Castro views. Some of Phillips's New Orleans infrastructure faded away after the CIA's ill-conceived "Operation Zapata" met its demise on the beaches of the Bay of Pigs at the hands of Castro's revolutionary forces.[40]

Oswald was jobless and alone when he arrived in New Orleans in April. Marina and their infant daughter, June, had remained behind at Ruth Paine's home in Irving, Texas. They were to join Lee when he found a job and a place for them to live. Oswald found a job with the William B. Reily Company as a greaser and lubricator of the coffee-processing machines for $1.50 an hour. The family was reunited a month later. Three months later Oswald was fired from his job for inefficiency and inattention to his work. His supervisor claimed that he spent too much work time hanging around the Capital City Garage next door. Oswald slipped next door during work hours to read gun magazines and talk about guns with Adrian Alba, one of the garage owners. Perhaps it was coincidence, but the Capital City Garage was where the FBI and Secret Service kept their cars.[41] The Newman building at 544 Camp Street was only a block away. The importance of the 544 Camp Street address will be discussed presently.

When Oswald lost his job the family, though accustomed to living close to the edge financially, was facing wrenching hard times. His weekly unemployment checks were not enough to cover the family's minimal needs. Compounding their dire economic plight was the fact that Marina was pregnant and the baby was due sometime in November. In September Marina took the infant June and returned to Ruth Paine's home because they could not afford proper prenatal care and she feared for the life of her baby. Oswald had a history of being a caring father, but uncharacteristically the breadwinner in the family did not actively seek employment. Instead, Oswald turned his efforts full time to politics. In retrospect, it appeared as though Oswald might have treated his job with the Reily company as a "between assignments" stand-down until he was activated by unnamed handlers.

On August 5 Oswald visited Carlos Bringuier's clothing store, Casa Roca, at 107 Decatur Street. Bringuier was a thirty-year-old former lawyer who had left Cuba shortly after Castro took power. When Oswald struck up a conversation with Bringuier it was clear that he was not interested in the merchandise. Oswald started by declaring that he was opposed to the Castro regime and wanted to help train Cuban exiles in guerrilla warfare. He told Bringuier that his Marine Corps experience was in small-arms tactics, infiltration, and "black operations." Bringuier was brought up short when his visitor mentioned that he knew about the secret training camp on the north shore of Lake Pontchartrain. Oswald let Bringuier know that he was aware that Bringuier was associated with the CRC and was actively engaged in anti-Castro activities in New Orleans. The Cuban exile suspected that Oswald was an FBI informer who wanted to infiltrate the Lake Pontchartrain camp, so he politely brushed off Oswald, claiming that he knew nothing about training camps and that the scope of his work with the CRC was confined to publicity and propaganda. The next day, while Bringuier was out of the store, Oswald showed up again at Casa Roca. Bringuier was away, so Oswald left his address and a copy of his Marine Corps handbook with an inscription, "Hope this helps you in your work," with Bringuier's brother-in-law.[42]

Of all the four thousand to five thousand first-generation members of *el exilio* (anti-Castro refugees) living in New Orleans in 1963, Bringuier was probably the one most closely connected to the CIA. He was a delegate to the New Orleans chapter of the Revolutionary Student Directorate (DRE). Bringuier's older brother, Juan Felipe, a member of Brigade 2506 ("La Brigada"), was captured on the beach when Castro's forces rolled up the CIA's invasion force at the Bay of Pigs in 1961. The founding father of the DRE was the former actor and CIA operative David Atlee Phillips. The directorate had gotten started in 1961 largely under the supervision and financial support of Phillips, whose base of operations was the CIA's JM/Wave station in Miami. By 1963 the DRE was the most outspoken, militant, and popular anti-Castro organization in Miami, with more than two thousand supporters. It had the deserved reputation among *el exilio* for carrying out daring raids against Castro's Cuba. In August 1962 the directorate carried out a "dark-of-the-moon" attack on the Rosita Hornedo Hotel in Miramar, Cuba, where Castro's advisers from the Soviet bloc countries were meeting. The CIA knew about the meeting because it had planted electronic devices in the hotel. Two DRE craft raked the Rosita with 20-mm cannon rounds before returning to their Miami base.[43]

The CIA's JM/Wave station in Miami was the center of the agency's covert war against Castro's Cuba. In early 1962 Richard Helms assigned a new contact officer to work with the directorate. George E. Joannides was a forty-year-old upwardly mobile CIA career officer who had been with the agency since 1951. A graduate of St. Johns University Law School in New York, Joannides was fluent in Greek and French and competent in Spanish. His previous posts had been in Greece and Libya. Joannides quickly demonstrated that he was able to skillfully handle the agency's most effective exile group, which had previously balked at too-close CIA hands-on control. While Joannides was stationed at JM/Wave in Miami, he kept abreast of Bringuier's activities in New Orleans.[44]

During the month of August 1963 New Orleans DRE members were "up to their necks" with Lee Harvey Oswald. On August 9, Bringuier was in his Decatur Street clothing store when a Cuban associate burst in with the news that a man was distributing pro-Castro literature a few blocks away. Joined by DRE members Celfo M. Hernandez and Miguel M. Cruz, Bringuier went looking for the man. They caught up with their quarry at the 700 block of Canal Street. It was Oswald. He was handing out FPCC fliers with the words "Hands off Cuba" and wearing a placard around his waist with "Viva Fidel" written in large black block letters. Oswald had noted in his address book the concentration of Cuban exile stores on Canal, Decatur, and Camp streets. If Oswald wanted to make sure to attract Bringuier's attention, he was in the very heart of New Orleans's *el exilio* community. Cruz tore the leaflets out of Oswald's hands and threw them on the ground. Bringuier confronted the man, who just four days ago had been in his store professing his hatred for Castro, shouting, "traitor" and "communist." A crowd had gathered, and some of the onlookers began to chant, "Go back to Cuba!" and "Kill him!" Oswald coolly dropped his hands in front of him, put his face close to the enraged, burly Cuban, and taunted, "OK, Carlos, if you want to hit me, hit me." At that point in the confrontation the police arrived and arrested all four men for creating a public disturbance.[45]

Oswald was taken to the First District Police Station, where he had to stay over the weekend because he refused to pay a $25 fine. According to the official story, while he was waiting in jail for his bench hearing the following Monday he asked to speak to an FBI agent. On the surface of things, it's difficult to understand why Oswald asked to speak to an FBI agent when he considered the FBI his enemy. As discussed earlier, when he returned from Russia and was interviewed by FBI agents, he showed them open hostility. On the day of the assassination, when FBI agent Hosty entered the room where he was being interrogated by the Dallas police, Oswald denounced him and the FBI in violent terms. Even if this previous display of animus was not an act, Oswald had his reasons on August 9 for wanting to speak to an FBI agent.

John L. Quigley, a twenty-seven-year FBI veteran, arrived on Saturday to interview Oswald. It was not exactly standard FBI practice to become involved with someone charged with being a public nuisance. However, at the time of his arrest Oswald's FBI dossier was "active" at the FBI New Orleans office. Milton R. Kaack was Oswald's case officer, but he had the weekend off, and, according to Quigley, he was filling in for Kaack. One of Kaack's preassassination reports on Oswald indicated that a "confidential informant" had informed the FBI that on June 26, 1963, Oswald had written a letter to the *Worker,* the American Communist Party's East Coast paper. The letter was intercepted and photographed for the FBI. On August 5, 1963, four days before Oswald's altercation with Bringuier, Kaack had interviewed Oswald's landlady. This visit might have been triggered by a report that two weeks earlier Oswald had been ushered off the Dumaine Street Wharf for distributing "Hands off Cuba" fliers to navy personnel attached to the aircraft carrier USS *Wasp,* which was temporarily berthed at the wharf. Some of the *Wasp*'s crew complained, and since the wharf was private property Oswald was peacefully sent on his way.[46] But the FBI mail cover on Oswald was in place before the *Wasp* incident, indicating that the New Orleans office had a dossier on Oswald created after the bureau learned of his reported 1959 defection to the Soviet Union. The "slug line" (character of report) on Kaack's submitted reports was IS-R (Internal Security—Russia). Opening a file on an American defector was standard FBI procedure and denoted nothing sinister; anything less would have been a dereliction of bureau responsibility.

Quigley spent more than an hour and a half with Oswald. Oswald told the FBI agent that he was the secretary of the FPCC New Orleans chapter, that the president was A. J. Hidell (whose only contact with Oswald had been by phone), and that there were thirty-three members in the chapter. When Quigley asked for specifics—members' names, meeting places, Hidell's phone number—Oswald's memory failed on all counts. Oswald had asked for the interview and then proved uncooperative. What little he did tell Quigley was the kind of information he probably assumed the FBI already knew about him. Oswald spun a tale that was a rich confection of misinformation, misstatements, and evasions. Quigley knew he was being used, but he took notes that ultimately ended up in Agent Kaack's case file on Oswald.[47] Aside from Oswald, there was no FPCC chapter in New Orleans. He represented no one but himself and possibly other principals who had an operational interest in him but who have so far remained unnamed. He used his own funds to purchase the "Hands off Cuba" fliers and never recruited a single member.[48]

When Quigley testified before the Warren Commission he was less than straightforward. He said that when he was introduced to Oswald at the jail that Saturday morning, Oswald's name did not ring a bell; that the interview was conducted without benefit of familiarity with Oswald's background and history. None of this could have been possible. Quigley would have known that the New Orleans office had a file on Oswald that had been opened in

1959. Some of the material in that file originated from the ONI Naval District Records Station in Algiers, Louisiana. Most of the documents dealt with Oswald's defection in 1959. There was a specific reference to Oswald's abrasive confrontation with U.S. Embassy senior counselor Richard Snyder and his threat to turn over to the Soviets "any information he acquired as Enlisted Radio Operator." This investigative lead in the Oswald file was preceded by a "Flash by Bureau" dated November 4, 1959, when the FBI first learned of Oswald's defection. The notation went on to direct that all further information on Oswald be forwarded to the FBI's Espionage Section, Division 5, at Washington headquarters ("IS-R"). Quigley was the New Orleans agent who reviewed the ONI file and reported its contents to the FBI's Dallas office.[49]

Agent Quigley was following instructions from FBI Washington when he intentionally gave the Commission the impression that he had never heard of Oswald until that Saturday when he showed up at the First District Police Station. In December 1963 Assistant Director William Sullivan had instructed the New Orleans office to distance itself from Oswald. Sullivan strongly indicated that all New Orleans records that might come before the Commission should show "in effect that Oswald was a non-entity": that Oswald had no official connection with the Fair Play for Cuba Committee in New York; that he had appointed himself as the New Orleans chapter's chairman; and that he "had no financial backing, no group to support him [and] even had to hire somebody to pass out his leaflets." In short, Sullivan's orders were to depict Oswald as a "cipher."[50] It would be pure unfounded speculation to attribute the bureau's efforts to distance itself from Oswald as part of a stratagem, as some critics have suggested, to hide the fact that Oswald was an FBI undercover informer, and that he asked to speak to an FBI agent to get him released from jail without blowing his cover.

There is yet to be unearthed any evidence that Oswald was an FBI source or informer. The most likely reason for the FBI's attempts to depict Oswald as a nullity, a "nonentity," was to cover up a devastating FBI secret: the failure of the bureau to have placed Oswald's name on its Security Index and the subsequent history-altering blunder of not alerting the Secret Service and the Dallas Police Department of Oswald's presence in Dallas prior to President Kennedy's Texas trip. Sullivan, as well as Hoover's other assistant directors, was aware that the director had ordered a secret in-house investigation into this intelligence-sharing disaster. Hoover enjoined James H. Gale from the Inspection Division to turn over every stone and cite names of those, from assistant directors to street agents, who were responsible for this intelligence failure. Given these circumstances it was only natural that FBI Washington wanted to minimize as much as possible any attention given to Oswald and his FBI contacts. Sullivan was particularly sensitive on this issue because Gale's report cited him for dereliction of responsibility and named him as one of seventeen candidates for administrative action.[51]

Oswald's pro-Castro pretext and his clever maneuvering of Bringuier into the Canal Street confrontation was all part of his effort to create a false biography. Oswald's provocative practice of handing out pro-Castro FPCC handbills in a Cuban refugee neighborhood ruled out any suspicion that he was trying to infiltrate New Orleans's anti-Castro movement. The day following his arrest, at about 5:20 P.M., Oswald was "paroled for a Mr. A. Heckman, a Jury Commissioner, State of Louisiana, Orleans Parish, New Orleans."[52]

The Friday incident with the DRE members and his jailhouse visit from an FBI agent excited media attention, and newsmen and a TV crew from WDSU in New Orleans, an NBC affiliate, were in the courtroom when Oswald was released. A month later Oswald used the press clipping from the *Times Picayune* as part of his pro-Castro credentials when he visited the Cuban Consulate in Mexico City and tried to get a visa to Cuba.[53] A few days after he was released from jail Oswald was still drumming up self-promotional schemes. David Chandler, a reporter for the *New Orleans States-Item,* told the FBI that Oswald came to his office and told him that Bringuier was "training guerillas for fighting in Cuba." According to Chandler, Oswald then advanced the idea that the paper should do a story on "his arrest and him personally." Chandler was not interested and terminated the interview. Undeterred, Oswald called Bern Rotman, the senior news editor of WDSU-TV, Channel 6, in New Orleans. Oswald asked Rotman when he would like him to show up and picket outside the International Trade Mart (ITM). Always on the lookout for a newsworthy story—and Oswald, the self-advertised Castro sympathizer, had established himself as a colorful and contentious local personality after his arrest—Rotman reported that he told Oswald to let him know the time and Channel 6 would be there. On August 16, when Oswald turned up outside the ITM to hand out FPCC handbills, Channel 6 was there. A WDSU-TV photographer who filmed Oswald handing out his pro-Castro fliers was Johann Rush. Rush, as it turned out, was also an FBI informant. This may have been coincidental, but it does reinforce the pattern of government interest in Oswald's New Orleans activities. When Rankin asked Hoover for a copy of the film of Oswald outside the ITM on August 16, Hoover made it available but volunteered nothing about Rush's status as an FBI informer.[54]

There was an intriguing sequel to Oswald's contrived and splashy confrontation with Bringuier and his DRE comrades that should have elicited some explanation from the Commission but was never addressed. The day after Kennedy's assassination two Secret Service men showed up at the First District Police Station, where Oswald had been held overnight after his arrest for being a public nuisance. They wanted to speak with Lt. Francis L.

Martello, who had had several long conversations with Oswald while he remained in the lockup waiting for his bench hearing. Martello told the agents he had never met anybody with Oswald's "socialist" ideas. His curiosity was aroused when he found out that Oswald had lived in the Soviet Union. When Martello asked what life was like behind the Iron Curtain, Oswald, the professed Marxist, said, "It stunk." According to the police lieutenant, Oswald was bitterly anti-Soviet, claiming that the country was run "by fat stinking politicians" and that "the leaders have everything and the people are still poor and oppressed." Martello had a folder with the literature in Oswald's possession the day he was arrested. Upon request he turned the folder over to Secret Service agent Adrian G. Vail.[55]

When Secret Service agents examined the material in Oswald's folder they found that some of the literature bore a rubber-stamped address, "FPCC 544 Camp Street, New Orleans, La." After what the Secret Service called an "extensive investigation," it found no evidence that the Fair Play for Cuba Committee had ever occupied any of the office space at that address. The owner of the building, Sam Newman, told the Secret Service that he did not know Oswald and had never leased any space to the pro-Castro committee. However, Newman reported that back in 1961–1962 he had rented an office on the second floor of the 544 Camp Street address to the Cuban Revolutionary Council, the most visible of the anti-Castro organizations in New Orleans. After four or five months, Newman recalled, the CRC fell into arrears in the rent and he evicted the organization. Prominent and activist anti-Castro elements in New Orleans were affiliated with the CRC. Sergio Arcacha Smith had been the New Orleans delegate to the CRC before he was removed for misappropriation of funds. Manuel Gil, production manager for Edward Butler's CIA front, the Information Council of the Americas, was a member of the CRC. The Secret Service report noted that Guy Bannister was a frequent visitor to the 544 Camp Street address when the CRC had offices in the building.[56]

There is a simple and straightforward explanation for why the Commission never provided any explanation of why Oswald's pro-Castro FPCC literature bore the return address of anti-Castro Cubans. The FBI kept the Commission in the dark about the significance of the 544 Camp Street address. This was part of the Hoover bureau's systematic postassassination campaign to suppress any possible link among Oswald, the CIA, and the Kennedy assassination. It was essential that there was nothing in the record to throw a shadow of doubt over the official conclusion that Oswald had not been an agent, informer, or employee of any government agency.

When FBI agent Quigley finished his interview with Oswald at the First District Police Station, Oswald gave him copies of the FPCC materials he was handing out when Bringuier confronted him. As Quigley recorded in his report of the interview, one of the pieces of literature was a forty-page pamphlet written by Corliss Lamont titled, "The Crime Against Cuba." The Lamont tract was a critical essay on U.S. policy toward Cuba before and during the Bay of Pigs invasion. Quigley's copy bore the rubber-stamped impression "FPCC/544 Camp Street/New Orleans, La." When the Commission questioned Quigley about his interview with Oswald, the FBI agent never mentioned the 544 Camp Street address. On September 12, 1963, FBI New Orleans asked the New York office to "furnish an appropriate characterization of Corliss Lamont." FBI New York's "characterization" of Lamont as a fellow traveler (communist sympathizer) and Quigley's Oswald interview report were included in two larger reports: Kaack's and de Brueys's for October 31 and October 25, respectively. In neither report was the Camp Street address mentioned. Three days after the assassination, the FBI did what can charitably be called a cursory investigation into the 544 Camp Street address. The results were incorporated into the FBI's Commission Document (CD) 1 summary report to the Commission. The salient information was: "Also at the time of his August, 1963, arrest, Oswald had been passing out publications bearing the stamp 'FPCC, 544 Camp Street, New Orleans, La.'" The Commission was never informed that at one time the CIA-funded Cuban Revolutionary Council's New Orleans chapter had occupied offices at this address. This was not an FBI oversight. When Secret Service agent John Rice, the agency's special agent in charge of the New Orleans Office, requested from his FBI counterpart information about where Oswald had had his FPCC handbills printed and also about the 544 Camp Street address, FBI Washington abruptly advised him that it had checked "this angle thoroughly but with negative results." In short, Rice was warned off the case.[57]

Before the month of August was over Oswald had had another encounter with New Orleans's anti-Castro infrastructure. Oswald's public support for the Cuban revolution attracted the attention of William Kirk Stuckey, a local radio host for WDSU radio. Stuckey was responsible for a five-minute spot called "Latin Listening Post" covering current economic and political developments in Latin America. His radio spot tilted heavily toward accounts of the repressive nature of life in Castro's Cuba. This was hardly surprising since he relied heavily on the anti-Castro community for his material. Bringuier and Edward Butler were among his main sources.[58] In July 1962 Stuckey wrote an article that appeared in the *New Orleans States-Item* about the anti-Castro training camp on the north shore of Lake Pontchartrain. The piece featured Gerald Patrick Hemming and the "International Anti-Communist Brigade." Like Hemming, most of the training cadre was made up of former marines. Stuckey must have had proven anti-Castro credentials to have had access to Hemming.[59]

With prompting from Bringuier, Stuckey sought out Oswald and invited him to participate in a debate on the Castro revolution. The day before the scheduled debate Oswald met with Stuckey at WDSU's station in the French Quarter to become familiar with the format of the program. Stuckey explained that the debate would be a twenty-five-minute public affairs program called "Conversation Carte Blanche." Although they exchanged pleasantries, Oswald, in what Stuckey characterized as a "jocular way," asked, "How many of you am I going to have to fight?" Oswald anticipated a setup, that the purpose of the debate was to discredit him and the Fair Play for Cuba Committee. Probably not to his surprise, Oswald learned from Stuckey that his opponents were Carlos Bringuier and Edward Butler.[60]

The debate took place during the evening of August 21. Before the debate Bringuier had contacted DRE headquarters in Miami to request background on Oswald and whatever the directorate had in its files on the FPCC. As Oswald was delivering his opening statement in defense of Castro's policies, Stuckey cut in and asked him if it was true that Oswald had lived in Russia. Oswald had not shared this piece of his biography with Stuckey during their meeting the day before. This revelation came from the Miami DRE, and Bringuier had passed it on to Stuckey before the debate. Oswald seemed taken aback. He tried to recover, admitting that it was true and that this experience gave him "excellent qualifications to repudiate charges that Cuba and the Fair Play for Cuba Committee is communist controlled." Bringuier chimed in at this point and asked if Oswald represented the Fair Play for Cuba Committee or the Fair Play for Russia Committee. Oswald was seemingly deflated, and little more was heard from him while Butler and Bringuier dominated the remainder of the program.[61]

After the debate Bringuier prepared a press release that he planned to place with the UPI and the local papers urging patriotic Americans to "write your congressmen asking for a full investigation of Mr. Lee Harvey Oswald, a confessed Marxist." He had no success in placing his open letter, but he sent a copy of the prepared release to the Secret Service. Butler's CIA-front organization, the Information Council of the Americas, made a record of the tape of the debate for circulation. The record was labeled "Self-Portrait in Red." Stuckey proudly told the Warren Commission that the debate finished Oswald in New Orleans. "I think that after that program the FPCC," Stuckey boasted, "if there was one in New Orleans, had no future there, we had publicly linked the FPCC with a fellow who lived in Russia . . . and was an admitted Marxist."[62] If Oswald had been a passionate advocate of the Cuban revolution, then the "Conversation Carte Blanche" debate was a personal debacle, poisoning the ground for any future legitimate attempts to root the FPCC in New Orleans. However, if the public notoriety he received was part of his operational plan for building a cover, then Oswald succeeded. Five weeks after the August 21 debate, Oswald left New Orleans for Mexico City.

The Oswald painted in the Warren report bears little resemblance to the Oswald who emerges from evidence ignored by the Commission. Forty years after the assassination the nature of Oswald's relationship with the government remains an unanswered question. It was not enough for the Commission to claim it could not prove a negative. The record revealed that it really sought to prove nothing, to brush the "Agent Oswald" question aside.

Commission general counsel Rankin, during the January 27 executive session, told the commissioners that they had to "wipe out" this "dirty rumor" insofar as they were able. Three days earlier Rankin and Warren had met secretly with members of the Texas Court of Inquiry. Most of that lengthy session centered on Oswald as a possible CIA informer or source. Henry Wade, the highly respected Dallas district attorney, volunteered that he had learned from a source that Oswald's CIA number was 110669, a number that was consistent with the CIA's system of identifying informers and sources. The Commission learned later, after Helms forwarded to Rankin the CIA's heavily sanitized Oswald preassassination 201 Personality File, that Oswald's agency number on this sanitized file was 289248. When the Commission met on January 27, Rankin and Warren withheld from the other members the fact that the Texas delegation had spent most of their session discussing whether or not Oswald had CIA connections.

During the January 27 executive session Rankin never mentioned 110669 to the commissioners. Instead, he paraded before them "S-172" and "S-179," symbols of reputed FBI informer numbers he knew to be bogus. There was nothing in Rankin's memorandum for the record about the meeting with the Texas Court of Inquiry representatives. His record of that meeting—the only record of it—does not indicate whether Rankin ever asked Wade to identify the source of the 110669 number. The CIA may have had more than one file on Oswald. Even more telltale was the fact that the Commission counsel never called as witnesses those sources he knew had brought forth the bogus numbers and 110669—reporters Lonnie Hudkins and Joseph Goulden, Dallas Sheriff Allen Sweatt, and Secret Service agent Lane Bertram. It was Bertram who included the 110669 number in a report that ultimately made its way to Rankin's desk. There is no record of any Commission attempt to identify the Secret Service agent's source. Apparently Rankin decided that the safest way to wipe out a "dirty rumor" was by not calling witnesses who might have aided the Commission in pursuing this question to a final conclusion.[63]

Instead, the Commission's conclusion that Oswald had no relations with government agencies was based on pro forma assurances in the form of affidavits from the heads of the FBI and the CIA. In response to an April letter from Rankin, both agencies also affirmed that Oswald had had no contact with the Russians, subversive groups, or any criminal elements.[64] What this inquiry did not seek, and what assurances the Commission knew it should have asked for, was whether or not Oswald had any connections with Cubans who had agency affiliations. In each instance, the Hoover and McCone affidavits and Commission testimony and Rankin's April letters to these agency heads, the CIA and FBI conferred before responding to the Commission's requests and questions. William C. Sullivan, the head of the FBI's Domestic Intelligence Division, and James J. Angleton, the CIA's counterintelligence chief, were in league to make sure that both agencies were on the same page when it came to questions relating to Oswald's government relations. Commissioner Allen Dulles, the former CIA director, was Angleton's pipeline into the deliberations and inner workings of the Commission. He let Angleton know beforehand about Commission concerns and how Rankin was going to proceed with the "Agent Oswald" matter, aware that the CI chief would contact his FBI counterpart. Despite all of Hoover's enduring jealousies and distrust of the CIA, over the years he had formed a strong professional bond with Angleton. The CIA's CI chief even had a special FBI signature symbol ("100"). In matters of deep mutual concern they exchanged intelligence to avoid any embarrassment to their respective agencies.[65]

To be fair, the Commission cannot be held responsible for not acting on information about Oswald that was withheld. However, the Commission, and Rankin in particular, gave every indication that it was satisfied not to have its preordained case against Oswald derailed by unruly facts or suspicious circumstances. When CIA deputy director Helms and McCone appeared before the Commission, Helms, speaking on McCone's behalf, assured the Commission that the agency had made a thorough examination of its "card files and personnel files" to make certain that there "was no material in the Central Intelligence Agency, either in the records or in the mind of any of the individuals, that there was any contact had or even contemplated with him [Oswald]."[66]

Helms's strategy in handling the Warren Commission when it came to the question of whether Oswald was a government agent or asset was to employ the charade of distance. The DDP tipped his hand early on with what he represented to Commission counsel Rankin as the CIA's preassassination Oswald file. Almost all of the thirty documents in the CIA's Oswald 201 Personality File originated with other agencies and branches of the government. The point Helms intended to underscore was that the CIA's preassassination interest in Oswald was of distant secondary importance to that of the FBI, the U.S. Navy, and the State Department. Still, there were key junctures in Oswald's life when, either by unplanned chance or design, his political activities had brought him into contact with CIA operatives and sources. None of these contacts were revealed in Helms's assurances and guarantees to the Commission.

The American public first learned of Oswald's defection to the Soviet Union in a two-column story appearing in the Washington *Evening Star* in November 1959. The byline was Priscilla Johnson. Johnson was an accomplished freelance writer in Moscow, fluent in Russian, with a master's degree from Harvard in Soviet area studies. She was also a part-time CIA contact during her three years in Russia under the agency's legal traveler program. Johnson had access to Oswald while he was staying at Hotel Metropole in Moscow waiting to learn whether Soviet officials would grant him citizenship. Her piece in the *Star* was based on a five-hour interview with Oswald in her Moscow apartment that started late at night and stretched into the early-morning hours. John McVickar, the assistant counsel in the U.S. Embassy in Moscow, arranged for this exclusive interview. According to CIA documents, when Johnson returned to the United States she made herself available to the agency through its Domestic Contact Division.[67]

Oswald's first contact with an American official in Moscow was with Richard Snyder, a CIA operative under diplomatic cover, when he showed up at the U.S. Embassy to announce his intention to seek Soviet citizenship. Probably the last U.S. government employee Oswald met with before leaving the Soviet Union in 1962 was Dr. Alexis H. Davison. Davison was assigned to the U.S. Embassy in Moscow and assumed a dual role: He was an officer in the U.S. Air Force, serving as assistant air attaché, and was the resident embassy physician. One of Dr. Davison's medical responsibilities was to examine people who were leaving the Soviet Union for entry into the United States. Before the Oswalds left Russia they reported to the U.S. Embassy in Moscow and were examined by the doctor. For reasons that Dr. Davison never fully explained, he gave Oswald his mother's name and address in Atlanta, Georgia. Davison's mother was born Natalia Alexseevna, a citizen of tsarist Russia. As a young woman she witnessed the Bolshevik Revolution and the Allied intervention in the Russian civil war between the Reds and the counterrevolutionary White armies. Davison's mother was a staunch anti-Bolshevik. She met Davison's father, an American officer with the U.S. military contingent, in the Russian Maritime Provinces. They were married there, and she left with him for the United States when the American interventionist forces withdrew in 1920.

The FBI became interested in Davison after they found his mother's name and address in Oswald's notebook. When the FBI located the doctor in 1964 he was on the staff of Grady Memorial Hospital in Atlanta, Georgia. Under FBI questioning, Dr. Davison gave the impression that he had been moved by Oswald's attractive young wife and, thinking of his mother's emigration from Russia to a new country, had given the young couple his mother's name and address in the hope that she might help Marina adjust to her new circumstances. He told his FBI questioner that he could not recall ever giving his mother's name to anyone else while he was assigned to the embassy in Moscow.[68] Since his mother was and remained bitterly anti-Soviet, Davison must have been absolutely certain that Lee Oswald shared her politics or he would never have made what he himself characterized as this unique gesture.

There is good reason to believe that Davison had access to the embassy's intelligence file on Oswald because he was either CIA or was recruited by the agency as part of the Moscow station's top-secret operation "CHICK-ADEE." This encourages the speculation that Oswald's 1959 defection to the Soviet Union was staged, that the former marine was a low-level "sleeper" government agent or asset put in place for intelligence purposes.

A year after the Oswalds left Russia, Davison and four other Americans, including the CIA's deputy chief of station, were declared persona non grata and expelled from Russia. Davison and the others were caught up in one of the Cold War's great spy sagas. In the spring of 1963 the KGB broke up the so-called Penkovsky spy ring (code-named "CHICKADEE"). Red Army Col. Oleg Penkovsky had turned over to British intelligence (MI 6) and the CIA detailed intelligence about the Soviets' rocket and missile programs. When Penkovsky needed to make contact with his CIA handlers he left a charcoal mark on lamppost No. 35 near the Kutuzovsky Prospect bus stop. The CIA deputy chief of station assigned Davison to check the lamppost every day.[69]

Earlier in this chapter I discussed what has sometimes been called Oswald's "Cubanization." During his New Orleans summer of 1963 Oswald's staged political persona was that of a fervent pro-Castro supporter and self-professed secretary of the nonexistent chapter of the New Orleans Fair Play for Cuba Committee. However, all his contacts were with militant anti-Castro types with CIA connections, including the DRE's Carlos Bringuier and Ed Butler, who was of interest to the CIA's Domestic Contact Division. Some of Oswald's FPCC literature even bore the address 544 Camp Street, the Newman Building, which had once housed the headquarters of the CIA's generously funded Cuban Revolutionary Council and the address of Guy Bannister and Associates. Bannister was the former FBI agent recruited by David Atlee Phillips as part of the New Orleans infrastructure in the agency's campaign to topple Castro in 1961.

On September 17, 1963, in preparation for his Mexico City trip, Oswald showed up at the Mexican Consul's Office in New Orleans. He was one of six Americans who presented themselves that day for tourist visas, or FM8 cards. According to Mexican immigration records Oswald was the fourth person to receive his tourist card that day. His FM8 card was number 24085. The names of the other people who received their tourist cards that day were recorded as part of the Commission's record except for the name of the person who received tourist card FM824084, the one immediately preceding Lee Harvey Oswald's. In the Warren report's record for history, alongside FM824084 is the citation "No record."[70]

It was the FBI's decision to bury the name of the person who went before Oswald. In order to check on Oswald's movements prior to his Mexico City visit, the FBI questioned everyone who was at the Mexican Consul's Office in New Orleans on September 17 to see if anyone recalled seeing Oswald in the office. The FBI field office reported on the interviews of all those named in the consul's files for September 17. The only one the FBI questioned whose name was not listed along with the other five was a William George Gaudet, who had to be FM824084.[71] Gaudet's name was confirmed in 1972, when, almost certainly as the result of a bureaucratic blunder during declassification, the National Archives released a stack of documents including CD 75 (page 573) that provided the complete list of persons who were issued tourist cards in New Orleans on September 17, 1963. Gaudet's name and FM8 number (24084) appeared on the list just above that of Lee Harvey Oswald.

The reason the FBI suppressed Gaudet's name was that he was CIA connected. The FBI was so determined to keep Gaudet's name out of the official record that it even dropped his name from the Dallas Field Office Index, the bureau's in-house database for the investigation into the JFK assassination. Because Hoover suspected that the CIA, particularly the Mexico City station, had been using Oswald in some operation, the FBI had a strong interest in Gaudet. Years later Gaudet admitted that the FBI had questioned him before there was a Warren Commission. His bureau interrogators wanted to know why his path had crossed Oswald's at the New Orleans Mexican Consul's Office and in Mexico City. According to Gaudet, the FBI guaranteed his anonymity and assured him that whatever information he provided would remain within the FBI.[72]

For almost twenty years (1950–1969) Gaudet had what the CIA termed a "special relationship" with the government. He was the editor and publisher of a newsletter titled *Latin American Report.* Gaudet had established contact with many key political figures in Latin America. He was highly regarded by the agency as a professional observer of political and economic trends and received valuable intelligence from highly placed correspondents. Much of Gaudet's information was the intelligence staple found in the CIA's 00-3 secret reports covering the Caribbean and all of Latin America from Mexico to Chile. During the twenty years that Gaudet was connected with the agency he had a "Secret" clearance.[73]

The offices of Gaudet's *Latin American Report* were located in the International Trade Mart building in New Orleans. The newsletter was a CIA cover that Gaudet used for almost twenty years. Most of his dealings with the CIA were through the Domestic Contact Division, which had an office in the ITM. There were occasions, however, Gaudet claimed, when he was called upon to perform errands for the CIA largely in a covert capacity. There is some indication that he played a role in the CIA's 1954 operation in Guatemala to topple the social democratic government of Jacobo Arbenz Guzman.[74]

Gaudet insisted that it was pure coincidence that he was directly in front of Oswald on September 17, 1963, at the Mexican Consul's Office. He claimed that he could not recall having seen Oswald that day at the consul's office. Furthermore, he had no information concerning the omission of his name from the list published in the Warren Commission Report. The time that Gaudet spent as a tourist in Mexico City coincided with part of the week that Oswald was in Mexico's capital city.[75] If this was all random and unplanned coincidence, then why did the Commission and the FBI connive to withhold it from the public for eight years? The more likely explanation was that Gaudet's name was originally suppressed from the record because the circumstances indicated that the CIA was directing and using Oswald.

One of the most closely held of Helms's secrets had to do with George E. Joannides, the JM/Wave contact officer for the DRE in 1963. Helms never revealed that the CIA was funding the directorate when the DRE had contact with Oswald, who was publicly agitating in favor of the Castro revolution in New Orleans during the months of July and August. Joannides probably knew more about Oswald and his relationship with the DRE and other anti-Castro exile groups in New Orleans than anyone else in the government. It was Helms who assigned Joannides to the CIA's Miami station because he was skilled in psychological warfare and disinformation operations. It was Helms who assigned veteran clandestine officer John Whitten to head up the CIA's in-house investigation of the Kennedy assassination and then with-held from him important information from Oswald's preassassination file. When Whitten protested, Helms removed him and turned the investigation over to Angleton.[76] It might have been just another awkward coincidence that David Atlee Phillips, the DRE's first contact officer, was chief of covert action in the Cuban Section of the CIA's Mexico City station when Oswald arrived in Mexico City in September 1963.[77]

Thomas Powers's biography of Richard Helms, *The Man Who Kept the Secrets,* could not have had a more fitting title. Helms kept Joannides and his DRE connections secret through four investigations into the Kennedy assassination.[78] Joannides's name did not publicly surface until the 1990s, when the so-called JFK Act led to the establishment of the Assassination Records Review Board (ARRB). Over a four-year period the ARRB, empowered to declassify JFK files, dislodged somewhere between four and five million pages of declassified documents. Joannides's record was one of those files, and his personnel records revealed that he had been the DRE's contact officer when the CIA claimed it had no contact with the directorate in 1963. But his file was purged, according to the *Washington Post*'s Jefferson Morley, who is the researcher responsible for introducing Joannides into the historiography of the JFK assassination. Morley described the file as "thin." There were no reports in the Joannides file for the entire seventeen months that he was the DRE's contact officer. All that his personnel file revealed is that Joannides was paying the directorate for "intelligence" and "propaganda." John Tunheim, now a federal judge in Minneapolis, chaired the ARRB. After reviewing all the CIA suppression and stonewalling surrounding the Joannides story, Tunheim remarked to Morley, "[This] shows that the CIA wasn't interested in the truth about the assassination."[79]

All the indicators strongly point toward Oswald having been connected to an American intelligence source. There is persuasive circumstantial evidence that Oswald was building a pro-Castro cover as part of an intelligence plan that ultimately took him to Mexico City. What we know today of his activities in Mexico City far exceeds what the Warren Commission chose to include in its report, out of design but more significantly because the CIA saw to it that the evidence was not available to the Commission and its staff lawyers.

As discussed in Chapter 3, there is a hard certainty that someone was impersonating Oswald while he was in Mexico City, linking him with a KGB officer in the Soviet Embassy when, in fact, there was no connection. The Soviet officer in question, Valery Vladimirovich Kostikov, was alleged by the CIA's Mexico City station to be the KGB's chief assassination and espionage agent in the Western Hemisphere. Later Helms assured Rankin that a "reliable source" had reported that Oswald had met with Soviet Embassy official Pavel Yatskov, not Kostikov.

The CIA Mexico City station's explanations about the erased tapes of Oswald's telephone conversations with Soviet Embassy officials were, at best, implausible. This leaves the question hanging of whether Oswald or his impersonator was calling the embassy using Oswald's name, especially the call he allegedly made on October 1, when he was supposed to have spoken with Kostikov. There are indications that this same "false Oswald" might have visited the Cuban Consulate, impersonating Oswald. Moreover, CIA Mexico City's insistence that its comprehensive photo-surveillance coverage of the Soviet and Cuban diplomatic compounds failed to capture Oswald on film is simply not true. The Lopez Report established that Oswald made a total of at least five visits to the Soviet and Cuban diplomatic compounds during his seven days in Mexico City. A more likely explanation is that the Mexico City station caught Oswald on film, but since he was in the company of others, the CIA had to suppress the photographic evidence. All of this, in addition to the inherently unbelievable Alvarado Ugarte affair—possibly a deliberate CIA disinformation setup to divert attention away from an operation that the CIA needed to conceal—pointed an accusing finger at officers within the CIA who were using Oswald as an asset in some clandestine operation of which President Kennedy's accused assassin was unaware. And all of this took place only weeks before President Kennedy made his fateful trip to Dallas.[80]

13   JFK, Cuba, and the "Castro Problem"

Cuba seems to have the same effect on American administrations as the full moon used to have on werewolves.
—Wayne Smith, former U.S. State Department officer in Havana

Arthur Schlesinger, Jr., President Kennedy's special assistant for Latin American affairs, observed that for the Kennedy White House Latin America emerged as the focal point of the communist threat and was perceived in the same terms as the Nazi-Fascist menace in the 1930s.[1] For the American intelligence community and the nation's senior military leaders Castro's government was at the very heart of that threat, and the only remedy was the immediate overthrow of his regime. For the CIA, there was an added urgency that took on aspects of a grudge fight. The agency's tarnished image and its diminished status with the Kennedy White House could be traced back to the Bay of Pigs debacle. Every day that Castro remained in power was an intolerable reminder of the CIA's fall from grace. This festering humiliation inspired a greater incentive among some CIA old hands to adopt any means necessary to topple its nemesis and revenge the Bay of Pigs.

Most students of the Kennedy assassination and historians writing about the post–Cuban missile crisis world of 1962–1963 do not seriously entertain the possibility that Kennedy was the victim of a communist conspiracy. Neither Moscow nor Havana would have chanced such an undertaking without anticipating that the American counteraction would be swift and remorseless.[2] Moreover, there was every indication of a sea change in relations among the heads of the three states, who maneuvered against threatening odds to resolve this Cold War crisis diplomatically, thereby avoiding a nuclear Armageddon. Kennedy's American University Speech in June 1963 and accompanying mutually agreed-upon initiatives between Washington and Moscow pointed toward a future politics of détente and peaceful competition between the two giant powers. The 1963 Nuclear Test Ban Treaty was a landmark agreement. It was followed by the removal of U.S. Jupiter missiles from Turkey in April 1963 and the introduction of a "hotline" between Moscow and Washington. These were tentative movements toward, if not ending the global rivalry between Washington and Moscow, then at least making it safer. During the fall of 1963 Kennedy held talks with Soviet foreign minister Andrei A. Gromyko about increased trade, possible collaboration on a moon project, and mutual arms reduction.[3] Havana's best guarantee against a U.S. invasion was Kennedy's no-invasion pledge as part of the deal with Khrushchev to get the Soviet premier to remove his missiles from Cuba. Despite his initial hostile reaction to the settlement, Castro understood that his revolution's interests were best served by the continuation of the Kennedy presidency and the American leader's post–missile crisis willingness to experiment with a policy of accommodation.

All history is not a conspiracy, but conspiracies do take place and do shape history and its outcomes. Conspiracies in recent U.S. history are a matter of record, and some were of important political significance. The break-in at the Watergate and the subsequent cover-up are one example. After more than twenty years the jury is still out on whether or not in 1980 the Reagan camp pulled off an "October Surprise" to wrest the White House from President Carter. Iran-Contra was a conspiracy of such immense scope that some of the machinations still have not been sorted out. The current corporate scandals associated in the public mind with Enron, Arthur Andersen, and WorldCom involved a thousand politically linked conspiracies of fraud, theft, and bribery. The contention that Kennedy was a victim of a conspiracy deserves serious consideration and cannot be dismissed out of hand as spectacular ballyhoo cooked up by conspiracy buffs and amateur sleuths suffering from assassination conspiracy obsession. The strongest counterargument against the conspiracy phobia that still plagues the Kennedy assassination is the fact that every official involved in investigating the crime knew that it was too complicated to be the work of a single gunman. Moreover, those in government who had more intimate and unfiltered access to the evidence and witness testimony in the case knew that Oswald could not have been the assailant.

Although there is every reason to keep examining the events that brought us as a people to November 22, 1963, in the hope of uncovering new truths about Kennedy's murder, there is little likelihood that after forty years we will ever know with cold certainty the specific "who" of Dallas. There is, however, implicit circumstantial evidence that America's thirty-fifth president was a victim of a conspiracy that does point toward the "why" of the assassination. There are enough dots available to provide a working explanation once they are connected. When the dots are connected the picture that begins to emerge (as through a glass darkly) is that JFK was the victim of a domestic conspiracy that was a direct outgrowth of the Cuban issue in American politics. Dallas was the consequence of extremist Cold War elements who were convinced that Kennedy was a "no-win" leader when it came to the "Castro problem" and therefore had to be removed from office before the communist government in Cuba could be uprooted.

During the months following the peaceful resolution of the Cuban missile crisis in 1962, Kennedy's senior military advisers on the Joint Chiefs of

Staff (JCS), CIA officials, anti-Castro Cubans, and other right-wing extremists arrived independently at a common consensus: that Kennedy could not be trusted with the nation's security. Military-civilian relations during the early Cold War years were rocky. The Truman-MacArthur confrontation had put to the test the constitutional principle of civilian control over the military. During his two terms in the White House former general Dwight D. Eisenhower had been engaged in a running battle with the JCS over the size and shape of the defense budget. During the Kennedy years, relations within the command system broke down completely. The JCS were contemptuous of the Ivy League intellectuals and Robert S. McNamara's "Whiz Kids" that Kennedy brought to Washington to confront the challenge of the international communist conspiracy. General Thomas Power, Strategic Air Command commander and a protégé of General Curtis LeMay, complained that the "computer types" Kennedy had installed in the Pentagon "don't know their ass from a hole in the ground."[4] The chiefs feared that the youthful inexperience of JFK's New Frontiersmen and their perceived naïveté and softness on communism would lead to war at a time and place not of the Pentagon's choosing.

For their part, the Kennedy team members increasingly became disillusioned with the Pentagon brass. They deplored the lack of sophistication among the military leaders, especially their inability to approach the international "hot spots" Kennedy had inherited from the Eisenhower administration, with any imaginative contingency planning other than large-scale war and an all-too-reckless readiness to resolve any confrontation with the communist camp by employing nuclear weapons.[5]

From the Bay of Pigs through the Nuclear Test Ban Treaty, the Kennedy administration came increasingly to instinctively distrust Pentagon recommendations. JFK's first foreign policy venture ended in the Bay of Pigs debacle. With some justification, the Kennedy team blamed the JCS for this embarrassing setback. When Kennedy asked the chiefs to review the CIA's plans for the invasion of Cuba, the Pentagon advised that it had a "fair chance of ultimate success." What the JCS failed to explain to their new commander in chief was that "fair" meant no more than a 30 percent chance of a favorable outcome. When the Pentagon endorsed "Operation Zapata," the CIA's code name for the invasion, it helped to dispel the president's reservations about the invasion. Kennedy did not know that the chairman of the JCS, Gen. Lyman L. Lemnitzer, privately believed that the CIA plan had "self-destruct" written all over it. Other chiefs, such as Adm. Arleigh Burke and Gen. David Shoup, commandant of the U.S. Marine Corps, thought the CIA plan was "sloppy" and "weak," but, like Lemnitzer, they left their strong reservations back in the Pentagon's Joint War Room. Consequently, Kennedy went ahead with the invasion plan, confident that it was fully staffed and generally approved by everybody who had a need to know about the operation.[6]

Lemnitzer and the chiefs signed off on the venture expecting the CIA to fail. Then Kennedy would have to turn to the military professionals in the Pentagon to save the day—to launch a full-scale military invasion to topple the Castro regime. Although Kennedy took full responsibility for the botched invasion, he put the JCS on notice that in the future he expected advice from the chiefs to come to him "direct and unfiltered." He pointedly reminded them that in all Cold War operations he looked to his senior uniformed officers "to contribute dynamic and imaginative leadership" in all future "military and paramilitary aspects of Cold War programs."[7]

The Bay of Pigs debacle did not dampen the Kennedy administration's fixation on Cuba and the removal of the Castro government. As the Democratic Party's presidential candidate in 1960, JFK had campaigned on the promise that as president he would not tolerate a communist regime ninety miles from American shores. During a campaign stop in Miami he pledged to help Cuban exiles and rebels to overthrow Castro and return to a free Cuba. Convinced that the CIA had sold him a bill of goods with its "Operation Zapata," Kennedy turned to his senior military advisers to take a leadership role in solving the Cuban problem. In November 1961 the major responsibility for dealing with Castro was shifted from the CIA to the Pentagon, where the Cuban project would be known as "Operation Mongoose." Convinced beyond argument that the "Communist regime in Cuba is incompatible with *minimum* security requirements in the Western Hemisphere," the JCS were anxious to succeed where the CIA had so spectacularly failed. Lemnitzer and the other chiefs saw this as an opportunity to do what they had had in mind all along: prepare for a full-scale invasion.[8]

In March 1962 the JCS submitted to Secretary of Defense McNamara a plan that would justify the United States launching a war against Cuba under the name "Operation Northwoods." The operational premise was that since all CIA attempts to provoke a civilian uprising inside Cuba had failed and the Castro regime showed no inclination to attack Americans or their property, dramatic steps would need to be taken to demonstrate to the American public and world opinion that a cabal of gangsters ruled in Havana whose "rashness and irresponsibility" were a palpable and intolerable threat to world peace.[9]

The eleven-page document forwarded to McNamara that was the product of the chiefs' "dynamic and imaginative leadership" contained a series of invented provocations designed to "place the United States in the apparent position of suffering defensible grievances" from an outlaw regime to "develop an international image of a Cuban threat to peace in the Western Hemisphere." A few examples from "Operation Northwoods" are offered here to underscore the extreme lengths to which the war-gaming chiefs were willing to go to justify an invasion of Cuba:

- A series of manufactured incidents against the US military base at Guantanamo City carried out by friendly Cubans disguised as Castro forces. These coordinated incidents included lobbing mortar shells over the fence into the base, blowing up an ammunition dump inside the base, burning aircraft inside the base, and staging riots at the main gate. The chiefs were recommending using U.S.-sponsored Cubans to kill American servicemen. There is no way to refine what JFK's senior military advisers were recommending with these extraordinary efforts to provoke an excuse for full-scale military action against Cuba.
- Blow up a ship in Guantanamo Bay and blame it on Cuba. (Shades of the U.S.S. *Maine* incident that precipitated the Spanish-American War in 1898!)
- Develop a Cuban terror campaign in the Miami area and in Washington, D.C., killing and wounding innocent American citizens and blaming these criminal acts on the Castro government.
- The sinking of a boatload of Cuban refugees en route to Florida ("real or simulated").[10]

The Kennedy administration rejected "Operation Northwoods." The president let Lemnitzer know there was no possibility that he would authorize any preemptive attack to overthrow the Castro government. The administration's rejection of the chiefs' plans did not deter Lemnitzer and the Pentagon brass. A month later, after submitting "Operation Northwoods" to the secretary of defense, the JCS shot off a strong memorandum to McNamara. It minced no words in stressing the urgency of moving quickly to rid the Western Hemisphere of the communist beachhead in Cuba. Lemnitzer was adamant in his view that covert action against the Cuban economy and diplomatic isolation would never succeed in provoking an internal uprising against the Castro regime. The only solution to the "Castro problem," the chairman persisted, was for the Kennedy administration to adopt as a national policy an early military intervention "before the release of National Guard and Reserve forces presently on active duty."[11]

Kennedy's dismissal of the chiefs' recommendations only confirmed in Lemnitzer's mind that the current administration was "soft" on communism and reinforced his conviction that it could not be trusted with the nation's security. The general was convinced that the nation would be better protected if the military ran the government. Lemnitzer's extreme views about civilian-military relations were rooted in his own military career and in a larger context: the sometimes overlooked fact that the entire history of the

Cold War, its assumptions and positions, converged upon the Cuban issue during the Kennedy years.

Lemnitzer was a protégé of Dwight Eisenhower. One of Eisenhower's last acts was to name him to the highest-ranking position in the armed forces. The old general wanted to move against Castro before he left office if the Cubans were rash enough to give him a good excuse. On January 3, 1961, just weeks before the inauguration of the new administration, Eisenhower met with Lemnitzer and floated the idea of manufacturing some kind of provocation against the United States, blaming Cuba, and using it as a pretext for launching a military invasion. Lemnitzer revered his former commander and patron. For the chairman of the JCS, it was insupportable that Kennedy, a junior officer in World War II, rejected out of hand "Operation Northwoods," whose inspirational godfather was Eisenhower, one of twentieth-century America's most celebrated military figures and popular presidents.[12]

Kennedy's initial enthusiasm for the CIA as a proven countercheck to Moscow's clandestine Cold War plans and designs was shattered by the Bay of Pigs disaster. Emphasizing that CIA intelligence reports revealed that a significant element of the Cuban population was hostile to the Castro government, senior agency officers "sold" JFK on the invasion plan by guaranteeing that any successful landing would ignite an uprising of the Cuban people, though they knew that this was a lie. Kennedy had made it clear to the CIA that if "La Brigada," the invasion force of almost 1,200 Cuban anti-Castro fighters, faced defeat, he would not send in the marines. The new president was determined that this American-sponsored invasion of Cuba by Cubans would be disclaimed if it went sour. CIA Director Allen Dulles and his deputy, Richard Bissell, expected that when the brigade met with overwhelming resistance, Kennedy would be forced to reconsider and authorize the use of U.S. military force rather than allowing the invasion to be rolled up on the beach.[13]

Like the JCS, the agency's senior professionals held the new administration in contempt. Kennedy was furious that he had been deceived. He told one top aide that he wanted "to splinter the CIA in a thousand pieces and scatter it to the winds." The new president had learned the hard way that old lesson: Intelligence analysis should be kept out of the hands of those with a vested interest in the result. Kennedy moved to remedy this problem by establishing the President's Foreign Intelligence Advisory Board (PFIAB) because, as Clark Clifford informed the board's members, the president had told him that he "could not make correct decisions without correct intelligence and he could not endure another Cuba."[14] After a decent interval, President Kennedy asked for the resignations of the two key insubordinate agency heads, Dulles and Bissell. He appointed a high-level committee to look into the agency's past misdeeds. He tried to curtail the CIA's power and restrict its future actions by turning the responsibility for paramilitary actions over to the Pentagon. He also threatened to reduce the CIA's budget.[15]

During the year following the peaceful resolution of the October 1962 missile crisis Kennedy vacillated between the old hard-line approach he had supported before the crisis and a more accommodating line. Despite the no-invasion pledge, he did not give up on the possible use of force as a last resort if circumstances in Cuba suddenly changed. If civil uprisings erupted on the island or if evidence was uncovered that Castro-inspired guerrilla war broke out in other Latin American countries, the White House was prepared to grasp the nettle and resort to a full-scale military invasion to uproot the Castro regime. Short of these developments, Kennedy showed no intention of authorizing another invasion. For those elements that saw Cuba as the front line in the Cold War struggle against international communism—most notably, the JCS, CIA, and militant anti-Castro exiles in the United States—the administration's position dashed their hopes that Cuba would be liberated. The unspoken but unmistakable message emanating from the White House was that Cubans would have to liberate themselves.[16]

The president continued to support government-directed harassment raids against Cuba, but after the resolution of the missile crisis "Operation Mongoose" was greatly attenuated. Kennedy authorized the CIA to go ahead with "dark-of-the-moon" sabotage raids but with the provision that they be carried out without a high noise level, and with no direct knowledge that they were government sponsored. Security was at a premium but problematic because six or seven government agencies were working with four or five Cuban exile groups. Most of these "exile raids" were conducted by the more hard-core anti-Castro exile groups such as Alpha 66 and the Revolutionary Student Directorate (DRE) under the nominal control of the CIA's JM/Wave station in Miami. The raids continued with periodic interruptions until September 1963. Although these harassment operations were an annoyance to Castro, they posed no serious threat to his regime.[17] In addition to these sabotage raids the CIA sent U-2s crisscrossing Cuba at twelve-hour intervals, and conducted radio propaganda and leaflet drops in an attempt to stir up anti-Castro sentiment among the island's population. The CIA also used its agents inside Cuba to promote disaffection among the Cuban military's high command, a project Director John McCone was frank to admit might take two or more years before it bore fruit, if ever.[18]

The restraints the Kennedy administration placed on "Operation Mongoose" were a bone in the throat of those determined cold warriors who wanted to resolve the "Castro problem" once and for all. JFK's skillful management of the missile crisis counted for little in their judgment. His no-invasion pledge meant that although the missiles had been removed peacefully, Castro remained in power. William Harvey, the CIA's chief of

Task Force W, the senior operative in charge of the agency's Cuban operations, had no confidence in "Mongoose." For Harvey, Kennedy's no-invasion assurances ruled out "invading Cuba on the pretext of a contrived provocation such as an attack on Guantanamo." The Task Force W chief was in complete agreement with Lemnitzer and the JCS. He wanted to loosen the restraints and make full use of agency and JCS resources to manufacture a provocation against U.S. lives and property to support a full-scale military retaliation.[19] At an October 1963 CIA briefing General LeMay dismissed "Mongoose" as too small to overthrow Castro. The general could not understand why the government did not just bomb Castro into submission.[20] In April 1963 the president of the Cuban Revolutionary Council (CRC), Dr. Jose Miro Cardona, ignited a public convulsion of anti-Kennedy feelings within Miami's Cuban exile community. Dr. Miro announced that he was resigning because the White House had no concrete plans for the liberation of Cuba. He accused the Kennedy administration of hewing to a policy of peaceful coexistence with the Castro regime.[21]

One of Miro's specific indictments against President Kennedy's policy of accommodation toward Castro was the administration's antiraid decree. In March the Alpha 66 exile group launched a raid against a Soviet ship and installations inside Cuba. This raid was followed by another a week later that did serious damage to a Russian vessel. It is very likely that these raids were carried out without the direct support of the exiles' CIA contact officers. The State Department officially deplored these acts of "hit-and-run" terrorism and assured Moscow that the United States had no involvement in them. The White House was concerned about the "exile raids" because they were complicating relations with Moscow and the upcoming talks between Secretary of State Dean Rusk and Soviet Premier Khrushchev.[22]

A month after the Alpha 66 raids on Soviet ships the DRE was planning an elaborate scheme to destroy the Nazabal sugar mill in central Cuba when word came down from CIA headquarters in Langley, Virginia, to the CIA station in Miami to abort the action. Not wanting a return of the tensions that had ushered in the missile crisis, the White House had decided to crack down on the exile groups in Miami. That April the administration ordered the Immigration and Naturalization Service to prohibit twenty-five of the most militant exile leaders from leaving Dade County without permission. These activist Cuban exiles, some with relatives and family members in Castro's jails, were already convinced that JFK had betrayed them and their cause twice. The first time was in 1961, when he refused to send in the marines to rescue the brigade at the Bay of Pigs. The second time was a year later, when Kennedy dashed their hopes of ever returning to Cuba by giving his pledge not to invade Cuba again. By 1963 Cuban exiles hated Kennedy almost as much as they did Castro. After the spring 1963 crackdown went into effect, Ted Shackley, chief of the CIA's Miami station, cabled Langley that the DRE's attitude toward American architects of the Cuban policy "was one of contempt repeat contempt." Jose Antonio Lanusa, the main spokesman for the DRE, one of the Cuban exile groups most affected by the Kennedy administration's crackdown, charged that these "coercive measures" were part of a secret White House deal with the Soviets during the settlement of the missile crisis.[23] Since the DRE was handsomely funded by the CIA, Lanusa's statement was almost certainly first cleared through the directorate's Miami station contact officer, George Joannides.

By September 1963 the administration's secret campaign to remove Castro had lost whatever allure it had had for Kennedy as he seriously considered an accommodation with Castro. A central figure in the following two months of secret talks was William Attwood. As editor of *Look* magazine in 1959, Attwood had interviewed Castro and come away with a lasting interest in Cuban affairs. Attwood's reporting of the 1960 election caught JFK's attention, and after the Democratic candidate became president he appointed Attwood as U.S. ambassador to Guinea. In 1963 Attwood was seconded to the United Nations as a special adviser to Ambassador Adlai Stevenson while the ambassador was recovering from a bout of polio. The first indication that Castro was looking to normalize relations with the United States came from Lisa Howard, a correspondent with ABC TV News. On September 5 Howard spoke to Attwood about her April conversation with Cuba's maximum leader, in which Castro had let her know that he was anxious to reduce his dependence on Moscow and interested in exploring the possibility of a rapprochement with the Kennedy administration.[24]

Kennedy was interested in exploring a possible démarche in U.S.-Cuban relations, and he encouraged Attwood to pursue the possibility of an exchange of views. For the next two months Attwood, with Lisa Howard's help, met secretly with Cuban officials close to Castro. Howard made her New York apartment available for Attwood to have a private talk with Carlos Lechuga Hevia, Cuba's ambassador to the UN. Lechuga favored any initiative that might lead to a change in course in Cuban-American relations. The Cuban ambassador and Attwood developed a friendly relationship that continued into the 1970s, after Attwood retired from government service. But since hard-liners in Castro's inner circle, notably Che Guevara and Raul Castro, opposed any accommodation with the United States, it was decided that Lechuga was too high-profile and that continued contact might tip Castro's hand that he was seeking an opening with the American president. Howard was instrumental in putting Attwood in touch with Dr. Rene Vallejo, Castro's physician and aide-de-camp, one of the so-called pro-Americans close to Castro and one of his trusted advisers. On November 12 it was agreed that Vallejo would come to the United States to meet privately with Attwood and discuss an agenda that would prove fruitful for any future dialogue and later meeting with Castro. Attwood reported back to Ambassador Stevenson, who relayed his progress back to the White House. Kennedy scheduled a meeting with Attwood for November 19 to go over the agenda and decide on what steps to take next.[25]

Kennedy knew from other sources that Castro had some anxiety over the mounting intensity of the exile raids. Even more pressing was the freezing of Cuban assets and the economic hardships caused by the embargo. For JFK all of Castro's concerns were negotiable, even the lifting of the embargo and establishment of trade between the two countries. One of Kennedy's unofficial go-betweens who played an important role in all these secret discussions was the French journalist Jean Daniel. Attwood recalled sometime after October 2 that Daniel, just back from Havana, related that Castro "seemed ripe for a conversation." The president met with Daniel on October 24, when Kennedy made it clear that relations between the two countries need not remain locked in implacable hostility. According to Daniel, the president invited him back to the White House after he returned from his upcoming visit to Cuba.

The president gave every indication that he was serious about Attwood's mission. According to Pierre Salinger, JFK's press secretary, on November 17 the president met again with Daniel right before he was to leave for Havana and a scheduled interview with Castro. Kennedy gave Daniel a letter to deliver to Castro that called for negotiations to normalize relations between the two countries.[26] Just days after he met with Attwood and Daniel, Kennedy left with the First Lady for a whirlwind political fence-mending visit into the heart of Texas. The assassins who cut down Kennedy also brought down the Attwood mission. The rapprochement initiative petered out with little fanfare when Lyndon B. Johnson took over the White House.

During his 1975 top-secret testimony before the House committee Attwood sought to encourage the committee to investigate whether Kennedy's efforts to normalize relations with Castro might have been the motive behind his assassination. "The interesting thing," Attwood mused, was that while he was pursuing these secret discussions with Cuban officials on one track, the CIA was simultaneously committed to another track, the "quick-fix" solution to the "Castro problem": assassinating Castro.

Attwood was convinced that JFK was serious about moving Cuban-American relations forward along an accommodation track. He therefore could not accept that the president was so deeply cynical about keeping his options open that JFK would encourage negotiations while secretly sanctioning covert operations to liquidate the Cuban leader.[27] Attwood was of course referring to the agency's covert "Executive Action" program, which included sabotage and assassination. More specifically, he had in mind the

AMLASH conspiracy that was unearthed during the Church Committee's investigation into the CIA's alleged assassination plots.

In January 1963 Desmond FitzGerald replaced Bill Harvey as CIA chief of covert operations for Cuba. Like Harvey before him, FitzGerald did not expect the Castro regime to be toppled by a civil war or insurrection inside Cuba. FitzGerald looked to recruit someone who was close to Castro but secretly disaffected and willing to take lethal risks to eliminate Cuba's president. In the fall of 1963 he thought he had found a reliable "delivery system" in a Cuban major, Dr. Rolando Cubela Secades. Cubela (code name AMLASH) qualified on two counts: As a student revolutionary in 1959 he had assassinated the Cuban dictator Fulgencio Batista's chief of military intelligence at point-blank range, and he had access to Castro.[28]

Before FitzGerald met with Cubela he discussed the planned meeting with his boss, Richard Helms. According to the agency's 1967 inspector general's report, Helms gave FitzGerald the green light for the operation and insisted that "it was not necessary to seek approval from Robert Kennedy for FitzGerald to speak in his name." When Helms was later questioned about what had prompted him to tell FitzGerald that there was no need to tell the attorney general about AMLASH, he made the astonishing assertion that the CIA had "preexisting" authority to bring about "a change in government." It was Helms's distinctly unconvincing contention that AMLASH was a political action operation to bring about a regime change, not a potential assassination.

On October 29 FitzGerald met with AMLASH in Paris, and three weeks later he gave the go-ahead for the operation, notifying Cubela that a cache would be made available inside Cuba, including high-powered rifles with scopes. The day Kennedy was gunned down in Dallas, a CIA contact officer was meeting with AMLASH in a safe house in Paris, where the CIA's hit man was provided with additional "technical support": a poison pen, a Paper Mate fitted out with a hypodermic syringe primed with Black Leaf 40, an insecticide fatal to humans.[29]

There is no evidence that Kennedy either authorized or knew about FitzGerald's plans for Castro. As Attwood remarked to his congressional questioners, it flew in the face of just plain common sense to imagine that JFK would have endorsed a CIA plot to assassinate Castro, who was the object of the White House's rapprochement diplomacy. On the question of authorization, Attwood's conviction received a chorus of support from officials in the Kennedy administration, including Dean Rusk, Maxwell Taylor, John McCone, and McGeorge Bundy, all of whom denied that Kennedy had ever approved or been informed any assassination plots. Attwood told his House Select Committee questioners that only a handful of people were knowledgeable about these secret discussions. In addition to the president, he mentioned Bobby Kennedy; Averell Harriman; McGeorge Bundy; Gordon Chase, Bundy's assistant; Arthur Schlesinger, Jr.; and Lisa Howard. He was pretty certain that Rusk had been excluded from these contacts with Castro because the secretary disapproved of any rapprochement initiatives with Cuba. Attwood first broached the subject of these back-channel talks with representatives of the Castro government with Schlesinger. The president's assistant for Latin American affairs liked the idea and said he would take it up with the White House. But Schlesinger let drop the cryptic comment, "The CIA, unfortunately, is still in charge of Cuba." At the time it obviously made an impression on Attwood because he quoted Schlesinger's exact words to the committee twelve years later.[30]

Schlesinger's comment raised some unanswerable questions. In order to achieve some kind of in-house truce with the CIA, did President Kennedy or his brother Bobby give the impression that the agency had carte blanche in its dealings with Cuba? Or was Kennedy so desperate to rid his administration of the nettlesome "Castro problem" that he engaged in a two-faced policy—to defuse the Castro threat by diplomacy or the elimination of Castro, whichever came first? It would not have been the first time that this president, who displayed two characteristics in the exercise of power, opportunism and realism, kept his options open when confronted with a seemingly intractable political problem. Or was Attwood's unswerving certainty that the White House was sincere in pursuing a démarche with Castro an accurate assessment of these top-secret overtures? In his own mind, Attwood was convinced that Kennedy's essential and indivisible goal was to wean Cuba away from the Soviet orbit and that his tightly held mission was a casualty of the Dealey Plaza conspiracy.

Although the public record does not resolve this uncertainty, there is documentary proof that the Kennedys never knew about the CIA's pre–Bay of Pigs attempts on Castro's life until about sixteen months after JFK first occupied the White House. President Kennedy and the attorney general only gained entree into this "need-to-know" world because FBI director Hoover accidentally discovered that the CIA had contracted a trio of formidable mafia bosses to get rid of Castro. Hoover reported this intelligence tidbit to the White House, and Bobby Kennedy demanded an explanation from Langley.[31]

It is highly improbable that Kennedy knew about AMLASH and FitzGerald's scheme to assassinate Castro. The greater likelihood is that FitzGerald, a product of the CIA's culture of assumed privileged insights and special understanding, believed that he knew the requirements of national security better than the transient elected officials to whom the agency was nominally accountable. FitzGerald enjoyed a certain reputation among agency old hands of being something of a "knuckle-dragger," a devotee of paramilitary solutions to nettlesome problems. During the Dulles era CIA division chiefs such as FitzGerald had been encouraged to take the initiative, be buccaneers, endorse projects, and create plans without consulting other sections of the agency that should have been informed. It was not too much of an exaggeration to characterize the CIA as a law unto itself while Director Dulles held sway during the 1950s.

When it came to the Cuban issue, the chief of Cuban covert operations thought the AMLASH plot was at best a long shot. Like Bill Harvey before him, FitzGerald had little confidence that the Cuban people would rise up and overthrow the Castro government. It was something of an article of faith with FitzGerald that the best way to increase the odds for an internal insurrection was to eliminate the charismatic embodiment of the revolution and the country's political strongman. An assassination-inspired insurrection or civil war was a development that could force Kennedy to abandon his policy of accommodation and do what the CIA and the president's uniformed service advisers had intended all along: launch a full-scale military invasion of Castro's Cuba.[32]

Both the CIA and the Joint Chiefs of Staff blamed Kennedy's failure of nerve for the Bay of Pigs disaster. But this humiliating setback was felt most acutely by the CIA, especially among those career professionals in the business of covert operations. During the Eisenhower presidency the CIA had emerged as the chief instrument for carrying the war to the perceived enemies of America's overseas interests. Those were heady times for Langley as the CIA made a habit of success. In 1953 the CIA and the British joined in a collaborative effort to remove Muhammad Mossadegh, Iran's elected head of state, because he had nationalized the country's oil resources. The following year the CIA brought down the mildly left-wing Jacobo Arbenz Guzman in Guatemala because he threatened American-owned business interests in that Central American country. Langley's success in getting a genuine copy of Khrushchev's Twentieth Congress secret speech on Stalin's crimes was a spectacular intelligence coup. In 1956 Dulles's assistant, Richard Bissell, the agency's supreme technocrat, brought the CIA into the new age of intelligence when he brought online the U-2 spy plane. Bissell guided the project from the blueprint stage to operational readiness in just seventeen months and brought it in $3 million under budget! The old general in the White House had nothing but praise for the agency, and Dulles had Ike's complete trust.[33]

The CIA's pride of place in America's Cold War arsenal ended abruptly with the Bay of Pigs debacle. Although President Kennedy still enthusiastically embraced the notion and practice of clandestine operations, the CIA never enjoyed the Kennedy White House's unqualified trust as it had during the "golden age" of the Eisenhower presidency. The man JFK brought in to replace Dulles and reform the CIA was John McCone, a wealthy California businessman. McCone was an outsider. He had no special insight or experience in the arcane world of intelligence and the shadow wars that tested the agency's mettle against the forces of international communism. McCone took over as director of Central Intelligence (DCI) in December 1961. Although he was a newcomer to the field of intelligence, the new DCI made an immediate and dramatic impact. He was the only senior member of the Kennedy administration who suspected that the Soviet Union had placed offensive strategic missiles in Cuba. It was largely due to his urgings that the CIA stepped up its U-2 flights over Cuba. U-2 photographs of suspected missile sites provided irrefutable evidence that Khrushchev had placed missiles with offensive capabilities in Cuba. Although McCone was clearly more than a figurehead DCI, the professional management of the agent networks, case officers, and chiefs of the CIA stations was handled by Richard Helms, the deputy director of plans, whose career in intelligence went back to World War II days. For the duration of his tenure as DCI, McCone claimed that he was never told about the agency's "Executive Action" program and the CIA's attempts on Castro's life. However, since McCone was the agency's chief he was not spared the sting of the president's displeasure over what JFK perceived as the CIA's shortcomings.[34]

In January 1963, a year after McCone assumed the post of DCI, the CIA came under criticism for failure to develop an aggressive clandestine intelligence collection operation in Cuba. The CIA had become fixated on "mechanical" intelligence collection, the U-2s and photographic satellites, while neglecting to develop human sources on the ground to interpret or give the true significance to the mind-boggling haul from the technical intelligence-gathering operations. The criticism came from the PFIAB, the part-time board of distinguished private citizens Kennedy had set up to report to him on the performance and problems of U.S. intelligence.[35]

Several weeks later McCone threatened to resign. The object of the DCI's ire was a PFIAB report that documented some thirty-five early indicators of Soviet offensive weapons in Cuba in 1962 that the CIA had failed to detect. The central thrust of the board's criticism was that there had been numerous missed opportunities for advance warnings of Soviet intentions that would have provided the White House with more lead time to decide on a response. The DCI told the board that if the report went forward to the White House he and five of the other top people in the CIA would have to tender their resignations.[36]

McCone was tied up with business in New York, but he relayed his emotional reaction in a phone conversation with a board member. The next day, March 8, 1963, McCone was still in New York when the board met with President Kennedy. The board's chair, Dr. James R. Killian, Jr., the president of MIT, brought to the floor the report on the investigation of the Cuba situation and CIA intelligence coverage. Kennedy thought that the report on the missed thirty-five indicators was "pretty thin," too easy on the CIA. He found it "extraordinary" that the intelligence community had failed to come up with "advance information" on the "Berlin Wall" and Khrushchev's risky gamble of placing missiles in Cuba. JFK also voiced his disappointment that the CIA had not been able to penetrate Castro's inner circle.[37]

The day before Kennedy was assassinated McCone complained to the PFIAB that the CIA's image was being eroded by adverse publicity appearing in the press. He singled out the *New York Times*'s Scotty Reston, "who would destroy the CIA if he had his way." The DCI also included the *Washington Post,* "from top to bottom," in this camp of "extreme liberals" who wanted the agency scattered to the winds. From its inception the CIA had been a magnet attracting the best and brightest. Now, McCone feared, if this campaign was not stopped, the CIA's ability to recruit "good men"—the country's valedictorians and the sons of the establishment—was in jeopardy. The agency's roles in the Diem assassination and the overthrow of the democratically elected Arbenz government in Guatemala were some of the reasons he offered for this reversal of fortune. But the "turning point," according to McCone, was "traceable back to the Bay of Pigs." According to the agency's chief, the only way the pall hanging over the CIA could be lifted was for President Kennedy to make this matter the subject of a major speech and several press conferences.[38]

The government's own documents establish the transparent truth that Oswald did not kill President Kennedy. What role, then, if any, did he have in the assassination? The Warren Commission devoted more than one-third of its 888-page report to biography-related material about Oswald. Despite the attention it lavished on Oswald, the picture that emerged was a manqué portrait, bearing only a superficial and distorted resemblance to the real Oswald or the world in which he acted and was acted upon. The Commission's version of Oswald was a carefully circumscribed view of the alleged assassin, as though he were being viewed through the wrong end of a telescope. The real life and times of Lee Harvey Oswald were dramatically different.[39]

The weight of the evidence pointed to the fact that most of the still unanswered questions stemming from Oswald's politics, activities, and contacts, from his tour in the military and fraudulent discharge to his possible staged defection to the Soviet Union, the suspicious circumstances surrounding his redefection, his bogus Fair Play for Cuba Committee theatrics in New Orleans, culminating in the nagging and unresolved reasons behind his Mexico City trip, coalesce around one unavoidable conclusion: that Oswald was an asset of the U.S. government's intelligence community. If we put aside the official version of Oswald as a "lone nut," a discernible pattern to his adult life begins to emerge. Some interested clandestine operators were directing Oswald in the business of building a cover, a false biography. The government agency most skilled and practiced in the legend-manufacturing business was the Central Intelligence Agency.[40]

This contention is not just another exercise in conspiracy-mongering. Hoover knew over the weekend following the assassination that, as he told President Johnson, the case against Oswald was "not very, very strong." The FBI director's reservations stemmed, in part, from the Dallas field office's revelations that there had been an Oswald imposter in Mexico City making contact with the Soviet Embassy and the Cuban Consulate at the same time that the real Oswald was believed to be in Mexico's capital city. Hoover's suspicions that the CIA had an interest in Oswald set in the day of the assassination, when the bureau's legat in Mexico City, Clark Anderson, informed the director that the CIA had withheld the information that Oswald had visited the Cuban Consulate in September. Hoover knew this was not an administrative oversight on the CIA's part. These suspicions deepened when the director, who appreciated the political value of information better than anybody else in Washington, had access to the CIA's preassassination file on Oswald, which Langley had turned over to the Warren Commission. The FBI director knew that the CIA must have debriefed Oswald when he returned from the Soviet Union, but the record of that debriefing was not in Oswald's 201 file that Helms had sent to Commission counsel Rankin. This compulsion of the CIA to intentionally and systematically withhold essential information about JFK's alleged assailant deepened Hoover's suspicions that Oswald was a CIA asset.

The case of William George Gaudet was a strong indicator that FBI Washington believed that the CIA had an operational interest in Oswald. Gaudet was a longtime CIA contact with a "Secret" clearance. The FBI suspected that he was "baby-sitting," or monitoring, Oswald just before he left for Mexico City. Gaudet was in Mexico City at the same time as Oswald and might have performed other services for the CIA, such as briefing Oswald or reporting on his movements. It cannot be overlooked that in 1954 Gaudet had been an asset of the CIA's most celebrated disinformation specialist, David Atlee Phillips, in "Operation Success," the code name for the CIA's successful overthrow of the Arbenz government in Guatemala. Phillips's contribution to that operation earned him the CIA's Intelligence Medal of Merit.[41] When Oswald visited Mexico City, Phillips was the Mexico City station's chief of covert operations.

For reasons that can only be speculated upon, the most obvious being Hoover's determination to preserve the official mythology that Kennedy's assassination was the act of a "lone nut," the FBI suppressed Gaudet's name from the list of witnesses it interviewed even before Johnson established the

Warren Commission. In 1963, when the FBI interviewed him, Gaudet was still a very active CIA source. He agreed to an interview only after a briefing from "Bill," his CIA contact officer in New Orleans. Bill immediately came to Gaudet's New Orleans office at the ITM to confirm that the two FBI agents were legitimate. According to Gaudet's account, his CIA contact officer then called CIA Washington for the ground rules for any interview. Gaudet was subsequently informed that he could tell the agents that he "had a connection with the CIA but was under no obligation to reveal anything that I had ever done for the CIA." During the ensuing interview his FBI questioners kept coming back to the purpose behind his trip to Mexico in September 1963 and whether he was "on a CIA assignment when he went to Mexico." According to Gaudet's account, he told the FBI that he "would rather not answer that question." It was clear that Hoover suspected that Oswald's Mexico trip was part of a CIA operation, and he had his agents bear down hard on Gaudet to confirm his suspicions. Gaudet related that his FBI interrogators offered a deal: If he would reveal the true purpose of his Mexico trip the FBI would keep his identity and statement within the FBI. Whatever Gaudet told the FBI was reported back to FBIHQ and was probably filed away in a "do not file" file. The FBI kept its promise to Gaudet, and Hoover had obtained high-grade political intelligence that he could exploit at some future date.

FBI Washington upheld its promise to Gaudet. Its determination to turn him into a nonperson went to such extremes as to eliminate his name from the Dallas Field Office Index, the FBI's mammoth control file of the investigation, to deny Gaudet's name to the Commission and prevent it from calling him as a witness. Hoover was so suspicious of the CIA's interest in Oswald and leery about the Cuban angle in the assassination that he excluded all of the FBI's Cuban experts and supervisors from the investigation. Instead of the Cuban section of the General Investigative Division (GID), the director assigned the GID's Soviet experts to handle the investigation into whether Oswald had either been an agent or been encouraged by a foreign government to assassinate the president.[42]

As discussed in an earlier chapter, the impression the CIA left with the Commission that it had only a cursory preassassination interest in Oswald was untrue. The so-called Lopez Report made the point that at the time of the assassination the CIA headquarters section at Langley that held Oswald's 201 file (or Personality File) was Counterintelligence/Special Investigation Group (CI/SIG), which CIA veteran John Whitten acknowledged confined itself to sensitive counterintelligence operations.[43] CI/SIG had a legitimate interest in Oswald's activities off and on from 1959 to 1963. If for no other reason, the agency's counterintelligence chief, James J. Angleton, would have needed to be certain that the redefecting former marine, if his

1959 defection had not been staged, had not been "turned" while he was in the Soviet Union and returning as a KGB "sleeper" agent. Unless Angleton had no reason to doubt Oswald's bona fides, he would have insisted on having Oswald aggressively debriefed, probably even before he was allowed back into the country. As far as we know, the record of that debriefing was not one of the thirty documents that Helms turned over to the Warren Commission. The Lopez Report also made clear that the CIA station chief in Mexico City, Win Scott, left a written record underscoring the fact that the Mexico City station had a "keen" interest in Oswald from the moment he arrived in Mexico City.[44]

The most significant and intriguing turn in this paper trail is the recent revelations that some senior CIA officers in the Special Affairs Staff (SAS) had an operational interest in Oswald just weeks before the Kennedy assassination.[45] At the end of 1962 the Kennedy team essentially shelved "Operation Mongoose" as ineffective in its determined campaign to oust Cuba's communist regime. In January 1963 the SAS was created to direct the secret campaign to bring down the Castro government and replace it with a pro-American government in Havana. The SAS's executive officer was Desmond FitzGerald, who ten months later was the chief action officer of operation AMLASH, a freelancing operation that did not have the White House's blessing.[46]

This keen interest in Oswald just weeks before JFK left for Dallas was closely held by FitzGerald and a handful of other senior SAS staff officers.[47] It was such a tightly held secret that Win Scott, Mexico City's chief of station, and John Whitten, the career officer Helms picked to head the agency's investigation into the Kennedy assassination, were never told. Whitten's exclusion from FitzGerald's highly compartmentalized "need-to-know" SAS group, and his subsequent abrupt removal from directing the CIA's in-house investigation, were anything but a routine administrative matter or a case of coming out on the losing end of some messy bureaucratic power struggle. Whitten, as discussed earlier, was a twenty-three-year professional in the clandestine service. His credibility was unquestioned. Early in his CIA career he had introduced the polygraph to the agency and put it to skillful use in some of the CIA's most sensitive espionage investigations.[48] Deputy Director of Plans Helms, chief of the CIA's covert operations division, removed Whitten not on the alleged grounds that his two-week investigation was going nowhere but out of concern as to where it might lead. Helms replaced Whitten with the chief of counterintelligence, and Angleton immediately turned the investigation over to his division's Soviet experts. As was the case with the FBI, the CIA's senior officers diverted all attention away from the Cuban angle in the Kennedy assassination. Always the professional, Whitten quietly stepped aside and held his own counsel until 1978, when he was called to testify before a House committee. At the time Whitten had retired and was living outside the country. Minnesota federal judge John Tunheim, the chairman of the JFK Assassination Records Review Board, was of the opinion that Whitten's 1978 testimony (not released until 2001) "was perhaps the single most important document we uncovered."[49]

Whitten testified that when he took over the CIA's in-house investigation his team of thirty agents was provided with no details about "Oswald's political activity in the United States, especially the 'pro-Castro activity' and autobiographical sketches . . . found among his effects."[50] These "autobiographical sketches" included Oswald's accounts of his encounters with Carlos Bringuier and the CIA-funded DRE group in New Orleans in August 1963. This information was readily available in some version of Oswald's 201 file that was held by Angleton's CI/SIG section at Langley. Whatever intelligence FitzGerald's select SAS group had on Oswald must remain in the realm of speculation. Whitten told his congressional questioners that if he had known about Oswald's activities in New Orleans and contacts with the DRE Cubans, he would have focused his investigation on the "possible involvement of the Miami station."[51] Although Whitten did not believe Oswald was connected to the CIA, after that year's chilling revelations about the CIA's "Executive Action" programs, which was the first time Whitten learned of these assassination operations, he told the committee he could not rule it out.[52]

Whitten was a man of uncompromising professional integrity. During his 1978 secret testimony he unburdened himself when the topic turned to political assassinations. He was appalled that Helms had endorsed such a program and appointed a "thug like [Bill] Harvey to hire some criminal to commit assassinations." He accused Helms of violating every "operational precept, every bit of operational experience, every ethical consideration." When the committee counsel asked if he thought Harvey had been involved in the Kennedy assassination, all Whitten would allow was that he "did not have any reason to believe it." A few minutes later the general counsel asked what Whitten made of the fact that Harvey had instructed his wife to burn all his private papers after his death, implying that there might be a "smoking gun" tying Harvey to the killing of the president. The generally gentlemanly and collected Whitten shot back, "He was too young to have assassinated McKinley and Lincoln. It could have been anything." In short, Whitten was ready to believe that Harvey, the CIA's former head of Task Force W, the action officer in charge of Cuban covert operations before FitzGerald replaced him in 1963 to head up the SAS, was capable of anything and that his nominal boss, the then DDP, Richard Helms, knew it and had taken no steps to restrain him.[53]

During the short time that Whitten was engaged in his investigation he never heard of operation AMLASH. The name Rolando Cubela Secades first came to his attention in the 1970s after the Senate's Church Committee brought it to light.[54] There was never a remote possibility that Whitten's team of investigators would have turned up anything about FitzGerald's plans to assassinate Castro. What unnerved Helms was the prospect that Whitten might have turned his attention to the CIA's Miami station (JM/Wave) operating out of South Dade and uncovered the CIA's connections with the DRE, the most militant of the anti-Castro exiles.

As developed earlier, in 1962 Helms had assigned George E. Joannides, a young, well-educated, and experienced junior officer on a fast track inside the agency, to take over as the DRE's contact officer.[55] Helms picked Joannides because the contact officer he replaced, Ross Crozier, had failed to earn the respect of the DRE and therefore had little control over these CIA assets. When Joannides took over, all of this changed. Joannides was the chief of the Psychological Warfare Branch of the Miami station for more than a year before Kennedy's assassination. He was the directorate's paymaster, keeping the exile group in funds to the tune of $25,000 a month.[56] More than any other CIA officer, Joannides (code name "Howard") knew about the real operational purpose behind Oswald's staged pro-Castro activities in New Orleans and his carefully scripted contacts with the DRE during the month of August 1963, just weeks before he left for Mexico City.

This was the reason Helms worked so assiduously to keep Joannides's name from ever surfacing in any of the investigations into the JFK assassination. Even when the so-called 1992 JFK Records Act forced the CIA to surrender Joannides's 201 file, the file was purged.[57] It was Helms's concern that if Whitten was allowed to continue his investigation he would discover the FBI reports on Oswald's "pro-Castro" activity in New Orleans and concentrate the in-house investigation on the CIA's JM/Wave station. With a team of thirty agents and a staff of thirty clerical workers Whitten might have shaken loose any operational secrets involving Joannides and the DRE and exposed a clearer picture of the CIA's interest in Oswald. Helms was determined to keep these "family jewels" securely locked away and out of reach of a colleague whose ethical integrity made him a poor risk as a co-conspirator. It was this looming threat that prompted Helms to remove Whitten from the investigation and turn it over to Angleton. Angleton, like his professional counterpart, Hoover, dropped the Cuban angle in the assassination and turned the investigation over to Counterintelligence's Soviet Division to determine whether the KGB had influenced Oswald in any way.[58]

As a stunned nation tried to cope with the news of Kennedy's murder and what it portended for the future, CIA assets and contacts were busy over the weekend following the assassination with press releases and assertions filtered into government circles responsible for internal security matters, claiming that Oswald had been a communist and a stooge of the Castro regime. Jose Antonio Lanusa, who handled the regular reports from the anti-Castro DRE delegates in Miami and New Orleans, released to the press the story of Carlos Bringuier's account of Oswald's August 5 visit to his clothing store at 107 Decatur Street in New Orleans. It was Bringuier's contention that Oswald, a covert pro-Castro supporter, was trying to infiltrate the DRE's New Orleans cell. Lanusa released the story, but only after first clearing it with his CIA control, George Joannides.[59] The story ran in the *Miami Herald* under the eye-catching title "Oswald Tried to Spy on Anti-Castro Exile Group." Bringuier's tale of Oswald as a Castro stooge also made the *Washington Post:* "Castro Foe Details Infiltration Effort." Both of these stories appeared the day after the assassination.[60] The unappreciated irony in this whole business was that the first JFK conspiracy theory to find its way into print was paid for by George E. Joannides, a CIA psychological warfare specialist.

On November 22, Lanusa contacted Daniel James, chief officer for the Citizens Committee for a Free Cuba, and told James that Oswald was "definitely a Communist and supporter of Castro." The DRE press secretary also alleged that a month before Kennedy's assassination, Castro had boasted to a diplomat during a party at the Brazilian Embassy in Havana that if the Kennedy administration continued to cause him difficulties he had facilities to "knock off United States leaders." Lanusa told James that his source, whom he did not name, was a friend and a CIA contact. The next day James reported Lanusa's account to the bureau's Washington field office, and Hoover ordered the FBI Miami office to interview Lanusa. On November 24, Edward S. Butler, the chief executive officer of the New Orleans–based Information Council of the Americas, a CIA front organization, appeared before the Senate Internal Security Subcommittee during an unusual Sunday session. Butler told the committee that based on his debate with Oswald in August on WDSU, a New Orleans radio station, Oswald was an "indoctrinated pro-communist" and a supporter of the Castro government.[61]

It is an unamendable fact that some historical issues are never answered beyond a shadow of a doubt. However, the assassination of John F. Kennedy, arguably a pivotal point in our history, should not be accepted as a dramatic, albeit a painful and frustrating, example of this truism. From the White House on down, every official who had any role in the investigation either knew or suspected that Kennedy was the victim of a conspiracy. This realization explains why they all conspired to rush to judgment with a counterfeit version of the assassination. Undoubtedly, some acted out of some self-imposed sense of a "higher good" that persuaded them to keep the truth of Dallas from the ordinary understanding of the American people in order to reassure a traumatized public that the system of government would endure despite this national crisis. Others in government either had guilty knowledge or well-grounded suspicions about the reasons why Kennedy was assassinated.

All the repeated assurances from official voices and the unprecedented volume of the written record compiled by the Warren Commission insisting that Oswald alone committed the crime will not stand when tested against the evidence in the case and when considered against the backdrop of the forces in play during the thousand days of the Kennedy administration. Kennedy's assassination was a direct outgrowth of the Cuban issue in American politics. Although the Cold War was global in its reach, the front lines of this confrontation during the Kennedy years centered on Cuba and the unwavering urgency among elements inside the government to do whatever it took to solve the "Castro problem."

There is convincing evidence that Castro's immediate reaction to the news of Kennedy's assassination was fear verging on terror. The news that the assailant in the case was a self-professed Marxist with pro-Castro sympathies convinced Cuba's premier that Kennedy's death would provoke an invasion of his country. The National Security Agency (NSA), the government's superspy intelligence organization, eavesdropped on all electronic traffic out of Cuba. The NSA picked up Castro's emotional and tremulous November 23 televised speech to the Cuban people in which he accused the "extremist racists of the Pentagon" of orchestrating the crime to justify the invasion of Cuba. Expecting a possible U.S. invasion, Castro placed his military forces on full alert. The French journalist Jean Daniel was having lunch with Castro at his summer residence fronting Varadero Beach when they heard that Kennedy had been struck down in Dallas. Castro's immediate reaction to early reports that Kennedy was still alive and there was hope of saving him was: "If they can, he is already re-elected." Daniel noted, "He pronounced these words with satisfaction." This hopeful mood was quickly eclipsed when the radio transmission from Miami reported that JFK's wounds were fatal. According to Daniel, a somber Castro stood up and declared, "Everything is changed. Everything is going to change." The Cuban leader told his journalist guest, "I'll tell you one thing: at least Kennedy was an enemy to whom we had become accustomed. This is a serious matter, an extremely serious matter."[62]

Castro's fear was genuine. Even though Castro knew about CIA plots to take his life during the Eisenhower and Kennedy administrations, there is no argument worth entertaining that he resorted to assassinating JFK in retaliation.[63] The prospect of a U.S. invasion and the resulting assured destruction of Cuba was enough of a deterrent to dissuade him from such a foolhardy course of action. There was no reason for Castro to believe that if Kennedy was removed, Lyndon Johnson's Cuban policy would be different; changing the leadership does not necessarily change the system. Furthermore, Castro could not count on LBJ to honor the no-invasion pledge that Kennedy had promised as part of the deal to get Soviet missiles out of Cuba. The strongest countercheck to any Castro "retaliation theory" was JFK's genuine encouragement of William Attwood's mission to open up talks with Havana. Castro, who initiated this possible change of course in U.S.-Cuban relations, told Daniel that he believed Kennedy was sincere in wanting to coexist with a socialist regime. Lightening the conversation with a little humor, Castro had told Daniel he "was willing to declare Goldwater my friend if that will guarantee Kennedy's re-election."[64]

The growing prospect of a détente with the United States that would include the unfreezing of Cuban assets, the lifting of the embargo, and the end of U.S.-sponsored hit-and-run sabotage raids was a diplomatic consummation that Castro wanted to achieve, even at the risk of facing sharp dissent within his own inner circle. For Kennedy the fruits of such a détente would be the satisfaction of wooing Castro away from the Soviet orbit and shifting the domestic balance of power inside Cuba away from the hard-liners such as Raul Castro and Che Guevara.

In 1978 Castro agreed to an interview with a handful of members of the House Select Committee on Assassinations, who were preparing the finishing touches on their own investigation into the Kennedy assassination. The congressional delegation came to Havana to see if Castro could clear up some of the mystery surrounding Oswald's trip to Mexico City. The committee's most tenacious investigators, Dan Hardway and Eddie Lopez, persuaded Chief Counsel Robert Blakey that there was enough evidence that the CIA had an interest in Oswald to take the trouble to elicit Castro's views.[65]

When it came to the mystery of Mexico City, the Warren report concluded that the seven days Oswald spent in that city had no significant bearing on the assassination. The report's conclusion was largely the product of information that had been first filtered through the CIA. Although the Cuban premier was not a disinterested party when it came to the Kennedy assassination, he gave the congressmen an alternative explanation. Castro directed his response to committee chairman Louis Stokes, who asked him to speculate on why Oswald had wanted a Cuban visa: "You see, it was always very much suspicious to me that a person who later appeared to be involved in Kennedy's death would have requested a visa from Cuba. Because, I said to myself—what would have happened had by any chance that man come to Cuba—visited Cuba—gone back to the States and then appeared involved in

Kennedy's death? That would have been a provocation—a gigantic provocation. . . . That is why it has always been something—a very obscure thing—something suspicious—because I interpreted it as a deliberate attempt to link Cuba with Kennedy's death."[66]

Castro's insightful explanation of course did not sweep away all the shadows of doubt and unanswered questions surrounding the reasons behind the Kennedy assassination. But in these four sentences he provided Stokes and his congressional colleagues with a prima facie motive for the assassination. Castro's comments might have intrigued the visiting congressional delegates, but when the House Select Committee released its findings, the report insinuated that the mob—Chief Counsel Blakey's pet thesis—had had something to do with the Dealey Plaza conspiracy. If we are to move the Kennedy conspiracy out of the shadows, any future investigation would do well to consider Castro's explanation for Oswald's Mexico City activities as a "gigantic provocation" to justify an American invasion of Cuba.

Conclusion

*"No, don't dig up the past! Dwell on the past and you'll lose an
eye." But the proverb goes on to say, "Forget the past and you'll
lose both eyes."*
—Alexander Solzhenitsyn, *The Gulag Archipelago*

After forty years the "who" and "why" of Dallas longs
for an answer that cannot be given definitively and responsibly. A clear explanation was made impossible by the official conspiracy to see to it that
there could be no other answer as soon as it was known that Lee Harvey Oswald, then the only suspect in the crime, had been assassinated and there
would be no trial. Since there was no good-faith effort to investigate JFK's
murder, there are few leads from the official evidence that the private researcher can use as a basis for solving the crime.

Despite the official mythology that Oswald acting alone killed President
Kennedy, government documents and records reveal that there were two
conspiracies. The first was the one that took Kennedy's life. The other was
the bloodless one engaged in by officialdom—President Johnson, FBI director Hoover, the Justice Department, the Secret Service, the U.S. Navy, the
CIA, and the members of the Warren Commission. All of them conspired to
foist a counterfeit solution to the assassination of President John F. Kennedy
on the American public. Although they all conspired, to one degree or another, to hide the truth that Kennedy was the victim of a conspiracy, it does
not necessarily follow that any of them were guilty of the original crime—
the planning and execution of JFK's murder. At the same time, that possibility cannot be excluded.

With the crime now four decades in the past, no researcher can possibly
truthfully answer the "who" and "why" of the JFK assassination. So far
there has been no "smoking gun" uncovered among the four or five million
pages of government documents released into the public domain and currently housed at the National Archives and Records Administration at College Park, Maryland; nor is there likely to be since those responsible for
uncovering the facts of the assassination never investigated the crime. Unlike pulp-fiction mysteries, in real life there usually is no smoking gun. Although this book has not uncovered any such clue, it has unearthed out of
the massive official record of the crime unanswered questions and impossi-
bilities galore regarding ballistics, the nature of JFK's wounds, the ignored
testimony of key witnesses, the suppression and destruction of evidence,
and a pattern of official lies and cover-up that continues to this day despite

national legislation that calls for full disclosure and release of documents and records relating to the JFK assassination.

A thread of recognition runs through the record, exposing the hard truth that all those responsible for reporting on the crime knew at one point or another in the investigation that Kennedy was the victim of a conspiracy. President Johnson was never in doubt that his sudden and accidental elevation to the presidency was the result of a conspiracy to take the life of John F. Kennedy. The weekend following the assassination, early intelligence from DCI McCone and Director Hoover persuaded Johnson that the tragedy in Dallas was the result of a "Red plot" hatched in Mexico City. This alone was reason enough for LBJ, Hoover, and Katzenbach to agree that a higher national purpose would be served by "settling the dust of Dallas" as quickly as possible. Like most Americans at the time, LBJ accepted at face value the existence of an international communist conspiracy. With Director Hoover's assistance the White House moved quickly to discourage all official talk of a "Red plot," with the attendant unthinkable consequences of missiles flying and forty million American lives hanging in the balance. Years later LBJ entertained the likelihood that the CIA had had something to do with Kennedy's assassination.[1]

As early as the weekend after the assassination the FBI suspected that there was a conspiracy when it learned of an Oswald imposter in Mexico City. By January, if not before, these suspicions had hardened into a dead certainty when FBI photoanalysts examined the Zapruder film and slides made from this historic film. The FBI interpreters concluded that the first shot at the presidential limousine had come before Zapruder frame 170, before a shot could have come from the "sniper's nest" because the view would have been obstructed by a live oak tree in full foliage in front of the Texas School Book Depository. Based on these findings, the only tenable conclusion confronting the FBI was either that Oswald had not been the assassin or that he had had an accomplice. Anticipating the FBI, the CIA's National Photographic Intelligence Center (NPIC) ran its own analysis of the Zapruder film over the weekend following the assassination. Like their FBI counterparts, the NPIC interpreters established that the first shot came before Oswald could have had a clear view of the presidential limo and that there were at least two shooters.[2]

The Secret Service and FBI agents who were present at the Bethesda Hospital morgue and witnessed the Kennedy autopsy were never able to reconcile the official version of the shooting with the wounds they saw on the president's body. The most stunning and puzzling disconnect derived from an X-ray of JFK's head revealing something on the order of thirty to forty dustlike particles that showed up on the light screen like the "Milky Way" (Agent Roy Kellerman's characterization). The immediate reaction from

both FBI and Secret Service onlookers was that Kennedy's massive lacerated head wound had been caused by a dum-dum bullet, that is, a hollow-
nosed ammunition that explodes when it enters the body. Although not
conclusive, this speculation about an exploding bullet was consistent with
FBI firearms expert Robert Frazier's diagrams of the distribution of bullet
fragments, blood, brain matter, and tissue in the presidential limousine. Frazier's report noted the scattering of blood and JFK's brain matter in front of
and *behind* the right visor and, more importantly, on the hood of the car. All
of this indicated that the bullet or bullets that had struck the president in the
head had exploded upon impact. The official story, of course, was that Oswald was using metal-jacketed, military-type ammunition that did not explode inside the human body. The wounds to JFK's back and throat were
consistent with nonexploding military-type ammunition. The Warren Commission never entertained the possibility that the president had been struck
by some bullets that were explosive and others that were not. That would not
have been consistent with the shooting scenario of a lone assassin.[3]

The Warren Commission pretended to dispel all doubts about the ammunition used in the crime when it reported that a bullet allegedly found in
Governor John Connally's hospital stretcher matched the type of ammunition that could have been fired from Oswald's Mannlicher-Carcano rifle. It
was the Commission's contention that this 6.5-mm copper-jacketed bullet
(Commission Exhibit [CE] 399) was the iron-clad ballistic evidence that
tied Oswald and his rifle to the murder of President Kennedy. But this presumption of fact failed to clear the hurdle of witness testimony. Despite his
best courtroomlike efforts, Commission counsel Arlen Specter, the Philadelphia assistant district attorney, was unable to get Parkland Memorial Hospital staff to agree that CE 399 had come from the governor's carriage. Much
to Specter and the Commission's dismay, all the recorded witness testimony
convincingly pointed to the greater likelihood that the missile in question
had come from a stretcher that had nothing to do with either Kennedy or
Connally. The Commission ignored this awkward turn of events because it
subverted its prima facie case against Oswald as the lone assassin. The most
credible explanation for the discovery of a virtually pristine 6.5-mm bullet
in a stretcher that had no association with either Kennedy or Connally was
that it had been planted by conspirators to put Oswald in the frame. The circumstances surrounding the so-called Connally stretcher bullet further
strengthened the case for conspiracy in the assassination of America's
thirty-fifth president.[4]

Putting the pieces of evidence together, a pattern emerges that points to a
more realistic hypothetical explanation than the official version. Kennedy
was removed from office by powerful and irrational forces who opposed his
revisionist Cuba policy. By 1963 senior military and CIA officers had ar-

rived at the conclusion that Castro's Marxist government was not about to fall if a "higher authority" did not intend to overthrow it. For a Bill Harvey, a Desmond FitzGerald, a Lyman Lemnitzer, and other like-minded highly placed professionals in the military and intelligence communities, Kennedy's 1962 no-invasion pledge was tantamount to giving Castro an intolerable degree of sanctuary. The CIA, its influence with the Kennedy White House already compromised because of the Bay of Pigs imbroglio, seethed at the prospect of becoming even more marginalized. If the White House would not commit to a military solution of the "Castro problem," the morale and motivation of the antiregime Cubans would be irreparably damaged. CIA agents specializing in covert operations, the celebrated secret warriors of the Eisenhower years who carried out the vital and dirty work for freedom, braced themselves, expecting increasing difficulty in recruiting agents and sources, keeping already recruited agents, and continuing or intensifying intelligence-gathering and other clandestine operations against the Castro regime.[5] For these CIA hard-liners, stalwarts of the Harvey-FitzGerald faction, bent on revenging the humiliation of the Bay of Pigs by getting rid of Castro, Kennedy may have crossed his Rubicon when he gave the green light to Attwood and a policy of accommodation with Cuba's leader.

One certain way to scuttle a policy of rapprochement and move directly to retaliation was to show that Kennedy's assassination was linked to the Castro government. Was this what Oswald's handlers had in mind when they coached him in building a pro-Castro legend during the three months he spent in New Orleans just before he left for Mexico City? What we know (which isn't very much) about Oswald's alleged activities and associations in Mexico City and the CIA's Special Investigations Group's (SIG) and Special Affairs Staff's (SAS) interest in Oswald just weeks before JFK's assassination indicates that some very serious people at Langley were keenly interested in Oswald. It seems hardly credible that this twenty-four-year-old ex-marine warranted this high-level attention from a small and elite circle of CIA operational officers because he was the self-professed secretary of a nonexistent Fair Play for Cuba Committee chapter in New Orleans. Was Oswald an unwitting tool in what Castro characterized as a "gigantic provocation"?

There is evidence that as soon as Oswald was charged with Kennedy's murder the CIA surreptitiously launched a disinformation campaign in the national press to convince the public that the assassin was linked to the Castro government. Was CIA director John McCone acting out of assassination hysteria or calculated design when he tried to push the Alvarado story on Commissioner Gerald Ford even after the FBI had proved the Nicaraguan agent's account to be bogus? Were these developments isolated and independent of one another or interlocking elements in some plan to create an incriminating story about Oswald as part of a Havana-KGB conspiracy to assassinate President Kennedy and provoke U.S. military action against Cuba?

If hard-line elements within the CIA conspired to force the new president's hand or provide Johnson with the grounds to settle the "Castro problem" by an invasion of Cuba, they were quickly disappointed. Two weeks after the assassination the White House sent a clear signal to the CIA to abandon its agitation about a "Red plot" behind the tragedy of Dallas. On December 6, 1963, Katzenbach invited John Whitten and Birch O'Neal, Angleton's trusted deputy and senior SIG officer, to the Justice Department to review a copy of the FBI's report (Commission Document [CD] 1) on the Kennedy assassination. At that point CIA Langley knew that the "official truth" of Dallas would be that Oswald, acting alone, had killed the president. President Johnson used CD 1 to impress upon the CIA that he wanted all rumors and allegations about a "Red plot" squelched.[6]

Hoover was quick to take the initiative in backstopping Johnson's determination to shut down the Mexico City rumor mill. On November 27 the director ordered Laurence Keenan, a Spanish-speaking supervisor in the bureau's Domestic Intelligence Division, to take the first available flight to Mexico City. Keenan was instructed to "coordinate the entire investigation" into the "Red plot" allegations and "pursue them vigorously until the desired results are obtained." Keenan left that evening on the first flight available to Mexico City. He had no passport or visa, but FBI legat Clark Anderson met him at the airport and whisked him through Mexican Customs and Immigration to an awaiting embassy car. When Keenan arrived at the U.S. Embassy there were five or six officials waiting for him, including Ambassador Thomas Mann and Win Scott, the CIA's station chief. According to Keenan, he relayed to the group that it was "Hoover's conviction that Lee Harvey Oswald was the lone assassin and in view of Oswald's untimely death no further investigation was deemed necessary."[7]

The FBI and CIA diverted their respective investigations away from probing into any connection between Oswald and his public pro-Castro activities during the three months before Kennedy's assassination. The day following the assassination Hoover canceled orders to contact the FBI's Cuban sources. The director narrowed the focus to Oswald and any alleged Cuban connections even further when he excluded all of the bureau's Cuban experts and supervisors from the investigation. Abandoning any Cuban angle in the assassination, Hoover turned the investigation over to the bureau's Soviet experts.

Senior CIA officers, in concert with the FBI, maneuvered to keep the public in the dark about any possible connection between the agency and Oswald's movements in Mexico City or his staged pro-Castro activities in New Orleans. In late December Deputy Director of Plans Richard Helms removed John Whitten from the CIA's investigation and replaced him with James Angleton, the chief of the agency's counterintelligence staff. According to Whitten, Angleton had "direct ties" with Hoover.[8] Angleton quickly concluded that Cuba was unimportant and focused his internal investigation on Oswald's life in the Soviet Union. Whitten later told his House Select Committee interrogators that had he remained in charge of the investigation and been fully informed of the FBI's and CIA's preassassination files on Oswald, he would have concentrated his attention on the CIA's JM/Wave station in Miami, Florida, to uncover what George Joannides, the station chief, and operatives from the SIG and SAS knew about Oswald. However, when Angleton took over the investigation the CIA had clear sailing in covering up any connection between it and the Kennedy assassination. Commissioner Allen Dulles, who had been CIA director before the Bay of Pigs fiasco prompted Kennedy to remove him, was Angleton's ex parte pipeline into what took place inside the Commission's executive sessions. For instance, when Hoover and McCone testified before the Commission they knew beforehand what line the questioning would take, allowing them to coordinate their responses. "Was Oswald ever an agent?" And "Does the CIA/FBI have any evidence showing that a conspiracy existed to assassinate President Kennedy?" When Hoover and McCone made their separate May 1964 appearances before the Commission they were on message with a "No" to both questions.[9]

These were the kinds of generic questions that the government should have made every effort to answer in order to be true to its solemn obligation to uncover the reasons behind the Dealey Plaza conspiracy. Where there is no mystery, no shadow of doubt, is that planning for provocation to justify major U.S. military action against Cuba was a persistent theme in some government circles, most notably the Joint Chiefs of Staff and the CIA, during the Kennedy presidency.

Another persistent theme during the Kennedy years was the deadly business of assassination of political leaders. "Executive Action" operations against foreign leaders posed no moral dilemma for some of the CIA's senior officers if the removal of those people would advance U.S. aims. In May 1961, Rafael Trujillo, the dictator of the Dominican Republic, was ambushed and killed by coup plotters with guns furnished by the CIA. Trujillo was on the CIA's hit list, and the agency was associated with the plotters who assassinated the Dominican strongman.[10]

The Trujillo assassination occurred on Kennedy's watch, but at the time the president knew nothing of the CIA's "Executive Action" operations and history. Kennedy learned about the program by happenstance a year after he entered the White House when FBI director Hoover brought it to his attention. When the Kennedys learned of these pre–Bay of Pigs CIA-mafia plots, the attorney general demanded an explanation. On May 7, 1962, Robert Kennedy met with Lawrence Houston, the CIA's general counsel, and Col. Sheffield Edwards, director of the Office of Security, for a briefing on the CIA's contacts with gangster elements. When the attorney general insisted that there be no more contact with mafia chieftains without first consulting him, Edwards assured Kennedy that all CIA-mafia plots had been terminated. But the CIA's own 1967 inspector general's report noted that Bobby Kennedy was never told that after the May meeting the "CIA had a continuing involvement with U.S. gangster elements." Edwards had lied to the attorney general.[11]

In February 1963 the CIA masterminded the overthrow of Iraq's prime minister, General Abdul Karim Qassem. His pro-Soviet policies were deemed a threat to Middle East stability. Qassem and his supporters resisted the coup forces for two days before he surrendered unconditionally. The toppled general received a summary trial and faced a firing squad, all within one hour after he surrendered. His bullet-riddled body was shown on Iraqi television night after night to assure the populace that he was indeed dead. James Critchfield, the CIA's division chief of the Middle East, was elated with the outcome, regarding it "as a great victory." Years later Critchfield boasted, "We really had the Ts crossed on what was happening."[12]

Just weeks before Kennedy was assassinated, the first crucial death that same November was the assassination of South Vietnamese prime minister Ngo Dinh Diem. DCI McCone and William Colby, the CIA's Far Eastern Division chief, had made it clear within U.S. government circles that they were adamantly opposed to the removal of Diem, so the CIA could be assumed to be guiltless in this assassination. But as historian John Prados has convincingly established, "in the broader context of U.S. government encouragement," CIA street agents in Saigon were in league with the military junta that toppled Diem, so the CIA's hands were not altogether clean.[13]

By the fall of 1963 President Kennedy was the greatest obstacle preventing hard-line government elements from getting rid of Castro. As late as November 18 the White House told William Attwood to go forward with his mission. It was agreed that Attwood would meet with the Cuban ambassador to the United Nations, Carlos Lechuga, to set up an agenda for a future dialogue.[14]

As Kennedy prepared for his Texas trip, differing plans within the government for handling the "Castro problem" were moving along separate tracks and heading pell-mell for the same crossing. Kennedy had committed to exploring a diplomatic solution. Desmond FitzGerald, the SAS's executive officer, was employing CIA resources and contacts to assassinate the head of Cuba's revolutionary regime. If "Operation AMLASH" went ahead without Kennedy's knowledge, as the lack of evidence to the contrary indicates, then this was indeed dramatic proof that when it came to dealing with Castro some CIA bitter-enders were prepared to act as a law unto themselves and finish their grudge fight with Castro. AMLASH exposed the utter contempt that some CIA elements had for Kennedy as well as their fundamental lack of trust in the White House's ability to advance the nation's interests, as they perceived them, and assure the country's security in an unruly and dangerous world.[15]

Given all the previous CIA attempts to assassinate Castro, the odds against the success of a childish plot such as AMLASH were off the books. Moreover, the fact that the CIA did not have the White House's endorsement for this risky attempt to hijack JFK's Cuban policy meant that if the operation was blown, careers would have been ruined and Kennedy might had been furious enough to carry through his earlier post–Bay of Pigs threat to splinter the CIA and scatter it to the four winds. This situation raises the unavoidable suspicion that CIA hard-liners, conceivably in league with other disaffected institutional forces, planned to remove Castro by first getting rid of Kennedy. After forty years, Castro's "gigantic provocation" still remains a credible template for any future investigation determined to probe the shadows surrounding the Kennedy assassination.

Short of uncovering the proverbial "smoking gun," no seamless explanation as to the "who" and "why" of Dallas is possible. Ideally, the time for uncovering answers to these questions was forty years ago, had the Warren Commission enjoyed the full cooperation of government agencies and a clear mandate from the Johnson White House to pursue the truth no matter where it led. Instead, "settling the dust" of Dallas as quickly as possible was the course the executive branch settled upon. For those involved in the investigation, this decision made at the highest level of government was tantamount to national policy. As a consequence, the Warren Commission went through the motions of an investigation that was little more than an improvised exercise in public relations. The government did not want to delve into the heart of darkness of the Kennedy assassination because it feared what it might uncover: the brutal truth that Kennedy was a victim of deep divisions and visceral distrust over how to solve the "Castro problem," and that his assassination was carried out by powerful and irrational forces within his own government.

Appendix A.
FBI Damage Control Tickler

This FBI damage control tickler reveals how the agency went about investigating the assassination. The tickler is not dated and provides no indication of purpose but was probably drafted in the 1970s in anticipation of the necessity of defending its investigation into the Kennedy assassination. During the 1970s Congress launched the first systematic investigation into the U.S. intelligence community, including uncovering disturbing FBI abuses of power—dubbed the "Hoover horrors" by some in the national press. This tickler was one of numerous documents released to Mark Allen in April 1985 in an FOIA lawsuit directed by his attorney, James Lesar. It presents a remarkable record of improper acts ranging from potential blackmail threats to revelations that the FBI opposed and impeded the Warren Commission while failing to conduct any semblance of a good-faith investigation. A colorful description of the FBI's investigative efforts is Assistant Director Alex Rosen's characterization of the FBI "standing with pockets open waiting for evidence to drop in." (Capitalization and punctuation are as in the original; interlined written notations are in brackets.)

Federal Bureau of Investigation
   1. Early Bureau Responses to the President's Assassination
      A. November 22–23, 1963
         1. Early teletypes; instructions to field;
         2. Jenkins memo of Nov. 24; Hoover says Oswald alone did it. Bureau must "convince the public Oswald is the real assassin"
         3. Hoover memo on Nov. 26: "wrap up investigation; seems to me we have the basic facts now" 62-109060-1490
         4. Hoover memo on Nov. 29: "Hope to have investigation wrapped up next week"
      B. Lee Harvey Oswald
         1. Establishing chain of evidence, bullet to gun, etc.
         2. November 29 memo; basic acts, yet contradictions on Oswald in Mexico; [redacted] photo not him
         3. Hosty note destruction: handling by Bureau on Nov 24 and effect in subsequent days
         4. Inteviews with Oswald associates, Marina wiretap [m=marines, etc.]
      C. Jack Ruby
         1. Basic facts, early memos
         2. Hoover suspicion of basement entry and assistance
         3. extensive teletypes and reports on organized crime connections, also Hoover's own memos
         4. contacts in 1959 as P. C. I – for use as informer on criminal element in Dallas
   2. Structure and Methods of the Bureau Investigation
      A. Basic Organization and Jurisdictions
         1. Legal basis of the FBI involvement

2. Hoover and Belmont memos
3. Organization Chart
B. General Investigative Division (GID)
   1. Rosen testimony on "ancillary nature" of probe; lack of Meetings; assignment to bank robbery desk
   2. Supervisors Senate testimony on physical evidence chain
   3. Sullivan on lack of communication with Domestic Intelligence – the Division running the probe of LHO [lack of coordination between Div 5 & 6]
   4. Rosen characterization of FBI "standing with pockets open waiting for evidence to drop in"
   5. Supervisors testimony on LHO not being included in G.I.D. probe other than in relation to physical evidence
   6. Rosen didn't know of "Gale Report" which found deficiencies in Bureau coverage of Oswald [DID no initial it.]
C. Domestic Intelligence Division [D.I.D. Div. 5]
   1. LHO background established, prior coverage
   2. Sullivan testimony on chaotic process, lack of input
   3. Soviet experts handled Oswald investigation
   4. Secret disciplining of DID officials who handled pre-assassination investigation of Oswald
   5. Incident of Sullivan's people copying GID files
   6. Hosty note destruction; Sullivan lack of knowledge
   7. Assignment of Ruby probe to Civil Rights Division – outside of DID jurisdiction, thus not a part of general Oswald investigation.
D. Investigation of Potential Cuban Aspects
   1. Cancellation of orders to contact Cuban sources on Nov 23
   2. [redacted]
   3. Deletion of [redacted] from memo provided to Commission
   4. Cuban experts and supervisors excluded from investigation
   5. Church Committee findings on narrow Cuban focus
   6. [redacted]
E. Investigation of Potential Organized Crime Aspects
   1. Hoover memos and teletypes on Ruby connections
   2. Ruby phone records
   3. Justice Dept. interest in probing O.C. aspects
   4. Chicago interview with Ruby associates
   5. Evans and Staffeld (and Danaby and Stanley) statements on not being consulted
   6. Use of Ruby as informant on Dallas criminal element
   7. LC[N?] sources available at time
3. Bureau Relationship with Warren Commission
A. Formation of Warren Commission
   1. Hoover opposition: memo and Jenkins memo
   2. Katzenbach testimony and Sullivan statement
   3. Early memos – adversary relationship
   4. Hoover blocking Warren's choice for general counsel
   5. Preparation of dossiers on staff and members
B. Assistance to Warren Commission
   1. Basic scope of official relationship
   2. Early friction over informant allegations (LHO)

3. Withholding of Hosty name from Oswald notebook
4. Hoover instructions to agents not to volunteer info. To WC
5. Destruction of Hosty note: implications
6. Withholding of secret "Gale Report" on Bureau mistakes in earlier Oswald probe; disciplining of officials
7. Hoover instructions ordering that no Bureau official attend earliest WC session, despite Katzenbach request
8. Delay in sending information to Commission regarding Bureau's past nine contacts with Ruby
9. Apparent withholding of "Oswald imposter" memos of 1960–1961
10. Handling of information pertaining to Oswald-Kostikov contact
11. Handling of Ruby polygraph

C. Related Bureau Actions and Activities
1. Preparation of dossiers on WC staff after the Report was out [Sept. 24, 1964]
2. Hoover's leaking of early FBI report (Sullivan statement)
3. Hoover views on Communism and Oswald (Kronheim letter)
4. Sullivan relationship with Angleton: pre-arranging of answers to Commission questions
5. Secret plan to distribute Oswald-Marxist posters in Bureau plan to discredit Communist Party; prejudicial aspects
6. Hoover reaction to Warren Report
7. Subsequent preparation of sex dossiers on critics of probe
8. Questions regarding FBI's continual pledge that "case will remain open for all time;" actual designation of it as "closed" in internal Bureau files.

Appendix B.
J. Lee Rankin's Memorandum

J. Lee Rankin's "Memorandum for the Files" is the only record of the January 24, 1964, meeting of the chief counsel and Earl Warren with members of the Texas Court of Inquiry. Most of the three-hour meeting centered on speculation as to whether Oswald was a CIA asset. Rankin was so determined to kill this "dirty rumor" that he did not even date the memorandum. Neither did he share what transpired during this secret session with the rest of the Commission's members or staff lawyers. (For context and further information, see Chapter 6.)

MEMORANDUM FOR THE FILES

FROM: Mr. J. Lee Rankin, General Counsel

SUBJECT: Rumors that Oswald was an undercover agent.

Allegations have been received by the Commission to the effect that Lee Harvey Oswald was an undercover agent for the Federal Bureau of Investigation or the Central Intelligence Agency prior to the assassination of President Kennedy on November 22, 1963. This memorandum reviews these allegations and summarizes the action taken to date by the Commission.

On Wednesday, January 22, 1964, I received a telephone call from Waggoner Carr, Attorney General of Texas. Mr. Carr stated that he had received on a confidential basis an allegation to the effect that Lee Harvey Oswald was an undercover agent for the Federal Bureau of Investigation since September of 1962 and that he had been paid $200.00 a month from an account designated as No. 179. Mr. Carr indicated that this allegation was in the hands of the press and defense counsel for Ruby and suggested that his information came ultimately from District Attorney Henry Wade, although he stated that he had not discussed this matter directly with Wade.

After a discussion with the Chairman of the Commission and Mr. Leon Jaworski, I contacted Attorney General Carr. I asked the Attorney General to contact District Attorney Wade and try to ascertain more definitely the source of this allegation. At the request of the Chairman of the Commission, I also asked Mr. Carr to ask Wade and his assistant, Bill Alexander, to come to Washington as soon as possible to discuss this matter.

A meeting of the Commission was called for 5:30 P.M. on Wednesday, January 22, 1964. All the members of the Commission were present with the exception of John J. McCloy and Senator Richard B. Russell. This specific allegation was discussed in detail by the Commission. It was recognized by all members of the Commission that, although this allegation was probably not accurate, this matter had to be regarded seriously by the Commission. It was agreed that the Commission would have to take whatever action necessary to pursue this matter to final conclusion. During the meeting efforts were made to contact Attorney General Carr again. When he was contacted, Attorney General Carr stated that the District Attorney Wade had been unable or unwilling to specify the source of this allegation in more detail. He informed me that he and Messrs. Wade, Alexander, Jaworski, and Storey would come to Washington the next day.

On Thursday, January 23, 1964 Secret Service Report No. 767 was brought to my attention. This report is dated January 23, 1964 and summarizes an interview by Agent Bertram with Houston Post reporter Alonso H. Hudkins III. A pertinent paragraph of the report reads as follows:

> On December 17, Mr. Hudkins advised that he had just returned from a weekend in Dallas, during which time he talked to Allen Sweatt, Chief Criminal Division, Sheriff's Office, Dallas. Chief Sweatt mentioned that it was his opinion that Lee Harvey Oswald was being paid $200 a month by the FBI as an informant in connection with their subversive investigation. He furnished the alleged informant number assigned to Oswald by the FBI as "S172".

The report concludes with the request that Chief Allen Sweatt of the Dallas Sheriff's office be interviewed regarding the above allegation. Upon being informed by representatives of the Secret Service that this subsequent interview had not yet taken place, I requested that it be done immediately.

On Friday, January 24, 1964, the Chairman of the Commission and I met with Attorney General Carr, District Attorney Wade, Assistant District Attorney Alexander, Mr. Jaworski and Dean Storey. We reviewed the situation to date. District Attorney Wade and others of the Texas representatives stated that the rumors to the effect that Oswald was an undercover agent were widely held among representatives of the press in Dallas. They stated also that Mr. Belli, attorney for Jack L. Ruby, was familiar with these allegations. Wade stated he was also aware of an allegation that Oswald was an informant for the CIA and carried Number 110669.

District Attorney Wade and Alexander stated that the sources for these allegations or rumors were several reporters, including Houston Post reporter Hudkins. They did not pinpoint Hudkins as being the source of this information, but they did not name any other individual reporters. They both indicated that they would not vouch for the integrity or accuracy of these reporters. They did inform us that this information was not disclosed in chambers during the bail hearing on Monday, January 20, 1964. District Attorney Wade stated that, based on his experience as an FBI agent during the years 1939–1943, he did not think that the number would be either a payroll or voucher number carried on the Bureau records. He suggested that the records are not kept that way and would not show the name of the informer, who would probably be paid by the FBI agent in cash. He further stated that in his experience it was customary for the agent to carry the informer on his books as a number.

There was a general discussion regarding other information disclosed in the investigative reports which lend some degree of credibility to these allegations. Among other matters discussed at the meeting, the following were stressed: (1) the use by Oswald of Post Office boxes; (2) use by Oswald of aliases; (3) the lengthy 2-hour interview conducted by the FBI of Oswald in August of 1962; (4) interviews conducted by Special Agent Hosty in Dallas regarding Oswald's whereabouts and the failure to notify Secret Service of this information; (5) the comment after the assassination of Special Agent Hosty that Oswald had contacted two known subversive agents about 15 days before the assassination; (6) Oswald had Special Agent Hosty's car license and telephone numbers in his notebook; (7) Oswald's mother has stated that her son was an agent for the FBI or some other agency; (8) Special Agent Hosty was transferred from Dallas two weeks after the assassination.

The Chief Justice decided to present the results of this meeting to the entire Commission on Monday, January 27, 1964 and decided to propose tentatively that necessary inquiries be made concerning these allegations and that this memorandum be prepared for the record.

On the evening of Friday, January 24, 1964, a member of my staff was informed by representatives of Secret Service that Allen Sweatt, Chief of the Criminal Division of the Sheriff's office in Dallas, had been interviewed regarding the allegations made in Secret Service Report No. 767. According to this oral report, Sweatt stated that he received the allegation from Mr. Alexander in District Attorney Wade's office. He also mentioned Houston Post reporter Hudkins as a source of the information. When Sweatt was informed that the number in a similar allegation was 179 rather than 172, as he had indicated initially, Sweatt indicated that he would accept 179 as the correct number. Secret Service Inspector Kelley expressed his view that Hudkins was not very reliable, based on previous unfounded reports which he had furnished to Secret Service.

Appendix C.
A Brief Chronology and
Summary of the Commission's
Case against Oswald

9/25/63   White House sources tell the *Dallas News* that President Kennedy will visit Texas on November 21–22. Although no specific details had been worked out, it is considered likely that Kennedy will visit San Antonio, Houston, Fort Worth, and Dallas.

10/3/63   After a seven-day trip to Mexico City, Lee Harvey Oswald—a 24-year-old ex-marine, husband and father of two children, former defector to the Soviet Union, and self-proclaimed pro-Castro Marxist—returns to Dallas.

10/14/63   Oswald is hired as a book order-filler at the Texas School Book Depository. He rents a room at 1026 N. Beckley Avenue, in the Oak Cliff section of the city.

11/19/63   The Dallas papers announce for the first time the route the presidential motorcade will travel from Love Field to the Dallas Trade Mart, including a stretch of highway passing the Texas School Book Depository (TSBD) on Elm Street.

11/22/63   *11:55 A.M. (CST)*   The presidential motorcade leaves Love Field in Dallas and begins the 10-mile route (designed by the Secret Service) through downtown Dallas to the Trade Mart, where Kennedy will address a luncheon gathering.

12:29 P.M.   As the president's limousine begins to pass the TSBD on Elm Street, only minutes away from the Trade Mart, gunshots are fired. Both Kennedy and Governor John Connally are hit. Kennedy, with a massive laceration to the right side of his head, is rushed to nearby Parkland Memorial Hospital and treated by a team of doctors.

1:00 P.M.   After their failed attempts to revive the unconscious president, including a tracheotomy procedure, Kennedy is declared dead. Dr. Kemp Clark makes the announcement, which is verified by Admiral George G. Burkley, Kennedy's White House physician.

1:50 P.M.   Oswald is arrested at the Texas Theatre in connection with, initially, the shooting death of Dallas police officer J. D. Tippit shortly before 1:30. Shortly thereafter he becomes a suspect in the assassination of the president.

3:16 P.M.   The Parkland Memorial doctors who worked on Kennedy hold a press conference at the hospital. In response to reporters' questions, Dr. Malcolm Perry, the emergency room physician who performed the tracheotomy, notes three times that Kennedy's neck wound is an entrance wound. Dr. Clark, who assisted Perry, agrees with that assessment. But testifying before the Warren

Commission in March 1964, they reverse this opinion to claim that this wound was actually an exit wound.

About 7:30 P.M. (EST)   Lyndon Johnson, the new president, returns to the White House, calls FBI Director J. Edgar Hoover, and officially turns over to his agency full responsibility for investigating the assassination. The FBI, however, had already seized control of the case from the Secret Service and had in fact interrogated Oswald at the Dallas city jail earlier that afternoon.

11/23/63   *1:30 A.M. (CST)*   Lee Harvey Oswald is charged with the president's murder. Officially, Oswald is the only "true suspect" in the government's investigation into the assassination.

Later that day, Dr. Burkley drafts Kennedy's Certificate of Death, which describes the cause of death as "gunshot wound, skull." He also notes that the president sustained a second wound "in the posterior of the back at about the level of the third thoracic vertebra." But he is never questioned about this assessment by the Commission, the FBI, or the Secret Service, and the Commission excludes the actual death certificate from its final report and its twenty-six volumes of Hearings and Exhibits.

11/24/63   *About 11:20 A.M. (CST)*   Oswald is murdered by a handgun-wielding Jack Ruby, a Dallas nightclub owner, in the city jail's basement as he is being transferred to the Dallas County jail. He is rushed to Parkland Hospital but never regains consciousness and is pronounced dead at 1:07 P.M. Ruby is arrested and later claims his act was meant to save the president's widow from having to relive the assassination through Oswald's trial.

LBJ, Hoover, and acting attorney general Nicholas B. Katzenbach agree that the FBI should produce a public report on the assassination that concludes that Oswald killed the president and that he acted alone. The new president insists that the FBI report be finished by Wednesday, 11/26/63. But circumstances conspire to force Johnson to appoint a commission of eminent men, all either currently or formerly active in government, to evaluate the FBI's investigation and report their findings to the American people.

11/30/63   The press announces the names of the men who will make up what comes to be called the Warren Commission, named after Supreme Court Justice Earl Warren, who heads the commission's investigation.

9/64   After nine months of investigations and testimony the Commission issues a 912-page report, in which the heart of its case against Oswald is laid out in Chapters III and IV: Oswald secreted his rifle in the TSBD on November 22 and, when the floor-laying crew broke for lunch at noon, he positioned himself at the southeast corner window on the sixth floor and waited for the presidential motorcade. When it swung past the TSBD, he opened fire, expending a total of three shots. One bullet hit Kennedy in his posterior neck and exited the front of his throat and entered Governor Connally. Another shot missed the motorcade altogether. The Commission was never clear as to whether the missed shot was the first or the second shot. Neither did the report venture to indicate the location of the missed shot. A third and fatal shot struck Kennedy in the back of the head. All of the shooting took place in a span of six to eight seconds.

The report continues: After Oswald shot the president he left the TSBD and made his way back to his N. Beckley Avenue rooming house, arriving there at about 1:00 and leaving several minutes later after picking up a lightweight jacket. Roughly 15 minutes and one mile later, he was stopped by Dallas patrolman J. D. Tippit, apparently because he matched the description of the president's assailant broadcast over the police dispatcher's radio at 12:34. Some words were exchanged and, when Tippit left his patrol car and advanced toward Oswald, with his revolver still holstered, Oswald shot and killed him—at 1:16 P.M. according to the report, which cited five witnesses who testified that they saw Oswald shoot Tippit.

The broadcast description of the president's assailant was based on the claims of Howard L. Brennan, who had been located on Elm Street directly across from the TSBD and, upon looking up, saw a man at the southeast corner window pointing and then firing a rifle at the motorcade. Brennan's description to the police was a model of specificity: the shooter was a slender white man about 5 feet 10 inches in height, in his early thirties. Brennan even described the clothes the gunman was wearing, including his pants.

Shortly after the assassination the police discovered a Mannlicher-Carcano rifle hidden behind a barricade of cartons in the northwest corner of the TSBD's sixth floor. The FBI traced the rifle's purchase (by Oswald) to a sporting goods store in Chicago, while the Dallas police lifted a palm print off the rifle that allegedly belonged to Oswald. FBI ballistics analysis of a bullet, in virtually pristine condition and allegedly retrieved from Governor Connally's stretcher at Parkland Hospital, indicated that it matched Oswald's rifle. Clearly the case against Oswald looked airtight.

Nevertheless, the Warren Commission acknowledged that it could not provide a definitive explanation for why Oswald killed President Kennedy. Nothing in Oswald's personal papers indicated any festering animus toward Kennedy. To the contrary, all those who knew Oswald indicated that he had been favorably disposed toward Kennedy and admired the First Family. In its final report, however, the Commission concluded that Oswald was a "loner" at odds with the world around him, especially authority figures. That view was reinforced for the Commission through the testimony of Oswald's Russian wife, Marina, who provided the only evidence linking Oswald to the attempted murder of right-wing extremist Major General Edwin A. Walker, seven months prior to the Kennedy assassination. That failed attempt, the killing of Patrolman Tippit, and the murder of Kennedy all suggested to the Commission that Oswald's hatred of authority figures fueled the psychological motivation for his acts of violence.

Notes

Introduction

1. Daniel Patrick Moynihan. *Secrecy: The American Experience* (New Haven, Conn.: Yale University Press, 1998), 219–220. Moynihan was not espousing a conspiracy explanation for the assassination. But he did point out that as time passed, the polls revealed that an increasing number of people surveyed believed there was a conspiracy behind the murder of President Kennedy.

2. Edward Jay Epstein, *Inquest: The Warren Commission and the Establishment of Truth* (New York: Viking Press, 1966). For the commissioners' attendance record, see Epstein's chapter 6, "The Commission Hearings."

3. Richard Whalen, "The Kennedy Assassination," *Saturday Evening Post* (January 4, 1967), 20.

4. Warren Commission, April 30, 1964, executive session transcript, National Archives and Records Administration, College Park, Maryland (hereafter cited as NARA), 42.

5. Lyndon Johnson telephone conversation with Russell, 9/18/1964 (7:54 P.M.), White House Telephone Transcripts, Lyndon Baines Johnson Library, Austin, Texas. For Judge Griffin's testimony and opinion about the Commission's findings about Oswald's motive, see *Investigation of the Assassination of President John F. Kennedy: Hearings before the Select Committee on Assassination of the U.S. House of Representatives,* 95th Congress, 2d session, Vol. 5 (Washington, D.C.: U.S. Government Printing Office, 1979), 494.

6. Memo to file, Inspector James R. Malley, 11/24/1963, Main Dallas JFK Assassination File, 89-43-440. For Hoover's 11/26/1963 memo, see Appendix A, 1. Early Bureau Responses to the President's Assassination, A. November 22–23, 1964, no. 3.

7. For the Warren report's description of the shooting, see chapter 4 of *The Warren Commission Report: Report of the President's Commission on the Assassination of President John F. Kennedy* (Washington, D.C.: U.S. Government Printing Office, 1964) (hereafter cited as *WCR*), 11.

8. For Hoover's response to a news story in the *Washington Post,* November 21, 1966, titled "'Life' Urges Review of JFK Death," see Rosen to DeLoach, 11/22/1966, FBIHQ JFK Assassination File, 62-109060-4267. When the story was brought to Hoover's attention he wrote on the bottom of the memo, "We don't agree with the Commission as it says one shot missed entirely & we contend all three shots hit." As far as the public record is concerned the Secret Service never changed its adherence to the three-shots, three-hits shooting scenario. For the closing of the JFK case see Appendix A, 3. Bureau Relations with Warren Commission, C., Related Bureau Actions and Activities, no. 8.

9. The reasons for Commissioner John McCloy's carefully brokered language are discussed in Chapter 10. For the quotation, see *WCR*, 19.

10. *WCR*, 92–95 and 557.

11. For a summary of the Olivier-Dziemian Report, see *WCR*, 584–585. The report is

identified as CRDLR 3264 and titled "Wound Ballistics of 6.5mm Mannlicher-Carcano Ammunition (U), Edgewood Arsenal, Md." A copy of the report can be found by checking the JFK Collection under Record Group 272, Series 53, NARA.

12. CRDLR 3264, 35.

13. George MacCalin to James B. Rhodes, 9/14/1965, ONI Files, box 3, RG 526, folder JFK Documents, 173-10002-10101 to 10125, NARA.

14. For the results of NPIC's photo analysis of the Zapruder film, see E. H. Knoche, assistant counsel to the CIA director, to Robert Olsen, 5/14/1975, CIA Document Number 1641-450, released May 18, 1982. A copy can be found in the Harold Weisberg Archive, Hood College, Maryland. For more details on this, see Chapter 8. The NPIC's chief analyst of the Zapruder film, Dino A. Brugioni, recalled that the center received the 8-mm film from two Secret Service agents several days after the assassination. CIA Director (DCI) McCone requested that the center do a special job on the film. The NPIC made two large briefing boards of the Zapruder film with notes for McCone. The DCI kept one set of the photo analysis and returned one to the center. The film was returned to the Secret Service. Author interview with Brugioni, May 2, 2003.

15. See Chapter 7.

Chapter 1. Assembling the "Official Truth" of Dallas

1. For the Kennedy and Connally quotes, see Christopher Matthews's piece in the *San Francisco Examiner,* December 6, 1998, A4.

2. D. J. Brennan to W. C. Sullivan, 12/2/1963, FBIHQ JFK Assassination File, 62-109060-1336; Brennan to Sullivan, 12/1/1963, FBIHQ JFK Assassination File, 62-109060-Not Recorded (NR).

3. Accounts by Secret Service agents can be found in the Warren Commission, Commission Record Group 7, National Archives, Washington, D.C. The security problems confronting the Secret Service for JFK's Texas trip are discussed at length in Chapter 10.

4. In the FBI's lexicon "Seat of Government" stood for FBI headquarters in the nation's capital. "SOG" was the frequently used acronym.

5. C. D. DeLoach to Mohr, 6/4/1964, FBIHQ JFK Assassination File, 62-109060-NR; Cartha "Deke" DeLoach, *Hoover's FBI: The Inside Story by Hoover's Trusted Lieutenant* (Washington, D.C.: Regnery Publishing, 1995), 115.

6. Richard Gid Powers, *Secrecy and Power: The Life of J. Edgar Hoover* (New York: Free Press, 1987), 383; Hoover memo, 11/22/1963, FBIHQ JFK Assassination File, 62-109060-59.

7. DeLoach, *Hoover's FBI,* 115.

8. For this testament to Hoover's confusion and run of erroneous information, see FBIHQ JFK Assassination File, 62-109060, serials 56, 57, 58, and 59.

9. Hoover memo, 5:15 P.M. (EST), 11/22/1963, FBIHQ JFK Assassination File, 62-109060-57.

10. DeLoach, *Hoover's FBI,* 135. For a sampling of some of the wild stories originating from the FBI's Dallas field office, see Shanklin to file, 11/22/1963, Main Dallas JFK Assassination File, 89-43-1. See San Antonio, Texas, to Dallas, 11/22/1963, 3:15 P.M. (EST), FBIHQ Oswald File, 105-82555-NR; SAC, San Antonio, to Director, FBI, and SAC, Dallas, 11/22/1963, FBIHQ JFK Assassination File, 62-109060-811.

11. Hoover memo, 5:15 P.M. (EST), 11/22/1963, FBIHQ JFK Assassination File, 62-109060-57; DeLoach, *Hoover's FBI,* 136; Manning C. Clements to SAC (special agent in charge), Dallas, 11/22/1963, Main Dallas JFK Assassination File, 89-43-804; Branigan to Sullivan, 11/22/1963, FBIHQ JFK Assassination File, 62-109060-NR. During Oswald's first

interrogation while in custody at the Dallas Police Department he expatiated at length and without inhibition about his anti-Soviet "Marxist" philosophy and politics. It can safely be assumed that any fine distinctions Oswald made, if in fact he was even clear in his own mind, between a Marxist point of view and Soviet communism would have been lost on Hoover. See *The Warren Commission Report: Report of the President's Commission on the Assassination of President John F. Kennedy* (Washington, D.C.: U.S. Government Printing Office, 1964), 599ff, for a transcript of Oswald's remarks (hereafter cited as *WCR*).

12. For the Richardson, Texas, memo, see I. C. Renfro to SAC, Dallas, 11/22/1963, Main Dallas JFK Assassination File, 89-43-84; Heitman report, FBIHQ Marina Oswald File, 105-126032-NR. See FBIHQ Oswald File, 105-82555-505, Section 23, for the time at which Oswald was charged with JFK's murder. For a balanced treatment of Hoover's heavy-handed, authoritarian management tactics, see William W. Keller, *The Liberals and J. Edgar Hoover: The Rise and Fall of a Domestic Intelligence State* (Princeton, N.J.: Princeton University Press), 24–27. Keller makes the forceful argument that hierarchy rather than functional status and trust in subordinates was Hoover's administrative style. Many students of the Hoover FBI agree that Hoover's authoritarian personality was the unchecked force that dominated the nation's preeminent law enforcement agency. For FBI Washington's directive to the New Orleans office, see SAC to file, 11/23/1963, Main New Orleans Oswald File, 89-69-29 and 89-69-54.

13. There are literally hundreds of these letters and telegrams in the FBI files. For a sampling, see serials 1–45 of FBIHQ JFK Assassination File, 62-109060. Understandably, Hoover, worried about the FBI's greatest asset—its public image—made it a point that his office responded to all of these communications. Most of the responses were boilerplate, form letters explaining that the FBI was on the case and that protecting the president was not the bureau's responsibility. But more than a few letters were personalized and tried to assuage the specific expressed concerns of the sender, indicating that Hoover took this outpouring of public feelings seriously.

14. DeLoach to Mohr, 12/2/1963, FBIHQ JFK Assassination File, 62-109060-NR; Drew Pearson, "FBI, Secret Service Need Study," *Washington Post,* December 2, 1963, B27. For the best treatment of Hoover as derring-do G-man and cultural icon, see Richard Gid Powers, *G-Men: Hoover's FBI in American Popular Culture* (Carbondale: Southern Illinois Press, 1983).

15. Belmont to Tolson, 11/22/1963, FBIHQ Oswald File, 105-82555-77; Branigan to Sullivan, 11/22/1963, FBIHQ Oswald File, 105-82555–section 1 (serial obliterated); Brennan to Sullivan, 11/25/1963, FBIHQ JFK Assassination File, 62-109060-NR (section 3). For more on the Gale investigation and the FBI's monumental blunders and cover-up in the JFK assassination, see Chapter 10.

16. Shanklin to file, 11/22/1963, Main Dallas JFK Assassination File, 89-43-1. Rosen to Belmont, 11/22/1963, FBIHQ JFK Assassination File, 620-109060448. See DeLoach to Mohr, 6/4/1964, FBIHQ Liaison with Commission File, 62-109090-NR, for the record of Manchester's interview with Hoover. One of the consequences of the Kennedy assassination was the enactment of Public Law 89-141 (August 28, 1965), making it a federal crime to kill a president. See John C. Kennedy, Acting Assistant Attorney General, to James H. Hutchinson III, 7/3/1975, Justice Department, Criminal Division, 129-11.

17. See Warren Commission Document 7, National Archives, Washington, D.C. (hereafter cited as CD with number), for the numerous reports of threats to President Kennedy.

18. See To All Agents (105-406), SAC, Little Rock, 12/12/1963, Little Rock, Arkansas Field Office Main JFK Assassination File, 105-406-39. It was FBI practice to circulate instructions from headquarters to all FBI field offices by using Little Rock as the designated office.

See also Appendix A, 1. Early Bureau Responses to the President's Assassination, C. Jack Ruby, for Hoover's suspicions of basement entry and assistance. For Ruby as an FBI PCI, see Hoover to Rankin, 2/27/1964, FBI Liaison with Commission File, 62-109090-NR, or Rosen to Belmont, 4/6/1964, FBI Liaison with Commission File, 62-109090-NR.

19. *Investigation of the Assassination of President John F. Kennedy: Hearings before the President's Commission on the Assassination of President Kennedy* (Washington, D.C.: U.S. Government Printing Office, 1964) (hereafter cited as *Hearings before Commission*), Vol. 5, 98–99. Hoover told the Commission that it was not until LBJ returned to Washington that he instructed "the Bureau to pick up the investigation of the assassination."

20. Secret Service report, 11/23/1963, serial number co-2-34030, Secret Service Records, File 24, Lyndon B. Johnson Library, Austin, Texas (hereafter cited as LBJ Library).

21. SAC, New Orleans, to SAC, Dallas, and Director, 12/3/1963, FBIHQ JFK Assassination File, 62-109060-1447; FBI FD-302 interviews for 12/3 and 12/4/1963, FBIHQ Oswald File, 105-82225, Section 15, 393, 395; SAC (New Orleans) to file, 12/6/1963, Main New Orleans Oswald File, 100-16601-119. SA Rice noted in his report that Robert I. Bouck, head of the Secret Service's Protective Research Section, ordered him to drop his investigation into the printing of the Fair Play for Cuba pamphlets. Bouck stated that FBI Washington regarded Rice's efforts as a "duplication of efforts." See John W. Rice report, New Orleans, 12/9/1963, Document 517, file no. co-2-34,030, 3, LBJ Library. For the FBI's leaking of its report, see Chapter 2.

22. Milton D. Newsom to SAC, Dallas, 11/25/1963, Main Dallas Assassination File, 89-43-518; Newsom to SAC, Dallas, 11/25/1963, Main Dallas JFK Assassination File, 89-43-493; Richard B. Trask, *Pictures of the Pain: Photography and the Assassination of President John F. Kennedy* (Danvers, Mass.: Yeoman Press, 1994), 280–281. It was FBI practice to keep unwanted potential photographic evidence about the assassination that could contradict the official version of the crime from being forwarded to the FBIHQ. For instance, when Dallas agent Ivan D. Lee took pictures of the crime scene showing locations from which a shot might have been fired, or, in this case, where a bullet was later reported at "the railroad area," HQ's photographic expert, Lyndal L. Shaneyfelt, told Lee he did "not want those photos in the Bureau." Lee advised he "will file them in Dallas office." See Shanklin to file (100-10461), 6/2/1964, Main Dallas Oswald File, 100-10461-6464.

23. A listing of the films showing the shooting of Kennedy and Oswald sent by the FBI to the Warren Commission does not include the Bronson film or his slides. See N. P. Callahan to Mohr, 12/17/1963, FBIHQ JFK Assassination File, 62-109060-NR (section 28). See also David R. Wrone, *The Zapruder Film: Reframing JFK's Assassination* (Lawrence: University Press of Kansas, 2003), 151–154.

24. The most useful and detailed news stories about the Bronson film can be found in the *Dallas Morning News,* November 26, 1978; *New York Times,* November 27, 1978; *Dallas Times Herald,* November 27, 1978; *Washington Post,* November 27, 1978; and Harold Weisberg, *Never Again!* (New York: Carroll and Graf, 1995), 29–30. See also Trask, *Pictures of the Pain.* Trask's work is an indispensable history of the Bronson film and explores how the FBI and Warren Commission consciously misrepresented the photographic record of the assassination revealed in the Robert J. E. Hughes film when circumstances forced them to deal with Hughes's pictures of the "sniper's perch." Trask was the most prominent historian of the Bronson film and slides, and his final words on the failure of the government to avail itself of current computer digital image-enhancing techniques to determine once and for all whether there were one or two individuals stationed at the so-called sniper's nest deserve reporting. "One of the most unsettling aspects of this Bronson film matter is the failure of the government to do what citizens have been forced to attempt themselves. To understand that with a

potentially important piece of evidence available, people within our government did not think it worth the effort or the expense to attempt by all legal means possible to examine that evidence, is abhorrent" (301–302). The FBI even suppressed the Bronson film from the Secret Service. When J. Gordon Shanklin, the agent in charge of the FBI's Dallas field office, turned over to his Secret Service counterpart, Forrest V. Sorrels, the list of names of those who had taken pictures of the motorcade, Bronson's name was not on the list. See Shanklin to Sorrels, 12/19/1963, Main Dallas Oswald File, 100-1046-1502.

25. For a detailed accounting of the FBI's suppression of films taken in Dallas on the day of the assassination, see Harold Weisberg, *Photographic Whitewash—Suppressed Kennedy Assassination Pictures* (Frederick, Md.: Harold Weisberg Publisher, 1967); and Sylvia Meagher, *Accessories after the Fact: The Warren Commission, the Authorities, and the Report* (New York: Vintage Books, 1992), 22, n13. In 1975 an FBI agent who was assigned to the Dallas office in 1963, Robert M. Barrett, was questioned by Paul Wallach, a staff lawyer with the Senate Select Committee on Intelligence Activities. Wallach, after a routine line of questioning about Barrett's duties in Dallas, suddenly shifted his questioning to the situation in the office immediately after the Kennedy assassination. At this point Wallach asked if Shanklin or some other FBI official "had given explicit directions that the investigation was to establish that Oswald acted alone in connection with the assassination." Before Barrett could answer, Wallach shot back at him "that such information had been received from other FBI agents." Wallach, of course, never mentioned these agents' names and Barrett denied that anything like that had ever occurred. Whether Wallach was on a fishing expedition or had solid reasons for confronting Barrett with this line of questioning was left unresolved. See FBI Letterhead Memorandum, 12/24/1975, released to the House Select Committee on Assassinations, item 81.

26. For some idea of Johnson's hectic assassination weekend schedule, see Secret Service Phone Logs for November 23–November 24, 1963, Collection: White House Telephone Transcripts, LBJ Library.

27. Michael Beschloss (ed.), *Taking Charge: The Johnson White House Tapes, 1963–1964* (New York: Simon and Schuster, 1997), 22.

28. Secret Service Phone Logs for November 24, 1963, LBJ Library; Hoover memo, 11/24/1963, FBIHQ JFK Assassination File, 62-109060-1490. For Malley's record of this Hoover-LBJ telephone conversation, see Malley to file (44-1639), 11/24/1963, Main Dallas JFK Assassination File, 89-43-440.

29. For the initial results of the paraffin tests on Oswald, see Kyle G. Clark to SAC, Dallas, 11/23/1963, Main Dallas JFK Assassination File, 89-43-89-430(? Serial number somewhat obscured). For more on the FBI's handling of the paraffin test results, see Chapter 10. J. L. Handley to Rosen, 4/27/1963, FBIHQ JFK Assassination File, 62-109060-6. See Hoover memo for 11/24/1963, FBIHQ JFK Assassination File, 62-109060-1490, or see Appendix A, 1. Early Bureau Responses to the President's Assassination, A. November 22–23, 1964, no. 3, for Hoover's haste to "wrap up" the investigation. Alex Rosen, assistant director of the FBI's General Investigative Division, would later note that the bureau's "basic investigation was substantially completed by November 26, 1963." See Rosen to DeLoach, 11/12/1966, FBIHQ JFK Assassination File, 62-109060-NR.

30. Inspector James R. Malley to file, 11/24/1963, Main Dallas JFK Assassination File, 89-43-440; Handley to Rosen, 11/27/1963, FBIHQ JFK Assassination File, 62-109060-6; DeLoach, *Hoover's FBI,* 127–128; A. H. Belmont to Sullivan, 11/26/1963, FBIHQ JFK Assassination File, 62-109060-NR.

31. For Katzenbach's comments, see *Investigation of the Assassination of President John F. Kennedy: Hearings before the Select Committee on Assassinations of the U.S. House of*

Representatives, 95th Congress, 2d session (Washington, D.C.: U.S. Government Printing Office, 1979), Vol. 3, 644–645.

32. Telephone call from Dean Rostow to William Moyers, 11/24/1963, White House Telephone Transcripts, LBJ Library; Jeff Shesol, *Mutual Contempt: Lyndon Johnson, Robert Kennedy, and the Feud That Defined a Decade* (New York: W. W. Norton, 1997), 149. For a review of the letters received by the Justice Department, see Foley to Miller, 12/5/1963, Justice Department, Criminal Division, 129-11. For a sampling of foreign reporting on the assassination, see Justice Department, Internal Security Division, 146-1-73 File.

33. For samples of the foreign press reportage on the JFK assassination, see Memorandum to William Moyers, 11/25/1963, National Security File, Intelligence File, box 17, Lee Harvey Oswald File, National Archives and Records Administration, College Park, Maryland.

34. C. A. Evans to Belmont, 11/25/1963, FBIHQ JFK Assassination File, 62-109060-1399. Katzenbach wrote his memo in longhand on Sunday, November 24, when he had no secretarial help. A copy of the memo can be found in FBIHQ JFK Assassination File, 62-109060-NR, as part of serial 1399. The Justice Department copy of the memo was withheld from the file for eighteen months. It did not reach the Records Branch until May 21, 1965. See Memorandum to Moyers, November 25, 1963, Justice Department, Criminal Division, 129-11, Records Branch. For the holographic copy written on Sunday night (after Oswald's assassination), see Justice Department, Criminal Division, file 129-11, section 1A, for the five-page summary. Hoover's copy of the Katzenbach memo reached FBIHQ on November 25, 1963. See Evans to Belmont, 11/25/1963, FBIHQ JFK Assassination File, 62-109060-1399.

35. Secret Service Phone Logs, 11/24/1963, LBJ Library; Hoover memo, 11/25/1963, FBIHQ JFK Assassination File, 62-109060-63. On LBJ's meeting with Carr, see LBJ to Joseph Alsop, 11/25/1963 (10:40 A.M.), White House Telephone Transcripts, LBJ Library.

36. Evans to Belmont, 11/24/1963, FBIHQ JFK Assassination File, 62-109060-1490; Hoover memo, 11/25/1963, FBIHQ JFK Assassination File, 62-109060-61; Evans to Belmont, 11/26/1963, FBIHQ JFK Assassination File, 62-109060-1491; Belmont to Tolson, 11/27/1963, FBIHQ Oswald File, 105-82555-NR (section 3).

37. Evans to Belmont, 11/26/1963, FBIHQ Oswald File, 105-82555-NR; Belmont to Evans, 11/24/1963, FBIHQ Oswald File, 105-82555-95. For Katzenbach's importuning, see DeLoach to Mohr, 11/25/1963, FBIHQ JFK Assassination File, 62-109060-176; Evans to Belmont, 11/26/1963, FBIHQ Oswald File, 105-82555-NR; Evans to Belmont, 11/27/1963, FBIHQ JFK Assassination File, 62-109060-1669; Evans to Belmont, 12/2/1963, FBIHQ JFK Assassination File, 62-109060-1715. For the Criminal Division's outline, see Herbert J. Miller, assistant attorney general, to Katzenbach, deputy attorney general, 11/27/1963, Justice Department, Criminal Division, 129-11. For the FBI's leaking of the report's conclusions, see Chapter 2.

38. For Hoover's briefing of LBJ about an Oswald imposter, see Hoover to the president, 11/23/1963, FBIHQ JFK Assassination File, 62-109060-433.

39. Hoover to Legat Mexico, 11/25/1963, FBIHQ Oswald File, 105-82555-NR (section 1); Hoover memo, 11/26/1963, FBIHQ JFK Assassination File, 62-109060-189 for the McCone briefing; Sullivan to Belmont, 11/27/1963, FBIHQ JFK Assassination File, 62-109060-455; and Hoover memorandum, 11/27/1963, FBIHQ JFK Assassination File, 62-109060-216. Larry Keenan wrote the author that by the time he departed for Mexico City everyone at SOG involved in the JFK probe realized that Hoover "had set everything in concrete within a couple hours" after the assassination. Keenan's May 19, 2003, letter to the author. For the alleged Mexico City Red plot, see Chapter 3.

40. LBJ phone conversation with Joseph Alsop, 11/25/1963 (10:40 A.M.), White House Telephone Transcripts, LBJ Library. For Reston's think piece, see *New York Times,* Novem-

ber 25, 1963; Hoover memo, 11/25/1963 (10:25 A.M.), FBIHQ JFK Assassination File, 62-109060-63.

41. LBJ phone conversation with Hoover, 11/25/1963 (10:25 A.M.), White House Telephone Transcripts, LBJ Library; Hoover memo, 11/25/1963 (10:25 A.M.), FBIHQ JFK Assassination File, 62-109060-63.

42. Kenneth O'Reilly, *"Racial Matters": The FBI's Secret File on Black America, 1960–1972* (New York: Free Press, 1989), 198–199; DeLoach to Mohr, 11/25/1963, FBIHQ JFK Assassination File, 62-109060-NR; Hoover memo, 11/25/1963 (11:30 A.M.), FBIHQ JFK Assassination File, 62-109060-61; DeLoach to Mohr, 11/25/1963, FBIHQ JFK Assassination File, 62-109060-NR. The following day there was a *Post* editorial titled "A Full Inquiry." It called for an investigation to assure "the most objective, the most thorough and most speedy analysis and canvass of every scrap of relevant information." The editorial supported Johnson's announcement of a Department of Justice inquiry as the instrument to assure "that all of the facts are made public." See the *Washington Post,* November 26, 1963, A18.

43. Belmont to Tolson, 11/27/1963, FBIHQ JFK Assassination File, 62-109060-1492; for Hoover's marginalia, see Evans to Belmont, 11/27/1963, FBIHQ JFK Assassination File, 62-109060-1670; Evans to Belmont, 11/27/1963, FBIHQ JFK Assassination File, 62-109060-1673; for Katzenbach's appraisal of the FBI report, see Belmont 12/6/1963 addendum; Evans to Belmont, 12/5/1963, FBIHQ JFK Assassination File, 62-109060-1673, 3.

44. Katzenbach underscored these two points in his cover letter with the FBI report to Chief Justice Earl Warren, whom LBJ appointed to chair the presidential commission investigating the Kennedy assassination. See Katzenbach to Warren, 12/9/1963, FBIHQ JFK Assassination File, 62-109060-15, for the FBI copy of the Katzenbach letter.

45. See "Investigation of Assassination of President John F. Kennedy, November 22, 1963," Federal Bureau of Investigation, United States Department of Justice, J. Edgar Hoover, Director. (This is the first Warren Commission document and is referred to as CD 1.) For more on the Tague bullet, see Chapter 9.

46. Rosen to Belmont, 11/29/1963, FBIHQ JFK Assassination File, 62-109060-426; Thomas J. Kelley Memorandum to file, 10/3/1966, Secret Service Report, file 24, LBJ Library. The FBI received a copy of the JFK autopsy report from the Secret Service on December 23, 1963, some eighteen days *after* it turned its report (CD 1) on the assassination over to the Warren Commission. For the December 23 date, see Rosen to DeLoach, 11/15/1966, FBIHQ JFK Assassination File, 62-109060-NR, 4.

47. Hoover memo to Tolson et al., 11/29/1963, FBIHQ JFK Assassination File, 62-109060-NR.

48. See Appendix A, 3. Bureau Relations with Warren Commission, C. Related Bureau Actions and Activities, no. 2. For discussion of the leaking and its impact on the commissioners, see Chapter 2.

Chapter 2. Creating the Warren Commission

1. Joe Alsop to LBJ, 11/25/1963 (10:40 A.M.), White House Telephone Transcripts, Lyndon B. Johnson Library, Austin, Texas (hereafter cited as LBJ Library); Hale Boggs to LBJ, 11/29/1963 (11:35 A.M.), White House Telephone Transcripts, LBJ Library; Edward Kennedy to LBJ, 11/23/1963 (7:40 P.M.), White House Telephone Transcripts, LBJ Library; and Whitney Young to LBJ, 11/24/1963 (5:55 P.M.), White House Telephone Transcripts, LBJ Library.

2. The account of the formation of the Warren Commission found in the House Select Committee on Assassinations records is incomplete and inaccurate. See *Investigation of the Assassination of President John F. Kennedy: Hearings before the Select Committee on Assas-*

sinations of the U.S. House of Representatives, 95th Congress, 2d session (Washington, D.C.: U.S. Government Printing Office, 1979) (hereafter cited as *HSCA*), Vol. 11, 3–9. The 1993 release of the White House Telephone Transcripts makes a more accurate account possible. A source that has used them to good advantage is Donald E. Gibson, "The Creation of the Warren Commission," *Mid-America: An Historical Review* 79, no. 3 (Fall 1997): 203–254.

3. Dean Eugene D. Rostow to Bill Moyers, 11/24/1963, White House Telephone Transcripts, LBJ Library; Joe Alsop to LBJ, 11/25/1963 (10:40 A.M.), White House Telephone Transcripts, LBJ Library. For the Rostow-Katzenbach connection, see Nelson Lichtenstein (ed.), *Political Profiles: The Johnson Years* (New York: Facts on File, 1963), 319–320.

4. Katzenbach to Moyers, 11/25/1963, Justice Department, Criminal Division, File 129-11, section A. For Jenkins-Hoover 11/24/1963 phone conversation, see *HSCA*, Vol. 3, 471–472. For the two-hour meeting in Hoover's office on Saturday, November 23, see Director, FBI, to the Attorney General, 10/1/1975, FBIHQ JFK Assassination File, 62-109060-7302X, 20. For more on Gale's investigation, see Chapter 10.

5. For Alsop's influence with LBJ, see Carol Felsenthal, *Power, Privilege, and the Post: The Katharine Graham Story* (New York: G. P. Putnam's Sons, 1993), 175, 184; Alsop to LBJ, 11/25/1963 (10:40 A.M.), White House Telephone Transcripts, LBJ Library; Gibson, "The Creation of the Warren Commission," 238.

6. LBJ to Senator Eastland, 11/28/1963 (3:21 P.M.) and LBJ to Speaker McCormick, 11/29/1963 (4:55 P.M.), White House Telephone Transcripts, LBJ Library. See Chapter 3 for the "Mexico City Plot."

7. Evans to Belmont, 11/29/1963, FBIHQ Liaison with Commission File, 62-109090-2; FBI memo, 11/29/1963, FBIHQ Liaison with Commission File, 62-109090-1; Clyde Tolson to Director, 11/27/1963, FBIHQ Oswald File, 105-82555-2894. The FBI report (CD 1) was never published, as one might conventionally assume, but remained only in manuscript form. Moreover, CD 1 was not part of the Warren report and was not included in any of the Commission's volumes of exhibits.

8. Hoover memo on his conversation with Rankin, 12/12/1963, FBIHQ JFK Assassination File, 62-109060-14.

9. LBJ to Hoover, 11/29/1963 (1:40 P.M.), White House Telephone Transcripts, LBJ Library. On the Johnson-DeLoach relationship, see Arthur M. Schlesinger, Jr., *Robert Kennedy and His Times* (New York: Ballantine Books, 1978), 678; and Curt Gentry, *J. Edgar Hoover: The Man and the Secrets* (New York: W. W. Norton, 1991), 582–583. For an insight into the extensive social relations between LBJ and Deke DeLoach, see Cartha D. DeLoach in White House Central File (WHCF), box D117, LBJ Library.

10. LBJ to Alsop, 11/29/1963 (7:00 P.M.), White House Telephone Transcripts, LBJ Library.

11. That was the core of Alsop's argument in his Monday-morning phone conversation when he urged LBJ to appoint a body of eminent public figures to summarize the FBI's findings and report them to the American people. "What I'm really honestly giving you," Alsop clarified for the president, "is public relations advice and not legal advice." See Alsop to LBJ, 11/25/1963 (10:40 A.M.), White House Telephone Transcripts, LBJ Library.

12. Hoover to LBJ, 11/29/1963 (1:40 P.M.), White House Telephone Transcripts, LBJ Library. McCloy had shown commendable aptitude as an investigator in the 1916 Black Tom Island wartime sabotage case, but that was almost thirty years before his selection to the Warren Commission. See Kai Bird, *The Chairman: John J. McCloy and the Making of the American Establishment* (New York: Simon and Schuster, 1992), 78–95.

13. For Johnson's maneuvering of Senator Russell and Chief Justice Warren, see LBJ to Russell, 11/29/1963 (4:05 P.M.), White House Telephone Transcripts, LBJ Library; Alfred

Goldberg (the Warren Commission's historian) interview with Chief Justice Earl Warren, March 26, 1974, Manuscript Division, Library of Congress, Washington, D.C., 1–2; *Washington Post,* September 23, 1993, A6; DeLoach to Mohr, 12/17/1963, FBIHQ Liaison with Commission File, 62-109090-37; Warren Commission, January 21, 1964, executive session transcript, NARA, 12–13. For more on LBJ's use of the Red plot in forming the Commission, see Chapter 3.

14. Evans to Belmont, 12/5/1963, FBIHQ Liaison with Commission File, 62-109090-Not Recorded (NR); LBJ to Hoover, 11/25/1963 (10:30 A.M.), White House Telephone Transcripts, LBJ Library; Alsop to LBJ, 11/25/1963 (10:40 A.M.), White House Telephone Transcripts, LBJ Library; Waggoner Carr with Byran D. Varner, *Texas Politics in My Rearview Mirror* (Plano, Tex.: Wordware Publishing, 1993), 89–91; DeLoach to Mohr, 11/25/1963, FBIHQ JFK Assassination File, 62-109060-55; Evans to Belmont, 11/27/1963, FBIHQ JFK Assassination File, 62-109060-1669.

15. Carr, *Texas Politics in My Rearview Mirror,* 94.

16. See Carr's statement in the *Washington Post,* December 7, 1963. See Warren's statement on the Texas Court of Inquiry in the Warren Commission, December 6, 1963, executive session transcript, 7, and for December 12, 1963, National Archives and Records Administration, College Park, Maryland (hereafter cited as NARA), 13–18; Evans to Belmont, 12/5/1963, FBIHQ Liaison with Commission File, 62-109090-NR, addendum 3.

17. DeLoach to Mohr, 12/6/1963, FBIHQ Liaison with Commission File, 62-109090-6; DeLoach to Mohr, 12/6/1963, FBIHQ JFK Assassination File, 62-109060-1993 for attached Justice Department statement; DeLoach to Mohr, 12/6/1963, FBIHQ Liaison with Commission File, 62-109090-NR.

18. All the source citations for the Texas Court of Inquiry came from the Sylvia Meagher Collection at Hood College, Frederick, Maryland (hereafter cited as Meagher Collection). Meagher was one of the few early responsible critics of *The Warren Commission Report.* Her pioneering work in this area included an early but insightful piece on the Texas Court of Inquiry, "Wheels Within Deals: How the Kennedy 'Investigation' Was Organized," *The Minority of One,* July–August 1968, 23–27. For Carr's rebuttal to "eastern writers" who branded Texas a state of "political extremism," see "Remarks of Attorney General Waggoner Carr before the Rotary Club of Tyler," January 23, 1964, in "Notes of General Carr on Court of Inquiry," Meagher Collection; Waggoner Carr correspondence can also be found in the Texas Court of Inquiry File, National Archives, Washington, D.C.

19. Carr to Chief Justice Warren, 12/5/1963, Meagher Collection.

20. Carr to Warren, 2/3/1964, Meagher Collection.

21. Carr to Rankin, 2/4/1964; Carr to Rankin, 3/20/1964, Meagher Collection.

22. Carr to Rankin, 8/14/1964; Carr to Rankin, 8/7/1964; Rankin to Carr, 8/25/1964, Meagher Collection.

23. See "Texas Supplemental Report on the Assassination of President John F. Kennedy and the Serious Wounding of Governor John B. Connally, November 22, 1963," 10, 17–18. A copy of Waggoner's summary report can be found in FBIHQ JFK Assassination File, 62-109060-3831. See also *The Warren Commission Report: Report of the President's Commission on the Assassination of President John F. Kennedy* (Washington, D.C.: U.S. Government Printing Office, 1964) (hereafter cited as *WCR*), 41, 196, 231, and 458. The Texas Court of Inquiry also published twenty-one volumes of documents (some 5,600 pages), many but not all of them repetitive of the Warren Commission's twenty-six volumes.

24. "Notes of Attorney General Waggoner Carr Concerning the Investigation Conducted in Dallas, Texas, on May 9, 1964, of the Texas School Book Depository Building and Surroundings," Meagher Collection.

25. Goldberg interview with Chief Justice Earl Warren, March 26, 1974, 1–2; Telford Taylor, *The Anatomy of the Nuremberg Trials* (Boston: Little, Brown, and Company, 1992), 419–421; Chief Justice Earl Warren, *The Memoirs of Earl Warren* (New York: Doubleday, 1977), 355–358; *Washington Post,* September 23, 1993, A6.

26. Edward Cray, *Chief Justice: A Biography of Earl Warren* (New York: Simon and Schuster, 1997), 72.

27. Quoted in ibid., 418.

28. "What Crime Wave?" *Fortune* magazine, January 1955; L. Nichols to Tolson, 2/24/1955, FBIHQ Warren Olney File, 63-317-10; Olney to Director, FBI, 5/3/1957, FBIHQ Warren Olney File, 63-317-NR. The FBI file on Olney is highly seasoned with Hoover invectives and loathing for the man.

29. Cray, *Chief Justice,* 418; FBIHQ Olney File, 63-317-10.

30. Belmont to Tolson, 12/3/1963, FBIHQ Liaison with Commission File, 62-109090-8; Evans to Belmont, 12/5/1963, FBIHQ Liaison with Commission File, 62-109090-7; DeLoach to Mohr, 2/7/1964, FBIHQ Liaison with Commission File, 62-109090-480.

31. LBJ to Hoover, 11/29/1963 (1:40 P.M.), White House Telephone Transcripts, LBJ Library; Gentry, *J. Edgar Hoover,* 384, for Ford asking for a pay raise for Hoover; Frank J. Donner, *The Age of Surveillance: The Aims and Methods of America's Political Intelligence System* (New York: Alfred A. Knopf, 1980), 254–258; DeLoach to Mohr, 12/12/1963, FBIHQ Liaison with Commission File, 62-109090-37.

32. DeLoach to Mohr, 12/17/1963, FBIHQ Liaison with Commission File, 62-109090-37; Hoover to My Dear Congressman (Ford), 4/17/1964, FBIHQ Liaison with Commission File, 62-109090-NR.

33. For Ford's testimony before the House Select Committee, see *HSCA,* Vol. 3, 9/28/1978, 561–599. For some of the press stories generated by the released FBI documents, see George Lardner, "Documents Show Ford Promised FBI Data—Secretly—about Warren Probe," *Washington Post,* January 20, 1978, A10; Jeremiah O'Leary, "Ford Reported to FBI on Warren Panel," *Washington Star,* December 8, 1978, 1–6; Mike Feinsilber, "Files Reveal Ford as FBI Conduit on Panel Probe," *Sacramento Bee,* January 19, 1978, AA2; *New York Times,* "Files Show Rift with Warren Panel," January 19, 1978; and UPI wire service for January 18, 1978.

34. Rosen to Belmont, 7/3/1964, FBIHQ Liaison with Commission File, 62-109090-185. This monumental lapse on the FBI's part is discussed in Chapter 10.

35. Warren Commission, December 5, 1963, executive session transcript, NARA, 69–82, 90–91. For Warren and Russell's strained relationship, see Goldberg interview with Chief Justice Warren, March 26, 1974, 7.

36. Goldberg interview with Chief Justice Warren, March 26, 1974, 9; Cray, *Chief Justice,* 376–377, 418.

37. DeLoach to Mohr, 12/12/1963, FBIHQ Liaison with Commission File, 62-109090-36; Hoover memo, 6/22/1964, FBIHQ Liaison with Commission File, 62-109090-36, in which Hoover piously denied to his old friend Assistant Circuit Judge Edward A. Tamm that he had anything to do with the sabotaging of Olney's appointment as general counsel.

38. Director to Herbert J. Miller, Sr., Assistant Attorney General, 12/6/1963, FBIHQ Liaison with Commission File, 62-109090-5. A biographical sketch of Rankin can be found in the J. Lee Rankin Papers, box 4, folder 20, NARA. This impression about Rankin derives from examining the Rankin Papers. There is virtually nothing in those forty thousand pages that provides any insight into Rankin as a person.

39. Mike Ewing interview with Samuel A. Stern, *HSCA,* Kennedy Collection (RG 233), NARA.

40. Gerald R. Ford and Frederick E. Stiles, *Portrait of the Assassin* (New York: Ballantine Books, 1965), 15.

41. Les Whitten, "Report to LBJ Calls Oswald the Assassin," *New York Journal-American,* November 27, 1963; Jerry O'Leary, "Piece of Oswald's Shirt Found 'Snagged in Rifle,'" *Evening Star* (Washington), December 5, 1963; Sterling Green, "Oswald Alone Shot Kennedy," *Evening Star,* December 3, 1963; and Jim Lucas, "Soviet File Is No Help," *Washington Daily News,* December 5, 1963.

42. LBJ to Russell, 11/29/1963 (4:05 P.M.), White House Telephone Transcripts, LBJ Library; Warren Commission, December 5, 1963, executive session transcript, NARA, 8.

43. Warren Commission, December 5, 1963, executive session transcript, NARA, 8–9. For more on the Commission members' expressed feelings that the FBI leaks had boxed them in, see Warren Commission, January 22, 1964, executive session transcript, NARA, 11–13. For solid proof that Hoover ordered the leaking of CD 1, see Appendix A, 3. Bureau Relations with Warren Commission, C. Related Bureau Actions and Activities, no. 2.

44. Evans to Belmont, 12/2/1963, FBIHQ JFK Assassination File, 62-109060-1715; DeLoach to Mohr, 12/7/1963, FBIHQ JFK Assassination File, 62-109060-762. For the proposed Katzenbach press release, see attachment to DeLoach to Mohr, 12/7/1963, FBIHQ JFK Assassination File, 62-109060-762.

45. Evans to Belmont, 12/5/1963, FBIHQ JFK Assassination File, 62-109060-7; DeLoach to Mohr, 12/9/1963, FBIHQ Liaison with Commission File, 62-109090-16; DeLoach to Mohr, 12/17/1963, FBIHQ Liaison with Commission File, 62-109090-37.

46. DeLoach to Mohr, 12/17/1963, FBIHQ Liaison with Commission File, 62-109090-37. Hoover's paranoia about Warren was so hair-triggered that he accused the chief justice of leaking Rankin's appointment to Les Whitten of the *New York Journal-American.* The wily director may have been establishing a charade of distance, writing for the record. But his suspicions were so deeply ingrained that he could have believed that Warren was feeding stories to the press. See Hoover's note, "Looks like Warren is still 'leaking,'" FBIHQ Liaison with Commission File, 12/23/1963, 62-109090-48. For Hoover on Katzenbach, see DeLoach to Mohr, 12/20/1963, FBIHQ Liaison with Commission File, 62-109090-38.

47. Belmont to Tolson, 12/6/1963, FBIHQ JFK Assassination File, 62-109060-1623. For Walker's record of extremist political activity, see his obituary in *New York Times,* November 2, 1993.

48. *Investigation of the Assassination of John F. Kennedy, November 22, 1963* (Commission Document Number 1 [CD 1]), 20–22; Belmont to Tolson, 12/6/1963, FBIHQ JFK Assassination File, 62-109060-1623.

49. DeLoach to Mohr, 12/6/1963, FBIHQ JFK Assassination File, 62-109060-1691. For Sandy Smith as a "cooperating" media source, see Kenneth O'Reilly, *Hoover and the Un-Americans: The FBI, HUAC, and the Red Menace* (Philadelphia: Temple University Press, 1983), 200; and Cartha D. DeLoach, *Hoover's FBI: The Inside Story by Hoover's Trusted Lieutenant* (Washington, D.C.: Regnery Publishing, 1995), 315–316; DeLoach to Mohr, 12/6/1963, FBIHQ JFK Assassination File, 62-109060-1691.

50. Jevons to Conrad, 4/1/1964, FBIHQ JFK Assassination File, 62-109060-NR (section 8). Dallas Police Department, Edwin A. Walker File, Vol. 12, Dallas Records and Archives, City of Dallas (hereafter cited as Dallas Police Files); Gemberling Report, 12/23/1963, FBIHQ Oswald File, 105-82555-1212, Section 55, 169–170. In the thirty-eight-page report on the Walker shooting by FBI Inspector Robert Gemberling, not a single witness questioned could provide a scintilla of eyewitness evidence connecting Oswald to the shooting on April 10, 1963. Gemberling Report, 7/2/1964, FBIHQ Oswald File, 105-82555-4354X, 92–130. The bullet's path is described in SAC, Dallas, to Director, FBI, 6/11/1964, FBIHQ Oswald

File, 105-82555-4107; see FBI Letterhead Memorandum, 6/10/1964, Ivan D. Lee and Robert M. Barrett report to the director, 2–3. For the FBI's early ballistics report on the Walker bullet, see L.W. Conrad to Belmont, 12/4/1963, FBIHQ JFK Assassination File, 62-109060-1132.

51. *Dallas Morning News,* December 7, 1963.

52. *HSCA,* Vol. 3, March 31, 1964, 414.

53. Ibid., 438–439.

54. Jevons to Conrad, 3/27/1964, FBIHQ JFK Assassination File, 62-109060-2845. For Heilberger's report, see FBIHQ JFK Assassination File, 62-109060-1719.

55. Warren Commission, April 30, 1964, executive session transcript, NARA, 10; Curry's remarks reported in Shanklin to file, 2/19/1964, Main Dallas Oswald File, 100-10461-3537, 6.

56. SAC, Dallas, to Director, 12/7/1963, FBIHQ Oswald File, 105-82555-1407; Director to SACs Oklahoma City and Dallas, 1/6/1964, FBIHQ Oswald File, 105-82555-1407.

57. FBI Report of SA J. A. Grimes, 1/10/1964, FBIHQ Oswald File, 105-82555-(section 65 of serial 1367); Hoover to Rankin, 1/17/1964, FBIHQ Oswald File, 105-82555-1414.

58. For Hoover's comment, see attachment to Dallas to Director, 2/18/1964, FBIHQ Oswald File, 105-82555-2070; Belmont memo, 1/8/1964, FBIHQ Oswald File, 105-82555-1459. Hoover ordered the Dallas and Oklahoma offices to "expedite" a search for Duff and question him about any contact he had had with Oswald or Jack Ruby. After three weeks of intensive searching, the Oklahoma City FBI found Duff in a U.S. Army hospital at Fort Sill, Oklahoma, where he was recovering from a hernia operation. Shortly after leaving Walker's employ Duff had joined the army. He insisted that he had never known Oswald or Ruby. At the time of the Walker shooting Duff was stationed at Fort Polk, Louisiana. After checking on Duff's story the FBI concluded its inquiry, eliminating Duff as a suspect in the Walker case. See Oklahoma City to Director and Dallas, 1/24/1964, FBIHQ Oswald File, 105-82555-1592; Hoover to Rankin, 2/15/1964, FBIHQ Oswald File, 105-82555-1788.

59. Dallas to Director, 2/18/1964, FBIHQ Oswald File, 105-82555-2070.

60. Walker to Russell, 1/21/1970; Hoover to Russell, 3/30/1970. Copies found in the Justice Department Criminal Division File, 62-117290.

61. For Walker's Commission testimony, see *Investigation of the Assassination of President Kennedy: Hearings before the President's Commission on the Assassination of President John F. Kennedy* (Washington, D.C.: U.S. Government Printing Office, 1964), Vol. 12, 404ff. A photograph of CE 573 (designated by the FBI as Q-188) can be found in *HSCA,* Vol. 7, 390.

62. Walker's correspondence with the Justice Department was filed under the Criminal Division File, 62-117290-1473. His letters may also be found at the Harold Weisberg Archive, Hood College, Frederick, Maryland, under "Edwin A. Walker" Subject Index File.

63. *WCR,* 406.

64. *WCR,* 184–185. The entire eleven numbered points in the note are reproduced in *WCR,* 183–184. In repeating this account over and over again to the FBI and Secret Service, some of the details changed in the retelling. Marina's multiple accounts can be found in "Investigation and Evidence File," Rankin Papers, "Walker Shooting," box 6, NARA.

65. For the Warren Commission testimony of the four Homicide-Robbery Bureau detectives, Richard S. Stovall, John P. Adamcik, Henry M. Moore, and Guy F. Rose, see *Investigation of the Assassination of President John F. Kennedy: Hearings before the President's Commission on the Assassination of President Kennedy* (Washington, D.C.: U.S. Government Printing Office, 1964) (hereafter cited as *Hearings before Commission*), Vol. 7, 188–189 (Stovall), 209–210 (Adamcik). The FBI inventory of the Oswalds' possessions removed from both residences can be found in SAC, Dallas, to Director, FBI, 10/6/1964, FBIHQ Oswald File, 105-82555-NR (section 214). Inventory item D74 is described as

"Russian book on cooking and other useful information in which was found the Walker note written in Russian by Oswald," 42. For a description of the dust cover of Marina's Russian housekeeping book, see Thomas Mallon, *Mrs. Paine's Garage and the Murder of John F. Kennedy* (New York: Pantheon Books, 2002), 83.

66. On finding the note, see Forrest V. Sorrels to Jesse Curry, Chief of Police, Dallas, Texas, 12/26/1963, serial no. co-2-34-34,000, copy found in Dallas Police Files, Vol. 12; Mallon, *Mrs. Paine's Garage,* 83. For the pressure the FBI applied to Marina, see Shanklin to file, 11/29/1963, Main Dallas JFK Assassination File, 89-43-1297; and Heitman to file, 11/30/1963, Main Dallas JFK Assassination File, 89-43-1421.

67. *WCR,* 183–184; Leon I. Gopadze, Dallas, to Chief, 12/3/1963, serial co-2-34.030, Secret Service Document 322, Secret Service File, LBJ Library.

68. For Latona's Commission testimony, see *Hearings before Commission,* Vol. 4, 5–48. For the results of his examination of Oswald's alleged "Walker Note" to Marina, see Latona to Trotter, 12/5/1963, FBIHQ JFK Assassination File, 62-109060-2151. For Cadigan's testimony, see *Hearings before Commission,* Vol. 7, 420–437. When the House Select Committee on Assassinations called on three independent document analysts to examine the "Walker Note," only one of the three was willing to affirm that Oswald had written it. See *HSCA,* Vol. 3 (March 1979), 225–249.

69. Shanklin to file, 12/6/1963, Main Dallas JFK Assassination File, 89-43-2613a.

70. *WCR,* 22–23, 187.

71. Shanklin to file, 2/19/1964, Main Dallas Oswald File, 100-10461-3537; Rankin to Hoover, 5/20/1964, FBIHQ Oswald File, 105-82555-3 [7?]92; Shanklin to file, 6/10/1964, Main Dallas Oswald File, 100-10461-6620.

72. Hoover to Rankin, 6/16/1964, FBIHQ Oswald File, 105-82555-4107.

73. For Coleman's and Surrey's accounts, see Lee and Barrett Report to FBI, Director, FBI Letterhead Memorandum, 6/10/1964, FBIHQ Oswald File, 105-82555-4107, 8–13. There is nothing in the Lee-Barrett thirty-two-page investigative report that even suggests that Oswald was the assailant in the Walker case.

Chapter 3. Oswald in Mexico—Seven Days That Shook the Government

1. Priscilla J. McMillan, *Marina and Lee* (New York: Harper and Row, 1977), 465; Robert L. Oswald with Myrick and Barbara Land, *Lee: A Portrait of Lee Harvey Oswald* (New York: Coward-McCann, 1967), 46–47. For the Commission's July 9, 1964, session with three psychiatrists, see Chapter 4, note 37.

2. *The Warren Commission Report: Report of the President's Commission on the Assassination of President John F. Kennedy* (Washington, D.C.: U.S. Government Printing Office, 1964) (hereafter cited as *WCR*), 658–659, 730–736. There are two monographs that disagree with the Commission's conclusion that Oswald's Mexico City trip was "inconsequential": Mark Riebling, *Wedge: The Secret War between the FBI and the CIA* (New York: Alfred A. Knopf, 1994); and John Newman, *Oswald and the CIA* (New York: Carroll and Graf, 1995). Both agreed that there was a Mexico City plot, but they assigned blame to different government agencies for failure to react in a way that might have foiled the Dallas assassination. Riebling found the FBI at fault; Newman's candidate for dereliction of responsibility was the CIA.

3. *WCR,* 732–733; (FBI) Legat, Mexico City, to Director, FBI, 5/11/1964, FBIHQ Oswald File, 105-82555-3772. In tracing Oswald's itinerary to Mexico City, the FBI utilized eight "symbol" or paid informants (symbol informants provide high-grade intelligence and are paid on a regular basis; they are identified under a special bureau numbering system).

4. The Cuban Embassy and Cuban Consulate in Mexico City were located in separate buildings. All of Oswald's contacts with Cuban government consular officers and staff took place in the Cuban Consulate. For Mexico's procedures and regulations controlling U.S. citizens' travel to Castro's Cuba, see Warren CD 944 and see also To Director (CIA) from Mexico City Station, 5/6/1964, CIA document no. 683-2(?)91, CIA releases 6/1976, Harold Weisberg Archive, Hood College, Frederick, Maryland (hereafter cited as Weisberg Archive). This CIA document notes that these Mexican regulations allowing travel for U.S. citizens to and through Cuba had been in effect since May 3, 1963.

5. For detailed treatment of Oswald's political odyssey, see Chapter 12. Oswald's hostile views of the Soviet political system can be found in the 150 pages of his notes in *Investigation of the Assassination of President John F. Kennedy: Hearings before the President's Commission on the Assassination of President Kennedy* (Washington, D.C.: U.S. Government Printing Office, 1964) (hereafter cited as *Hearings before Commission*), Vol. 16, 283–434. The Soviet state was equally disenchanted with Oswald and had no wish for him to return. See Warren CD 451 or note 31 for this chapter; To Director from Mexico City Station, 5/6/1964, CIA document no. 683-2(?)91, Weisberg Archive.

6. For a summary conclusion of Oswald's motivations according to the Commission, see *WCR,* 423–424. Se also William T. Coleman, Jr., and W. David Slawson to Rankin, 2/14/1964, J. Lee Rankin Papers, box 17, folder 285, National Archives and Records Administration, College Park, Maryland (hereafter cited as NARA), or see copy found in the FBI's Lee Harvey Oswald, Post-Russian Period, 1–2, FBI FPCC (Fair Play for Cuba Committee) File (hereafter cited as FBI FPCC File) for questions raised about Oswald's finances. The FBI's FPCC file can be found in the Weisberg Archive. For the Lopez Report, see House Select Committee on Assassinations staff report, 180-10110-10484, "Lee Harvey Oswald, the CIA and Mexico City," NARA (hereafter cited as Lopez Report), 245–246. This document is a three hundred–page report by HSCA staffers Dan Hardway and Eddie Lopez.

7. Lopez Report; Gaeton Fonzi, *The Last Investigation* (New York: Thunder's Mouth Press, 1994), 267.

8. *WCR,* 734–735. See the transcript of Silvia Turado Duran's June 6, 1978, deposition by Gary Cornwell, House Select Committee on Assassinations, JFK Collection, Record Group (RG) 272, tape one, NARA. There is some confusion about when Oswald visited the Cuban Consulate. Duran insisted that he made three visits on Friday, September 27. The Lopez Report contends that Duran was probably truthful on this matter. See Lopez Report, 246.

9. Coleman and Slawson to Rankin, Memorandum on Oswald's Foreign Activity, 1/24/1964, Rankin Papers, box 17, folder 285, NARA; Coleman and Slawson to Rankin, Memorandum on Oswald's Mexican Trip, FBI FPCC File; Helms to Rankin, 2/21/1964, Translation of Interrogation Reports of Sylvia Duran, CD 426 (hereafter cited as CD 426); Slawson to Records, 3/12/1964, Conference with CIA on March 12, 1964, Rankin Papers, box 17, folder 289, NARA; Slawson to Rankin, 3/27/1964, Memorandum on Conference with CIA, March 27, 1964, Rankin Papers, box 18, folder 290, NARA; Helms to Rankin, 5/19/1964, CD 944.

10. For an overview of the CIA's extensive surveillance of the Soviet and Cuban diplomatic compounds in Mexico City, see John Whitten deposition, NARA (hereafter cited as Whitten deposition), 52–53, 58. Whitten was the CIA official who headed WH-3 (Western Hemisphere Branch) when he was deposed by the HSCA in 1978 in executive session. In order to hide his identity the House committee used the name "Scelso." His deposition was not released until after his death in 2001, but it is now available at NARA. I want to thank Jim Lesar for drawing my attention to Whitten's deposition. See also Lopez Report, 8, 13, and 33.

11. *David Atlee Phillips v. Donald Freed, et al.,* Civil Action No. 81-1407, U.S. District Court for the District of Columbia, November 26, 1984, 315–316. John Newman identified

Luis Alberu, one of the Cuban Embassy's cultural attachés, as the source. Newman, *Oswald and the CIA,* 388.

12. Lopez Report, 73–76. See page 117 of the report for a handy summary of all Oswald-related phone calls for the seven days he was in Mexico City.

13. Warren Commission testimony of Pamela Mumford, *Hearings before Commission,* Vol. 11, 217; Evanisto Rodrigues, Vol. 11, 341; and John E. Donovan, Vol. 8, 294.

14. Lopez Report, 77–79, 184. Just how and under what circumstances Oswald became proficient in the Russian language remains one of the mysteries associated with the JFK assassination. When Marina first met Lee at a social and cultural event held at the Palace of Culture in Minsk, they spent the evening conversing and dancing. She recalled that Oswald's Russian "although good, bore a definite accent." Marina thought he was from one of the Russian-speaking Baltic countries. It was not until later in the evening that a friend told her that her companion was an American. Lee's older brother, Robert Oswald, noted that Lee spoke Russian fluently. For Marina's comments, see Gemberling Report, 12/2/1963, FBIHQ Oswald File, 105-82555-454, Section 12, 561–565. For Robert Oswald see ibid., 105-82555-1567, Section 72, 193.

15. Lopez Report, 73.

16. See CD 2564.

17. Lopez Report, 91–93; CIA document, The CIA Does Not Have Picture of Lee Harvey Oswald Entering/Leaving Cuban Consulate, JFK Record Series, record no. 104-10118-10290, NARA.

18. Lopez Report, 105–115.

19. Robert Dallek, *Flawed Giant: Lyndon Johnson and His Times, 1960–1973* (New York: Oxford University Press, 1998), 51–52; Lyndon Baines Johnson, *The Vantage Point: Perspectives on the Presidency, 1963–1969* (New York: Holt, Rinehart, and Winston, 1971), 26–27; *Time* magazine, February 10, 1975, 16.

20. McCone Memorandum for the Record, 11/25/1963, John McCone's Discussions with President and Dean Rusk, November 23, 1963, Meeting Notes File, Lyndon Baines Johnson Library, Austin, Texas (hereafter cited as LBJ Library). See Mexico City to CIA Director, 10/9/1963, CIA document no. 5-1A, FOIA releases, June 1976, Weisberg Archive, for CIA Mexico City station's first mention of a Kostikov meeting with Lee Harvey Oswald on October 1, 1963. The Oswald identified in this classified message was the imposter. For Bagley's memo, see Acting Chief, SR Division, to Assistant Deputy Director, Plans, 11/23/1964, record no. 104-10119-10378, JFK record series, NARA.

21. Johnson phone conversation with Hoover, 11/23/1963, 10:01 A.M., White House Telephone Transcripts, LBJ Library; Hoover to Rowley, 11/23/1963, FBIHQ JFK Assassination File, 62-109060-104. For an accounting of the transfer of the tape recording and photographs, see Kyle G. Clark to SAC, Dallas, 11/22/1963, Main Dallas JFK Assassination File, 89-43-346. FBI Washington received from the Dallas office on November 23, 1963, two photographs of the "mystery man" of eight separate poses obtained by the FBI Legat in Mexico City from the Mexico City CIA. The FBI record noted that the pictures were not to be "disseminated outside the Bureau." See SAC, Dallas, to Director, FBI, 6/1/1964, FBIHQ Oswald File, 105-82555-4039 (CIA Referral).

22. Legat Mexico City to Director, 4/6/1964, FBIHQ Oswald File, 105-82555-327 (last digit obliterated); Legat Mexico City to Director, 4/3/1964, FBIHQ Oswald File, 105-82555-2978; Whitten deposition, 40–45; Lopez Report, 123–124.

23. Hoover to Rankin, 5/4/1963, FBIHQ Oswald File, 105-82555-3561, item 61; Director to FBI Legat Mexico City, 4/3/1964, FBI Mexico City File, 105-3702-586.

24. Legat Mexico City to Director, 4/6/1964, FBIHQ Oswald File, 105-82555-327 (last digit obliterated); or see FBI Referrals, CIA, State, and Navy, FBI Referral File, NARA.

25. For the CIA's physical description of the man in the photographs, see CIA Mexico City cable to Director, 10/8/1963, Mexi 6453, CIA Historical Review Program Releases, 1995, NARA. Dallas County Medical Examiner Dr. Earl Rose's autopsy report on Oswald can be found in *Hearings before Commission,* Vol. 16, 638, and Vol. 20, 691. Although the Commission felt obliged to exhibit the pictures to satisfy the record, they do nothing to dispel the mystery because they are accompanied by no explanation. Copies of these photos can be found in CIA documents 929-927A through series up to 929-927H, CIA releases for July 1976, NARA; or see CIA files in the Weisberg Archive.

26. For Scott's professional reputation within the CIA, see Whitten deposition, 22–23; and Jefferson Morley's piece on Scott, "The Spy Who Loved Him," *Washington Post,* March 17, 1996, Sunday Style section.

27. Lopez Report, 137–138.

28. For the CIA requests to the navy, see CIA to Department of the Navy, 10/24/1963, CIA document no. 10-6, CIA releases, April 1976, NARA; CIA Director to Mexico City Station, 11/23/1963, CIA document no. 56-20, CIA releases, April 1976, NARA.

29. For Stern's comments, see Memorandum for the Record, 4/2/1964, Meeting with Representatives of the President's Commission on the Assassination of President Kennedy, 3/27/1964, Langley, CIA document no. 633-792, CIA releases, June 1976, NARA.

30. Lopez Report, 138–139, 141.

31. Oswald's pictures accompanied stories of his defection in the *Washington Post,* November 16, 1959, and the *Evening Star.* These pictures in the CIA's preassassination Oswald file are identified as CIA document nos. 593-252C and 594-252D, respectively. Or see the handy facsimile edition *Lee Harvey Oswald: CIA Pre-Assassination File,* edited by Louis B. Sckolnick (Leverett, Mass.: Rector Press, 1993).

32. Christopher Andrew, *The Sword and the Shield: The Mitrokhin Archive and the Secret History of the KGB* (New York: Basic Books, 1999), 362.

33. CIA document, Valery Vladimirovich Kostikov, JFK Record Series, record no. 104-10109-10147, NARA.

34. For the CIA's surveillance reports on Kostikov's embassy contacts, see (CIA) Mexico City to Director, 11/24/1963, Assassination Records Review Board CIA releases, 1995 (hereafter cited as ARRB), record no. 104-10015-10080, Agency File no. 201-189248, NARA; Director (CIA) to Mexico City Station, 11/23/1963, CIA document no. 41-15, Weisberg Archive; Mexico City to Director, FBI, 11/27/1963, CIA document no. 150, Weisberg Archive; Mexico City to Director (CIA), 12/5/1963, CIA document no. 312-117, Weisberg Archive. All CIA Mexico City was able to report was that it was "convinced beyond reasonable doubt" that Kostikov was a KGB staff officer. See CIA memo, 11/27/1963, CIA document no. 179-71, Weisberg Archive.

35. Helms to Rankin, 7/2/1964, CD 1216, NARA; CIA releases to Harold Weisberg, CIA folder 492, Weisberg Archive. Helms's "reliable" informer was a CIA source very close to Pavel Yatskov. See CIA cable traffic, 6/6/1964, box 57, para. 350, Mexi 9948, NARA, 79.

36. In February 1964 a Soviet staff officer in the Counterintelligence Directorate of the KGB, Yuri Nosenko, defected to the CIA. Nosenko had had an opportunity to see the KGB Minsk file on Oswald shortly after the assassination. The CIA allowed the FBI to interview Nosenko about Oswald and what he had gleaned from the Minsk file. According to Nosenko, the KGB regarded the American as "not being completely normal mentally." After the suicide attempt, Nosenko claimed the KGB "washed its hands of Oswald." He also commented that the KGB kept Oswald under periodic surveillance through its Intourist sources and suspected that the ex-marine might be a "sleeper agent" for American intelligence. It was Nosenko's department that recommended that Oswald's application for a reentry visa be denied.

Nosenko's bona fides became the subject of a poisonous conflict within the CIA that threatened to tear the agency asunder. But in time sanity prevailed, and Nosenko was recognized as an authentic defector and not a Soviet plant. For Nosenko's February 26 and 27, 1964, FBI interviews, see Warren CDs 434 and 451. For a useful account of the "Nosenko wars" inside the CIA, see Tom Mangold, *Cold Warrior: James Jesus Angleton: The CIA's Master Spy Hunter* (New York: Simon and Schuster, 1991). In a 1967 letter Hoover wrote Secret Service Chief James J. Rowley that the FBI was satisfied that Oswald had no connections with Fidel Castro or officials of the Cuban government. Hoover to Rowley, 2/15/1967, FBIHQ JFK Assassination File, 62-109060-4538.

37. Oswald's postdefection political activities consistent with creating a "cover" are discussed in Chapter 11. A photocopy of the registry of Hotel del Comercio was acquired by the FBI for examination. The bureau concluded that the signature on the registry was Oswald's. See Legat, Mexico, to FBI, Dallas, 12/18/1963, FBI Mexico City File, 105-3702-132.

38. President to J. Edgar Hoover, 11/25/1963, 10:30 A.M., White House Telephone Transcripts, LBJ Library. See also Hoover memorandum to Tolson et al., 11/25/1963, FBIHQ JFK Assassination File, 62-109060 serials 61–63. A harried Johnson probably heard about Rostow's recommendation from Bill Moyers, who reported to LBJ his conversation with the Yale dean on Sunday the 24th. Johnson mistakenly assumed that Rostow was some interfering lawyer in the Justice Department. For Rosen's comment, see Rosen to DeLoach, 11/12/1966, FBIHQ JFK Assassination File, 62-109060-Not Recorded (NR).

39. CIA to White House, Attn: McGeorge Bundy, FBI, and Department of State, Attn: U. Alexis Johnson, 11/26/1963, record no. 104-1005-10157, ARRB, NARA.

40. CIA to White House (McGeorge Bundy), FBI, and Department of State, 11/28/1963, CIA document no. 207-84, Weisberg Archive; Mexico City Station to Director, 11/26/1963, CIA document no. 125-52, Weisberg Archive. This is just a brief composite of what Alvarado claimed he witnessed on 9/18/1963 at the Cuban Consulate. His account to the CIA and the Mexican security forces was interlarded with a wealth of detail to authenticate his story. See Richard Helms to Rankin, 6/14/1964, CE 3125; Deputy Director (Plans) to Director, FBI, 12/13/1963, FBIHQ Oswald File, 105-82555-954, for the translation of the Mexican police's interrogation report of Gilberto Nolasco Alvarado Ugarte, a composite report of their September 28 and 30 sessions with the Nicaraguan.

41. CIA cable no. 85089, 11/26/1963, to White House, Department of State, and FBI, with copy to Secret Service, ARRB, NARA.

42. Hoover note attached to a Domestic Intelligence Division memo, 11/27/1963, FBIHQ Oswald File, 105-82555-460; Hoover memo to Tolson et al., 11/25/1963, FBIHQ JFK Assassination File, 62-109060-61; Rosen to Belmont, 11/27/1963, FBIHQ JFK Assassination File, 62-109060-211 (or 216).

43. President to House Speaker John McCormick, 11/29/1963, White House Telephone Transcripts, LBJ Library; Johnson to Charles Halleck, 11/29/1963, White House Telephone Transcripts, LBJ Library; Johnson to Senator Russell, 11/29/1963 (8:55 P.M.), White House Telephone Transcripts, LBJ Library; *Washington Post,* September 23, 1993, A6.

44. For summaries and paraphrases of CIA cable traffic, all ARRB releases, 1995, 11/26/1963, box 57, Mexi 7069, 21; CIA to White House, FBI, and State Department, 11/26/1963, record no. 104-10015-10157, Agency File no. 210-289248, all NARA; Director (CIA) memo, 11/26/1963, CIA document no. 117-583, Weisberg Archive; Fonzi, *The Last Investigation,* 280.

45. Fonzi, *The Last Investigation,* 284–285.

46. Lawrence Freedman, *Kennedy's Wars: Berlin, Cuba, Laos, and Vietnam* (New York: Oxford University Press, 2000), 230–233; Evan Thomas, *The Very Best Men: Four Who*

Dared: The Early Years of the CIA (New York: Simon and Schuster, 1995), 299–304, 309–310; Mark J. White (ed.), *The Kennedys and Cuba: The Declassified Documentary History* (Chicago: Ivan R. Dee, 1999), 324–330; David Corn, *Blond Ghost: Ted Shackley and the CIA's Crusades* (New York: Simon and Schuster, 1994), 105–119. For Chairman Lyman L. Lemnitzer and the Joint Chiefs' off-the-table plans to incite a war against Cuba, see James Bamford's *Body of Secrets: Anatomy of the Ultra-Secret National Security Agency from Cold War through the Dawn of the New Century* (New York: Doubleday, 2001), 80–91, especially 82–85, for the provocative scenarios the nation's military elites were contemplating.

47. W. R. Heitman to SAC, Dallas, 11/22/1963, Main Dallas JFK Assassination File, 89-43-103; Mexico City (Mann) to Secretary of State, 11/23/1963, cable no. 1180, Weisberg Archive, in folder "CIA in Mexico."

48. For Kennedy liberals' view of Mann, see Arthur Schlesinger, Jr., *Robert Kennedy and His Times* (New York: Ballantine Books, 1978), 680; and Richard N. Goodwin, *Remembering America: A Voice from the Sixties* (Boston: Little, Brown, and Company, 1988), 245–246. For McCone's cable, see Director to Mexico City Station, 11/27/1963, CIA document no. 145-56, released April 1967, NARA.

49. Mann's secret (Roger Channel) cable to Rusk, 11/28/1963, "Mexico-CIA" file, Weisberg Archive; U. Alexis Johnson to AmEmbassy, 11/28/1963, cable no. 1201, Weisberg Archive.

50. For Oswald's role in creating a pro-Castro false biography, see Chapter 12.

51. McCone to Mexico City, 11/23/1963, record no. 104-10040, Agency File no. 201-28924, ARRB, NARA; Director to Mexico City Station, 11/27/1963, CIA document no. 158-610, CIA releases, April 1976, Weisberg Archive; CIA cable traffic, 11/23/1963, box 57, para. 46, 9, Weisberg Archive. That same day McCone called Secretary of State Dean Rusk to inform him of the arrest of a "Mexican employee of the Cuban Embassy" by Mexican security police. McCone did not use Silvia Duran's name, but he left the impression with Rusk that the arrest was solely on the initiative of the Mexican authorities. See Memorandum for the Record, 11/23/1963, John McCone's Discussion with LBJ and Dean Rusk, Meeting Notes File, LBJ Library; COS to Director, 11/25/1963, record no. 104-10086-10002, Agency File no. 80T013 57A, ARRB, NARA.

52. Deposition of Silvia Duran taken by Gary Cornwell, June 6, 1978, HSCA, JFK Collection, RG 272, tape 2, NARA, 2, 20; CIA to White House Situation Room, State, and FBI, 11/26/1963, National Security File, Intelligence File, box 17, Lee Harvey Oswald File, NARA. For proof that Scott provided the questions, see CIA cable traffic, 11/23/1963, box 57, para. 59, Mexi 7076, NARA, 11.

53. CIA cable traffic, 11/26/1963, box 57, para. 72, Mexi 7054 and para. 73, Mexi 7055, NARA, 14, 15. *Excelsior* appeared on the streets at about 6 A.M. See Legat Mexico City to Director, 1/13/1964, FBI Mexico City File, 105-3702-181. The CIA's Whitten, who handled all the cables about the Alvarado matter, noted that the sum of $6,500 that Oswald allegedly received to kill JFK was a rumor on Mexico City radio, and "everyone in Mexico City believed it." Whitten deposition, 89.

54. CIA cable traffic, 11/26/1963, box 57, para. 97, Mexi 7072, NARA, 22; Branigan to Sullivan, 11/27/1963, FBIHQ Oswald File, 105-82555-122; CIA cable traffic, 11/25/1963, box 57, para. 88, Mexi 7065, NARA, 20; CIA cable traffic, 11/26/1963, box 57, para. 97 and 110, Mexi 7072 and 1839, NARA, 22, 25; CIA document titled "We Discover Lee Oswald in Mexico City," initially written 12/13/1963, ARRB, NARA, 21–23, for the Dorticos-Hernandez exchange.

55. CIA cable traffic, 11/26/1963, box 57, para. 99, Mexi 7084, NARA, 23; CIA cable traffic, 11/27/1963, box 57, para. 126, Mexi 7104, NARA, 28.

56. CIA to White House, State, and FBI, 11/28/1963, National Security Intelligence Files, Intelligence Files, box 17, Lee Harvey Oswald File, NARA.

57. Belmont to Tolson, 11/26/1963, FBIHQ Oswald File, 105-82555-55; Legat, Mexico City, to Director, 11/25/1963, FBIHQ Oswald File, 105-82555-380; Hoover memorandum for Tolson et al., FBIHQ JFK Assassination File, 62-109060-216; Branigan to Sullivan, 6/5/1964, FBIHQ Liaison with Commission, 62-109090-NR; Belmont to Tolson, 11/27/1963, FBI Internal Security File, 67-473513-200. My phone interview with Laurence Keenan, February 27, 2003. Keenan was an intimate of Anderson, and the FBI Legat had specifically requested him for this assignment to help rein in Ambassador Mann.

58. Sullivan to Belmont, 11/27/1963, FBIHQ JFK Assassination File, 62-109060-455; C.A. Evans to Belmont, 11/27/1963, FBIHQ JFK Assassination File, 62-109060-1493; Robert W. Adams, Counselor of Embassy, to Department of State, 12/2/1963, 146-1-73-181, NARA; Mann (Mexico City) to Secretary of State, 11/27/1963 (Roger Channel), "CIA-Mexico" file, Weisberg Archive.

59. Branigan to Sullivan, 11/29/1963, FBIHQ Oswald File, 105-82555-246; ASAC Joseph T. Sylvester to SAC, New Orleans, 11/27/1963, Main New Orleans JFK Assassination File, 89-69-407A. The New Orleans Library recorded that Oswald took out three books on 9/19/1963: Ian Fleming's *Moonraker,* Aldous Huxley's *Ape and Essence,* and Huxley's *Brave New World.* See Richard M. Mosk to Wesley J. Liebeler, 6/18/1964, memo Oswald's Reading, Russell Papers, Series 13, Subseries A, box 4, Assassination Commission—Evidence re: Oswald, Richard B. Russell Papers, Athens, Georgia. Branigan to Sullivan, 11/27/1963, FBIHQ Oswald File, 105-82555-122; Branigan to Sullivan, 11/29/1963, FBIHQ Oswald File, 105-82555-246. The FBI first learned from Marina that Lee was in New Orleans on September 18, 1963. See Shanklin to file, 11/28/1964, Main Dallas JFK Assassination File, 89-43-1297.

60. CIA cable traffic, 11/28/1963, box 57, para. 140, State Telegram Sent SECSTATE 2101 Flash, NARA, 31; CIA cable traffic, 11/28/1963, box 57, para. 141, DIR 85371, NARA, 31; CIA cable traffic, 11/28/1963, box 57, para. 142, DIR 85653, NARA, 32; CIA cable traffic, box 57, para. 141, DIR 85469, NARA, 32; U. Alexis Johnson to AmEmbassy, 11/27/1963, cable nos. 965 and 969, Weisberg Archive, file drawer 76; AmEmbassy to SecState, 11/28/1963, cable no. 1201, Weisberg Archive.

61. Branigan to Sullivan, 11/27/1963, FBIHQ Oswald File, 105-82555-122; CIA cable traffic, 11/27/1963, box 57, para. 120, DIR 85198, NARA, 26; Branigan to Sullivan, 2/13/1964, FBIHQ Oswald File, 105-82555-2237.

62. Branigan to Sullivan, 12/12/1963, FBIHQ Oswald File, 105-82555-953; CIA cable traffic, 11/30/1963, box 57, para. 176, Mexi 7168, NARA, 39; CIA cable traffic, 12/2/1963, box 57, para. 170, Mexi 7203, NARA, 41; Mann to Secretary of State, 11/30/1963, FBIHQ Oswald File, 105-82555-2234; CIA cable traffic, 12/1/1963, box 57, para. 180, DIR 86064, NARA, 39.

63. CIA cable traffic, 11/28/1963, box 57, para. 160, DIR 85667, NARA, 36; Birch O'Neal, Memorandum for the Record, 12/3/1963, CIA document no. 287-690, ARRB, NARA.

64. CIA cable traffic, 12/4/1963, box 57, para. 212, Mexi 7229, NARA, 46; CIA cable traffic, 12/4/1963, box 57, para. 215, DIR 86659, NARA, 47; CIA cable traffic, 12/5/1963, box 57, para. 224, Mexi 7256, NARA, 48; D. E. Moore to Sullivan, 12/10/1963, FBIHQ Oswald File, 105-82555-242; Branigan to Sullivan, 12/12/1963, FBIHQ Oswald File, 105-82555-953. See FBI report released to the Commission on December 13, 1963, titled "Investigation of the Assassination of President John F. Kennedy: Hoaxes, False Reports, and Irresponsible Reporting," FBIHQ JFK Assassination File, 62-109060-1987.

65. Jeremiah O'Leary and James R. Dickerson, "Assassination Sparked Bitter Quarrels," *Washington Star,* December 8, 1977, A1; DeLoach to Mohr, 12/12/1963, FBIHQ Liaison with Commission File, 62-109090-36. DeLoach and O'Leary enjoyed a close friendship, and DeLoach was godfather to one of O'Leary's children. See Cartha "Deke" DeLoach, *Hoover's FBI: The Inside Story by Hoover's Trusted Lieutenant* (Washington, D.C.: Regnery Publishing, 1995), 181. Branigan to Sullivan, 12/19/1963, FBIHQ Oswald File, 105-82555-NR. The FBI had good reason to suspect that McCone had some nefarious purpose in mind in pushing the "Red plot" story on Capitol Hill when his own agency was debunking any Soviet involvement in the Kennedy assassination. See, for example, CIA memorandum for December 11, 1963, CIA document 376-154, and Priority Director, 11/27/1963, CIA document 151-60, ARRB, NARA.

66. Dallek, *Flawed Giant,* 92.

67. Whitten deposition, 113–114.

68. Summary of Oswald Case Prepared for Briefing Purposes, ca. 12/10/1963, CIA document no. 367-726, ARRB, NARA, 15. See Chapter 11 for more detail on this issue. A reproduction of Oswald's November 9, 1963, letter can be found as CE 15.

69. Lopez Report, 167–171. See also Chapter 12.

70. See the three-page addendum to footnote 614 located at the front of the Lopez Report.

71. Evans to Belmont, 11/24/1963, FBIHQ JFK Assassination File, 62-1090601490; Hoover memo, 11/25/1963, FBIHQ JFK Assassination File, 62-109060-1491. For Hoover's November 26, 1963, memo, see Appendix A, 1. Early Bureau Responses to the President's Assassination, A. November 22–23, 1964, no. 3.

72. For Hoover's suspicions about the circumstances surrounding Oswald's murder, see Appendix A, Early Bureau Response to the President's Assassination, C. Jack Ruby, no. 2.

73. Rosen to DeLoach, 11/12/1966, FBIHQ JFK Assassination File, 62-109060-NR.

74. See Appendix A, 2. Structure and Methods of the Bureau Investigation; B. General Investigative Division, nos. 1 and 4; C. Domestic Intelligence Division, no. 3; and D. Investigation of Potential Cuban Aspects, nos. 1, 2, and 3.

75. Whitten deposition, 111–115, 134–135.

76. Ibid., 114. For Oswald's supposed pro-Castro activities in New Orleans, see Chapter 12.

77. Whitten deposition, 72–73; Lopez Report, 142, for location of Oswald's 201 Personality File.

78. Whitten deposition, 17, 61, 138–139.

79. Ibid., 137–142. Years later, some of the ugly revelations about the CIA's "Executive Action" programs surfaced during the Church Committee investigation in the 1970s. Whitten spoke frankly and passionately to the HSCA about his disgust with the assassination program. He condemned Helms for using hired killers to go after Castro. Ibid., 143–144, 153–154.

80. Ibid., 113–115.

81. Ibid., 73–74. See also Thomas Powers, *The Man Who Kept the Secrets: Richard Helms and the CIA* (New York: Pocket Books, 1979), 361–365. For the FBI-CIA wars, see Riebling, *Wedge.*

82. Whitten deposition, 136–138. In the ancillary matter of the so-called mystery man, the CIA was candid with the Commission when Helms assured Rankin that, "as far as the Agency is aware," the unidentified man "had no connection with Lee Harvey Oswald or the assassination of President Kennedy." Helms to Rankin, 7/23/1964, CIA document no. 775-337, CIA releases, June 1976, Weisberg Archive. In all likelihood the man in the picture was either a Russian sailor or a KGB officer. See Lopez Report, 179.

Chapter 4. The Warren Commission Behind Closed Doors

1. Foreshadowed in earlier Commission executive sessions, this recognition was the dominating topic of the Warren Commission's January 22, 1964, executive session transcript, National Archives and Records Administration, College Park, Maryland (hereafter cited as NARA).

2. Warren Commission, December 5, 1963, executive session, NARA, 1–2, 35. Despite not having any independent classifying authority, Rankin went ahead to classify Commission documents as "Top Secret." See Rosen to Belmont, 12/18/1963, FBIHQ JFK Assassination File, 62-109060-Not Recorded (NR); James B. Rhodes, archivist of the United States, comments to U.S. Representative and Chairperson Bella Abzug in House of Representatives, Committee of Agriculture, Subcommittee on Government Information and Individual Rights, November 11, 1975. See also *Washington Post,* November 12, 1975, for the story on these hearings and Rhodes's admission that Rankin overstepped his authority in classifying Commission documents as "Top Secret."

3. Kai Bird, *The Chairman: John J. McCloy and the Making of the American Establishment* (New York: Simon and Schuster, 1992).

4. Warren Commission, December 5, 1963, executive session transcript, NARA, 36–38; Bird, *The Chairman,* 549. Russell, on the other hand, suspected a foreign conspiracy.

5. Warren Commission, December 5, 1963, executive session transcript, NARA, 38, 41.

6. Gilbert C. Fite, *Richard B. Russell, Jr., Senator from Georgia* (Chapel Hill: University of North Carolina Press, 1991), 423; Warren Commission, December 5, 1963, executive session transcript, NARA, 36; LBJ call to Russell, 11/28/1963 (8:55 P.M.), White House Telephone Transcripts, Lyndon B. Johnson Library, Austin, Texas (hereafter cited as LBJ Library); *Washington Post,* November 12, 1975, A1 and A4; Peter Grose, *Gentleman Spy: The Life of Allen Dulles* (Boston: Houghton Mifflin, 1994), 544–545. The failure of Dulles and the CIA to disclose the agency's assassination attempts on Castro was an issue that emerged intermittently with the House Select Committee on Assassinations. See *Investigation of the Assassination of President John F. Kennedy: Hearings before the Select Committee on Assassinations of the U.S. House of Representatives,* 95th Congress, 2d session (Washington, D.C.: U.S. Government Printing Office, 1979) (hereafter cited as *HSCA*), Appendix to Hearings, Vol. 11.

7. Warren Commission, December 5, 1963, executive session transcript, NARA, 11; Katzenbach to the Chief Justice, 12/9/1963, copy found in FBIHQ Liaison with Commission File, 62-109090-15, 2.

8. Warren Commission, December 16, 1963, executive session transcript, NARA, 11, 42, 43.

9. Rosen to Belmont, 11/26/1963, FBIHQ JFK Assassination File, 62-109060-426. For a detailed treatment of the Kennedy autopsy, see Chapter 7.

10. Warren Commission, December 16, 1963, executive session transcript, NARA, 12; Francis X. O'Neill and James W. Sibert, FBI Report, 11/26/1963, JFK 4-1 File, National Archives, Washington, D.C., 2–3, or SAC, Baltimore, to Director and SAC, Dallas, 11/23/1963, FBIHQ JFK Assassination File, 62-109060-459. A copy of the official autopsy report can be found in *The Warren Commission Report: Report of the President's Commission on the Assassination of President John F. Kennedy* (Washington, D.C.: U.S. Government Printing Office, 1964), (hereafter cited as *WCR*), 538–543.

11. Warren Commission, December 16, 1963, executive session transcript, NARA, 33, 48–49, 54–55; Warren Commission, January 21, 1964, executive session transcript, NARA, 5, 20.

12. For more on McCloy and the Commission's suppression of the medical evidence, see Chapter 7.

13. Warren Commission, December 16, 1963, executive session transcript, NARA, 43–44, 48–49.

14. Warren Commission, December 16, 1963, executive session transcript, NARA, 51–52; Bird, *The Chairman,* 549; Arthur Schlesinger, Jr., memorandum for Honorable Robert Kennedy, December 9, 1963, Department of Justice, Criminal Division, 129-11 File. See Staughton Lynd and Jack Minnis, "Seeds of Doubt: Some Questions About the President's Assassination," *New Republic,* December 21, 1963.

15. Warren Commission, December 16, 1963, executive session transcript, NARA, 35.

16. Edward Jay Epstein, *Deception: The Invisible War between the KGB and the CIA* (New York: Simon and Schuster, 1989), 14; Rosen to Belmont, 12/17/1963, FBIHQ Liaison with Commission File, 62-109090-20.

17. There are some grounds for suspecting that the FBI may have wiretapped Commission members. Historian Kenneth O'Reilly, whose work on the FBI has received scholarly acclaim, has been quoted as saying that wiretapping during the Hoover years was so pervasive that "virtually everyone was overheard" whom the FBI deemed important in Washington politics. See "FBI Kept a File on Supreme Court," *New York Times,* August 21, 1988.

18. Hoover memorandum, 12/12/1963, FBIHQ Liaison with Commission File, 62-109090-14.

19. For a detailed discussion of this question, see Chapter 10; see also Bird, *The Chairman,* 554–555.

20. Shanklin to file, 2/28/1964, Main Dallas Oswald File, 100-10461-3863; Rankin to Hoover, 2/25/1964, FBIHQ Liaison with Commission File, 62-109090-NR; Hoover to Rankin, 2/28/1964, FBIHQ Liaison with Commission File 62-109090-NR.

21. Hoover memorandum, 12/16/1963, FBIHQ Liaison with Commission File, 62-109090-13. For Warren's statement, see the *Evening News* (Washington), December 17, 1963. For Hoover's comment, see FBIHQ Liaison with Commission File, 62-109090-49.

22. See Chapter 7.

23. Rosen to Belmont, 12/18/1963, FBIHQ Liaison with Commission File, 62-109090-NR.

24. The quotation is from hard-line Reagan loyalist and judicial appointee Judge Lawrence H. Silberman. See "Strange Tale of Judge and Hoover Files," *National Law Journal,* June 8, 1998, A10.

25. See Chapter 6 for evidence of the Commission's fear of Hoover.

26. Hoover memorandum to Tolson, 12/26/1963, FBIHQ Liaison with Commission File, 62-109090-50; Rosen to Belmont, 1/23/1964, FBIHQ JFK Assassination File, 62-109060-2275. Had Hoover wanted to go to extremes and send the Commission all the FBI's "nut" files, he could have brought the work of the Commission to a standstill. The FBI had over 500,000 "nut" files; the New York field office alone kept over 25,000 names on file. See Hoover memorandum, 12/14/1963, FBIHQ Liaison with Commission File, 62-109090-NR.

27. Brennan to Sullivan, 12/19/1963, FBIHQ Liaison with Commission File, 62-109090-73; Branigan to Sullivan, 12/26/1963, FBIHQ JFK Assassination File, 62-109060-2096; Staughton Lynd and Thomas Hayden, *The Other Side* (New York: New American Library, 1966), 118–119.

28. Brennan to Sullivan, 12/19/1963, FBIHQ Liaison with Commission File, 62-109090-73. For Hoover's long-standing dislike of Yarmolinsky, see Frank J. Donner, *The Age of Surveillance: The Aims and Methods of America's Political Intelligence System* (New York: Alfred A. Knopf, 1980), 119, 249n; and Robert Dallek, *Flawed Giant: Lyndon Johnson and His Times, 1960–1973* (New York: Oxford University Press, 1998), 110–111.

29. L. J. Gauthier to Belmont, 12/1/1963, FBIHQ JFK Assassination File, 62-109060-991;

Curt Gentry, *J. Edgar Hoover: The Man and the Secrets* (New York: W. W. Norton, 1991), 725–726, 743–744; Gauthier to Callahan, 12/9/1963, FBIHQ JFK Assassination File, 62-109060-2049; Gauthier to Callahan, 6/23/1964, FBIHQ JFK Assassination File, 62-109060-3468; Hoover to Rankin, 1/20/1964, FBIHQ JFK Assassination File, 62-109060-2294. In 1978 the Justice Department issued a forty-page report detailing Hoover's abuse of FBI services and agents to do special favors in his house and property. See *Washington Post*, January 12, 1978.

30. Gauthier to Callahan, 1/14/1964, FBIHQ JFK Assassination File, 62-109060-2313; Gauthier to Callahan, 1/2/1964, FBIHQ Liaison with Commission File, 62-109090-55; Gauthier to Callahan, 1/28/1964, FBIHQ Liaison with Commission File, 62-109090-NR; Gauthier to Callahan, 1/28/1964, FBIHQ JFK Assassination File, 62-109060-2366.

31. The FBI produced an impressive manual with a step-by-step narrative account of the shooting. The manual also contained photographs of the Dealey Plaza model. See The Assassination of President John F. Kennedy, November 22, 1963 and the Killing of Lee H. Oswald, November 24, 1963. Visual Aids, J. Lee Rankin Papers, "Investigation and Evidence," 1963–1964, box 8, folder 7, NARA. For the Secret Service's views on the shooting, see Gauthier to Callahan, 1/28/1964, FBIHQ JFK Assassination File, 62-109060-2366 and Warren Commission Document 5; see Gemberling Report, 11/29/1963, FBIHQ Oswald File, 105-82555-505, Section 21, 117, for Secret Service SA John J. Howlett's agreement on the theory of three shots and three hits.

32. Walther's report can be found in the Waggoner Carr Collection, National Archives, Washington, D.C. See also James T. Tague affidavit in Harold Weisberg's civil action suit, no. 75-226, U.S. District Court for the District of Columbia; *Dallas Morning News,* November 23, 1963, and December 13, 1963. See also Dallas to Bureau, 6/19/1964, FBIHQ Oswald File, 105-82555-4149.

33. The FBI report of Tague interview, 12/14/1963, was a standard FBI FD 302 interview form by agents Henry J. Oliver and Louis M. Kelley, Main Dallas Oswald File, 100-10461-NR; FBI report, 12/14/1963, Exhibit C from civil action suit no. 75-226; Gemberling Report, 7/2/1964, FBIHQ Oswald File, 105-82555-4584, 27–39; Rosen to Belmont, 6/8/1964, FBIHQ JFK Assassination File, 62-190960-NR.

34. For a full development of the implications of the "missed shot," see Chapter 9. See FBI Manual, Rankin Papers, "Investigation and Evidence," Record Group (RG) 12, box 8, folder 7, NARA, 14–15.

35. See FBI Manual, Rankin Papers, "Investigation and Evidence," RG 12, box 8, folder 7, NARA, 14–15.

36. W. D. Griffith to Conrad, 1/28/1964, FBIHQ JFK Assassination File, 62-109060-2405; Rosen to Belmont, 1/29/1964, FBIHQ JFK Assassination File, 62-109060-2367; Rosen to Belmont, May 11, 1964, FBIHQ Liaison with Commission File, 62-109090-NR.

37. Dulles, McCloy, Rankin, and the Commission staff held what could be called a "rump" session on July 8, 1964, with three psychiatrists to plumb the reasons behind Oswald's motives and actions. The meeting lasted the entire day and ended to no one's satisfaction. Oswald had a reading problem (dyslexia was one psychiatrist's diagnosis) that was proved, according to the good doctor, by his extensive reading. Another ventured that Oswald had shot JFK to prove his manhood, meaning that his motive was to prove something to Marina, his emasculating wife. At one point or another in the day-long session every staff member disagreed, sometimes strongly, with the trio of doctors. After 245 pages of transcript, this analytical marathon discussion ended without agreement. The July 8 session was so explicit about Lee and Marina's marital relations that the National Archives suppressed it rather than violate the Oswalds' privacy; at least, that was the rationale offered. I do not count this July 8

meeting as one of the thirteen Commission executive sessions. See Jack Anderson and Les Whitten, "The Washington Merry-Go-Round," *Washington Post,* November 8, 1975.

38. See Warren Commission, January 21, 1964, executive session transcript, NARA, for Rankin's decision to classify all the Commission sessions as "Top Secret."

39. See Warren Commission, June 4, 1964, executive session transcript, NARA.

40. Melvin A. Eisenberg to file, 2/13/1964, Rankin Papers, box 34, folder 443, NARA.

41. Ibid.; see also Samuel Stern interview with Mike Ewing, HSCA, JFK Collection, RG 233, 4, NARA.

42. For the working or tentative outline, see Rankin Papers, box 1, folder 5, NARA.

43. For McCloy's remarks, see Warren Commission, December 5, 1963, executive session transcript, NARA, 37.

44. For Rankin's remarks, see Warren Commission, December 16, 1963, executive session transcript, NARA, 43. Other negative comments about the FBI are pervasive throughout this session.

45. For Warren's concern, see Warren Commission, December 6, 1963, executive session transcript, NARA, 9.

46. Warren Commission, December 16, 1963, executive session transcript, NARA, 43–44. Actually, before the Commission began taking testimony Rankin had at his command a sizable staff. Counting assistant counsels, staff members, and a small army of lawyers, clerks, and secretaries, the final figure came to eighty-four, including the general counsel himself. See *WCR,* v and 481–482.

47. Rosen to Belmont, 12/18/1963, FBIHQ Liaison with Commission File, 62-109090-NR.

48. See Appendix A, 3. Bureau Relations with Warren Commission, A. Formation of Warren Commission, no. 3.

49. Rankin to Hoover, 3/26/1964, FBIHQ Liaison with Commission File, 62-109090-NR; Warren Commission, December 16, 1963, executive session transcript, NARA, 43–44.

50. See Chapter 10 for a detailed treatment of the Oswald note and its subsequent destruction on orders from FBIHQ.

51. Belmont to Tolson, 3/7/1964, FBIHQ Liaison with Commission File, 62-109090-114; Branigan to Sullivan, 4/3/1964, FBIHQ Liaison with Commission File, 62-109090-NR; Rosen to Belmont, 3/26/1964, FBIHQ Liaison with Commission File, 62-10909-NR.

52. Warren Commission, December 16, 1963, executive session transcript, NARA, 44; Shanklin to file, 3/18/1964, Main Dallas Oswald File, 100-10461-4524; Director, FBI, to SAC, Dallas, 3/18/1964, FBIHQ Liaison with Commission File, 62-109090-121; Joseph J. Loeffler to SAC, Dallas, 3/19/1964, Main Dallas Oswald File, 100-10461-serials 4751 and 4750.

53. SAC, New Orleans, to Director, FBI, 4/8/1964, FBIHQ Oswald File, 105-82555-3169; Dallas to Director, 3/20/1964, FBIHQ Oswald File, 105-82555-2762; Rosen to Belmont, 3/24/1964, FBIHQ Oswald File, 105-82555-2761; Hoover to Rankin, 4/7/1964, FBIHQ Oswald File, 105-82555-3026; Rosen to Belmont, 4/4/1964, FBIHQ Liaison with Commission File, 62-109090-124.

54. Edward Jay Epstein, *Inquest: The Warren Commission and the Establishment of Truth* (New York: Viking Press, 1966), 90–95; Samuel Stern interview with Mike Ewing, *HSCA,* 2. Not all of the Commission's staff lawyers were smitten with the image of an infallible and superhuman Hoover agency. For instance, Burt Griffin had worked with the FBI for two years before he joined the Commission. He later told the House Select Committee on Assassinations that he never found the bureau "very creative" or "imaginative." His impression of FBI ham-handedness coincided with Stern's after-the-fact assessment. Griffin did not have much

confidence in the FBI, and he volunteered that Rankin did not trust it either. Speaking for himself to the same congressional body, Rankin was not as caustic as Griffin, but he did allow that his personal relationship with Hoover was far from cordial by the time September rolled around and the Commission had finished its work. Rankin stopped short of characterizing the relationship as adversarial. Hoover, on the other hand, clearly came to regard the Commission as an adversary. See *HSCA*, XI, 273 (Griffin), 366, 372, and 385 (Rankin), and Appendix A, 3. Bureau Relations with Warren Commission.

55. Warren Commission, December 16, 1964, executive session transcript, NARA, 44; Stein interview with Ewing, *HSCA*, 2.

56. SAC, Dallas, to Director, FBI, 4/17/1964, FBIHQ Liaison with Commission File, 62-109090-NR; Brennan to Sullivan, 4/23/1964, FBIHQ Liaison with Commission File, 62-109090-NR.

Chapter 5. The Warren Commission Confronts the Evidence

1. *The Warren Commission Report: Report of the President's Commission on the Assassination of President John F. Kennedy* (Washington, D.C.: U.S. Government Printing Office, 1964) (hereafter cited as *WCR*), 145. For Brennan's statement to the Sheriff's Department, see J. Lee Rankin Papers, "Investigation and Evidence" (Cancelled Exhibits File), box 10, folder 3, National Archives and Records Administration, College Park, Maryland (hereafter cited as NARA); or see *Investigation of the Assassination of President John F. Kennedy: Hearings before the President's Commission on the Assassination of President Kennedy* (Washington, D.C.: U.S. Government Printing Office, 1964) (hereafter cited as *Hearings before Commission*), Vol. 19, 470; Gerald R. Ford, "Piecing Together the Evidence," *Life* 57 (October 2, 1964): 47; *Hearings before Commission*, Vol. 3, 154 (Brennan).

2. Gemberling Report, 1/15/1965, FBIHQ Oswald File, 105-82555-5375, 3.

3. Brennan's description of the man in the "sniper's nest" can be found in box 5, folder 2, John F. Kennedy/Dallas Police Department Collection Records Related to the Assassination of John F. Kennedy, City of Dallas Municipal Archives and Records Center, Dallas, Texas (hereafter cited as JFK Collection, Dallas Police Department). Rosen to Belmont, 11/13/1964, FBIHQ Liaison with Commission File, 62-109090-Not Recorded (NR), 2; Rankin to Hoover, 11/2/1964, FBIHQ Liaison with Commission File, 62-109090-NR; Hoover to Rankin, 11/12/1964, FBIHQ Oswald File, 105-82555-5262; Rosen to Belmont, 11/13/1964, FBIHQ Liaison with Commission File, 62-109090-NR. Sergeant Gerald D. Henslee, a sixteen-year veteran of the Dallas Police Department, was the dispatcher for all transmissions with the motorcycle officers escorting the presidential motorcade on November 22. It was Henslee who broadcast the description that the Warren Commission attributed to Howard Brennan: "male, approximately 30, slender build, height 5 feet 10 inches, weight 165 pounds, reported to be armed with what is believed to be a .30 caliber rifle." For the transcript of the radio log, see FBI Letterhead Memorandum, 8/11/1964, FBIHQ JFK Assassination File, 62-109060-(serial obliterated but record can be found in Section 83). For Henslee's Commission testimony, see *Hearings before Commission*, Vol. 6, 324–327, or see SAC, Dallas, to Director, FBI, 3/23/1964, FBIHQ JFK Assassination File, 62-109060-2725, 8, for a copy of Henslee's description of the suspect in the shooting of President Kennedy.

4. See Chapter 12 for the FBI's response to the Warren report. For Hoover's remarks, see Rosen to Belmont, 11/13/1964, FBIHQ Liaison with Commission File, 62-109090-NR; Gemberling Report, 1/15/1965, FBIHQ Oswald File, 105-82555-5375, 9.

5. For Brennan's sworn statement to the Dallas Sheriff's Department on 11/22/1963, see Warren Commission, Decker Exhibit, *Hearings before Commission*, Vol. 19, 469–470. That

Brennan's testimony cannot stand up to scrutiny is revealed by the Zapruder film, which showed that Brennan was looking at the presidential limousine as it moved onto Elm Street until he heard the first shot at Z frame 204. Then he did not look up at the depository, as he testified, but over his right shoulder in the direction of the Dal-Tex Building on Houston Street. That his Commission testimony was a lie prompts the speculation that he was coached by the FBI, Secret Service, or Commission staff lawyers. See David R. Wrone, *The Zapruder Film: Reframing JFK's Assassination* (Lawrence: University Press of Kansas, 2003), 166; and my conversation with Professor Wrone, August 28, 2004.

6. *WCR*, 3, 143. For CE 1311, see *Hearings before Commission*, Vol. 22, 484; Rankin's request for this FBI photograph can be found in Rankin to Hoover, 7/24/1964, FBIHQ Liaison with Commission File, 62-109090-3631. See Robert Lee Studebaker Exhibit D, one of four pictures of the so-called sniper's nest. This picture refutes key statements made by Howard Brennan.

7. *WCR*, 3, 143; *Hearings before Commission*, Vol. 3, 147; *WCR*, 145. For Brennan's statement to the FBI that he could not positively identify Oswald, see Gemberling Report, 11/30/1963, FBIHQ Oswald File, 105-82555-505, Section 21, 11, 13.

8. *WCR*, 145–147. The other person the Commission connected with the description of the alleged assassin was Inspector Herbert J. Sawyer, a twenty-three-year veteran of the Dallas Police Department. According to the FBI, Sawyer arrived at the depository building about seven minutes after the shooting. He spoke to a witness who said that shortly after the shooting he had seen "an unknown white male, approximately 30, slender build, 5 feet 10 inches, 165 pounds, *carrying* [my emphasis] what looked to be a .30-.30, or some type of Winchester rifle," running out of the depository building. According to the official account, it was Sawyer who relayed this description to Henslee. Sawyer said he could not remember the name of the man who provided the description of the fleeing gunman. In April 1964, when Sawyer testified before the Warren Commission, he still did not know the name of the eyewitness who had given him the primary description. See SAC, Dallas, to Director, FBI, 1/9/1964, FBIHQ Oswald File, 105-82555-1354. For Sawyer's Commission testimony, see *Hearings before Commission*, Vol. 6, 315–323. When Brennan testified before the Commission he never said he saw a man carrying a rifle running from the depository building. Moreover, if Brennan was the one who spoke to Sawyer for seven minutes and then spoke with Secret Service agents, as he testified, before Secret Service Agent Forrest Sorrels walked him to the Sheriff's Department so he could make his statement, Brennan would never have had time to provide the description that went out over the police radio at 12:45 P.M. (CST). The failure of the Commission and the FBI to resolve this confusion and provide a satisfactory explanation for the source of the gunman's description invites speculation that conspirators setting up Oswald as a patsy were the source of the description that so closely resembled Oswald. For Brennan's account of his movements after the shooting, see *Hearings before Commission*, Vol. 3, 148–158.

9. *WCR*, 145; *Hearings before Commission*, Vol. 3, 148, 150, 160. Assuming that Brennan came forward on his own and without coaching, he appears to be one of those self-promoting bystanders who because of shock and confusion or something much worse—the need to be associated with some great tragedy—pretend knowledge of the event when they actually have no information.

10. *WCR*, 143–144, 129–130.

11. *WCR*, 129–130; *Hearings before Commission*, Vol. 6, 375–377.

12. For the Commission's reenactment of Oswald's alleged movements, see *WCR*, 149–156. For Weitzman's and Boone's statements, see *Hearings before Commission*, Vol. 7, 106–108, and Vol. 3, 293. For the Commission's reconstruction of Oswald's movements after

he allegedly shot the president, see *WCR,* 149–156, 648. The FBI did a movement study to determine how long it would have taken the "assassin" to go from the sixth-floor "sniper's nest" to the front door of the book depository building. The study varied with the likely method of travel (normal pace, fast pace, running, etc.) and direction of a possible escape route to fix the time for each scenario. The study looked at ten different possible combinations, and in every one the FBI failed to factor in the time it would have taken to hide the alleged murder weapon. Gemberling Report, 11/30/1963, FBIHQ Oswald File, 105-82555-505, Section 21, 120–122. See Robert Lee Studebaker Exhibit C picture of the alleged murder weapon hidden under two boxes behind a barricade of boxes.

13. *Hearings before Commission,* Vol. 6, 387–392 (Adams). Actually, Adams would later report that she started down the stairs not thirty seconds to a minute but fifteen to twenty seconds after she saw the head shot. Adams corrected the Commission's account of her testimony when on February 17, 1964, she went to the U.S. attorney's office in Dallas to check the transcript of her testimony. See confirmation in Assistant Attorney Mary Jo Stroud's letter to Rankin in "Victoria Adams" subject index file, Harold Weisberg Archive, Hood College, Maryland (hereafter cited as Weisberg Archive).

14. For Adams's statement to Leavelle, see Record Group 91.001, box 3, folder 19, JFK Collection, Dallas Police Department.

15. *WCR,* 154. For Lovelady's and Shelley's April Commission testimony, respectively, see *Hearings before Commission,* Vol. 6, 329–330 and 339–340.

16. For Lovelady and Shelley's initial statements, see CE 2003, 36 (Lovelady), and CE 2003, 59 (Shelley); or see their affidavits, box 5, folder 2, JFK Collection, Dallas Police Department; Lovelady's November 22, 1963, FBI interview can be found in FBIHQ Oswald File, 105-82555-505, Section 22, 332.

17. The best treatment of the Commission's handling of Victoria Adams's testimony can be found in Sylvia Meagher's *Accessories after the Fact: The Warren Commission, the Authorities, and the Report* (New York: Vintage Books, 1992), 70–74. The Warren Commission never questioned Sandra Styles, but FBI records indicate that the bureau did. FBI Agent Thompson did the interview, but his report is not filed with the interviews of other Texas School Book Depository employees. Styles was with Adams and could have confirmed Adams's account of not seeing Oswald or hearing anyone on the stairs twenty to thirty seconds after they saw JFK assassinated. Styles was yet another witness who could have exonerated Oswald but was never called to testify, whose account disappears from the record and history. Copies of these interviews can be found in Gemberling Report, FBIHQ Oswald File, 105-82555-505, Section 21. For proof that Gaston C. Thompson did interview Styles, see SAC, Dallas, to Director, 3/25/1964, FBIHQ JFK Assassination File, 62-109060-2720, 3. Styles's recollection of what she witnessed was important because she could either corroborate or refute Adams's testimony.

18. For Harrison's altered FD-302 interview form, see CD 5:41. Arnold never saw the altered report. The proof that Arnold saw Oswald on the first floor at 12:25 P.M. can be found in an internal FBI document for 3/31/1964, FBIHQ JFK Assassination File, 62-109060-2783. When the Commission requested all the signed statements of the whereabouts of depository building employees at the time of the shooting, certain statements had to be corrected before they were turned over to the Commission. The FBI's first typed statement had Arnold leaving the building at 12:25 A.M. Before Arnold signed this statement she insisted that the FBI correct this "error" to make it read 12:25 P.M. For Arnold's corrected and signed statement, see CD 706(a). The five women who joined Arnold in front of the building were O. V. Campbell, L. C. Richey, Betty Drago, Virgie Baker, and Judy Johnson. None were ever questioned by the Commission.

19. Earl Golz, "Depository Chief Disputes Evidence of Filmed Image," *Dallas Morning News,* November 27, 1978.

20. For Oswald's statement to the FBI, see Gemberling Report, 11/30/1963, FBIHQ Oswald File, 105-82555-505, Section 21, 90, 97. His statement to Inspector Kelley can be found in Lee H. Oswald—Post-Russian Period—2–3, FBI FBI FPCC (Fair Play for Cuba Committee) File, 177, Weisberg Archive.

21. Allman's statement to the police can be found in box 3, folder 19, JFK Collection, Dallas Police Department. For Sorrels's report closing this area of the investigation, see CD 354. The Warren report spent two paragraphs on the testimony of Charles Douglas Givens, a black employee of the Texas School Book Depository who worked with the floor-laying crew on the sixth floor. The Commission asserted that Givens was the last person to see Oswald before the assassination. According to Givens's revised testimony, he saw Oswald on the sixth floor at about 11:55 A.M. See *WCR,* 142. But Kennedy assassination researcher and writer Sylvia Meagher presented documentary evidence that Givens revised his original testimony and that this revision might have been the result of coercion by the Dallas police and the FBI. Meagher also pointed out that Commission staff lawyers who questioned Givens knew he had changed his testimony, providing sufficient grounds for charges of subordination of perjury and falsification of evidence. For the full argument, see Sylvia Meagher, "The Curious Testimony of Mr. Givens," *The Minority of One,* August 13, 1971. For the documents supporting Meagher's argument, see SA Bill H. Griffin and Bradwell D. Odum's FD-302 report for 11/22/1963, Main Dallas JFK Assassination File, 89-43-(no serial number), and SA Robert P. Gemberling's FD-302 report, 2/13/1964, Main Dallas Oswald File, 100-10461-(no serial number).

22. SA Paul E. Wuff to Shanklin, 6/10/1964, Main Dallas Oswald File, 100-1041-6597; R. H. Jevons to Conrad, 11/23/1963, FBIHQ JFK Assassination File, 62-109060-368; Jevons to Conrad, FBIHQ Liaison with Commission File, 62-109090-NR; Gemberling Report, SAC, Dallas, to Director, FBI, 6/27/1964. FBIHQ Oswald File, 105-82555-4247, Section 180, 9, for date Dr. Rose removed the three slugs from Tippit's body.

23. SA Arthur E. Carter received a copy of the Tippit autopsy report on March 9, 1964; Main Dallas Oswald File, 100-10461-(no serial assigned).

24. Shanklin to file, Main Dallas Oswald File, 100-10461-4479; Vincent E. J. Drain to SAC, Dallas, 3/13/ 1964, FBIHQ JFK Assassination File, 62-109060-2624; SAC, Dallas, to Director, 3/14/1964, FBIHQ JFK Assassination File, 62-109060-2624. Fritz's gaffe with the missing Tippit bullets was apparently consistent with his general handling of evidence. According to Dallas District Attorney Henry Wade, the police captain had a reputation for being very poor in gathering evidence. See Wade's Commission testimony, *Hearings before Commission,* Vol. 5, 218.

25. Jevons to Conrad, 3/12/1964, FBIHQ Liaison with Commission File, 62-109090-NR; Rosen to Belmont, 3/17/1964, FBIHQ Liaison with Commission File, 62-109090-121; Stanford J. Unger, *FBI: An Uncensored Look Behind the Wall* (Boston: Little, Brown, and Company, 1975), 154.

26. Jevons to Conrad, 3/12/1964, FBIHQ Liaison with Commission File, 62-109090-NR. See internal memo by Conrad titled "Independent Examination of Evidence in Subject and Related Cases," 9, n.d.), FBIHQ JFK Assassination File, 62-109060-(no serial assigned); Rosen to Belmont, 3/17/1964, FBIHQ Liaison with Commission File, 62-109090-121.

27. See Chapter 9 for a detailed treatment of the Commission's "single-bullet" hypothesis.

28. Rankin to Hoover, 4/9/1964, FBIHQ Liaison with Commission File, 62-109090-2870; Hoover to Rankin, 4/16/1964, FBIHQ Liaison with Commission File, 62-109090-NR. A copy of the FBI's April 22, 1964, lab report (Lab. No. PC-80185 BX HB) is attached to the bureau's copy of the Hoover April 16, 1964, memo to Rankin. See also Dallas Report,

5/6/1964, FBIHQ Oswald File, 105-82555-3899, Section 63, 284, for the FBI's admission that it could not forensically establish whether Connally had been hit by an intact missile or missile fragments. If the latter were the case, then the Commission's "single-bullet" construction was impossible on those grounds alone.

29. For Mrs. Connally's account of her husband's clothes, see "A Matter of Reasonable Doubt," *Life* 61 (November 25, 1966), 48.

30. Shanklin to file, 11/28/1963, Main Dallas JFK Assassination File, 89-43-1121; Washington Field to Director, 11/22/1963, FBIHQ JFK Assassination File, 62-109060-27.

31. *WCR*, 94.

32. For Dr. Gregory's comments, see *Hearings before Commission,* Vol. 4, 125. Dr. Shaw's opinion can be found in the *Dallas Morning News,* April 21, 1977. Shaw was not only troubled by the holes in Connally's shirt; he was also skeptical about one bullet having caused all of the governor's massive wounds. When Commissioner Dulles asked him whether two bullets could have wounded Connally, Shaw responded without hesitation, "Yes, or three." For this exchange, see *Hearings before Commission,* Vol. 4, 108–109.

33. DeLoach to Mohr, 6/4/1964, FBIHQ Liaison with Commission File, 62-109090-NR, for a memorandum for the record of William Manchester's interview with the director.

34. In 1992 there was a strikingly similar case involving forensic interpretation of a bullet hole in the clothes of a shooting victim. The case was the shooting death of Sammy Weaver, the teenaged son of white separatist Randy Weaver, who was killed at Ruby Ridge, Idaho. The government contended that the boy had been unintentionally killed by a bullet from his father's rifle during a running gun battle with federal agents. The defense charged that he had been cut down by an FBI sniper. At first the FBI laboratory contended that since the fatal bullet had not been located, no tests were possible. Eventually, BuLab did tests on the bullet residue on Sammy Weaver's jacket and reported that the results were "inconclusive." Independent forensic experts were called. After examining the "bullet wipe" from the youth's coat and the casings of the spent shells in the area and testing the velocities of the different bullets in question, the team of experts concluded that the boy had been killed by an FBI sniper's bullet. Sometime after this report was filed, the authorities discovered the bullet that had felled young Weaver, making a positive ballistics match possible. Ballistics tests confirmed that the fatal shot had come from the rifle of the FBI sniper. See John F. Kelly and Philip K. Wearne, *Tainting Evidence: Behind the Scandals at the FBI Crime Lab* (New York: Free Press, 1998), 143–145.

35. For Frazier-McCloy exchange, see *Hearings before Commission,* Vol. 3, 391, 395.

36. Redlich to Dulles, 7/2/1964, "Investigation and Evidence" File, box 4, file 3 (Revolver), Rankin Papers, NARA. The Dallas police officer who apprehended Oswald in the Texas Theatre was M. N. McDonald. When McDonald was grappling with Oswald the two men tumbled into the seats. As McDonald fell, his hand still on Oswald's gun, he felt something graze his hand and heard what sounded like the tapping of the revolver's hammer. But the gun did not fire. After Oswald was subdued and removed from the theater, McDonald opened the revolver's cylinder and noticed that the primer on one of the shells had an indentation, but not enough to explode the charge in the bullet. In short, the firing pin in Oswald's handgun was defective. For McDonald's Commission testimony, see *Hearings before Commission,* Vol. 3, 300–301.

37. Joseph J. Loeffler to SAC, Dallas (89-43), 12/4/1963, Main Dallas JFK Assassination File, 89-43-2592; Jevons to Conrad, 12/2/1963, FBIHQ JFK Assassination File, 62-109060-916.

38. Jevons to Conrad, 3/26/1964, FBIHQ Liaison with Commission File, 62-109090-NR; Hoover to Rankin, 3/27/1964, FBIHQ JFK Assassination File, 62-109060-2823.

39. *Hearings before Commission,* Vol. 15, 746; Harold Weisberg, *Post-Mortem: JFK Assassination Cover-Up Smashed* (Frederick, Md.: Harold Weisberg Publisher, 1975), 449, for a facsimile of Gallagher's quantitative test results.

40. *Hearings before Commission,* Vol. 3, 434 (Frazier).

41. Rosen to Belmont, 4/4/1964, FBIHQ Liaison with Commission File, 62-109090-124.

42. *Hearings before Commission,* Vol. 5, 68 (Frazier).

43. Ibid., Vol. 5, 67, 69, and 74 (Frazier).

44. Jevons to Conrad, 5/14/1964, FBIHQ JFK Assassination File, 62-109060-3090.

45. *Hearings before Commission,* Vol. 15, 746ff.

46. Ibid., Vol. 5, 69 (Frazier).

47. Warren Commission, executive session transcript, NARA, 42 (Rankin). Dulles had his way on this matter. A reading of the Warren report reveals that almost half of the 912-page report, one way or another, is a biography of Lee Harvey Oswald. Whatever its merits, it is not evidence on the assassination of John F. Kennedy or an account of the murder. By sharp contrast, the space in the report allotted to the assassination and the JFK autopsy pales in comparison to the attention given to the life and times of Lee Harvey Oswald.

48. For the circumstances that forced the Commission to come to grips with the Tague curbstone shot, see Chapter 9.

49. Warren Commission, April 30, 1964, executive session transcript, NARA, 17–18.

50. Ibid., 38–39.

51. Robert Kennedy's biographer, Evan Thomas, noted that RFK had no interest in the public investigation into the murder of his brother. Although he had his own list of possible plotters who might have been responsible for the assassination, he provided no help to the Warren Commission, which he dismissed as largely a public relations exercise to tranquillize the public. See Evan Thomas, *Robert Kennedy: His Life* (New York: Simon and Schuster, 2000), 284.

Chapter 6. The Warren Commission's "Smoking Guns"

1. Because of their size and all too frequent bumbling nature, large bureaucracies sometimes tend to overlook the small things. This was the case with the January 22 transcript. According to a February 7, 1964, note by Rankin's Commission secretary, Julia Eide, "all the waste material" (reporter's notes, carbons, stenotypist's tape, etc.) was turned over to Elmer Moore of the Secret Service, who took the transcript to the White House "to be burned." Ms. Eide's note was attached to a Ward & Paul billing record. Ward & Paul was a reliable Washington firm that provided office stenographic reporters for congressional committees. It had been in business since the Great Depression. Chairman Earl Warren hired it to work for the Commission. A Ward & Paul record for March 10, 1964, noted for the January 22 Commission executive session, "No write-up (Reporter's notes confiscated by Commission) pages estimated 30." The paper record of the session was destroyed, but somehow the stenotypist's tape of the session was overlooked. Years later it was resurrected from archival limbo by assassination researcher Harold Weisberg under a Freedom of Information request and restored to the public and the historical record. The transcript was still cloaked in an aura of secrecy even upon its release. The copy I received from the National Archives in College Park noted that it was prepared by a Pentagon stenotypist with "proper security clearance." I wish to thank Harold Weisberg for allowing me to use his Ward & Paul file.

2. A copy of Rankin's summary of the January 24 meeting can be found in the CIA files under document number 487-195A, Record Copy 201-0289248. Or see Appendix B.

3. For a detailed study of the civil action suit (CA 2052-73) brought by Harold Weisberg to release the January 27 transcript, see David R. Wrone (ed.), *The Legal Proceedings of*

Harold Weisberg v. General Services Administration (Stevens Point, Wisc.: Foundation Press, 1978).

4. Warren Commission, January 22, 1964, executive session transcript, National Archives and Records Administration, College Park, Maryland (hereafter cited as NARA), 1.

5. Ibid., 2, 3; Alonzo F. Hudkins, "Oswald Rumored as Informant for U.S.," *Houston Post,* January 1, 1964.

6. For the Lane Bertram report, see CD 320. The report also carried the Secret Service file number 00-2-34,030.

7. Warren Commission, January 22, 1964, executive session transcript, NARA, 3.

8. See Rankin desk notes on his January 22, 1964, telephone conversation with Jaworski, J. Lee Rankin Papers, box 16, folder 245, NARA. There was some talk within Texas Democratic political circles about running Wade for governor.

9. For Oswald's "Crypto" clearance, see Chapters 5 and 12; Warren Commission, January 22, 1964, executive session transcript, NARA 6, 7, 8.

10. Warren Commission, January 22, 1964, executive session transcript, NARA, 6.

11. FBI typology makes a distinction between a human "source" and an "informant." A source is someone in a position to have logical access to information and is usually not paid. An informant, or more accurately a "symbol informant," is in effect a part-time FBI employee who has passed a period of probation, usually about six months, and who is identified in FBI communications by an arbitrary symbol rather than a name. The symbol consists of the FBI's abbreviation for the field office to which the informant reports (e.g., NO for New Orleans), plus the arbitrary four-digit number. An FBI symbol informant or informer supplies information on a regular basis and is usually paid.

12. Warren Commission, January 22, 1964, executive session transcript, NARA, 10, 11.

13. Ibid., 11.

14. Ibid., 12.

15. For more on the January 11, 1964, tentative outline, see Chapter 4.

16. Warren Commission, January 22, 1964, executive session transcript, NARA, 12–13.

17. Rankin desk notes, Rankin Papers, box 16, folder 245, NARA. Harold Feldman, "Oswald and the FBI," the *Nation,* January 27, 1964, 1; Dallas to Director, 1/25/1964, FBIHQ Liaison with Commission File, 62-1-9090-Not Recorded (NR); Dallas to Director, 1/25/1964, FBIHQ Oswald File, 105-82555-1766.

18. See Rankin Record Book for December 16, 1963, to May 31, 1964, for length of the January 24, 1964, meeting, Rankin Papers, box 8, folder 128, NARA.

19. Belmont to Tolson, 1/25/1964, FBIHQ Oswald File, 105-82555-1820. Ward & Paul records reveal that there was no billing for the January 24, 1964, meeting since there was no court reporter present.

20. See Appendix B.

21. Ibid., 2.

22. Based on my interviews with Harold Weisberg, who knew Sweatt and spoke with him about the Sheriff's Office's investigation into the assassination.

23. Belmont to Tolson, 1/25/1964, FBIHQ Liaison with Commission File, 62-109090-NR; Shanklin to file, 1/23/1964, Main Dallas Oswald File, 100-10461-2799; Belmont to Tolson, 1/25/1964, FBIHQ Oswald File, 105-82555-1820; M. A. Jones to DeLoach, 2/23/1964, FBIHQ Liaison with Commission File, 62-109090-NR; Dallas to Director, 2/24/1964, FBIHQ Oswald File, 105-82555-1749.

24. Belmont to Tolson, 1/25/1964, FBIHQ Oswald File, 105-82555-1820.

25. Dallas to Director, 1/25/1964, FBIHQ Oswald File, 105-82555-1706; Dallas to Director, 2/8/1964, FBIHQ Oswald File, 105-82555-1969; see Rankin memorandum for his reference to 110669, Appendix B, 3.

26. Dallas to Director, 2/8/1964, FBIHQ Oswald File, 105-82555-1969, 2; Bertram to Chief, 1/24/1964, CD 372.

27. SAC, Dallas, to Director, 12/9/1963, FBIHQ Oswald File, 105-82555-469; W. A. Branigan to W. C. Sullivan, 12/11/1963, FBIHQ Oswald File, 105-82555-470.

28. Hoover to Rankin, 2/11/1964, FBIHQ Oswald File, 105-82555-1906; Report of SA John R. Wineberg, 2/12/1964, CD 463. Goulden's story on Oswald appeared in the *Philadelphia Inquirer* on December 8, 1963.

29. Dallas to Director, 2/8/1964, FBIHQ Oswald File, 105-82555-1906; Hoover to Rankin, 2/11/1964, FBIHQ Oswald File, 105-82555-1906; Branigan to Sullivan, 2/10/1964, FBIHQ Liaison with Commission File, 62-109090-NR.

30. Dallas to Director, 1/25/1964, FBIHQ Oswald File, 105-82555-1906; Dallas to Director, 2/8/1964, FBIHQ Oswald File, 105-82555-1906, 3; Branigan to Sullivan, 2/28/1964, FBIHQ Oswald File, 105-82555-3087.

31. Dallas to Director, 2/13/1964, FBIHQ Oswald File, 105-82555-2020; Shanklin to file, 3/3/1964, Main Dallas Oswald File, 100-10461-3945.

32. Robert F. Gemberling to SAC, Dallas, 6/5/1975, Main Dallas JFK Assassination File, 89-43-9532. For Hudkins's story on the origins of S172, see his piece in the Baltimore *News-American,* "Reporters 'Had' the FBI, But Not Oswald's Number," March 10, 1975.

33. Appendix B, 5.

34. Warren Commission, January 27, 1964, executive session transcript, NARA, 129–130; Appendix B, 4.

35. Appendix B, 3; Dallas to Director, 2/8/1964, FBIHQ Oswald File, 105-82555-1969; Rankin's desk notes of his January 22, 1964, phone conversation with Leon Jaworski, Rankin Papers, box 16, folder 245, NARA; Warren Commission, January 27, 1964, executive session transcript, NARA, 136.

36. Warren Commission, January 27, 1964, executive session transcript, NARA, 139.

37. Ibid., 136. In a meeting with Rankin on January 28, 1964, Hoover pointed out that the FBI had turned over to the Commission more than ten thousand pages of investigative reports on the assassination. See Hoover memo, 1/31/1964, FBIHQ Liaison with Commission File, 62-109090-83.

38. Warren Commission, January 27, 1964, executive session transcript, NARA, 139, 158.

39. Ibid., 142, 146, 160, 164.

40. Ibid., 146; Jack Langguth piece in the *New York Times,* January 26, 1964, 58.

41. Hoover to Rankin, 1/27/1964, FBIHQ Oswald File, 105-82555-1517; Warren Commission, January 27, 1964, executive session transcript, NARA, 144; Belmont to Tolson, 1/25/1964, FBIHQ Liaison with Commission File, 62-109090-NR. See Appendix A, 3. Bureau Relations with Warren Commission, A. Formation of Warren Commission, no. 5.

42. Warren Commission, January 27, 1964, executive session transcript, NARA, 141–142, 144.

43. Appendix B, 4.

44. Warren Commission, January 27, 1964, executive session transcript, NARA, 142, 143, 144.

45. Ibid., 180–182.

46. Hoover memo, 1/31/1964, FBIHQ Liaison with Commission File, 62-109090-83, 2, 3.

47. Ibid.

48. The Warren report was made public in September 1964, and the FBI engaged in a "counterattack" on the Commission after it had disbanded. Hoover ordered a name check on all eighty-four Commission employees and had dossiers (files containing allegedly "derogatory" information) prepared on sixteen of the staff lawyers. Hoover also worked behind the

scenes with the House Un-American Activities Committee in a nasty Red-baiting campaign against Rankin's closest trusted assistant counsel, Norman Redlich. For a synopsis of the FBI's so-called derogatory information on Commission personnel, see Rosen to Belmont, 10/2/1964, FBIHQ Liaison with Commission File, 62-109090-385. See also Appendix A, 3. Bureau Relations with Warren Commission. The Norman Redlich Papers housed at NARA are the place to get a feel for Hoover's vindictiveness regarding the Commission's understated but deserved criticism of the FBI for failing to alert the Secret Service about Oswald.

49. Rosen to Belmont, 2/7/1964, FBIHQ Oswald File, 105-82555-1944; Rankin to Hoover, 2/10/1964, FBIHQ Oswald File, 105-82555-1907; Hubert to Rankin, 2/24/1964, Rankin Papers, box 17, folder 287, NARA; Sullivan to Belmont, 2/7/1964, FBIHQ Liaison with Commission File, 62-109090-94.

50. Memorandum for the Record, 3/12/1964, Meeting with the Warren Commission on 12 March 1964, CIA document 603-256, FOIA review June 1976, Harold Weisberg Archive, Hood College, Frederick, Maryland (hereafter cited as Weisberg Archive). For Dulles's comments, see Warren Commission, January 27, 1964, executive session transcript, NARA, 154; Rankin to McCone, 4/30/1964, Request from Warren Commission for affidavit stating Oswald was never associated with CIA, CIA document 672-286A, FOIA review, June 1976, Weisberg Archive.

51. In 1974 Chief Justice Warren granted an interview with the Commission historian, Alfred Goldberg. As might be expected, most of the interview was official boilerplate. What stands out, however, is Warren's astonishing ignorance and error when evidence is referred to, especially in the medical-autopsy area. This section of the interview shows that the Commission chairman was so detached from the work of the Commission that he never mastered or understood some of the critical facts of the investigation. For example, he told Goldberg that he had had no qualms about the "single-bullet" theory because the bullet (CE 399, which was in almost pristine condition) had not struck any bones in JFK or Governor Connally. In fact, the bullet that hit the governor sheared off part of a rib and smashed his wrist bone, one of the densest bones in the body. Warren also defended his decision to deny the Bethesda prosectors access to JFK's autopsy X-rays and pictures before they were scheduled to testify before the Commission, arguing that if Oswald had lived to go to trial "the court would not have permitted the X-rays [and pictures] to be introduced because it would have operated against the defendant." The truth is, of course, that not only would the court have permitted it but best evidence virtually required it, and the defense would have demanded that the X-rays and pictures be entered into the proceedings. See transcript of interview with Chief Justice Earl Warren by Alfred Goldberg, March 26, 1974, Manuscript Division, Library of Congress, Washington, D.C., 4–5.

52. Lane Bertram's report can be found in Rankin's summary of the January 24 meeting. See Appendix B, 3.

53. In 1967 Hudkins was a reporter for the *News-American,* a Baltimore city newspaper. He was contacted by representatives of *Newsweek* magazine, CBS, and NBC and asked if he had any additional information on the assassination that he could contribute to a program on Dallas that had a conspiratorial twist. Hudkins contacted the FBI's Baltimore office to alert it to this development. See SAC, Baltimore, to Director, FBI, 3/13/1967, FBIHQ JFK Assassination File, 62-109060-4770.

54. Hoover memo, 5/27/1964, FBIHQ Liaison with Commission File, 62-109090-160; *Investigation of the Assassination of President John F. Kennedy: Hearings before the President's Commission on the Assassination of President Kennedy* (Washington, D.C.: U.S. Government Printing Office, 1964) (hereafter cited as *Hearings before Commission*), Vol. 5, 99, 103–104. Hoover's assertion that Oswald demonstrated no propensity for violence is refuted by the fact

that a few weeks before the JFK assassination Oswald delivered a note to the FBI's Dallas office threatening violence against the FBI (blowing up the FBI office!) if it did not stop harassing his pregnant wife by repeated attempts to interview her. There is no dispute that there was an Oswald note; the only unresolved question is whether top FBI officials at Washington headquarters conspired to keep it from Hoover. For a detailed treatment of the Oswald note, see Chapter 10.

55. Belmont to Tolson, 5/21/1964, FBIHQ Liaison with Commission File, 62-109090-162; Sullivan to Belmont, 5/18/1964, FBIHQ Liaison with Commission File, 62-109090-152; Hoover memo, 5/27/1964, FBIHQ Liaison with Commission File, 52-109090-160; Belmont to Tolson, 5/15/1964, FBIHQ Liaison with Commission File, 62-109090-169; Belmont to Tolson, 5/19/1964, FBIHQ Liaison with Commission File, 62-109090-168. For the filming of Hoover's Commission testimony, see FBI Worksheet, FBIHQ Liaison with Commission File, 62-109090-169.

56. Belmont to Tolson, 5/21/1964, FBIHQ Liaison with Commission File, 62-109090-163; Belmont to Tolson, 6/2/1964, FBIHQ Liaison with Commission File, 62-109090-167. Rankin's additional sentences may be found in *Hearings before Commission,* Vol. 5, 102, and his paragraph in Vol. 5, 112. A time-consuming but useful exercise on how Hoover's Commission testimony was edited can be accomplished by comparing his testimony in Vol. 5 of the Commission hearings with the original text found in FBIHQ Liaison with Commission File, 62-109090-168, Evidence Behind File (EBF), Part I.

57. See Appendix A, 2. Structure and Methods of the Bureau Investigation, B. General Investigative Division (GID), no. 4.

58. *Hearings before Commission,* Vol. 5, 104–105.

59. *The Warren Commission Report: Report of the President's Commission on the Assassination of President John F. Kennedy* (Washington, D.C.: U.S. Government Printing Office, 1964) (hereafter cited as *WCR*), 105. See also *WCR,* 113, for CE 900 showing James W. Altgens's photo of the oak tree in front of the Texas School Book Depository at the time of the first shot. The clincher is a Secret Service picture taken from the sixth-floor "sniper's nest" looking down onto Houston Street. There is not a tree in sight. See Commission Exhibit 875.

60. William C. Sullivan with Bill Brown, *The Bureau: My Thirty Years in Hoover's FBI* (New York: W. W. Norton, 1979), 101–114; M. A. Jones to Wick, 9/12/1966, FBIHQ JFK Assassination File, 62-109060-NR.

61. *Hearings before Commission,* Vol. 5, 120–121; Sullivan to Belmont, 5/13/1964, FBIHQ Oswald File, 105-82555-3689. See also Appendix A, 3. Bureau Relations with Warren Commission, C. Related Bureau Actions and Activities, no. 4.

62. See section designated as B5, FBIHQ JFK Assassination File, 62-109060-4199, EBF, Part 3; W. D. Griffith to Conrad, 1/28/1964, for Hoover's disparaging remark. For the FBI Crime Laboratory's analysis of the Zapruder film, see section B6, FBIHQ JFK Assassination File, 62-109060-4199, EBF, Part 3.

63. My telephone interview, May 2, 2003, with Dino A. Brugioni, the center's chief analyst, who was in charge of NPIC's interpretation of the Zapruder film. The conclusions that follow are my own and should not be attributed to Brugioni. When Brugioni turned over to McCone or Helms the four photo-briefing boards with accompanying memoranda or explanations interpreting the calculations in the document, he had no knowledge of the "official truth" of JFK's assassination that had been decided upon over the weekend. See also Philip Melanson, "Hidden Exposure: Cover-Up and Intrigue in the CIA's Secret Possession of the Zapruder Film," *The Third Decade* 1, no. 1 (November 1984): 9. Melanson makes a strong circumstantial case that NPIC received a copy of the Zapruder film the day after the assassination.

64. See CIA document 1641-450 for NPIC's analysis of the Zapruder film of JFK's assassination. These results were pried loose from the CIA by a Freedom of Information Act re-

quest in 1982 by the assassination researcher Harold Weisberg. Or see Harold Weisberg, *Photographic Whitewash—Suppressed Kennedy Assassination Pictures* (Frederick, Md: Harold Weisberg Publisher, 1967), 302–303.

65. Hoover to Rankin, December 4, 1964. A copy of this letter appears in Weisberg, *Photographic Whitewash,* 143. In my conversation with Brugioni, he was absolutely clear that it was over the weekend following the assassination that McCone requested that NPIC submit the Zapruder film to analysis. Brugioni still recalls his shock when he witnessed the fatal shot that took off the right side of JFK's head. The former chief analyst for the center relayed the same account to the assassination researcher and author Gus Russo. See Gus Russo, *Live by the Sword: The Secret War against Castro and the Death of JFK* (Baltimore: Bancroft Press, 1998), 339–340.

Chapter 7. The JFK Autopsy

1. See phone interviews with Nicholas Katzenbach (May 31, 1978) and J. Lee Rankin (May 31, 1978) by House Select Committee on Assassinations interviewers, JFK Collection, Record Group (RG), National Archives and Records Administration, College Park, Maryland (hereafter cited as NARA), 233. Katzenbach sneered at the idea of FBI "cooperation" in the investigation, noting that it was "unbelievable some of the stuff they concealed." He described Hoover as a crafty tyrant whose "real talent was running over people and covering up in the process." Dulles, he volunteered, was carrying water for his old agency. Katzenbach charged that Dulles "was the CIA's spy on the Commission." Rankin found the FBI's performance "quite disturbing in hindsight. We would have found their conduct," alluding to the Hosty note destruction, "nearly unbelievable if we had known about it at the time." The Commission's former chief counsel even went so far as to conjecture that if the Commission had been aware of this "unconscionable" act it would have regarded the FBI as "suspect" and hired its own investigators. For the Hosty note destruction, see Chapter 10.

2. Henry Hurt aptly described JFK's autopsy as "the autopsy of the century." See Henry Hurt, *Reasonable Doubt: An Investigation into the Assassination of John F. Kennedy* (New York: Holt, Rinehart, and Winston, 1985).

3. A copy of the Oswald autopsy report is on file with NARA as Commission Exhibit (CE) 1981. The Warren Commission filed it as Commission Document (CD) 305. The original Oswald autopsy report is held by the National Archives at College Park.

4. Some of the more noteworthy critics of the JFK autopsy are Hurt, *Reasonable Doubt;* Sylvia Meagher, *Accessories After the Fact: The Warren Commission, the Authorities, and the Report* (New York: Vintage Books, 1992); David Lifton, *Best Evidence: Disguise and Deception in the Assassination of John F. Kennedy* (New York: Macmillan, 1981); and Harold Weisberg, *Post-Mortem: JFK Assassination Cover-Up Smashed* (Frederick, Md.: Harold Weisberg Publisher, 1975). Weisberg's powerful work still remains the most forcefully argued critique of the official autopsy. The official autopsy has its defenders. They usually argue that whereas the autopsy had startling deficiencies, it still arrived at the correct and valid conclusions. For example, see Gerald Posner, *Case Closed: Lee Harvey Oswald and the Assassination of JFK* (New York: Random House, 1993); David W. Belin, *November 22, 1963: You Are the Jury* (New York: Quadrangle/New York Times Books, 1973); David W. Belin, *Final Disclosure* (New York: Scribner's, 1988); Denis L. Breo, "JFK's Death" (Parts I–III), *Journal of the American Medical Association* 267, no. 20, and 268, no. 13; and John K. Lattimer, *Kennedy and Lincoln: Medical and Ballistic Comparisons of Their Assassinations* (New York: Harcourt, Brace, and Jovanovich, 1980).

5. *Investigation of the Assassination of John F. Kennedy, Hearings before the Select Committee on Assassinations of the U.S. House of Representatives,* 95th Congress, 2d session

(Washington, D.C.: U.S. Government Printing Office, 1979) (hereafter cited as *HSCA*), Vol. 2 (March 1979), 193–194. Despite this unflattering review the medical panel charitably concluded that these errors and deficiencies did not invalidate the official autopsy's conclusions. The Bethesda prosectors did not see Kennedy's clothes until March 1964, the day before they appeared before the Warren Commission. See *Investigation of the Assassination of President John F. Kennedy: Hearings before the President's Commission on the Assassination of President Kennedy* (Washington, D.C.: U.S. Government Printing Office, 1964) (hereafter cited as *Hearings before Commission*), Vol. 2, 364.

6. *Transcript of the Proceedings, Assassination Records Review Board,* NARA (hereafter cited as *ARRB*), Deposition of J. Thornton Boswell, February 26, 1996, 15–16; Boswell phone interview with Dr. Gary L. Aguilar, spring 1994, 7, copy of interview found in the Harold Weisberg Archive at Hood College, Frederick, Maryland (hereafter cited as Weisberg Archive); *ARRB,* Deposition of Pierre A. Finck, May 24, 1996, 69, 78; phone interview with Admiral David Osborne, June 20, 1978, *ARRB,* Master Set of Medical Exhibits, MD 66, 2.

7. Michael M. Baden, *Unnatural Death: Confessions of a Medical Examiner* (New York: Ivy Books, 1989), 12; Belmont to Tolson, 11/22/1963, FBIHQ JFK Assassination File, 62-109060-284; SAC, Baltimore, to Director and SAC, Dallas, 11/23/1963, FBI Main Baltimore JFK Assassination File, 89-30-7. According to Humes, the autopsy started at about 8 P.M. with certain X-rays and other necessary preliminaries that might have taken the better part of an hour. The actual autopsy procedures began at about 9, and the autopsy concluded at 11 P.M. See *Hearings before Commission,* Vol. 2, 349, 374.

8. James W. Sibert and Francis X. O'Neill to SAC, Baltimore, 11/26/1963, FBI Releases to the House Select Committee on Assassinations, Section 13, Serials 841–888; or see Sibert and O'Neill's five-page report on the autopsy, 11/26/1963, Main FBI Baltimore JFK Assassination File, 89-30-31, 4. Sibert was prompted to call BuLab because when Humes placed X-rays of JFK's head on the viewer Humes was astonished to see approximately forty dust-like particles of a disintegrated bullet. Sibert and Secret Service agent Kellerman described the configuration as looking like the "Milky Way." This gave rise to a discussion of whether soft-nosed ammunition might have been used in the shooting. The doctors were puzzled at the amount of fragmentation and questioned what kind of bullet completely "fragmentizes." See Sibert interview with Jim Kelly and Andy Purdy, 8/29/1977, and Francis X. O'Neill interview with Kelly and Purdy, 1/10/1978, HSCA, JFK Collection, RG 233, NARA.

9. Dr. John H. Ebersole testimony, HSCA, JFK Collection, document 01367, box 9, NARA, 54–55, 65.

10. Marshall Houts, *Where Death Delights: The Story of Dr. Milton Helpern and Forensic Medicine* (New York: Coward-McCann, 1967), 13, 27–30; Cyril Wecht, "A Critique of President Kennedy's Autopsy," Appendix C, in Josiah Thompson, *Six Seconds in Dallas: A Micro-Study of the Kennedy Assassination* (New York: Bernard Geis Associates, 1967), 278–279.

11. Francis X. O'Neill, Jr., and James W. Sibert, FBI Report, 11/26/1963, "Autopsy of Body of President John F. Kennedy," JFK 4-1 file, National Archives, Washington, D.C., 2–3. Or see their report 11/26/1963, FBI Baltimore JFK Assassination File, 89-30-31, 1–3. See also Appendix to *HSCA,* Vol. 7, 7–9; Dr. Robert F. Karnei, Jr., interview with Jim Kelly and Andy Purdy, August 29, 1977, *ARRB,* Master Set of Medical Exhibits, MD 61, 1–2. For Admiral Kinney's presence in the morgue, see Adm. George G. Burkley's statement, "report on my participation into the activities surrounding the assassination of President John Fitzgerald Kennedy," November 27, 1963, Warren CE 1126, National Archives, Washington, D.C.

12. On the qualifications of the JFK prosectors, see *HSCA,* March 1979, Vol. 7, 182; Houts, *Where Death Delights,* 55. In 1957 the American Board of Pathologists established that candidates for certification had to have participated in at least twenty-five homicide au-

topsies. Under this standard, none of the three prosectors would have qualified in the world of civilian forensic pathology. See James A. French, "Issuance of Certificates in Forensic Pathology," *Legal Medicine Annual 1969* (New York: Appleton-Crofts, 1969), 160.

13. *Hearings before Commission,* Vol. 2, 372–373.

14. *ARRB,* Deposition of James Joseph Humes, February 13, 1996, 227–228; *ARRB,* Boswell deposition, 207.

15. Harold Hirsh, "Tampering with Medical Records," *Medical Quarterly* annual, 1978, 454; Emmanuel Hayt, *Medicolegal Aspects of Hospital Records,* 2d ed. (Berwyn, Ill.: Physicians' Record Company, 1977), 166; Mary D. Helmelt and Mary Ellen Mackert, "Factual Medical Records Protect Hospitals, Practitioners, and Patients," *Hospitals,* July 1, 1977, 52. I want to thank medical records expert Betsy Neichter for her guidance with these sources.

16. "The Autopsy," *Armed Forces Institute of Pathology* (Washington, D.C., 1951), 64. When questioned by the ARRB, Humes admitted that he had "trained young doctors to do autopsies all my life." He was less than responsive when asked about what training manuals he used. Humes gave his questioner to believe that his approach was freewheeling, that he taught mostly from his own experience of many years. It is hard to accept that a military training hospital such as the Bethesda Naval Medical School did not insist on the standard AFIP manual for autopsy procedures done around the world. Failure to do so could only invite numerous legal actions and expensive litigation. See *ARRB,* Humes deposition, 40–44.

17. *Hearings before Commission,* Vol. 2, 372. For Warren CE 397, see *Hearings before Commission,* Vol. 17, Exhibits 392–884.

18. *ARRB,* Humes deposition, 129–131; Boswell interview with *HSCA,* 8/17/1977, JFK Collection, RG 233, NARA, 9; *ARRB,* Boswell deposition, 108–112.

19. Testimony of Pierre Finck, *State of Louisiana vs. Clay L. Shaw,* Criminal District Court, Parish of New Orleans, State of Louisiana, February 24, 1969 (hereafter cited as *State of Louisiana vs. Clay L. Shaw*), 96; *ARRB,* Finck deposition, 24, 56. For the account of Finck's angry outburst in the AFIP lunchroom, see affidavit of Dr. Leonard D. Saslaw, May 15, 1996, *ARRB,* Master Set of Medical Exhibits, MD 74.

20. Humes's testimony, *HSCA,* September 6, 1978, Vol. 1, 330.

21. See Humes's testimony, *HSCA,* March 1979, Vol. 7, 257–258; *ARRB,* Humes deposition, 125–128. Humes's "bloodstain" story verges, if it does not cross the line, on silliness when it is recalled that JFK's violent death was a frightfully bloody affair. There were bloodstains and body-fluid marks on Boswell's descriptive sheet, which Humes did not dare destroy. The presidential limousine was covered with blood, and there was even blood and brain tissue behind the visor on the driver's side. The lining of JFK's coffin was saturated with blood. The two motorcycle cops flanking the limo were splattered with blood and brain tissue. There were bloodstains on the gurney, mattress, and sheets; on the doctors and nurses who attended the dying president; and God knows where else in Emergency Room One at Parkland Memorial Hospital, where JFK was taken after the shooting. Humes had no way of controlling the disposition of any of this assassination gore that could (but never did) have ended up in some sideshow or hanging on the side of a barn somewhere in Kansas. The latter apparently, at least according to Boswell, was one of Humes's recurring nightmares. See *ARRB,* Boswell deposition, 14.

22. See *Hearings before Commission,* Vol. 17, Exhibits 392–884.

23. A copy of the final autopsy draft can be found in *The Warren Commission Report: Report of the President's Commission on the Assassination of President John F. Kennedy* (Washington, D.C.: U.S. Government Printing Office, 1964) (hereafter cited as *WCR*), 538–543.

24. I want to thank Harold Weisberg for helping me work through the traps and snares of the JFK autopsy. His autopsy file was invaluable, especially Howard Roffman's fifteen-page

study titled "Comparison of Medical Report and Data." See Weisberg, *Post-Mortem,* 255–256.

25. Justice Department, Criminal Division, 129-213-3, section 7, 1. For transfer of X-rays and autopsy photographs to the Secret Service, see Capt. J. H. Stover, MC, USN, Commanding Officer, U.S. Naval Medical School, to Roy H. Kellerman, Assistant Special Agent in Charge, U.S. Secret Service, November 22, 1963. Documents can be found in *ARRB,* Master Set of Medical Exhibits, MD 78 and 79. Roy Kellerman interview by Jim Kelly and Andy Purdy, August 24 and 25, 1977, *ARRB,* Master Set of Medical Exhibits, MD 56, 6.

26. See *ARRB,* Master Set of Medical Exhibits, MD 10.

27. (Admiral) C. B. Galloway to the White House Physician, November 25, 1963, CD 371, or see *ARRB,* Master Set of Medical Exhibits, MD 52. Galloway's receipt should have been filed with Warren CE 397, but it does not appear in the exhibits of the Commission's published report.

28. Bouck's receipt is filed as CD 371. Or see *ARRB,* Master Set of Medical Exhibits, MD 119. See also Humes's March 16, 1964, Commission testimony during which Assistant Counsel Specter elicited from Humes that CE 397 was identical with Commission File 371, which the Commission employed for internal purposes. Clearly, this was a blatant deception on Specter's part. If the JFK autopsy had not been corrupted, then the receipts for the autopsy notes and JFK's death certificate would have been part of CE 397. For Specter's dishonesty, see *Hearings before Commission,* Vol. 2, 373. The JFK death certificate signed by Dr. Burkley is not in *The Warren Commission Report* or any of the twenty-six volumes of hearings or exhibits. Researcher Harold Weisberg discovered the original copy in records the Commission sent to the U.S. Government Printing Office that were not to be copied. See Weisberg, *Post-Mortem,* 302–306. The reason for the suppression of the death certificate is discussed below.

29. *Hearings before Commission,* Vol. 2, 374; Humes's testimony, *HSCA,* March 1979, Vol. 7, 258.

30. Dr. Finck recalled that all three prosectors and Admiral Galloway, the commanding officer of Bethesda Naval Hospital, were all in Galloway's office when the final autopsy protocol was signed. For Finck's recollection, see *HSCA,* March 1979, Vol. 7, 192.

31. For the revised handwritten autopsy report, see *Hearings before Commission,* Vol. 17, Exhibits 392–884, Exhibit 397, 1.

32. Ibid., Exhibit 397, 1.

33. Ibid., Exhibit 397, 7, 8, 9.

34. Ibid., Exhibit 397, 9; *State of Louisiana vs. Clay L. Shaw,* February 25, 1969, 4–5. This edited version of "presumably of exit" and "presumably of entrance" was incorporated into the final official JFK autopsy protocol. See *WCR,* 541.

35. *Hearings before Commission,* Vol. 17, Exhibits 392–884, Exhibit 397, 3. For the editing in the final typed autopsy protocol, see the second page of the report in *WCR,* 539.

36. See Chapter 1.

37. *ARRB,* Humes deposition, 136–138. Humes died in May 1999. For his obituary, see *Newsday,* May 11, 1999.

38. *ARRB,* Humes deposition, 128–131.

39. See ARRB, "Staff Report to Accompany July Release of Medical and Autopsy Records," July 31, 1998, 1. A copy of the report can be acquired from the JFK Special Collections Branch, NARA.

40. Although the ARRB drew attention to the missing autopsy notes and the inexplicable destruction of the first holographic autopsy draft, other earlier government-selected medical panels established to review the official JFK autopsy findings never bothered to raise these

questions. The 1968 Ramsey Clark Panel (sometimes referred to as "the Panel") found technical errors along with procedures that were forensically unsound but made no mention of the fact that most of the autopsy facts in the final report had no identifiable source. The panel concluded, after only two days of examining some of the autopsy material, that it could find no reason to invalidate the Bethesda autopsy report. As mentioned before, the HSCA's Medical Panel, though more thorough and more wide-ranging in its professional critique, arrived at the same conclusion. Both buttressed *The Warren Commission Report.* For the Clark Panel report (February 26, 1968), see *ARRB,* Master Set of Medical Exhibits, MD 59.

41. News Conference No. 1, November 22, 1963, 3:10 P.M. (CST). This was the first news conference of the Lyndon Johnson presidency. For the White House transcript of the Dallas press conference, see *ARRB,* Master Set of Medical Exhibits, MD 41.

42. *Hearings before Commission,* Vol. 6, 18.

43. Humes, ibid., Vol. 2, 361–362; *ARRB,* Boswell deposition, 27, 31–32; Finck, HSCA testimony, March 11, 1978, JFK Collection, RG 233, 116117, NARA; Admiral Galloway, HSCA interview, May 17, 1978, JFK Collection, RG 233, 2, NARA.

44. See *WCR,* 540. Or see page 2 of the final typewritten autopsy protocol in *ARRB,* Master Set of Medical Exhibits, MD 3.

45. *ARRB,* Boswell deposition, 23–24; Ebersole interview, March 11, 1978, JFK Document 013617, JFK Collection, RG 233, box 239, 47 and 52, NARA.

46. James W. Sibert, HSCA interview, August 25, 1977, JFK Collection, RG 233, NARA, 3; Sibert affidavit, October 24, 1976, National Archives, Washington, D.C.

47. In 1993 a Dr. Robert B. Livingston testified for the plaintiffs in a lawsuit against the *Journal of the American Medical Association.* Livingston swore that on the day of the assassination he reached Dr. Humes at the Bethesda Naval Hospital and spoke to him before Humes autopsied the dead president. Dr. Livingston had an impressive medical career. He taught at the Yale and Harvard medical schools and was on the First Life Sciences Committee for the National Aeronautics and Space Administration in the 1950s. He was executive assistant to the president of the National Academy of Sciences and to the chairman of the National Research Council. When he retired he was professor of neurosciences at the University of California, San Diego. During the Okinawa campaign in World War II, Livingston was a medical officer and treated wounded Japanese prisoners of war. The navy later awarded him a Bronze Star. Livingston was working at the National Institutes of Health in Washington, D.C., the day Kennedy was assassinated. He followed the breaking news about JFK's wounds, especially the wound in the throat. From the media reporting he was certain that the neck wound had been caused by a shot from in front of the president. Because of his experience with bullet wounds, Livingston called Humes to advise him on the importance of dissecting the wound to avoid any medicolegal doubt about whether it was a wound of entry. Livingston swore that his conversation with Humes was cordial and that the navy pathologist was thankful for his concern and advice. But, according to Livingston, Humes left the phone and when he returned told Livingston, "I can't continue the conversation, and, in fact, the FBI won't let me." For Livingston's affidavit, see *ARRB,* Master Set of Medical Exhibits, MD 24, 1–30. Humes forcefully denied that he had spoken with Livingston, right before the autopsy or at any other time. He told ARRB questioner Jeremy Gunn that it was all "pure fantasy" on Livingston's part. See *ARRB,* Humes deposition, 45–49.

48. Dr. Malcolm Perry interview with D. A. Purdy, Jr., and T. M. Flanagan, Jr., January 11, 1978, *ARRB,* Master Set of Medical Exhibits, MD 58, 10.

49. Adm. George G. Burkley oral history interview, October 17, 1967, John F. Kennedy Library, Harvard University, Cambridge, Mass., 16, 21.

50. Ibid., 17–18.

51. Adm. Calvin B. Galloway, HSCA interview, May 17, 1978, JFK Collection, RG 233, NARA, 2.

52. *Baltimore Sun,* November 25, 1966; Weisberg, *Post-Mortem,* 35–37. I want to thank Harold Weisberg for bringing this story to my attention.

53. Ebersole, HSCA interview, March 11, 1978, JFK Documents, 013617, box 239, 4–5, 20, 51–52. Ebersole's testimony was not released to the public until after the passage of the so-called JFK Act of 1992; John Thomas Stringer, Jr., HSCA testimony, August 17, 1977, JFK Collection, RG 233, NARA, 5. Author William Manchester noted that Humes called Dr. Perry shortly after midnight. See William Manchester, *The Death of a President: November 20–November 25, 1963* (New York: Harper and Row, 1967), 433.

54. *Hearings before Commission,* Vol. 6, 16–17. Humes had certain knowledge by Saturday morning, if not by Friday night, that Perry had described the president's anterior neck wound as a gunshot wound of entry. This was reported in the November 23, 1963, morning edition of the *Washington Post,* which Humes cited in the official autopsy report. See *WCR,* 539, paragraph 2.

55. Humes, *Hearings before Commission,* Vol. 2, 371; Perry, ibid., Vol. 6, 16. The assassination researcher Harrison Edward Livingstone reported from an interview with Audrey Bell, the supervising nurse in Emergency Room One at Parkland Memorial Hospital, that when Dr. Perry showed up for duty on Saturday morning he "looked terrible, having not slept." According to Livingstone, when Bell asked the surgeon the reason for his troubled night, Bell reported that Perry said, "They called him from Bethesda two or three times in the middle of the night to change the entrance wound in the throat to an exit wound." Harrison E. Livingstone, *High Treason 2: The Great Cover-Up—The Assassination of President John F. Kennedy* (New York: Carroll and Graf Publishing, 1992), 121.

56. *Hearings before Commission,* Vol. 6, 16.

57. Ibid., Vol. 6, 14, 17.

58. Perry, ibid., 14; Clark, ibid., 127.

59. Charles A. Crenshaw with Jesse Hansen and J. Gary Shaw, *JFK Conspiracy of Silence* (New York: Signet, 1992), 155–156.

60. *Hearings before Commission,* Vol. 2, 364–365, 368.

61. Ibid., 351, 357, 361, 363, 367, 375.

62. For the Sibert and O'Neill list of persons in the morgue, see *HSCA,* March 1979, Vol. 7, 8–9. T. H. Ryberg's name is not on their list. Finck testified that Humes "supervised" the Ryberg illustrations. See *State of Louisiana vs. Clay L. Shaw,* February 24, 1969, 18.

63. Finck, *HSCA* testimony, March 11, 1978, 105–106.

64. Arlen Specter to J. Lee Rankin, April 30, 1964, Warren CD 10079, National Archives, Washington, D.C., 1–2; Specter to Rankin, 11/12/1964, J. Lee Rankin Papers, box 37, folder 473, NARA.

65. When John J. McCloy asked about the "raw material of the autopsy . . . the colored photographs of the President's body—do we have these?" Rankin acknowledged that they had the "raw materials," photos, and X-rays. See Warren Commission, January 21, 1964, executive session transcript, NARA, 35. Two years after the Commission submitted its final report on the assassination, former assistant counsels W. David Slawson and Norman Redlich reported to Burke Marshall that the Commission had not seen the X-rays and the autopsy photos. See W. David Slawson to file, 10/7/1966, Department of Justice, Criminal Division, file 129-11, 1–2.

66. McCloy's *Face the Nation* comments can be found in an FBI clipping of the Washington Capitol News Service, 7/6/1967, FBIHQ Liaison with Commission File, 62-109090-601.

67. Rosen to DeLoach, 12/7/1966, FBIHQ JFK Assassination File, 62-109060-4235.

Hoover was accurate as far as FBI records were concerned. A serial-by-serial search of the Baltimore field office's (the office of origin on this issue) Main JFK Assassination and Lee Harvey Oswald files uncovered no record that the Kennedy family had requested that the autopsy report be kept confidential. See J. Stanley Rotz to SAC, Baltimore, 10/18/1966, Main Baltimore JFK Assassination File, 89-30-268; 89-30-262 and 267.

68. SAC, Baltimore, to Director and SAC, Dallas, 11/23/1963, FBIHQ JFK Assassination File, 62-109060-459.

69. Francis X. O'Neill, HSCA interview, 1/10/1978, JFK Collection, RG 233, NARA, 4, 8; O'Neill affidavit, 11/8/1978, JFK Collection, RG 233, NARA, 5.

70. Clint Hill statement, *Hearings before Commission,* Vol. 18, 740ff.; see page 6 for Hill's statement.

71. Roy H. Kellerman, *Hearings before Commission,* Vol. 2, 93; Kellerman, HSCA interview with Jim Kelley and Andy Purdy, August 29, 1977 (see last page attachment for Kellerman's placement of the rear wound), *ARRB,* Master Set of Medical Exhibits, MD 56.

72. Chester H. Boyer, HSCA interview, November 25, 1978, JFK Collection, RG 233, NARA, 4; Jan G. Rudnicki, HSCA interview, May 18, 1978, JFK Collection, RG 233, NARA, 3.

73. Arlen Specter to J. Lee Rankin, 5/12/1964, Rankin Papers, box 37, folder 473, NARA; Specter to Rankin, 3/12/1964, Rankin Papers, box 37, folder 473, NARA; Francis W. Adams and Arlen Specter to J. Lee Rankin, 1/23/1964, Investigation and Evidence File, box 4, folder 3, page 1, of their "Memorandum of Things to Be Done and Some of the Problems Involved," Rankin Papers, box 37, folder 473, NARA.

74. The official autopsy protocol noted, "As far as can be determined this missile struck no bony structures in its path through the body." See copy of the autopsy report in *WCR,* 543, the sixth page of the report. The Ramsey Clark Panel report made the same claim at the top of page 3. For Clark Panel report (February 26, 1966), see *ARRB,* Master Set of Medical Exhibits, MD 59; Pierre A. Finck to Brig. Gen. J. M. Blumberg, "The Autopsy of President Kennedy Summary," January 25, 1964, Otis Historical Archives, National Museum of Health and Medicine, Armed Forces Institute of Pathology, 1.

75. Humes, *Hearings before Commission,* Vol. 2, 349; *ARRB,* Boswell deposition, 26; Finck's revised "Summary" to General Blumberg, Otis Historical Archives, National Museum of Health and Medicine, AFIP, 3. The HSCA identified the officer in question as Lieutenant Commander Humes. Guileless or not, the HSCA's assertion is suspect because Humes did not outrank Lieutenant Colonel Finck. The only officers in the morgue who did were two navy captains and the three medical admirals. The only other explanation that supports Humes as the officer in question is that Dr. Finck was an army officer on U.S. Navy turf and may have felt obliged to defer to a navy officer of comparable rank. See note 8 for the list of all military officers who were present in the morgue.

76. *WCR,* 92. This was one autopsy measurement over which there is no dispute. See also *HSCA,* Vol. 7, 85, for medical illustrator Ida Dox's drawing of JFK's back wound. It aligns exactly with the location of the missile holes in JFK's shirt and coat. That is, it is a wound in the back and not in the neck, as Humes insisted in his Warren Commission testimony.

77. See *WCR,* 541, or page 4 of the official autopsy report, where it reads, "The second wound presumably of entry is that described above in the upper posterior thorax."

78. Humes, *Hearings before Commission,* Vol. 2, 366; *ARRB,* Boswell deposition, 74. Kennedy's custom-made shirts, for example, came from Charles (Charles Dillon shirtmaker), Park Avenue, New York, and not the local K-Mart. Boswell and Humes argued that JFK's shirt and coat had been pushed up when he was in a sitting position because of his back brace and that when he raised his arms to wave, this action served to further bunch his shirt

and jacket up around his neck. JFK did wear a back brace that fit below the waist and above the hips. Had the brace been as ungainly and formidable a contraption as Humes and Boswell would have us believe, it is questionable whether Kennedy would have been able to sit down at all. On May 30, 1995, Arlen Specter was a guest on a popular Philadelphia nighttime talk show hosted by Tom Snyder. A caller asked the now Senator Specter if he had changed his views on the Kennedy assassination. During the course of his reply Specter launched into a defense of the Warren report and the controversial "single-bullet theory." In buttressing his case for the report's validity he trotted out the old canard of the back brace and the shirt and jacket that had ridden up the president's back. See Richard Bartholomew, "True Believers: Tom Snyder Talks to Arlen Specter," *Fourth Decade* 2, no. 5 (July 1995): 30. A useful, if not definitive, description of JFK's back brace was provided by Parkland doctor Charles J. Carrico to Arlen Specter. See Sixth Floor Museum, box 8, Carrico Collection 1044.00061, Dallas, Texas, 13. William Greer, the Secret Service agent who drove the presidential limo that day in Dallas, helped carry Kennedy into the Parkland emergency room. He described the back brace as "soft, maybe a kind of corset-type material" that Kennedy wore "below his belt." See *Hearings before Commission,* Vol. 2, 125 (Greer).

79. SAC, Baltimore, to Director and SAC, Dallas, 11/23/1963, Main Baltimore JFK Assassination File, 89-30-7. See also Francis X. O'Neill affidavit, 11/8/1978, 5, JFK Collection, RG 233, NARA.

80. For the series of press stories, see *Baltimore Sun,* November 25, 1966; an Associated Press story in the *Baltimore Sun,* November 24, 1966; *Washington Post,* November 25, 1966, A4; *New York Times,* November 25, 1966.

81. Boswell, interview with Jim Kelly and Kenneth Klein, August 17, 1977, *ARRB,* Master Set of Medical Exhibits, MD 26, 9, and MD 159 for the adjustment upward of the posterior wound.

82. Ford's editing of *The Warren Commission Report,* draft dated 6/26/1964, can be found in the Rankin Papers, box 26, folder 385, NARA.

83. Humes, *HSCA,* Vol. 7, 262.

84. Finck, *HSCA,* March 11, 1978, 73–75.

85. The postmortem authorization form signed by Robert F. Kennedy was part of the permanent navy record of the president's autopsy. As discussed earlier, it was one of the eleven items that Dr. Burkley received from Admiral Galloway and transmitted on November 26, 1963, to Robert Bouck, head of the White House Protective Research Section of the Secret Service. The original should have been part of the published Warren Commission records. The autopsy authorization form should have been one of the documents found in the CD 397 file, but it was suppressed by the Commission. The original form can be found in RG 87, Secret Service Records, NARA, in the Valuable Documents Collection.

86. See trip report written by Pierre A. Finck regarding *State of Louisiana v. Clay L. Shaw,* March 13, 1969, *ARRB,* Master Set of Medical Exhibits, MD 36, 1–2; *ARRB,* Finck deposition, 140–141. It should be noted that Garrison's case against Shaw was baseless, and he was ultimately acquitted.

87. *State of Louisiana vs. Clay L. Shaw,* February 24, 1969, 13. Finck persisted in his in-court spelling bee for much of this session.

88. Ibid., 115–116.

89. Ibid., 51–52.

90. Ibid., February 25, 1969, 4–6, 36–37. Galloway was later interviewed by the HSCA, but he was never questioned about what Finck had testified to in the Clay Shaw trial. See Calvin B. Galloway, HSCA interview, May 17, 1978, JFK Collection, RG 233, NARA.

91. Although the Garrison prosecution team thought that Finck's revelations gave legs to the JFK assassination story, they went largely unnoticed by the national press.

92. *ARRB,* Boswell deposition, 208–213. Exactly what business the federal government had in a local prosecution remains an intriguing mystery because the ARRB failed to pry from Boswell the story behind this story when it had him under oath. Nor did the ARRB make any real effort to subpoena the Boswell-Eardley correspondence cited in the transcript of the doctor's testimony.

93. See Burkley's nine-page statement, "report on my participation in the activities surrounding the assassination of President John Fitzgerald Kennedy," November 27, 1963, Warren CE 1126, National Archives, Washington, D.C. See also Kellerman to Chief, 11/30/1963, CD 3, 3–4, National Archives, Washington, D.C.; and statement of Special Agent Clinton J. Hill, 11/30/1963, CD 3, 4–5, National Archives, Washington, D.C.

94. Burkley oral history interview, 16; Manchester, *Death of a President,* 349–350.

95. D. J. Brennan to W. C. Sullivan, 6/4/1964, FBIHQ Liaison with Commission File, 62-109090-Not Recorded (NR); A. Rosen to Belmont, 6/8/1964, FBIHQ Liaison with Commission File, 62-109090-NR. In some ways Burkley's statement was one of the most remarkable single documents in the vast quicksand of the Warren Commission and its work. The statement said absolutely nothing about the president's wounds, their nature, or their number. He offered no observations about what had taken place in the Bethesda morgue. In fine, it is a literary monument to vapidity and innocuousness. For Burkley's nine-page statement, see *Hearings before Commission,* Vol. 22, 93–97.

96. See Death Certificate of President John Fitzgerald Kennedy, November 23, 1963, signed by George Gregory Burkley, Physician to the President, RADM (Rear Admiral Medical), *ARRB,* Master Set of Medical Exhibits, MD 6. Burkley's location of JFK's back wound at the third thoracic vertebra is anatomically consistent with its position on Boswell's body chart as it appears in CE 397. The medical admiral signed off on Boswell's face sheet with the rear wound unmistakably placed in the region of JFK's shoulder girdle. His signature, "GGBurkley," is clearly visible in the lower left-hand corner of the document. However, when the Warren Commission printed the body chart as part of CE 397, it falsified the document by stripping away Burkley's name as a witness. The likely, if not the only, explanation for this official corruption of the document was to allow the Commission and the Bethesda pathologists to insist that the nonfatal posterior wound was high enough in the neck region for the bullet to exit Kennedy's throat. The Kennedy assassination researcher Harold Weisberg found the original Boswell face sheet at the National Archives in a file where it was hidden. For the original face sheet, see the photograph section in this book. For Boswell's explanation as to why he placed the wound in the back and not the neck, see note 78 for this chapter.

97. For Burkley's November 24, 1963, receipt of the official autopsy report, see *ARRB,* Master Set of Medical Exhibits, MD 53.

98. It should be noted that there are two Dallas JFK death certificates. The one signed by Theran Ward on November 22, 1963, placed the nonfatal rear wound "just above the right shoulder," as cited in the text. A second death certificate signed by Ward on December 6, 1963, reported that the immediate cause of death was "multiple gunshot wounds of the head and neck." Since this later death certificate was executed after the official autopsy report was released, I regard this repositioning of the nonfatal posterior wound with great suspicion. For copies of these Dallas County death certificates, see *ARRB,* Master Set of Medical Exhibits, MD 42 and MD 43. The HSCA forensic panel opted to cite the December 6, 1963, version of the Dallas County death certificate in its critique of the official autopsy report because that version was compatible with its findings that the report, while sullied by gross errors and deficiencies, had arrived at "correct and valid conclusions." See *HSCA,* March 1979, Vol. 7, 189. See Weisberg interview with Dr. Charles Carrico, December 1, 1977, Southwestern Medical School, University of Texas, Harold Weisberg's autopsy file, Weisberg Archive.

99. Finck's measurements can be seen on the autopsy descriptive sheet, Warren CE 397; or see *WCR,* 540, page 3 of the official autopsy report.

100. *ARRB,* Finck deposition, 45.

101. Manchester, *Death of a President,* 445–446; George G. Burkley interview with T. H. Baker, December 3, 1965, 12–13, Lyndon Baines Johnson Library, Austin, Texas.

102. Burkley oral history interview, 18; George G. Burkley obituary, *Washington Post,* January 21, 1991; Hurt, *Reasonable Doubt,* 49.

Chapter 8. Birth of the "Single-Bullet" Fabrication

1. See Chapter 11 for Russell's dissent.

2. *The Warren Commission Report: Report of the President's Commission on the Assassination of President John F. Kennedy* (hereafter cited as *WCR*), 19. The use of sophistical language in the report is reminiscent of Admiral Galloway's editing of the official Bethesda autopsy report, where Galloway used the adverb *presumably* in describing JFK's anterior neck wound as "presumably" a wound of exit and his posterior neck wound as "presumably" a wound of entry. See Chapter 9.

3. Ibid., 96–106.

4. Ibid., 92–96. Despite the Olympic-like acrobatics the Commission attributed to Commission Exhibit (CE) 399, it needs pointing out that the bullet that entered Connally's wrist two inches up on the thumb side and exited at the wrist crease in the middle of the palm could not, anatomically, have been the same missile that exited the governor's chest below the right nipple. This was pointed out to me by Professor David Wrone, the author of the masterful study of the Zapruder film. See David R. Wrone, *The Zapruder Film: Reframing JFK's Assassination* (Lawrence: University Press of Kansas, 2003), especially 42–43.

5. *WCR,* 557. A picture of CE 399 can be found in *Investigation of the Assassination of President John F. Kennedy: Hearings before the President's Commission on the Assassination of President Kennedy* (Washington, D.C.: U.S. Government Printing Office, 1964) (hereafter cited as *Hearings before Commission*), Vol. 17, 49.

6. A restricted but illustrative sample of the "single-bullet wars" in the Kennedy assassination literature can be found in the writings of Drs. Cyril H. Wecht and John K. Lattimer. Wecht is a forceful critic of the so-called single-bullet theory. Lattimer, on the other hand, is one of its staunchest defenders. Wecht's attacks on the Commission's construction can be found in "A Critique of President Kennedy Autopsy," Appendix D of Josiah Thompson's *Six Seconds in Dallas: A Micro-Study of the Kennedy Assassination* (New York: Bernard Geis Associates, 1967); "The Medical Evidence in the Assassination of President Kennedy," *Forensic Science* 3 (1974); "JFK Assassination: A Prolonged and Willful Cover-Up," *Modern Medicine,* October 28, 1974; interview with Ken Rankin, "Part 1: The Evidence," *Physicians Management,* October 1975; "Part 2: The Cover-Up," *Physicians Management,* November 1975; "Pathologist View of the JFK Autopsy: An Unsolved Case," *Modern Medicine,* November 27, 1972; and "A Post-Mortem on the Warrenfeller Commission," *Juris,* December 1975. For Lattimer's contributions to the other side of the debate, see "An Experimental Study of the Backward Movement of President Kennedy's Head," *Surgery, Gynecology and Obstetrics,* February 1976; Gary Lattimer, John K. Lattimer, and Jon Lattimer, "The Kennedy-Connally One Bullet Theory: Further Circumstantial and Experimental Error," *Medical Times,* November 1978; "The Kennedy-Connally Single Bullet Theory—A Feasibility Study," *International Surgery,* December 1968; "Observations Based on a Review of the Autopsy, Photographs, X-Rays, and Related Materials of the Late President John F. Kennedy," *Resident Staff and Physician,* May 1972; "Factors in the Death of President Kennedy," *Journal of the American Medical Association,* October 24, 1966.

7. For more on this, see Chapter 4.

8. Gauthier to Callahan, 1/28/1964, FBIHQ JFK Assassination File, 62-109060-2366. See also Commission Document (CD) 5, Warren Commission Documents, National Archives and Records Administration, College Park, Maryland (hereafter cited as NARA); or see John B. Connally (JBC-1) File, National Archives, Washington, D.C., for Secret Service agent John J. Howlett's statement to this effect.

9. Gauthier to Belmont, 12/1/1963, FBIHQ JFK Assassination File, 62-109060-991. For the FBI brochure see Investigation and Evidence File, RG (Record Group) 272, Series 12, box 8, folder "Witnesses and Exhibits (November 1963-March 1964)," J. Lee Rankin Papers, NARA. For more detail on the FBI's Dealey Plaza scale model see Chapter 4.

10. W. D. Griffith to Conrad, 1/28/1964, FBIHQ JFK Assassination File, 62-109060-2367; Rosen to Belmont, 4/15/1964, FBIHQ JFK Assassination File, 62-109060-2933; Griffith to Conrad, 4/22/1964, FBIHQ JFK Assassination File, 62-109060-2985.

11. *WCR,* 117.

12. For Connally's testimony about the shots, see *Hearings before Commission,* Vol. 4, 135. It was the governor's unshakable conviction that he was hit by the second shot and that JFK alone was struck by the first shot. See Connally's statement to this effect in the *New York Times,* November 24, 1966, two years after the Warren report was released to the public. For Mrs. Connally's testimony, see *Hearings before Commission,* Vol. 4, 147.

13. Hoover to Rankin, 6/30/1964, Investigation and Evidence File, Record Group (RG) 272, Series 12, box 1, folder 3, NARA; Specter to Rankin, 6/11/1964, Rankin Papers, box 4, folder 063, NARA.

14. Eisenberg to file (First Staff Conference, 1/20/1964), Investigation and Evidence File, RG 272, Series 12, box 1, folder 2, NARA; Warren Commission, April 30, 1964, executive session transcript, NARA, 6.

15. Gauthier to Callahan, 1/28/1964, FBIHQ JFK Assassination File, 62-109060-2366; Eisenberg memo, 4/22/1964, Investigation and Evidence File, RG 272, Series 12, box 1, folder 3, NARA.

16. Rosen to Belmont, 4/15/1964, FBIHQ JFK Assassination File, 62-109060-2933; Gauthier to Callahan, 4/15/1964, FBIHQ JFK Assassination File, 62-109060-2998; Eisenberg memo, 4/22/1964, Investigation and Evidence File, RG 272, Series 12, box 1, folder 3, NARA. For the Bethesda doctors' Warren Commission testimony, see *Hearings before Commission,* Vol. 2, 374–375 (Humes), Vol. 2, 377 (Boswell), and Vol. 2, 382 (Finck).

17. Eisenberg memo, 4/22/1964, Investigation and Evidence File, RG 272, Series 12, box 1, folder 3, NARA; Griffith to Conrad, 4/22/1964, FBIHQ JFK Assassination File, 62-109060-2985.

18. Since Dolce was never deposed or called to testify before the Commission, most of what follows about his experience with the Commission lawyers during the April 21 conference is taken from an extended interview with Gerard "Chip" Selby, who interviewed Dolce at the doctor's home in West Palm Beach, Florida, on October 17, 1986. A short excerpt of this interview appeared in Selby's award-winning documentary *Reasonable Doubt.* The documentary won the Golden Eagle Award in the history division in the 1988 competition of the Council on International Non-theatrical Events. Gaeton Fonzi, an investigator for the House Select Committee on Assassinations (HSCA), spoke with Dolce and subsequently recommended that the committee interview him. According to Fonzi, Dolce was anxious to appear before the HSCA. Fonzi believed that "his testimony would be strong and sensational within limitations." However, Dolce was neither invited to testify nor deposed by HSCA staffers. See Fonzi to Tannenbaum, 3/23/1977, JFK Collection, RG 233, NARA. I want to thank Harold Weisberg for a copy of the transcript of the Selby-Dolce interview. For more on Selby's interview with Dr. Dolce, see Harold Weisberg, *Never Again!* (New York: Carroll and Graf, 1995), 291–299.

19. Selby interview with Dolce transcript, 2–4.

20. Ibid., 4–5; Eisenberg memo, 4/22/1964, Investigation and Evidence File, RG 272, Series 12, box 1, folder 3, NARA.

21. Selby interview with Dolce transcript, 9.

22. For their Commission testimony, see *Hearings before Commission,* Vol. 5, 84–90 (Olivier) and Vol. 5, 91–93 (Dziemian). A summary of their opinions can be found in *WCR,* 584–585.

23. Selby interview with Dolce transcript, 1.

24. For Light's May 6, 1964, Commission testimony, see *Hearings before Commission,* Vol. 5, 91–95.

25. Only one of the ten bullets recovered from the Dolce-Light tests was entered into evidence as CE 856. See *Hearings before Commission,* Vol. 17, 850. CE 856 exhibits the classic mushrooming effect—the peeling back of the metal at the nose of the bullet after striking a hard object such as the radius. These and the other tests carried out by Olivier and Dziemian at Edgewood Arsenal were written up in a fifty-five-page report bearing the date March 1965. The authors of the report were Drs. Olivier and Dziemian. Dolce's and Light's names do not appear on the document titled "Wound Ballistics of 6.5-MM Mannlicher-Carcano (U)," U.S. Army Edgewood Arsenal Chemical Research and Development Laboratories Technical Report. The report produces a photograph of four of the ten bullets Dolce and Light fired into cadaver wrists (see figure A14 of the report). The bullet showing the least deformation appears to be CE 856. The other three are even more mutilated than the one the Commission chose to enter into evidence. The Olivier-Dziemian report conferred a clean bill of health on the single-bullet theory. Classified by the government as "Confidential," the report was withheld from researchers for eight years. The Olivier-Dziemian report can be found in RG 272, Series 12, box 52 or entry 52, NARA. For a useful treatment of the report, see Howard Roffman, *Presumed Guilty: How the Warren Commission Framed Lee Harvey Oswald* (South Brunswick, N.J.: A. S. Barnes, 1976), 139–141.

26. Rosen to Belmont, 4/20/1964, FBIHQ JFK Assassination File, 62-109060-2999; Rosen to Belmont, 4/28/1964, FBIHQ JFK Assassination File, 62-109060-3008; Eisenberg memo, 4/22/1964, Investigation and Evidence File, RG 272, Series 12, box 1, folder 3, NARA. See also *WCR,* 97, 106, 107, 112, for the Commission's reasoning on which of the Zapruder frames shows the impact of the first and second shots. For results of the FBI lab's testing of Zapruder's Bell and Howell Zoomatic 8-mm movie camera, see Griffith to Conrad, 12/20/1963, FBIHQ JFK Assassination File, 62-109060-213.

27. The Oswald rifle was a bolt-action weapon not designed for use with a telescopic scope, yet an inexpensive Japanese scope had been added. FBI firearms expert Robert A. Frazier was at his convincing courtroom best when he testified before the Commission (March 19, 1964) that the telescopic sight considerably improved the marksmanship of the shooter, even for someone of amateurish standing. But he did allow that "you would have to be very familiar with the weapon to fire it rapidly, and to do this—hit the target at those ranges" (*Hearings before Commission,* Vol. 3, 413). Had the commissioners asked him to demonstrate rapid fire with the Oswald rifle, they would have had a graphic understanding of what Frazier meant by "very familiar." In order to reload and sight the rifle, the shooter has to take his eye away from the scope or risk the chance of putting his eye out when operating the bolt. This problem hindered accurate sighting and firing, factors making the time span of 2.3 seconds to recycle the Oswald rifle and stay locked in on a moving target demonstrably unrealistic, if not impossible.

Ronald Simmons, chief of the Infantry Weapons Evaluation Branch of the U.S. Army's Ballistics Research Laboratory, in his testimony before the Commission confirmed this point about the recycling of CE 139, the alleged murder weapon. Simmons supervised the testing of the Oswald rifle using shooters who had participated in national rifleman competitions sponsored by the National Rifle Association (NRA). Two of these three skilled riflemen required 7.0 and 6.75 seconds, respectively, to squeeze off three shots. The one who got off three shots within 4.6 seconds on his first attempt and 4.45 seconds on his last attempt, using the iron sights, was an NRA-designated "Master" marksman. Oswald could not have traveled in this select company even on his best day. See *Hearings before Commission,* Vol. 3, 449–450.

The firearms panel of the House Select Committee on Assassinations was more forthright on this point when it concluded, "An individual could attain better accuracy using the iron sights than the scope under circumstances involved in Dealey Plaza." See *Investigation of the Assassination of President John F. Kennedy: Hearings before the Select Committee on Assassinations of the U.S. House of Representatives,* 95th Congress, 2d session (Washington, D.C.: U.S. Government Printing Office, 1979) (hereafter cited as *HSCA*), Vol. 7, March 1979, 373. Having asserted this, the panel did not venture an opinion as to whether Oswald using the iron sights would have been able to accomplish the shooting attributed to him in the short span of five to seven seconds.

28. Rosen to Belmont, 4/20/1964, FBIHQ JFK Assassination File, 62-109060-2999; Griffith to Conrad, 1/28/1964, FBIHQ JFK Assassination File, 62-109060-2405; Rosen to Belmont, 4/20/1964, FBIHQ JFK Assassination File, 62-109060-2999.

29. Rankin to Hoover, 5/7/1964, FBIHQ JFK Assassination File, 62-109060-3118.

30. A copy of Specter's April 30, 1964, memo to Rankin can be found in *HSCA,* Vol. 11, 92–93.

31. Specter to Humes, 12/11/1967, 4 Series, box 50, NARA. For Belin's criticism of the Commission's treatment of the autopsy pictures and X-rays, see his testimony before Bella Abzug's Subcommittee on Government Information and Individual Rights, November 11, 1975 (Washington, D.C.: U.S. Government Printing Office), 20–25.

32. Warren made this admission in his posthumously published memoirs, *The Memoirs of Earl Warren* (New York: Doubleday, 1977), 371–372. For Warren's remarks, see Warren Commission, April 30, 1964, executive session transcript, NARA, 35.

33. Specter to Rankin, 4/12/1964, Rankin Papers, box 37, folder 473, NARA; Warren Commission, April 30, 1964, executive session transcript, NARA, 42.

34. Specter to Rankin, 5/12/1964 memo, "Examination of Autopsy Photographs and X-rays of President Kennedy," Rankin Papers, box 37, folder 473, NARA; "Overwhelming Evidence Oswald Was Assassin," interview with Arlen Specter, assistant counsel, Warren Commission, *U.S. News and World Report,* October 10, 1966, 53.

35. See *HSCA,* Vol. 11, March 1979, 92.

36. See *WCR,* Chapter 8, "The Protection of the President," for photograph number 12; *Hearings before Commission,* Vol. 5, 133 (Kelley).

37. Ibid., Vol. 16, 977.

38. Ibid., Vol. 2, 361, 363, 364, 365, 367, 368, 369. For the McCloy-Humes exchange, see Vol. 2, 368.

39. Ford's editing of the June 26, 1964, draft was mentioned in Chapter 7. See Rankin Papers, box 26, folder 385. See also George Lardner's story "Ford's Editing Backed 'Single-Bullet' Theory," *Washington Post,* July 3, 1977, A17.

40. Redlich to Rankin, 4/27/1964, Rankin Papers, box 34, folder 443, NARA.

41. Belin to Rankin, 5/14/1964, Rankin Papers, box 17, folder 285, NARA. See page 4 of Belin's report for his comment on Brennan.

42. Rankin to Hoover, 5/7/1964, FBIHQ JFK Assassination File, 62-109060-3139.

43. Griffith to Conrad, 6/10/1964, FBIHQ Liaison with Commission File, 62-109090-Not Recorded (NR).

44. For Adams's professional biography, see *WCR,* 476–477. The Commission payroll records for all staff lawyers disclose that Adams did not draw a check for February, and by May 1964 he was essentially no longer working for the Commission. See Comprehensive Payroll, General Services Administration. This document was released under the 1992 JFK Act. Adams's total number of days worked for the Commission was sixteen. See *HSCA,* Vol. 11, 78. See also Gaeton Fonzi, *The Last Investigation* (New York: Thunder's Mouth Press, 1994), 18–19.

45. For Specter's June 10, 1964, draft on Area I, see Rankin Papers, RG 200, box 4, folder 64, NARA. Dolce was disturbed that as a wound ballistics expert he was never called as a Commission witness. But he was even more exercised over the fact that what Drs. Olivier and Dziemian testified to under Specter's questioning was diametrically contradicted by the test results from the ten experiments Dolce and Dr. Light ran on human cadaver wrists. In every instance the 6.5-mm bullets were dramatically distorted after being fired into the cadavers. Dolce letter to HSCA, 12/20/1976, JFK Collection, RG 233, box 14, NARA. For a detailed treatment of the suppression of the critical CRDLR 3264 report, see the Introduction.

46. Dolce to Senator Lawton Chiles, 11/19/1976, HSCA, RG 233, JFK Collection, NARA. For Dolce's letter to Chiles, see HSCA, memorandum, 12/20/1976, HSCA, RG 233, box 14, JFK Collection, NARA; Chiles to Richardson Preyer, 12/1/1976, HSCA, RG 233, box 12, NARA; Andy Purdy memo to Bob Tannenbaum, 2/7/1977, HSCA, RG 233, box 19, JFK Collection, NARA.

47. Jevons to Conrad, 11/23/1963, FBIHQ Oswald File, 105-82555-NR; SAC, Dallas, to Director, 11/26/1963, FBIHQ JFK Assassination File, 62-109060-42; SAC, Dallas, to Director, 11/28/1963, FBIHQ JFK Assassination File, 62-109060-251. Robert Frazier testified that microscopic examinations and spectrographic analysis were run on CE 399 and fragments the Secret Service retrieved from the president's limo the day after the assassination. See *Hearings before Commission,* Vol. 3, 428, 435, and Vol. 5, 67.

48. SAC, Dallas, to Director, 11/26/1963, FBIHQ JFK Assassination File, 62-109060-42.

49. The Secret Service report with a cover letter from Treasury Secretary Douglas Dillon was sent to the Commission on December 18, 1963, Lyndon B. Johnson Library, Austin, Texas.

50. Rosen to Belmont, 11/22/1966, FBIHQ JFK Assassination File, 62-109060-4267.

51. *Hearings before Commission,* Vol. 3, 391.

52. Ibid., 394, 406, 411.

53. Ibid., 406–412. See also note 27 in this chapter.

54. Ibid., 430–431. For Dr. Gregory's stark description of Connally's chest wound, see ibid., Vol. 6, 101.

55. Ibid., Vol. 3, 428–429.

56. Redlich to Rankin, 4/16/1964, Rankin Papers, box 34, folder 433, NARA.

57. *Hearings before Commission,* Vol. 3, 437.

58. Ibid., 435; FBI laboratory report to Dallas Police Chief Jesse F. Curry, 11/23/1963, Baltimore JFK Assassination File, 89-30-52, 3. Pictures of these fragments can be found in *Hearings before Commission,* Vol. 17, 256–257.

59. Interviews with James W. Sibert, 8/29/1964, HSCA, RG 233, JFK Collection, NARA; Francis X. O'Neill and James W. Sibert, 11/26/1963, A. "Autopsy of President John Fitzgerald Kennedy, JFK 4-1 File, National Archives, Washington, D.C." For Humes's description of JFK's head fragments, see *Hearings before Commission,* Vol. 2, 353, 359.

60. SAC, Baltimore, to Director and SAC, Dallas, 11/23/1964, FBIHQ JFK Assassination File, 62-109060-459.

61. For Frazier's comment, see *Harold Weisberg vs. U.S. Department of Justice and U.S. Energy Research and Development Administration,* Civil Action 75-226, U.S. District Court for the District of Columbia, February 24, 1977, deposition of Robert A. Frazier, 76.

62. *Hearings before Commission,* Vol. 5, 67.

63. Ibid., 69.

64. Ibid., 72.

65. Ibid., 73–74. It is worth noting that when Frazier was giving firsthand testimony in the area of his own expertise, he was meticulous in his use of language. Frazier, after all, was senior FBI ballistics examiner and a skilled professional, and he was quick to showcase his years of experience when necessary. For instance, he lectured Eisenberg on the importance of exactitude in ballistics identification. Frazier informed the assistant counsel that in ballistics there was no such thing as an "apparent match" or "probable" identification. He emphasized that he "would not report any type of similarities unless they were sufficient" for a positive identification. In the FBI's Firearms and Toolmarks Unit, Frazier's turf, "there is no such thing," he was quick to point out, "as a probable identification. It either is or isn't as far as we are concerned." For the Frazier-Eisenberg exchange, see ibid., Vol. 3, 434.

66. Ibid., Vol. 5, 74.

67. Ibid., 69.

68. Jevons to Conrad, 7/6/1964, FBIHQ JFK Assassination File, 62-109060-3452; Rankin to Hoover, 2/4/1964, FBIHQ JFK Assassination File, 62-109060-NR; Hoover to Rankin, 2/7/1964, FBIHQ JFK Assassination File, 62-109060-1094(?) (obliterated).

69. Jevons to Conrad, 12/9/1963, FBIHQ JFK Assassination File, 62-109060-1663; Jevons to Conrad, 12/12/1963, FBIHQ JFK Assassination File, 62-109060-1990; Jevons to Conrad, 12/19/1963, FBIHQ JFK Assassination File, 62-109060-2095.

70. The Dallas police report on Oswald's paraffin test can be found in box 3, folder 27, RG 91-001, JFK Collection, Dallas Municipal Archives, Dallas, Texas. See also *WCR,* 560, for a report on the negative reaction of the paraffin test to Oswald's right cheek. See also Rosen to Belmont, 11/23/1963, FBIHQ JFK Assassination File, 62-109060-644. In this memo Rosen informed Belmont that the paraffin cast of Oswald's right cheek showed no traces of nitrates. For diagrams of the mapping of nitrate deposits on Oswald's hands, see Gemberling Report, 11/30/1963, FBIHQ Oswald File, 105-82555-505, Section 21, 148, and attachments.

71. See Hoover to Rankin, 3/18/1964, CD 525, NARA, for a list of all the items of common usage that could leave traces of barium and antimony on the skin. Or see *WCR,* 561, for a comparable list.

72. Jevons to Conrad, 12/2/1963, FBIHQ JFK Assassination File, 62-109060-916; Jevons to Conrad, 3/26/1964, FBIHQ JFK Assassination File, 62-109060-2781.

73. Jevons to Conrad, 11/27/1963, FBIHQ JFK Assassination File, 62-109060-427; Redlich to Dulles, 7/2/1964, Investigation and Evidence File, RG 272, Series 12, box 4, folder 3 (Revolver), NARA.

74. For Eisenberg's September 5, 1964, memo to Redlich, see Harold Weisberg, *Post-Mortem: JFK Assassination Cover-Up Smashed* (Frederick, Md.: Harold Weisberg Publisher, 1975), 447; Hoover to Rankin, 3/18/1964, CD 525, NARA.

75. For BuLab's misleading dismissal of the scientific efficacy of neutron activation testing, see R. H. Jevons to Conrad, 11/27/1963, FBIHQ JFK Assassination File, 62-109060-427.

76. For the FBI lab report, see attachment to FBI, Dallas (100-10461), to FBI Laboratory, Washington, D.C., 3/6/1964, FBIHQ Oswald File, 105-82555-2384. For Mason's Dallas City-County Criminal Investigation Laboratory results on Oswald's paraffin tests, see Kyle G. Clark to SAC, Dallas, 11/23/1963, Main Dallas JFK Assassination File, 89-43-(8?)00 (first digit in serial number partially obliterated).

77. Jevons to Conrad, 11/27/1963, FBIHQ JFK Assassination File, 62-109060-427. The FBI was so ultrasensitive about drawing any public attention to Oswald's paraffin casts and NAA testing that when Dallas SAC Gordon Shanklin was quoted, accurately or not, in the press as saying that he had seen the results of Oswald's paraffin tests and they showed that he had fired a rifle, general quarters sounded at FBIHQ. The bureau elite in Washington ordered that Shanklin immediately issue a statement that the "allegation is completely unfounded." See Shanklin to file, 8/12/1964, FBI Main Dallas Jack Ruby File, 44-1639-6008; Horton to SAC, Dallas, 8/19/1964, Main Dallas Oswald File, 100-10461-7663; Loeffler to SAC, Dallas, 8/20/1964, Main Dallas Oswald File, 100-10461-7664.

78. For the circumstances surrounding Russell's dissent and how it was suppressed, see Chapter 11.

79. See *Hearings before Commission,* Vol. 15, 746–752, for Gallagher's deposition. See especially 749–751 for his conclusions on Oswald's hand and cheek casts. The entire session with Redlich was only seven pages.

80. This list was compiled by FBI Director Clarence M. Kelley in response to Freedom of Information Act (FOIA) litigation. See Kelley to James H. Lesar, 4/10/1975. Lesar was Harold Weisberg's lawyer in Weisberg's FOIA case to get the FBI to disclose the results of NAA testing at Oak Ridge National Laboratory. The FBI release of fifty-four pages of the data can be found in the Harold Weisberg Archive, Hood College, Frederick, Maryland (hereafter cited as Weisberg Archive).

81. *Hearings before Commission,* Vol. 15, 746–752 (Gallagher).

82. R. M. Jevons to Conrad, 2/27/1964 (memo has no classification number). For the FBI's confidential informant on the history and defects of the "Model 91s," see Gemberling Report, 1/22/1964, FBIHQ Oswald File, 105-82555-1567, Section 71, 39–41.

83. Assassination researcher Harold Weisberg sued both the FBI and the AEC to gain disclosure of the results of the December-January Oak Ridge National Laboratory tests on the paraffin casts. He made no headway with the FBI, but the AEC's successor, the Energy Research and Development Administration (ERDA), anxious to avoid litigation, turned over the results to Weisberg in July 1981. The ERDA file can be found at the Weisberg Archive. The Commission turned to FBI firearms expert Cortlandt Cunningham, whose testimony was buried in Appendix X of the Warren Report under the rubric "Expert Testimony," to explain why Oswald's negative paraffin test on his right cheek was of no evidentiary value. Ignoring the results of the FBI's own authorized AEC tests on the rifle as well as Dr. Guinn's report to Gallagher, Cunningham testified that the chamber of the Mannlicher-Carcano was so tightly sealed that it prevented any blowback. It was Cunningham's professional opinion that given the construction of the weapon, "personally" he would not expect to find "any residues on a person's right cheek after firing" it. See *WCR,* 561.

84. *WCR,* 163–164 (Roberts). See also Earlene Roberts's FBI interview, Gemberling Report, 11/28/1964, FBIHQ Oswald File, 105-82555-505, Section 23, 354–355.

85. The extreme difficulty of washing away "contamination" of handgun and rifle residue is detailed in the following relevant studies: H. R. Lukens et al., "Forensic Neutron Activation Analysis of Bullet-Lead Specimens," Report by Gulf General Atomic, San Diego, California, June 30, 1970, distributed by National Technical Information Service, U.S. Department of Commerce, Springfield, Va.; Ralph T. Overman and Herbert M. Clark, *Radioisotope Techniques* (New York: McGraw-Hill, 1960), 391–392, 394; Department of Energy Study 1128.98, "Guide of Good Practices for Occupational Protection in Plutonium Facilities," 4-28, 4-29; Department of Energy, Idaho National Engineering Laboratory, "Health Physics Manual of Good Practices for Uranium Facilities," June 1988, 11-2; Idaho National Engineering and Environmental Laboratory, "Personnel Decontamination," July 6, 2000, 1–7. I

wish to thank Clay Ogilvie, an administrator for the Department of Energy's Emergency Management Program, for directing me to these sources.

Chapter 9. Politics of the "Single-Bullet" Fabrication

1. See the testimony of the Parkland Memorial Hospital nurses who were on duty when Connally was admitted, *Investigation of the Assassination of President John F. Kennedy: Hearings before the President's Commission on the Assassination of President Kennedy* (Washington, D.C.: U.S. Government Printing Office, 1964) (hereafter cited as *Hearings before Commission*), Vol. 6, 127, 116–117 (Standridge), 131 (Wester). See also Commission Document (CD) 379. A useful chronology of events at Parkland Memorial Hospital on the day of the assassination can be found in Andy Purdy to Belford Lawson and Patricia Orr, 1/14/1977, House Select Committee on Assassinations (HSCA), Series 4, box 12, National Archives and Records Administration (hereafter cited as NARA), College Park, Maryland.

2. *The Warren Commission Report: Report of the President's Commission on the Assassination of President John F. Kennedy* (Washington, D.C.: U.S. Government Printing Office, 1964) (hereafter cited as *WCR*), 95. For Tomlinson's testimony, see *Hearings before Commission,* Vol. 6, 130.

3. Purdy memo, "Chronology of Events at Parkland Hospital," HSCA, 4 Series, box 12, NARA; James J. Rowley, memorandum to file, 12/19/1963, Warren CD 320; SAC, Washington field office, to Director, 6/24/1964, FBIHQ Oswald File, 105-82555-4225.

4. This material is developed more fully in Chapter 7.

5. *WCR,* 81.

6. *WCR,* 81; *Hearings before Commission,* Vol. 21, 242 (Nelson); Vol. 6, 129 (Tomlinson).

7. Tomlinson's sketch of the corridor with the location of the two stretchers is helpful for orientation purposes. See ibid., Vol. 21, 673.

8. Ibid., Vol. 6, 131 (Tomlinson).

9. For the Parkland Hospital's admittance record, see Price Exhibit No. 5, ibid., Vol. 21, 157. See also Vol. 21, 156 (Guycion). For the Fuller boy, see Price Exhibit No. 27, Vol. 21, 218 (Randall), 226 (Richards), 208–209 (Lumpkin), 220 (Majors), 228 (Sanders). Based on the circumstantial evidence, Josiah Thompson made a strong case that the "stretcher bullet" came from the stretcher of the Fuller boy. See Josiah Thompson, *Six Seconds in Dallas: A Micro-Study of the Kennedy Assassination* (New York: Bernard Geis Associates, 1967), 161–165.

10. *Hearings before Commission,* Vol. 6, 133–134.

11. Ibid., 121–123 (Wester); 126 (Jimison).

12. Richard E. Johnsen to Chief James Rowley, 11/30/1963, *Report of the U.S. Secret Service on the Assassination of President Kennedy* (Washington, D.C.: U.S. Treasury Department), Lyndon Baines Johnson Library, Austin, Texas.

13. *Hearings before Commission,* Vol. 2, 374 (Specter). In his book *Six Seconds in Dallas,* Thompson offered another possible scenario. He speculated that some hospital employee might have found C1 either on the floor of Trauma Room One, in JFK's clothes, or on the president's stretcher and momentarily pocketed it as a souvenir, only to realize its importance and later secrete it on a carriage where someone else could discover it. Thompson's alternative explanation could be possible only if C1 entered Kennedy's back, made a path of only a few inches, and then fell out during cardiac massage, as Dr. Humes postulated. Sibert and O'Neill, the two FBI agents in the Bethesda morgue, reported that hand probing of the back wound "determined distance traveled by the missile was short as the end of the opening could be felt by the examining doctor's finger." Either Humes's finger probing correctly determined

the superficial nature of JFK's back wound or the bullet track had closed up and resisted all of Humes's efforts to determine the path. The confusion could have been resolved had the back wound been dissected. Dissection is the prescribed and standard procedure for tracking a bullet's path in the body. The Bethesda prosectors did not perform this procedure for reasons discussed in Chapter 7. Whether C1 (designated later as CE 399) was planted or fell out of Kennedy's back and was scooped up as a souvenir, the certainty remains that neither scenario supported the Commission's claim that C1 came from Governor Connally's stretcher. See Thompson, *Six Seconds in Dallas,* 168–169. For Sibert and O'Neill on the probing of JFK's back wound, see FBI teletype from SAC, Baltimore, to SAC, Dallas, 11/23/1963, FBI Baltimore Main JFK Assassination File, 89-30-7; SAC, Dallas, 11/23/1963, serial 105-7740-16 (file name unknown).

14. *WCR,* 91–92. Jevons to Conrad, 11/26/1963, FBIHQ JFK Assassination File, 62-109060-1086, for the results of BuLab's examination of JFK's clothes.

15. *WCR,* 92.

16. For Carrico's description of JFK's condition, see Sixth (6th) Floor Museum, box 8, Carrico Collection (044.0006), Dallas, Texas, 2, 3, and 12. For the Trauma Room Number One nurses, see *Hearings before Commission,* Vol. 6, 136 (Bowron), 141 (Hentchliffe).

17. The FBI laboratory's photograph of Kennedy's shirt collar with the slits can be found in Harold Weisberg's *Never Again* (New York: Carroll and Graf, 1995), 245. It is also included in the photograph section of this book.

18. *WCR,* 92. Carrico's deposition of March 21, 1964, Sixth (6th) Floor Museum, box 8, Carrico Collection (044.0006), Dallas, Texas, 4, 14.

19. *Hearings before Commission,* Vol. 3, 361–362 (Carrico).

20. See FBI report to Honorable James J. Rowley, Chief of U.S. Secret Service, 12/5/1963, FBIHQ JFK Assassination File, 62-109060-1781; Director FBI to SAC, Dallas, 11/26/1963, FBIHQ JFK Assassination File, 62-109060-42; Jevons to Conrad, 11/26/1963, FBIHQ JFK Assassination File, 62-109060-1086.

21. *WCR,* 91–92; Hoover to Rankin, 3/23/1964, FBIHQ JFK Assassination File, 62-109060-Not Recorded (NR); *Hearings before Commission,* Vol. 5, 61 (Frazier).

22. *Hearings before Commission,* Vol. 4, 156–174 (Stombaugh). For Frazier's February 1977 deposition, see *Harold Weisberg vs. U.S. Department of Justice and U.S. Energy Research and Development Administration,* Civil Action 75-226, U.S. District Court for the District of Columbia, February 24, 1977 (hereafter cited as *Weisberg vs. U.S. Department of Justice*), 61–62. In this deposition, Frazier inferred that JFK's tie had been cut off by a knife or scalpel, 60ff. Given the uncertainty about the slits in JFK's collar and whether they were caused by a bullet or a scalpel, the Commission should have insisted on nothing less than neutron activation analysis (NAA) of the material to establish whether or not it had been damaged by an "exiting" missile. There was nothing more essential to substantiate the Commission's case for the single-bullet construction and its conclusion that JFK had not been a victim of a conspiracy. If Stombaugh ran an NAA test on the shirt collar, the results were never made public, and, as mentioned before, the Commission never asked him about this matter when he testified under oath. By contrast, the Warren report cited Stombaugh at length about his hair and fiber analysis of Oswald's blanket found in Ruth Paine's garage. See *WCR,* 586–592.

23. *WCR,* 557. FBI ballistics expert Robert A. Frazier estimated that CE 399 lost about 2.5 grains.

24. *Hearings before Commission,* Vol. 4, 120. For Dr. Gregory's postoperative report, see 4 Series, box 4.02 (Ballistics/Forensics), NARA; *Hearings before Commission,* Vol. 4, 120.

25. *Hearings before Commission,* Vol. 4, 123 (Gregory).

26. Ibid., 113 (Shaw).

27. *WCR,* 557.

28. *Hearings before Commission,* Vol. 4, 125 (Gregory); Vol. 6, 106 (Shires); for Dr. Reynolds's November 27, 1963, and December 4, 1963, postoperative reports, see 4 Series, box 4.02 (Connally fragments), NARA; *Investigation of the Assassination of President John F. Kennedy: Hearings before the Select Committee on Assassinations of the U.S. House of Representatives,* 95th Congress, 2d session (Washington, D.C.: U.S. Government Printing Office, 1979) (hereafter cited as *HSCA*), Vol. 7 (March 1979), 149 (Shaw interview).

For Shaw's drawing of the actual size of Connally's chest wound, see ibid., 143. It requires noting that before President Kennedy was pronounced dead, some Secret Service agents washed blood and brain matter out of the presidential limousine in preparation for its return to Washington, D.C. Exactly what evidence was washed away along with the assassination gore—bullet fragments, for example—can only be guessed at. White House photographer Capt. Cecil W. Stroughton, who was assigned to cover Kennedy's Texas trip, caught on film the Secret Service agents cleaning up the limo outside Parkland Memorial Hospital. See Richard B. Trask, *Pictures of the Pain: Photography and the Assassination of President John F. Kennedy* (Danvers, Mass.: Yeoman Press, 1994), 41–42.

29. For the Ramsey Clark Panel report, see U.S. Justice Department, Criminal Division, 129-012-3, Enclosure 2, or Assassination Records Review Board, Master Set of Medical Exhibits, MD 59, NARA.

30. See Chapter 7.

31. *Hearings before Commission,* Vol. 6, 94; Vol. 4, 112, 114 (Shaw); Vol. 4, 127–128 (Gregory). Dr. Shaw's reservations did not change even after the Warren report was published. In 1977 the Dallas thoracic surgeon was quoted as saying that the bullet that struck Connally "was not consistent with the appearance of the bullet found on the governor's stretcher," *Dallas Morning News,* April 21, 1977.

32. *WCR,* 19.

33. J. Doyle Williams's interviews can be found in HSCA Record 180-10090-10270, NARA. For the weight assigned by the FBI to Q9, see Jevons to Conrad, 4/9/1964, FBIHQ Liaison with Commission File, 62-109090-NR.

34. *Hearings before Commission,* Vol. 17, 841; Dallas Municipal Archives and Records Center, box 5, folder 2, 130, Dallas, Texas; *WCR,* 95; for Specter's June 10 draft, see Rankin Papers, box 4, folder 64, 54, NARA.

35. For Bell's March 12, 1977, testimony before the HSCA, see 4 Series, box 12, NARA. Commission Exhibit (CE) 842 can be found in *Hearings before Commission,* Vol. 17, 841. For HSCA's CE 842, see *HSCA* Vol. 7 (March 1979), 392.

36. 4 Series, box 12, NARA. Bell's pencil sketch is attached to the five-page interview.

37. *HSCA* Vol. 7 (March 1979), 156.

38. Jesse E. Curry, *JFK Assassination File* (Dallas, Tex.: Jesse E. Curry and American Poster and Printing Company, 1969), 88–89.

39. *Hearings before Commission,* Vol. 17, 843–856.

40. Harbison's story can be found in the *Dallas Morning News,* April 21, 1977.

41. Walsh to Tannenbaum, Fenton, Hess, and Gay, 4/11/1977, HSCA, JFK Collection, Record Group (RG) 272, box 92, NARA.

42. *Dallas Morning Herald,* June 5, 1964; Shanklin to file, 6/5/1964, Main Dallas Oswald File, 100-10461-6537; Hoover to Rankin, 6/30/1964, RG 272, 13 Series, "Investigation and Evidence," box 1, folder 3, NARA.

43. For the drafts of June 13, 1964, and June 26, 1964, see Rankin Papers, box 5, folder 65, 1 of 5 for 6/13/1964, 70, and folder 2 of 5 for 6/26/1964, 65, NARA.

44. Interview with Harold Weisberg, July 13, 1999, Frederick, Md. Weisberg interviewed Dillard in Dallas in 1977. This is a summary of that interview.

45. Martha Joe Stroud to J. Lee Rankin, 6/9/1964, FBIHQ JFK Assassination File, 62-109060-3659.

46. Rankin to Hoover, 7/7/1964, FBIHQ Oswald File, 105-82555-4668X, or see FBIHQ JFK Assassination File, 62-109060-3657, for the original filing; Director to SAC, Dallas, 7/23/1964, FBIHQ JFK Assassination File, 62-109060-4999 EBF (Evidence Behind File).

47. Kyle G. Clark to SAC, Dallas, Main Dallas Oswald File, 100-10461-7467.

48. For the August 14, 1964, draft, see Rankin Papers, box 5, folder 65, 4 of 5, 67, NARA. The designated "Final Draft" can be found in ibid., box 20, folder 311, 79.

49. *WCR,* 116–117.

50. Ibid., 117.

51. Tague's December 14, 1963, FBI interview is attached to Rosen to Belmont, 6/6/1964, FBIHQ JFK Assassination File, 62-109060-NR. For Underwood's statement, see RG 272, 13 Series, "Investigation and Evidence," box 2, folder 2, NARA; Walthers's report originally filed with the County of Dallas, Sheriff's Department, under call numbers E 842.9/F27, Vol. 2; *Dallas Morning News,* November 23, 1963 (some of these details were discussed in Chapter 4). For Gemberling's 7/2/1964 report, see FBIHQ Oswald File, 105-82555-4584, 27–39.

52. *Hearings before Commission,* Vol. 7, 555–556 (Tague deposition). My phone interview with James Tague, September 23, 2002.

53. Rankin to Hoover, 7/7/1964, FBIHQ Oswald File, 105-82555-4668X.

54. Hoover to Rankin, 8/12/1964, FBIHQ JFK Assassination File, 62-109060-3657.

55. The FBI lab report (Lab. No. D-455927 HQ) is masked, but a copy can be found attached to Hoover's 8/12/1964 letter to Rankin, FBIHQ Oswald File, 105-82555-4668X. At the request of the Commission, Shaneyfelt calculated the distance from Z 313 to the mark on the curb at two hundred feet. Hoover to Rankin, 9/3/1964, FBIHQ Liaison with Commission File, 62-109090-NR.

56. The quotation from the FBI lab worksheet (Lab. No. D-455927 HQ) attached to Hoover's 8/12/1964 letter to Rankin, FBIHQ Oswald File, 105-82555-4668X, originally in FBIHQ JFK Assassination File, 62-109060-3659; *WCR,* 117.

57. Jose T. Fernandez to Sissi Maleki, March 17, 1983. This correspondence may be found in the Weisberg Archive Subject Index File under "Jim Tague" and in his Subject Index under "Henry Hurt." Weisberg was the one who suggested that *Reader's Digest* contract with a physical engineer to examine the curbstone.

58. When Harold Weisberg used an FOIA request for the spectrographic plate of the "smear" on the Main Street curbstone, the FBI went into stonewalling mode. It pretended that it had launched an "exhaustive search of the pertinent files and storage locations" but failed to "turn up spectrographic plates and the notes made therefrom." See J. Stack to Cochran, 6/18/1975, Freedom of Information Act Request of Harold Weisberg, 100-351938. William A. Heilman, the retired FBI spectrographer who allegedly ran the plate, advised that "it is probable that it was destroyed along with other plates which are disposed of periodically according to policy set down in BuFile 62-38539." See Stack to Cochran, 6/20/1975, FOIA Request from Harold Weisberg, 100-351938-31. Although FBI housekeeping efficiency has to be applauded, at the same time that the bureau disposed of key evidence it kept, for example, the three pieces of pressed board it used to simulate the package Oswald allegedly used to smuggle his rifle into the Texas School Book Depository on November 22, 1963. See *Weisberg vs. U.S. Department of Justice,* Exhibit 37.

59. For Hoover's "Dear Lee" letter of 12/13/1963, see FBIHQ JFK Assassination File, 62-109060-1987.

60. Director to SAC, Baltimore, 12/10/1970, FBIHQ JFK Assassination File, 62-109060-6983; SAC, Dallas, to Director, 2/20/1969, FBIHQ JFK Assassination File, 62-109060-6786; SA Alfred C. Ellington to SAC, Dallas, 2/15/1969, Main Dallas JFK Assassination File, 89-43-8869.

61. SAC, Dallas, to Director, 12/11/1967, FBIHQ JFK Assassination File, 62-109060-5898; Jevons to Conrad, 12/14/1967, FBIHQ JFK Assassination File, 62-109060-5908.

62. Jevons to Conrad, 12/14/1967, FBIHQ JFK Assassination File, 62-109060-5908; SAC, Dallas, to Director, 12/11/1967, FBIHQ JFK Assassination File, 62-109060-5898; report of FBI Crime Laboratory to FBI Dallas, 2/27/1969, FBIHQ JFK Assassination File, 62-109060-6787, 4.

63. *Hearings before Commission,* Vol. 5, 100 (Hoover).

64. Director to SAC, Dallas, 10/20/1964, FBIHQ Oswald File, 105-82555-5169; SAC, Dallas, to Director, 11/6/1964, FBIHQ Oswald File, 105-82555-5246.

65. SAC, Dallas, to Director, 11/6/1964, FBIHQ Oswald File, 105-82555-5246.

66. SAC, Dallas, to Director, 10/16/1964, FBIHQ Oswald File, 105-82555-5169. The scar Aldredge reported on the Elm Street sidewalk at the western end of the Texas School Book Depository coincided with the testimony of a young married couple, Arnold J. Rowland and his wife, both high school students, who were in Dealey Plaza to view President Kennedy's visit. Rowland reported to the Dallas Secret Service head Forrest V. Sorrels that before the motorcade approached Elm Street he happened to look up at two open windows at the west end of the depository, where he thought he saw a man standing with what appeared to be a rifle with a telescopic sight. The man was standing too far back from the window for Rowland to identify him. In fact, Rowland gave the matter little thought at the time, believing the man was a Secret Service agent. Sorrels believed that Rowland was truthful in coming forward with his story. If a shot or shots did come from the depository building, Aldredge's and Rowland's uninvestigated accounts leave room for speculation that a sniper was at the westernmost end of the depository and not the southeastern corner, from which Oswald allegedly fired on the presidential motorcade. For Rowland's account, see *Hearings before Commission,* Vol. 7, 350–351. Rowland's witness statement to the Dallas County Sheriff's Office can be found in box 5, folder 2, John F. Kennedy/Dallas Police Department Collection Records Related to the Assassination of John F. Kennedy, City of Dallas Municipal Archives and Records Center, Dallas, Texas, 55. For a picture of the Texas School Book Depository taken thirty minutes after the assassination that shows the open windows as reported by Rowland, see Trask, *Pictures of the Pain,* 519.

67. SAC, Dallas, to Director, 11/6/1964, FBIHQ Oswald File, 105-82555-5246.

Chapter 10. FBI Blunders and Cover-Ups in the JFK Assassination

1. Michael Dorman, *The Secret Service Story* (New York: Delacorte Press, 1967), 170–171.

2. Rosen to Belmont, 12/12/1963, FBIHQ JFK Assassination File, 62-109060-1970; John E. Campion to Chief, 12/5/1963, U.S. Secret Service Reports, Lyndon B. Johnson Library, Austin, Texas (hereafter cited as LBJ Library). Since 1961 the Secret Service had been trying to obtain a bubble-top for the presidential limo that was lightweight but strong enough to provide protection against a .45-caliber slug fired at a distance of ten feet. The Protective Research Section (PRS) of the agency had a number of conferences with a plastics manufacturing company, Swedlow, Inc., but the company was unable to develop a top that accommodated all of the PRS's requirements. See Douglas Dillon, Secretary of the Treasury, *Report of the U.S. Secret Service on the Assassination of President Kennedy,* December 18,

1963 (Washington, D.C.: U.S. Treasury Department) (hereafter cited as Dillon Report), LBJ Library, 22–23.

3. S. A. Stern and J. H. Ely to Rankin, 3/31/1964, Record Group (RG) 272, 13 Series, "Investigation and Evidence" files, National Archives and Records Administration, College Park, Maryland (hereafter cited as NARA); Dorman, *The Secret Service Story,* 174.

4. *Investigation of the Assassination of President John F. Kennedy: Hearings before the President's Commission on the Assassination of President Kennedy* (Washington, D.C.: U.S. Government Printing Office, 1964) (hereafter cited as *Hearings before Commission*), Vol. 7, 337–338, 342 (Sorrels); Lawson to James J. Rowley, Chief, U.S. Secret Service, 11/30/1963, U.S. Secret Service Reports, LBJ Library, 3, 5–7.

5. Bouck to Chief, 12/3/1963, Warren Commission Document (CD) 760, NARA; U.S. Secret Service, Protective Research Section, 10/30/1963, co-2-34, 007, U.S. Secret Service Records, LBJ Library. See also Warren CD 1316 (c4), NARA, for Dallas police lieutenant Jack Revill's report on the right-wingers of the Young Republican Club at North Texas State University. Revill had a source inside the Young Republican Club.

6. Bouck to Chief, 12/3/1963, Warren CD 760, NARA, 1.

7. *Hearings before Commission,* Vol. 4, 299 (Bouck); Dorman, *The Secret Service Story,* 240.

8. Warren Commission, April 30, 1964, executive session transcript, NARA, 16–17. See Hoover to Rankin, 5/4/1964, FBIHQ Oswald File, 105-82555-3561, for the ten-page inventory of the FBI's preassassination Oswald file consisting of sixty-nine items.

9. Brennan to Sullivan, 12/12/1963, FBIHQ JFK Assassination File, 62-109060-1862; Rosen to Belmont, 12/19/1963, FBIHQ JFK Assassination File, 62-109060-2139; Dillon Report, 6.

10. See summary of Oswald's U.S. Marine Corps record released to Mark A. Allen in his Freedom of Information Act suit for FBI records turned over to the House Select Committee on Assassinations. See *Mark A. Allen vs. Federal Bureau of Investigation, et al.*, Civil Action 81-1206, U.S. District Court, District of Columbia, March 19, 1982 (a copy may be found in the Weisberg Archive's Subject Index File under "Mark Allen") (hereafter cited as *Allen vs. FBI,* 1982); *Hearings before Commission,* Vol. 4, 311–313 (Bouck). For more on Oswald's activities that should have raised FBI suspicions, see Chapter 12.

11. Branigan to Sullivan, 11/22/1963, FBIHQ Oswald File, 105-82555-76; *Hearings before Commission,* Vol. 4, 410 (Fain). For more on Oswald's background and activities that convincingly supported the proposition that he was a government agent, see Chapter 12.

12. Branigan to Sullivan, 11/22/1963, FBIHQ Oswald File, 105-82555-76. For Fain's Fort Worth reports, see Warren Commission Exhibits (CEs) 822, 823, and 824.

13. The CIA picked up on Oswald's reference to his Ministry of Internal Affairs (MVD) contacts in the Soviet Union from his autobiographical papers in the Commission's possession. On page 313 of his writings about life in the Soviet Union, Oswald noted that he received a monthly salary of five thousand rubles supplemented by seven hundred rubles that came through the Soviet Red Cross. It was Oswald's belief that these additional monthly sums, while technically earmarked from the Soviet Red Cross, originated with the MVD as a "payoff" for his denunciation of American capitalism. Ultimately, the CIA was satisfied that it was a standard Soviet practice to subsidize foreigners, even unskilled laborers like Oswald, who came from countries with high standards of living. The purpose was to paint a picture of the Soviet Union as a workers' paradise. His salary of five thousand rubles a month as a "checker" metalworker at the Minsk Radio Factory plus the Red Cross supplement meant that Oswald's total monthly income was about equal to that of the factory director. Deputy Director (Plans) to Director of Central Intelligence, 12/6/1963, CIA release of documents to

Harold Weisberg, folder 135, Harold Weisberg Archive, Hood College, Frederick, Maryland; CIA document, "Excerpts of unpublished writings of Lee Harvey Oswald," ibid., folder 257; Memo to J. Lee Rankin, 9/10/1964, ibid., folder with documents 353 through 396; CIA draft of chronology of Oswald in the USSR, October 1959–June 1962, CD 321b, Part I. The CIA was convinced that these "MVD" interviews were actually conducted by officials from the Visa and Registration Department of the Directorate of Internal Affairs, a branch of the Soviet government that was closely connected with the KGB.

14. *Hearings before Commission,* Vol. 19, 567–580, for Oswald's fourteen pages of correspondence with the Socialist Workers Party (SWP) for its literature, including the writings of Leon Trotsky. The SWP was the fiercest of the die-hard enemies of Stalinist communism on the American political landscape. See also Warren CE 97, 22–23, for Oswald's diatribe against what he regarded as the U.S. Communist Party's betrayal of the American working class. During his first interrogation while in custody at the Dallas Police Department, Oswald expatiated upon his anti-Soviet "Marxist" philosophy and politics without inhibition. See *The Warren Commission Report: Report of the President's Commission on the Assassination of President John F. Kennedy* (Washington, D.C.: U.S. Government Printing Office, 1964) (hereafter cited as *WCR*), 599ff.

15. *WCR,* 439 (Paine); James P. Hosty, Jr., to SAC, Dallas, 11/24/1963, Main Dallas JFK Assassination File, 89-43-517, 2.

16. *WCR,* 288; *Hearings before Commission,* Vol. 19, 577.

17. *Hearings before Commission,* Vol. 20, 511–533; Branigan to Sullivan, 11/22/1963, FBIHQ Oswald File, 105-82555-79, 3; for Oswald's May 26, 1963, letter to the FPCC's New York office, see the FBI's Lee Harvey Oswald, Post-Russian Period, 2–3, FBI FPCC (Fair Play for Cuba Committee) File (hereafter cited as FBI FPCC File), Exhibit 62; FBI FPCC File, 393; de Brueys report to file, 10/25/1963, FBI FPCC File; de Brueys's summary of his testimony before the House Select Subcommittee on the Assassination of President John F. Kennedy, HSCA Correspondence File, 62-117290-996X5.

18. *WCR,* 23. Oswald openly discussed his politics in his first interrogation. Insofar as he and his interrogators understood what he was talking about, the record of this session can be found in Appendix 11 of the *WCR,* 599–632.

19. *Hearings before Commission,* Vol. 4, 425–427, 430 (Fain). See also Warren CE 824 for Fain's August 30, 1962, report.

20. Branigan to Sullivan, 11/23/1963, FBIHQ Oswald File, 105-82555-76; Dorman, *The Secret Service Story,* 201. For a useful chronology of Oswald's activities, see the Warren Commission staff's paper titled "Chronology of Events in the Assassination of President John F. Kennedy on November 22, 1963," RG 272, 13 Series, box 11, NARA; FBI, New Orleans, report, 7/22/1964, FBI FPCC File; Patrolman Girod Ray to Chief L. Deutschman, 6/16/1963, FBI FPCC File; SA John L. Quigley's report of interview with Oswald, 8/15/1963, FBI FPCC File; for Bringuier's statement, see SA Robert M. Whomsley's report, 11/30/1963, FBI FPCC File. For more on Oswald's New Orleans activities, see Chapter 12.

21. *Hearings before Commission,* Vol. 4, 442 (Hosty); Hosty to file, 9/10/1963 (Main Dallas Oswald File, 100-10461). For Lee's frequent and increasing violence against Marina, see Priscilla J. McMillan, *Marina and Lee* (New York: Harper and Row, 1977), 225, 235–235, 320–332. Marina testified before the Warren Commission that Lee had beaten her on numerous occasions. See *Hearings before Commission,* Vol. 5, 594, 597–598 (Marina Oswald). For Hosty's report that Lee beat his wife, see Warren CD 11, NARA; James P. Hosty, Jr., with Thomas Hosty, *Assignment Oswald: From the FBI Agent Assigned to Investigate Lee Harvey Oswald Prior to the Assassination* (New York: Arcade Publishing, 1996), 46, 111–113.

22. Brief of FBI Investigation of the Assassination of President John F. Kennedy, June 5,

1964, item 70, FBI referrals to the House Select Committee on Assassinations, *Allen vs. FBI,* 32–33.

23. Hosty to SAC, Dallas, 11/24/1963, Main Dallas JFK Assassination File, 89-43-517; Hosty to SAC, Dallas, 9/29/1964, Main Dallas Oswald File, 100-10461-8413, 2; Hosty to SAC, 12/3/1963, Main Dallas Oswald File, 100-10461-285a; ASAC Kyle G. Clark to SAC, Dallas, 9/29/1964, Main Dallas Oswald File, 100-10461-8410.

24. For a facsimile of the rough draft of Oswald's letter to the Soviet Embassy, see Warren CE 103.

25. For Fenner's account of Oswald's note delivery, see her July 15, 1975, affidavit, FBIHQ JFK Assassination File, 62-109060-7407X.

26. H. N. Bassett to Held, 8/17/1976 (file identification is masked), *Allen vs. FBI,* 1, 5. To confirm that Oswald's note contained a threat, see Bassett to Callahan, 9/29/1975, FBIHQ JFK Assassination File, 62-109060-7302X, 19, and the release of FBI Deputy Associate Director James B. Adams's 10/21/1975 statement before the Subcommittee of Civil and Constitutional Rights, House of Representatives, Committee on the Judiciary, FBIHQ JFK Assassination File, 62-109060-7582, 10. See also statement of William C. Sullivan, 9/17/1975, 5; statement of John V. Almon, 9/8/1975; statement of Ural E. Horton, Jr., 9/4/1975; statement of Charles T. Brown, Jr., 9/5/1975; statement of Joseph L. Schott, 9/3/1975. All of these statements and others can be found in the FBIHQ JFK Assassination File, 62-109060-7407X, Part 1. Other affidavits from those who were interviewed two or three times can be found in FBIHQ JFK Assassination File, 62-109060-serials 7229X, 7302X, 7314X, 2, and 7314X, part 2 of 2.

27. Hosty, *Assignment Oswald,* 185, 21, 29. Hosty affidavit, 9/22/1975, FBIHQ JFK Assassination File, 62-109060-7302X. Fenner affidavit for July 15, 1975, FBIHQ JFK Assassination File, 62-109060-7407X. For all three Fenner affidavits, see FBIHQ JFK Assassination File, 62-109060-7314X2, Part I. See also Fenner's December 11, 1975, testimony before the Subcommittee on Civil and Constitutional Rights, House of Representatives, Committee on the Judiciary, 1st and 2d sessions, serial 2, part 3, FBI Oversight Hearings, 37 (hereafter cited as FBI Oversight Hearings). Hosty defended his version of the Oswald note and claimed that Fenner was unreliable on almost every point, Hosty, *Assignment Oswald,* 199–200.

28. Fenner affidavit, 7/15/1975, FBIHQ JFK Assassination File, 62-109060-7407X, 2; Fenner testimony, FBI Oversight Hearings, 38, 48; Hosty affidavit, 9/22/1975, FBIHQ JFK Assassination File, 62-109060-7302X; Hosty, *Assignment Oswald,* 30; Fenner affidavit, 7/15/1975, FBIHQ JFK Assassination File, 62-109060-7407X.

29. James B. Adams's testimony, FBI Oversight Hearings, 2–3.

30. Adams's statement, FBI Oversight Hearings, 4ff.; see also FBI release of Adams's FBI Oversight Hearings statement, FBIHQ JFK Assassination File, 62-109060-7582, 11.

31. For the FBI mail cover on the Soviet Embassy, see Chronology of Events in the Assassination of President John F. Kennedy on November 22, 1962, RG 272, 13 Series, "Investigation and Evidence" file, box 11, NARA, 10.

32. For FBIHQ orders to destroy the note, see Appendix A, 1. Early Bureau Responses to the President's Assassination, B. Lee Harvey Oswald, no. 3; Hosty, *Assignment Oswald,* 42; Hosty affidavit, 9/22/1975, FBIHQ JFK Assassination File, 62-109060-7302X.

33. See FBI release of Adams's FBI Oversight Hearings statement, FBIHQ JFK Assassination File, 62-109060-7562, 11–12.

34. On publicizing the motorcade route, see S. A. Stern memo to Rankin, 2/17/1964, RG 272, 13 Series, "Investigation and Evidence" file, NARA, 49–50; Dorman, *The Secret Service Story,* 174. See also Dillon Report, 11.

35. FBI Oversight Hearings, 18; *Hearings before Commission,* Vol. 3, 18 (Paine). Marina

also testified before the Warren Commission that Lee was so enraged over Hosty's attempts to question his wife that he told Marina he would visit the FBI's Dallas office and have it out with Hosty. Marina said nothing about a note; she actually never thought her husband would have the courage to confront the FBI agent on his own turf. She called Lee her "brave rabbit." See ibid., Vol. 1, 57–58.

36. For Hosty's testimony, see *Hearings before Commission,* Vol. 4, 447, 459–460, 473. All three FBI agents who testified on May 6, 1974, were instructed by FBIHQ to repeat the party line that Oswald had never demonstrated any propensity for violence. See Belmont to Tolson, 5/5/1964, FBIHQ Oswald File, 105-82555-366(obliterated). See Warren Commission testimony of John W. Fain and John Quigley for May 6, 1964, *Hearings before Commission,* Vol. 4, 424–425, 429 (Fain), 436 (Quigley). See also Hosty, *Assignment Oswald,* 3–4.

37. For the instructions in the FBI Handbook, see Warren CE 836, section 83, subsection K, "Threats against the President of the United States."

38. Hosty, *Assignment Oswald,* 50; Hoover to Rankin, 5/4/1964, FBIHQ Oswald File, 105-82555-3561, item 68. FBI Dallas was informed on October 18, 1963, of Oswald's visit to the Mexico City Soviet Embassy. See Hosty to SAC, Dallas, 12/6/1963, Main Dallas Oswald File, 100-10461-(no serial number assigned). This information had to come from CIA Mexico City through the FBI legat, Clark D. Anderson. It's tempting to speculate whether a "red flag" would have gone up at FBI Dallas had the CIA also informed the FBI of Oswald's two or three visits to the Cuban Consulate.

39. Sanford J. Unger, *FBI: An Uncensored Look Behind the Wall* (Boston: Little, Brown, and Company, 1975), 128–129; Warren Commission, April 30, 1964, executive session transcript, NARA, 16–17; Hosty, *Assignment Oswald,* 21. For Hoover's case for the FBI's cooperation and assistance to the Secret Service in preparation for JFK's Dallas trip, see Hoover to Rankin, 3/31/1964, FBIHQ Liaison with Commission File, 62-109090-Not Recorded (NR); *Hearings before Commission,* Vol. 7, 340–341 (Sorrels). The Criminal Intelligence Division of the Dallas Police Department had infiltrated some of the more active extremist groups in the Dallas area. As a result of these proactive measures the police were able to prevent several planned demonstrations along the route of President Kennedy's motorcade. The fact that General Edwin Walker saw fit to leave Dallas on November 21 for a speaking engagement out of the state may have been prompted by the police's intelligence gathering, which thwarted any attempts to embarrass the presidential party. However, since the FBI never alerted the Dallas Secret Service or Police Chief Curry about Oswald, the Dallas police did not search or post officers in the TSBD or any of the buildings in the vicinity of the depository building. But in view of the precautionary efforts of Curry's department in preparing for the presidential visit, had the police known about Oswald and his place of employment overlooking the motorcade route, the Criminal Intelligence Division might have placed Oswald under surveillance or stationed officers in the TSBD. See FBI Agent A. Raymond Switzer's interview with Curry, 2/29/1964, FBIHQ Oswald File, Gemberling Report, 105-82555-4584, Section 197, 94–95.

40. Hosty, *Assignment Oswald,* 16.

41. *Hearings before Commission,* Vol. 5, 34–35 (Revill). See also Warren CEs 709 (Revill) and 711 (Brian) for their affidavits.

42. Hosty to SAC, Dallas, 4/13/1964, Main Dallas Oswald File, 100-10461-(obliterated); for Hosty's April 22, 1964, affidavit, see FBIHQ Liaison with Commission File, 62-109090-NR, or Warren CE 825.

43. See Hosty, *Assignment Oswald,* 7, 18, 28–29, for his disparaging comments about the Dallas police and the Secret Service. The inside flap of the dust jacket touted Hosty as "the lead investigator in the FBI's post-assassination investigation of Oswald." The reality was

that on the Monday following the assassination Hosty was taken off the Oswald case. Hosty interpreted his separation from the case as some dark conspiracy to protect those responsible for organizing the assassination. In his rewriting of the JFK assassination Hosty represented himself as the victim of a monster government-wide conspiracy to suppress the truth of Dallas, involving even the legendarily anticommunist Hoover as part of the cover-up of a Soviet-Castro plot to murder President Kennedy.

44. Ibid., 19.

45. J. R. Malley to SAC, Dallas, 12/11/1963, Main Dallas Oswald File, 100-10461-1381; Hosty, *Assignment Oswald,* 28–29; *Hearings before Commission,* Vol. 7, 355–356 (Sorrels); Stern to Rankin, 2/17/1964, RG 272, 13 Series, "Investigation and Evidence" File, NARA, 30.

46. Hosty to SAC, Dallas, 12/11/1963, Main Dallas Oswald File, 100-10461-1377; SAC, Dallas to Director, FBI, 12/11/1963, Main Dallas Oswald File, 100-10461-1378.

47. Hosty to Dallas, 11/28/1963, Main Dallas Oswald File, 100-10461-134; Bookhout to SAC, Dallas, 11/29/1963, Main Dallas Oswald File, 100-10461-135; Hosty, *Assignment Oswald,* 20–25.

48. *Hearings before Commission,* Vol. 5, 39 (Revill); Hosty, *Assignment Oswald,* 67–68, 26–27.

49. DeLoach to Mohr, 11/23/1963, FBIHQ JFK Assassination File, 62-109060-21; Shanklin to file, 11/22/1963, Main Dallas JFK Assassination File, 89-43-24.

50. For Gale's account of the November 23 meeting, see Director, FBI, to the Attorney General, 10/1/1975, FBIHQ JFK Assassination File, 62-109060-7302X, 20. For a copy of Gale's 12/10/1963 report, see *Investigation of the Assassination of President John F. Kennedy: Hearings before the Select Committee on Assassinations of the U.S. House of Representatives,* 95th Congress, 2d session (Washington, D.C.: U.S. Government Printing Office, 1979) (hereafter cited as *HSCA),* Vol. 3, 526; William C. Sullivan and Bill Brown, *The Bureau: My Thirty Years in Hoover's FBI* (New York: W. W. Norton, 1979), 52; *HSCA,* Vol. 3, 546 (Gale).

51. When members of the House select committee asked that question, Gale, who retired from the FBI in 1971, held firm to his opinion, even to the point of unreasonableness, that the one had nothing to do with the other. Gale contended that the bureau's failure to place Oswald's name on the Security Index was independent of what happened in Dallas. He insisted throughout his testimony that even if Oswald's name had been on the index, he was not sure that the FBI would have disclosed this information to the Secret Service. When some of his incredulous questioners asked Gale what would have prompted disclosure, an irritated Gale shot back that if Hosty had known Oswald was going to be in the TSBD with a rifle, then Hosty would have advised the Secret Service. See *HSCA,* Vol. 3, 552, 553–554 (Gale).

52. Sullivan, *The Bureau,* 53; see also Appendix A, 2. Structure and Methods of the Bureau Investigation, C: Domestic Intelligence Division (Div. 5), nos. 6 and 4, and B: General Investigative Division (GID), no. 6.

53. Gale report, *HSCA,* Vol. 3, 536. See also Gale to Tolson, 9/30/1964, internal memorandum, 494012-133, for Hoover's comments and the addendum for Belmont and DeLoach's dissent.

54. Hugh Aynesworth, "FBI Knew Oswald Capable of Act, Reports Indicate," *Dallas Morning News,* April 24, 1964; Rosen to Belmont, 4/24/1964, FBIH'Q Oswald File, 105-82555-3401. For the Alexander-Aynesworth-Hudkins scam, see Chapter 6.

55. Rosen to Belmont, 4/24/1964, FBIHQ Oswald File, 105-82555-3401; DeLoach to Mohr, 4/24/1964, FBIHQ JFK Assassination File, 62-109060-3004; DeLoach to Mohr, 4/24/1964, FBIHQ JFK Assassination File, 62-109060-NR; Dallas to Director, 4/24/1964,

FBIHQ Liaison with Commission File, 62-109090-NR; DeLoach to Mohr, 4/24/1964, FBIHQ JFK Assassination File, 62-109060-3004.

56. ASAC to SAC (67-5593), 4/2/1964 (no file name provided), 67-425-1734, *Allen vs. FBI,* 1982.

57. Dallas to Director, 4/24/1964, FBIHQ Liaison with Commission File, 62-109090-NR; Hoover to Rankin, 4/27/1964, FBIHQ Oswald File, 105-82555-3432; Belmont to Tolson, 4/24/1964, FBIHQ Liaison with Commission File, 62-109090-3552.

58. Curt Gentry, *J. Edgar Hoover: The Man and the Secrets* (New York: W. W. Norton, 1991), 181–182.

59. For an account of the incident with independent corroboration of Berger and Johnsen's reporting, see Warren CE 1024 and SA Johnsen to Chief James J. Rowley, RG 272, 13 Series, "Investigation and Evidence" file, box 4, folder 1, NARA.

60. United Press International, *Four Days* (New York: UPI Publications, 1963), 25; De-Loach to Mohr, 2/4/1964, FBIHQ JFK Assassination File, 62-109060-2424.

61. Jones to DeLoach, 2/3/1964, FBIHQ JFK Assassination File, 62-109060-2425; De-Loach to Mohr, 3/4/1964, FBIHQ JFK Assassination File, 62-109060-2424; Jones to De-Loach, 1/22/1864, FBIHQ JFK Assassination File, 62-109060-2314; Shanklin to file, 11/29/1964, Main Dallas JFK Assassination File, 89-43-1391; Brennan to Sullivan, 2/13/1964, FBIHQ JFK Assassination File, 62-109060-2437. Considering that the UPI and AP journalists sensationalized the incident out of all proportion, it is understandable that Hoover was wrought up about the treatment. At the same time, it's hard to avoid comparing FBIHQ's concerted efforts to "correct" the record of this minor contretemps to, for example, the Hoover bureau's neglect of Governor Connally's clothes while they still had critical evidentiary value.

62. Brennan to Sullivan, 12/10/1963, FBIHQ JFK Assassination File, 62-109060-1869.

63. Rosen to Belmont, 12/18/1963, FBIHQ JFK Assassination File, 62-109060-NR; Hoover to Rankin, 5/4/1964, FBIHQ Oswald File, 105-82555-3561. (The May 4 date re-flected the fact that this was a copy of an earlier filing that went to the Commission. The May 5 copy was prepared for Alan Belmont's appearance before the Warren Commission on May 5, 1964.) During the FBI's October 1975 investigation into the destruction of the Oswald note, FBI Dallas agent Joe A. Pearce stated, "Oswald was an informant or source of SA Hosty and it was not uncommon for sources to occasionally come to the office for the pur-pose of delivering some note to the contacting Agent." The House Select Committee referred Pearce's statement back to the FBI for clarification. Pearce's claim went no further; it was al-most certainly a misperception on his part. The FBI explained that the Warren Commission had investigated the story and found there "was no substance whatsoever to this particular claim." See Director to the Attorney General, 12/31/1975, FBI releases to the House Select Committee on Assassinations, document 66, *Allen vs. FBI,* 1982.

64. Clark to SAC, Dallas, 12/23/1963, Main Dallas Oswald File, 100-10461-1990; Stern to Rankin, 2/17/1964, RG 272, 13 Series, NARA, 27–28; *Hearings before Commission,* Vol. 4, 450, 453 (Hosty). Hosty made this admission in the presence of Sorrels, Inspector Thomas Kelley, and SA Max Phillips at Secret Service headquarters in Dallas after the interview team returned from questioning Marina Oswald at the Six Flags Inn. The following day Secret Ser-vice agents Leon Gopadze and Max Phillips and a trusted friend of Marina's, Peter P. Gre-gory, visited Marina without being accompanied by any FBI agents. Marina told them about Agent Hosty's attempts to question her on November 1 and 5. See U.S. Secret Service, U.S. Treasury Department, report by Leon Gopadze, 11/29/1963, document 319, file no. CO-2-34030, 2, 6, and 7,

65. Hosty to SAC, Dallas, 11/24/1963, Main Dallas JFK Assassination File, 89-43-710;

Hearings before Commission, Vol. 4, 449, 451 (Hosty). A facsimile of Oswald's address book appeared in the FBI Oversight Hearings, 211–227. It gave November 27, 1963, as the date that Fritz made the address book available to Hosty. Stern to Rankin, 2/17/1964, RG 272, 13 Series, NARA, 27. For some indication of Dallas police and Secret Service relations, see Griffith and Hubert to Rankin, 3/23/1964, Rankin Papers, box 18, folder 288, and Memorandum to the files, 4/10/1964, Rankin Papers, box 18, folder 291, NARA.

66. For a copy of Hoover's December 13, 1963, letter of censure, see FBI Oversight Hearings, 139; Hosty, *Assignment Oswald,* 103.

67. Stern to Rankin, 2/17/1964, RG 272, 13 Series, NARA, 26–27. Former FBI agent and chairman of the House Committee on the Judiciary Don Edwards took pains to make this point when he was questioning FBI witness James B. Adams. See FBI Oversight Hearings, 21.

68. Rankin to Hoover, 2/20/1964, FBIHQ JFK Assassination File, 62-109060-NR; Branigan to Sullivan, 2/10/1964, FBIHQ JFK Assassination File, 62-109060-NR; Harold Feldman, "Oswald and the FBI," the *Nation,* January 27, 1964, 86; Branigan to Sullivan, 2/10/1964, FBIHQ Liaison with Commission File, 62-109090-NR.

69. Warren Commission, February 24, 1964, executive session transcript, NARA, 4; Rankin to Hoover, 2/20/1964, FBIHQ JFK Assassination File, 62-109060-NR; Rosen to Belmont, 2/26/1964, FBIHQ Liaison with Commission File, 62-109090-116; Dallas to Director, 2/24/1964, FBIHQ Oswald File, 105-82555-2248. Hosty claimed that Gemberling and Kesler made the decision to keep the Hosty reference secret from Washington headquarters; see Hosty, *Assignment Oswald,* 234.

70. Dallas to Director, 2/24/1964, FBIHQ Oswald File, 105-82555-2248. For Gemberling's and Kesler's affidavits, see SAC, Dallas, to Director, FBI, 2/25/1964, FBIHQ Oswald File, 105-82555-2243.

71. Griffin and Hubert to Rankin, 3/23/1964, Rankin Papers, box 18, folder 288, NARA, 2; SAC, Dallas, to Director, FBI, 4/17/1964, FBIHQ JFK Assassination File, 62-109060-3065; Brennan to Sullivan, 4/23/1964, FBIHQ JFK Assassination File, 62-109060-3066. The "marked change" Sorrels noted might have been a reference to the FBI detailing forty agents, at Rowley's request, to assist the Secret Service at President Kennedy's funeral. When Johnson took over the presidency he reached out to the FBI on numerous occasions to provide protection when he left Washington. Hoover was always ready to make available one of his bulletproof limousines at White House request. See Belmont to Tolson, 11/24/1963, FBIHQ JFK Assassination File, 62-109060-962; Brennan to Sullivan, 12/10/1963, White House Security File, 94-4-3830-133; Brennan to Sullivan, 12/6/1963, White House Security File, 94-4-3830-135; New York to Director, 2/5/1964, White House Security File, 94-4-3830-143.

72. Stern memo to Rankin, 3/20/1964, Rankin Papers, box 18, folder 291, NARA, 4–5; Alonzo L. Hamby, *A Life of Harry S. Truman: Man of the People* (New York: Oxford University Press, 1995), 471–472; Dorman, *The Secret Service Story,* 64–65; Stern to Rankin, 3/30/1964, second interview with Bouck, Rankin Papers, box 18, folder 291, NARA, 2.

73. Stern to Rankin, 2/17/1964, RG 272, 13 Series, "Investigation and Evidence" file, NARA, 81–87; Stern to Rankin, 2/10/1964, Rankin Papers, box 18, folder 291, NARA.

74. Rosen to Belmont, 4/15/1964, FBIHQ Liaison with Commission File, 62-109090-NR.

75. Rosen to Belmont, 4/15/1964, FBIHQ Liaison with Commission File, 62-109090-132; Sullivan to Belmont, 4/17/1964, FBIHQ Liaison with Commission File, 62-109090-131; Rosen to Belmont, 4/22/1964, FBIHQ Liaison with Commission File, 62-109090-130.

76. *Hearings before Commission,* Vol. 4, 311–314 (Bouck).

77. Rosen to Belmont, 4/24/1964, FBIHQ Liaison with Commission File, 62-109090-133; Rosen to Belmont, 5/5/1964, FBIHQ Liaison with Commission File, 62-109090-NR; Belmont to Tolson, 4/24/1964, FBIHQ Oswald File, 105-82555-3552.

78. Rosen to Belmont, 5/5/1964, FBIHQ Liaison with Commission File, 62-109090-NR. In 1975, when the Hosty note destruction cover-up became public, former Commission assistant counsel Samuel A. Stern was troubled (Stern interview with Mike Ewing, HSCA, JFK Collection, RG 233, NARA, 5). It was Stern who had laid the groundwork for Hosty's Commission testimony, and Stern felt that he had fallen down on the job because he had failed to ask this key question during his several conferences with the FBI agent. It goes without saying that Hosty never volunteered anything about the Oswald note during his pretestimony sessions with Stern. See Bassett to Callahan, 12/3/1975, FBIHQ JFK Assassination File, 62-109060-7437X.

79. Hosty, *Assignment Oswald,* 151, 153–156; Hosty to Director, FBI (Personal and Confidential), 10/24/1975, Hoover's Personal and Confidential File, 62-494012-191.

Chapter 11. Senator Russell Dissents

1. *Investigation of the Assassination of President John F. Kennedy: Hearings before the President's Commission on the Assassination of President Kennedy* (Washington, D.C.: U.S. Government Printing Office, 1964) (hereafter cited as *Hearings before Commission*), Vol. 5, 99–101 (Hoover).

2. Gilbert C. Fite, *Richard B. Russell, Jr., Senator from Georgia* (Chapel Hill: University of North Carolina Press, 1991), 494–495.

3. LBJ phone conversation with Russell, 9/18/1964 (7:54 P.M.), White House Telephone Transcripts, Lyndon Baines Johnson Library, Austin, Texas (hereafter cited as LBJ Library); Edward Jay Epstein, *Inquest: The Warren Commission and the Establishment of Truth* (New York: Viking Press, 1966), 149–151.

4. LBJ phone conversation with Russell, 9/18/1964, White House Telephone Transcripts, LBJ Library; Kai Bird, *The Chairman: John S. McCloy and the Making of the American Establishment* (New York: Simon and Schuster, 1992), 565. President Johnson voiced the belief that JFK had been the victim of a conspiracy, but he wavered on whether the plot to kill Kennedy had been foreign or domestic. In the days and weeks after Dallas he entertained the possibilities that Castro and the Soviets were involved. All the rumors and allegations originating with the CIA and U.S. Ambassador to Mexico Thomas Mann about Oswald's contacts with the Cuban Consulate and Soviet Embassy in Mexico City influenced his early suspicions about a Red plot. See Robert Dallek, *Flawed Giant: Lyndon Johnson and His Times, 1960–1973* (New York: Oxford University Press, 1998), 51–53. By 1967, however, presumably after he learned about the CIA's "Executive Action" programs against Castro, LBJ told Marvin Watson, a White House staffer and liaison to the FBI, that he suspected the CIA was behind the assassination since it had been running a "Murder, Inc." in the Caribbean. See DeLoach to Tolson, 4/4/1967, FBIHQ JFK Assassination File, 62-109060-5075.

5. Fite, *Richard B. Russell, Jr.,* 405–406; Bird, *The Chairman,* 564–566; Lyndon B. Johnson telephone conversation with Russell, 9/18/1964 (7:54 P.M.), White House Telephone Transcripts, LBJ Library.

6. See Warren Commission, January 27, 1964, executive session transcript, National Archives and Records Administration, College Park, Maryland (hereafter cited as NARA), for Russell's concerns that the CIA and FBI were holding back information from the Commission. See also Chapter 6 for the senator's suspicions that the FBI was rigging some of the ballistics evidence in the case. Russell, like his fellow commissioners, was clearly frustrated with the FBI's leaking of Commission Document (CD) 1's conclusions. See Warren Commission, December 5, 1963, executive session transcript, NARA. For the Russell-Dulles exchange, see Warren Commission, January 27, 1964, executive session transcript, NARA, 143.

7. Handwritten notes found in Senator Russell's desk dated December 5, 1963, Richard B. Russell Papers, Series 2, Intra Office Communication, Special Collections Division, Richard B. Russell Memorial Library, University of Georgia, Athens, Georgia (hereafter cited as Russell Papers).

8. Ibid. Russell raised the need for a general counsel during the Commission's first meeting. See Warren Commission, December 5, 1963, executive session transcript, NARA. See also Warren Commission, January 27, 1964, executive session transcript, NARA, for Russell's expressed suspicions about Oswald's Mexico trip. Russell never relented in his suspicions that Oswald was linked in some way with Castro's Cuba and had received assistance from the Cuban government in the assassination. See Gary Diamond's May 8, 1989, edited transcript of Russell's interview with Hal Suit on February 11, 1970 (hereafter cited as Diamond compilation), "I think someone else worked with him," Russell Papers, 5–6.

9. See Russell's written statements, made two days before he read them to his Commission colleagues, Russell Papers, Series 1, Subseries H, box 84, Kennedy Assassination Commission Dictation—Kennedy Assassination, 1963–1964.

10. LBJ phone conversation with Russell, 11/29/1963, White House Telephone Transcripts, LBJ Library, in which Russell confided that he suspected Castro was the mastermind behind the Kennedy assassination.

11. See Russell's Cox TV transcript of interview broadcast on WSBTV, September 18, 1969, Russell Papers. Russell thought Warren too grandfatherly in his questioning of Marina and Rankin's interrogation "not very vigorous." See also Hal Suit interview with Russell, Diamond compilation, Russell Papers, 3.

12. Russell's Cox TV interview, September 18, 1969; *Hearings before Commission,* Vol. 5, 590ff. (Russell); Hugh Gates interview with Senator Cooper, oral history 40, John Sherman Cooper Papers, University of Kentucky, Lexington, Kentucky (hereafter cited as Cooper Papers), 3–4. Richard Helms to Rankin, 6/5/1964, Warren CD 1041, NARA. See also FBI releases to HSCA, 9/10/1964, item 430, NARA. For the CIA reports on Minsk, see Memorandum for J. Lee Rankin, 9/10/1964, "Secret Training Locations and Training Procedures in USSR," CIA document no. 826-430, Harold Weisberg Archive, Hood College, Frederick, Maryland (hereafter cited as Weisberg Archive); Richard Helms to Rankin, 6/4/1964, "Allegations Regarding Intelligence Training School in Minsk, USSR," CIA document no. 726-314, Weisberg Archive.

13. For Russell's statement to the Commission on September 18, 1964, see Russell Papers, Series I, Subseries H, box 19, Kennedy Assassination Dictation, 1963–1967; Cooper oral history interview, Cooper Papers. Connally remained adamant that he had been hit by a separate bullet. He was quoted in a 1966 *Life* magazine story that left no doubt about his views on the subject. Connally said, "They talk about the one bullet or two bullet theory but as far as I am concerned there is no theory. There is my absolute knowledge . . . that one bullet caused the President's first wound and that an entirely separate shot struck me. It is a certainty, I will never change my mind." See *Washington Post,* November 21, 1966, for the quotation from *Life.* For Russell's many comments on drafts of the Commission's Chapter 3, see Gary Diamond's "Richard Russell's Opinions Concerning the Kennedy Assassination," May 8, 1989, Diamond compilation, Russell Papers, 25–29.

14. Epstein, *Inquest,* 150; Bird, *The Chairman,* 565.

15. Epstein, *Inquest,* 150.

16. Warren Commission, December 5, 1963, executive session transcript, NARA, 38, 41 (McCloy). McCloy to Rankin, 6/24/1964, Rankin Papers, Record Group (RG) 200, box 1, folder 16, NARA. McCloy's biographer noted that McCloy "loved the outdoors all his life and took great pleasure in introducing his grandchildren to fishing and hunting." Bird, *The Chairman,* caption to photo 40 opposite p. 547.

17. Redlich, Rankin's most trusted staff lawyer, was on the rewrite committee, and the general counsel assigned him the task of rewriting Chapter 3. See *Investigation of the Assassination of President John F. Kennedy: Hearings before the Select Committee on Assassinations of the U.S. House of Representatives,* 95th Congress, 2d session (Washington, D.C.: U.S. Government Printing Office, 1979) (hereafter cited as *HSCA*), Vol.11, 463, for "Who Wrote What."

18. *The Warren Commission Report: Report of the President's Commission on the Assassination of President John F. Kennedy* (Washington, D.C.: U.S. Government Printing Office, 1964) (hereafter cited as *WCR*), 19. For Mrs. Eide's (Rankin's secretary) call to Russell later that same day, see Series 13, Subseries A, box 5, JFK Assassination Commission—Miscellaneous, Data 7, Russell Papers.

19. For example, after Cooper reviewed the penultimate draft of Chapter 3, he wrote Rankin that "he could not agree with the statement" that "the two shots caused all wounds." See Rankin Papers, 8/20/1964, box 1, folder 23, NARA.

20. *WCR,* 107, 109, 584–586. See also Chapter 7. The experiments carried out by Drs. Olivier and Dziemian at the Edgewood Arsenal proved that the Commission's single-bullet explanation was impossible. Consequently, the results of their tests were suppressed by the Defense Department and were not declassified until 1973, eight years later. See the Introduction.

21. *Hearings before Commission,* Vol. 2, 374–375 (Humes), 379 (Boswell), 382 (Finck). See also Chapter 7.

22. See Chapter 7 for Dolce's views.

23. *Hearings before Commission,* Vol. 4, 112, 114 (Shaw), 127–128 (Gregory). See also Chapter 8.

24. See Chapter 6 in Epstein's *Inquest* for a succinct but very useful treatment of the two nonconvergent worlds of the staff's investigation and the Commission's hearings.

25. Epstein, *Inquest,* 22, for some of the staff lawyers' sharply etched comments.

26. *HSCA,* Vol. 11, 217–218.

27. Epstein, *Inquest,* 110; Russell took exception to Epstein's calculation of his 6 percent attendance record, commenting to a Virginia admirer that he was sure he "was present more than 6% of the time." See Russell to Elizabeth Westgate, 11/1/1966, Series 13, Subseries A, box 1, JFK Assassination Commission—Correspondence, 1965–1966, Russell Papers; Russell's interview on Cox TV, ibid.; Fite, *Richard B. Russell, Jr.,* 498, 413–414.

28. For a copy of this letter of resignation from Russell to the president, 2/24/1964, see Dictation Series, Kennedy and Assassination Commission 1963–1966, Russell Papers; Diamond compilation, 15. See Epstein, *Inquest,* 105, for a breakdown of witnesses who appeared before the Commission as compared to the vast majority who were questioned one-on-one by the staff lawyers or submitted affidavits.

29. In 1968 Russell struck up a relationship with Harold Weisberg after Weisberg brought to the senator's attention Rankin's suppression of the record of the September 18 executive session. The quotation is from Weisberg's Richard B. Russell file, Weisberg Archive.

30. Quoted in Fite, *Richard B. Russell, Jr.,* 501.

31. *HSCA,* Vol. 11, 274 (Griffin). See Chapter 9 for more detail on the Tague bullet; *Hearings before Commission,* Vol. 7, 552–558, for Tague's deposition.

32. For the record of depositions that Russell reviewed, see "Depositions," Series 13, Subseries A, box 3, JFK Assassination Commission—Russell three-ring notebook, Russell Papers. I selected the Tague bullet to illustrate how Russell was unaware of and distanced from relevant evidence that could have made a significant difference in his coming to terms with the Warren report. The curbstone shot was just one item in a list that could grow impressively long. For example, Russell was convinced that Oswald was something of a crack shot. Had

he read or been aware of Ronald Simmons's Commission testimony that even some of the best marksmen in the country using the alleged assassination weapon could not duplicate the shooting the Commission attributed to Oswald, he might have been forced to reexamine his views. For Russell on Oswald as a skilled marksman, see LBJ phone call to Russell, 9/18/1964, White House Telephone Transcripts, LBJ Library. For Simmons's Commission testimony, see *Hearings before Commission,* Vol. 3, 449–450.

33. See comments of Senator Cooper on Chapter 3, 8/20/1964, Rankin Papers, box 1, folder 23, NARA; *WCR,* 111, for the paragraph headed "The Shot That Missed."

34. See Senator Cooper's interview with Bill Cooper (no relation), Cooper Papers, 29–30.

35. For full treatment of the curbstone shot, see Chapters 8 and 9.

36. LBJ phone conversation with Russell, 9/18/1964, White House Telephone Transcripts, LBJ Library.

37. *WCR,* 22.

38. Warren Commission, January 22, 1964, executive session transcript, NARA; Jesse L. Ward, Jr., to Hon. Earl Warren, 12/3/1964, RG 272, no. 20, box 5, File "Commission Reporting Service," NARA. For Russell's support of Ward & Paul for the Commission's stenographic recording, see Warren Commission, December 16, 1963, executive session transcript, NARA, 4–5.

39. See Ward & Paul file, Weisberg Archive.

40. Warren Commission, September 18, 1963, executive session transcript, NARA; or see Appendix F of Diamond compilation, "Richard Russell's Opinions Concerning the Kennedy Assassination," Russell Papers.

41. Rankin's meeting with the Texas delegation is covered in detail in Chapter 6.

42. Rankin's Memorandum for the Commission, 11/5/1964, attached to a copy of Warren Commission, September 18, 1964, executive session transcript, NARA. The Commission did not formally surrender its offices at the Veterans of Foreign Wars building until November 20, but the only office that was still occupied and functioning after the Commission submitted its findings to President Johnson on September 27 belonged to J. Lee Rankin. See CIA memo 11/20/1964, CIA document 926-365, Weisberg Archive.

43. For the Rhoads letter, see Weisberg's Richard B. Russell file, Weisberg Archive, or James B. Rhoads to Harold Weisberg, 5/20/1968, Series 13, Subseries A, box 1, Kennedy Assassination Commission—Correspondence 1969–1970, Russell Papers. For Russell's withdrawal from these Senate duties, see *Washington Post,* October 11, 1968. For Weisberg-Russell exchange of letters, see Weisberg's Richard B. Russell file, Weisberg Archive.

44. Russell to Weisberg, 1/7/1969, Richard B. Russell file, Weisberg Archive; Don Oberdorfer, "Russell Says He Never Believed Oswald Alone Planned Killing," *Washington Post,* January 19, 1970, A2. Gary Diamond's edited compilation dealing with Russell's dissent is most useful. See Diamond compilation, "I think someone worked with him," May 8, 1989. See also Dani E. Biancolli, "The First Dissenter: Richard B. Russell and the Warren Commission," M.A. thesis, College of William and Mary, Virginia, 2002, 66. I want to thank Ms. Biancolli for allowing me to read her thesis. She was one of my most promising students during my years at Hood College.

Chapter 12. Was Oswald a Government "Agent"?

1. See Chapter 11, "Senator Russell Dissents."

2. *The Warren Commission Report: Report of the President's Commission on the Assassination of President John F. Kennedy* (Washington, D.C.: U.S. Government Printing Office, 1964) (hereafter cited as *WCR,* 22; Kai Bird, *The Chairman: John J. McCloy and the Making of the American Establishment* (New York: Simon and Schuster, 1992), 565.

3. *WCR,* 22.

4. See Chapter 1, "Assembling the 'Official Truth' of Dallas."

5. *WCR,* Chapter 7 and 683–686; see Record Group (RG) 127, Records of the U.S. Marine Corps, JFK Collection Register, National Archives and Records Administration, College Park, Maryland (hereafter cited as NARA). For some anecdotal accounts of Oswald when he was stationed at El Toro in Santa Ana, see Warren Commission Document (CD) 113, NARA.

6. For Rankin's comments, see Warren Commission, January 27, 1964, executive session transcript, NARA, 164. Maj. Rufus C. Young, Jr., Correspondence Branch Judge Advocate Division, to Emory L. Brown, Jr., 9/18/1975; Capt. P. J. Harris, Adjutant Defense Language Institute, Presidio Monterey, California, to Brown, 2/11/1978; and Maj. Michael C. Mandel, U.S. Army, Public Affairs Officer, Defense Language Institute Foreign Language Center, to Brown, 1/17/1985. All of Brown's correspondence can be found in Harold Weisberg's "Agent Oswald" file, Harold Weisberg Archive, Hood College, Frederick, Maryland (hereafter cited as Weisberg Archive).

7. *WCR,* 684–685. For the record that Oswald was involved in "Operation Strongback," see Office of Naval Intelligence (ONI) Files, JFK Collection Register, RG 526, box 2, folder 173-10002-10031, NARA; Statement of Captain Francis J. Gajewski on Oswald's performance during "Operation Strongback," Paul Hoch's ONI Files, Weisberg Archive. For an account of the CIA's effort to overthrow the Sukarno regime, see Stephen E. Ambrose, *Ike's Spies: Eisenhower and the Espionage Establishment* (New York: Doubleday, 1981), 249–251.

8. For Rankin's request for the Schrand file, see Wilfred Hearn to Judge Advocate General, Commandant of the Marines, 4/30/1964, "Agent Oswald" files, Weisberg Archive. See the navy's fifty-four-page inquest into Schrand's death, Investigative File into the Death of Pvt. Martin D. Schrand, RG 526, box 2, JFK documents, folder 173-10002-10041 and box 3, JFK documents, folders 10101-10125 and 10126-10150, ONI Files, NARA (hereafter cited as Schrand investigation). *Investigation of the Assassination of President John F. Kennedy: Hearings before the President's Commission on the Assassination of President Kennedy* (Washington, D.C.: U.S. Government Printing Office, 1964) (hereafter cited as *Hearings before Commission*), Vol. 11, 82ff. (Thornley); Vol. 8, 232, 259 (Degado).

9. Director to St. Louis, 11/29/1963, FBIHQ JFK Assassination File, 62-109060-394. Security Officer to Commanding Officer, MACS-1, January 9, 1958, U.S. Naval Air Station, Cubi Point, Philippines, Schrand investigation; Judge Advocate General to Commandant of the Marine Corps, April 30, 1964, signed by Wilfred Hearn, Schrand investigation. Suspecting that the weapon issued to Private Schrand was unstable if improperly used, the navy did some tests on the type of riot gun issued for guard duty at the Cubi Point installation. The tests disclosed that if the weapon was dropped vertically on the butt end on the ground, which was one of the drill steps in the Manual of Arms, it might discharge. Schrand had a reputation among his fellow marines for being a "bug" on drill. The navy concluded that the weapon had accidentally discharged when he had diverted himself while on guard duty with repetitive Manual of Arms exercises. Filed by Special Agent W. C. Kuehl, 5/26/1964, Office of Naval Intelligence, ONI-25852(b), Weisberg Archive. See also Wilfred Hearn, JAG, to Commandant of the Marine Corps, 4/30/1964, ONI File, RG 526, box 22, JFK documents, folder 173-10002-10042 through 10090, NARA. Faced with disappointment in the Schrand matter, the FBI and Rankin bore down harder on Marina Oswald to provide testimony supporting the claim that her husband had been the assailant in the General Walker shooting.

10. Lt. Col. B. S. Kozak's August 17, 1959, report on Oswald's early hardship discharge, Records of the U.S. Marine Corps, JFK Collection Register, RG 127, NARA; *Hearings before Commission,* Vol. 19, 676, 680.

11. *Hearings before Commission,* Vol. 22, 77–79.

12. *WCR,* 746. See the 112 pages of photocopies of Oswald's Marine Corps records reproduced in *Hearings before Commission,* Vol. 19, 656–768. The most insightful analysis of Oswald's Marine Corps records is still Harold Weisberg, *Whitewash: The Report on the Warren Report* (Hyattstown, Md.: Harold Weisberg Publisher, 1965), 123–124.

13. Snyder was identified as CIA in Edward Jay Epstein, *Legend: The Secret World of Lee Harvey Oswald* (New York: McGraw-Hill, 1978), 94–95. Since it was pretty much an open secret that Epstein's major source for the book was James Jesus Angleton, the chief of the CIA's Counterintelligence Branch, it can be safely assumed that Snyder was with the agency when he encountered Oswald. For a copy of Oswald's note and McVickar's comments, see Edward L. Freers, Charge d'Affaires to Department of State, 11/2/1959, Warren Commission Exhibit (CE) 2685. See also ALUSNA, Moscow, cable to CNO, 11/3/1959, CE 717.

14. *WCR,* 752–754.

15. See Oswald's Marine Corps Records, *Hearings before Commission,* Vol. 19, 680, for his signature acknowledging the penalties for violating the 1950 Internal Security Act. For Spas Raikin's account, see CD 75. See also Weisberg, *Whitewash,* 123–124, 130–131, 200.

16. *Hearings before Commission,* Vol. 8, 297–298 (Donovan). Morrissey interview with Donovan, 12/4/1963, FBI Washington Field Office (WFO) 105-37111 (no serial number included).

17. Epstein, *Legend,* 53–56, 121–122. Epstein implied that Oswald might have provided the Soviets with critical information about the U-2, for example, the spy plane's altitude and its ultrasecret radar-jamming equipment, that gave the Russians the edge they needed to shoot down Gary Powers on May 1, 1960. The shoot-down led to a series of heated diplomatic exchanges between Eisenhower and Khrushchev and the subsequent collapse of their scheduled summit talks in Paris. See his chapter 5, "Wreck of Race Car." Later evidence revealed that the Soviets already knew how to track the U-2s, so all Oswald could have told them was that there were U-2 bases at Atsugi and Cubi Point, which the Russians certainly already knew.

What frustrated Moscow was the inability of their interceptor aircraft and surface missiles to reach heights of ninety thousand feet until they developed the SA-2 (Guideline surface-to-air missiles). The Guidelines had the capability of reaching the U-2s. By 1960 the Russians had SA-2s deployed around principal cities and strategic industrial installations across the Soviet Union. The CIA knew about the Guideline and its capabilities when it sent Powers aloft on May 1, 1960. His flight plan called for photo surveillance over Soviet missile test centers, nuclear plants in the Urals, the ICBM complex at Yurya, the submarine shipyards at Severadvinsk, and the naval bases at Murmansk. All of these points on Powers's itinerary were guarded by SA-2 missile sites. See Dino A. Brugioni, *Eye Ball to Eye Ball: The Inside Story of the Cuban Missile Crisis* (New York: Random House, 1991), 43–44.

18. ONI Files, NARA; Jackson's letter of transmittal with the enclosure listing the folders sent to the Commission, ONI File, RG 526, box 1, NARA.

19. For the circulation of Oswald's ONI file, see Molinari to file, 11/22/1963, a copy in Paul Hoch's ONI File, Weisberg Archive.

20. Rankin to McNaughton, 2/18/1964; Frank A. Bartimo memorandum, 2/25/1964; C. J. Roach, Special Agent, Atten: Captain Jackson, 11/23/1963; Rankin to Folsom, 5/19/1964. All in Paul Hoch's ONI File, Weisberg Archives.

21. For Stern's comments, see Memorandum for the Record, 4/2/1964, "Meeting with Representatives of the President's Commission on the Assassination of President Kennedy, 3/27/1964, Langley," CIA document no. 63-792, CIA release, June 1976, NARA.

22. This is not an irresponsible accusation when we consider that it was the navy that saw to it that there would not be a complete and competent autopsy. The record of the Bethesda

autopsy reeks of dishonesty, false swearing by navy officers, destruction of the first autopsy protocol, missing autopsy records, and a host of unanswered questions that do constitute an accusation against the navy, and a very serious one. See Chapter 7, "The JFK Autopsy."

23. Richard Helms, Deputy Director of Plans, to Rankin, 3/6/1964. See CD 692, NARA, for a list of the thirty documents.

24. John Whitten's deposition taken by the House Select Committee on Assassinations, 5/16/1978, 8–10. Since his testimony was classified, his identity was concealed by the Assassination Records Review Board (ARRB) until 2001. The House committee used the pseudonym "Scelso" to protect his identity. Whitten's deposition is available at NARA (hereafter cited as Whitten deposition). I want to thank James Lesar for calling this source to my attention.

25. Whitten deposition, 69–71. For Rocca's statement, see Lisa Pease, "James Angleton," in *The Assassinations: Probe Magazine on JFK, MLK, RFK, and Malcolm X,* edited by James DiEugenio and Lisa Pease (Los Angeles: Feral House, 2003), 153.

26. For a more detailed and forcefully presented treatment of the CIA's nonresponsive explanations to these questions raised by committees of the U.S. Congress see Pease, "James Angleton."

27. For more on Angleton and his conviction that JFK was the victim of a KGB plot, see Conclusion.

28. See Chapter 3, "Oswald in Mexico—Seven Days That Shook the Government."

29. Oswald's "Historic Diary" is part of the FBI's investigative record into the assassination. The FBI identified the 206-page manuscript simply as "Oswald's Writings." The document can be found at NARA.

30. Hoover to Director of Central Intelligence Agency, 4/13/1964, FBI Referrals, CIA, State, and Navy, part 2 of 3, serials 1852-3525; or see FBIHQ Oswald File, 105-82555-326? (last digit is obscured), or FBIHQ Oswald File, 105-82555-3831.

31. Hoover to Director of Central Intelligence Agency, 4/13/1964, FBI Referrals, CIA, State, and Navy, part 2 of 3, serials 1852-3525, NARA.

32. Mark Riebling, *Wedge: The Secret War between the FBI and CIA* (New York: Alfred A. Knopf, 1994).

33. Mexico City legal attaché Clark D. Anderson was so incensed over the CIA's withholding of key information that he reminded Hoover about it on two separate occasions. Legat Mexico City to Director, 4/3/1964 and 4/6/1964, FBI Referrals, CIA, State, and Navy, part 1 of 3 and part 2 of 3, NARA; or see FBIHQ Oswald File, 105-82555-2978 and 105-82555-327? (last digit obliterated).

34. Whitten deposition, 50–51; see also Chapter 10, "FBI Blunders and Cover-Ups in the JFK Assassination."

35. *Investigation of the Assassination of President John F. Kennedy: Hearings before the Select Committee on Assassinations of the U.S. House of Representatives,* 95th Congress, 2d session (hereafter cited as *HSCA*), Vol. 4. For the sanitizing of Oswald's 201 file, see CIA document 563-810, 208. For CIA documents indicating that the agency might have debriefed Oswald, see JFK Exhibits F 526, 208, and 210, NARA. On September 22 and 25, 1978, Richard Helms appeared before the HSCA. When a staff lawyer asked pointed questions about the agency's practice of creating "phony files," why it had taken the CIA a year after Oswald's defection before it opened a 201 file on him, and the meaning of the documents cited here, the most charitable thing that could be said about Helms's testimony is that it was nonresponsive. See Helms's testimony, *HSCA,* Vol. 4, 184–191.

36. Helms Memorandum to Director, Federal Bureau of Investigation, 5/15/1964, FBIHQ Oswald File, 105-82555-3831. Edward Epstein interviewed nine former marines who served

in the radar units at U-2 bases. Some of them knew that "Race Car" was a U-2 and others guessed that its mission was to gather intelligence. Epstein, *Legend,* 279–280.

37. Hoover to Rankin, 5/21/1964, FBI Referrals, CIA, State, and Navy, part 3 of 3, Weisberg Archive.

38. Harold Weisberg, *Oswald in New Orleans: Case of Conspiracy with the CIA* (New York: Canyon Books, 1967), 67.

39. See Stephen Schlesinger and Stephen Kinzer, *Bitter Fruit: The Untold Story of the American Coup in Guatemala* (New York: Anchor Books, 1983), 114, 167, for Phillips's successful efforts in spreading terror and panic in Guatemala. For the report of the Honor Awards Board, see CIA documents, JFK records series, 104-10128-10362, NARA.

40. Most of the information about the CIA's New Orleans preparation for the April 1961 invasion of Cuba was taken from the sworn testimony of Gordon Novel. See his lengthy deposition in *Gordon Novel vs. Jim Garrison and the HMH Publishing Company, Inc.,* U.S. District Court for the Northern District of Illinois, Western Division, May 1969, especially pages 377–599. For Novel's admitted CIA connection, see the *New Orleans States-Item,* April 25, 1967, and ASAC Sylvester to SAC, New Orleans, 4/20/1967, New Orleans JFK Assassination File, 89-69-2015. For the FBI's efforts to find out about the CIA's operational interests in Sergio Arcacha Smith, see SAC, New Orleans, to Director, FBI, 2/21/1967, FBIHQ JFK Assassination File, 62-109060-4707. For Butler's CIA connection, see CIA document, "Subj. Edward Scannell Butler," JFK records, 104-10106-10727, NARA. For Smith and his connection to the Cuban Revolutionary Council, a CIA-funded anti-Castro organization, see CIA documents, 104-10106-10793 and 10763. The CIA funneled about $250,000 a month into the Cuban Revolutionary Council. See Memorandum for Director of Security, 5/1/1967, JFK record series, record number 104-10115-10388, NARA.

41. *WCR,* 726; Weisberg, *Oswald in New Orleans,* 103.

42. *Hearings before Commission,* Vol. 10, 32–43 (Bringuier); Edward D. Kuykendall to SAC, Dallas, 6/18/1964, Main Dallas Oswald File, 100-10461-6723.

43. For Bringuier's DRE affiliation, see *Hearings before Commission,* Vol. 10, 34–35, and CIA documents, JFK record series, 104-10106-10783, 10019, and 10771, NARA. For the importance of the directorate to the CIA JM/Wave station's covert operations, see Jefferson Morley, "Revelation 19.63," *Miami New Times,* April 12, 2001, 5. I want to thank Jim Lesar for calling my attention to this important source. For the bugging of the Rosita, see Melvin Beck, *Secret Contenders: The Myth of Cold War Counterintelligence* (New York: Sheridan Square Publications, 1984), 51ff. Beck was the CIA officer who supervised the bugging of the Rosita.

44. Morley, "Revelation 19.63," 4.

45. For Oswald's address book and notation of Cuban-exile-owned stores, see CD 205, 28; *Hearings before Commission,* Vol. 10, 38 (Bringuier); Milton R. Kaack report, 10/31/1963, CE 826, Vol. 27, 753–774. Kaack was the New Orleans FBI agent in charge of the field office's Oswald file; Robert M. Whomsley and Richard E. Logan report, 12/6/1963, FBIHQ Oswald File, 105-82555-416.

46. *Hearings before Commission,* Vol. 4, 431 (Quigley); for Kaack's October 31, 1964, report, see CD 12, NARA, 3. See FBI report, "Lee Harvey Oswald," 7/22/1964, FBI Fair Play for Cuba Committee (FPCC) File, Weisberg Archive, for Oswald's activities on the Dumaine Street Wharf. This file is helpful for information on Oswald's New Orleans activities, but the number of serials missing raises the suspicion that the file was purged.

47. *Hearings before Commission,* Vol. 4, 431–438 (Quigley). Quigley's report on his August 10 interview with Oswald can be found in FBIHQ Oswald File, 105-82555, serials 1–51 in section 1.

48. The bureau's New Orleans field office interviewed sixty-nine owners of printing companies in the city to find out who had run off Oswald's FPCC handbills. Agent John M. McCarthy located the source, the Jones Printing Company at 422 Girod Street. Oswald ordered one thousand copies of the fliers and paid $9.89 for the completed job. FBI FPCC File, 393–409, Weisberg Archive. A December 1963 FBI canvas of bureau informants in New Orleans resulted in the information that they knew of no FPCC in the city or that anyone with the name of Lee Harvey Oswald or A. J. Hidell was connected with Communist Party activities in New Orleans. See CD 6, NARA.

49. *Hearings before Commission,* Vol. 4, 444 (Quigley); SAC, New Orleans, to SAC, Dallas, 4/27/1961, FBIHQ Oswald File, 105-82555-54; SAC John L. Quigley to SAC, New Orleans, 8/27/1963, New Orleans Main JFK Assassination File, 100-16601-18. See attachment for "Flash by Bureau," 11/4/1959.

50. ASAC to SAC, 12/2/1963, Main New Orleans Oswald File, 89-69-560.

51. For a full development of this matter, see Chapter 10.

52. "Paroled for a Mr. Heckman"; see CE 2216. This reference is the only time Heckman's name is mentioned in the Commission's records. Exactly why Heckman felt compelled to "parole" Oswald is a question that the Commission left unanswered.

53. *Hearings before Commission,* Vol. 10, 38–39 (Bringuier), 57 (Martello). The August 13, 1963, edition of the *Times-Picayune* carried the story of Oswald's arrest and his jailhouse interview with an FBI agent. See Chapter 3 for Oswald's attempts to convince Cuban consular official Eusebio Ascue Lopez that he was a "friend" of the Cuban revolution and should not be denied a visa to Cuba.

54. For Chandler's account, see Stephen M. Callender's report, 12/19/1963, FBIHQ Oswald File, 105-82555-970, 13; SA Richard A. Logan interview with Bern Rotman, 12/17/1963, New Orleans Main JFK Assassination File, 100-16601 (no serial no. provided); Furman G. Boggan to SAC, New Orleans, 11/26/1963, New Orleans Main Oswald File, 89-69-186; Branigan to Sullivan, 11/8/1968, FBIHQ Oswald File, 105-82555-Not Recorded (NR). This document redacts Rush's name, but the text makes it clear that Rush was the subject. The bottom left-hand corner of the document indicated where copies were to be filed. One of the files cited was 134-17762, the FBI's filing code for "security informants." Rankin to Hoover, 6/30/1964, FBIHQ JFK Assassination File, 62-109060-3481; Hoover to Rankin, 7/14/1964, FBIHQ JFK Assassination File, 62-109060-3481.

55. *Hearings before Commission,* Vol. 10, 53–56 (Martello).

56. Secret Service report by Anthony K. Gerrets and Roger D. Counts, 12/1–5/1963. A facsimile of their report can be found as Warren CE 1414, Vol. 22, 828–831.

57. For Quigley's report of the interview, see *Hearings before Commission,* Vol. 17, 758–762. His report contains Hidell's name and the bogus FPCC PO Box 3006 address, but not the 544 Camp Street address; *Hearings before Commission,* Vol. 4, 437; Vol. 17, 811. For Kaack, see CE 826, and for de Brueys's October 25, 1963, report, see CD 1114, VI-29, 24–41. For the FBI's questioning of Sam Newman, see CD 75, 680–681; see CD 75, 682–683, for Guy Bannister. The quotation from CD 1 can be found on p. 64 of that document. For the FBI's closing off of Rice's investigation, see *Hearings before Commission,* Vol. 22, 831. For more on closing Rice off the case, see Chapter 1. Early JFK assassination researcher Paul Hoch established beyond question that the pamphlet that Quigley received from Oswald bore the 544 Camp Street address. Hoch's persistence with the Justice Department was finally rewarded with a Xerox copy of the original FBI record copy that Quigley filed with the FBI's New Orleans office. This copy of the record held by the FBI contained the rubber-stamped 544 Camp Street address. The copy of the Lamont pamphlet that appeared in the official record as CE 3120 did not carry the 544 Camp Street address. See Paul

Hoch's lengthy correspondence with the Justice Department under "Paul Hoch, 544 Camp Street," Weisberg Subject Index, Weisberg Archive.

58. *Hearings before Commission,* Vol. 11, 166–167 (Stuckey).

59. CIA Memorandum for the Record, 6/10/1975, CIA's Howard E. Hunt File, Subject Index File under Howard E. Hunt, Weisberg Archive. For indications that Hemming was associated with CIA personnel, see CIA document, JFK series, 104-10106-10665, NARA.

60. *Hearings before Commission,* Vol. 11, 166–167 (Stuckey).

61. Morley, "Revelation 19.63." For the Warren Commission's transcript of the tape of the debate, see "Stuckey Exhibit No. 3," *Hearings before Commission,* Vol. 21, 633–641; Vol. 11, 171 (Stuckey).

62. *Hearings before Commission,* Vol. 10, 44–45 (Bringuier); Vol. 11, 171 (Stuckey).

63. See Chapter 6, "The Warren Commission's 'Smoking Guns.'"

64. For these letters, see *Hearings before Commission,* Vol. 17, 857–858 (FBI), 864 (CIA).

65. Sullivan to Belmont, 5/13/1964, FBIHQ Oswald File, 105-82555-3689. For the close relationship between Hoover and Angleton, see Whitten deposition, 74, 169. For Angleton's FBI symbol "100," see box "Bureau Source 100" (James Angleton) in "Additional Requests" series, NARA. I want to thank Jim Lesar for directing me to this source.

66. *Hearings before Commission,* Vol. 5, 120ff. (Helms).

67. See Johnson's piece in *Evening Star* (Washington), November 25, 1959. For her CIA contacts, see Memorandum for the Record, 4/8/1964, CIA document, 10159 record series, NARA; Memorandum for the Record, 3/3/1964, Partial Contact Report on Meeting with Priscilla Johnson, January 30–31, 1964, CIA document, 104-10135-10089, JFK record series, NARA; Memorandum for the Record, 2/4/1964, Partial Contact Report on Meeting with Priscilla Johnson, January 30–31, 1964, CIA document, 104-10135-10088, JFK record series, NARA. For more detail about her interview with Oswald see piece in *Harper's* (April 1964). After she returned to the United States, Johnson befriended Oswald's widow, Marina, and wrote the book *Marina and Lee* (New York: Harper and Row Publishers, 1977). The book appeared under her married name, Priscilla Johnson McMillan. Johnson's work was praised for its insights into the mind and the motives of Lee Oswald, President Kennedy's assassin.

68. SAC, Denver, to Director, FBI, 1/13/1964, FBIHQ Oswald File, 105-82555-1383; SA Charles S. Harding interview with Dr. Alexis H. Davison, 1/29/1964, FBIHQ Oswald File, 105-82555-1791, section 77.

69. The CIA's Office of Security had a file on Davison. See Memorandum for Files, OS Review of Names #41–45 (Subj.: Penkovsky, Davison, Alexis), CIA document 104-10112-10421, JFK record series, NARA; David Wise and Thomas B. Ross, *The Invisible Government* (New York: Random House, 1975), 250–251; David Wise, *Molehunt: The Secret Search for Traitors That Shattered the CIA* (New York: Random House, 1992), 60, 117–120. In September 1963 McCone was lamenting the fact that the American Embassy in Moscow was so closely monitored by Soviet counterintelligence that the few CIA employees still in place were at high risk. The director noted that the "several CIA operatives" who had been forced out of Russia more than a year earlier when the Penkovsky case blew up had left the current CIA embassy complement drastically understaffed. President's Foreign Intelligence Advisory Board (PFIAB) Memorandum for the File for 9/12–13/1963 Meeting, PFIAB Files, NARA, 75.

70. *Hearings before Commission,* Vol. 24, 685, and Vol. 25, 18, for the list of names provided by the inspector for Mexican immigration, Jose Marcio Del Valle.

71. SAC, New Orleans, to Director and SAC, Dallas, 11/28/1963, FBIHQ JFK Assassination File, 62-109060-129.

72. Interview of William George Gaudet, May 13, 1975, with Bernard Fensterwald and Allan Stone, 22–26. I want to thank Jim Lesar for bringing this document to my attention. A transcript of the interview is available at the Assassination Archives and Research Center, Washington, D.C.

73. For Gaudet's CIA relationship over the years, see CIA document, "Secrecy Agreement, 3/2/1950, William G. Gaudet," 104-10135-10025, JFK record series, NARA; CIA document, Project Review Committee, Subj.: William G. Gaudet, 12/29/1949, CIA document no. 104-10116-10092, JFK record series, NARA.

74. Memorandum for the Record, 1/23/1976, Subj.: William George Gaudet, CIA document, 104-10116-10063, JFK record series, NARA; Jackson R. Horton, Memorandum for Special Assistant to the CDC, 1/23/1978, Subj.: William G. Gaudet, CIA document, 104-10135-10026, JFK record series, NARA; Schlesinger and Kinzer, *Bitter Fruit,* 82.

75. See the two interviews Gaudet gave to Allan Stone, radio station WRR, Dallas, Texas, on May 7, 1975, and with Stone and Bernard Fensterwald on May 13, 1975. Transcripts of these interviews are available at the Assassination Archives Research Center, Washington, D.C.

76. This is developed in some detail in Chapter 3.

77. Morley, "Revelation 19.63," 2, 4; for Phillips's Mexico City responsibilities, see Whitten deposition, 21.

78. Helms saw that Joannides and his DRE connections were kept secret not only from the Warren Commission but from the Garrison investigation, the Rockefeller investigation, and the House Select Committee on Assassinations.

79. Tunheim quoted in Morley, "Revelation 19.63," 2–8.

80. All of this was developed in Chapter 3, "Oswald in Mexico—Seven Days That Shook the Government."

Chapter 13. JFK, Cuba, and the "Castro Problem"

1. Arthur M. Schlesinger, Jr., *A Thousand Days: John F. Kennedy in the White House* (Boston: Houghton Mifflin, 1965), chapter 7, "Latin American Journey."

2. If the Pentagon's general nuclear war plan had been carried out in 1963, the Pentagon estimated that the number of deaths in Russia and China would range from 250 million at the lowest end of the megadeath scale to a higher figure of 325 million. Fallout deaths in the NATO countries from a full-scale nuclear attack would have run to 100 million deaths. The Pentagon calculation did not factor in the effects of retaliatory nuclear attacks on the United States, Western Europe, and U.S. bases elsewhere. See Daniel Ellsberg, *Secrets: A Memoir of Vietnam and the Pentagon Papers* (New York: Viking Press, 2002), 58–59.

3. Mark J. White, "The Cuban Imbroglio: From the Bay of Pigs to the Missile Crisis and Beyond," in *Kennedy: The New Frontier Revisited,* edited by Mark J. White (New York: New York University Press, 1998), 78–85.

4. Quoted in John Gaddis Lewis, *Strategies of Containment* (New York: Oxford University Press, 1982), 25n.

5. Richard Reeves, *President Kennedy: Profile of Power* (New York: Simon and Schuster, 1993), 111–113; Richard Rhodes, "The General and World War III," *New Yorker,* June 19, 1995, 51–59; Heather A. Purcell and James K. Galbraith, "The U.S. Military Plan: A Nuclear First Strike for 1963?" *American Prospect* (Fall 1994): 88–96. For a useful overview of deteriorating civilian-military relations, see George C. Herring, *LBJ and Vietnam: A Different Kind of War* (Austin: University of Texas Press, 1994), chapter 2, "No More MacArthurs"; Howard Jones, *Death of a Generation: How the Assassination of Diem and JFK Prolonged*

the Vietnam War (New York: Oxford University Press, 2003), 39, 41, 47, 49, 60, 63, 114; Robert Dallek, "JFK's Second Term," *Atlantic Monthly* (June 2003).

6. Lawrence Freedman, *Kennedy's Wars: Berlin, Cuba, Laos, and Vietnam* (New York: Oxford University Press, 2000), 132; James Bamford, *Body of Secrets: Anatomy of the Ultra-Secret National Security Agency from Cold War through the Dawn of the New Century* (New York: Doubleday, 2001), 73–74. For Shoup and Burke's comments, see Trumbull Higgins, *The Perfect Failure: Kennedy, Eisenhower, and the CIA at the Bay of Pigs* (New York: W. W. Norton, 1988), 84.

7. For Kennedy's stiff language and unmistakable chastisement of the JCS, see his National Security Memorandum No. 55 addressed to the Chairman, Joint Chiefs of Staff, June 28, 1961, National Archives and Records Administration, College Park, Maryland (hereafter cited as NARA).

8. For the quotation reflecting the JCS's urgency over Cuba, see "Operation Northwoods" documents, box 4, Record Group (RG) 218, folder 3 of 3, page 3, NARA; Bamford, *Body of Secrets*, 79.

9. Memorandum for the Secretary of Defense, Enclosure, 3/5/1962, "Operation Northwoods" documents, box 4, RG 218, folder 3 of 3, NARA; Bamford, *Body of Secrets*, 83.

10. For the eleven-page document of provocation scenarios, see "Operation Northwoods" documents, box 4, RG 218, folder 3 of 3, NARA. James Bamford deserves plaudits for bringing this seminal Cold War document to public attention. For the fully developed details and chilling account of what he characterized as "the most corrupt plan ever created by the U.S. government in the name of anti-communism," see his chapter 4, "Fists," in *Body of Secrets*.

11. Quoted in Bamford, *Body of Secrets*, 87, 67, 82–83.

12. Ibid., 67, 82–83.

13. Freedman, *Kennedy's Wars*, 138. The CIA's investigation into the reasons for the failure of the Bay of Pigs was conducted by Lyman Kirkpatrick. His report essentially blamed Dulles and Bissell for the debacle; see John Ranelagh, *The Agency: The Rise and Decline of the CIA* (New York: Simon and Schuster, 1986), 381. Ranelagh raised serious doubts about the objectivity of Kirkpatrick's report, warning that Kirkpatrick had his own political reasons for focusing on the DCI and his deputy director of plans. But historian John Prados found Kirkpatrick's criticisms of the Dulles and Bissell "perfectly appropriate." John Prados, *Lost Crusader: The Secret Wars of CIA Director William Colby* (New York: Oxford University Press, 2003), 138.

14. Clifford's comments can be found in Memorandum for the file, 2/4/1964, Board Meeting with the President, January 30, 1964, President's Foreign Intelligence Advisory Board (PFIAB), NARA, 4.

15. This transfer of responsibility is laid out in National Security Memorandum 55. The transfer of paramilitary responsibility from the CIA to the Pentagon fell under "Operation Switchback." The CIA turned over its program with the montagnard project in Vietnam's Central Highlands to the U.S. Army's Green Berets. Later the CIA handed over control of its maritime base at Da Nang to the U.S. Navy. Prados, *Lost Crusader*, 134, 138; Jones, *Death of a Generation*, 166, 449.

16. Freedman, *Kennedy's Wars*, 226; White, "The Cuban Imbroglio," 84–85.

17. Desmond FitzGerald Memorandum for the record, 6/19/1963, CIA Files on JFK and Cuba, released 1998, NARA; McGeorge Bundy Memorandum for members of the Special Group, 9/23/1963, PFIAB, NARA, 22; FitzGerald Memorandum for the record, 8/5/1963, CIA Files on JFK and Cuba, released 1998, NARA.

18. Memorandum for the file, PFIAB, 4/23, 6/11, and 11/21–22/1963, NARA.

19. Harvey's seventeen-page Memorandum for the Director of Central Intelligence, 11/27/1962, CIA Files on JFK and Cuba, released 1998, NARA, 2–3.

20. Notes from DCI weekend reading, 10/1/1963, by Walter Elder, CIA Files on JFK and Cuba, released 1998, NARA.

21. For Dr. Miro's resignation, see FitzGerald Memorandum to Director of Central Intelligence, 4/11/1963, CIA Files on JFK and Cuba, files released 1998, NARA. For Miro's attack on JFK, see the *New York Times,* April 19, 1963.

22. *New York Times,* April 19, 1963; Freedman, *Kennedy's Wars,* 230.

23. Jefferson Morley, "Revelation 19.63," *Miami New Times,* April 12, 2001, 5. For the White House's restriction on the most prominent militant exile leaders, see the *New York Times,* April 1, 1963. There was a host of stories in the *New York Times* during the first week of April 1963 on Kennedy's determination to rein in the activities of Cuban exile raiders.

24. Most of this account of a possible U.S.-Cuba démarche comes from William Attwood's top-secret testimony before the U.S. Senate on July 10, 1975. *Report of Proceedings: Hearings Held before U.S. Senate Select Committee to Study Government Operations with Respect to Intelligence Activities,* Vol. 1 of 3, SSCI, box 231, folder 11, NARA (hereafter cited as Attwood testimony).

25. Ibid., 5–10.

26. Ibid., 7. For Daniel's October 24 White House meeting with Kennedy, see Jean Daniel, "Unofficial Envoy: An Historic Report from Two Capitals," *New Republic,* December 14, 1963, 14–20. For Pierre Salinger's op.-ed. piece "JFK Moved to Lift the Embargo Just Five Days before He Was Killed," see *Washington Post,* August 29, 1994. For more detail on the Attwood mission, see Freedman, *Kennedy's Wars,* 240–245. If Attwood's memory can be trusted, Daniel must have had two meetings with Castro: one in October 1963 and the other in November, just days before the assassination. In his personal account of his work as an unofficial White House go-between, Daniel only admitted to one meeting with Castro and contended that on November 17 he had already been in Cuba for several weeks waiting for his second interview.

27. Attwood testimony, 10.

28. Evan Thomas, *The Very Best Men: Four Who Dared: The Early Years of the CIA* (New York: Simon and Schuster, 1995), 292, 295–299.

29. The most detailed account of "Operation AMLASH" during the Kennedy administration can be found in *Alleged Assassination Plots Involving Foreign Leaders: An Interim Report of the Select Committee to Study Government Operations with Reference to Intelligence Activities,* U.S. Senate, 94th Congress, 1st session (Washington, D.C.: U.S. Government Printing Office, 1975) (hereafter cited as Church Committee Report), 170–176. Later Helms further defended FitzGerald's AMLASH operation by contending that Kennedy's accommodation policy toward Castro had been such a tightly held secret within the administration that the CIA was never aware of the Attwood mission. Helms held firm on these points to the very end. See Richard Helms with William Hood, *A Look over My Shoulder: A Life in the Central Intelligence Agency* (New York: Random House, 2003), 229–231. The Church Committee caught Helms dissembling when he reported to President Johnson's secretary of state that AMLASH had not been an assassination plot against Castro. Helms confessed to the Senate committee that his 1966 memo to Dean Rusk was "inaccurate" and inconsistent with the actual facts. It is hard to avoid the conclusion that all of Helms's statements concerning AMLASH were transparent flimflam. See Church Committee Report, 178.

30. See Attwood testimony, 18, 8. For the denials from Rusk and others, see Church Committee Report, 154–161.

31. Attorney General Kennedy made his request to the CIA for specifics about the CIA-mafia relationship on May 11, 1962. For the CIA's response, see Lawrence R. Houston, General Counsel CIA, to Honorable Robert F. Kennedy, the Attorney General, 5/15/1962, Department of Justice, file no. 82-46-5. The attached three-page communication is titled

"Arthur James Balletti, et al.—Unauthorized Publication or Use of Communications," Memorandum for the Record, 5/14/1962, submitted by Sheffield Edwards. My copy came from the Harold Weisberg Archive, Hood College, Frederick, Maryland. For more on this, see Conclusion.

32. For the characterization of FitzGerald as a "knuckle-dragger," see Prados, *Lost Crusader,* 192; Ranelagh, *The Agency,* 272–273; Thomas, *The Very Best Men,* 296–298.

33. The general information in this paragraph can be found in any history of the CIA. My source was Ranelagh, *The Agency.*

34. For McCone's alert about Soviet strategic missiles in Cuba, see Jerrold and Leona Schecter, *Sacred Secrets: How Soviet Intelligence Operations Changed American History* (Dulles, Va.: Brassey's, 2002), 271–272; Thomas, *The Very Best Men,* 307.

35. Memorandum for the Director of Central Intelligence, 1/21/1963, PFIAB, NARA. The entire fifteen-page memo was devoted to what the board assessed as a "grave" loss of capability in the field of clandestine intelligence operations. See also McGeorge Bundy to the Chairman of PFIAB, 2/27/1963, PFIAB, NARA.

36. Memorandum to the file, 3/8 and 3/9/1963; Meeting of PFIAB, 3/11/1963, PFIAB, NARA.

37. Memorandum to the file, Board Meeting with the President, 3/9/1963, PFIAB, NARA.

38. Agenda for Meeting of November 21–22, 1963, PFIAB, NARA, 34.

39. A summary of the Commission's findings about Oswald can be found in *The Warren Commission Report: Report of the President's Commission on the Assassination of President John F. Kennedy* (Washington, D.C.: U.S. Government Printing Office, 1964), 22–23.

40. See Chapters 3 and 12.

41. See Chapters 3 and 12.

42. For the name of Gaudet's CIA Domestic Contact Division officer in New Orleans, see Anthony Summers, *Conspiracy* (New York: McGraw-Hill, 1980), 363. For Gaudet's interview with the FBI, see Interview with William George Gaudet, May 13, 1975, Waveland, Mississippi, with Bernard Fensterwald and Allan Stone, WRR Radio, Dallas Texas, 1, 17, 26. A transcript of this interview is available at the Assassination Archives and Research Center, Jim Lesar, President, 1003 K Street, Suite 204, Washington, D.C. 20001. A check of the Dallas Field Office Index reveals that William George Gaudet's name did not appear in the FBI's central control file with the names of the witnesses that the FBI interviewed during its investigation. The Dallas Field Office Index is available at NARA.

43. House Select Committee on Assassinations staff report, 180-10110-10484, "Lee Harvey Oswald, the CIA and Mexico City," a three hundred–page report by HSCA researchers Dan Hardway and Eddie Lopez (a.k.a. the Lopez Report), 73. For more on the Lopez Report, see Chapter 3. Whitten's sworn deposition was one of the records that the JFK records review board wrested from the CIA. Because of the sensitive nature of Whitten's testimony he was known only as John "Scelso." His deposition was not released into the public domain until October 2002. The Whitten deposition is available at NARA (hereafter cited as Whitten deposition).

44. See Chapter 3.

45. Jefferson Morley, "The Oswald File: Tales of the Routing Slips," *Washington Post,* April 2, 1995. At the time Morley was the editor for the *Post*'s Sunday Outlook section. He later expanded on this excellent piece of investigative reporting with his as yet unpublished "What Jane Roman Said." This piece was based on an interview he and John Newman had with Jane Roman, the senior liaison officer on the counterintelligence staff of the CIA. In 1963 she handled communications between the counterintelligence staff and other federal agencies. A copy of this interview is available through Jim Lesar, President, Assassination

Archives and Research Center, 1003 K, N.W., Suite 204, Washington, D.C. 20001. I want to thank Jim Lesar for bringing this article to my attention.

46. For FitzGerald's emergence as SAS chief in 1963, see Thomas, *The Very Best Men,* 291, 299.

47. Morley, "What Jane Roman Said," 16.

48. For more on Whitten, see Chapter 3.

49. Quoted in Morley, "What Jane Roman Said," 24.

50. Whitten deposition, 114.

51. Ibid., 132.

52. Ibid., 129–131.

53. Ibid., 148, 146, 149–150.

54. Ibid., 142.

55. For more on Joannides, see Chapter 12.

56. Morley, "What Jane Roman Said," 25.

57. See Chapter 12.

58. See Chapter 12.

59. Gaetano Fonzi, *The Last Investigation* (New York: Thunder's Mouth Press, 1994), 57–58.

60. These press stories are cited in Morley, "What Jane Roman Said," 27.

61. SAC, Washington Field Office (WFO), 11/23/1963, FBIHQ Oswald File, 105-82555-506; Wannall to Sullivan, 11/25/1963, FBIHQ JFK Assassination File, 62-109060-1725; SAC (WFO) to Director, 11/23/1963, FBIHQ JFK Assassination File, 62-109060-157; De-Loach to Mohr, 11/26/1963, FBIHQ Oswald File, 105-82555-208; Wannell to Sullivan, 11/29/1963, FBIHQ Oswald File, 105-82555-209

62. George Lardner, Jr., "Frightened Castro after JFK Killing," *Washington Post,* August 20, 1997, A9. Lardner's story was based on released NSA documents, especially a two-page report code-worded "TOP SECRET DINAR." For Daniel's account, see his piece "When Castro Heard the News," *New Republic,* December 12, 1963, 7–8.

63. Castro handed visiting U.S. Senator George McGovern a list of twenty-four CIA attempts on his life during the senator's visit to Havana; see *Washington Star,* July 30, 1975, A6. The Church Committee, relying on records that then DCI William Colby turned over to it, identified some half-dozen "Executive Action" programs targeted at the Cuban premier. See also Don Oberdorfer, "Church Says CIA Tried to Kill Castro," *Washington Post,* October 16, 1975, A2.

64. Quoted in Daniel, "When Castro Heard the News," 7.

65. Fonzi, *The Last Investigation,* 284.

66. From the transcript of an interview of Fidel Castro Ruz on April 3, 1978, by Congressman Louis Stokes et al., House Select Committee on Assassinations, NARA, 13. See also Fonzi, *The Last Investigation,* 284–285.

Conclusion

1. In an off moment LBJ confided to White House aide Marvin Watson that he was "convinced that there was a plot in connection with the assassination," and according to Watson's account, "the President felt that the CIA had something to do with this plot." DeLoach to Tolson, 4/4/1967, FBIHQ JFK Assassination File, 62-109060-5075. Sometime in February 1967 Hoover sent to the White House the FBI file on the CIA's attempts in 1963 to recruit the mafia to assassinate Fidel Castro. Why the director held back this information for almost four years is still a mystery, but LBJ began to growl about a kind of "Murder Incorporated" running

rampant in the Caribbean. See John Prados, *Lost Crusader: The Secret Wars of CIA Director William Colby* (New York: Oxford University Press, 2003), 190. Johnson also dismissed the so-called blowback, or retaliation, theory of the Kennedy assassination that found favor among some CIA officers. The idea was that Castro had gotten to JFK before the CIA was able to get to him. In March 1967, when Attorney General Ramsey Clark raised this theory with LBJ after the president had read the FBI file on the CIA-mafia machinations, Johnson told Clark that the Cuban theory was as preposterous as if he were told that Lady Bird "was on dope." See *New York Times*, April 17, 1994, 16.

2. See Chapter 6.

3. See Chapter 7. A copy of Frazier's report was submitted to the Senate Select Committee to Study Government Operations with Respect to Intelligence, 11/6/1975, item 4, SSCI, box 337, folder 12, National Archives and Records Administration, College Park, Maryland (hereafter cited as NARA). The possibility that Kennedy was struck by an exploding bullet cannot be summarily dismissed. A qualified neuropathologist with access to JFK's brain and the serially sectioned damaged brain tissue might have been able to rule in or out the likelihood that a dum-dum, or exploding missile, had struck the president in the head. This possibility is thwarted by the startling fact that JFK's brain and the photographs of those sections are missing from the Archives. There is overwhelming forensic evidence that Kennedy's brain was replaced by a surrogate brain.

Douglas P. Horne, a former officer in the U.S. Navy before taking up duties as analyst for military records for the Assassination Records Review Board (ARRB), submitted a report to the board forcefully setting forth the argument for two different brain specimens. Horne's hypothesis, based on careful examination of the autopsy records, was so convincing that the ARRB's general counsel, Jeremy Gunn, was persuaded that it was "highly plausible" that there had been two different brain exams after the autopsy. That is to say, every official investigation that relied on the brain photographs held by the National Archives was actually examining images of a substitute brain. These included the Clark Panel (1968), the Rockefeller Commission (1975), and the House Select Committee on Assassinations (1977–1978). See Douglas P. Horne, "Evidence of a Government Cover-Up: Two Different Brain Specimens in President Kennedy's Autopsy," in *Murder in Dealey Plaza: What We Know Now That We Didn't Know Then About the Death of JFK,* edited by James H. Fetzer (Chicago: Catfeet Press, 2000), 299–310; and David W. Mantik and Cyril H. Wecht, "Paradoxes of the JFK Assassination: The Brain Enigma," *The Assassinations: Probe Magazine on JFK, MLK, RFK, and Malcolm X,* edited by James DiEugenio and Lisa Pease (Los Angeles: Feral House, 2003), 250–271.

4. See Chapter 9.

5. For these concerns inside the CIA, see [William Harvey], Chief of Task Force W to Director CIA, 11/27/1962, CIA's JFK and Cuba File, released 1998, NARA, 3. Bill Harvey, a classic example of the agency's culture of arrogance, assumed privileged insights, and special understanding, believed that he knew the requirements of national security better than the transient elected officials to whom the CIA was nominally accountable. For example, on October 16, 1962, at the outset of the Cuban missile crisis, Harvey dispatched ten teams of raiders to Cuba to be in place with beacons and signal flares in preparation for an invasion when President Kennedy gave the order. Harvey took this highly dangerous and provocative action without White House authorization or knowledge. When Bobby Kennedy, by accident, learned of the operation, he ordered the mission scrubbed. Harvey's days as head of Task Force W came to an end, but his CIA career was temporarily salvaged when Richard Helms appointed him CIA station chief in Rome, Italy. See David C. Martin, *Wilderness of Mirrors: Intrigue, Deception, and the Secrets That Destroyed Two of the Cold War's Most Important Agents* (New York: HarperCollins, 1980), 143–144.

6. John Whitten deposition, NARA, 113–114. LBJ was in no way committed to a hands-off-Cuba policy, but, as he told Senator J. William Fulbright, he was "not getting into any Bay of Pigs deal." Johnson asked the Arkansas Democrat to put on his thinking cap and come up with some ideas on how he "could pinch their nuts more than we're doing." LBJ phone call to Fulbright, 12/2/1964, Michael R. Beschloss (ed.), *Taking Charge: The Johnson White House Tapes, 1963–1964* (New York: Simon and Schuster, 1997), 87–88.

7. Sullivan to Belmont, 11/27/1963, FBIHQ JFK Assassination File, 62-109060-455; Belmont to Tolson, 11/27/1963, FBI serial 67-473513-200; Keenan to Ambassador Thomas C. Mann, 2/3/1994; Keenan to the author, 5/19/2003. I want to thank Larry Keenan for copies of these documents.

8. See Chapter 12, note 65, for Angleton's FBI informant symbol, "100."

9. See Chapter 12, note 65.

10. John Ranelagh, *The Agency: The Rise and Decline of the CIA* (New York: Simon and Schuster, 1986), 336.

11. *Investigation of the Assassination of President John F. Kennedy: Hearings before the Select Committee on Assassinations of the U.S. House of Representatives,* 95th Congress, 2d session (Washington, D.C.: U.S. Government Printing Office, 1979), Vol. 4, 106, 118–120, for quotation from the CIA's IG Report.

12. Con Coughlin, *Saddam: King of Terror* (New York: Ecco, 2002), 40.

13. Prados, *Lost Crusader,* chapter 8, "Death in November."

14. Attwood's top-secret testimony before the U.S. Senate, July 10, 1975, *Report of Proceedings. Hearings Held before U.S. Senate Select Committee to Study Government Operations with Respect to Intelligence Activities,* Vol. 1 of 3, SSCI, box 231, folder 11, NARA.

15. For the best evidence that neither JFK nor Bobby Kennedy was aware of or authorized AMLASH, see Chapter 13.

Selected Bibliography

Books

Ambrose, Stephen E. *Ike's Spies: Eisenhower and the Espionage Establishment.* New York: Doubleday, 1981.

Andrew, Christopher. *The Sword and the Shield: The Mitrokhin Archive and the Secret History of the KGB.* New York: Basic Books, 1999.

Baden, Michael M. *Unnatural Death: Confessions of a Medical Examiner.* New York: Ivy Books, 1989.

Bamford, James. *Body of Secrets: Anatomy of the Ultra-Secret National Security Agency from Cold War through the Dawn of the New Century.* New York: Doubleday, 2001.

Belin, David W. *Final Disclosure.* New York: Scribner's, 1988.

———. *November 22, 1963: You Are the Jury.* New York: Quadrangle/New York Times Books, 1973.

Beschloss, Michael R. (ed.). *Taking Charge: The Johnson White House Tapes, 1963–1964.* New York: Simon and Schuster, 1997.

Bird, Kai. *The Chairman: John J. McCloy and the Making of the American Establishment.* New York: Simon and Schuster, 1992.

Carr, Waggoner, with Bryan D. Varner. *Texas Politics in My Rearview Mirror.* Plano, Tex.: Wordware Publishing, 1993.

Corn, David. *Blond Ghost: Ted Shackley and the CIA's Crusades.* New York: Simon and Schuster, 1994.

Cray, Edward. *Chief Justice: A Biography of Earl Warren.* New York: Simon and Schuster, 1997.

Crenshaw, Charles A., with Jesse Hansen and J. Gary Shaw. *JFK Conspiracy of Silence.* New York: Signet, 1992.

Curry, Jesse E. *JFK Assassination File.* Dallas, Tex.: Jesse E. Curry and American Poster and Printing Company, 1969.

Dallek, Robert. *Flawed Giant: Lyndon Johnson and His Times, 1960–1973.* New York: Oxford University Press, 1998.

DeLoach, Cartha "Deke." *Hoover's FBI: The Inside Story by Hoover's Trusted Lieutenant.* Washington, D.C.: Regnery Publishing, 1995.

Donner, Frank J. *The Age of Surveillance: The Aims and Methods of America's Political Intelligence System.* New York: Alfred A. Knopf, 1980.

Dorman, Michael. *The Secret Service Story.* New York: Delacorte Press, 1967.

Ellsberg, Daniel. *Secrets: A Memoir of Vietnam and the Pentagon Papers.* New York: Viking Press, 2002.

Epstein, Edward Jay. *Deception: The Invisible War between the KGB and the CIA.* New York: Simon and Schuster, 1989.

———. *Inquest: The Warren Commission and the Establishment of Truth.* New York: Viking Press, 1966.

———. *Legend: The Secret World of Lee Harvey Oswald.* New York: McGraw-Hill, 1978.

Felsenthal, Carol. *Power, Privilege, and the* Post: *The Katherine Graham Story.* New York: G. P. Putnam's Sons, 1993.

Fetzer, James H. (ed.). *Assassination Science: Experts Speak Out on the Death of JFK.* Chicago: Catfeet Press, 1998.

———. *Murder in Dealey Plaza: What We Know Now That We Didn't Know Then About the Death of JFK.* Chicago: Catfeet Press, 2000.

Fite, Gilbert C. *Richard B. Russell, Jr.: Senator from Georgia.* Chapel Hill: University of North Carolina Press, 1991.

Fonzi, Gaeton. *The Last Investigation.* New York: Thunder's Mouth Press, 1994.

Ford, Gerald R. *A Time to Heal: The Autobiography of Gerald R. Ford.* New York: Harper and Row, 1979.

Ford, Gerald R., and Frederick E. Stiles. *Portrait of the Assassin.* New York: Ballantine Books, 1965.

Freedman, Lawrence. *Kennedy's Wars: Berlin, Cuba, Laos, and Vietnam.* New York: Oxford University Press, 2000.

French, James A. "Issuance of Certificates in Forensic Pathology." *Legal Medicine Annual 1969.* New York: Appleton-Crofts, 1969.

Gentry, Curt. *J. Edgar Hoover: The Man and the Secrets.* New York: W. W. Norton, 1991.

Goodman, Richard N. *Remembering America: A Voice from the Sixties.* Boston: Little, Brown, 1981.

Goodman, Walter. *The Committee: The Extraordinary Career of the House Committee on Un-American Activities.* New York: Farrar, Straus and Giroux, 1964.

Grose, Peter. *Gentleman Spy: The Life of Allen Dulles.* Boston: Houghton Mifflin, 1994.

Hamby, Alonzo L. *A Life of Harry S. Truman: Man of the People.* New York: Oxford University Press, 1995.

Hayt, Emmanuel. *Medicolegal Aspects of Hospital Records.* Berwyn, Ill.: Physicians' Record Company, 1977.

Herring, George C. *LBJ and Vietnam: A Different Kind of War.* Austin: University of Texas Press, 1994.

Hosty, James P., Jr., with Thomas Hosty. *Assignment Oswald: From the FBI Agent Assigned to Investigate Lee Harvey Oswald Prior to the Assassination.* New York: Arcade Publishing, 1996.

Houts, Marshall. *Where Death Delights: The Story of Dr. Milton Helpern and Forensic Medicine.* New York: Coward-McCann, 1967.

Hurt, Henry. *Reasonable Doubt: An Investigation into the Assassination of John F. Kennedy.* New York: Holt, Rinehart, and Winston, 1985.

Kelley, Clarence M., and James Kirkpatrick Davis. *Kelley: The Story of an FBI Director.* Kansas City and New York: Andrews, McMeel, and Parker, Universal Press Syndicate, 1987.

Kelley, John F., and Phillip K. Wearne. *Tainting Evidence: Behind the Scandals at the FBI Crime Lab.* New York: Free Press, 1998.

Lewis, John Gaddis. *Strategies of Containment.* New York: Oxford University Press, 1982.

Lichtenstein, Nelson (ed.). *Politicial Profiles: The Johnson Years.* New York: Facts on File, 1963.

Lifton, David. *Best Evidence: Disguise and Deception in the Assassination of John F. Kennedy.* New York: Macmillan, 1981.

Livingstone, Harrison E. *High Treason 2: The Great Cover-Up—The Assassination of President John F. Kennedy.* New York: Carroll and Graf, 1992.

Lynd, Staughton, and Thomas Hayden. *The Other Side.* New York: New American Library, 1966.

Mailer, Norman. *Oswald's Tale: An American Mystery.* New York: Ballantine Books, 1995.

Manchester, William. *The Death of a President: November 20–November 25, 1963.* New York: Harper and Row, 1967.

Mangold, Tom. *Cold Warrior: James Jesus Angleton: The CIA's Master Spy Hunter.* New York: Simon and Schuster, 1991.

McCullough, David. *Truman.* New York: Simon and Schuster, 1992.

McMillan, Priscilla J. *Marina and Lee.* New York: Harper and Row, 1977.

Meagher, Sylvia. *Accessories after the Fact: The Warren Commission, the Authorities, and the Report.* New York: Vintage Books, 1992.

Moynihan, Daniel Patrick. *Secrecy: The American Experience.* New Haven, Conn.: Yale University Press, 1998.

Newman, John. *Oswald and the CIA.* New York: Carroll and Graf, 1995.

O'Reilly, Kenneth. *Hoover and the Un-Americans: The FBI, HUAC, and the Red Menace.* Philadelphia: Temple University Press, 1983.

———. *"Racial Matters": The FBI's Secret File on Black America, 1960–1972.* New York: Free Press, 1989.

Oswald, Robert L., with Myrick and Barbara Land. *Lee: A Portrait of Lee Harvey Oswald.* New York: Coward-McCann, 1967.

Overman, Ralph T., and Herbert M. Clark. *Radioisotope Techniques.* New York: McGraw-Hill, 1960.

Posner, Gerald. *Case Closed: Lee Harvey Oswald and the Assassination of JFK.* New York: Random House, 1993.

Powers, Richard Gid. *G-Men: Hoover's FBI in American Popular Culture.* Carbondale: Southern Illinois University Press, 1983.

———. *Not without Honor: The History of American Anti-Communism.* New York: Free Press, 1995.

———. *Secrecy and Power: The Life of J. Edgar Hoover.* New York: Free Press, 1987.

Powers, Thomas. *The Man Who Kept the Secrets: Richard Helms and the CIA.* New York: Pocket Books, 1979.

Prados, John. *Lost Crusader: The Secret Wars of CIA Director William Colby.* New York: Oxford University Press, 2003.

Reston, James. *Deadline: A Memoir.* New York: Random House, 1991.

Riebling, Mark. *Wedge: The Secret War between the FBI and the CIA.* New York: Alfred A. Knopf, 1994.

Roffman, Howard. *Presumed Guilty: How the Warren Commission Framed Lee Harvey Oswald.* South Brunswick, N.J.: A. S. Barnes, 1976.

Schlesinger, Arthur M., Jr. *Robert Kennedy and His Times.* New York: Ballantine Books, 1978.

Schlesinger, Stephen, and Stephen Kinzer. *Bitter Fruit: The Untold Story of the American Coup in Guatemala.* New York: Anchor Books, 1983.

Shesol, Jeff. *Mutual Contempt: Lyndon Johnson, Robert Kennedy, and the Feud That Defined a Decade.* New York: W. W. Norton, 1997.

Sullivan, William C., with Bill Brown. *The Bureau: My Thirty Years in Hoover's FBI.* New York: W. W. Norton, 1979.

Taylor, Telford. *The Anatomy of the Nuremberg Trials.* Boston: Little, Brown, 1992.

Thomas, Evan. *Robert Kennedy: His Life.* New York: Simon and Schuster, 2000.

———. *The Very Best Men: Four Who Dared: The Early Years of the CIA.* New York: Simon and Schuster, 1995.

Thompson, Josiah. *Six Seconds in Dallas: A Micro-Study of the Kennedy Assassination.* New York: Bernard Geis Associates, 1967.

Trask, Richard. *Pictures of the Pain: Photography and the Assassination of President John F. Kennedy.* Danvers, Mass.: Yeoman Press, 1994.

Trent, Joseph J. *The Secret History of the CIA.* Roseville, Calif.: Primia Publishers, 2001.

Unger, Stanford. *FBI: An Uncensored Look Behind the Wall.* Boston: Little, Brown, 1975.

Warren, Earl. *The Memoirs of Earl Warren.* New York: Doubleday, 1977.

Weisberg, Harold. *Never Again!* New York: Carroll and Graf, 1995.

———. *Oswald in New Orleans: Case of Conspiracy with the CIA.* New York: Canyon Books, 1967.

———. *Photographic Whitewash—Suppressed Kennedy Assassination Pictures.* Frederick, Md.: Harold Weisberg Publisher, 1967.

———. *Post-Mortem: JFK Assassination Cover-Up Smashed.* Frederick, Md.: Harold Weisberg Publisher, 1975.

———. *Whitewash: The Report on the Warren Report.* Hyattstown, Md.: Harold Weisberg Publisher, 1965.

———. *Whitewash II: The FBI–Secret Service Cover-Up.* Hyattstown, Md.: Harold Weisberg Publisher, 1966.

White, Mark J. (ed.). *The Kennedys and Cuba: The Declassified Documentary History.* Chicago: Ivan R. Dee, 1999.

Wrone, David R. *The Zapruder Film: Reframing JFK's Assassination.* Lawrence: University Press of Kansas, 2003.

——— (ed.). *The Legal Proceedings of Harold Weisberg v. General Services Administration.* Stevens Point, Wisc.: Foundation Press, 1978.

Zelizer, Barbie. *Covering the Body: The Kennedy Assassination, the Media, and the Shaping of the Collective Memory.* Chicago: University of Chicago Press, 1992.

Articles

"The Autopsy," *Armed Forces Institute of Pathology* (Washington, D.C.), 1951.

Blyth, Myrna, and James Farrell. "Marina Oswald: Twenty-Five Years Later." *Ladies' Home Journal,* November 1993.

Department of Energy, Idaho National Engineering Laboratory, "Health Physics Manual of Good Practices for Uranium Facilities." June 1988.

Feldman, Harold. "Oswald and the FBI." *Nation,* January 27, 1964, 1.

Ford, Gerald R. "Piecing Together the Evidence," *Life* 57 (October 2, 1964): 47.

Gibson, Donald E. "The Creation of the Warren Commission." *Mid-America: An Historical Review* 79, 3 (Fall 1997): 203–254.

Helmelt, Mary D., and Mary Ellen Mackert. "Factual Medical Records Protect Hospitals, Practitioners, and Patients," *Hospitals,* July 1, 1977, 52.

Hirsh, Harold. "Tampering with Medical Records." *Medical Quarterly* annual, 1978, 454.

Idaho National Engineering and Environmental Laboratory. "Personnel Decontamination." July 6, 2000.

"JFK: The Untold Story of the Warren Commission." *U.S. News and World Report,* August 17, 1992.

Lardner, George. "Documents Show Ford Promised FBI Data—Secretly—About Warren Probe." *Washington Post,* January 20, 1978, A10.

———. "Ford's Editing Backed 'Single-Bullet' Theory." *Washington Post,* July 3, 1977, A17.

Lattimer, John K. "An Experimental Study of the Backward Movement of President Kennedy's Head." *Surgery, Gynecology and Obstetrics,* February 1976.

———. "Factors in the Death of President Kennedy." *Journal of the American Medical Association,* October 24, 1966.

———. "The Kennedy-Connally Single Bullet Theory—A Feasibility Study." *International Surgery,* December 1968.

———. "Observations Based on a Review of the Autopsy, Photographs, X-Rays, and Related Materials of the Late President John F. Kennedy." *Resident Staff and Physician,* May 1972.

Lattimer, John K., and Jon Lattimer. "The Kennedy-Connally One Bullet Theory: Further Circumstantial and Experimental Error." *Medical Times,* November 1978.

Lukens, H. R., et al. "Forensic Neutron Activation Analysis of Bullet-Lead Specimens." Report by Gulf General Atomic, San Diego, California, June 30, 1970.

Lynd, Staughton, and Jack Minnis. "Seeds of Doubt: Some Questions about the President's Assassination." *New Republic,* December 21, 1963.

"Marina's Story." *Ladies' Home Journal,* May 1993.

"A Matter of Reasonable Doubt." *Life* 61 (November 25, 1966).

Meagher, Sylvia. "The Curious Testimony of Mr. Givens." *The Minority of One,* August 13, 1971.

———. "Wheels within Deals: How the Kennedy 'Investigation' Was Organized." *The Minority of One,* July–August 1968, 23–27.

Morley, Jefferson. "The Oswald File: Tales of the Routing Slips." *Washington Post,* Outlook section, April 2, 1995.

———. "Revelation 19.63." *Miami New Times,* April 12, 2001, 5.

———. "The Spy Who Loved Him." *Washington Post,* March 17, 1996, Sunday Style section.

———. "What Jane Roman Said." Unpublished manuscript, 2003.

Newman, John. "Oswald, the CIA, and Mexico City: Fingerprints of Conspiracy." *Probe Magazine,* October 1999.

Smith, Sandy. "The Oswald Cover-Up." *Time,* September 15, 1975.

"Strange Tale of Judge and Hoover Files." *National Law Journal,* June 8, 1998, A10.

Summers, Anthony and Robbyn. "The Ghosts of November." *Vanity Fair,* December 1994.

Szulc, Tad. "The Warren Commission in Its Own Words." *New Republic,* September 27, 1975.

Thomas, D. B. "Echo Correlation Analysis and the Acoustic Evidence in the Kennedy Assassination Revisited." *Science and Society* 41 (2001): 21–32.

Wecht, Cyril. "A Critique of President Kennedy Autopsy," Appendix C of Josiah Thompson, *Six Seconds in Dallas: A Micro-Study of the Kennedy Assassination. Warren.* New York: Bernard Geis Associates, 1967.

———. "JFK Assassination: A Prolonged and Willful Cover-Up." *Modern Medicine,* October 28, 1974.

———. "The Medical Evidence in the Assassination of President Kennedy." *Forensic Science* 3 (1974).

———. "Part 2: The Cover-Up." *Physicians Management,* November 1975.

———. "Pathologist View of the JFK Autopsy: An Unsolved Case." *Modern Medicine,* November 27, 1972.

———. "A Post-Mortem on the Warrenfeller Commission." *Juris,* December 1975.

Government Documents and Reports

Warren Commission Executive Session Transcripts.

Warren Commission Record Group 7, National Archives, Washington, D.C.

Warren Commission Documents.

The Warren Commission Report: Report of the President's Commission on the Assassination of President John F. Kennedy (Washington D.C.: U.S. Government Printing Office, 1964).

Investigation of the Assassination of President John F. Kennedy: Hearings Before the President's Commission on the Assassination of President Kennedy (Washington, D.C.: U.S. Government Printing Office, 1964), 26 volumes.

Investigation of the Assassination of President John F. Kennedy: Hearings before the Select Committee on Assassinations of the U.S. House of Representatives, 95th Congress, 2d session (Washington, D.C.: U.S. Government Printing Office, 1979).

U.S. House of Representatives, Committee on Agriculture, Subcommittee on Government Information and Individual Rights, November 11, 1975.

U.S. House of Representatives, Committee on the Judiciary, Subcommittee on Civil and Constitutional Rights, 1st and 2d sessions, serial 2, part 3, FBI Oversight Hearings, 1975.

U.S. Senate, *Alleged Assassination Plots Involving Foreign Leaders: An Interim Report of the Senate Committee to Study Governmental Operations with Respect to Intelligence Activities,* 94th Congress, 1975.

Report of Proceedings: Hearings Held before U.S. Senate Select Committee to Study Government Operations with Respect to Intelligence Activities, 3 volumes, SSCI, box 231, folder 11, National Archives and Records Administration, 1975.

Texas State Supplemental Report on the Assassination of President John F. Kennedy and the Serious Wounding of Governor John B. Connally, November 22, 1963.

John F. Kennedy/Dallas Police Department Collection Records Related to the Assassination of John F. Kennedy, City of Dallas Municipal Archives and Records Center, Dallas, Texas.

Files of the Federal Bureau of Investigation and Justice Department Files

The FBI Dallas Field Office Index. Essentially this was the FBI's control file in that it was used by FBIHQ to track the documents that the bureau sent to the Warren Commission. This massive index is an invaluable research tool. No work on the Kennedy assassination can be considered serious unless it has made use of the Dallas Index.

Investigation of the Assassination of John F. Kennedy, November 22, 1963, Federal Bureau of Investigation, U.S. Department of Justice, J. Edgar Hoover, Director (CD 1)

FBI Investigation of the Assassination of President John F. Kennedy, November 22, 1963, Supplemental Report, January 13, 1964

Lee Harvey Oswald, Post-Russian Period, 1–2, Fair Play for Cuba Committee File

Main Dallas Jack Ruby File, 44-1639

Hoover's Official and Confidential File, 62-27799

Presidential Protection File, 62-28799

FBIHQ JFK Assassination File, 62-109060

FBIHQ Liaison with Commission File, 62-109090

Warren Olney File, 63-317

Dallas ("June Mail") File on Marina Oswald, 66-1313A

Personnel Matters File, 67-425

Administrative Matters File, 67-494012

Main Baltimore JFK Assassination File, 89-30

Main Dallas JFK Assassination File, 89-43

Main Dallas Oswald File, 100-10461

FBIHQ Oswald File, 105-82555

FBI Mexico City File, 105-3702

FBI HQ Marina Oswald File, 105-126032
Norman Redlich File, 140-292391
U.S. Department of Justice, Criminal Division, 129-11 File
U.S. Department of Justice, Criminal Division, JFK Assassination 51-16 File
U.S. Department of Justice, Internal Security Division, 146-1-73 File

Central Intelligence Agency Documents

These are available at the National Archives and Records Administration, College Park,
Maryland.
CIA Documents released in 1976
CIA Documents released in 1992
CIA Documents released in 1995 (especially box 57)

Libraries, Archives, and Manuscript Divisions

Lyndon B. Johnson Library
Secret Service Phone Logs
White House Telephone Transcripts
Secret Service Report on JFK Assassination with Cover Letter from Treasury Secretary
Douglas Dillon
White House Central File (WHCF)

National Archives, Washington, D.C.
Waggoner Carr Correspondence
Texas Court of Inquiry File
JFK 4-1 File (autopsy file)
FBI's Norman Redlich File

Manuscript Division of the Library of Congress
Earl Warren Papers

National Archives and Records Administration
CIA Documents, JFK Record Series
CIA Cable Traffic with Mexico City (Box 57)
National Security File, Intelligence File
HSCA Report, "Lee Harvey Oswald, the CIA and Mexico City" (the Lopez Report)
J. Lee Rankin Papers
Kennedy Collection, Record Group 233
Kennedy Collection, House Select Committee on Assassinations, Record Group 272
Master Set of Medical Exhibits
Office of Naval Intelligence File
Records of the U.S. Marine Corps, JFK Collection Registrar
Russ Holmes Work File
Assassination Records Review Board Depositions of J. Thornton Boswell, Pierre A. Finck,
and James Joseph Humes
James P. Hosty, Jr., File
John Whitten Deposition

Hood College Archive
Harold Weisberg Archive (250,000 pages of JFK documents)
Sylvia Meagher Papers
CIA's Howard Hunt File
FBI's Fair Play for Cuba Committee File
FBI Referrals, CIA, State, and Navy Files

Court Cases

David Atlee Phillips v. Donald Freed, et al., Civil Action 81-1407, District of Columbia, November 26, 1984

Gordon Novel vs. Jim Garrison and the HMH Publishing Company, Inc., U.S. District Court of Northern District of Illinois, Western Division, May 1969

Harold Weisberg v. U.S. Department of Justice and U.S. Energy Research and Development Administration, Civil Action 75-226, U.S. District Court, District of Columbia, February 24, 1977

Mark Allen v. Federal Bureau of Investigation, et al., Civil Action 81-1206, U.S. District Court, District of Columbia, March 19, 1982

State of Louisiana v. Clay L. Shaw, Criminal District Court, Parish of New Orleans, State of Louisiana, February 24, 1969

Personal Papers

John Sherman Cooper Papers, University of Kentucky, Lexington
Richard B. Russell Papers, Special Collection Division, Richard B. Russell Memorial Library, University of Georgia, Athens

Oral Histories

George G. Burkley oral history, John F. Kennedy Oral History Project, John F. Kennedy Library, Harvard University, Boston, Massachusetts
John Sherman Cooper oral history, University of Kentucky, Lexington

Newspapers

Baltimore Sun
Baltimore News-American
Boston Globe
Dallas Morning Herald
Dallas Morning News
Evening Star (Washington)
Houston Chronicle
Houston Post
New Orleans States-Item
New York Daily News
New York Journal American
New York Times
Palm Beach Times
Philadelphia Inquirer

Sacramento Bee
San Francisco Examiner
Times-Picayune (New Orleans)
Washington Daily News
Washington Post
Washington Star

Index